Knight without Armor

J. CISNEROS '90

KNIGHT WITHOUT ARMOR
Carlos Eduardo Castañeda, 1896–1958

FÉLIX D. ALMARÁZ, JR.

TEXAS A&M UNIVERSITY PRESS
College Station

The paper used in this book meets the minimum requirements
of the American National Standard for Permanence
of Paper for Printed Library Materials, z39.48-1984.
Binding materials have been chosen for durability.

*Assistance with the funding of this book was
provided through generous grants from*

The Kathryn Stoner O'Connor Foundation
and
The Program for Cultural Cooperation Between
Spain's Ministry of Culture and United States Universities

LIBRARY OF CONGRESS CATALOGING-IN-PUBLICATION DATA
Almaráz, Félix D. (Félix Díaz), 1933–
    Knight without armor : Carlos Eduardo Castañeda, 1896–1958 / Félix D.
Almaráz, Jr.
      p.   cm.
    Includes bibliographical references and index.
    ISBN 0-89096-890-X
    1. Castañeda, Carlos Eduardo, 1896–1958.   2. Historians—United
States Biography.   3. Mexican Americans Biography.   4. Mexican-
American Border Region—Historiography.   5. Southwest, New—
Historiography.   6. Mexican Americans—Historiography.   7. Catholic
Church—Texas—Historiography.   I. Title.
E175.5.C275A46   1999
972.007′202—dc21   99-24693
[B]   CIP

IN LOVING MEMORY OF MY PARENTS,

Antonia Rodríguez de Almaráz (1900–1984)

AND

Félix D. Almaráz, Sr. (1899–1968)

The shadow fell for a moment upon the hour that marked his death then passed leaving his name and memory illuminated by the eternal sunshine.

—INSCRIPTION ON SUNDIAL,
BRUTON PARISH CHURCH, WILLIAMSBURG, VIRGINIA

Contents

Illuɔtrationɔ

Rev. Dr. Paul J. Foik

Our Lady of the Lake College

Sister M. Angelique Ayres

Winnie Allen

Rev. Dr. Peter P. Forrestal

Frederick C. Chabot

Harry Yandell Benedict

Rev. Francis Borgia Steck

Carlos on graduation day, 1932

PHOTO SECTION 2
following page 252

Superintendent Castañeda

Most Rev. Mariano S. Garriga

Donald Coney

Milton R. Gutsch

Castañeda with Rev. James P. Gibbons

Carlos and Elisa with Rosemary

Castañeda's investiture as Knight of the Equestrian Order of the
Holy Sepulchre of Jerusalem

Castañeda in Knights of Columbus procession

Homer Price Rainey

Most Rev. Robert E. Lucey

Castañeda at San Jacinto Monument

Rev. Monsignor Francis J. Haas

Most Rev. Laurence J. FitzSimon

Rev. Monsignor Patrick J. McCormick

Aerial view of Catholic University of America

Most Rev. Louis J. Reicher

Texas Knights of Columbus members with *Our Catholic Heritage in Texas*

Carlos, Rosemary, and Josefina Ella in San Antonio

Presentation of the Junípero Serra of the Americas Award

Backyard family photo

Castañeda in Caracas, Venezuela

Preface

In the annals of southwestern historiography, the name Carlos E. Castañeda stands prominently as a hallmark of sound scholarship and inspirational teaching. No Mexican American historian in the twentieth century has approximated his solid publishing record of eighteen books and nearly fifty articles. No educator of Mexican descent in the United States has received as many honors and distinctions as were conferred on Don Carlos in his lifetime. From the hierarchy of the Catholic Church in Rome, Castañeda received knighthood in the prestigious Equestrian Order of the Holy Sepulchre of Jerusalem; from the Academy of American Franciscan History the Junípero Serra Award of the Americas; and from the government of Spain knighthood in the Order of Isabel the Catholic. Moreover, he attained recognition as a bona fide Pan Americanist with membership in the Texas Philosophical Society, the Hispanic Society of America, the Academy of History of Mexico, the Sociedad de Geografía e Historia de Guatemala, and the Centro de Estudios de Argentina.

Physically, Castañeda was of medium stature; intellectually, as his students (such as Ray F. Broussard of the University of Georgia) testified, he was a giant. Of his prodigious bibliography, two titles have withstood the rigor of time: *The Mexican Side of the Texan Revolution* and the seven-volume *Our Catholic Heritage in Texas, 1519–1936*. All the same, the publication about which Castañeda manifested genuine enthusiasm, probably because it earned for him the coveted doctoral degree, was his annotated translation of Fray Juan Agustín Morfi's long-lost *History of Texas, 1673–1779*, published as a handsome two-part edition by the Quivira Society of New Mexico.

In the world of academe Castañeda led a quiet and productive life, continually striving to perfect his style and technique as a Texas borderlands historian of first rank. Few individuals today, scholars and nonspecialists, are aware of Castañeda's incredible struggle to overcome serious financial barriers and ethnic discrimination that threatened his ambition of becoming a university teacher and historian. As a lone, yet courageous, precursor of the civil rights movement of later decades, Carlos clearly personified the ideal from which evolved the title for his biography—a knight without armor.

The biographical search for Castañeda began in the spring of 1970, when a retired businessman and civic-minded educational reformer of west-side San Antonio, Eleuterio Escobar, invited three professors and a graduate student from Saint Mary's University to recommend a system for organizing an extensive collection of materials relating to social action movements on behalf of Spanish-surnamed students in Texas. Among the voluminous documentation in the Escobar Papers were letters written by Carlos E. Castañeda, superintendent of the San Felipe Public Schools in Del Rio, Texas. This batch of Castañeda correspondence focused on a reform initiative in the 1930s and 1940s in San Antonio to which Don Carlos pledged his moral support to upgrade the condition of schools in the west-end barrios. An immediate question was: Why was a historian of Castañeda's caliber involved in public school administration in a small community adjacent to the Rio Grande? Finding answers to that inquiry in turn raised other questions which ultimately led to an awareness of Castañeda's tenure as a regional director of President Franklin D. Roosevelt's Committee on Fair Employment Practice during World War II.

The encounter with the Escobar Papers coincided with an invitation from Pan American College (now the University of Texas—Pan American) to deliver a series of guest lectures on the sweeping topic of the greater American Southwest. The prospect of speaking to audiences in the lower Rio Grande Valley, scene of Castañeda's youthful years, suggested a title for one of the lectures—"Profile of a Reformer." Conceivably the search might have ended with that oratorical exercise, except that the response from Castañeda's friends and relatives in the audience (including his youngest sister, Josefina, who drove sixty-two miles from Brownsville for the occasion) was so encouraging that the quest for documentary evidence became an odyssey of twenty-five years' duration.

The outcome of the search for Castañeda has been a self-rewarding experience. It involved extended visits to public and private archives, university libraries, and newspaper files as well as interviews with resource persons who knew Don Carlos intimately or casually. The odyssey approximated the theme of Robin W. Wink's *The Historian as Detective* (Harper, 1969). As research material accumulated, the odyssey transformed itself into a personal commitment to place in perspective Castañeda's growth and development as a student, teacher, librarian, and borderlands historian and to use his life story as an instructional model with undergraduate and graduate students in history.

In reconstructing the life and times of Carlos E. Castañeda, the most helpful records, in terms of content and volume, were the correspondence files in the possession of his widow, Elisa, and in the depositories of the Catholic Archives of Texas (Chancery of Austin) and the Latin American Collection (now named for its longtime director, Dr. Nettie Lee Benson) at the University of Texas at Austin. Other windfalls were the Eugene C. Barker Papers in the Texas Collection at the University of Texas at Austin; the Herbert E. Bolton Papers in the Bancroft Library of the University of California, Berkeley; the Henrietta Henry Papers in the files of the Texas Old Missions and Forts Restoration Association, Waco; the Sister Angelique Ayres Letter Folder at Our Lady of the Lake University in San Antonio; the Francis Borgia Steck Papers in the Brenner Library of Quincy College, Illinois; the Chandler-Castañeda correspondence file in the Earl Gregg Swem Library, College of William and Mary, Williamsburg, Virginia; and in Washington, D.C., the Castañeda Files in the Academy of American Franciscan History and in the Archives and Manuscripts Collection at Catholic University of America, and the records of the President's Committee on Fair Employment Practice in the National Archives.

Personal interviews with knowledgeable individuals filled in many of the gaps and provided a human dimension to the story. The scrapbooks of news clippings in the Castañeda Biographical File in the Barker Texas History Center reduced significantly the amount of time required to examine diversified journalistic sources. The comprehensive collection of *The Southern Messenger* and *The Alamo Register* in the Texas Room of Incarnate Word College Library, San Antonio, and at Our Lady of the Lake University Library complemented the scrapbook materials.

With the exception of the earliest writings, Saint Mary's University Library of San Antonio contained practically all of Castañeda's published works, and the library staff extended unrestricted use of its materials and facilities. The late Rev. Benjamin B. Hunt, C.S.P., Saint Paul's College in Washington, D.C., contributed copies of Don Carlos's initial magazine articles to the project.

Preliminary versions of chronological chapters in the biography, read as formal papers at historical conferences, later appeared in professional journals. For instance, the initial essay on Castañeda's formative years (1896–1927) was the lead-off presentation at the 1971 meeting of the Texas State Historical Association in Austin. Subsequently, at the suggestion of Professor José Roberto Juárez (then at the University of California, Davis, and now in postretirement teaching at Texas A&M International University at Laredo), Norris Hundley, Jr., the editor of *Pacific Historical Review,* invited me to submit the manuscript for a topical issue on Mexican Americans in August, 1973. Regional interest in the Castañeda story gained momentum at the Conference on the Borderlands (October, 1973), sponsored by Southwest Texas State University, with a sequential essay on Carlos's ideological affiliation with Herbert E. Bolton's school of Spanish American frontier history. Modestly revised to fit the schematic design of the biography in progress, the manuscript was published in the winter, 1974, issue of *Red River Valley Historical Review* as "The Making of a Boltonian—The Early Years." Then another essay focusing on the initial volumes of *Our Catholic Heritage in Texas* (presented in El Paso at the 1974 convention of the Rocky Mountain Social Science Association) appeared in the spring, 1976, issue of *The Social Science Journal*. Finally, for a special edition on libraries and culture in 1980, Donald G. Davis, Jr., editor of *The Journal of Library History,* invited me to participate in a seminar session; afterward he published my contribution as "Carlos E. Castañeda's Rendezvous with a Library: The Latin American Collection, 1920–1927." To appeal to younger audiences, I included a cameo profile of Don Carlos in a co-authored endeavor, *Reading Exercises on Mexican Americans* (Continental Press, 1977), which attracted the attention of educators, some of whom identified a common bond in the biographical sketch. Overall the timing, location, distribution of these publications, and occasional guest lectures on the subject enlarged the scope of interest in the life of Carlos Eduardo Castañeda.

As with most creative endeavors, researching and writing a worthwhile book is comparable to trudging in a pilgrimage. The journey is long, and the road often meanders through a varied environment of sunny fields, rustic wastelands, humid forests, highland crossroads, and rolling hills. All the same, the gallant personalities who accompany the sojourner for short distances or render assistance at occasional rest stops make the trek tolerable and even memorable.

In the initial stages of investigation for this biography, numerous individuals donated generously to the undertaking, either in the form of documentary and secondary materials or in the nature of helpful commentary and encouragement. Grateful acknowledgment is given to my family for comfort and security in the wearisome phases of writing. I especially appreciate the loyal support and sensitive counsel of my wife, Dolores Marie Cardona de Almaráz, who promptly learned to understand the rigors of historical scholarship. Next, I am grateful to my brother, Robert, in Racine, Wisconsin, who provided moral support of long duration and designed the format for the working title page. Then, to my late parents I owe a debt far greater than I am capable of repaying for their steadfast presence in my formative years and particularly in the training period for a career in teaching. Not to be overlooked, my son, Antonio O. Almaráz, I thank for traveling with me in his early childhood as I pursued the call of the profession in the classroom, in the archives, and on the public circuit. Hopefully through this book Antonio will gain insight and understanding of the hardships and achievements of Mexican Americans for whom Castañeda became a beacon of pride and inspiration. Finally, my young daughter, Felisia Dolores, contributed to the productivity of this enterprise when, in her early childhood, I took advantage of postmidnight hours to advance the composition.

The late Eleuterio Escobar, who shared primary materials from his private collection, was the first person to suggest the need for a full-length biography of Castañeda. Before leaving Saint Mary's University to join the faculty of Pan American College (now a component of the University of Texas system), my friend and colleague Hubert J. Miller quickly endorsed the concept for a biography and offered supportive criticism. The late Joe B. Frantz, former director of the Texas State Historical Association, widely publicized the research project in *Riding Line,* which resulted in several beneficial contacts. Likewise, his successor, L. Tuffly Ellis, consistently encouraged the enterprise, particularly during seasons of slow progress. James A. "Tug" Wilson, of Southwest Texas State University, showed genuine interest through his regular inquiries about the evolving biography. For the counsel and friendship of these colleagues I am thankful.

From the outset the members of the Castañeda family expressed positive interest in the biographical study. Throughout the long, dry years of extended research they manifested remarkable patience and understanding. For sharing their personal recollections and family photographs I wish to thank Don Carlos's daughters, Consuelo Dolores Castañeda de Artaza and Rosemary Castañeda de Folks.

Affiliated with the initial oral history and photography aspects of the research in 1971 was O. Wayne Poorman, now a resident of Rosenberg, Texas, whose assistance I especially recognize because of the infectious enthusiasm with which he aided the project in its nebulous origins at UT-Austin. Another student at the University of Texas at San Antonio, Juan J. Ortiz, in 1974 contributed to the oral history with follow-up interviews with Castañeda's widow in Houston.

With nostalgic reflection I respectfully thank the cadre of dedicated students at UT-Austin who assisted me in extracting research data at the Catholic Archives of Texas (before its impressive remodeling) during the spring semester of 1971: Marshall W. Denson, Anita Marie Faubion, Samuel C. Ferguson, Will Stribling Moursund, Della Louise McLean, John David Richter, Paul Vélez, and Sue Yerger. For sharing their colorful reminiscences I owe deep gratitude to Raymond Estep, Fernando Guerra, José Roberto Juárez, José Rubén Moreno, Joe W. Neal, E. Victor Niemeyer, James Presley, Philip J. Sheridan, and Valdemar Rodríguez. Reverend Edward Peters, C.S.P., at Ohio State University, likewise provided taped recollections.

I also acknowledge the courtesy and kindness of Dr. George S. Ulibarri, who located and identified the extensive records of the President's Committee on Fair Employment Practice at the National Archives. Dr. Ulibarri's interest in Castañeda, whom he considered "one of the unsung heroes of our people," sparked renewed motivation in the research effort. Another acquaintance in Washington, D.C., Dr. J. Manuel Espinosa, whose earlier biography of Diego de Vargas has become a minor classic in New Mexico, always offered encouragement and fellowship during my intermittent visits to the nation's capital.

Corpus Christi physician Clotilde P. García surprised me with a gift of volumes 2, 3, and 4 of Castañeda's *Our Catholic Heritage in Texas*. Another close friend, Dr. Severo Gómez, retired associate commissioner of education in the Texas Education Agency, donated several volumes of the series to the project. To these admirers of Castañeda I wish to express heartfelt gratitude for their unwavering support. In this context, I would be woefully negligent if I did not recognize the friendship and counsel of another scholar and traveling companion to history conferences, the Reverend Dr. Barnabas C. Diekemper, O.F.M., former director of the Franciscan Provincial Archives of the Sacred Heart in Saint Louis, Missouri. Father Barney opened the way for me to obtain copies of the Steck-Castañeda correspondence at Quincy College in Illinois.

For their interest, criticism, and motivation I am indebted to the Reverend Dr. John Francis Bannon, S.J. ("Father Jack"), of Saint Louis University; Dr. Ralph H. Vigil of the University of Nebraska at Lincoln; and Dr. Marc Simmons of Cerrillos, New Mexico, all three of whom shared sound advice derived from vast experience in creative writing. Father Jack discovered important Castañeda letters at the Bancroft Library while conducting research for his biography of Herbert E. Bolton. A transplanted Texan in New Mexico, Marc Simmons contributed personal reminiscences of Don Carlos. Ralph H. Vigil, a regular participant at historical conferences before his retirement, has followed the progress of the Castañeda story from its inception to its completion.

The quality of any writer remains hidden until a talented secretary produces a readable manuscript. Thus, I wish to pay tribute to Elisa Valderas de Jiménez, in the Division of Behavioral and Cultural Sciences, University of Texas at San Antonio (now retired), who typed the working drafts of the initial chapters with the same efficiency that she prepared a multitude of examinations.

A former student and now my daughter's *padrino,* Homer D. Muñoz, president of Alamo Computer Consulting in Dallas, patiently introduced me to the realm of rapid communication, for which I am very grateful. Mary M. Standifer, an expert editor, transformed a hefty manuscript into a readable biography. Her succinct queries and adroit revisions helped to clarify many obscure points. Fred S. Roucloux, longtime friend and former classmate at South

San Antonio High School, generously shared tasty food and lively conversation during my periodic visits to Austin.

Various supporters of the project died before the book was finished. I will always remember Cristóbal P. Aldrete, Rev. John Francis Bannon, S.J., Dr. Nettie Lee Benson, Sister Frances Xavier Brannen, C.C.V.I., Dan Bus, Robert C. Cotner, Jack Autrey Dabbs, Joe B. Frantz, Sam Liberto, Sister Mary Clare Metz, C.D.P., Rev. Antonine S. Tibesar, O.F.M., and especially Miss Josefina E. Castañeda and Mrs. Elisa R. Castañeda with a profound gratitude I should have offered sooner.

As with other historical projects in the Southwest, the high standards in the art of José Cisneros definitely enhance the quality of any publication. Cisneros's earlier friendship with Castañeda, combined with a beneficence of several drawings to the latter volumes of *Our Catholic Heritage in Texas,* inspired the premier artist of El Paso to create two exquisitely elegant illustrations for the biography—a coat-of-arms and a portrait—that manifest the twin concepts of knighthood and scholarship. For keeping faith in the project and for his magnificent artistic contribution, I affectionately salute my friend José Cisneros *con cariño y alegría.*

With a befitting sense of fairness and inclusion, I wish to recognize the courteous assistance I received from the following individuals, whose names are listed alphabetically:

Robert "Kelly" Acosta, Washington, D.C.; James D. Ashe, Knights of Columbus Council 759, Fort Worth, Texas; Raymond R. Baird, former director, Division of Behavioral and Cultural Sciences, University of Texas at San Antonio; Melleta Bell, archival assistant, Archives of the Big Bend, Bryan Wildenthal Library, Sul Ross State University, Alpine, Texas; Thomas J. Bellows, Office of International Programs, University of Texas at San Antonio; Frances Bennett, district clerk, Brazoria County Courthouse, Angleton, Texas; Martha A. Boyd, News and Information Office, University of Texas at Austin; C. M. Calderón, Jr., Del Rio, Texas; W. E. Cooper, Austin–Travis County Collection, Austin Public Library, Austin, Texas; Gilbert R. Cruz, Glendale Community College, Glendale, Arizona.

Toni Daniel, Archives of the Big Bend, Bryan Wildenthal Library, Sul Ross State University, Alpine, Texas; Sister Therese Deplazes, S.C.L., Special Collections, De Paul Library, Saint Mary College, Leavenworth, Kansas; Kay Domine, college archivist, Earl Gregg Swem Library, College of William and Mary, Williamsburg, Virginia; William H. Dunn, C.S.C., Saint Edward's University, Austin, Texas; Earl H. Elam, director emeritus, Center for Big Bend Studies, Sul Ross State University, Alpine, Texas; Ralph L. Elder, head of public service, Barker Texas History Center, University of Texas at Austin; Most

Reverend Patrick F. Flores, Archbishop of San Antonio; C. Patrick Foley, editor, *Catholic Southwest: A Journal of History and Culture,* Azle, Texas.

Herbert Ganter, former archivist, College of William and Mary, Williamsburg, Virginia; Francisco Javier García III, NcNair Scholar, University of Texas at San Antonio; Reverend Msgr. Raymond V. García, Archdiocese of San Antonio; Marie Antoinette Garza, library director, Our Lady of the Lake University, San Antonio, Texas; Martha Germany, district clerk, Val Verde County, Del Rio, Texas; Yolanda Z. González, reference librarian, Arnulfo L. Oliveira Memorial Library, Brownsville, Texas; Robert D. Green, former county clerk of Bexar County, San Antonio, Texas; Glynda Kay Groomer, Del Rio, Texas; Laura Gutiérrez-Witt, head librarian, Nettie Lee Benson Latin American Collection, University of Texas at Austin; Jeff Luis Haddock, student assistant, San Antonio College Library; Edward M. Hellenbeck, regional director, Bureau of Reclamation, Lower Colorado Regional Office, Boulder City, Nevada; Sidney Heitman, Colorado State University, Fort Collins, Colorado; Henrietta Henry, Texas Old Missions and Forts Restoration Association, Waco, Texas.

Reverend Msgr. Balthasar J. Janacek, San Francesco Di Paola Church, San Antonio, Texas; Jennifer Jukes, archives assistant, Archives and Manuscripts, Catholic University of America, Washington, D.C.; Michael F. Kelly, director of libraries, University of Texas at San Antonio; Chester V. Kielman, former librarian-archivist, Barker Texas History Center, University of Texas at Austin; Rev. Victor Kingery, O.F.M., Brenner Library, Quincy College, Quincy, Illinois; Robert D. Kinnally, Jr., Assumption Seminary, San Antonio, Texas; Sr. Martina Krenek, O.P., Catholic Archives of Texas, Austin, Texas; J. Wilfred Lambert, vice president of student affairs emeritus, College of William and Mary, Williamsburg, Virginia; Albert T. Lowman, San Marcos, Texas; Betty Lozano, associate archivist, Diocese of Corpus Christi Archives, Corpus Christi, Texas.

Lucy T. Mares, vital statistics clerk, City of Brownsville, Brownsville, Texas; Lisa May, archivist, Diocese of Galveston—Houston Archives, Houston, Texas; Most Reverend John E. McCarthy, Bishop of Austin; B. Michael Miller, Center for Southwest Research, University of New Mexico General Library, Albuquerque, New Mexico; Irene Moran, head of public services, Bancroft Library, University of California, Berkeley; Rev. Dennis W. Morrow, archivist, Archives of the Diocese of Grand Rapids, Michigan; Rev. Luis Narro Rodríguez, S.J., Saint Mary's Seminary, Houston, Texas; Brother Philip Odette, C.S.C., archivist, Saint Edward's University, Austin, Texas; Laura Frances Parrish, assistant university archivist, Earl Gregg Swem Library, College of William and Mary, Williamsburg, Virginia; J. B. Peña, San Felipe–Del Rio Consolidated Independent School District, Del Rio, Texas; Amali Runyon Perkins,

San Antonio, Texas; Kinga Perzynska, archivist, Catholic Archives of Texas.

J. Gilberto Quezada, associate superintendent, South San Antonio Independent School District, San Antonio, Texas; Brother David Richardson, O.S.C., secretary to the archivist, Archives, Manuscripts & Museum Collections, Catholic University of America, Washington, D.C.; William H. Richter, former assistant archivist for public service, Barker Texas History Center, University of Texas at Austin; Betty Quinn Riley, former librarian, Saint Mary's University, San Antonio, Texas; Richard A. Ritter, The Catholic Church Extension Society of the United States, Chicago, Illinois; Paul H. Rodríguez, Division of Life Sciences, University of Texas at San Antonio; Agapito Santos, O.M.I., former pastor, Immaculate Conception Church, Rio Grande City, Texas; Marcie Savage, reference librarian, Val Verde County Library, Del Rio, Texas; Anita Saxine, former director of libraries, Saint Mary's University, San Antonio, Texas; William J. Shepherd, assistant archivist, Catholic University of America, Washington, D.C.; Very Rev. Msgr. Lawrence J. Stuebben, vicar general, Archdiocese of San Antonio; Jerry Don Thompson, dean of arts and humanities, Texas A&M International University, Laredo, Texas; Jerry Van Voorhis, assistant to the president, College of William and Mary, Williamsburg, Virginia; Clarence C. Walton, former president, Catholic University of America, Washington, D.C.

Knight without Armor

The Formative Years, 1896–1923

At midmorning on Saturday, November 19, 1977, a sizable crowd of dignitaries, administrators, faculty, students, and invited guests assembled at the University of Texas (UT) at Austin to hear former governor Allan Shivers, chairman of the UT system board of regents, dedicate a large new social science and humanities research library. The regents had named the facility in memory of two distinguished professors at the Austin campus, Dr. Ervin Sewell Perry, a civil engineer and the first African American appointed to the University of Texas faculty, and Dr. Carlos Eduardo Castañeda, a historian and respected authority on the colonial and republican history of Mexico and Texas. Among the family members and friends invited as special guests for the occasion, two in particular were inclined to reminisce as the ceremony unfolded. Elisa Ríos de Castañeda, Carlos Eduardo's widow, and Josefina E. Castañeda, his youngest sister, allowed their thoughts to drift in time and southward to the Rio Grande as they recalled the life of their husband and brother and reflected on the cultural heritage they shared.[1]

In the decade following the end of Reconstruction in Texas, as part of a continuing influx of immigrants from Mexico, Timoteo C. Castañeda, a native of Yucatán, journeyed to San Antonio to attend private school, likely Saint Mary's Institute, operated by the religious community of the Society of Mary. The fact that the boys' school enjoyed the approbation of the Catholic hierarchy in Monterrey, Nuevo León, probably would have influenced Timoteo to apply for admission. In time he met Elisa Andrea Leroux, a French émigré in her early twenties who resided in San Antonio. Following a respectable period of courtship, they exchanged marriage vows in San Fernando Cathedral on February 3, 1881, in a ceremony conducted by the bishop-designate of San Antonio, Most Reverend Jean Claude Neraz. After the ceremony the newlyweds established their household in Camargo, Tamaulipas, across the border from Rio Grande City, where they eventually reared a large family. Owing to the education he had received in San Antonio, Timoteo became a schoolteacher.[2]

Gradually at first and then with energetic determination, Timoteo combined teaching and politics, attaining recognition in Camargo as spokesman for the long-standing administration of President Porfirio Díaz. Eventually he earned appointment to a few "positions of trust" by which he supplemented his salary to support a growing family. On Wednesday, November 11, 1896, at seven o'clock in the morning Timoteo and Elisa celebrated the arrival of their seventh child, Carlos Eduardo, whose birth they registered with the civil authorities in Camargo the next day. Six weeks later, when the mother was able to travel outside the home, the family took the baby into Texas for christening at Rio Grande City, an act indicative of the bicultural ambiance of the border region. Rev. Evaristo Repiso, O.M.I., pastor of Immaculate Conception Church, greeted Carlos's parents and his *padrinos* (godparents)—Jacobo C. Guerra and Isabel Cox de Guerra—and then performed the rite of baptism.[3]

As Carlos advanced from infancy to early childhood, his father became even more involved in partisan politics along the border. In 1902 he launched an ambitious campaign for governor of the state of Tamaulipas. According to family tradition, Timoteo's progressive views on the social issues of the time—education and poverty—annoyed the local political machine loyal to President Díaz. As a consequence, Timoteo lost the race by a narrow margin. Disappointed but not dejected, the elder Castañeda evaluated his personal situation. Aware of a budding disenchantment with the Díaz administration in many parts of the country and convinced that the end of Porfirian rule was imminent, Timoteo decided to move his family downriver to the large city of Matamoros, opposite Brownsville, Texas.[4] There he became a full-time teacher at the Colegio de San Juan, a public institution that provided instruction for students who advanced from two primary schools in the vicinity. Carlos enrolled in the Escuela Oficial de Párvalos, a kindergarten, where he acquired rudimentary skills in Spanish phonics and reading readiness.[5]

In the last decade of the nineteenth century Matamoros was the dominant municipality on the right bank of the Rio Grande, with an aggregate population of ten thousand people. A community of Spanish colonial origins, it featured nine watchtowers along its southern limits and accommodated an impressive town square, Plaza de Hidalgo, where residents celebrated events of national history with military processions, patriotic orations, musical renditions, and fireworks displays. On the east side of the plaza stood the Cathedral of Matamoros, Nuestra Señora del Refugio, whose twin towers dominated the central area of the city. Broad streets, laid out in a grid pattern and fairly well paved, sloped gently in all directions away from the main plaza. Sidewalks constructed of flagstone and brick adorned the streets in the commercial and residential districts.[6]

Brownsville, across the river from Matamoros, had developed around a

United States Army fort established in 1846 at the beginning of the Mexican-American War. A lucrative, cart-drawn trade that flowed between Saltillo, Matamoros, and the nearby port of Brazos Santiago quickly attracted Anglo merchants to the area. By the late 1800s, however, the completion of a railroad link between Corpus Christi, Laredo, and Monterrey effectively eclipsed the Brownsville-Matamoros trade. Thereafter commercial activity in Brownsville declined, until Anglo farmers arrived in the region in the early twentieth century. Until that time a local oligarchy of intermarried Anglo and Mexican families ruled the town and surrounding region.[7] When Carlos Eduardo was a young teenager, three English-language and four Spanish-language newspapers served this diverse community.[8]

In 1906, not long after the Castañedas' move to Matamoros, the family became binational as some of its members, Carlos included, traversed the Rio Grande "on the Santa Cruz Ferry Boat" and established residency in a two-story house at 1517 Madison Street in the northeast sector of Brownsville. Although Carlos had crossed an international border, the move hardly signified a total break with the culture into which he had been born. In the Texas environment, however, he learned to face adversity and opportunity in a bicultural setting that embraced both banks of the Rio Grande Valley.[9]

Just before the turn of the century Brownsville had an estimated population of seven thousand inhabitants. The city's north-south streets bore the names of distinguished persons, such as early American presidents or saints of the Catholic Church. While urban planners restricted the north and west ends to residential housing, they promoted development of the southern extremity as the business district. At the east end the city planners allowed construction of homes for an expanding "suburban population," along with the railroad station, repair shops, and warehouses. Interspersed here and there among the oldest buildings were Mexican *jacales* (shacks) that offered protection to the dwellers from sun, wind, and rain. Shade trees and tropical plants abounded in the residential areas. In December the fragrance of Christmas roses intermingled with the sweet scent of orange and banana blossoms, filling the air with delightful aromas.[10]

On October 12, 1909, when he was almost thirteen years old, Carlos, along with his siblings, sustained a traumatic shock with the death of his mother at the age of fifty-two. Following a customary *velorio* (evening vigil), the bereaved family buried Elisa in the old City Cemetery in Brownsville. Two years later, on October 2, 1911, during a merchandising trip to San Antonio, fifty-two-year-old Timoteo Castañeda died suddenly of heart failure. After the coroner's examination, Elisa's relatives arranged for his body to be shipped home to Brownsville. In one of the longest funeral processions the neighborhood had seen, a horse-drawn hearse carried Timoteo's coffin to the City Cemetery. At a reserved plot next to Elisa, six pallbearers gently lowered the coffin into the grave.[11]

The impact of dual parental loss instilled in Carlos a deep sense of family loyalty and responsibility that he retained throughout adulthood. Since four of the eldest siblings no longer lived at home, only Carlos, Josefina, and two older sisters continued to reside at the house on Madison Street. To supplement the household income, Carlos worked throughout most of his high-school years at Adolpho Garza and Brothers, a general merchandising store at the corner of Fifteenth Street and Madison. On the average he earned three dollars a week, income with which he purchased basic commodities for the family. Initially his duties at the store varied, but ultimately the owners, aware of his penchant for mathematics, assigned him clerical tasks in the office. By the age of fifteen, according to Josefina, he monitored "all purchases and sales."[12]

When Carlos had first moved to Brownsville, because he did not know any English, the teachers in the public schools required him to repeat two primary grades. After attending summer sessions, however, he skipped the second and fourth grades and moved forward to a class of students his own age. In the summer of 1912 Carlos entered the freshman class at Brownsville High School. Josefina recalled that he "studied hard and his school work always came first." She also described him as a frequent visitor at the local Learners' Public Library. "Our oldest sister would say, 'You're just going to get sick reading.' And we did not have electric lights over in that part of town in those years. So he would stay up and read till eleven or twelve o'clock—with a lamp."[13]

Between school assignments, house chores, and part-time work at the grocery/clothing store, somehow Carlos managed to reserve hours for recreational activities. Josefina remembered that "he loved to go swimming, horseback riding, and hunting." Occasionally he made weekend excursions into Matamoros to visit family members who still resided there. He also attended events at El Casino, a social club in Matamoros, which regularly invited him to gala dances at Christmas, the sixth of January (El Baile de los Compadres), and Easter. On those special occasions he typically escorted his sisters. In the summer, usually in August, the Castañedas locked up the house on Madison Street and traveled sixteen miles out of town to Blue Lake Plantation, site of an old sugar mill, where they rented a cabana for leisurely enjoyment. These vacations, the most they could afford, included side trips to South Padre Island and family cookouts on the beach.[14]

As Carlos advanced in age from adolescence into adulthood, a decade-long period of revolution in Mexico caused thousands of refugees to flee northward, seeking haven in towns along both sides of the Rio Grande. Once, when the fighting reached Matamoros, Carlos found himself in a tense situation. In

June, 1913, after rebel forces, led by Lt. Col. Luciano Blanco supporting Constitutionalist leader Venustiano Carranza, had captured Matamoros, Carlos and three young ladies, in the midst of a crowd of Americans, strolled across the international bridge for a sight-seeing tour of the battlefield. Encountering some officers of the rebel army, the four young people spontaneously found themselves invited to a celebratory gala. Apprehensive about attending, Carlos refused to speak in Spanish at the party until he accidentally spilled coffee onto the map of the army chief of staff. Forgetting his pose as a foreigner, he apologized profusely in Spanish. Officers who feared he might be a spy immediately surrounded and interrogated him. With an engaging smile, however, Carlos soon convinced them that he posed no threat to rebel security.[15]

Among the Mexican refugees seeking asylum in Brownsville was a widow, Dolores Alvarado de Ríos, who had emigrated from Monterrey with her family in 1914. Through the network of families in the Spanish-speaking barrios of Brownsville, refugees obtained useful information regarding sources of basic human services. It was through this medium that the widow learned about Adolpho Garza and Brothers, to which she would dispatch her attractive, petite daughter Elisa on errands. As the months passed, Elisa's acquaintance with Carlos developed into friendship. Whenever she entered the store, Elisa recalled many years later, everyone, especially the owners, became aware of Carlos's hyperactivity. He would "come out [of the office] and look around and they'd tell him, 'Carlitos, go back to your books.' I was just twelve years old and he was a high school student." [16]

Carlos found Elisa so attractive that he would look for her at church services or socials just for the opportunity to exchange glances and perhaps even faint smiles. To demonstrate his interest in Elisa, but not to arouse unnecessary speculation on the part of elders, he casually strolled by her house on his way to and from other destinations. Carlos's courtship of Elisa followed prescribed Hispanic custom and tradition. The boy "would write a letter," explained Elisa, "telling me how much he liked me, how much he admired me, how much he loved me. . . . He asked to come to the house; he lived close by. *Then* we went together." [17]

In the meantime Carlos continued to progress academically. As he approached his senior year in high school, he began tutoring fellow students and even a few university freshmen, mainly in mathematics and Spanish, subjects in which he excelled. Toward the end of the following spring semester school administrators announced that the valedictorian of the graduating class of nine would be Carlos Eduardo Castañeda.[18]

News of the honor to be bestowed upon a Mexican-born student circulated rapidly in the border town of Brownsville. A few days before graduation an ugly rumor surfaced to the effect that only those boys who owned a suit would be allowed to participate in the ceremonies. Carlos did not own a suit, and his sisters, with their property taxes overdue, could not afford to buy one for him. Whatever the truth of the rumor, one of Carlos's schoolmates, Nora Kelly, appealed to her father, William Kelly, to intervene discreetly with the gift of a suit so that Carlos could receive the public recognition that was due him.[19]

Partly due to his outstanding designation as valedictorian but mostly on the strength of superior grades in mathematics and science, Carlos's teachers counseled him to apply for admission to the University of Texas and to concentrate on training for a career as a civil engineer. Sound as the advice may have been, Carlos, for shortage of funds, decided to postpone attending the university for at least a year. Meanwhile he negotiated employment as an uncertified teacher at Las Palmas, a nearby rural school in Cameron County. Throughout the fall semester he worked hard to earn sufficient income to settle unpaid taxes on the family homestead. In the spring term, after contributing to the household account, he saved whatever money he could for the eventual move to Austin. In the interim Elisa Ríos's family left Brownsville and relocated in San Antonio. Whatever emotions Carlos experienced, he maintained stoic silence, keenly aware that time and distance would test the durability of the relationship he shared with Elisa. For the moment Castañeda's primary goal was finding resources to attend the university.[20]

While Carlos taught disadvantaged students at Las Palmas, an experience that made him contemplate entering "social-welfare work," [21] his sisters whenever possible conveyed the message to anyone who listened that they were determined to enroll their brother at the University of Texas. In between preparing lessons for his classes Carlos charged fifty cents an hour to tutor students at home in history, Spanish, and English. Midway through the 1916–17 school year Carlos informed the local parish priest that meager resources prevented him from attending the university. Although the pastor was unable to help financially, he wrote a strong letter of introduction to Rev. John Elliot Ross, a Paulist priest assigned to Saint Austin's Church in Austin. In his reply Father Ross offered support in the form of modest living quarters in the garret of the church.[22]

In late summer of 1917 Castañeda arrived in Austin with about sixty dollars and a firm determination to earn a degree in engineering. Austin at the time had a population of nearly forty-seven thousand, 90 percent of whom were Caucasian. In addition to the University of Texas, the city was home to Saint Edward's University, Texas Wesleyan College, Tillotson College, and Sam Houston College for Colored Children. Enrollment at the University of Texas, described as the "largest in the South," exceeded twenty-five hundred students.[23]

Notwithstanding its size, the university, then in its thirty-fourth year of operation, consisted of one landmark building (affectionately called "Old Main") and a cluster of "miserable shacks." While local authorities agreed that those "shacks were a humiliation to the University and an eyesore to the citizens," a workable solution to finance more adequate structures eluded everyone concerned with the problem.[24] As young Castañeda acquainted himself with Austin in the final days of August, 1917, the political story that dominated the news was the impeachment trial of Gov. James Edward Ferguson. For nearly four years the embattled state executive had antagonized the university community by interfering in the internal management of the institution. Thwarted in an attempt to dictate administrative policy to campus leaders, the governor in June, 1917, retaliated by vetoing the entire appropriation for the University of Texas. The power struggle, compounded by other issues, shifted back and forth until it culminated in Governor Ferguson's conviction and removal from office in September, 1917.[25]

Isolated from the political furor and eager to commence engineering studies, the student from Brownsville surveyed his immediate surroundings and wondered what adjustments he would be compelled to make. For Catholic students at the University of Texas, numbering fewer than a hundred, Saint Austin's Church served as a convenient meeting center. Founded as a chapel in 1907 by the Paulist Fathers of New York, a religious order of men dedicated to communicating with the laity, Saint Austin's occupied a site near the corner of Twenty-first and Guadalupe Streets. By the time young Castañeda arrived, diocesan leaders had elevated Saint Austin's status to that of a full-fledged parish. Of several Paulists who were associated with Saint Austin's in the early years, few were as influential in the community as John Elliot Ross. Renowned as "a brilliant scholar," Ross quickly gained respect and recognition as "one of the best known priests" in the Austin area. Catholic students who came under his influence, Castañeda among them, always remembered Father Ross's labors in the development of the Newman Club, a fraternal off-campus center, as well as his presence on the university campus.[26]

Castañeda arrived at the Newman Club with modest personal belongings and extremely limited resources. In exchange for his room at Saint Austin's, he performed janitorial work at the church after Sunday services. He also washed dishes at the university commons, whereby he secured his meal ticket.[27]

Apart from subsistence work, adjusting to campus life required great effort on the part of incoming freshmen, especially those from remote parts of Texas. The Newman Club sponsored social activities to help its members get through this difficult transition. Vera Struve Lamm, who met Castañeda at a Newman Club dance and convocation at the beginning of the 1917 fall semester, described him as "very polite and shy . . . very friendly and pleasant."[28]

Uplifted by the spiritual support of the Newman Club and enthralled by vi-

sions of engineering as a prestigious career, Castañeda plunged into the specialized curriculum during the fall term with courses in trigonometry, algebra,
analytic geometry, plane surveying, and engineering drawing. He also enrolled
in rhetoric and English composition, physical training, reading and speaking, and educational psychology. Exactly what motivated Carlos to include a
course related to teaching is unknown, but the recent experience at Las Palmas may have caused him to think of a contingency plan for the future. In any
case, for the next semester in 1918 he added to his already heavy engineering
load classes in English literature, principles of teaching, and school and class
management.[29]

In a composition course conducted by Professor Killis Campbell the student
from Brownsville acquired the basic skills that enabled him to earn his "first
writing money." Although disappointed at receiving "only a B in the course,"
Castañeda later submitted one of his essays, "Indian Problems in Mexico," for
publication in a literary magazine.[30] Clearly, the choice of a topic reflected the
intellectual ferment that percolated in Carlos's mind.

Encouraged by Father Ross, whose campus ministry brought him into contact with prominent faculty members, Carlos hesitantly introduced himself to
Dr. Eugene Campbell Barker, eminent Texas scholar and chairman of the history department.[31] At the time Professor Barker urgently needed a student assistant with bilingual capability to help him organize and translate nineteenth-
century correspondence written in Spanish by Stephen F. Austin on which
to base a definitive biography of the Anglo American colonizer of Mexican
Texas. Castañeda, who got the job, later noted that the opportunity provided
him with his "first real insight into the field of history."[32] The intellectually
stimulating experience of helping a renowned historian such as Barker thrust
Castañeda into a quandary. Aside from the small stipend he earned as a student assistant, how could he reconcile the loyalty he owned to the engineering school with the intangible reward of self-satisfaction he gained by working with the eminent scholar? Several years elapsed before he resolved the
dilemma.[33]

At the beginning of his sophomore year at the university, Castañeda enrolled in only three courses (popular astronomy, general chemistry, and descriptive chemistry), while he contemplated volunteering for active duty in the
United States Army. To be sure, as a Mexican national he was not legally obligated to enlist in the armed forces for combat in World War I. Nonetheless,
cognizant that a record of honorable military service would be helpful in
applying for naturalized citizenship,[34] he reported to Camp Mabry, a Texas
National Guard facility in northwest Austin, for training in machine-gun war-
fare.[35] In an effort to get assigned to the European battlefield, so as to be eligible for rapid promotion, he requested transfer to the navy or to the artillery,

where officers with a background in engineering were needed. His foray into military service was cut short, however, by the signing of the Armistice on November 11, 1918, Castañeda's twenty-second birthday.[36]

Following the cessation of hostilities in Europe, in the winter of 1918–19 Castañeda enrolled and then, for unexplained reasons, promptly withdrew from three courses. In the spring he carried a fairly light load of only two chemistry courses. To compensate for the losses in credit hours created by his withdrawals, Carlos signed up for three courses in the summer session, one of which was the American colonial period and the Revolution—his first formal encounter with history at the university.[37]

The intensive nature of summer school instruction, combined with a prolonged exposure to history as a discipline of the humanities, further piqued Carlos's interest in the subject. Father Ross, who had been an engineer prior to his ordination, persistently counseled Castañeda to abandon "engineering as a career and take up history." Years later Carlos acknowledged the profound influence Father Ross had exerted on him: "He pointed out how my Latin extraction, my knowledge of Spanish as my native tongue, and my formal training in the University all would fit me to interpret more effectively the history of Latin America to the people of the United States. The idea took shape in my mind and began to grow. Perhaps there was something to it."[38]

Firmly planted and nurtured, the idea germinated in Castañeda's mind, but it also conflicted mightily with the family's conviction that an engineering degree was tantamount to financial security and social prominence. In fact, plagued by the specter of inadequate funds before the end of the 1919 spring semester, Castañeda appealed to the dean of the engineering school, Thomas Ulvan Taylor, for assistance. Without full-time summer employment, Carlos pleaded, he would not be able to enroll in school the coming year. In a few weeks Dean Taylor summoned Castañeda to his office for consultation. "I've got a job for you," the dean announced, "building a highway from Hillsboro to Fort Worth, and you are to superintend a crew." Dumbfounded, Carlos replied: "Dean, I don't know anything about building a highway." Acknowledging the truth of Carlos's statement, Taylor informed him that it was the only available job and that if he had any sense he would say nothing and "presume that the people on the job, . . . will know what they're doing." As parting advice, the dean told Carlos: "And you'll just kind of hold them together and stay out of the way."[39]

With understandable trepidation, tempered by gnawing borderline poverty, Castañeda accepted the job. Taking an overnight train to Hillsboro, he arrived about 5:30 in the morning. He met the crew at the depot and then asked to be transported to the work site. In the first light of dawn Castañeda recognized among the workers Rufus Carroll Thaxton, a fellow student he had known at the University of Texas who, although a graduate of the engineering school, lacked practical field experience to apply for a supervisory position. With a flair for authority and professionalism, the twenty-two-year-old Carlos walked confidently up to the alumnus, shook his hand, and appointed him second in command. Glancing into the distance as daylight made objects more visible, the new superintendent saw the train he had ridden from Austin. "Where does that railroad go?" he asked. Promptly one of the workers responded, "It goes from Hillsboro to Fort Worth." Satisfied with the answer, Carlos curtly addressed the crew: "All right, gentlemen, I have one instruction—keep that railroad in sight at all times."[40]

Castañeda's positive self-image as superintendent to the contrary, midway into the summer he contracted an infection that inflamed his lungs. Diagnosing the illness as pleurisy, a physician advised him "never to work out of doors."[41] During convalescence Carlos mused at the irony of an engineer in training being unsuited to the work environment. Still, the resilience of youth motivated him to overcome seemingly minor setbacks.

The salary Castañeda earned superintending construction of the Hillsboro–Fort Worth highway fulfilled two objectives for the upcoming 1919–20 academic year. Carlos used part of the money to pay university expenses and then sent the remainder to his sisters in Brownsville for their household needs. Castañeda maintained such close contact with his hometown that for nearly every major holiday or special occasion such as a birthday or feast day he journeyed to the lower valley for family reunions, or else relatives would visit him. During his holiday excursions to Brownsville, Castañeda eagerly scheduled brief stopovers in San Antonio to visit Elisa Ríos. By then both families acknowledged the serious nature of the relationship.[42]

Partly because of a growing concern over finances, Castañeda enrolled in only two courses in the fall of 1919 and then withdrew. Although both courses were offered in the history department, Carlos expressed particular interest in the one on the history of Latin America, largely because it was taught by a dynamic adjunct professor, Charles Wilson Hackett, who had studied in California under Herbert Eugene Bolton, celebrated scholar of the borderlands and former teacher at the Austin campus.[43] So profound was the impact that Hackett made upon the impressionable Carlos that it resurrected his inner conflict over the choice of a career. While Barker had planted the seeds of interest in history, Hackett's teaching accelerated the student's "desire and opened new panoramas."[44]

In the spring of 1920 the need to earn enough money to complete his studies impelled Carlos to ignore earlier medical advice against working outdoors and prompted him to accept a job with the engineering department of the Mexican Gulf Oil Company in Tampico. Grateful for the opportunity to earn a superior salary, Carlos viewed this sojourn as a time for pensive reflection and hard work. All through the summer he labored in the remote wilderness, "away from even the out-of-town camps," gaining practical experience in railroad engineering, pipeline surveys, land surveying, construction work, and other aspects of the profession and content in the thought that his savings were increasing. At the beginning of August he arrived at the stark conclusion that civil engineering was not the romantic career he had envisioned. Hesitantly but with a newly discovered level of maturity, Castañeda informed the historian whom he considered his mentor, Eugene C. Barker, of his decision to "take up my school work with a little more enthusiasm, and a broader attitude than last fall." Inquiring into the possibility of securing "typewriting work" in the upcoming academic year, Carlos plunged into the core of the issue and asked, "Is there any opportunity of getting an assistan[t]ship in the History Department?"[45]

In view of the windfall salary he had earned working for the Mexican Gulf Oil Company, it was not likely that Carlos wanted an assistantship purely for the modest stipend it provided. At this point in his life—on the threshold of his senior year, having abandoned engineering for history—Carlos earnestly sought the security of acceptance by the faculty who would train him, foremost among whom were Barker and Hackett.

Returning home to Texas, Castañeda paused briefly in Brownsville to visit his sisters and other relatives. En route to Austin he stopped in San Antonio to discuss with Elisa Ríos tentative plans for their wedding after his graduation. Finally he arrived back at Saint Austin's Church, where he reoccupied the room in the garret. Through meticulous strategies, aided by friendly counseling from Professor Barker and Father Ross, Carlos arranged his class schedule for the senior year. Encouraged by the award of the first George Tarleton Scholarship, he enrolled in four history courses plus two additional classes in Latin American government and Spanish classical prose. To compensate for credit-hour losses when he withdrew from the university, Castañeda satisfied the requirements for a course in contemporary Spanish literature through advanced placement examination. In the winter and spring semesters Carlos improved his overall scholastic average enough to become eligible for membership in Phi Beta Kappa. At last, in the spring commencement of 1921, overcoming economic hardship and medical setbacks, Castañeda received a bachelor of arts degree with a declared major in history.[46]

Exhilarated by his academic success, Carlos contemplated the prospect of a career as a college professor. In order to begin preparing himself, he enrolled in three graduate history courses during the 1921 summer session. Additionally, he signed up for a course in state government and administration, which was required for all public-school teachers. For while he aimed ultimately at teaching at the college level, Castañeda realized that his immediate need was to find full-time employment. When his search for a job as a history teacher met with continued rejection, Carlos as a matter of practical necessity turned to Spanish, a discipline for which he had a natural aptitude and affinity. Receiving a lead from the Texas State Teachers Bureau about an instructor's position in Beaumont, he submitted an application, and within a few days he accepted a contract to teach Spanish language classes at Beaumont High School at a starting salary of sixteen hundred dollars.[47]

A few days prior to the opening of the school year, Castañeda traveled to Beaumont, where he found lodging in a boardinghouse at 1035 Broadway. Making the transition from full-time student to professional teacher was something of a jolt to Carlos. About six weeks into the 1921–22 academic year he wrote to Barker that he was "getting used to high school ways again. I had a hard time at first, for I expected the students to behave something as University men. I do not hold that delusion anymore."[48] Having always worked beyond normal capacity, probably to earn extra income to share with his sisters in Brownsville, Castañeda told Barker about his nighttime teaching. His schedule now included a Spanish class at the YMCA and another at the high school, which together added up to "four nights' work a week, besides the regular day school."[49]

Carlos also bombarded Barker with long-range plans for advancing the graduate study he had initiated during the summer.

> This [forthcoming] summer, . . . I certainly will be back [at the university] again. My intention has been, . . . to do some work on my thesis, but up to the present I have been too busy getting my teaching work started to think very much of anything else. I intend to begin doing some reading before this month [October, 1921] is over. Dr. Hackett, [sic] had promised to send me the book I need from time to time and I am going to avail myself of the opportunity. I am sure there is . . . very interesting material in the García Library. If it is not too much trouble, I expect to consult with you now and then as to my work.[50]

Shortly after arriving in Beaumont, Castañeda drafted and revised an essay entitled "The Early Missionary Movement in Texas." With the help of Father Ross in Austin, he submitted the manuscript to *The Missionary,* a journal sponsored by the Paulist congregation, which accepted the article for publication in December. Modest at best in scope and content, the article immensely brightened Carlos's outlook as a scholar. It also presaged what would become his chief research interest. As he recalled many years later, "The devoted patience of the unselfish sons of St. Francis, their deep concern for the natives of

Texas in their heroic efforts to found the first missions, made a deep impression on my mind." [51]

In mid-November Carlos wrote to Barker to tell of his imminent marriage to Elisa. "I do not know what you are going to think about it, but I have just decided to try to do one more thing in addition to the others and that is to get married. Perhaps this will not be a very great surprise, for I have been contemplating this step for some time and at last I have made up my mind to do it." [52] Castañeda mixed a few details about the wedding with a bold invitation to the professor to participate in the liturgy during the Christmas holidays. "I do not know the exact date yet," he admitted, "but it will be some time during Christmas week and I would appreciate your presence. You have always shown such great interest in me that I feel that in taking this step, your presence would add much to the meaning of the ceremony. I dare not hope that you will accept, though I most sincerely wish that you would." [53] Unable to attend because of a prior commitment with the American Historical Association, Barker replied: "I wish you all the happiness in the world and am sure you will 'get away' with this enterprise as efficiently as you have done with all your other undertakings in the past." [54]

Once the school in Beaumont recessed for the yuletide season, Castañeda hurried to San Antonio to assist Elisa with final arrangements. On the morning of Christmas Eve they applied for a marriage license at Bexar County Courthouse. The next day they joined relatives and friends at Sunday worship and celebrated Christmas in a round of festivities. They devoted Monday to last-minute rehearsals and preparations. Finally, on Tuesday, December 27, 1921, in a nuptial mass officiated by Father John Elliot Ross, Carlos and Elisa exchanged solemn vows in San Fernando Cathedral, the site where forty years earlier his parents had celebrated their spousal ceremony. [55]

After the reception the newlyweds boarded an eastbound train for Beaumont. Making a honeymoon stopover in Houston, they registered at the Ben Milam near the depot. Because they were on a tight budget, they confined their sight-seeing to places within walking distance of the hotel. [56]

When Carlos and Elisa arrived in Beaumont just before classes resumed in January, they moved into 1493 Hazel Street. Since administrative rules for night classes were not as rigid as at the high school, Elisa frequently accompanied her husband. During class breaks she enjoyed meeting some of the people there, a few of whom "were French." [57]

As before, Castañeda continued to assume responsibility for the welfare of his sisters in Brownsville. Mindful of this obligation, he wrote to Barker in the fall of 1921 and again the following spring, inquiring about part-time campus employment during the summer. Barker conveyed discouraging news concerning the possibility of work in the history department: "All our funds are used up and there seems little likelihood that we can get any additional money." However, since there was always a possibility of an unexpected vacancy occurring in the Spanish department, the historian advised Carlos to contact the faculty administrator, Miss Lilia Casis. Barker also reiterated advice he had given earlier regarding Castañeda's speaking pattern.

> *I wonder if you have gotten rid of some of your rapid enunciation and have learned to separate words. You know I have insisted many times that you must slow down your speech if you were ever to become a successful teacher. I hope that your experience in the high school has helped you to remedy that trouble. I suppose that it is a simpton [sic] of your nervous disposition, aggravated by the tremendous pressure under which you have always worked. Now that you have become a settled married man, I hope that you will not live at such high speed.*[58]

Given the bleak employment prospects for the summertime at the University of Texas, Castañeda remained ever vigilant for timely opportunities. From several sources he learned that the Mexican government would provide "a free trip to all teachers" who would enroll at the National Autonomous University of Mexico "during the summer." Tempted by the offer, he informed Barker that the program "pays the transportation expenses from the border to the capital as well as the return trip to the border." Excited about the possibility of visiting Mexico City, he asked Barker if there were any specific course work for which he should enroll that would "count towards my M.A." Undecided and anxious for his mentor to indicate a direction, Carlos eagerly invited Barker's opinion: "Would it be worth my while to go? Or would it be better that I stay in Austin this summer and try to do as much as I can there? There is another question I wanted to ask you. Could I do any work for the University of Texas while I am in Mexico in the archives or something like that? I will appreciate your suggestions on this matter."[59]

In his reply Barker advised Carlos that there would be ample summer courses offered at the Austin campus that definitely would apply toward the degree plan. Moreover, he pointed out that the primary sources (Spanish and Mexican colonial records) for a thesis were closer to home—in San Antonio, actually—than in far-off Mexico City. In addition to the arguments offered by Barker, a recent medical report confirming Elisa's early stages of pregnancy caused Carlos and his wife to look favorably upon San Antonio as their next home. Finally, there was the priority of securing employment for the following year once he and Elisa decided to leave Beaumont. Accordingly, in June when the semester ended, the Castañedas packed their few possessions and headed for San Antonio.[60]

Within a relatively short period after arriving in San Antonio, Carlos and Elisa rented living accommodations above a grocery store on Yellowstone Street.[61] By happy coincidence the election of Elvira Pizzini de Guerra as vice president of the board of trustees of the San Antonio city schools encouraged Carlos to apply for a teaching position in Spanish at George W. Brackenridge, a prominent high school with an enrollment of 2,184 students. In recognition of prior service in Las Palmas, combined with his year in Beaumont, Superintendent Jeramiah Rhodes allowed Castañeda credit for three years' experience and recommended to the board a salary of $1,410.[62]

Relieved at having obtained employment for the 1922–23 academic year and secure in the knowledge that Elisa's close relatives lived nearby in case of an emergency, Carlos hurried to Austin to attend summer school. In the first session Castañeda enrolled in two classes (on the Texas Revolution and on the history of the West to 1850); in the second he took a history class, a Spanish literature course, and an introduction to sociology. Indeed, it was an arduous curriculum to fulfill in twelve weeks, but Carlos continued to post high grades.[63]

At the conclusion of the summer sessions Castañeda reported to Brackenridge High School to begin the new academic year as one of six teachers in the Spanish department. Lamenting a reduction in salary when he accepted the job in San Antonio, Carlos wrote to Barker that he hoped to offset the difference in pay by offering a Spanish class for teachers two afternoons a week. In the classroom Castañeda devised plans to stimulate student interest in Spanish as a foreign language. Recalling that one of his professors, Charles W. Hackett, had compiled a series of transparencies of Mexico, he asked Barker to inquire with the administrator of the visual extension department about procedures for borrowing the slides.[64] Next, Carlos organized a student club, "strictly and definitely" honorary, replete with a formal initiation and an annual banquet at which either "a prominent member of the faculty or of the school board" was guest of honor. Convinced that the club's name should be "short, significant, and picturesque," Castañeda suggested Los Hidalgos, indicating persons in a Spanish community who had attained a rank of lower nobility.[65]

With the classroom situation under control, Castañeda turned his attention to his thesis project, an inventory of Spanish-language documents at the Bexar County Courthouse. Of inestimable value to him was an introduction to Thad Smith, the county clerk's chief assistant, whom Carlos described as "a very interesting old man" endowed with an ability to speak Spanish "as fluently as a native." On account of Smith's friendliness, Castañeda confidently reported to Barker: "I expect I will be able to do the work I want to without difficulty."[66]

Devoting a few hours a day after school and during Thanksgiving and

Christmas vacations, Castañeda maintained steady progress inventorying extant Spanish documents in the courthouse. The material included official papers, such as land grants, transfers, wills, and mission records, as well as miscellaneous documents. Shortly before Christmas he suspended research for several days to celebrate the religious holiday with family and friends. That particular Christmas was memorable indeed, because amid the festivities Elisa complained of suffering labor pains. At a half-hour past midnight, on the eve of their first wedding anniversary, Elisa gave birth to a daughter whom they named Irma Gloria.[67]

After the new year commenced, Carlos returned to the classroom and whenever possible compiled entries for the records inventory. To accommodate the needs of a growing family, the Castañedas moved into larger quarters at 416 West Elmira Street. Toward the end of the school term Carlos learned of a faculty vacancy in foreign languages at historic William and Mary College in Virginia. Dispatching an unusually terse letter to Professor Barker asking for a recommendation, Castañeda noted that the position would give him a "first opportunity" to advance into college teaching and that quite naturally he was "very anxious to try to secure it."[68] Meanwhile, on Sunday, June 3, 1923, Carlos and Elisa invited relatives and friends to San Fernando Cathedral for Irma Gloria's baptism. For the occasion Carlos's older sister María and Elisa's brother Abraham served as godparents, as Father Ross solemnized the rite of baptism.[69]

Elated when William and Mary finally offered him the position, as the temperate climate of June yielded to the scorching heat of July, Carlos took his family on an extended automobile tour of Mexico. For several weeks Castañeda combined pleasure with business. Cognizant of the benchmark contribution made by Herbert E. Bolton in his *Guide to Materials for the History of the United States in the Principal Archives of Mexico,* Castañeda attempted to probe the treasure troves of colonial records in a similar manner. He informed Barker: "While in Querétaro I made a special effort to locate some of the records of the famous Querétaro college of the Franciscans. I was not quite successful, but I located a man who I think will be able to give me a great deal of information as to what became of the library of the college of the Holy Cross [Nuestra Señora de la Santa Cruz de Querétaro]. I am sure that there ought to be some interesting documents there with regard to the Missions of Texas, since the missionaries started [their journeys] from there."[70]

The visit to Mexico City and other regional archival depositories fired Castañeda's imagination with ideas about future research possibilities. In addition to searching for colonial records, he also interviewed state superintendents of education in Nuevo León, Coahuila, San Luis Potosí, and Querétaro, with a view to writing a series of essays on Mexico's public school system. In the course of this work he became personally acquainted with some of Mexico's outstanding intellectuals, such as José Vasconcelos, then secretary of public instruction in the cabinet of Alvaro Obregón.[71] These contacts became invaluable to him in the years ahead.

Castañeda returned home in the middle of the third week in July. He found "a little note" from Barker recommending that he read Herbert E. Bolton's article "Spanish Mission Records in San Antonio," published in the *Southwestern Historical Quarterly*. Feeling a bit guilty for neglecting the inventory project, especially in view of the fact that the William and Mary professorship required that he have a master's degree in hand, Castañeda quickly regained confidence and momentum for meeting the graduation deadline. He informed Barker, "I assure you that I intend to work day an[d] night from now on in order . . . to finish the thesis. I fully appreciate the fact that I have a real job ahead of me, but . . . if perseverance and steady work can accomplish it I will finish." [72]

By early August, as he tried to reconcile the magnitude of his thesis with an imminent deadline, he became temporarily frantic. Confessing to Barker that he was "almost sick with worry," Carlos rendered a detailed accounting of his inventory. "I have been working steadily every day since I saw you and I am not anywhere near through yet. I have over 1300 cards made out already, and there must be at least 400 more manuscripts to be gone over." In fact, he estimated that the "index data alone" would require 150 pages.[73]

Seizing the initiative without waiting for a response, Carlos wrote to Barker again, explaining the plan he had devised for organizing his material and asking for prompt approval.[74] By the end of the month, but a few days before the deadline, he submitted the required number of copies of the thesis to his supervising professor.[75]

At the summer commencement Castañeda received the master of arts degree. The formative period of his development as a historian, which began in Brownsville with the aspirations of an immigrant Mexican student, covered six long years. Now, as the former scholar and teacher looked ahead, another eventful journey beckoned.

Sojourn in Virginia, 1923–1927

After Labor Day in September, 1923, Carlos Eduardo Castañeda started out alone in the family automobile for Virginia, having arranged for Elisa and the baby to follow later by train. No doubt the humid timberlands east of the Mississippi River, so different from the landscapes he had known for most of his life, alternately inspired and depressed him. Arriving in Williamsburg, where the restoration of the colonial district would not begin for another six years, Carlos found the haphazard juxtaposition of modern buildings and historic structures somewhat jarring. Excitedly he meandered through the rustic old city until he found the sprawling campus of William and Mary at the juncture of Jamestown and Richmond roads.

Hailed as the second oldest institution of higher learning in the United States, William and Mary, founded in 1693, comprised several compact red-brick buildings in a wooded terrain that once accommodated an Episcopalian seminary. Castañeda, joining the faculty at the rank of associate professor, resolved to expand the intellectual horizons of his Anglo-American students about the Hispanic culture through the medium of the language courses he had been hired to teach, both on campus and through the extension division in nearly communities. Assessing the enrollment statistics of the college, he discovered that, out of a campus population of approximately a thousand, "the Spanish branch" of the modern languages department had fewer than forty students.[1] With the encouragement and support of Professor Arthur George Williams, departmental chairman, Castañeda proceeded at full tilt to increase class enrollments and to foster appreciation of the Hispanic culture.[2] His dedication to the department quickly earned for him the respect of other colleagues, one of whom remembered that he "did not sulk nor weep over unfamiliar conditions but proceeded to get to work."[3]

Saddened by the fact that only a tiny minority of the student body were practicing Catholics, Carlos recalled his own insecurity as an undergraduate at the University of Texas and especially how the Newman Club had filled a void in his spiritual life. Consequently, working with a nucleus of twelve students and capitalizing upon regional history, he organized the Gibbons Club, named in memory of James Gibbons, the first American cardinal, who during the 1870s had served briefly as bishop of the Diocese of Richmond before being transferred north to Baltimore.[4] Defining modest objectives for the first year, the club leaders, with Castañeda as faculty adviser, planned a monthly liturgical service on campus, celebrated by a priest who drove thirty-five miles from Newport News. The success of the initial year motivated the Catholic students and their sponsor to expand the program in 1924 to include two masses a month.[5]

To generate student interest in his academic courses, as well as to stimulate an awareness and appreciation of the Hispanic culture, in the fall semester of 1923 Castañeda founded the Club Honorario, Los Quixotescos, named in admiration of the renowned and aged knight created by Miguel de Cervantes. Indicative of the pride that Castañeda instilled in the club members, a page in the college yearbook listed the various categories—club colors, flower, membership, motto, and officers—entirely in Spanish.[6]

Late in October, Castañeda wrote to Eugene C. Barker that for six weeks he had "been enjoying a sort of rest" because classroom duties took up "very little" of his time. With the exception of composing a paper, entitled "The Aims of a Two-Year High School Course in Spanish," to be presented in absentia at the convention of the Texas State Teachers Association, he claimed he had not committed himself to extra work. Resolving not to remain idle too long, however, he eagerly accepted an invitation to read an original essay "on some contemporary Mexican writers" at the meeting of the Virginia Modern Language Association in Richmond during the Thanksgiving holiday. Turning to his teaching load and sponsorship of the Gibbons Club and Los Quixotescos, Castañeda judged that the quality of his work at William and Mary was "satisfactory for the powers that be, for everything has been going on smoothly." Still, there were the perennial financial woes that continuously plagued him. "Although I have been diligently scouting for private tutoring with a view of getting some extra spending money, I find there is none here. Of course, translations are out of the question in this small town, and in Norfolk, where I go once a week on extension work, I have not succeeded in finding anything either." Castañeda informed Barker that as a result he had decided to search for "other pursuits" in which to utilize his "spare time." To be sure, "other pursuits" signified historical research. Carlos recalled that during a graduate course he had taken on the Texas Revolution, Barker had casually mentioned a report compiled by Mexican colonel Juan Nepomuceno Almonte, who had conducted a thorough inspection of Texas in 1834, about a year before the outbreak of hostilities. Now Castañeda asked Barker to send him a printed copy of Almonte's report.[7] At this time Barker served as editor of the *Southwestern Historical Quarterly* in addition to his faculty duties, and Carlos hoped to submit a translation of the report to the journal for publication. With chagrin, however, Barker replied that the university's circulating copy "had disappeared," as had the one belonging to the State Library. Unable to locate a copy in Austin that could be loaned out, Barker turned to contacts in Mexico City. Meanwhile, to maintain Carlos's interest in Texas history projects, Barker promised, "It may be that I will be able to find a manuscript that . . . [is] worth the effort of translation, and if so will let you hear from me shortly." [8]

Expressing regret at the trouble Barker had encountered trying to secure a copy of Almonte's report, Castañeda willingly agreed to translate any alternate manuscript his mentor suggested. In the meantime Carlos commenced writing "a detailed sketch" of a resourceful Franciscan missionary of eighteenth-century Texas, Antonio Margil de Jesús.[9]

As winter descended upon Williamsburg, Castañeda's wife contracted a serious illness that required long-term hospitalization. During Elisa's confinement in the hospital Carlos entrusted their daughter to the care of a family who lived in the country. To reduce expenses in automobile maintenance, as well as to meditate on solutions to life's problems, in the evenings when weather permitted he frequently walked the mile and a half to visit his little girl.[10] On other occasions, not inclined to dwell on the temporary misfortune that had upset his household, Carlos continued working on the Fray Margil sketch while waiting for a reply from the Library of Congress about the availability of Almonte's report. So anxious was he to begin translating that he even contemplated requesting a photocopy of the rare book, but the prospect of having to pay "15¢ a double page" restrained him. Uncertain as to the number of pages in the Almonte diary, which Barker had agreed to annotate, Carlos suggested to the historian a flexible deadline, forecasting completion of the translating phase by summer when he could devote adequate time to the project. In the midst of these developments Castañeda drew sudden inspiration from a local claim that William and Mary had hired the first modern-language professor. To prove their assertion Carlos initiated research "regarding the early teaching of modern languages in the United States." Accordingly, he mailed inquiries to "the thirty oldest colleges and universities in this country." By early January of the new year he told Barker: "I have gathered a good deal of very interesting material on the subject." [11] Without the pressure of a deadline Carlos worked intermittently on the new project, casting around for a suitable conference at which to present the results of his research.

In mid-February the hospital released Elisa for further convalescence at home. Overjoyed at her return, Carlos shared a hope with Barker that "in a few weeks" she would "be almost back to normal again." Another event that uplifted the young husband's morale was the recent visit to William and Mary of his longtime friend Father J. Elliot Ross. Aware that the Paulist theologian would deliver public addresses in the region, speaking first in Richmond and then to an American Legion audience in Newport News, Castañeda invited the priest "to make a talk" to members of the Gibbons Club. Proud of the campus group he had organized, Carlos informed Barker that the Gibbons Club was "the first of its kind in this institution and naturally Father Ross is much interested." [12]

At about this same time complaints from students about the paucity of library holdings in the area of Spanish language and culture also engaged Castañeda's attention. Aware that the normal process from requisition to accession would require a long time, he turned to student leaders in Los Quixotescos for suggestions. Their group solution was to conduct "a series of three public entertainments," including lectures by Don Carlos, to raise "funds to buy Spanish books for the library." For his lectures Carlos chose the titles "Mexico and Its History," "Industrial Opportunities of Spanish America," and "Education in Mexico." [13] With the consent of their moderator, the students slated the programs for three consecutive Tuesday evenings, beginning in the last week in January. To inaugurate the series "a large audience" gathered in the chapel to hear Castañeda's lecture on Mexico history, which he illustrated with "stereoptican views of Mexico City." [14] At the conclusion of the final program, the club president announced that the series had raised fifty dollars. Not to be upstaged, President Julian Alvin Carroll Chandler contributed a matching amount and asked Castañeda to "select the books which will be purchased with this money." An editorial in the student newspaper, The Flat Hat, acknowledged the accomplishments of the club's moderator: "Professor Castañeda with his lectures under the auspices of the Spanish Club has done his part in bringing about a better understanding of Mexico. There has been too little sympathy and knowledge of things Mexican in this country, lack of which, no doubt, has contributed a great deal toward America's unwholesome relations with its Southern neighbor." [15]

While Castañeda's work on campus proceeded apace, mounting bills associated with Elisa's stay in the hospital presented a new source of financial pressure. To regain partial fiscal solvency Carlos agreed to teach both summer terms at William and Mary for a compensation of $450. Reluctantly he canceled plans for a vacation in Texas. So desperate was Carlos about his financial situation that he sounded out the college administration about "a slight possibility" of obtaining rent-free housing on campus, which would mean an additional saving on his "fuel and light bill." [16] At this juncture, with a view toward future supplemental income, he approached an established publishing house in New York—D. C. Heath and Company—about the prospect of writing a Spanish textbook for junior-high-school students.[17]

Gradually through the winter months Elisa recovered fully from her illness. By mid-April, having survived their first winter in Virginia (which he described as not "particularly severe" but "long"), Castañeda wrote to Barker that he and his family were "just beginning to thaw out and enjoy the balmy spring weather." Concerning future plans, Carlos confided that he would remain in Virginia "this summer and all of next year," after which he wanted to return to Texas. To achieve that goal Carlos sought Barker's advice on appropriate steps for "securing a position either in a college or normal school, whether in History or Spanish." Not surprisingly, at the crux of Castañeda's desire "to go back to some school in Texas" was the welfare of his sisters in Brownsville, who lamented that Carlos was "so far away." Among the "many inconveniences" of residing in southeastern Virginia was "the impossibility" of visiting his sisters "even once a year." "I must get nearer home," he told Barker, "and to do so I must get work somewhere in Texas or one of the neighboring states. Perhaps I ought not to trouble you with these matters but you have always taken so much interes[t] in my welfare that I feel like consulting somebody whose advise I have always followed." [18] Carlos then informed the Texas historian that in anticipation of pursuing work leading to a doctoral degree, he had determined to initiate study in German and French. "Just where I will do my graduate work I have not decided yet," he admitted, "but I know that I must do it in the next two or three years." Meanwhile, acknowledging that there was "not much money in it" but that it made for "good advertisement [publicity]," Carlos disclosed that he had succeeded in getting five short articles published.[19]

Barker advised Carlos to be selective in searching for a teaching position. Firing "a broad side at all of the Texas colleges," the historian counseled, would not "be a good idea," because it would create an impression that the applicant, desperate for employment, would accept just about any position. In the meantime Barker promised he would "try to get something definite" from Miss Lilia Casis of the foreign languages department, "looking towards employment here." More specifically, he held out hope "that we may be able to place you in history and enable you to go on with your Doctor's degree in History." For the time being he complimented Carlos's initiative "in finding a medium of publication" and encouraged him to keep a file of published articles to append to job "applications in the future." [20]

With the advent of the summer session, Carlos directed his restive energy toward an accelerated teaching schedule. Midway into the semester he bid farewell to his wife and daughter at the railway station. Unable to accompany them on a modest vacation trip to San Antonio, Carlos contented himself at the close of summer school with a short train ride to Washington, D.C., for research purposes. Whatever pleasure Castañeda derived from a visit to the nation's capital quickly vanished in early September when he received word from Texas that Elisa had "caught a very bad cold" that developed into "a case of bronchitis." Reacting to the crisis, Castañeda traveled south by train as far as New Orleans, where he met Elisa and Gloria. Upon their return to Williamsburg, the family physicians prescribed "absolute rest" for Elisa, who became "practically an invalid." Once again a bleak fiscal situation almost overwhelmed Castañeda. Acknowledging that Elisa's illness had thrown him "completely out of balance financially," Carlos frantically looked for opportunities to supplement his annual salary of twenty-two hundred dollars. He wrote Barker: "At the College I will have only three classes, but there are not extras here because the College is small and the town is too small for anything. There are no opportunities in the way of private tutoring, or translation, or correspondence work." [21]

No matter how dreary the immediate outlook appeared, Carlos usually discovered tiny signs of hope. While his articles had not resulted in substantial monetary gain, he looked forward, he told Barker, to the publication of a new essay in the October, 1924, issue of *Educational Review*.[22] In this article Castañeda examined the "general reorganization" of Mexico's "entire educational system" since the overthrow of the Porfirio Díaz regime in 1910, arguing that the results of this little-noticed revolution would be "infinitely more lasting" than those of the political upheaval that absorbed most observers. "If," he declared, "the character of the schools builds the character of the coming generations, then we can safely assert that Mexico's future is assured." [23]

Buoyed by the forthcoming publication of his essay, Castañeda initiated a bold plan for a summer program, patterned after William and Mary's successful vacation school in Europe, to be conducted in association with the National Autonomous University of Mexico. Convinced of the merits of the proposal, on October 1, President Chandler invited Carlos to "call by the office" at the earliest opportunity to discuss his appointment as project director.[24] By early November, Castañeda announced that all major arrangements for the summer school had been made.[25] Much of his attention then turned to promoting the new program, both on campus and throughout the country. Aware of Carlos's energetic commitment to the college, Chandler authorized the department to hire a student grader for one of his classes in order to relieve part of the teaching burden.[26]

Although sincerely committed to the foreign languages department and its new ancillary project, Castañeda seldom missed an opportunity to indulge his interest in history. In November he joined Richard Lee Morton of the history faculty and student Earl Gregg Swem in organizing a campus affiliate of the

International Relations Club, a fraternity dedicated to the study of foreign affairs, to be known formally as the History Club of the College of William and Mary. The club, an honorary society, invited qualified students who were either majoring or minoring in the discipline to apply for membership.[27] By virtue of their regular contacts as cosponsors Morton became better acquainted with Castañeda's talents in history. In fact, Carlos created such a favorable impression that Morton extended an unprecedented invitation for him to cross departmental lines as "an honorary member" of the latter's history problems class, which was then in progress. With a strong foundation in Texas and southwestern history, the Spanish professor provided an ideal counterpoint to Morton's American perspectives. Toward the end of the fall semester the campus newspaper commented on the "unusual" team-teaching approach: "In presenting his problems to the class, Mr. Castañeda gives very interesting and reliable accounts of events which have occurred between the United States and Mexico. His views are somewhat different from those of the students, but they give new lights on the issue."[28]

In late December, Castañeda attended the annual meeting of the American Historical Association, which convened that year in Richmond. The meeting doubtless lifted his spirits, because Elisa's health had once more compelled her to check into a Richmond hospital. After visiting his wife Carlos meandered through the corridors of the Jefferson Hotel, introducing himself to delegates and attending sessions where participants read formal papers.[29] On the last day of the conference over 250 of those in attendance gathered to tour Jamestown, Yorktown, and Williamsburg, where Carlos joined them in the college dining room for a luncheon of traditional Virginia dishes.[30]

When the new year of 1925 commenced, Castañeda found ample justification to celebrate. First, Barker in Texas dispatched several copies of the January issue of the *Southwestern Historical Quarterly,* which featured Carlos's translation of Colonel Almonte's report. To his mentor Castañeda replied, "I assure you that I deeply appreciate your publishing it and annotating it so carefully."[31] Carlos then asked Barker to suggest "something new" on which he could work during the year. "It is my intimate desire to keep up my history [research] if possible," he continued, "and I shall be glad to do anything that will keep me in touch with history."[32]

Cognizant of Castañeda's constant financial panic, Barker outlined a plan for translating historical documents that would accrue benefits of recognition for his protégé. "There are several other little books of the period of Almonte's report which, I think, would be well worth translating. I am wondering, however, about the feasibility of a more ambitious project—namely, a translation of [General Vicente] Filisola. This, as you know, is a two-volume history of the Texas Revolution. I intend to make some inquiries about the possibility of publishing such a translation. It might be that a publisher would be willing to undertake its publication and allow you a royalty for your work." [33]

At the same time that the Almonte report appeared in print the *Catholic Education Review* published another essay by Castañeda on the early teaching of foreign languages.[34] The article, which Carlos had submitted with the aid of Father Ross, confirmed the status of William and Mary as the first college to offer modern-language instruction. It also vindicated the academic reputation of Carlos Bellini, the school's first teacher of modern languages. This contribution created such a positive impression on the William and Mary community that President Chandler agreed to pay for "500 reprints and distribute them with the compliments of the College." Castañeda unabashedly confessed to Barker that he was "quite elated over the matter." [35] In late spring Castañeda published yet another article, an essay about Argentine educator Domingo Faustino Sarmiento, which appeared in *Current History*.[36]

Appreciative of the exceptional work Carlos had "done in Spanish," in May, President Chandler offered Castañeda a raise of one hundred dollars for the 1925–26 academic year. In addition to the new salary of twenty-three hundred dollars, the college administration continued providing a grader for one of his classes. After waiting several days to reply, Carlos accepted the offer, pledging to "do all I can to continue to keep the good name of the College and the standards of the modern language department." [37]

Along with writing, teaching, and discharging his other responsibilities Castañeda also worked industriously preparing for the summer school in Mexico City. In an early budget he calculated that an enrollment of twenty students would cover his salary, travel costs, and per diem, as well as other operating expenses, and still leave the school a net profit of $450.[38] "If the thing is a success," he wrote to Barker in February, 1925, "and I manage to get a good crowd of students to go with me, I will make a little money besides the advertisement [publicity] which I will get. If the plan fails it will not be for lack of advertisement for I am doing all I can to keep it before the public." [39]

To promote the summer school Carlos submitted an informative article to *La Prensa*, a Spanish-language newspaper in New York that enjoyed widespread circulation among high school and college educators. He also distributed brochures to colleagues in the profession, mailing copies to about a hundred teachers, in addition to a reprint of his recent article on Mexican education.[40] His barrage of correspondence with various editors resulted in published notices (as in the *Bulletin* of the Pan American Union and in *Hispania*, official journal of the American Association of Teachers of Spanish) and timely recognition in articles of current interest (as in "International Relations of the United States," issued by the American Council of Education). Leaving no stone unturned, Castañeda also cultivated the support of newspaper editors in

Mexico City and Havana, where his group would stop over, who rewarded his initiative by publishing reports of the upcoming educational tour. With every breakthrough, no matter how minor, Carlos kept Chandler apprised.[41]

On June 20 Castañeda and most of the summer school contingent set sail from New York City on the S.S. *Mexico,* bound for Veracruz. The group included Castañeda's wife and daughter, two other William and Mary faculty members—Cary F. Jacob, a Shakespearean scholar, and Cecil R. Ball, an English professor—and fourteen students. In Havana, a routine port of call for their ship, the Cuban secretary of public instruction welcomed Carlos and his companions and entertained them with an official tour of historic places. Reaching Mexico City on July 1, the group checked into the Hotel Metropolitano, their summer quarters, where "four other members" joined the delegation. The latter group included Carlos's older sister María B. Castañeda who served that summer as chaperone.[42]

Castañeda found the task of administering the summer school not without its share of minor problems, occasioned by exaggerated American newspaper accounts of revolutionary violence south of the border. Arriving in Mexico City shortly after President Alvaro Obregón's loyal forces had effectively suppressed an attempted coup d'état by followers of disgruntled Gen. Adolfo de la Huerta, Castañeda and the Virginia delegation encountered many journalistic reports that tended to sensationalize every incident. One morning two young ladies surprised Carlos by curtly informing him that their mothers wished them to return home "at once because of unsettled conditions" in Mexico City, as reported by one of the leading dailies in Washington, D.C. Rather than yielding to pressure created by what he considered irresponsible journalism, Castañeda read one of the published accounts to his class on international relations. The students, protesting against "unfounded publicity," drafted a resolution and sent it to the editor.[43]

To offset the negative effects of strained diplomatic relations between Mexico City and the United States, university administrators scheduled "social Thursdays," based on the Spanish tradition of the informal *tertulia.* On these evenings students under the direction of the department of fine arts presented a variety of regional entertainment for the four hundred–plus enrollees affiliated with the summer program, almost a quarter of whom were American.[44] Castañeda, too, endeavored to increase his students' exposure to Mexican history and culture. On weekends he led excursions to such sites as the National Palace and the castle of Chapultepec; the Desert of the Lions, an old monastery situated approximately two thousand feet above Mexico City; the Shrine of Guadalupe; the Pyramids of San Juan Teotihuacán; and Cuernavaca, which he described in his later report on the summer school as "the beautiful summer resort of the aristocracy and wealthy class."[45]

While working hard to ensure that William and Mary students profited from the summer program, Castañeda also used the time in Mexico to his own advantage. In addition to two classes he had taught before (on governments of Spanish America and on diplomatic relations of the United States and Mexico), he assigned himself to teach a third offering—history of Spanish America to 1820—to enhance both his curriculum vita and his earning power.[46] He also continued to establish contacts in Mexican libraries and archives, where he was developing a reputation as an indefatigable researcher. It was during this trip that he renewed a friendship with Charles W. Hackett, the Latin American historian who had sparked his enthusiasm for history at the University of Texas.[47]

Just before the close of the session, the American students, including the William and Mary delegation, hosted a reception and dinner in honor of the faculty in appreciation for all the courtesies extended to them. The rector of the National University of Mexico, Dr. Alfonso Pruneda, expressed profound satisfaction with the academic segment offered by William and Mary. "Such a movement of international co-operation between old institutions," he declared, "will result in a better understanding and a stronger friendship between the intellectual classes of the two countries."[48] Tomás Montaño, director of the Universidad Nacional Autónoma de México summer school, also praised "the idea of mutual cooperation," while Castañeda expressed appreciation and gratitude on behalf of the American students.[49]

Back in Williamsburg, his mind filled with fertile ideas for another excursion into Mexico in 1926, Carlos promptly sent an annotated report on the summer school program to the college president. "I am glad to say that it was a success far exceeding my fondest expectations," he assured Chandler, "and that the good name of the College will be gratefully remembered in Mexico City because of the work we did there this summer." As an afterthought he promised to dispatch later "a detailed account of expenses showing the balance left in the bank."[50] Although his intentions were honorable, Castañeda, while not forgetful, tended to allow tedious details of basic bookkeeping to overwhelm him. Consequently, as teaching and club monitoring duties took up most of his time, he kept pushing the expense account further down on his list of priorities. In mid-September, acknowledging the value of the annotated memorandum, Chandler congratulated Castañeda's "splendid work" and provided a gentle reminder: "I prefer an itemized statement of money received and how [it was] expended."[51]

Confident that he possessed the financial data, but not necessarily an ideal reporting format, Carlos serenely pursued other interests of the moment. When several of his students, for example, informed him of their desire to reserve "a Spanish table" in the dining hall, similar to what members of the

French class had organized, Carlos immediately approached Chandler with a request that the president promptly approved.[52] By early November, having exhausted the supply of college stationery that in the upper-left-hand corner promoted the Summer School in Mexico and its director, Castañeda asked the president for permission to reorder. Annoyed by the request, on account of Carlos's failure to submit the financial report, Chandler dictated a curt response: "My dear Professor Castañeda, I am not in a position to give approval to any matters relating to this Summer School until I have received a reply to my letter of September 17th."[53] Castañeda waited a week before compiling an abbreviated financial statement showing a balance of $115. Not to be outdone, Carlos began his cover letter with an equally deferential "My dear Dr. Chandler."[54]

While Chandler pondered the contents of the statement Castañeda shifted part of his attention to guiding the Spanish Club, whose members had decided to host an annual banquet off campus at the Colonial Inn on December 12, 1925. With Castañeda acting as intermediary, the students invited Frank L. Crone, former director general of education in Peru, to be the featured speaker. Seemingly unruffled by the recent exchange of letters with the executive suite, Carlos extended an invitation to President Chandler, explaining that club leaders were trying to arrange for Crone to deliver "a public talk in English" in the afternoon of the banquet date on the topic of "Educational Conditions in Perú" for a general audience. The president, a consummate southern gentleman, replied, "I shall put this date on my calendar, but I cannot assure you that it will be possible for me to be present as it may be necessary for me to be out of town at that time."[55]

Adroitly separating the social from the business priorities of the college, Chandler, while not outrightly rejecting Castañeda's financial report, found several ambiguities that prompted him to assess the document as unsatisfactory in its present format. The president affixed the proverbial carrot to his prodding stick: "I cannot authorize your school for the summer of 1926 until I have a satisfactory report for 1925."[56] Hard-pressed to win presidential approval for 1926 and unable to procrastinate any longer, within twenty-four hours Castañeda compiled a detailed two-page report accounting for every conceivable expenditure, including $35, entered under miscellaneous, for "stickers, identification cards, one automatic pistol, one pair field glasses, etc." Evidently the large amount of cash that he carried with him to cover sightseeing tour fees, baggage handling, gratuities, and other incidentals convinced Carlos that a handgun was essential. From his honorarium as project director he subtracted salaries paid to his colleagues ($80 to Jacob for one course; $250 to Ball for three courses), leaving him a net gain of only $223. The overall balance for William and Mary remained at $115, as previously reported. Com-

pletely satisfied, Chandler issued a terse command: "You are instructed to conduct your summer school for next year with the same arrangement with the
College as for the previous year."[57]

While planning for the 1926 summer school, Castañeda continued his
active involvement in Los Quixotescos and the Gibbons Club. In the spring
of 1926 Los Quixotescos hosted two nights of public entertainment to raise
money again for the purchase of library materials. As before, the program featured lectures by Castañeda and "several musical numbers." For his second
lecture Carlos chose to speak on "Bolshevism in Mexico," at that time a matter of some public concern in the United States. The topic coincided with an
essay he was then preparing. Castañeda also assisted leaders of the Gibbons
Club in scheduling the third outdoor field mass. On this occasion he invited
his old friend Father J. Elliot Ross to officiate.[58]

During this year Carlos steadily added to his list of published articles. His
annotated translation of a Mexican lieutenant's diary, which chronicled an
1828 scientific and surveying expedition in Texas, appeared in the April, 1926,
Southwestern Historical Quarterly. Carlos sent a courtesy copy of the article
to President Chandler with the observation that the report was "an important
source for Texas history."[59] In June the *North American Review* published
Castañeda's discussion of the First Pan American Congress, held in Panama in
1826. That same month *The Catholic World* carried Carlos's article "Is Mexico Turning Bolshevik?" In this piece Castañeda addressed the gargantuan
struggle for supremacy then being waged between the hierarchy of the Catholic Church and the national government of Mexico, personified by President
Plutarco Elías Calles.[60] Considering Castañeda's staunch Catholicism, it is interesting to note that in writing the essay he avoided polemics and the pitfalls
attendant on choosing sides. Carlos realized he could not jeopardize the success of the summer school program by writing an article even moderately critical of the host government. Still, as a scholar and intellectual he felt morally
obligated to comment on a subject with which he was familiar. Accordingly,
he focused on the causes of Mexico's state-versus-church conflict as it had
evolved across the centuries rather than on recently reported atrocities, no
matter how deplorable. This long-range examination of church-state relations
led him to conclude that the present strife was political and not religious in
nature.[61] The editors paired Castañeda's article with another by Charles Phillips, an English professor at Notre Dame. Phillips, a former newspaper editor,
had visited Mexico the previous summer and interviewed nine of the Mexican
bishops as an observer for the National Catholic Welfare Conference in Washington, D.C. He slashed Carlos's essay for being too lenient with the Calles
regime, which the journalist condemned as secular, Godless, materialistic, and
Bolshevik.[62]

Although the swirl of scholarship extracted a full measure of his time, Castañeda was not one to slight social gatherings. Immersed as he was in the heartland of the tobacco industry, he gradually developed a partiality for fine cigars and lively conversation. In Newport News, for example, where he conducted extension courses, periodically after class he would become so engrossed in discussions with students that he lost track of time. Or in "sleepy old Williamsburg," amid cigar smoke, he frequently participated in traditional "bull sessions" with friends and colleagues.[63] Illustrative of these excursions was a Thanksgiving dinner in 1925 at Fort Eustis, served on a "bountiful table" and hosted by an army captain in charge of recreation on the post.[64]

Notwithstanding the pleasant life in Virginia, Castañeda privately nursed dreams of returning to Texas. Certainly Barker, his mentor, implied in his letters that serious scholarship in Texas history required hands-on research in archival materials. For the time being, however, Carlos impatiently waited for his Texan friends to initiate tantalizing proposals. Charles W. Hackett, in particular, conducted inquiries within the university community, and by early March these gentle probes resulted in an exploratory letter to Castañeda from Ernest William Winkler, the director of libraries.

Straightforward and almost devoid of ceremony, Winkler approached Castañeda with an offer: "A vacancy exists in the librarianship of the García Collection. Dr. Hackett has informed me that you are planning to continue your studies in history. Does the place named above interest you? It pays an annual salary of $1800. Librarians are expected to work seven hours a day, and are allowed four weeks vacation. Besides being work in which you would be very much interested, it would be right in line with your plans, therefore I've ventured to lay it before you."[65]

While Castañeda pondered Winkler's offer, a totally separate development, one that would have enormous significance for his career, gradually took shape in Texas. The State Council of the Knights of Columbus, a fraternal order of Catholic laymen, had resolved at its 1923 convention to produce a comprehensive history of Catholicism in Texas. The fraternity chose Joseph I. Driscoll, an influential El Paso lawyer and state deputy of the organization, to give direction to the project, which the governing council conceived as a contribution to the 1936 centennial celebration of Texas' independence from Mexico. Driscoll subsequently recruited, as charter members of the Knights' Texas Historical Commission, Rev. Dr. Paul J. Foik, C.S.C., of Saint Edward's University, Austin (chairman); Rev. Dr. Peter Guilday of Catholic University of America, Washington, D.C.; Rev. John Murphy; and himself. After three years of relative inaction, the commission determined in 1926 to implement a long-range plan to research, write, and publish such a study. Aware of Castañeda's interest in archival research on topics related to Texas history, Driscoll invited him to prepare recommendations on procedural methods for the project.[66]

Preoccupied with planning the second summer in Mexico, Castañeda filed Driscoll's inquiry for later consideration and postponed a decision on the curatorship of the García Collection. Determined to stake out the summer school as his exclusive domain, Carlos lodged a complaint with the president's office against a faculty member who had advertised a rival project in Spain. Although William and Mary was not officially associated with a summer school in Burgos, Chandler explained that if students desired to travel abroad the administration could not "take the position that no opportunity will be given them to study Spanish in European countries."[67]

Undaunted by the competition and drawing upon the experience of the previous summer, Carlos recruited Louise B. Hill of the Bennett School of Liberal and Applied Arts in Millbrook, New York, to assume the sensitive duty of dean of women and to teach an American government and politics course, a decision Chandler quickly sanctioned.[68] Another faculty member who joined the excursion was Walter Alexander Montgomery of William and Mary, who accepted assignment to teach three courses (contemporary drama, effects of the Roman Empire and its decline on Spain, and English and American poetry of the twentieth century). Not inclined to repeat an indiscretion of the previous summer, Castañeda prudently reserved only two courses for himself—diplomatic relations between the United States and Latin America, and governments of Latin America.[69] Cognizant of academic protocol, especially in Mexico, Carlos drafted appropriate letters of introduction, for President Chandler's signature, to Tomás Montaño and Alfonso Pruneda, chief administrators at the National University of Mexico.[70] A faculty colleague in the Department of Biblical Literature and Religious Education provided a letter of introduction to the American consul general in Mexico City, describing Carlos as "a charming fellow" and asking that courtesies and kindnesses be extended "to him and to the other members of his party."[71] In view of mounting tensions in Mexico, an introduction to a member of the American diplomatic corps was a precautionary measure. At the suggestion of immigration authorities, Castañeda also asked President Chandler to issue a special document "on official stationery" and embossed with "the seal of the College" identifying him as leader of the William and Mary program affiliated with the National University of Mexico who had resided in Williamsburg for three years as a faculty member and who intended "to return upon the conclusion of the summer session of the said University."[72]

To promote his summer school project among a wider audience, Carlos published an article in *Hispania,* the journal of the American Association of

Teachers of Spanish. Providing a "short summary" of the University of Mexico's Escuela de Verano "from 1920 to the present," Castañeda discussed "the value of the English courses offered there" and emphasized the summer program's "international character." [73]

As he wrapped up preparations for the summer school, Castañeda paused to answer Driscoll's letter concerning the Knights of Columbus project. The publication of a comprehensive history of the Catholic Church in Texas, he agreed, was an "excellent idea": "Nowhere within the limits of the present United States, did the Catholic missionaries work harder, showed [*sic*] greater abnegation, build more permanently, than in Texas, yet when anyone speaks of missions, they never think of Texas, but of California and even Florida. A work such as you have undertaken is greatly needed to bring to the attention of the American people the great work accomplished and the greater still, which was undertaken, by the early missionaries in Texas." [74] Hesitating to go into much detail without knowing the composition and wishes of the Historical Commission, Carlos merely outlined some broad, yet helpful, guidelines for Driscoll's consideration, allowing that the research "naturally divides itself into distinct periods such as the early missionary work under the Spanish Regime, the abolition of the missions, the church from 1810 to 1836, covering both the revolutionary period and the period after independence was obtained from Spain, . . . from this point on the modern history of the church in Texas would begin." [75]

Castañeda then informed Driscoll of his background and research experience, particularly in San Antonio, Austin, and more recently in Mexico City. "At the present time," Carlos wrote, "[I am] collecting some material on the early relations between the Church and the Government in an endeavor to trace the distant causes for the present trouble in Mexico." After suggesting a skeletal plan for compiling and cataloging a massive amount of primary research data to support the scope of the work the Knights envisioned, Carlos offered his assistance: "I am more than willing to cooperate with you in any way possible. I am a graduate of the University of Texas, and though a Mexican by birth, I feel I am a Texan in spirit." [76]

In mid-June, about a week before Castañeda's departure for Mexico, Chandler informed him that the college governing board had approved his reappointment to the faculty with a salary of twenty-four hundred dollars for the 1926–27 academic year. [77] With the promise of that modest increase, Castañeda and his family embarked for the second William and Mary summer school. Capitalizing upon his experience from the previous year, Carlos devoted less time this session to administrative duties and more to teaching and research. He also indulged in social reunions with relatives and friends, such as Luis Castañeda, a cousin who was a physician, and Daniel Cosío Villegas, one of Mexico's outstanding historians.[78]

During the summer term Castañeda received a second letter from Driscoll, who unilaterally authorized Carlos, on behalf of the Texas project, "to secure and send such materials" as he might locate in archival collections in Mexico City and which were not already discussed in secondary sources.[79] Although the invitation to participate lacked contractual security, the letter nonetheless informally associated Carlos with the ambitious project in Texas.

Driscoll's invitation unquestionably became a topic of lively discussion when Carlos once again met Charles Wilson Hackett. During the summer he had several "interviews" with his former professor, who had introduced him to Latin American history. Hackett likely pointed out the possibility of conducting research for the Catholic history project while serving as librarian of the Genaro García Collection. Carlos, however, with two years of teaching experience at the college level, preferred to remain in the classroom where interaction with students was more stimulating. Hackett, a more mature scholar, no doubt viewed the library job in practical terms, an easy chair for a graduate enrollee to occupy while pursuing doctoral studies. At their final meeting the two friends agreed to remain in contact through exchanges of correspondence.[80]

While Castañeda and his group were in Mexico City, the conflict between leaders of the Catholic Church and partisans of the Calles administration continued to escalate. In retaliation for oppressive legislation directed against the clergy, the Mexican episcopate decided to suspend indefinitely all forms of public worship throughout the nation. On Sunday morning, August 1, 1926, for the first time in over four hundred years, the Catholic Church bolted its doors and withheld the sacraments. In several states around the federal district an armed movement known as the Cristero Rebellion rallied Catholics in defense of the church.[81] No doubt newspaper accounts of this revolt, with grim details of destruction and fatalities, alarmed Castañeda. As soon as the summer school ended in late August, amid hasty farewells to relatives and friends, he escorted his group of students, faculty, and family down to the coastland of Veracruz for the homeward voyage to the United States.[82]

With the start of the fall semester Castañeda renewed contact in earnest with his Texas friends. First, he reminded Hackett of their "last conversation regarding the García Library" and the likelihood of securing the appointment. Reluctant to lose the flexibility of classroom instruction, Carlos admitted that the "library position" was not his first preference. Still, anxious as he was to return to "dear old Texas," he asked the Latin American historian to keep him "in mind" for that job or "any other possibility." [83] Then, after a long delay of six months, he dispatched a lengthy response to Ernest Winkler. Instinctively courteous, Carlos avowed that the librarianship offer was deeply interesting; he even admitted that doubtless "the work could be most congenial and pleasant." There were, nonetheless, "several considerations" that needed clarification. Accustomed by nature to maintaining a rigorous schedule at his own pace, Carlos complained that the librarian's job description, particularly the part about the seven hours, was a bit rigid. What concerned him the most was not having time "for any personal work" on his graduate studies. Another issue was the salary of $1,800, which he considered inadequate and definitely not an inducement for him to surrender his "present position" as associate professor at William and Mary. "I am getting $2700 a year here and have only three classes a day. Under the circumstances, you see, it would mean a loss to me of $900. It is true that I would have some time to work on my doctorate, but if I put in seven hours a day, I hardly see when I could do much work for myself." [84] Since the school year was already under way, Castañeda worried about an honorable transition. Specifically, his contract with William and Mary required a sixty-day notice to allow the administration time to hire a replacement. Even under optimum conditions, Carlos noted, the earliest date that he could leave Virginia was not "before December 1st." Finally, to generate serious discussion, he countered with an alternative salary. "Now if you can give me say $2400," he proposed, coupled with two months' latitude to terminate affairs in Williamsburg, "I would be inclined to consider your offer." [85]

In rapid sequence Carlos appealed to Eugene C. Barker, asking him to intervene with Winkler in the matter of a higher salary. Reiterating the main points presented to the library director, Castañeda thanked the senior historian for whatever adjustment might be attained, conceding that he "would love to return to Texas even at a sacrifice." [86]

Barker replied promptly with several observations. First, Winkler needed more time to consider his options. Next, the librarian opined that Castañeda was "too good a man" to remain indefinitely at William and Mary "at a salary of $2400." Then, the historian promised he would endeavor "to reconcile" Winkler to offer a "better salary." Lastly, with regard to the doctoral program, Barker advised Castañeda to weigh carefully the alternatives of saving money from his "present income," no matter how stringent the budget, to enable him to take a year off and pursue full-time study so as to advance the date of graduation versus part-time enrollment after regular work hours for an indefinite period. "Think soberly about the matter," Barker counseled, "and let me have your conclusions while Winkler is puzzling over it." [87]

Keenly aware that in less than two months in November he would celebrate his thirtieth birthday, Carlos concluded that he had reached a crucial juncture in his career. Agreeing with Barker that toiling in the library seven hours daily for eleven months would virtually drain his reserve of energy, he admitted that the "chief inducement" for enduring such an ordeal was "the possibility of working on my doctorate." If such a goal were "practically non-existent" or incompatible with the librarianship, then it would be hardly worthwhile, he concluded, to leave William and Mary "just now." However, if the curatorship permitted him to achieve a "good start" on doctoral studies, then he would not hesitate to postpone the decision "one minute" because the prospect he greatly feared was that every year he delayed would assuredly lower his chances for successful completion. Shifting quickly from guarded pessimism to controlled optimism, Carlos speculated that "once back in Texas, something else may turn up" that would provide "the desired opportunity." One nebulous alternative that tantalized Castañeda for a while was the possibility of searching for "a part-time teaching job" at "some large" unnamed university, presumably in the North or Northeast, where he could pursue graduate study and earn "sufficient" income to support himself and his family. Feigning mild desperation, he promised Barker, "I am determined to get a start somewhere next fall at all costs." Then slowly but with a sense of urgency he informed Barker of the "one possibility" that might enable him to earn supplemental income, the history project of the Texas Knights of Columbus based at Saint Edward's University in Austin. "Now my idea is to try to get the job of editing the material or some such work. You know that in an undertaking of this kind, some person has to do the actual work of getting the material together, copying, rewriting, etc., the real grind." Asking if Barker "could do something to help" secure the appointment with the Knights of Columbus, Castañeda disavowed interest in titles, admitting that he only wanted the job. "I don't particularly care to be editor, call it clerk of the commission, or any other name, the question for me would be the money in it." Not certain whether to approach Driscoll or to write directly to the Historical Commission, Carlos decided to rely on the counsel of the two friends who had influenced him the most in his undergraduate years, Barker and Father John Elliot Ross.[88]

Meanwhile, in Austin the gears of the university bureaucracy crunched slowly. Genuinely concerned about his former student, Barker learned from confidential sources that Winkler would request a twenty-four-hundred-dollar salary for the librarianship of the Genaro García Collection. Promptly he notified Castañeda: "I expect it to be all right. The delay of two months can be arranged if you need it."[89] Also knowledgeable about the intricacies of university administration, Winkler patiently waited for an informal consent before submitting an elaborate document to President Walter Marshall William Splawn formally recommending the employment of Carlos Eduardo Castañeda "as librarian of the Latin American Collection at an annual salary of twenty-four hundred dollars to begin January 1, 1927." A central paragraph in Winkler's recommendation provided a glimpse of the role two senior historians had played in the selection process: "It has been no easy task to find a suitable person to recommend for this place. Mr. Castañeda's age, education, and experience more nearly qualify him for this work than those of any other candidate known to me. He is well known to a number of those who use the Latin American material most, and is recommended by them." [90]

Transmitting the good news in mid-October, Winkler congratulated Carlos, adding, "if my information about you is correct, it means the beginning of a very interesting, valuable and congenial service for you near home." [91] Barker also affirmed: "Winkler tells me he has offered you the place. I hope we can help you toward the Ph.D. in History." Recalling Carlos's earlier plea for special assistance, the elder historian commented: "You are right in thinking that something may turn up if you are on the ground." [92]

As the foregoing events transpired at the university, Castañeda worried that an absence of mail from Austin signified a breakdown in negotiations. [93] By mid-October the arrival of letters from Barker and Winkler quickly brightened his outlook. With utmost courtesy Carlos informed President Chandler of his decision to accept the Texas offer. Somewhat taken by surprise, the president reluctantly agreed to release Castañeda on the first of January "if absolutely necessary," but he preferred for the professor to remain another month to terminate the semester. Besides administrative logic there was another incentive that persuaded Carlos to ask Winkler for a slight delay. By completing the school term, he confided to Barker, "I get half of the summer's salary which means about $300 additional since the salary is paid on a nine months basis but in twelve installments and in case of leaving before the close of the semester I forfeit my summer allowance." [94]

Borrowing a line from Shakespeare's *Julius Caesar,* Carlos shared with a former colleague, Havila Babcock, his hopes for the future. "'There is a tide in the affairs of men, which, taken at the flood, leads on to fortune.' . . . well, it seems like a tidal wave has suddenly arisen on my barren shore of life, and it threatens to sweep by frail bark into unknown and trackless seas." Intertwining memories of his recent excursion into Mexico with thoughts of the librarianship in Texas, Castañeda indulged in a rare flight of fancy: "Even as the swallow returns at the close of winter, have I returned at the close of summer, more like the butterfly that after . . . [its] glorious rioting in the bright sunlight of the tropics, fades and pines away with the first cold winds of winter. But I am no butterfly and much less a sparrow, even for a large stomach. I am back, that is all, back at the old grind, to dream and build in fantasy until next summer." [95] The reality was that the season was neither summer nor

winter but autumn, with less than twelve weeks remaining in which to prepare
for the transition. Whereas in 1923 the trip to Virginia had required modest
planning, accompanied by stress and sorrow, the prospect of returning home
to friends and relatives in early 1927 filled Castañeda and his family with
mixed emotions. Elisa's illnesses and financial setbacks notwithstanding, the
Castañedas, through friendships begun and nurtured, gradually had learned
to like Virginia.[96] Carlos had found satisfaction, too, in his endeavors at the
college. Reflecting on his experiences of the last few years, Castañeda wrote
to a younger colleague that fall: "I cannot help but feel a tinge of sadness in
giving up my work here, for I really enjoy it. I look upon the Spanish Library
of this college as my own creation." In spite of disappointment that "some administrative sources" had not adequately recognized the value of his contributions to the institution, Castañeda confessed he had "become attached to
the old place in many ways." [97] Now, as Texas beckoned, the reality of leaving
Williamsburg formed a concourse of anxiety, joy, and sadness.

With a renewed sense of purpose Castañeda plunged into the tasks at hand
secure in the knowledge that Winkler had obtained an extension for his initial
reporting date, allowing him leeway to depart Williamsburg on January 24,
1927.[98] Carlos met briefly with the college president and the departmental
chairman for an informal round of farewells. "Anyway," he wrote to a friend
in Mexico, "I must say in all justness that the president and Professor Williams
were very nice . . . and we outdid each other in mutual compliments on the
pleasantness of the work at William and Mary, etc." [99]

Carlos's pace accelerated after he received a letter of inquiry from Rev.
Paul J. Foik, chairman of the Knights of Columbus Historical Commission and
librarian and professor of history at Saint Edward's University. Encouraged by
Joseph Driscoll to contact Castañeda, Foik carefully crafted his message to
achieve at least two objectives: first, to lure Carlos into volunteering his professional services to the fledgling project; second, to forge a link in a chain
of communication as the undertaking expanded. His strategy worked. Carlos
dispatched a voluminous reply reiterating his interest in the "praiseworthy"
enterprise, suggesting topical outlines for research, and explaining his upcoming role as librarian of the García Collection. Regarding his own qualifications
to participate in such an ambitious project, he credited simply his "life-long
interest in the early history of Texas and particularly the early missionary
movement in Texas," which he noted "is a great epic in the gallant efforts to
spread our holy faith to the farthermost ends of the trackless wilds of New
Spain." [100]

Castañeda's reply to Foik and a belated note of gratitude to Hackett for his
help in landing the library job manifested curious facets of his personality. On
the one hand, with the priest of the Congregation of the Holy Cross, Carlos

behaved like an obedient Catholic parishioner talking with a benevolent pastor. With Hackett, on the other hand, he assumed a more secular stance, separating religious doctrine from civic life. Referring to a negative response the Latin American historian had received from certain Catholics in Austin and elsewhere in Texas in regard to a lecture he had given on the church-state conflict in Mexico, Castañeda noted his agreement with Hackett's analysis of the issue and apologized for the criticism he had encountered. "I am very sorry that they took it that way, but it only goes to prove the extent of prejudice that exists among Catholics in this country. I fully agree with you though I am a Catholic, and I can only deplore that more Catholics are not more open minded." [101]

Castañeda's own continuing engagement with issues concerning Hispanics and Latin American–U.S. relations became evident in two essays he composed that fall. Squeezed into a heavy burden of commitments was an opinion piece on the plight of Mexican Americans in the Southwest. Published in mid-November in *Commonweal*, the essay implored American Catholics to widen their vision of charity by extending assistance not only to the uprooted in Mexico but also to American citizens of Mexican descent. [102] In December, Castañeda tried but failed to get another of his "timely" essays, entitled "Diplomatic Aspects of the Mexican Tangle," accepted by either *The Forum* or *The New Republic*. [103]

As his stay at William and Mary drew to a close, Castañeda also continued to watch over the affairs of his two student organizations with undiminished solicitude. In November he planned with the officers of Los Quixotescos an annual banquet scheduled for December 11. Carlos canvased friends in foreign language instruction for suggestions on a guest speaker who could make a short presentation "in Spanish or in English on Spain or Spanish America." Ultimately the club invited a "man from Washington," Dr. Antonio Alonzo, assistant chief of the Division of Education of the Pan American Union, who delivered a provocative speech on "U.S. Dollar Diplomacy" and its potential for arousing "masked antagonism" in the hemisphere. Lending prestige to the event at the Colonial Hotel in Williamsburg, President Chandler attended the banquet to welcome the guest of honor. Castañeda, the proud faculty adviser, later described the memorable gathering as "quite a sumptuous affair." [104]

Not inclined to bequeath any outstanding problems to his successor, Castañeda next planned with members and officers of the Gibbons Club the annual field mass for the following May. Under Carlos's guidance the Gibbons Club had flourished, its membership increasing from twelve at its inception to "about fifty" at the time of his departure. Although he would not be present for the field mass in the spring, Castañeda wanted a priest with celebrity status to attract sizable attendance for the outdoor liturgy. Hence, he invited the editor of *The Catholic World* in New York, Father James M. Gillis, C.S.P. In fact, Carlos devoted so much attention to details that he even suggested a complete itinerary for the guest of honor which he expected the Gibbons Club to implement.[105]

With teaching duties, involvement in student activities, and household chores associated with the upcoming move, December was a busy month for Carlos. In addition, as a member of Phi Beta Kappa he accepted an invitation to speak at the organization's 150th anniversary celebration, to be held on the campus of "the mother chapter," William and Mary. Sharing the platform with "such stalwarts" as John Erskine, professor of English at Columbia University, and Henry Van Dyke, recent professor of English literature at Princeton University, Castañeda presented an address entitled "Modern Language Instruction in American Colleges." Shortly thereafter the essay appeared in *Catholic Educational Review.* As a tribute to both Carlos and William and Mary, President Chandler authorized a reprint of the essay for complimentary distribution.[106]

In one of the last social events of the season, just prior to dismissal of classes for the holidays, the students in Eta Circle of Omicron Delta Kappa national fraternity voted to confer honorary membership on Carlos, making him the second individual at William and Mary, after President Chandler, to be so honored. The student presenter declared that Eta Circle followed "the policy of selecting for honorary membership, men who have rendered distinguished service to the college in their branch of activity." [107] It was a fitting tribute with which to close the old year.

The opening weeks of 1927 found Castañeda juggling the calendar to accommodate as many commitments as possible. Reluctantly he began to cancel prior appointments.[108] Before the semester ended, the student newspaper, *The Flat Hat,* rendered yet another accolade: "In the going of Professor Carlos Eduardo Castañeda, William and Mary loses one of its most popular faculty members and one of the most prominent workers connected with the college in recent years. This will not only be a distinct loss but will create a vacancy in faculty ranks which will be difficult to fill." Focusing specifically on Castañeda's contribution to the "Spanish branch" of the modern languages department, the editorial writer summarized the growth in enrollment during his tenure and acknowledged the new prestige that Spanish enjoyed at the college as a result of his efforts. "The excellence of his teaching," the writer continued, "is testified to in the statement made here some time ago upon the . . . visit of the Latin American diplomats when one of their number told a member of the faculty that William and Mary was the only college or university they had visited where students of the Spanish Department had been able to conduct a fluent conversation above common or set forms of address." The student editor concluded: "*The Flat Hat* believes that it speaks for the entire student body and of the alumni who have worked under Professor Castañeda when it says that it regrets beyond expression that he is to leave William and Mary for other fields. It is our sincerest wish that he may look with pleasure upon his stay here. Adios[,] Señor Castañeda."[109] President Chandler reiterated the sentiment: "Your absence will be felt by the members of the faculty, but more by the students, with whom you worked so closely and by whom you were loved."[110]

On Wednesday, January 19, after the semester closed, Castañeda took Elisa and their daughter Gloria, with as many personal belongings as he could pack into their suitcases, to Richmond, where they boarded a southbound train with connections to Texas.[111] Returning to Williamsburg, Carlos finished clearing out his office and packed the family automobile for the "long and tiresome" journey home. "I wish I had some company," he had lamented earlier, "but I guess it will not be easy to find anyone going that far at that time [of the year]."[112]

On Saturday morning, January 22, with the family Ford completely loaded, Castañeda drove by the campus for a final glance at the place where for three and a half years he had invested his intellectual energy. The familiar landmark of Lord Berkeley's statue in front of the Wrenn Building slowly receded from view as he followed the narrow road leading out of quaint colonial Williamsburg. Leaving behind the lower peninsula, he chose a major highway that stretched across the entire length of Virginia. Near Charlottesville, site of Monticello, home of Thomas Jefferson, he admired the Blue Ridge Mountains standing like silent sentinels to the west. Cautiously he turned left to another highway that gradually meandered through Tennessee and Arkansas.[113] As Carlos approached the state line at Texarkana, assuredly he rejoiced and wept at the same time. The tall pines of east Texas undoubtedly reminded him of Virginia, but he knew for certain he had returned home.

The Making of a Librarian, 1927–1929

In the last week of January, 1927, Carlos E. Castañeda, travel weary from the long drive from Virginia, finally arrived in Austin. After renting a modest house at 2304 Red River,[1] he alternated the remaining days of the month between multiple household chores and driving to San Antonio to pick up his wife and daughter. On Tuesday morning, February 1, he promptly reported to Ernest William Winkler for duty as librarian of the Latin American Collection.[2]

The magnificent trove of research materials now given over to Castañeda's care had been a stunning acquisition for the university. In late November of 1920 four delegates from Texas had journeyed to Mexico City to attend the inauguration of President Alvaro Obregón. The quartet included Charles W. Hackett, then an adjunct professor of Latin American history at the university, and board regents Joseph Alexander Kemp, H. J. Lutcher Stark, and H. A. Wroe.[3] Typical of most historians in a foreign city, Hackett, accompanied by Kemp, stopped at a *librería* that specialized in rare editions. In the course of buying a copy of Bernal Díaz del Castillo's *Historia Verdadera de la Conquista de la Nueva España* (1632) for the university library, the two men learned from the bookstore owner that Genaro García, a prominent historian and bibliophile, had died. When Hackett visited the family to express condolences, García's widow informed him that the Mexican government had declined to purchase her husband's collection. As she was in dire need of money to support herself and her ten children, Señora García inquired about prospective buyers in the United States. Hackett hurriedly advised Stark and Kemp of the windfall opportunity to acquire the "finest and most extensive historical and literary collection" in Mexico. Before returning to Texas the regents executed a formal option to purchase the library from the widow, the executrix of the estate. Early in 1921 university president Robert E. Vinson assigned Winkler, then reference librarian and curator of Texas books, the enviable task of conducting a preliminary assessment of the García library. In February, with Winkler's favorable report in hand and Kemp's strong advocacy in support of the purchase, the board of regents voted to acquire the García Collection. Following legal and financial transactions, the university assigned a library employee to accompany two members of the García family aboard a special train that transported "the precious shipment" from the high central plateau to the lowlands of the Rio Grande at Laredo.[4]

When Castañeda returned to Austin in 1927, the García Collection constituted the heart of the Latin American section of the library. Assigned to a desk "in the back of the catalog room," Carlos immediately began compiling a comprehensive inventory of the materials in the original García Collection. The work plunged him into a cornucopia of historical riches. Winkler, describing the collection earlier to Eugene C. Barker, recorded this observation: "In the U.S., Sr. García was the best known of contemporary Mexican historians. He was, perhaps, the only Mexican historian who faithfully adhered to the principles of the modern school of historians, who insist that history must be based upon fact gleaned from the most reliable sources. Sr. García formed his library with the view of making it his workshop. It is the library, therefore, of an industrious, productive, ambitious, and moderately wealthy student of the history of Mexico."[5] This "workshop," Castañeda later reminisced, consisted of twenty-five thousand printed items, "including numberless bibliographical treasures, important files of newspapers, fundamental sets of documentary sources, and rare editions." Among three hundred thousand pages of manuscripts were the personal archives of outstanding personalities in Mexican history, such as Antonio López de Santa Anna, Vicente Guerrero, Valentín Gómez-Farías, Ignacio Comonfort, Lucas Alamán, Mariano and Vicente Riva Palacio, and Teodosio Lares.[6]

Understandably, during his initial days on the job Castañeda experienced a feel of euphoria he likened to being "puffed up," but quickly the reality of hard work removed "all the puffiness" out of him. After a week he calculated that the entire collection consisted "of about 20,000 volumes plus as many manuscripts," a total that he acknowledged was not a "light matter." With one-fifth of the collection inventoried, Carlos projected completion within a month.[7] Ten days later he confided to a friend in Mexico that being librarian was not a "soft job" but that to his surprise he enjoyed the work "much more than teaching," and he vowed that soon he would "get it well in hand."[8]

In addition to the seven hours a day he spent in the library, Castañeda also devoted time to an evening graduate course on the history of Mexico and Spanish South America, offered by Dr. Hackett.[9] All in all, Carlos found his new situation greatly to his liking. "My work here," he declared to an acquaintance in Baltimore, "is wonderful for it is just what I love, books, and the opportunities for study and research could not be better. It is truly a great good fortune for me and I am trying to make the best out of it."[10]

In the ten years since Castañeda first arrived as a freshman, the University of Texas had nearly doubled in size, now boasting a "great throng" of more than five thousand students and a faculty that was "correspondingly large." While tending to his job and class work, Castañeda also reserved time for many of the activities available at a large university. "It is certainly wonderful," he wrote another friend in late April, "to be in a big institution [such] as this. I have heard over a dozen excellent lectures on all sorts of subjects. Among them, I heard Dr. [Rudolph] Schevill of California, who is considered one of the leading Hispanicists in this country. I have also heard some excellent music and seen some very good shows. Life here is much richer and fuller than in Williamsburg." [11]

Even as he immersed himself in his new environment, Carlos kept in touch with various correspondents about projects he had initiated at William and Mary. To one friend he wondered about the Spanish club, Los Quixotecos, which he had left "in excellent condition." "I hope the boys will keep it up," he wrote, "now that I am gone." [12] In August, 1927, Castañeda lamented the decision by diocesan authorities at the Catholic Chancery in Richmond to discontinue the annual field mass. The liturgy had been "doing a lot of good," he wrote to a former member of the Gibbons Club, and its cancellations made him sick at heart. "It was a great opportunity we had to have started the club," he continued, "and to make it a success as we did. I sincerely hope that its good work goes on. When you get to Washington keep in touch . . . with the Gibbons Club." [13]

In his first year back in Austin, Castañeda became involved in similar activities. Soon after his return he accepted an invitation to address the members of Sigma Delta Pi, the honorary Spanish society on campus. Amused at being introduced as "a distinguished speaker," Carlos recalled that only six years before he had been a member of the organization's predecessor, known affectionately as "the old Spanish club." [14] Early in the year Castañeda also found time to assist Professor Hackett in establishing El Club Mexicano. Remembering his loneliness as an undergraduate, Castañeda, now as adult adviser, no doubt influenced the club's statement of purpose, which was "to bring together the students from Mexico . . . to develop a spirit of comradeship and to foster better relations between the two countries." Open to anyone interested in promoting "sympathetic understanding" between citizens of the United States and its neighboring country, the club convened every two weeks for "open discussions" about contemporary problems in Mexico and related topics. Although he could barely afford the gesture, to help El Club Mexicano in its fledgling start-up period Carlos contributed five dollars to its treasury. [15] Castañeda also resumed his Newman Club connection. Two weeks after Thanksgiving, 1927, he made a trip to Baton Rouge for a Newman Club conference, combining the visit with a research foray into some rare documents at Louisiana State University.[16]

While El Club Mexicano and the Newman Club offered students moral, intellectual, and spiritual support, Castañeda often lent personal assistance to Mexican students in financial need. In one instance he wrote to Father William Blakeslee, chaplain of the Newman Club, on behalf of "another deserving Mexican student who is in a hard fix just at present." He continued: "Could you arrange to allow him to stay upstairs with [Edmundo] Mireles as Rubio and I used to do[?] I think the room is . . . [adequate] enough for two and I believe this . . . [student] would get along very well with Mireles. He, like Mireles[,] is getting a small loan from the Rotarians of Eagle Pass. The saving of his room rent will be of great help. Talk to him a while and if you think he deserves to be helped to the extent of giving him quarters with Mireles, do so. I feel that he is all right." [17] At other times he directed Mexican students in search of employment to Sister Agatha at Seton Infirmary.[18]

Removed from regular contact with students in the classroom, Castañeda often compensated by offering assistance and encouragement to those persons who entered the premises of the Latin American Collection. Aware of the friendship Carlos shared with senior professors, Agnes Charlton, a graduate student from Canyon, Texas, consulted him for suggestions on how to proceed with a thesis. "Seriously," she wrote later, "I want to thank you for the many times you have stopped your work to answer questions and give me assistance of various kinds. You have given me much more help in the preparation of my thesis than anyone else. Dr. Hackett was willing enough, but somehow I did not know how to ask him—besides I always rather stood in awe of him." [19] Llerena B. Friend, who worked in the Archives Room adjoining the Latin American Collection, became acquainted with Carlos in meetings of the Graduate History Club. She recalled: "I remember I was having a hard time getting off the ground—simply could not begin with sentence 1 in my thesis, and so I complained to Castañeda. In his excitable volubility he said—'Why just say'—and went on improvising an opening. I laughed and was able to start. Oh, Dr. Barker had me redo that initial start, but at least I had started—and to Carlos I was eternally grateful." [20]

Alert to the various needs of library patrons, and rapidly adjusting to administrative routine within the labyrinth of the university, Castañeda petitioned Winkler in early April, 1927, to install awnings "on the windows in the west side of the section occupied by the Latin American Collection." By reason of the tables' alignment "next to the window[s]," he explained, it was virtually impractical "for . . . students . . . to work in the afternoon after three o'clock, because . . . the sun makes it impossible to read or to write." [21]

While he had resumed graduate study and begun work in a new field, the spring of 1927 found Castañeda, in typical fashion, with still other irons in the fire. Midway through the spring semester, anxious to test the merit of his scholarship outside of the academy, Carlos volunteered to present a paper, "The Veto in Latin American Constitutions," at a conclave of the Southwestern Association of Political Sciences.[22] He also kept abreast of the monumental historical project being launched by the Knights of Columbus. At Saint Edward's University, Rev. Paul J. Foik, chairman of the Knights' Texas Historical Commission, began the task of recruiting a cadre of researchers for the projected history of Catholicism in Texas. "If my wires don't break in pulling them too hard," Castañeda remarked to a former student, "I shall soon be a corresponding member of the Texas Catholic Historical Commission with which I have been cooperating most actively, and ad infinitum."[23] For a while Carlos worried that his *Commonweal* article, in which he had seemingly sided with the government of Mexico in that country's church-state conflict, might jeopardize his chances of securing an affiliation with the Knights of Columbus (KC) project. He gave a thankful sigh of relief, therefore, when he learned in a roundabout manner, just before the spring term ended, that Foik had bestowed on him the coveted membership.[24] In mid-June he predicted confidently to a friend that he would "very likely edit the first volume on the missionary period." However, due to an oversight it was not until early November that Castañeda received formal notification of his appointment as a corresponding member. In his letter to Carlos conveying the belated news, an apologetic Father Foik expressed the hope that Castañeda would "accept this honor as an appreciation coming to you by the unanimous consent of the active members of the commission."[25] The honor was the second bestowed on Castañeda that year, for in the spring the Texas State Historical Association had designated him a Fellow. That recognition, based on his contributions to the organization's *Quarterly,* evolved largely through the influence of Eugene C. Barker.[26]

When summer school commenced, Carlos decided not to enroll in any graduate courses in order to work on other self-imposed tasks, including selected readings that would put him ahead of schedule in the fall semester.[27] Family responsibilities also required his time, as Elisa was recovering from a tonsillectomy she had undergone in the late spring.[28] Whereas, over the years, Castañeda had learned to accept Elisa's delicate health as a way of life, with his little girl it was another matter. Around late May, Gloria contracted measles. She was showing signs of recovery when she ate something that disagreed with her system, in her weakened condition, and serious complications ensued. "The poor child suffered a good deal," Carlos wrote to a friend later, and while she finally seemed well again at the end of three weeks, he expressed the hope that she would "not have a relapse."[29]

During Gloria's illness the work of the Texas legislature compounded Castañeda's worries. Then meeting in special session, the legislature considered,
among other things, appropriations for the University of Texas. For a while
Carlos's salary of twenty-four hundred dollars rested on the chopping block.
"Luckily for me," he wrote a former colleague in Virginia, "they finally decided to leave my salary without cutting. At first the bill passed the lower house
with a $600.00 reduction in my salary and I was naturally alarmed and almost
regretted leaving old Virginia, but in the committee conference it was finally
put back at its former figure so I am no better off, but there is no hope of advancement (in salary of course) during the next two years." [30]

Annoyed at the politicians' theatrics and aware of his own vulnerability because of his status as a Mexican national working in Texas, Castañeda, with
understandable anger, lashed out at critics of the university community.

> The politicians always play to the backwoods people by condemning higher
> education in general and praising the multitudinous blessings of free ru[r]al
> education and the little red school house on the hill. Well, you know what
> Barnum says, "one a minute" and that makes a grand total. It seems that
> people cannot realize that a little education is dangerous. The best proof of
> this old adage is the way the legislat[ors] act. Most of the members are "self-
> made" and had little advantages beyond the grammar school. They point
> proudly at their achievement but never realize how far short it falls of what
> it should be. [31]

With the Texas legislature in adjournment for at least eighteen months and
Gloria's health back to normal, Castañeda, not inclined to remain pessimistic
or forlorn, eagerly looked toward an upcoming vacation. A prospect for
teaching summer school in Mexico, because of money shortages south of the
border, failed to materialize. [32]

In mid-July, however, Castañeda, accompanied by Elisa and Gloria, journeyed to Brownsville, his first visit since 1923. Carlos looked forward to the
visit in part because of the opportunity it would give Gloria to learn Spanish
in the company of her aunts. [33] After a joyful reunion with sisters and brothers and renewing "old acquaintances," Carlos wandered through the town
observing numerous changes. To Earl Gregg Swem, librarian in far-off William
and Mary, he reported, "The old home band did not come out to greet me,
nor were there any public demonstration[s] for the prodigal son." [34] Not long
thereafter he walked across the international bridge into Matamoros to satisfy a researcher's curiosity about extant archival records of historical value.
A preliminary discovery prompted Winkler in Austin to counsel: "This kind

of work is of great importance; do it thoroughly, and stay as long as it is worthwhile." [35]

Encouraged by Winkler's support, coupled with news that the board of regents had approved plans for enlarging the library at the University of Texas, allowing the Latin American Collection to "spread," Castañeda first visited the Archivo del Ayuntamiento of Matamoros, adjacent to the town square. Upon entering the Palacio del Ayuntamiento (city hall), Carlos found a sizable collection of public records "kept in the front room of the Palacio . . . facing the small office of the Secretario on the second floor and immediately to the right of the head of the stairway. They are kept on shelves built along the south wall protected by large glass doors." [36] Devoting more than a week to superficial sorting, reading, and arranging original manuscripts, dating from 1797 to 1925, Carlos succinctly summarized the outcome of his discovery to a friend:

> I found a lot of excellent material related to the early relations between Texas and Tamaulipas and the border troubles that developed later, after 1836 and subsequent to the Mexican War. I did not have time to go over the whole collection, but there is a lot of material relative to the relations of Mexico and the [Southern] Confederacy, for until 1863, when the federals took Brownsville, Matamoros was the chief port of exit for the cotton of the south. I am going to make another trip a little later and finish the revision [evaluation]. We are going to try to get copies of all those [documents that] we may decide are of sufficient historical value. [37]

Satisfied with the preliminary outcome in the municipal archive, Carlos compiled a "rough transcript" to identify the records he had separated in a bundle for future copying. Like a mining prospector staking out a claim, he appended a notation: "Material relative to the Early History of Texas . . . selected by C. E. Castañeda, of the University of Texas, to be copied later." [38]

Proceeding east across the municipal plaza to the Catholic cathedral of Matamoros, Castañeda surely experienced curator's shock as he entered a small room, immediately to the right of the main door of the church, that served as an ecclesiastical archive. For lack of better facilities, church officials had stored the records "in two large wooden boxes set on a table and covered [with] a *petate* [straw mat] to protect them from rain in case the roof should leak which from the appearances of the room is certain. The arrangement is very poor." [39] In view of the documents' rich historical value, combined with haphazard methods of conservation, Carlos urgently recommended photocopying the major portion of both state and church records, ending on a note of concern: "I hope, though, that it is done soon, before something happens that may destroy or make unavailable if not all, at least some of them."[40] To the librarian friend in Virginia he reverted to his usual posture of infinite optimism: "All in all, I think I have a gold mine."[41]

At the end of a two-week working vacation in Brownsville and Matamoros, Castañeda and his family returned to Austin. With a new semester looming, Castañeda faced again an admixture of satisfaction and frustration that his situation entailed. In mid-June he had written to a friend: "My work here is very pleasant but it certainly takes a great deal more time than I had imagined. It is the most curious phenomenon to me. I thought I would have a great deal of time to read and study while in the Library but I find that being librarian means an endless amount of unavoidable routine and trifling duties that take up all the time and leave very little to show for your pains. Nevertheless, I like my work and am learning a great deal incidentally about library work and bibliography in general."[42] After his archival foray into Mexico, he found even stronger terms for his predicament. "My work is fascinating, for I always have loved books and have some of the rarest and loveliest books known in the world on Mexican history. The thing that exasperates me now and then is the fact that the work in the library absorbs my interest so much that I have not been able to do anything outside of my regular routine. In other words, like a great love, the library has consumed all my energies and left me lifeless for anything else."[43]

At the beginning of the new academic year Castañeda enrolled in three graduate courses plus a special reading class in German in preparation for satisfying a foreign language requirement.[44] On top of the library work and graduate studies, and at the urging of historian friends such as Daniel Cossío Villegas and Jesuit Father Mariano Cuevas, Carlos also dedicated extra hours on the job to publication projects involving material in the Latin American Collection. One particular item that attracted his attention, a manuscript from the original García Collection, was a history of colonial colleges in Mexico City by Félix Osores de Sotomayor, a nineteenth-century priest, essayist, and politician. In October the Mexican Ministry of Education informed Castañeda of its decision to publish the Osores manuscript, using the format of the García documents—a series published by Genaro García—and promising to secure permission of the deceased bibliophile's family to continue the numerical sequence of the set with the number 37. Most surprising of all to Carlos was the government's offer to reimburse him for his work at the rate of fifty dollars for three months, mostly to offset the cost of hiring a professional typist, and to provide him multiple copies of the book for personal distribution.[45] While waiting for a decision from the Ministry of Education on the Osores manuscript, Castañeda turned to a project that Barker had suggested during his tenure at William and Mary.[46] The volume that resulted contained Carlos's translation of five documents by the chief Mexican participants in the Texas campaign of 1835–36 along with his introduction and annotations. Published the following year as *The Mexican Side of the Texan Revolution,* the work represented an intellectual triumph for a scholar trying to interpret history from a different perspective.

The whirlwind nature of Castañeda's routine made an indelible impression on historian Joe B. Frantz, who many years later recalled that "Castañeda's life was cluttered. It was just like every morning somebody took it all, threw it up in the air and let it scatter. It landed where it could. He did *everything* [at] just a racetrack pace. There wasn't any time to put up or tidy up." [47] Driven by an insatiable ambition to succeed as a scholar and historian, Castañeda energized his motivation with love for members of his extended family who, through the years, had provided him with unfailing emotional support. Therefore, his desire to accrue royalties, no matter how modest, for his relatives' benefit as well as his own partly fueled his consuming drive to publish.

Castañeda's finances were clearly on his mind in October, 1927, when he advised his elder brother Timoteo, who had opened a grocery store in Laredo, to be extremely cautious in extending credit to customers. For his own part, he wrote: "My work is very distinct from yours, but do not think that I live in the midst of opulence or that I possess a lot, because the truth is that you have saved more than I. I live from hand to mouth, but my social situation requires me to make many indispensable expenditures and, therefore, my salary barely covers all necessities. I do not lack anything, that is certain, but I do not have extra money. Next year I expect to begin saving a little, but at the moment with my studies and frequent trips I have been unable to save anything." [48]

By early November, Castañeda had completed translations of four documents for "The Mexican Side of the Texan Revolution." Work, however, was not the only area in which his full-throttle approach manifested itself. Inclined to celebrate life joyfully and abundantly, Carlos overindulged at Thanksgiving. Serving himself generous portions of every dish, especially turkey, he ate so much that in the evening he suffered what he thought was "a slight attack of appendicitis." Fortunately the pain subsided and did not develop "into anything serious," but the experience forced him to moderate his eating and smoking habits. Momentarily convinced his health was not infallible, Castañeda admitted he dreaded "the very idea of having the surgeon become intimately acquainted with my interior." [49]

As the Christmas holidays approached, Carlos reluctantly accepted Winkler's counsel to delay a trip to Brownsville until photocopying of the Matamoros documents commenced in earnest. Consequently, on Christmas Eve the three Castañedas climbed into the family Ford, badly in need of a paint job and

new front tires, and headed for nearby San Antonio. At the town of Selma, on
the northern fringe of metropolitan San Antonio, a police officer stopped the
vehicle and issued a speeding citation to Carlos. Denying the allegation, Castañeda promptly informed a justice of the peace at Marion that remarkably he
had driven the three-year-old Ford from Williamsburg to Austin without
arousing the wrath of police in the states through which he had traveled. He
could not believe, he told the judge, that his old car possessed the capacity of
accelerating up to "42 miles as the officer claimed." Unequivocally certain he
could not win in a rural traffic tribunal, Carlos threw himself "upon the mercy
of the court." [50]

Back in Austin, no doubt to ease the stress of that unfortunate encounter
with police at Selma, Castañeda reverted to a prior habit of immoderate smoking. To celebrate the final days of 1927 he opened a box of cigars mailed to
him from Virginia. "Those good cigars arrived safe and sound and every ring
of blue smoke that curls up in gentle curbs [curves] and floats away into space,
leaving behind the fragrant aroma of the magic weed brings back sweet memories of not forgotten 'bull sessions' in sleepy old Williamsburg. Now, I think
that sentence is a masterpiece, and I will not spoil it by writing another one
like it. Enough is as much as a feast." [51]

With the holidays over, reinforced by a resolution to achieve marked progress in whatever he attempted, Carlos returned to the library, his schoolwork,
and his myriad projects. Joe B. Frantz, who periodically saw Castañeda walking furiously from one appointment to another, described a colorful sight: "He
was always running into his own cigar ashes. You know, there wasn't time.
[There was] no such thing as a leisurely cigar. This was furious puffing. He
didn't have time to knock the ashes off; he used to let them dribble down . . .
[in] front. Too big a hurry." [52]

No sooner had the new year begun than Castañeda bumped hard into library politics, a nettle against which he would brush more than once in his career. On this occasion the university regents' approval of plans for expanding
the library incited the maneuvering. In the middle of the third week in January, during the lunch hour, Carlos encountered fellow library staffers animat-
edly discussing possible reorganizational changes. Curators of other sections
randomly recommended shuttling parts of collections to different wings of the
building, and the Latin American component became a focal point of the discussion. Angered by the audacity of some coworkers, Castañeda promptly dispatched a lengthy memorandum to Winkler advising against destroying the
thematic unity of the resource. [53] Although the wisdom of his counsel prevailed
at the upper echelon of the library administration, some staffers continued to
harbor a resentment of Carlos that was both personal and territorial.

In the meantime, Winkler asked Castañeda to assess the space currently occupied by both the Latin American Collection and the Texana Collection, as

well as the room both depositories would likely need in the future. Encouraged by the confidence Winkler had placed in his acquired competence in librarianship, Carlos responded with a detailed report. Cognizant of the thematic compatibility of the two collections, he also urged that they be given an entire floor of their own in the renovated library.[54] It cannot be determined with any degree of certitude if Castañeda, in submitting a practical needs assessment to Winkler, realized that parochial jealousies within the library community were bound to surface once it became clear that the head librarian intended to implement his proposal. For the moment the assessment remained an internal working document.

At about the same time he was defending the integrity of the Latin American Collection, Castañeda tried to launch another summer-school program in Mexico. Without consulting university policy on such ventures, he proceeded to plan an excursion that would use San Antonio as a point of departure and return. Determined to broaden the scope of recruitment and publicity, he asked the State Department of Education for a checklist of "high schools, junior colleges, colleges and universities," including addresses of faculty administrators responsible for foreign-language instruction.[55] In addition to drafting a "prospectus" for distribution, he also worked out alternative itineraries as practical options. To a friend at the University of South Carolina he promised a definite answer about the possibility of teaching in the summer program in Mexico within two weeks, hoping in the meantime that the University of Texas administration would bestow its official "stamp of international cooperation in educational lines."[56] After completing final examinations he requested appointments with high-echelon administrators, who in the end ruled against the proposal, even a compromise version of the plan with Carlos leading "an independent group," which would have necessitated "a leave of absence."[57] Disappointed and perhaps a bit peeved, Carlos wrote to Havila Babcock in South Carolina, who earlier had expressed interest in the enterprise.

> The Summer school in Mexico is all off. I tried my D—best to get it going, but there is no chance here. The University is opposed to my undertaking it under the auspices [of the school] and it does not look with favor upon . . . it as a private venture. It is Hell to be poor but worse [yet] to be unable to act even when you have a good idea and know that you can swing it.
>
> Sorry, Old Boy, to have aroused your enthusiasm. If you want to go on, I can give you all the information you . . . [will need] and letters to old friends in Mexico, but I hardly see how you could carry it out without somebody who can speak the lingo.[58]

While the university administrators' decision to deny permission for Castañeda to lead the tour may have stemmed from an inflexibility normally found in large public institutions, as opposed to private corporations like William and Mary, there is also a distinct possibility that smoldering resentment in intralibrary management spilled into the channels of communication, causing some authorities to question Carlos's priorities and commitment to the Latin American Collection. In any case, no sooner was this episode over when Castañeda conceived another educational tour plan, this time to the Caribbean. To Babcock in South Carolina he declared: "Well, I am ready to sail for Panama!" Ultimately, as Castañeda redirected his energies toward a more challenging venture in Mexico—locating and photocopying archival material for the university library—the Caribbean excursion never materialized.[59]

In mid-March, 1928, Carlos sent his sisters in Brownsville a progress report on his various endeavors. He wrote:

> I am very busy. This part [of the] semester that ended in February I did not do badly at all; I took three courses and earned two A's and a B. My book of translations is in press and will be out in October of this year. By January or February of 1929 I shall begin to receive a little commission if it sells well. We shall see. Now I am working on two other books which I expect to publish by the end of this year or the beginning of the next. One of them will be published by the government of Mexico and the other by the University [of Mexico]. We shall see what happens. Neither of the two [books] will earn money for me, but [they] will give me name recognition which later, perhaps, [will help me] to earn money through another endeavor.

Unconsciously amusing when he tried to be serious, given his penchant for a fast-paced lifestyle that sometimes excluded lunch, Carlos counseled his sisters to slow down their work schedule and to safeguard their health by eating a balanced diet that included "vegetables, fruit and milk, which is the best."[60]

For his own part, Castañeda carried forward in a style characteristic of a circus juggler, weaving and leaning as he attended to his multiple commitments. Besides his work as curator and his enrollment in three graduate classes, he agreed—unquestionably owing to the influence of Eugene C. Barker—to present a paper at the annual meeting of the Texas State Historical Association in April. To stimulate interest in his upcoming book of translated documents pertaining to the Texas Revolution, he chose to speak on the subject of "Santa Anna as Seen by His Secretary."[61] After the program, mingling with the audience, he distributed copies of his "publisher's notice" promoting *The Mexican Side of the Texan Revolution (1836).*[62]

That spring Castañeda enthusiastically promoted his first book with friends in distant places as well as closer to home. To an army captain at Fort Eustis, Virginia, he mailed greetings and a sales pitch: "I will send you a personal copy, autographed and everything, but I expect the Fort Eustis library or read-ing club, or whatever you call it, to buy a copy. It is very interesting reading, nothing dry about the book. Even an ignorant private may read it with joy and profit. Now, you see, the old booster spirit has asserted itself." Optimistic in the belief that the future possessed better days for everyone, Carlos tried to uplift the captain's sagging morale: "You say you haven't a ni[c]kle to your name. Well, don't worry, I haven't either. I have an absolute faith in the bible for I understand that somewhere it says that the Lord provideth for the birds of the air and the fish of the sea. As I am a bird of air if not of the air and not such a bad fish at that, I have implicit faith that the Lord will provide." [63]

The spring semester also found Castañeda working to strengthen his ties with the Knights of Columbus. As a corresponding member of the group's Texas Historical Commission, Carlos little by little sought new opportunities to be of service to the small band of researchers. From periodic visits to San Antonio, as well as through other sources, he learned of discussions among conservationists relating to the reconstruction of the church at Mission San José, specifically the dome and north wall that had collapsed in 1868. Concern about the physical deterioration of the missions had prompted the Knights to form a committee in the early 1920s to try to save them. In a related move, by 1928 the Knights had also established the Texas Catholic Historical Society to promote research and writing on selected topics in early Spanish colonial Texas history. Castañeda, whose interest in San José had been stimulated by his research into the contributions of the missionary friars, perceived the res-toration of the mission as a project that could galvanize the Historical Society. He also saw an opportunity for the Knights' Historical Commission to exert moral and intellectual authority in the decision-making process with respect to the proposed restoration. [64]

In April, 1928, Castañeda contacted Dr. Foik, chairman of the Historical Commission, to say that Samuel Charles Phelps Vosper, a professor in the School of Architecture at the university, had offered his services free of charge "in drawing plans and making the necessary sketches" for rebuilding the mis-sion. Vosper had a keen interest in the history of the Lone Star State and had studied the Spanish vernacular architecture of south Texas. Castañeda assured Foik that the architect was a competent scholar who would exert "special care" to ensure that the restoration was "historically correct." "The San José Mission," Castañeda wrote Foik, "will have to be rebuilt and in the very near future. If it is rebuilt without due regard for the historical facts so as to make it a true and correct reproduction of the original structure, it will stand for many years as a monument of Catholic carelessness and lack of regard for their antiquities in Texas. I hope that you can do something towards arousing in-terest in the project in order that we may take advantage of the enthusiasm and good will which prompted Prof. Vosper to make his l[i]beral offer to me." [65] In the end, serious work on San José lagged behind until 1932, but Castañeda had underscored for Foik his interest in the Knights' projects and his willingness to help. Moreover, he had clarified that he had definite ideas regarding architectural integrity and the importance of historically accurate restoration.

Castañeda followed up his San José proposals with an offer to present "a special illustrated lecture" on "the wonderful García Collection" at the Knights' annual meeting in San Antonio in mid-May. In addition to advertising the contents of the collection, and demonstrating before a large audience his knowledge of bibliography and historiography, Castañeda perceived in the conference an opportunity to meet personally with Joseph I. Driscoll, who with Foik was chiefly instrumental in guiding the affairs of the Texas Historical Commission. "It seems to me," he wrote Driscoll, that a presentation on the García Collection "would be a very effective way of interesting all the Knights of Columbus in the work of the Historical Commission; and that seeing the slides and hearing of the García Collection will bring the matter home to many who have not fully grasped the magnitude and significance of the work undertaken by the Historical Commission." [66]

In April, 1928, Castañeda accepted an offer from Sister Mary Angelique Ayres, academic dean of Our Lady of the Lake College in San Antonio, to teach a general survey course in Spanish literature during the summer session. Carlos welcomed this chance to earn supplemental income, an opportunity made possible by his accumulation of a full month's vacation plus compensatory leave for his work in the Matamoros records the previous summer. [67]

The present summer promised to be a full one, for in addition to his teaching position at Our Lady of the Lake, Castañeda envisioned supervising the copying of large portions of the archives in Matamoros. An expeditious copying of such documents, as Castañeda had recommended, obviously excluded direct participation by the University of Texas because of the bureaucracy's sluggish nature. Accordingly, with Winkler's consent, Carlos and Winnie Allen, a library coworker in charge of the archives, entered into a flexible partnership to which they gave the impressive name The Mexican Photo Print Company. As opposed to Allen, who provided working capital and monitored clerical duties in Austin, Castañeda invested personal services, on-site supervision whenever necessary, and "the use of all my influence" in Mexico on behalf of the company. [68] Planning ahead, Carlos recruited an elder brother, Fernando A. Castañeda of Matamoros, as a library employee to perform the actual work of copying the records. Then he ordered a "No. 1 Photostat with Bookholder" from Rochester, New York. To acquaint Fernando with technical aspects of the equipment, Carlos arranged to spend an entire week in

Brownsville, before the opening of summer school at Our Lady of the Lake. Timing the trip to the Rio Grande Valley to coincide with the delivery of the copying apparatus, shipped via Railway Express by the Photostat Corporation, Carlos and family left Austin on May 24 in their new Chevrolet Coach.[69]

Shortly after arriving in Brownsville, Carlos and Fernando stopped at the railroad depot to pick up a wooden crate with the Photostat equipment and then drove across the bridge into Matamoros. At the Ayuntamiento the brothers obtained permission to assemble the machine in a corner of the archival depository where the copying would not impede normal office operations. Next, the resourceful Carlos visited the American Consulate, where in the midst of jovial discussions he persuaded Vice Consul H. H. Leonard to lend assistance to the copying enterprise. Just before leaving for San Antonio, Carlos wrote a letter of introduction for Fernando to deliver to Leonard personally. Reminding the diplomat of his "kind offer" of support, Castañeda asked that Fernando be permitted to utilize a bathroom which was "not in use" to wash the photostatic copies. Concerning the frequency of Fernando's visits to the consulate, Carlos estimated: "He will attend to everything and will very likely have to go in twice a day, once at noon and once at five in the afternoon. He will have to return about nine o'clock to hang the proof[s] to dry. I sincerely hope that . . . [his visits] will not inconvenience you too much." [70]

Trying to anticipate every conceivable problem, both mechanical and procedural, Carlos drafted a set of meticulous guidelines for Fernando to consult for routine matters and emergencies.[71] Before leaving Brownsville, Castañeda borrowed a hundred dollars at a local bank to meet incidental expenses related to the project. In view of his growing reputation as a scholar and librarian, coupled with hometown connections, the bank extended a short-term loan based on Castañeda's personal signature, confident that Winnie Allen would wire repayment within a few days.[72]

Having attended to all operational details of The Mexican Photo Print Company and apparently satisfied with the local arrangements, Castañeda bid farewell to his relatives and headed north with his family to San Antonio. When they arrived at Our Lady of the Lake College, situated on a spacious campus accented by large trees at the western edge of the city, the Sisters of Divine Providence accorded to them a warm and gracious welcome.[73] Castañeda, and to a lesser degree Elisa and Gloria, enjoyed the attention for as long as they resided on campus. The nuns, Elisa later recalled, "furnished a house for the [other UT] faculty member who was teaching at the time—a Dr. [Lloyd L.] Click . . . of the English Department and us. We had a duplex. They [the Clicks] had one part of the duplex and we had the other. . . . We ate our dinner [on campus]. We were furnished home and fare and needs. They [the Sisters] used to have the professors [sit and eat] with the priests, you know, in one dining room. Women teachers and wives of the professors, we had our own dining room. We didn't mix." [74]

After one week on the job at Our Lady of the Lake, Carlos received an urgent telegram from Fernando reporting that municipal officials in Matamoros were reluctant to allow him to photostat records without express authorization from the governor of Tamaulipas.[75] Castañeda immediately informed Winnie Allen about the delay, promising to make "a flying" trip to Ciudad Victoria, capital of Tamaulipas, if necessary, to consult the governor.[76] Meanwhile, he submitted a sales proposal to Sister Angelique recommending that the college library acquire a set of the Matamoros archives. Estimating that the set would contain "about 10,000 pieces" dating from 1797 to the late 1870s, Carlos assured the academic dean that the photostatic materials could "be delivered every two months beginning August 1st, 1928." Altogether, he calculated a cost to the college of three thousand dollars, for which he offered "a special understanding" of a 10 percent discount.[77] Obviously to build up depressed morale caused by the temporary suspension of work in Matamoros, Carlos informed Allen that the nuns were "very enthusiastic about the project" and that he felt "confident that they will get the means some day. It is a question of time." [78]

Always planning for the future, Castañeda capitalized upon his affiliation with the Knights of Columbus Texas Historical Commission to use a room at Saint Edward's University as an intermediate work site for transforming photostatic negatives into positive prints. Happily he reported to Allen: "They will let me use the machine and give me the key to the room whenever I want it. No charges, no expenses, everything lovely. We have to supply the operator and helper." [79]

No matter how attractive the arrangement appeared at Saint Edward's, however, unless the governor of Tamaulipas granted approval, no substantive progress would occur.[80] As Allen pondered Carlos's messages, and the college dean studied his sales proposal, Castañeda telegraphed an appeal to the Tamaulipas executive in Ciudad Victoria, located approximately 150 miles southwest of Brownsville, requesting formal permission to photostat the Matamoros archives. To his brother Castañeda sent special instructions to remain actively occupied cleaning the machine while waiting for a response from the gubernatorial office. "When we begin to work in earnest," he counseled Fernando, "you should devote additional hours on the job to make up the time lost through no fault of your own." As an afterthought he appended an addendum: "Advise me as soon as the governor's permission arrives. Stop by the municipal president's office every day to inquire if the governor's order has arrived." [81]

Wearily impatient at the end of the second week of summer school, Castañeda reassessed the situation in Matamoros. From Fernando word came that evidently a reason for the delay was that the governor had been away from the state capital on official business in Mexico City. On the edge of frustration, he told his partner Winnie Allen: "I am going to telegraph tonight again as a last resort." If that inquiry failed to receive a reply, then he would "make ready to go" the following weekend: "My man in Matamoros [as he called Fernando to avoid the stigma of nepotism] has everything in readiness and is more than anxious to start just as soon as the permission arrives. The uncertainty makes it necessary to keep the man waiting and that is an additional worry to us just now. He has promised to put in extra time at night . . . to make up in part for the lost time. This is not bad." [82] Striking out boldly with another strategy, Carlos drafted a letter commending the photocopying project for the signature of Harry Yandell Benedict, university president; Ernest W. Winkler, director of libraries; and Gov. Daniel J. Moody, Jr. In the event Castañeda had to lobby the governor in Tamaulipas in person, he intended to present these letters to him written in Spanish with appropriate deference to protocol, along with another obtained from the consul general of Mexico in San Antonio. "I hope that we can face the crisis," he told Allen, "and weather the storm." [83]

After asking Allen to secure the signatures for the letters, Castañeda traveled to Austin, apparently to inspect the premises of the family's new quarters at 2008 Red River, just a few blocks from the house he initially rented when he arrived from Williamsburg. That weekend Fernando sent him a telegram to the Austin address: "YESTERDAY THE ORDER ARRIVED. TODAY I RECEIVED WRITTEN PERMISSION. EXPECT TO RECEIVE BY MAIL THE WORK FOR THIS WEEK. ADVISE ME ON REDOING COPIES WITH FLAWS." [84]

Relieved that the impasse had been resolved, Castañeda hurriedly briefed Fernando on a number of pending matters. First, he discussed the problem of stained copies. "I would like for you to review everything you have done," he cautioned, "and re-do everything that is of inferior quality or stained." After Fernando had done that Carlos wanted him "to send all that is finished, via express collect," so that the process of making positive prints could commence at Saint Edward's. With regard to supplies Fernando would need for the work in Matamoros, Carlos promised to order rolls of special paper. "Tell me with ample time what you will need," he counseled, "so that nothing is lacking." Concerning the work itself, Castañeda advised that it was best to copy the documents with great care to avoid making flawed negatives, even if it required more time, because in the long run correcting stained copies would be more expensive. To expedite requests for reimbursement, Carlos asked Fernando to submit itemized accounts on the twenty-fifth of each month so that remuneration and salary checks could be simultaneously processed; otherwise, reimbursement would be held over until the next pay period. Finally, trying to anticipate every technicality of the last phase of work at Saint Edward's, Castañeda cautioned Fernando to make certain the photostated documents had wide margins on the left side for binding. Castañeda advised Fernando that if he encountered difficulties with customs agents while transporting wrapped bundles of copied documents across the international bridge he should contact a family friend, Crisanto Villarreal, who would render prompt assistance.[85]

Gratified that Fernando, despite a frustrating two-week delay, was "working with such a vim" that he had compiled nearly a thousand photostatic copies, Castañeda now concentrated on what was needed to complete the first six volumes of documents for delivery by the self-imposed deadline of August 1. "Everything," he reassured Allen, "is going along fine. I will come up next Saturday early to complete arrangements at St. Edwards [sic] to make the positive copies. The thing now is a go! Drop the letters of recommendation." Listing materials for Allen to order post haste from Rochester, Carlos then indulged in poetic fantasy as he proclaimed to his partner that the business was under way and, "like the proverbial avalanche, it will sweep everything before it, carrying in its wake the rich alluvial deposits of our easy dividends."[86] Meanwhile, in Austin, working in a "terribly depressing" heat wave, Allen collected the letters of recommendation. Notwithstanding the ongoing work in Matamoros, she mailed them to Castañeda at Our Lady of the Lake College for final routing to Ciudad Victoria. She wrote: "Mr. Winkler thinks that it would be a good idea to send them on and let the Governor of Tamaulipas file them in his office for future reference, and it might be a good idea. Anyway they will show you how your project stands in the 'favor of the mighty.'"[87]

On the last Sunday in June, in an evening program at Our Lady of the Lake, Castañeda presented an illustrated lecture on "the García or Latin American Library" to a "large and appreciative audience" in the college auditorium.[88] His multiple activities notwithstanding, Carlos continued from afar to monitor events in the library. "Every two weeks," he told a friend, "I go to Austin at least on Sundays." Although he was preoccupied with summer school teaching in San Antonio and the supervision of the Matamoros project, he never lost sight of the García library, which he "carefully watched" from a distance.[89]

Since the end of the summer term, commencement, and his return to Austin all coincided around July 14, a date that loomed on the horizon, Castañeda rushed to attend to other pending obligations. Notified that one of his married sisters, Elisa Castañeda de Villarreal, was ailing with a heart condition, Carlos promised his other siblings at the homestead in Brownsville that the first Saturday in July he would arrive "around noon" for a whirlwind visit, at which time they could discuss all outstanding matters. Meanwhile, he reassured them: "I am in good health and my classes are progressing satisfactorily at the college, and so I do not have anything about which to complain." [90]

Before long, however, Carlos found plenty about which to worry. In Matamoros brother Fernando, in haste to normalize the work occasioned by the unexpected delay, submitted numerous negatives that were defective, which, in turn, slowed down the final process at Saint Edward's. To save time at both ends of the project, Carlos asked Winnie Allen to return to Brownsville all defective copies and then to contact a faculty member at Saint Edward's, Father Peter P. Forrestal, C.S.C., for assistance in recruiting two male students for her to train in converting negative prints into positive copies.[91] Next, to Fernando he sent an enumerated checklist of work steps to follow in producing photostatic negatives, including suggestions for adjusting the exposure lamp, using pewter basins, painting with enamel the tubs used for washing negatives, and careful handling of chemicals poured into the vats. Aware that Fernando was older than he, Carlos gently offered praise and encouragement: "The University considers you a new employee on the job, and therefore, it is making allowances for your work up to now, but it expects the work to improve in the future. Follow the instructions which I send and everything will turn out fine." [92]

Evidently convinced that the family situation in Brownsville had stabilized, and concerned because final examinations for his students were imminent, Castañeda canceled plans for a hurried trip to the lower Rio Grande Valley. He took the family instead to Austin for a long weekend. Allowing Elisa and Gloria to enjoy a leisurely rest at home on Red River, Carlos took off, dervishlike, for a round of appointments at Saint Edward's and the University of Texas. Undoubtedly he stopped at his "little corner" in the library and affectionately caressed complimentary copies of his first book, *The Mexican Side of the Texan Revolution,* which had just arrived. A quarter of a century later, no longer striving for recognition as an emerging historian, Castañeda described the emotion he experienced when he gazed on the finished product of his labor: "The thrill of that first book will ever remain a treasured and vivid memory. Only those who have had a first book printed can understand this strange sensation of elation. It is akin to the joy of bringing a new being into this world. My line of future endeavor was now clearly drawn. I would continue to work in the field of history, more particularly the early history of Texas and Mexico." [93] Among Carlos's scheduled visits at Saint Edward's was one with Father Forrestal, who offered "kind hospitality" and practical advice for paying the student assistants an hourly wage (of fifty cents to the machine operator and thirty cents to the helper) as opposed to a monthly salary.[94] With that arrangement settled, the final stage of the Matamoros project, from a management point of view, seemed certain of completion.

Rushing back to San Antonio to conclude the summer session at Our Lady of the Lake, Carlos distributed a lengthy study guide to prepare his pupils for examinations.[95] No doubt the experience of evaluating students' test papers reminded Castañeda of his philosophy of grading at William and Mary. Reacting to a teacher who reputedly was "a much closer grader" than he, Carlos opined: "I suppose I was inclined to benevolence in general, but then too much severity in grading kills interest in the subject. The ideal, of course, is to steer a middle course." [96] At the conclusion of the term Castañeda participated in every activity expected of him, including commencement, for which Gloria and another little girl made "the best bows" for decorating the stage in the auditorium.[97]

Back in Austin, Castañeda was pleased to hear from a friend, Father Mariano Cuevas, who had recently dined in San Francisco "with the great" Herbert Eugene Bolton, "illustrious scholar and historian of the Spanish Southwest." Of special delight was the fact that Cuevas had informed Bolton about Carlos's work in the Latin American Collection, including the photocopying project in Matamoros. Earlier, through courses taught by Hackett, Castañeda had formed an intellectual kinship with Bolton; now, through the kind offices of a Mexican Jesuit, he enjoyed a solid connection with the renowned father of borderlands history. Immensely pleased and flattered, Castañeda assured Cuevas that he was "very grateful for what he had done." [98]

Unforeseen at the time, Father Cuevas's reentry into Carlos's life, even from a distance, opened a long period of frustration with a project Castañeda had earlier accepted. This endeavor was Cuevas's multivolume history of the church in Mexico. Unable to continue research in that country because of "unsettled conditions," Cuevas had escaped from the persecution of President Calles's partisans and migrated to Texas by way of El Paso. Eventually making his way to Austin, he introduced himself to Castañeda, who guided the cleric through the Latin American Collection. Describing Cuevas as "one of Mexico's leading historians," Carlos expressed deep satisfaction assisting the Jesuit in finding "excellent material for his fifth volume." An intangible reward for the librarian had been the evolution of a friendship. Father Cuevas, he wrote a friend in late spring of 1927, "will probably stay here about a year. He is a charming man and certainly knows his field. It is a pleasure to come in contact with such a scholar." [99] By the summer of 1928 Castañeda had become editor in chief of an English translation of Cuevas's work.

From an intellectual perspective, the theme of Father Cuevas's history genuinely interested Carlos. At the time his own experience translating and editing historical documents for *The Mexican Side of the Texan Revolution* assuredly boosted his level of confidence. Not entirely without reason, therefore, in the spring and early summer of 1928 Castañeda viewed the editorial task as a simple matter of finding talented translators in San Antonio or elsewhere and later evaluating their manuscripts. Consequently, he had taken the honor of editor in chief in natural stride and proceeded to divide his time between summer school teaching and directing the Matamoros project from a distance.

In late summer, 1928, however, Carlos started to feel the discomfort of his position, especially since the Jesuit persistently emphasized meeting a publication deadline within six months. Under that type of pressure Castañeda recruited several translators, each working with varying momentum and productivity. Supervising this unwieldy editorial troupe, on top of other ongoing commitments, forced Carlos to suspend undertakings of higher authority, if not permanently then certainly for the autumn season. Initially he worked with three translators: Jovita González, who later married Edmundo E. Mireles; Isabel Fineau; and Priscilla H. Buckley. One member of this group produced a copy that was nearly a word-for-word translation of the text, forcing Carlos to rewrite nearly every page of manuscript. Another, who had a "good 'Command' of the English language," performed independently and produced readable translations. A third translator, a faculty member at the State School of Mines and Metallurgy in El Paso, gladly accepted the challenge but soon encountered problems reconciling full-time duties and the pressing deadline. Accordingly, in an effort to expedite the work, Castañeda contracted with a fourth translator, Father Forrestal at Saint Edward's, with whom he shared a special bond of corresponding membership in the Knights of Columbus Texas Historical Commission.[100]

For several months Castañeda also tried to recruit another translator, Frederick C. Chabot, whom he knew only by reputation as a competent student of Spanish-language documents relating to colonial Texas history. At the time Chabot, working on a manuscript about old-line families in San Antonio, asked Castañeda during the summer to provide him with an introduction to the clergy of San Fernando Cathedral, which permitted the genealogist to consult church records. Although the two scholars kept missing each other during Castañeda's periodic visits to San Antonio, occasioned by Elisa's desire to see her relatives, Carlos encouraged Chabot in his work and offered advice relative to publication.[101] Finally, in October, Carlos virtually conscripted Chabot into service after receiving a demanding telegram from Father Cuevas: "ARRIVE MONDAY MORNING . . . PREPARE ROOM IF POSSIBLE THE ONE I HAD LAST FIX THE WINDOWS."[102] Under increasing pressure from Cuevas, who now wanted the translation finished by the end of November, Castañeda asked Chabot to complete the fourth volume, which had been started by Fineau in El Paso.[103] Hoping to encourage Jovita González's productivity, he augmented her honorarium by $100, putting it on a par with Chabot's fee of $250.[104] However, to expedite the revision of Jovita's translation, Carlos secured the services of a faculty member at Our Lady of the Lake, Sister Angela Fitzmorris, authorizing her "to pay the typists 35 cents an hour and get an extra one if necessary." As an added inducement he volunteered to review Sister Angela's thesis and to make suggestions for improving it in anticipation of future publication, possibly in the *Quarterly* of the Texas State Historical Association.[105]

Around the third week of October, before leaving Austin for Saint Louis, Father Cuevas emphatically insisted on including in the fifth volume an illustrated appendix, photographs of atrocities perpetrated by government partisans in the Cristero Rebellion.[106] To Fineau in El Paso, who had notified Carlos of her decision to continue translating the volume that had been assigned to her, Castañeda wrote: "I have tried to demonstrate to Father Cuevas that it is wrong to rush the translation, but he had his mind made up. There have been other issues, such as the inclusion of the appendix to the fifth volume, which is nothing but a collection of horrible, gruesome pictures of the recent outrages committed in Mexico . . . which . . . [detract] greatly from its scholarly merit." For Carlos there were also mundane political issues that compelled him to oppose the appendix. He wrote Fineau, "Under the circumstances, I will have to give up the editorship of the work. It would mean that my name would be placed on the proscribed list in Mexico and I would close the doors upon my return to that country for several years. The whole thing is in a turmoil just now." [107]

As Castañeda struggled with a decision over the editorship, Cuevas's November deadline for the work came and went. With the approach of Christmas, Carlos finalized plans to attend the annual meeting of the American Historical Association (AHA) in Indianapolis. Since the American Catholic Historical Association traditionally met jointly with the AHA, Castañeda invited the peripatetic Father Cuevas, then in Detroit, to join him in Indianapolis for a consultation about the project.[108] Although Cuevas failed to attend, Carlos publicized the forthcoming work among his colleagues and encountered "wide interest" in the project, with several "prominent historians" asking about the target date of publication.[109]

As the work on the book moved haltingly forward, Cuevas confronted difficulties within his religious community that reverberated all the way to the Jesuit superior general in Rome.[110] Essentially, the difficulties involved issues of escalating publication costs and the possibility that the book would exacerbate, rather than placate, the turbulent church-state struggle in Mexico.[111]

In the face of continuing frustration with the pace of the project, Castañeda drew encouragement from the news that the Macmillan Company had indicated a willingness to review the manuscript as soon as it could be completed.[112] The prospect of being associated with an imprint from such a prestigious firm prompted Carlos to reevaluate an earlier decision. "It may be," he told Cuevas in January, 1929, "that I will opt for my name to appear as editor of the English edition. I presume this will not be inconvenient, since after all, I have performed that task."[113]

Progress on the work, however, continued to be torturous. Some translations dropped below standard, necessitating substantial revision, and all five translators fell behind schedule in submitting finished manuscripts.[114] In January, 1929, Cuevas complained that he stood on the verge of appearing "ridiculous" to publishers, who would interpret the delay as *mexicanada*.[115] At the helm of the project Carlos sought to encourage and sustain the author while coaxing and prodding the translators.[116] Meanwhile, the only actual control he exercised was limited to revising the manuscripts the translators submitted after endless delays. Having begun the work, however, Carlos found it impossible to extricate himself from the enterprise without losing status with colleagues who had heard him promote the new edition at conferences. Under the circumstances, there was no other honorable recourse but to proceed sluggishly toward completion.[117]

If the Cuevas project burdened Castañeda with unforeseen labor and frustration, it failed nevertheless to exhaust his energies. At the AHA convention in December, 1928, ever mindful of the interests of the Latin American Collection, Carlos sought out members of the American Bibliographical Society in an effort to "learn what was being done in other Libraries that have large manuscript collections." Motivated by the highly charged atmosphere of intellectual exchange in which he met and conversed with professionals in diverse fields, Carlos secured appointment as Consulting Editor of Social Science Abstracts for the section on Spanish American history. In a subsequent report to his boss, Ernest W. Winkler, he noted: "This will imply additional work, but it will be to the benefit of our Latin American Collection to be officially identified with this new Abstract sponsored by the National Social Science Research Council."[118] Altogether, the experience of attending the AHA convention invigorated Castañeda's dedication to Latin American and borderlands history.

On paper in the graduate school, however, Castañeda ultimately claimed American history as his major field. Earlier, responding to a routine request to identify the members of his supervisory committee for the doctorate, Carlos had instinctively listed Professor Eugene C. Barker, an American historian, as chairman. By the fall of 1928 that arrangement no longer coincided with Castañeda's primary academic interests, which had shifted to Latin American history. Faced with his quandary, Carlos postulated a solution to Henry Winston Harper, dean of the graduate school.

> *I deeply regret that I did not see this anomaly before, but in view of the cir-cumstances there are only two alternatives: Either I make my major Ameri-can History, which can be done by regrouping my courses, and my minor Latin American History, in which case Dr. Barker would be my chairman, or I keep my major as I have it and make Dr. Hackett the chairman, which is the only logical solution. I am perfectly willing to make American History my major if you think it is the best solution of the embarrassing situation which has resulted in part through an oversight of mine.*

Two days later, taking advantage of the dean's absence from the office because of illness, Castañeda withdrew the petition. Undoubtedly, in deference to the help Barker had rendered during his formative years on campus, and also in recognition of the fact that the senior historian was a power broker in uni-versity affairs, Carlos allowed his mentor to remain as the designated chair-man of the Supervisory Committee.[119] Seemingly minor on the surface, the di-lemma signified Castañeda's struggle to emerge as a respected Latin American historian.

This quest for professional identity as a Latin Americanist had been an im-portant factor in Castañeda's amiable opposition to Father Cuevas's proposed appendix for volume 5. In spite of Carlos's position on this matter, sometime around the beginning of 1929 Cuevas secured for Castañeda an honorary membership in the Sociedad Mexicana de Geografía y Estadística. Castañeda, Cuevas wrote, could confirm for his benefactors the wisdom of their decision by sending to them "a glowing description" of the Genaro García library.[120]

In January of the new year Castañeda addressed a large assembly of the Knights of Columbus in Austin, where he also endeavored to promote inter-est in the García Collection. His lecture, "College Life in Mexico in the Six-teenth and Seventeenth Centuries," was based on an Osores manuscript in that collection, *Historia de todos los colegios de la Ciudad de México desde la con-quista hasta 1780,* which he was editing for publication. Motivated by the lec-ture to the Knights of Columbus, Carlos apprised an old friend in South Car-olina of recent accomplishments in scholarship, accentuated by deliberate yet lethargic progress in doctoral studies. He told Havila Babcock: "I have been so busy trying to 'keep the wolf from the door' since I came to Texas or as you might say 'making hay while the sun shines' or again trying *to provide for a rainy day* that I have advanced but slowly on the way to my ultimate goal, my Ph.D. which you conquered so gracefully and with such apparent ease (I say apparent for I realize it is not easy) at South Carolina." [121]

At about this same time Castañeda wrote to inquire about hotel facilities and rates in the Federal District. A contact in Mexico City advised that Hotel Metropolitano, where Carlos had stayed before, anticipated an influx of Rotarians in the summer. As alternate choices the friend recommended the Bristol or the Independencia, both of which had tubing for hot and cold water.[122] As casual and tentative as the inquiry appeared, it signified that Castañeda had initiated plans (at least in his mind) for returning to Mexico in search of documents to duplicate.

Occasionally Castañeda interrupted his schedule, no matter how heavy, to go to Brownsville for a potpourri of activity. In mid-February he made such a trip, partly to consult with Fernando about the Matamoros records and partly to lend moral support to his sisters, who had taken in their niece and nephew after the death of the children's mother, Elisa Castañeda de Villarreal, the previous month.[123] On this trip Castañeda also met briefly with state representative José Tomás Canales and a cadre of leaders who were working to end discrimination in education and employment against Spanish-surnamed Americans.

In the decade of the 1920s, while Castañeda resided in Virginia, Hispanic business and civic leaders, disgusted with pockets of discrimination and segregation that existed throughout south and central Texas, formed alliances with various names in different towns to combat the problem. Representing divergent groups with similar goals (such as the Order of Sons of America in Corpus Christi, the Knights of America in San Antonio, and the Loyal Mexican American Citizens of Brownsville), a loose coalition of leaders met in the coastal city of Corpus Christi during the same weekend in mid-February, 1929, that Castañeda visited his hometown. The Corpus Christi group, guided by Benjamín Garza, proprietor and manager of Metropolitan Café on Chaparral Street, fraternally welcomed the delegations from Brownsville and San Antonio at a labor center called Obreros Hall. From that historic unification meeting of February 17, 1929, evolved the modern League of United Latin American Citizens (LULAC), led originally by Ben Garza as president and Luis Wilmot as treasurer.[124]

Another commitment in San Diego, county seat of Duval, which required more time than had been anticipated, prevented Carlos from attending the organizational meeting of February 17. Instead he opted to proceed northward to Austin, where he arrived at four o'clock in the morning. In a February 17 letter to Canales endorsing the goals of the new group, Castañeda wrote that it was "a sacred duty of all Latin American citizens to take an active part in the social, economic and political development of their adopted country or the country where God has willed they be born." Reflecting the problems that confronted pioneer LULAC leaders, he praised "the splendid work" of the

Brownsville group and extended encouragement to Canales in resolving internal dissension within the Hispanic community of south Texas. He wrote Canales, "Once more let me wish you success in the worthy undertaking of unmasking those who are trying to use the new organization for their own mean and personal ends."[125] Although Castañeda generally remained aloof from internal squabbling, in giving unequivocal support to the objectives of LULAC he earned the respect of a cavalcade of leaders, including Clemente N. Idar and M. C. Gonzales, who continually looked to him for counsel and encouragement.[126]

In the aftermath of the LULAC organizational meeting, Ben Garza invited Castañeda to attend an upcoming convention scheduled for the third weekend in May in Corpus Christi. Not having been present at the February conclave, Carlos consulted Oliver Douglas Weeks of the political science faculty for firsthand impressions of that landmark meeting. Grateful for the briefing, Castañeda sent to Garza a glowing endorsement of the university professor: "Dr. Weeks told me he had been royally treated by you and all the men he had met at the Convention. He is a good friend of mine and is interested in the welfare of the Mexican and his activity in politics. . . . He is making a special study on the situation of the Mexicans in Texas who are American citizens. He is an impartial observer. He is very well impressed with everything and said that he thought you were doing something which is absolutely essential for the improvement of the Mexico-Texan in this State."[127]

Acutely aware of the sensitive nature of his professional employment yet morally committed to social justice, Carlos endeavored to balance zeal with moderation. Illustrative of the latter tendency was his February 28 reply to Garza concerning the possibility of establishing a LULAC chapter in Austin: "I believe it would be an excellent thing, but the element [of support] we have here is far inferior to that of almost any other city. I will study the question and look into the matter before I decide whether it is worth while to try to organize a Council here. If I find there is sufficient interest, I shall try to bring down to the [May] Convention two or three of the leaders here."[128]

Castañeda's involvement with LULAC, although peripheral, constituted an important milestone in his life, for the new civil rights movement would continue to crisscross his pathway in the future. On the one hand, as a Mexican national residing in Texas, and particularly as an employee of the state government, he went to great lengths to remain apolitical. On the other hand, as librarian, teacher, and historian he manifested a deep interest in public affairs, especially in events affecting the hemisphere. Frequently he expressed opinions on current developments, as evidenced by his essays in *Commonweal*, *North American Review*, and *Catholic World*.[129] Intellectually he was courageous; in public action he was cautious and prudent. Activities such as the

LULAC movement were sporadic interludes to which Castañeda directed tremendous outbursts of energy, after which he returned to normal pursuits within the academic environment.

At the end of his second year as librarian of the Latin American Collection, Castañeda compiled a comprehensive report for Winkler that demonstrated his mastery of virtually every detail of library administration for which he was responsible. With regard to the Matamoros project, he noted succinctly that sixty-seven volumes of records had been copied to date, each containing two hundred prints, and that thirty of these had "been delivered to the library and added to the Archives." Citing "various reasons," paramount of which were "lack of time and adequate space," Castañeda admitted, "little or nothing has been done towards calendaring the numerous manuscripts of the [García] Collection." If he could have a library page for three afternoons a week, Carlos wrote, it would give him "much more time for the calendaring of the manuscripts and the arrangement of the maps and illustrations, all of which should receive immediate attention." Castañeda also recommended the creation of

> a special fund to purchase the more recent publications that are appearing and to fill in books which we do not have as they come on the market. I cannot urge too strongly the necessity of a small fund for this purpose, say $500.00 or less that may be used for the acquisition of materials for the García Collection. During the last two years, we have had to depend on the departmental funds for our additions entirely. The serious inconvenience encountered in this respect is that the various departments, when they order a book on Mexico, whether library, historical, or statistical, if such a book is placed in the García Collection, it means that their classes can only use it in the Library as most of our books do not circulate. To permit greater circulation would require more clerical help.

Although the number of graduate students conducting investigations in the García library had declined, there were several serious researchers whose names Carlos was especially proud to include in the report—Wilfrid H. Callcott, Mariano Cuevas, J. Frank Dobie, Dorothy Schons, Jefferson R. Spell, and Gabriel Tous—to which he appended a summary of his own scholarly activity resulting in publications.[130]

Toward the end of spring, during Winkler's absence while at a convention, a serious problem erupted in the library. Lingering resentment of Castañeda ignited in criticism of his multiple external projects, including the Cuevas volumes, which some viewed as "a Catholic work that was wholly unrelated to duties in the Library." The gossip also maligned Castañeda for being a Mexican national and a Catholic. "I never imagined there was so much prejudice," he lamented to Cuevas in Philadelphia, "but now I am convinced. I do not know where this uproar will end, but hopefully it will result in nothing." [131] His tranquillity disturbed, Carlos contacted a political scientist at Bucknell University who had been his office mate in Virginia, exploring possibilities for future employment in Pennsylvania: "Less fortunate than yourself, I have not succeeded in getting my Ph.D. yet, though I am getting near it every day. I have to[o] much work in the Library and as usual I am engaged in two or three different activities besides, so I make little headway in any one direction though I keep advancing on a far flung battle front." Summarizing publications and other professional activities, Castañeda assessed his personal situation at the University of Texas: "I have changed but little, though I have gained much in weight with the consequent solidity of mind. I am beginning to feel aged or mature, but I try to keep engaged in as many activities as before." Then he guardedly asked: "By the way don't you want a good man at Bucknell? Have you a chance to get me in the History or Spanish departments there? Not that I am anxious to move, but I am always ready and open to suggestions that may lead to improvement." [132] Determined to neutralize criticism in the library, Castañeda seized the initiative and asked Winkler for a private meeting: "Certain conditions have arisen during your absence which make it imperative that I see you as soon after your return as you can allow me a few minutes of your time, preferably before you come to your office." [133] Apparently the strategy succeeded, because in less than a week Carlos calmly appraised Cuevas that upon Winkler's return the controversy subsided.[134] Not entirely eradicated, merely submerged, the seeds of controversy and prejudice remained hidden, waiting for an opportunity to haunt their victim again.

Relieved of anxiety over the library situation, Castañeda hurriedly terminated as much unfinished business as possible prior to leaving for Mexico. Cuevas's *Historia,* of course, was a constant thorn. Unable to make further progress with editing the translations, he simply suspended the work for the time being.[135] Excitedly Carlos planned an itinerary of six weeks that included Ciudad Victoria, Monterrey, Saltillo, and Monclova. On the weekend of June 12 the Castañedas loaded the Chevrolet and drove out of Austin toward the Rio Grande Valley.[136] Hardly did they realize that at the end of a long journey tragedy awaited.

Stopping for an overnight rest in Brownsville, Carlos happily combined pleasure with business by inviting two of his sisters, plus the Villarreal children, to accompany them on a family vacation into Mexico. As the family members interacted and amused themselves without his presence, Carlos attended to the primary purpose of the trip, interviewing directors of archives, drafting inventories of documentary materials, and obtaining approval for making photostatic copies. After nearly three weeks on the road Castañeda, not at all exhausted but rather rejuvenated by archival discoveries, sent an incisive report to Winnie Allen.

> I had complete success in Monterrey. They gave me every facility and we can get anything we want from the crowd there. It was just as easy as taking milk away from a baby. Here in Saltillo everything is going on fine. I am getting a list of documents as long as from here to New York. Bolton did not list half of the materials [in his Guide] and though Dr. Barker used most of what he was interested in, he did not copy everything and we should have a complete copy in the Archives here bearing on Texas. Of particular interest is a report of Almonte on conditions in Texas in 1834 which I do not believe Barker used. It is very good. There are so many things of interest I have found that I cannot go into them now.

Delighted by the windfall discoveries in regional depositories, along with news from Austin that galley sheets for an article in the *Hispanic American Historical Review* had arrived for proofreading, Castañeda predicted that following a visit to Monclova the family would return home "in a week or so." [137]

The Castañeda party returned to Texas by way of the Matamoros-Brownsville bridge in mid-July. Intending to rest at the homestead only overnight, the Castañedas prepared to leave for Austin the following day. Unexpectedly, Gloria complained of a stomach ailment which confined her to bed. Worried but not overly concerned since the child usually suffered minor illnesses of a temporary nature, Carlos reluctantly agreed to drive alone to Austin, leaving Elisa to take care of Gloria with the help of the Castañeda sisters. Six days later he received an emergency call that Gloria was in critical condition. Rushing back to Brownsville, Carlos learned from attending physician James L. Rentfro that Gloria had heocolitis, an intestinal infection probably contracted in Saltillo. Although the physician reassured them that the situation was "critical but not hopeless," Gloria's condition deteriorated. Anxious and distraught, the parents summoned a second physician and hired nurses to look after Gloria around the clock, all to no avail. On Sunday, July 28, 1929, Gloria Irma Castañeda died. Shocked with disbelief, Carlos later confided to close friends in Virginia: "She suffered the most painful death I ever saw a human being suffer. When I think of it, I almost go wild. She was conscious almost to the end. My God, what a horrible death for so sweet a child!" The burial occurred the next day at the city cemetery.[138]

After the funeral the Castañedas drove northward to central Texas. Stopping off in San Antonio, Carlos left Elisa, inconsolable, in care of her mother for a couple of weeks, as he had to leave almost immediately for a conference. At noon on Saturday, August 3, Castañeda boarded a train for Charlottesville, where he was to represent the Universidad Nacional Autónoma de México at a two-week seminar sponsored by the Institute of Public Affairs at the University of Virginia. Carlos welcomed the trip as a temporary escape from his grief. In spite of the recent tragedy he acquitted himself well. Later he wrote Chabot that he had "had a very successful trip to Virginia. I covered myself with glory at the Institute, but what was the use of it? I did not go to Chapel Hill, though I had some correspondence with friends there." Not in the mood for professional networking following the conclusion of the seminar, Castañeda returned directly to Texas. In San Antonio he rested for a day and then he and Elisa sadly returned home to Austin.[139]

Heavy of heart, Carlos resumed work in the library sustained by his Christian faith and the support of compassionate colleagues, some of whom, such as Winnie Allen, understood the pain of losing a beloved family member. Allen wrote: "I have been thinking of you so much and wanting you to know how I have felt, but words seem inadequate. Will it be any comfort in your sorrow to have the thought that you have known the most beautiful human relation in the love and devotion you felt for Gloria—always anxious to do everything for her . . . and deriving only pleasure from serving her—no matter what cost to yourself. If you can but feel that the relation has been translated from the human to a spiritual one, then it will be with you always and will continue to grow and thrive as in life." [140] While Castañeda was able to find some relief in his work, Elisa, surrounded at home by haunting memories, succumbed to depths of despair. So serious was her spiritual depression that Carlos pleaded with Father Cuevas to give her Christian counseling.[141]

As Castañeda resumed his old routine in the late summer and fall of 1929, circumstances forced him to deal with an assortment of professional disappointments. One frustration concerned his salary, which the state legislature, meeting in special session, had frozen again at twenty-four hundred dollars for the next biennium.[142] Then, almost immediately after Gloria's death, Castañeda received bad news about the Cuevas project.[143] During Carlos's absence while in Mexico, Father Cuevas, still anxious to rush the work into print, had submitted an imperfect manuscript to an El Paso publisher. Encouraged by the ease with which volumes 1 and 2, carefully revised by Castañeda, had passed critical assessment, Cuevas hoped that the press would indicate those passages in need of revision, thus saving time in a lengthy process.[144] The submission was unfortunately premature because Castañeda, owing to his departure for a conference in Virginia, had thoroughly evaluated only the first seventy-five pages of volume 5. To the dismay of both Cuevas and Castañeda, the publisher, which had issued the original Spanish edition, rejected the manuscript for the fifth volume because of faulty English.[145]

On September 11, bemoaning the fact that publishing arrangements in

El Paso had abruptly terminated, the Jesuit advised Castañeda to prepare an itemized invoice for the balance of the work to be completed while he explored new printing prospects in New York.[146] From that point on the project, in which Castañeda had invested tremendous energy and emotion, rapidly declined to an ignoble end. Successful in locating a new publisher in New York, *America National Catholic Weekly,* Father Cuevas lost editorial control of the entire project, leaving Castañeda and his cadre of translators without input for the final product. Virtually superseding Castañeda as editor in chief without portfolio, Father Wilfrid Parsons, S.J., unilaterally decided to publish "in toto" the first volume as it had been initially accepted in El Paso. However, for the sake of economy in production costs, he condensed volumes 2, 3, and 4 into an abridged tome. Finally, the controversial fifth volume, now tightly edited and renumbered, closed out the trilogy.[147] Obviously hurt by the arbitrary decision and not even being given an opportunity to consult, Castañeda admitted that a condensed publication of Cuevas's *Historia* was preferable to an unfinished project. Trying to salvage a modicum of professional recognition for the long months he had devoted to the enterprise, Carlos asked if he merited a credit line for his editorial contribution. To settle accounts and to answer questions Cuevas, a week before Thanksgiving, arrived in Austin. The Jesuit conceded sadly that Parsons in New York exercised ultimate authority in editorial matters; therefore, only Father Peter P. Forrestal, who had translated the first volume, would receive full recognition for his work. Intermittently in the course of a four-day stopover, Castañeda and Cuevas conducted "a number of long talks" in an attempt to resolve all "past accounts." Personal feelings aside, Cuevas, in light of restrictions imposed on him by Jesuit superiors, presented "all sorts of arguments" and then compensated Castañeda a meager $150 for work rendered, of which two-thirds went to Chabot. With bruised feelings and wounded pride, Castañeda withdrew altogether from the project. Not pleased with the outcome but somehow reenergized by the experience, the former editor in chief of a "famosa historia" succinctly assessed the modified project's chances of success under the rubric of America Press of New York: "I cannot tell for sure that it will be carried out because I have lost all faith in the matter." [148]

In the meantime an ancillary project on which Carlos had collaborated with Chabot attained less than modest results. The two partners had invested energy, money, and time in a high-risk speculative venture to publish a volume of "handsome photographs," limited to fifty copies, which appeared in late summer, 1929. Originally priced at under ten dollars and now considered rare and very expensive, their *Early Texas Album: Fifty Illustrations with Notes* sold haltingly during the Great Depression. Signifying Castañeda's fear of insolvency was a "Bad news!" comment to Chabot regarding refusal notices for

Early Texas Album from libraries in Chicago and New York: "Well, as long
as there is life there is hope, but without a little cash life gets mighty lean!" [149]

Nor was the news good with regard to another of Carlos's books, *The
Mexican Side of the Texan Revolution.* Sales, which had peaked at "over 500
copies" in the first six months, exceeding expectations, declined drastically to
about ninety for the next reporting period. "I do not expect to get a large royalty from the book of this sort," he explained on August 26 to P. L. Turner,
president of Southwest Press, "but it seems to me it should sell at a rate of more
than zero in six months." A strong believer in creating opportunities, he asked
the publisher if there was anything he could do "to help market the book." [150]
Eager to promote the volume in journals of national distribution, as far back
as January, Castañeda had requested that a copy be sent to J. Fred Rippy,
whom he had met in Indianapolis, for an evaluation in a forthcoming issue of
the *Hispanic American Historical Review (HAHR).* [151] Now he wrote to James
A. Robertson, *HAHR* managing editor, offering to provide book reviews for
this journal in exchange for an assessment of his own work in an upcoming
issue. Although replete with reservations, Robertson's response greatly encouraged Castañeda. The *HAHR* editor wrote: "Of course, I will give the book
a good review, if I really think it merits it. You would not have me do otherwise. I imagine it is a first rate book if you have had anything to do with it.
But I could not agree before seeing any book to give a good review of it—that
is a laudable review." [152]

Carlos also turned periodically to promoting the photostats from Mexican
archives. Since the University of Texas was paying Carlos's brother Fernando
to photocopy the materials, one set rightfully belonged to the Latin American
Collection. The second and third sets went to the Bancroft Library in California and the Newberry in Chicago, leaving a fourth aggregate that Castañeda
consistently tried to persuade another institution, either Our Lady of the Lake
College or Catholic University of America, to acquire. [153] In a September, 1929,
letter to Sister Angelique of Our Lady of the Lake, Castañeda broached the
subject by summarizing his recent accomplishments in Mexico: "This summer
I located a great deal of very interesting material in Saltillo, Monterrey, and
Monclova. We expect to begin copying the Saltillo archives within two weeks.
The material is of the most vital nature for the history of Texas, as Saltillo was
the capital of Coahuila and Texas. I found a good many secret reports on conditions in Texas, among other materials. I hope that you can make arrangements to subscribe to our Matamoros Archives and to all of the rest in the near
future." [154]

If Castañeda experienced frustration with various projects, he also enjoyed
some successes in the fall of 1929. By late September he stood less than three
courses away from fulfilling a major requirement, exclusive of the disserta-

tion.[155] Still experiencing much pain over Gloria's death, he confided to his former department chairman at William and Mary: "I expect to do a lot of work this winter. I must bury myself in work to forget and I am determined to do it." [156] Intellectually committed to Latin American history but reconciled to keeping Barker as his adviser, Castañeda apprised the Texas historian of his status in course work and of tentative plans for the future: "By the end of the present year I will have fulfilled my required class work for the Doctor's degree and will have taken my preliminary examinations. I would very much like to be considered for a place in the Summer School as I need the actual experience in teaching history, all my previous teaching having been in Spanish . . . I will appreciate being given an opportunity to teach in the Summer School." [157]

While finishing his course work Castañeda likewise logged additions to his curriculum vita. Besides his *Early Texas Album* he saw the release of *Historia de Todos los Colegios de la Ciudad de México,* which he had edited, and the publication of an article, "The Corregidor in Spanish Colonial Administration," in the November *Hispanic American Historical Review.* He also agreed to evaluate two titles for the *Catholic Historical Review*—J. Lloyd Mecham's *Francisco de Ibarra and New Vizcaya* and Irving A. Leonard's *Don Carlos de Sigüenza y Góngora.* By the first week of December, moreover, he had completed a Spanish-language translation of a report on contemporary issues in the Western Hemisphere. Issued by the Latin-American Relations Committee of the Catholic Association for International Peace, the document aimed at influencing readers in the United States as well as securing placement in libraries of Mexico and Central and South America.[158]

In the nearly three years since his return to the university Castañeda had progressed considerably in his quest to become a historian. No less important, he had gained a conspicuous mastery of librarianship. Proud and protective of the collection under his custody, in December he dispatched a lengthy rejoinder to the Reverend Dr. Foik, chairman of the Texas Historical Commission of the State Council of the Knights of Columbus, who, he felt, had slighted the library at the group's last meeting. Politely but firmly Carlos criticized Foik for "sadly" neglecting to enumerate, or at least to acknowledge, "the 400,000 pages of manuscripts in the García Collection . . . relative to the early history of Texas and a great deal of indispensable background for the missionary movement that resulted in the founding of the permanent missions." Although not as well "housed" as the renowned Bancroft Library, he asserted, the Latin American Collection was "far superior" and more "usable." [159]

Just before Thanksgiving, slowly healing from their grief, Carlos and Elisa reached a major decision in their lives when they signed closing papers for the purchase of a town lot in the Lakeview Addition on West Thirty-seventh

Street, located north of the university campus and bounded on the east by Red River—site of the rented house—and on the west by Guadalupe Street. To consummate the transaction with a solid down payment, the Castañedas withdrew a thousand dollars from savings and then negotiated a vendor's lien note for the balance of two thousand dollars, payable in monthly installments of fifty dollars.[160]

For Thanksgiving, Carlos and Elisa traveled to San Antonio. After the traditional dinner, leaving Elisa with his mother-in-law, Carlos hurried back to Austin to concentrate on studies during the long weekend. In between, catching up on correspondence, he commented wryly to Chabot: "I have been so D. . . . busy that I hardly have had time to breath[e]. I hope that by the end of the year I will have finished all the odds and ends and that I can concentrate on one or two things only."[161] Fully in control of his emotions five months after the death of his daughter, Carlos Eduardo Castañeda philosophically weighed his achievements and setbacks. On the final day of the year, anticipating greater challenges ahead, he shared a cogent resolution with his friend Frederick C. Chabot: "1929 has come to an end, but I have a thousand and one things unfinished. . . . Here is hoping that next year will see both of us near the completion of our ambitious plans."[162]

Appointment with History, 1930–1932

By 1930 Carlos Eduardo Castañeda had reached a watershed in his life. During three years of full-time service to the Latin American Collection, he had learned the intricacies of librarianship. By enrolling in two or three graduate courses each semester he had systematically satisfied several major requirements for the coveted doctorate. The previous year he had received an Edward Disney Farmer Fellowship to support archival research for a dissertation. Finally, with the purchase of a town lot north of the university campus, Carlos and Elisa began once again to move forward with their lives. For Castañeda the new year seemed full of bright promise.

Highly pleased with the improved quality of the negatives being sent from Saltillo, Castañeda frequently visited Saint Edward's University "to use the photostat machine."[1] With the start of another year he resolved to turn "a new leaf" and initiate a "vigorous" sales campaign to dispose of the extra sets of the documentary series. In early February he asked Sister Angelique Ayres, academic dean of Our Lady of the Lake College in San Antonio, for the names of three or four patrons whom he might persuade "to donate the Archives to the College."[2] During Castañeda's visits to Saint Edward's he consulted with the Reverend Dr. Paul J. Foik, chairman of the Texas Historical Commission. Indicative that the two historians were not completely at ease with each other, in a letter to Peter P. Forrestal, another Holy Cross priest and friend then in Spain, Castañeda disclosed that Foik "has become rather confidential with me, but he is always looking out for himself." Whatever personal reservations Castañeda may have had, he nevertheless sought a minimum of professional compatibility with the chairman. "We had a little tilt in December," Carlos wrote Forrestal in another letter, "because in the report to the commission no mention was made of the Garcia Library[,] of my *famous* Matamoros and S[a]ltillo Archives, nor the valuable services I have rendered the Commission in many ways." One positive outcome of Castañeda's insistence on receiving proper recognition for his services was that he and Foik arrived at a common ground of understanding.[3]

Not even a sudden shift in climate in January deterred Castañeda from his work. With a bit of bravado he described to an acquaintance in Chicago the effects of a cold front that swept across Austin and the south-central region of Texas: "You have nothing on us when it comes to the weather. We had over a week of near-zero weather. It went down to four imagine!" While most Texans had "shivered and shivered," Carlos had reported daily for work "at the García," which he aptly equated to "a refrigerating plant."[4]

During this time Castañeda also remained busy with publication projects. When his essay "The Corregidor in Spanish Colonial Administration" appeared in the November, 1929, issue of the prestigious *Hispanic American Historical Review,* he sent a copy to a friend in Brownsville, José Tomás Canales, inviting criticism. Canales, the recently appointed city attorney and a founder of the League of United Latin American Citizens, commented that the article was not only "valuable" but should be required reading for "every lawyer in Texas," particularly "those who practice real estate law."[5]

Buoyed by Canales's comments, Castañeda renewed contact with Father Mariano Cuevas in Mexico City. Exiled from Mexico by the government of Plutarco Elías Calles during the turbulent Cristero Rebellion in the mid-1920s, Cuevas had returned to his homeland "without difficulties" and conducted a spiritual mission at a chapel dedicated to the Virgin of Guadalupe in San Luis Potosí.[6] Remembering that Cuevas was the first scholar who had encouraged him to publish selected documents from the Genaro García Collection in the University of Texas Library, Carlos notified the Jesuit that the next edition would contain the correspondence of Gen. D. Manuel Doblado concerning Mexico's War of La Reforma.[7] This struggle (1858–61) had pitted President Benito Juárez's liberal partisans against the forces of conservatism and the status quo. The publisher, *La Prensa* of San Antonio, scheduled production of *La Guerra de Reforma según el Archivo del General D. Manuel Doblado* for February. This Spanish-language newspaper, published by Ignacio E. Lozano, addressed "upper-class Mexican refugees" who had "settled in the Southwest by the thousands" during the revolutionary upheaval of the 1910s.[8] Before *La Prensa* actually began publication, however, it desired written permission from the university. Castañeda thus petitioned Ernest W. Winkler, director of the library, for authorization to continue the Documentos series that García had begun shortly before his death. He wrote, "This [news]paper will undertake to publish a volume in serial form first and in a separate edition of 1000 copies upon conclusion of the serial publication. The same format used by García will be followed as nearly as possible." Castañeda volunteered to edit the documents, promising that they would be "presented in the proper form and in accordance with American standards for such publications." [9]

In mid-February, Winkler authorized the printers at *La Prensa* to begin daily serialization of the Doblado correspondence, and Castañeda optimistically predicted publication of the book edition by April.[10] Castañeda then initiated a subtle campaign to promote the Documentos series. First, he asked Herbert E. Bolton to write "a brief notice" in the *American Historical Review* announcing "the renewal of this important series of source material." [11] Next, to stimulate interest in the project, he shared with Bolton and Father Peter Guilday, editor of *Catholic Historical Review,* copies of *Historia de Todos los Colegios de la Ciudad de México,* recently published by the Secretaría de Educación. "This volume," Carlos explained to Guilday, "is of particular interest to Catholics in that it is the history of all the . . . [schools] of Mexico City which were in the main . . . Catholic colleges." "It is the best refutation," he concluded, "to the repeated accusation that the Church did nothing for education in Mexico." [12] In response to educators who sent him copies of their theses, Castañeda occasionally shared softback editions of his Documentos series. Apologizing to a nun of Incarnate Word College for not binding one of his editions, Carlos lamented that "a poor librarian" lacked the means "to dress his intellectual children in the garb they deserve." The grateful recipient replied, "The fact that it lacks a binding does not make it less valuable in my estimation." [13]

Meanwhile, in Mexico City, Mariano Cuevas endeavored to repress unpleasant memories of the translating venture in which he and Castañeda had been associated. On the basis of the "Corregidor" article and other meritorious work, Cuevas nominated Castañeda for induction into the Sociedad Mexicana de Geografía y Estadística. Conveying this news to Castañeda in January, Cuevas observed that in his opinion the society had elevated its standards for membership. Pleased with the friendly gesture, Carlos promised to mail clippings from *La Prensa*'s serialization of the Doblado correspondence.[14] The following month Cuevas notified Castañeda that the Sociedad Mexicana de Geografía y Estadística had conferred membership provisionally, pending formal acceptance with the presentation of a scholarly essay. Castañeda discussed the matter with Winkler, after which he informed Father Cuevas that April seemed like a feasible time to travel to Mexico to receive the diploma and deliver a guest lecture. Father Cuevas volunteered to read the essay in the event unforeseen circumstances should prevent Castañeda from making the trip.[15] The honor of membership in the society, which ranked with the Royal Academy of Spain, was a significant measure of Castañeda's emerging status as an international scholar. For Carlos personally, however, an even greater honor was an invitation from the editors of the *Catholic Historical Review* to evaluate a new book, *Mexico and Texas, 1821–1835,* by his mentor Eugene C. Barker. Castañeda readily accepted, and his review appeared in a forthcoming issue.[16]

In February, briefly interrupting his work routine in the library, Castañeda attended a meeting of the League of United Latin American Citizens (LULAC) in Brownsville. One reason for Carlos's decision to make the trip may have been his desire to confront his emotions in the place where his daughter had died. On the trip to the Rio Grande Valley he stopped in San Antonio to pick up an editor of *La Prensa* who was going to cover the gathering and with whom he discussed progress on the Doblado edition. The preliminary sessions of the meeting, during which Carlos had an opportunity to converse with numerous friends and acquaintances, served as a barometer of rising tensions within the organization. Basically the tensions evolved from differences of opinion about strategy and dispatch to reach common goals. Leaving the valley early in order to resume work at the library, Castañeda was absent when José Tomás Canales verbally flogged ideological opponents for lacking the courage of conviction. Renowned for his public battle against the legendary Texas Rangers, whom he had investigated in 1919 as a state representative on charges of reprehensible treatment of Mexican Americans, attorney Canales enjoyed the excitement of political debate. Days later he summarized for Castañeda the outcome of the LULAC meeting, pointing out that if Carlos had remained in Brownsville a half-hour longer he "would have seen the prettiest fight for righteousness in your life." Canales continued: "This was [a] greater fight than the one I made against the State Rangers in 1919, because this was against the traitors who were rendering aid and comfort to our enemies, . . . I licked them good and proper, and there was no dissension among our councils. All remained after the fight and all are loyal to our cause. Isn't this a great triumph? For the first time we have a big fight, and then part friendly after we have punished the disloyal element. This is great!" [17]

Castañeda subsequently found himself in a quandary over LULAC. Philosophically he supported the goals of the organization, but in political matters, including internal struggles for power, he had a temperamental preference for persuasion as opposed to sharp confrontation. Meanwhile, in recognition of their moral support, the LULAC councils conferred honorary membership upon Carlos Eduardo Castañeda and Oliver Douglas Weeks, a political scientist at the University of Texas.[18]

In appreciation of the honor Castañeda suggested to Canales the importance of appointing a committee to compile statistical data about educational conditions, a focus of interest on the part of councils in Falfurias, San Diego, and Rio Grande City. In the course of exchanging views on strategies and tactics, as well as drafts of English translations of LULAC proceedings, Castañeda proposed starting a Spanish-language newspaper in the Rio Grande Valley.[19] Dissatisfied with the lukewarm attention *La Prensa* had given to LULAC events, based on that newspaper's conservative opposition to revolutionary trends in Mexico, Castañeda asked Canales for an "honest and candid opinion." "For some time," Carlos wrote, "I have been watching developments and I have become convinced that there is a real need for a good independent Mexican daily that represents the interests of the Latin American element in the Rio Grande Valley. One of a hundred incidents that I could cite you is . . . your article. LA PRENSA has . . . no news of interest. It is anti-American and anti-Mexican, that is, anti-Mexican Government, thus keeping up the ill feeling between the two countries."[20]

Encouraged by pledges of support from several friends, Castañeda explored legal and technical aspects of the enterprise. From a Dallas company he requested quotations of "best prices and terms" for "a plane duplex printing press, various kinds of types, and general printing equipment."[21] Choosing the town of Mercedes as headquarters for the newspaper, Castañeda asked a correspondent in Dallas for "detailed information" about fees for affiliation with "the Associated Press Service."[22] Finally, with Canales as legal counsel, Castañeda scheduled a meeting in San Diego for mid-April to discuss the newspaper venture with a prominent local physician, J. G. García, whom they needed as principal investor.[23] Despite the great energy they devoted to the project, the Depression made it impossible for Castañeda and his friends to obtain adequate financial backing to inaugurate the venture.

Alongside his work with the library and LULAC, Castañeda also had to contend with graduate school. In February he applied to President Harry Yandell Benedict for renewal of an Edward Disney Farmer Fellowship. Established by the benefactor to foster "the growth of friendship and goodwill between the State of Texas and the Republic of Mexico," the Farmer Fellowships supported field research for theses and dissertations. As one of the initial recipients of this award, Castañeda knew that there was a question within the administration as to whether renewals should be permitted. "When I accepted the appointment for the present year," he wrote Benedict, "it was with the hope that I would be given an opportunity to pursue my studies here for two or three years. I believe that in order to carry out the spirit that inspired the establishment of these fellowships it is advisable for students to remain [in the program] at least two years."[24]

In early March, Elisa suddenly became ill and had to be hospitalized for minor surgery. She remained in the infirmary for over a week, and a harried husband scrambled to find resources to pay unanticipated expenses. The hospital charges "looked like a mountain," he told Frederick Chabot, "and the Doctor has not presented me with his bill yet." Chabot replied that everyone's finances were "rather pressed," thanks to "the famous Republican Prosperity!" When Elisa was released from the hospital, the attending physician advised that she be confined to bed "for a week or ten days more," and Carlos confided to Father Cuevas that it would probably be one or two months before she fully recovered.[25] A factor that seemed to be hindering Elisa's recovery was not physical but emotional. Although his wife was "getting along fairly well," Carlos told a history colleague in Chicago, she still grieved "excessively," and he was unable to lift her spirits. He said, "I have tried everything, but I cannot make her take a new interest in life."[26]

While Elisa was recuperating, Father Peter Guilday extended an invitation for Castañeda to participate in the annual conference of the American Catholic Historical Association (ACHA) in Boston in December. As a faculty member at Catholic University of America in Washington, D.C., Guilday recognized the time constraints that frequently encumbered academicians: "No doubt like the rest of us, you have to weigh such invitations from two standpoints of time and money. . . . but I hope you can see your way to overcome both difficulties."[27]

Flattered by the invitation to perform at a national convention before some of the leading Catholic historians, Castañeda carefully evaluated his precarious financial situation. Perennially optimistic even in the most trying circumstances, he promptly accepted. "I have thought the matter over," he informed Guilday in early April, "and believe that I will be able to get the University to pay either part or the whole expense of the trip." Associating himself with Bolton's borderlands, he proposed as a tentative title for his essay "The Spanish Southwest and the Cross." He explained, "It is my intention to take up the openings of the Spanish Southwest, pointing out the prominent part played by the religious fervor and the [Spaniards'] strong desire to spread the faith to the tribes of the unexplored wastes of Norther[n] and eastern New Spain."[28] Subsequently Castañeda changed the title to "Influence of Missionary Fervor in the Exploration of the Southwest"[29] and then later to "Earliest Catholic Activities in Texas." The essay, he told Guilday in September, would be based on "original accounts" in the Latin American Collection revealing missionary initiatives that predate by at least fifty years the exploration of Alonso de León and Fray Damián Massanet in 1689, an expedition scholars previously had accepted as "the first effort to establish and preach the Catholic faith in Texas."[30]

In the spring, accompanied by the chairman of the Spanish department, Elmer Richard Sims, Castañeda drove north to Temple to deliver a keynote address to the Central Texas chapter of the Association of Secondary Teachers of Spanish. In the auditorium of Temple Junior College, Castañeda expounded on the topic of "Problems in the Instruction of Modern Languages." At a banquet afterward he exchanged views and greetings with the teachers. Recalling his teaching experience at William and Mary, Carlos avowed to a friend in Chicago, "You see, I am getting recognized as a leader in the Spanish field." [31]

At about this time Castañeda slightly reformed his lifestyle by abandoning cigars and taking up pipe smoking. "It is more pleasant," he admitted to Father Forrestal in Spain, "at least for the pocket." As he prepared for his trip to Mexico City, where he would deliver his paper on Texas cartography to the Sociedad Mexicana de Geografía y Estadística, he commented: "It is getting pretty hot now. I have to force myself to work, but I am keeping my nose right down to the grind stone." [32]

In late April, with modest but adequate financial support from the library, Castañeda boarded a train for the border. Elisa had decided not to make the trip. At Laredo, where all passengers bound for Mexico City transferred to another train, Carlos sent a telegram to Father Cuevas advising the Jesuit of his imminent arrival. Upon reaching "the old Aztec capital" Castañeda plunged into a swirl of social events, taking advantage of inexpensive cabs to get around the sprawling metropolis. Among the "scores of interesting people" Carlos met was Luis González Obregón, a prominent historian and author of *México Viego* and *Las calles de México,* who invited him to visit his library and office. Comfortable among Mexico's intellectual elite, Castañeda remained in the capital an entire week, never at a loss for company or entertainment.[33]

Afterward, describing his recent trip to Father Guilday, Carlos wrote: "I was most agreeably impressed with conditions in Mexico. I found the church question practically settled. The churches are crowded, Catholic schools are operating without interference, and there is a decided effort on the part of the government officials to avoid and to check all radical action." [34]

In May, Castañeda was highly pleased to learn that the university administration had given him an appointment to teach in the first session of summer school. The opportunity occurred, in part, because Professor Hackett was spending the year in California at Stanford University. In order to accept the job, which paid three hundred dollars for two courses, Castañeda asked Ernest Winkler for a leave of absence for six weeks. Eager to acquire teaching experience in history, Carlos agreed to offer a course on France under the Bourbons and colonial Latin America.[35]

As he waited for the start of summer school the burden of full-time librarianship, studying for the "last two examinations" in course work, and family responsibilities bore down heavily upon Castañeda. A week before the examinations he confided to a close friend in Williamsburg: "I do not know whether it is because I am tired or whether experience is beginning to sour me. I feel downcast and despondent. I am not as optimistic as I used to be. Mrs. Castañeda has not been in very good health. Her old trouble is not bothering her, but her nerves are all unstrung and she persists, . . . in grieving for our little girl. I try to forget all my troubles by burying myself in work, but it is getting to be a losing fight, because . . . the strain is beginning to tell on me." [36] Some of Castañeda's despondency obviously stemmed from Elisa's delicate mental health, but most of it emanated from his tendency to overburden himself with commitments. In addition to all his other work he served as faculty sponsor for El Club Latino Americano and belonged to three supervisory committees in the Spanish department related to master's theses. "I am spreading myself too much," he admitted. [37] To another friend in Virginia, with whom he discussed the possibility of a return engagement in late summer with the Institute of Public Affairs in Charlottesville, Castañeda speculated that conceivably he was having an "off day." Nevertheless, he promised to moderate his work schedule: "I am going to cut . . . my superfluous occupations and settle down to the essentials." Since he had completed "class requirements for the doctorate," the principal challenge would be writing the dissertation. [38]

Coincidental with final exams and the start of summer school, Castañeda succumbed to an ailment that confined him to sickbed for a whole week. Although the malady did not restrict his activities for long, it was serious enough to require the consultation of a physician. A few weeks later, not fully recovered but trapped by the intensity of summer school, Castañeda informed Chabot: "I am not very peppy since I got up. Work has crowded up and I cannot dig out of it." For an individual accustomed to an active schedule, recuperation was probably worse than the sickness. Admitting he was "almost lifeless," Castañeda worried about his low "vitality" level. [39]

Contributing further to his anxiety was the depressed condition of the American economy. If Chabot thought that he was in a "hard financial" bind, Carlos wrote that he was in a virtual "panic." Listless though he was, Carlos offered sympathy to his friend: "There is no question that financial crash affected the big and little fry alike. Sorry you were caught." [40] Still struggling to advance financially, Castañeda at some point invited Early Martin, Jr., to collaborate in another speculative venture, the publication of *Three Manuscript Maps of Texas by Stephen F. Austin*. The book was released in 1930 in an edition limited to fifty-five copies, which Carlos had to promote single-handedly. [41]

During the summer of 1930 Castañeda developed an interest in applying for a vacant faculty position in Spanish at the College of William and Mary, an opening created by the sudden resignation of his friend and former chairman Arthur George Williams. Responding to an alert from a friend in Newport News, Virginia, Castañeda promptly sent a telegram to President J. A. C. Chandler in Williamsburg. In a letter of application he reminded Chandler that he had "been working steadily" toward the doctorate and had finished "all work" except the dissertation. At the University of Texas, Carlos informed the president, he had "continued the study of Spanish and Latin American history." As to the quality of his work, Chandler had become "acquainted with it during the three and a half years" Castañeda taught at William and Mary.[42] Despite a concerted effort, time and distance worked against Castañeda's desire to return to southeastern Virginia. While Carlos preferred waiting until August to schedule an interview in Williamsburg, when he would be in Charlottesville at the Institute of Public Affairs, Chandler wanted to make a decision as soon as possible. The president terminated the search in mid-July when he hired an experienced instructor at Randolph-Macon College in nearby Ashland.[43]

Disappointed but not distressed, Castañeda pushed aside the William and Mary episode and concentrated on his travel plans to professional meetings. His chief concern was getting released time from the library. The trip to Mexico constituted one major absence from work on official business; the December conference of the American Catholic Historical Association in Boston represented another leave. If he attended the upcoming institute at the University of Virginia, it would be a third trip, which meant that "altogether" he would be absent from the Latin American Collection for "about a month and a half."[44] With these considerations in mind, during his sojourn in Mexico City, Castañeda had drafted an agreement with officials of the Universidad Nacional Autónoma de México concerning sponsorship and travel support to Virginia, which he held in reserve. While convalescing from his illness Castañeda advised President Benedict that during his vacation he planned "to attend the Institute of Public Affairs held in Charlottesville under the auspices of the University of Virginia as a representative of the University of Mexico at the Round Table on 'Our Latin American Relations.'" Benedict approved of Carlos's suggestion that he also be appointed to represent the University of Texas,[45] thus giving Castañeda dual credentials. Additionally, Carlos tried to persuade an editor of La Prensa in San Antonio to appoint him as correspondent at the conference, reporting either by air mail or telegram.[46]

To reduce expenses Castañeda decided to drive his "faithful Chevy" to Virginia, accompanied by Elisa and her sister Carmen Ríos.[47] Exhausted by the long journey, the trio arrived in Charlottesville on August 5. So weak he could barely stand, Castañeda managed to register at the conference and obtain accommodations for Elisa and Carmen. Unable to proceed further, he asked to be taken to a local hospital, where attending physicians diagnosed his illness as typhoid fever. Carlos had evidently contracted the typhoid bacillus either in Mexico or in Austin shortly after his return. In any case, since the incubation extended over a period of several weeks, physicians could not treat it un-

til the symptoms became apparent in Charlottesville. Confined to a hospital
bed, Castañeda became exasperated and livid that the medical staff would not
grant him temporary leave to present his paper. Near the end of the two-week
conference Elisa Castañeda, aware of her husband's determination to keep
the appointment, hid his clothes the day before his session. An hour before he
was scheduled to speak she arrived at the hospital and "found him, in paja-
mas and dressing gown, in a wheelchair preparing to leave for the Institute."
With firm determination she and the nurses prevented Carlos from leaving the
premises.[48]

Under the circumstances institute directors recruited Clarence Haring of
Harvard to read Castañeda's paper, which was written in longhand. The essay dealt with problems related to Mexican immigration, which the author
declared were "neither social nor moral" but "purely economic" and required
resolution by the American public. Castañeda's postulations were so forceful
that they attracted the attention of Associated Press journalists, who transmitted a synopsis of his essay via wire service to newspapers in Texas. On the
same day that Haring read Castañeda's remarks in Charlottesville, Ernest
Winkler and others in the library read them in a late edition of the San Antonio Express: "It is a nation's right and duty to protect the interests of its nationals. If Mexican immigration is in fact prejudicial to the best American
interests, if it is unnecessary, if it threatens to fill the Southwest with an undesirable class such as Europe did in 1920, the United States has not only the
right but the obligation to adopt any measure it sees fit to protect the interests
of its nationals." Castañeda suddenly shifted gears and sharply denied that
the Mexican laborer was inferior to other immigrants or that the Mexican
American made a poor citizen. "It cannot be proved," he asserted, "that the
average Mexican American is inferior, either mentally or physically." The
source of such irresponsible charges, he concluded, was American organized
labor, which stereotyped the Mexican, as it did all other immigrants, as "a
menace."[49] Confined to the hospital, Castañeda missed the lively interaction
among the participants as well as the "chance to get into the arguments."[50]
In Austin, Winkler clipped the Associated Press article, which he mailed to
Carlos with cryptic approval: "Thought you would like to know the Express
took notice of this paper." Concerned about the health of his peripatetic librarian, Winkler appended a note of advice: "Hope you are doing well—
it may seem to you [like] doing nothing—but when one has his foot in a trap
like typhoid there's no good in rearing and scotching. You're up against an en-
durance test—your patience and will power against the germs."[51]

A few days after the close of the institute hospital physicians, satisfied with
Castañeda's progress, released him for outpatient convalescence. Referring to
himself as "a knight errant trekking through Virginia,"[52] Carlos compensated

in spirit for what he lacked in strength. Gradually, for a few minutes each day, he devoted attention to correspondence that had piled up during his illness. In mid-August, still in Virginia, he informed Winkler, "Today is the first time I am allowed to use the typewriter." Although debilitated, he avowed he was "raring to get back to work." Mindful that twice within a single season he had become ill, Castañeda admitted to Winkler that his health imposed limitations: "I am glad . . . [to be] out of the hospital, though pretty weak yet. I believe that by the end of the week I will be able to start back [to Texas], but I am going to have to take it easier [than before] as the doctor advised that I take care of myself for a while." [53]

Before Castañeda left Charlottesville for a tour of Washington he heard from Winnie Allen, who had visited the Castañeda house periodically to ensure that the property was in satisfactory order. His partner in the Mexican Photo Print Company also brought him up-to-date on their business venture. Evaluating the final sets of documents from Brownsville, she noted with pleasure the high quality of work performed by Carlos's brother Fernando. As she had not had to send back a single document since completion of the fourteenth volume, Allen concluded that Fernando had "struck his pace in good fashion." The documents he had produced, she said, contributed to "a good looking and usable set." Meanwhile a second installment check for the Matamoros Archives from the Bancroft Library at Berkeley, California, had stabilized the company's "financial status." [54]

Castañeda postponed decisions about business problems until his return to Austin. Driving at a normal rate of speed to avoid exhaustion and stopping regularly to rest and ward off road fatigue, Castañeda's party leisurely toured through Virginia, Tennessee, and Arkansas. After arriving home Carlos rested for several days before going to the library in September. [55]

Uppermost among the tasks facing Castañeda on his return was a review of a history of Mexico that he had promised to write for *Mid-America,* a journal founded by Jesuit historians in the Saint Louis–Chicago corridor. [56] Next he carefully reviewed Winnie Allen's ledgers for the Mexican Photo Print Company. According to Carlos's calculations, the University of Texas library still owed the company a total of $874.20. With Allen away in Houston on family business, it became Castañeda's turn to shepherd the company's interests. Castañeda's own bank account had been hit heavily by his recent illness, which had forced him, as he told a friend, to dig "down into my little pile." [57]

Soon other developments caught Castañeda's attention. In the autumn of 1930 Latin American scholars were drawn to a wealth of unclassified Spanish colonial documents lately acquired by the National Library of Mexico. Castañeda's interest stemmed partly from his need to find a topic for his dissertation. Moreover, as the driving force behind the Mexican Photo Print Company, his curiosity was naturally piqued by sketchy information about sizable bundles of documents randomly stacked at the National Library. Observing a code of honor among scholars which condemned encroaching on other people's projects, he wrote to France V. Scholes about the status of work being conducted at the National Library by Lansing B. Bloom for the University of New Mexico. About his own plans Castañeda announced his decision to return to Mexico City, possibly as early as "the first of November," to photocopy all of the Texas material "in the Biblioteca Nacional." [58] Castañeda also endeavored to persuade Scholes to become a subscriber to documents reproduced by the Mexican Photo Print Company. Casting blame upon "a thousand details" for not responding earlier, Scholes, for economic reasons, declined Castañeda's proposal to photostat New Mexico documents in the Archivo General de la Nación. An affable and crusty codger, Scholes had already negotiated an intricate business pact between the Library of Congress and the University of New Mexico whereby employees of the two institutions worked independently in Mexico City copying documents of regional significance but careful not to encroach upon spheres of special interest to the other. Directors of the two libraries had agreed to exchange extra sets of documents, thus reducing the per-page cost to less than thirty cents, which was Castañeda's price. Nonetheless, Scholes assured Castañeda that the American woman he had hired to select New Mexico materials in the Biblioteca Nacional would not touch "the Texas, Sonora, Coahuila stuff which you want." Scholes explained to Carlos that as a university administrator he had a "duty to make the best arrangement" for the institution in light of the fact that they were "sorely pressed for funds." He told Castañeda, "I regret that we can't come into your plan for personally I'd like to assist you" [59]

Undeterred by Scholes's response, Castañeda finalized his plans for traveling to Mexico City either in late November or early December "for a couple of weeks," first to select documents pertaining to Texas and adjacent provinces and then to begin the technical process of producing negatives. Highly complimentary of what Scholes had been able to achieve through resourceful contacts, Castañeda asked for information about the "type of machine" and the less expensive method of photostating that New Mexico employed, which he might consider adopting. "I know how busy you are," he told Scholes, "but I need this information and shall be deeply indebted . . . if you take a minute to jot it down for me." [60] Surprisingly, Scholes, who enjoyed a reputation for procrastinating, promptly sent an elaborate commentary filled with numerous variables, not one of which Castañeda could modify for his own operation.[61] Still the response encouraged Carlos to proceed with his modest system, which had yielded satisfactory results.

In the fall, shortly after finishing his language proficiency and qualifying examinations, Castañeda received notification from Father Guilday that his essay for the ACHA meeting had been selected for the January, 1931, issue of the *Catholic Historical Review*. Adding pressure to an already crowded schedule, Guilday asked for the manuscript "within a fortnight."[62] Blaming his summer illness for a lag in scholarly productivity, Castañeda replied, "I have not quite finished my paper, though I have all my material together and am writing it up as fast as I can." Carlos assured Guilday he would finish the essay by the end of November and added, "I hope it will not be too late for the January issue of *CHR*."[63] Hoping to arrange work and travel schedules to accommodate as many appointments as possible, Castañeda failed to mention his upcoming trip to Mexico City, business that would surely conflict with the December meeting of the American Catholic Historical Association.

By Thanksgiving, Castañeda found himself "in the midst of a great rush" as he prepared to leave Austin for Mexico City. "I expect to stay for a month working in the archives," he told Frederick Chabot in San Antonio, "arranging for some photostat work we are planning." As on other occasions, Carlos asked his in-laws in San Antonio to let Elisa stay with them. His itinerary included a two-day rest stop in San Antonio, where he would board a train for Mexico.[64]

On the eve of his departure Castañeda caught up on a number of obligations, one of which was mailing the essay for the American Catholic Historical Association. Excited about the prospect of copying documents in the interior of Mexico, he reconciled himself to the fact that he would not travel to Boston as he had intended.[65] "I hope that you can get someone to read it for me," he told Father Guilday. Concerning the essay's publication, Castañeda acknowledged that it might "be too late for the January number." He told the editor, "If you decide to use it in March, let me know, for in case you do not use it I have planned to publish it somewhere else." In the event the *Catholic Historical Review* did publish the article, Father Foik of Saint Edward's University wanted to order "a number of reprints" for distribution among members and benefactors of the Texas Historical Commission.[66]

For the first time since 1927, liberated from the burden of graduate courses, Castañeda enjoyed flexibility in linking the purpose of his journey to Mexico with the broader goals of the Texas Historical Commission of the Knights of Columbus. In late November the commission chairman, Rev. Dr. Paul J. Foik, telegraphed the state deputy of the Knights of Columbus, Joseph I. Driscoll, in El Paso asking for authorization to defray part of Carlos's travel expenses: "CASTANEDA LEAVES . . . FOR MEXICO CITY TO PHOTOSTAT QUERETARO ARCHIVES TWENTY THOUSAND PAGES THEN GUAD[A]LAJARA TO PHOTOSTAT FOUR ARCHIVES. TEXAS UNIVERSITY PAYS MEXICO CITY TRIP BUT NOT GUAD[A]LAJARA. ASKS COMMIS-

SION TO HELP [DEFRAY] EXPENSES AMOUNTING TO ONE HUNDRED
FIFTY DOLLARS. BELIEVE IT REASONABLE EXPENDITURE. WIRE AN-
SWER CONFIRMING OR REJECTING OFFER."[67] Driscoll responded: "AP-
PROVE CASTANEDA PROPOSAL. KINDLY FORWARD VOUCHER AND DI-
RECTIONS FOR PAYMENT."[68]

While Foik and Driscoll resolved the logistics of transmitting expense
money, Castañeda left San Antonio with a portfolio of letters of introduction
for use at opportune times during his sojourn in Mexico. With a bit of pride
in his resourcefulness, Carlos described to Scholes his anticipation of success
in the archdiocesan records in Guadalajara: "I expect to find much material
of interest and to arrange to copy it after we finish the Mexico City job. . . .
Bolton admits that his examination of the archives there was very cursory and
I believe that the Church archives, which will be thrown open to me as [a] result of letters from the [Catholic] hierarchy in this country, should contain a
lot of material on the Southwest."[69]

In Mexico City, Castañeda rented a room in a private home located on
Calle Moreno in a residential area known as Colonia del Valle. Then he set to
work, joining other scholars who had come to examine a vast quantity of documents that had been found in total disarray in a massive and cavernous Augustinian church that the Mexican government had appropriated as facilities
for the National Library. As Carlos later recalled: "Several scholars in the
Latin-American field came from the United States to help put them in order.
It was at this time that I met Dr. Herbert E. Bolton. We were all given tables
by the librarian and instructed to pick out a bundle of documents at random
from the immense heap on the floor to find out what it contained, sort out
the documents and put them in some kind of order."[70] After a week in the library Castañeda reported to Foik that considerable "new material" relating
to Texas had "been added" to the Biblioteca Nacional. More importantly,
working through friends "in influential positions," he had "secured exclusive
rights" to photocopy documents relating to Texas and other northern Mexican states, beating requests submitted by an employee of the Library of Congress.[71] The intense competition to duplicate documents stemmed from a
growing awareness that the scope of the records was of greater magnitude than
Castañeda and his colleagues had originally anticipated. Three days after his
first letter to Foik, Carlos filed another progress report.

> The Archive I have been examining is not, as I thought once, that of Queré-
> taro, but the complete archive of the Colegio Grande de San Francisco de
> México, where Father [Antonio] Margil [de Jesús] died and the head and
> center of all the Franciscans in Mexico. Both the College of Querétaro and

Zacatecas were subordinate to it and sent full and complete records of
everything. For this reason I have found it a veritable treasure trove for
Texas Material. There are 110 large legajos [bundles] of over 1000 pages
each and I have had to go through the whole of it to find the material I
wanted. I have it all sorted out and I am going to arrange it in chronologi-
cal order and calendar it for copying. As soon as I have my calendar com-
pleted . . . I will send you a copy that will amaze you.[72]

During the period of Spanish rule Fray Francisco Antonio de la Rosa Figueroa,
librarian of the Convento Grande and archivist for the Franciscan Province of
the Holy Gospel, had compiled an extensive collection of papers relating to
missionary activities of the order. Lost since 1867, following the collapse of
Maximilian's empire, they were assessed by scholars as being "of the highest
value for the history of the Franciscans in the Southwest."[73]

On December 11, the eve of Mexico's notable religious observance, the ap-
parition of Our Lady of Guadalupe, Castañeda was engaged in this work of
sifting and organizing documents. Just before noon, entirely by chance and
good fortune, he discovered a significant and long-lost manuscript that advanced his professional career in a matter of months. Years later he reminisced
about that unforgettable day: "I picked out a bundle and took it to my table
only to find that one of the first documents, consisting of some three or four
hundred pages, written in a small but very legible hand, appeared to be an un-
published history of Texas." With curiosity aroused, he minutely examined
the manuscript. Familiar by now with the calligraphy of early Franciscan missionaries in Texas, Castañeda realized suddenly that the manuscript in his
hand had been written by Fray Juan Agustín Morfi, chaplain and chronicler
of the 1777–78 expedition led by Commandant General Teodoro de Croix.
"Could this be his lost history?" he asked himself, since the document was un-
signed and lacked a "title page to indicate authorship."[74] The next day Castañeda wrote Father Foik to inform him about his overall progress and, in particular, about his stunning discovery.

Your heart will dance with glee when you see the complete calendar of the
material I have found. I almost had heart failure . . . when I unexpectedly
ran into the long-lost and much searched after "Historia de la Provincia de
los Tejas" by no[ne] other than Father Morfi. This is a real find. . . . There
are two other works of Morfi known. The Diary published in the Third se-
ries of Documentos, and the Memorial of which you have a copy, made
from our copy from [the] Library of Congress, but this history I have dis-
covered is the one that was found in his cell after his death [in 1783] with

eight or ten other works, the list of which is given by Bolton but the origi-
nals of which have been lost ever since. Bolton will be surprised to hear I
have found it.[75]

On the day of his discovery Castañeda, not wishing to disclose the news to
his associates just then, discreetly invited a researcher sitting at an adjacent
table (whose name he forgot) to join him for lunch. At an elegant restaurant
Carlos selected "the best six-course dinner on the menu" and ordered "the
corresponding wines." That afternoon, highly elated and incapable of "any
systematic effort," he decided not to return to work in the library.[76] For relaxation he walked along the tree-lined boulevards for which Mexico City
is renowned, reliving the events of the memorable morning. At nightfall
he purchased a bottle of wine and retired to his room on Calle Moreno to
celebrate.[77]

Castañeda's desire to explore also the archives of Guadalajara was reinforced when someone who had recently returned from that city reported "a
veritable mine of material" there, including "a good part of the original Au-
diencia de Guadalajara Archive," in which Carlos anticipated making "some
real finds."[78] The news of Castañeda's archival discoveries stirred Foik's in-
quisitive nature. As a historian and librarian, the priest appreciated Carlos's
great adventure exploring unknown realms of documentary evidence. As
chairman of the Knights of Columbus project, however, Foik worried that
there was nothing legally binding that obligated Castañeda to safeguard the
research interests of the Texas Historical Commission. The priest ultimately
relied on trust: "Contract or no contract," he counseled Driscoll, "we must
depend on Mr. Castañeda's integrity to fulfill his mission to the best of his
ability."[79] Wishing Castañeda "every success" in his undertaking, Foik urged
him to "keep a sharp eye out for Texas material" in Mexico City, especially
"new material that will clear up some of the dark corners of our Mission history."[80] With specific reference to Castañeda's pending trip to Guadalajara,
Foik wrote: "In attempting to serve the interests of your clients please remember that you pay special attention to the interests of the Commission and
of the Catholic Church in Texas. I know that you have the historical acumen
to ferret out all the material that may be of value to us. Please remember that
we may never have the opportunity to make a second investigation so make
hay while the sun shines."[81]

Although in previous years Castañeda and Foik had exchanged pleasant-
ries on the campus of Saint Edward's University, the two scholars had maintained a polite distance from each other. The relationship might have remained unchanged except that in the autumn of 1930 Castañeda's project in
Mexico City pushed him closer to the research objectives of the Knights of

Columbus Texas Historical Commission. For neglecting to cultivate Carlos's friendship earlier, Foik now paid a small penalty in nervous anxiety. But just as Foik had to rely on Carlos's professional integrity, Castañeda had to place trust in the chairman's goodwill. As he grew restless in Mexico City waiting for Driscoll to wire the money for travel expenses to Guadalajara, the chairman sent an urgent telegram to the lawyer in El Paso: "RUSH DRAFT TO CASTANEDA. RECEIVED GOOD NEWS TODAY. LETTER FOLLOWS." Then he mailed a copy of Carlos's description of finding Fray Morfi's priceless manuscript and said that the archival discoveries were "very encouraging" and would "place the Commission before the American public in a most favorable light." Surely, Foik reasoned, a report of the discoveries would have a "salutary effect" upon the Knights of Columbus, who provided "financial support" to the project, and would furthermore "arouse interest among scholars of Southwestern history." [82]

Gradually through an exchange of letters Castañeda and Foik learned to trust each other. From this experience evolved a solid friendship between two scholars. Unlike Driscoll, who viewed life from the drab perspective of what was legal, Foik enjoyed the vicarious excitement of discovery as Castañeda blazed new trails in a virgin field. "Carlos," he wrote, "I am proud of your work and I hope that you will continue to reveal documents that will amaze the mightiest." Aware of the significant leap Castañeda had taken in field research, the priest offered a friendly disclosure: "You see how envious I am for some of the glory that must surely come to you among the scholars when you return." [83] To alleviate Castañeda's anxiety about the trip to Guadalajara, Foik bombarded Driscoll's office with letters and telegrams. Upon returning to El Paso from a business trip, the lawyer, to avoid delay within the Knights of Columbus organization, tapped his personal resources and dispatched a check drawn on a "New York exchange." [84]

Castañeda arrived in Guadalajara on the day after Christmas. After finding a comfortable room at Calle Corona 243 he immediately paid a courtesy call at the Arzobispado, the Catholic chancery. Upon seeing his portfolio of letters of introduction Archbishop Francisco Orozco y Jiménez received Castañeda "most kindly." [85] Satisfied with the credentials and a candid explanation of the research mission, the archbishop allowed Carlos to delve into the chancery archives, where he worked until the facility closed for the weekend. Afterward Castañeda happily reported to Foik that he had encountered "the highest mountains of mixed papers," which he likened to "a virgin tropical forest." Among the ecclesiastical records he found the "famous Zacatecas documents" relating to the work in Texas of the eighteenth-century missionary Fray Antonio Margil de Jesús "nicely packed up in a box in his worship's office." Monseñor Orozco possessed "a complete calendar" of the Margil papers and offered to share with Castañeda a copy together with permission to photocopy the collection later. The prelate also invited Carlos to investigate the papers in the episcopal archive, which sadly had "been sacked twice" during the turbulent past, leaving few items of historical value. The following week, through a junction of personal ingenuity and charisma, Castañeda befriended the director of the Jalisco State Library, who invited him to examine the remainder of the ecclesiastical archive in the public depository. "Everything is working fine," he assured Foik, "and I believe it was almost miraculous that I came at this time and located the various remnants of the ecclesiastical records under such auspicious circumstances for their copying." [86]

Evaluating his notes and reflecting on future needs, Castañeda prepared a calendar of the papers in the Biblioteca Nacional that he sent to Winnie Allen along "with instructions" for her to make copies for individuals, such as Foik and Winkler, who needed to be apprised of his work in Mexico. In fact, Castañeda kept Foik constantly informed. Alluding to the forthcoming calendar, Carlos reported: "You will readily see how much mission material I have unearthed and its great importance." With regard to his present research, he predicted finding "much more" in Guadalajara. Completing his archival work by the end of the week, Castañeda arranged for the selected documents to be copied, and returned to Mexico City. [87]

Back in his rented quarters on Calle Moreno, Carlos assessed the work of the preceding month. Using Mexico City as his standard, Castañeda now rated his findings in Guadalajara as "disappointing." "I worked like a Trojan for ten days and went over veritable mountains of documents in the various archives," he confided to Foik, "but found only about 2500 folios or 5000 pages of . . . [manuscript] material pertinent to our interests." Nevertheless, he had made some significant discoveries, including the documents of Fray Antonio Margil "in the archbishop's office" and, among "the most interesting," several papers of explorer Alonso de León that he estimated as being "very valuable." [88]

The disappointing results of the Guadalajara research stemmed from "the poor condition" of the archival facilities and not from a lack of personal initiative. During the violence of the Cristero Revolt the depositories in Guadalajara had not only sustained "mutilation and destruction in some instances" but, as Castañeda noted, had been "horribly disarranged and often ransacked." In contrast, his work in Mexico City exceeded expectations. Castañeda inventoried "over 8,000" new documents relating to Texas, which he arranged chronologically for copying and for which he also prepared a calendar. Apart from the discovery of the Fray Juan Agustín Morfi manuscript, he found an "original diary" of the extraordinary expedition led by the marqués de Aguayo, governor of the Province of Texas, which a notary public had certified in Monclova in 1722 at the conclusion of the journey. Among other papers Castañeda included in the inventory were "numerous documents" pertaining to the Franciscan missions of San Sabá and San Xavier in the hill country north of San Antonio de Béxar. Altogether Carlos reported finding copies of diaries of virtually every important expedition into Texas "from 1673 to 1778."[89]

As soon as a copying machine operator arrived in Mexico City, Carlos completed "all arrangements" for the work to be done after his departure. He promised that he would show Foik "a complete list of documents" reserved for copying in Guadalajara and provide "details about the situation" in Mexico as he had "found it."[90]

After returning to Austin, Castañeda reported to Winkler in the library the outcome of his recent trip. Next he devoted considerable attention to papers, letters, journals, and other printed materials that staff members had stacked on his desk in the Latin American Collection. One evening he met with Father Foik at Saint Edward's University, and the two scholars cemented their friendship with dinner and several toasts. Assisted by his calendars, Castañeda launched into "a verbal report" on the archival discoveries. The two then engaged in a "long conversation" that lasted "until after midnight." Foik later summarized the results of the meeting. "Suffice it to say," he told Driscoll, "the harvest is rich and there is much more to be reaped."[91]

Unlike previous years, when Castañeda's schedule of activities resembled a swirling tornado, 1931 appeared mild in comparison. Returning to work in the Latin American Collection, where he performed his "own typing" without benefit of secretarial assistance, Castañeda noticed that since his six weeks' sojourn in Mexico his fingers had become "a little refractory," providing results that were replete with "typographical errors."[92] Attending diligently to his duties, Carlos handled routine matters with efficiency in order to reserve time for the process of writing a dissertation. With Professor Barker's consent he chose as his project the translation and annotation of Morfi's *Historia*.

Occasionally an extraordinary event would disrupt the tranquillity of the library, such as the arrival of "a casual note" from Michael M. Russel, a retired book dealer in Galveston. Russel told Castañeda to expect delivery of "a trunk full of papers." Eventually a work crew arduously hauled the trunk, decorated with many "foreign seals," to the Latin American Collection. When Castañeda and other library staff opened it they found "about eight thousand pages of documents and notes, some original," others typed or in longhand, relating to the Mexican War and compiled by a prominent historian, Justin H. Smith. Castañeda later narrated the experience to an attentive audience: "Here were the sources collected so diligently in the archives of Spain, France, England, the United States, and Mexico during a life time." Castañeda and the staff meticulously examined the trunk's contents hoping to learn why the donor had insisted the materials be deposited in the former Genaro García library. "Valuable to any library," Carlos explained: "the Justin H. Smith papers have a peculiar interest to Texas because of its close association with the Mexican War. As a matter of fact, . . . a few years before, [the University of Texas had made] an unsuccessful attempt . . . to acquire by purchase, gift, or as a trust this important collection of sources. Now they came unsolicited and without even the expense of transportation." [93]

Meanwhile the Texas legislature, which convened in regular session in January, adopted a budget that once again locked in Castañeda's salary at the rigid level of twenty-four hundred dollars for another biennium.[94] The plight of the national economy was one reason for the austerity of the budget; another and more significant explanation was an arbitrary decision by the comptroller of public accounts. Years before, about the time Castañeda had moved to Virginia, Ernest Winkler had recommended application of a "twelve-month rule," which classified all librarians at the University of Texas "as administrative staff." For at least a decade that interpretation prevailed, although according to a reliable source the status of librarians seemingly deteriorated as Winkler's "tenure progressed." With the start of the legislative session in 1931, to attain flexibility in fiscal matters the comptroller reclassified "all librarians, whether professional or non-professional, as clerical workers." In all fairness to Winkler, when the policy decision became public knowledge he protested the decision vigorously to the university president, arguing that librarians should remain in the category that put them on par with "members of the teaching staff." Winkler's protestations notwithstanding, President Benedict decided the reclassification was not "grave enough" to justify official intervention with the comptroller's office.[95] The president's decision not to intervene rendered the librarians, and Castañeda in particular, vulnerable to hostile attack in the future. Resuming scholarly activities with renewed determination, Castañeda drafted an essay, based on materials in the Latin American Collection, on the Indians of Texas for publication in *Mid-America*.[96] Motivated by the challenge of writing a dissertation, Carlos gradually reduced the number of commitments on his calendar. Assurances that administrators of the Universidad Nacional Autónoma de México would invite him to represent the school at the annual Institute of Public Affairs in Virginia presented a temptation, however, to deviate from his new path. Determined to uphold his latest resolution, Castañeda tried to persuade a fellow scholar, Alfred Barnaby Thomas at the University of Oklahoma, to consider serving as alternate delegate. "The University of Mexico will pay your expenses," he informed Thomas, "that is, it will allow you about $225.00 . . . [which] more than pays them." [97] No matter how much Castañeda tried to reduce commitments, new ones continued to dot his calendar. In response to Herbert Hoover's proclamation of Pan American Day, President Benedict appointed a special committee, chaired by Charles W. Hackett with Castañeda and three other persons as members, "to work out suitable plans" for an appropriate observance of the event in April.[98] As a favor to Jovita González, president of the Texas Folk-Lore Society, whom he had met earlier at Our Lady of the Lake College, Castañeda also accepted an invitation to speak at the seventeenth annual meeting of the group in San Antonio. For the conference, which had Pan American Day as its general theme, Carlos modified the essay he had submitted to *Mid-America,* titling it "Indian Folk-Lore of East Texas." [99]

Near the end of spring the Knights of Columbus, at their annual convention in Dallas, announced the appointment of Rev. Dr. Francis Borgia Steck, a distinguished Franciscan specialist in sixteenth-century Mexico, as "historiographer" to write the volume covering "the mission era." Impressed with Dr. Steck's sterling credentials, Foik told Carlos that "the time is not far distant when the real work of compiling the history will be [at] hand." However optimistic they may have been, there was no way either Foik or Castañeda could have known the many years that would be required to produce a history of the magnitude envisioned by members of the Texas Historical Commission. For the moment, without a doctorate to his credit, it is doubtful if the selection committee would have considered Carlos for the position of "historiographer." Foik realized, however, that Castañeda's candidacy for the doctorate combined with his firsthand knowledge of Mexican archives and documents made him an important resource person to have around for consultation. As Foik was planning a trip to Mexico City in December to represent the State Council of the Knights of Columbus at the four hundredth anniversary of Our Lady of Guadalupe, he invited Carlos to join the group as their guide.[100]

With the arrival of summer Castañeda once again took a leave of absence from the Latin American Collection in order to teach in the summer session, this time in the Spanish department.[101] Between lesson plans, examinations, and lectures he translated a few passages of Morfi's *Historia* and conducted research to clarify obscure points in the manuscript. He also spent some time assessing his business venture. In a letter to Frederick Chabot he declared, with some exaggeration, that the Mexican Photo Print Company, due to sluggish sales of its documents, was "about to go into the hands of the receiver." Carlos hoped to keep alive another line of business, the publication of special editions, but his own financial situation made outside help a necessity.[102] Meanwhile, in San Antonio, Frederick Chabot had successfully organized the Yanaguana Society, a civic group dedicated to the promotion and preservation of local history. For the society's initial project Chabot recommended to the membership the publication of Castañeda's thesis, "A Report on the Spanish

Archives in San Antonio, Texas." "This is an invaluable record," Chabot informed the president of the influential San Antonio Conservation Society, "for local business interests, for research workers, and for the County itself." [103]

During a lull in the summer Castañeda received a letter from an old friend, Father J. Elliot Ross, who was stationed in Champaign, Illinois, that lifted his spirits. Except for "a seasonal greeting" now and then, Carlos had not heard from the Paulist priest who had played such a meaningful role in his undergraduate years at the University of Texas, especially in counseling him to switch career paths from engineering to history. Now on the brink of finishing the doctoral program, Carlos shared the good news with his mentor of yesteryear: "I have been pretty busy with one thing and another. I have positively completed all my work towards a doctorate except the dissertation which I should finish before Christmas. I have already taken my preliminary examinations and fulfilled the language requirements. I surely should get it by next June without any further delay." [104]

When summer school ended in August, Castañeda notified university administrators that he would take his accrued vacation the following month. Because of rising temperatures in Austin, where it was "actually hotter in September and October than in July and August," Carlos decided to take a leisurely tour of the Gulf Coast and around Galveston. Combining pleasure with business, he stopped at various places along the route, "looking over old documents." About sixty miles from Galveston and the famous Rosenberg Library, in the vicinity of "old Peach Point," he received an urgent message to return to the Latin American Collection to attend to work that had "piled up" and required prompt attention. Castañeda obediently abandoned his vacation and hurried back to Austin.[105]

In the fall, as Castañeda scrutinized publications received in the library, he discovered mention of a friend from his Brownsville school days, William Ekin Birch, now a resident of Nueva Gerona, Isle of Pines, Cuba. Recalling his own visit to Cuba in 1926, Carlos provided Birch with a summary of his professional activities, ending with a rare personal comment on his expectations as a family man: "I had a baby girl, but unfortunately the Lord called her to Himself when she was almost seven years old, it was a tremendous blow, the only child, like dazed I struggled on, and am still hoping that someday I'll have another child. My wife is well, though not strong and the doctors advise that she do not try to have a family for some time." [106] The importance of the contact with Birch was that it motivated Carlos to express himself about a painful memory that he had blotted from his mind. Neither he nor Elisa suspected that, contrary to medical advice, their loneliness would end shortly after graduation.

With other matters on his mind, Castañeda gave only scant attention to memories of the past. Of immediate concern were upcoming meetings of the National Council for the Social Studies in Minneapolis and the American Historical Association in Indianapolis, both scheduled for December. Because of severe cutbacks in travel allowances, Castañeda, unable to participate in the conventions, arranged for surrogates to read his papers. At the Minneapolis meeting, Burr Phillips of the University of Wisconsin substituted for him on the panel; at the AHA conference Samuel Flagg Bemis presented Castañeda's essay "Teaching History in the Secondary Schools of Mexico." [107] In between projects, notwithstanding prior experience, Carlos unsuccessfully endeavored to secure financial assistance from the Guggenheim Foundation to continue research in Mexican archives.[108]

For the first time in several years Castañeda spent the Christmas holidays at home, although he continued working in the Latin American Collection.[109] Right after New Year's Day, Carlos received several packages from Guadalajara containing Photostat documents relating to Antonio Margil de Jesús. Sending the unopened parcels on to Foik, he asked the priest to keep each package separate and not to "destroy the wrappings as these have some notations that will enable me to identify the documents that were copied and permit me to find out which were omitted when I check up with my original lists." [110]

Reconciled to the fact that a more experienced scholar had been hired to write at least the initial tome of a multivolume history of Texas, Castañeda submitted to Foik a detailed eight-point proposal for extensive research in Spain's principal archives (Sevilla, Madrid, and Simancas). The proposal generated a flurry of letters between Foik and Driscoll, on the one hand, and between Barker, Benedict, and Winkler, on the other, with Castañeda lodged in the middle of the discussion. The proposal ultimately lost momentum when it became too cumbersome to reconcile contractual obligations, salaries, leaves of absence, and travel schedules, all of which were affected by other considerations, not the least of which were an invitation for Castañeda to teach history courses during summer school and Elisa's surprise pregnancy.[111]

In January, 1932, Castañeda realigned his priorities for the first half of the new year. Foremost on the list was completing the writing, revising, typing, and proofreading of his dissertation in time for graduation in late spring. Accordingly, after agreeing to teach in the summer program, Carlos started turning down speaking invitations. He sent a polite refusal to Alfred B. Thomas, chairman of the history sessions for the Southwestern Social Science Association: "I am in the midst of Morfi at present . . . so deep in the arduous task of finishing my dissertation by June that I will not be able to accept your invitation at this time." Citing financial constraints, Castañeda softened the rejection by recommending Rudolph Leopold Bisele, a faculty member in the history department and an authority on German immigration in the Mississippi Valley and Texas.[112] Still hoping to persuade Carlos to participate in the program, Thomas suggested "a brief talk" around the topic of "The García Library Resources for the History of the Southwest."[113] Unable to convince Castañeda to make the trip to Dallas for the convention, Thomas settled for inviting him to review his book *Forgotten Frontiers: A Study of the Spanish Indian Policy of Don Juan Bautista de Anza, Governor of New Mexico, 1777–1778*, if not in the *Southwestern Historical Quarterly*, "then in some Catholic" journal. "There is so much Catholic material in the volume," Thomas informed Castañeda, "that I thought you might wish to call attention to the documents translated therein."[114] Impressed with the contents of *Forgotten Frontiers*, Carlos congratulated the author and agreed to write a critique for the *Catholic Historical Review*. In the meantime he assured Thomas that "from a hurried inspection" of its contents the book made a "pleasing impression" and was "a real contribution" about which any press would feel proud.[115]

Among the essays Castañeda had continued to draft while working on his dissertation was one titled "The First American Play," which was published in the January, 1932, issue of *The Catholic World*. An army captain whom the Castañedas had known years before in Virginia read about the piece in the *Honolulu Advertiser* and mailed a clipping to Carlos together with a note stating, "Your fame has even spread to the Hawaiian Islands." The article reported Castañeda's challenge to the commonly held belief that the first performance of a drama in North America occurred in 1718 in Williamsburg, Virginia. Basing his "conviction on ancient documents" in the Latin American Collection at the University of Texas, Castañeda explained that "as early as 1526" Tlaxcalan Indians in colonial Mexico had performed the "first American play" as a religious pageant accented by ample "pomp and splendor."[116] Grateful for the publicity, Castañeda nonetheless wondered why, in view of events of truly "great magnitude" such as war in the Orient, the kidnapping of "the Lindberg Baby," and rampant crime in Honolulu, a leading newspaper in the islands had devoted space to such a "remote" topic "as the First American Play." To him, a more lively subject for discussion was his candidacy for the degree of doctor of philosophy, which Carlos described as "the grand finale." He wrote to Walsh, "Now let the band sound off and pass in review. It will soon be all over."[117]

Castañeda's work schedule was disrupted in the spring when he was asked to intervene in an extremely delicate matter involving the Texas Historical Commission and Dr. Francis Borgia Steck, who was residing temporarily at Saint Edward's University. Owing to the vague guidelines that he had been given, Steck had run into difficulties with the commission chairman. Essentially what Steck demanded was unhampered freedom to write the history without guidance or interference from Foik. Unable to win over the Franciscan to his point of view, Foik called on Castañeda to act as mediator in the dispute. As a longtime admirer of the Franciscans' place in borderlands history, Carlos found the task of confronting a scholar of Steck's stature highly distasteful and discomforting. Accordingly, he avoided discussing the merits of the contending arguments, most of which centered on editorial control by the commission. Instead he emphasized the point that Foik would enjoy the full backing of the Historical Commission if the issue of editorial supervision should be put to a formal vote. Castañeda persuaded the friar to accept in principle the notion of a friendly editor giving helpful counsel. Humiliated by the episode but never blaming Carlos, Steck withdrew from Texas for several months to attend to personal and professional matters in the North.[118] After teaching a six-week course in Saint Francis, Wisconsin, the friar spent the rest of the summer in Ashland, on Lake Superior, working on volume 1 for the commission. During the autumn Steck spent some time conducting research in the Library of Congress; then in late fall he returned to Texas.[119]

Unknown to Castañeda, during the mediation sessions Foik recommended him to Driscoll as a possible successor historiographer. The lawyer rendered a cautious reply: "Your discussion of the qualifications of Dr. Castañeda are noted, and as I am fairly well acquainted with these guidelines, I believe no mistake would be made in his selection, . . . while at the same time I think we should be on the alert to select others who may be needed." [120]

Finally, after years of work, Castañeda delivered the prescribed number of copies of his dissertation to the dean of the graduate school, fulfilling the last requirement for the doctorate.[121] On Sunday morning, June 7, as was his custom, he attended mass in thanksgiving at Saint Austin's Church. No doubt he reminisced about his long journey from Brownsville and his special relationship with the Paulist fathers who had guided his spiritual growth. That evening on the campus of the University of Texas he joined classmates in a traditional procession. Although he had participated in commencement before, there was nothing comparable to the grand march of the doctoral candidates. With mixed emotions he relished the triumph alone because Elisa, pregnant, had to remain at home. At the conclusion of the ceremony Castañeda formally appended the title of doctor to his name.[122]

The day after commencement Castañeda embarked on a leave of absence of seven weeks to teach history courses in the summer program.[123] Although assigned to the classroom, he stayed close to the library to give assistance to visiting researchers. One of these was Donald Mackenzie Brown, a political scientist from Stanford University, who inquired about the effects of the Mexican Revolution of 1910 upon the agrarian society. Castañeda described the primary sources pertaining to the subject in the García Collection and offered a candid assessment of the contributions of scholars Ramón Beteta and Herbert Ingram Priestley. "I am inclined to side with Priestley," he told Brown, "and feel confident that a careful study of the facts will show that the 'Indianism' . . . has been superficial and merely a political pretext, . . . and that in the final analysis the agrarian agitation has benefitted the Indian nothing." [124] That summer he also critiqued the thesis of a graduate student in the Spanish department and assumed responsibility for conveying copies of the manuscript to the appropriate offices. When all details had been completed, Castañeda thanked Frances Louise Reast for the privilege of serving on her committee: "I can sincerely say that your thesis is a real nice piece of constructive work." [125]

At the conclusion of summer school Castañeda returned full-time to the Latin American Collection, but, owing to Elisa's advanced pregnancy, he reduced the number of his outside commitments. One project that did not require much effort was shipping a copy of his dissertation to the Quivira Society of California for publication in early 1930. [126] In September, with deep disappointment in the outcome of the business, Carlos terminated the operations of the Mexican Photo Print Company. Enlisting the help of "a Catholic student," he carefully boxed the copying machine for storage and then neatly stacked the documents on inventory in a room at the Newman Club that had served as an office address since 1928. Carlos postponed closing out the account books until later, when he could devote careful attention to details. [127] Aside from these activities, nothing disturbed his concentration on the domestic scene, not even the smoldering politics within the library or the spirited political campaign between Republicans and Democrats for the American presidency. On September 16, coinciding with the anniversary of the battle cry of Mexican independence, the Castañedas welcomed the arrival of a baby daughter whom they named Consuelo Dolores, signifying present comfort and past sorrow. For nearly three weeks Carlos neglected scholarly work, his normal schedule shattered "by the wild and thrilling yells" of his "little 'Injun' girl," who became "the center of attention for some time." [128] Friends who knew about the parents' grievous loss in 1929 sent congratulatory messages. Arthur G. Williams wrote from Virginia: "May Consuelo's future be bright and happy and may she be an endless source of joy and happiness to her parents, is my heartfelt wish." [129] Another friend in Virginia, Frank L. Crone, sent a dress and a toy rabbit, which Castañeda assessed as "too cunning for words." Five weeks after her arrival Carlos described his daughter's progress to Crone: "So far she is getting along just fine. She is growing and gaining steadily and gives promise of being a strong and healthy baby. I hope that she will grow real soon. She will be a great consolation to her mother who has been inconsolate since the loss of Gloria."[130] Joseph I. Driscoll in El Paso mailed a brief but thoughtful communication: "I congratulate you and bespeak for yourselves and for your daughter God's blessing, and every wish for increased happiness by this enlargement of your family."[131]

For a Columbus Day observance Castañeda drove south to San Antonio, leaving Elisa and Consuelo at his in-laws' home, while he delivered an address, "replete with authentic information" gleaned from archival sources, at Mission San José. Once again in charge of the historic mission after an absence of more than a century,[132] the Franciscan friars had obtained permission to erect six flagpoles at the entrance of their new residence to commemorate the governments that had claimed sovereignty over Texas: Spain, France, Mexico, the Republic of Texas, the United States of America, and the Southern Confederacy. At the conclusion of his lengthy speech Castañeda paid tribute to the friars with whose deeds he had become familiar through archival research: "It is significant that the pioneers in the real beginnings of civilization in the state were the humble and pious Franciscan missionaries who almost three centuries ago, when there were no material incentives to stimulate interest in the country, braved the hardships of the wilderness, risked their lives, and gave the best they had in them to save the souls of the natives and to implant the seeds of Christian civilization."[133] After the ceremony a modern Franciscan inscribed in the community journal: "The address was excellent. In the near future a thousand copies of the address will be printed and one copy sent to us for our archives. The weather for the occasion was most ideal."[134]

Afterward, as a hedge against criticism within the library, Castañeda asked a contact in foreign languages at the University of Virginia, James C. Bardin, about the possibility of temporary employment: "How has the depression affected Virginia? I would like very much to get an offer to teach either in the Spanish or history department there during the summer and to have an opportunity to participate in the Institute of Public Affairs."[135] Bardin responded promptly, offering a bit of encouragement but nothing definite: "We are not able to offer much work in Spanish in the summer and hence I think your best chance would be in History." As a courtesy Bardin volunteered to take Carlos's inquiry to "the proper quarters" and wait for developments to unfold.[136]

On the fourth of November, Castañeda and his family celebrated his *dia de santo* (patron saint's day), the feast day of Saint Charles Borromeo. On that festive occasion Carlos remembered a nun in Riverside, California, Sister Mary Borromeo, with whom he shared a kinship in name. Affectionately called "Aunt Borromeo," the nun regularly welcomed news about the Castañeda family in Austin. "I hope you had a very pleasant day," Carlos wrote to Sister Borromeo, "and that your new friends helped to make it more enjoyable." With regard to his daughter's progress, Carlos commented: "Little Consuelo is doing fine. She is sick now and then with the Colic, but on the whole she is doing as well as could be expected. She will soon be two months old. We are going to baptize her Sunday. I wish you were here to attend the ceremony as she will miss her 'Aunt Borromeo.'" [137]

A week after the American voters elected Franklin Delano Roosevelt as president of the United States, Carlos Eduardo Castañeda observed his thirty-sixth birthday. The following month, for the second time in two years, he celebrated the Christmas season at home. Mixing light work with the holidays, he evaluated Samuel H. Lowrie's *Culture Conflict in Texas,* a controversial study of English-speaking immigrants in Mexican territory, for the *Hispanic American Historical Review.*[138] And in the tranquillity of his home he contemplated his blessings. By sheer determination he had completed the doctoral program. In California another of his book manuscripts, Morfi's *Historia,* progressed toward publication. On the personal side, after a seemingly endless sorrow Carlos and Elisa had enlarged their family. Admittedly, the financial outlook was bleak, but when had prosperity ever brightened his path? All things considered, Carlos E. Castañeda possessed ample reasons for celebrating life with gusto.

Wedding photo of Castañeda's parents, Timoteo C. Castañeda and
Elisa Andrea Leroux. *Courtesy Josefina E. Castañeda/O. Wayne Poorman.*

The Castañeda family. *Back row, left to right:* Luis, Timoteo, Constanzo,
Elisa Leonila; *middle row:* María, Andrea Elisa, Don Timoteo and Doña Elisa
(holding Reymundo, who later died); *front row:* Josefina Ella, Fernando, and
Carlos Eduardo. *Courtesy Josefina E. Castañeda/O. Wayne Poorman.*

Carlos, age five, in "official"
Matamoros kindergarten photo.
Courtesy Josefina E. Castañeda/
O. Wayne Poorman.

Carlos on a Sunday outing in
Brownsville. *Courtesy Josefina E.*
Castañeda/O. Wayne Poorman.

Carrancista forces, led by Gen. Lucio Blanco, captured Matamoros
September 16, 1913; they remained in control of the city until March, 1915.
Courtesy Robert Runyon Collection, The Center for American History,
The University of Texas at Austin, CN 08553.

St. Austin's Church and Newman Hall.
Courtesy Austin–Travis County Collection, Austin Public Library.

Rev. J. Elliot Ross, C.S.P., Newman
Club chaplain at the University of
Texas at Austin. *Courtesy Paulist Fathers
Archives, New York, N.Y.*

Eugene Campbell Barker.
*Courtesy Prints and Photographs Collection,
The Center for American History,
The University of Texas at Austin,
CN 00536.*

Charles Wilson Hackett.
*Courtesy Prints and Photographs Collection,
The Center for American History,
The University of Texas at Austin,
CN 00530A.*

Carlos at graduation,
University of Texas at Austin, 1921.
*Courtesy Josefina E. Castañeda/
O. Wayne Poorman.*

Wedding of Carlos E. Castañeda and Elisa G. Ríos, 1921.
Courtesy Josefina E. Castañeda/O. Wayne Poorman.

Partial group picture of Catholic field Mass celebrated at William and Mary.
Note celebrant at far right conducting old-style liturgy.
Print courtesy University Archives, Swem Library, College of William and Mary.

Aerial view of Williamsburg, Virginia;
in the foreground is part of the College of William and Mary.
Print courtesy University Archives, Swem Library, College of William and Mary.

Carlos and Elisa in Williamsburg,
ca. 1924. *Courtesy Rosemary C. Folks and
Consuelo C. Artaza, Houston.*

Irma Gloria Castañeda, age three.
*Courtesy Rosemary C. Folks and
Consuelo C. Artaza, Houston.*

Julian Alvin Carroll Chandler,
president of the College of William
and Mary. *Print courtesy University
Archives, Swem Library, College
of William and Mary.*

Ernest William Winkler.
*Courtesy Prints and Photographs
Collection, The Center for
American History, The University
of Texas at Austin, CN 05758.*

Interior view, Latin American Collection. *Courtesy Prints and Photographs Collection,
The Center for American History, The University of Texas at Austin, CN 05732.*

Librarian Castañeda, Latin American Collection.
Courtesy Prints and Photographs Collection,
The Center for American History,
The University of Texas at Austin, CN 05728.

Texas Knights of Columbus Historical Commission at its first meeting at Saint
Edward's University in Austin, November 23, 1926. *Front row, left to right:* Rev.
Joseph G. Donohoe, Rev. Dr. Paul J. Foik, C.S.C., Rev. Monsignor Mariano S.
Garriga; *middle row:* Rev. Daniel Laning, Rev. Dr. Peter K. Guilday, Rev. H. D.
Buchanan; *top row:* William P. Galligan, Rev. John S. Murphy, Joseph I. Driscoll.
Courtesy Catholic Archives of Texas.

Rev. Dr. Paul J. Foik, C.S.C., chairman of the Texas Knights of Columbus Historical Commission and editor of *Our Catholic Heritage in Texas. Courtesy Saint Edward's University Archives, Austin.*

Sister M. Angelique Ayres, C.D.P., academic dean, Our Lady of the Lake College. *Courtesy Archives, Congregation of Sisters of Divine Providence, San Antonio, Tex.*

Administration Building   Our Lady of the Lake College   San Antonio, Texas

Our Lady of the Lake College, San Antonio. *Courtesy Archives, Congregation of Sisters of Divine Providence, San Antonio, Tex.*

Winnie Allen.
*Courtesy Prints and Photographs
Collection, The Center for
American History, The University
of Texas at Austin, CN 05700.*

Rev. Dr. Peter P. Forrestal, C.S.C.
*Courtesy Indiana Province Archives,
Congregation of the Holy Cross,
Notre Dame, Indiana.*

Frederick C. Chabot.
*Courtesy The San Antonio Light
Collection, Institute of Texan
Cultures, University of Texas at
San Antonio, #0119-N.*

Harry Yandell Benedict, president of
the University of Texas at Austin,
1937–47. *Courtesy Prints
and Photographs Collection, The Center
for American History, The University of
Texas at Austin, CN 06247.*

Rev. Dr. Francis Borgia Steck, O.F.M., Ph.D.
Courtesy Archives of the Franciscan Province
of the Sacred Heart, Saint Louis, Missouri.

Carlos on graduation day, 1932.
Courtesy Rosemary C. Folks and
Consuelo C. Artaza, Houston.

Involuntary Exile to Del Rio, 1933–35

In the electoral tide that swept the Democratic Party to victory in 1932, Miriam A. Ferguson recaptured the governor's office in Texas. Following her inauguration in January, 1933, the state legislature, reflecting the nativist tendencies that permeated some pockets of American politics, considered adopting measures directed against foreign-born workers.[1] Almost oblivious to the political maneuvering in Austin, Carlos Eduardo Castañeda welcomed the new year with spunky optimism, buoyed in part by the achievements of recent months. Before long he sustained a rude awakening when rumors circulated about the intentions of some solons to introduce legislation to ban "the employment of aliens in state-supported schools."[2] Concerned but not unduly alarmed, since the legislative process was long and tortuous, Castañeda routinely performed his duties in the Latin American Collection.

Restrictive legislation, born perhaps of a depression-era frenzy to protect domestic jobs for Americans workers, was only one danger confronting Castañeda, however. In the labyrinth of Ernest Winkler's library dissension spread rapidly into the corridors. Not well organized but troublesome, partisans in the Wrenn Library (curated by Fannie Elizabeth Ratchford) complained that other components of the system, most prominently the Latin American Collection, received constant attention. With a modicum of justification the university president, Harry Yandell Benedict, concluded that in allowing "some of his subordinates" to operate loosely without "proper" direction Winkler had created an untenable situation in which "the vaulting ambition" of individuals in the special libraries fomented friction and dissension.[3]

Unquestionably, through his determination to make things happen, Castañeda contributed his share to the disharmony that reigned in the library. An obvious nub of discord concerned the Mexican Photo Print Company that he and Winnie Allen, assistant archivist, had organized with a quasi-connection to the library. In an effort to clarify obscure points in that relationship, including expenditure of public funds and acquisitional benefits to the library, Presi-

dent Benedict asked Eugene C. Barker, Castañeda, and Winkler to give an accounting of all transactions.[4] Discussing the role of the history department,
Barker described the internal mechanics of channeling support for special projects, some of which had recently included Castañeda's photostatic reproductions from Mexican archives.

> *Two years ago Mr. Castañeda undertook to make photostatic copies of some
> of the archives in Saltillo. He counted on partial compensation from that
> fund [an annual allocation of five hundred dollars by the university's board
> of regents] that had been appropriated to the History Department since
> 1906 for copying historical documents. After that fund was discontinued,
> he found himself faced with the difficulty of paying for the documents al-
> ready copied for which the university had no funds, and in the emergency I
> wrote . . . to the Rockefeller Executive Committee of the University of Texas
> requesting it to make an allowance of five hundred dollars for the purchase
> of materials already photostated by Castañeda. The appropriation was made
> by the Rockefeller Committee and the material was delivered, and it is pos-
> sible that I OK'd the voucher for that purchase.[5]*

Barker's response manifested the appreciation and esteem of a senior faculty
member, and department chairman, for Castañeda's contribution to the Latin
American Collection. Backed by Barker's reputation as a paragon of integrity,
the reply also evidently satisfied Benedict as to the involvement of the history
department. For his part Carlos wrote a lengthy account outlining a history of
the innovative project and explaining how the Latin American Collection had
acquired documents at below cost (fifteen cents per page) while out-of-state
subscribers paid a higher rate to absorb the difference. Notwithstanding all the
cost-cutting efforts that Castañeda introduced to make the enterprise a success,
the gloomy status of the national economy had forced him and Allen by 1932
to terminate the business, particularly after the Bancroft Library of Berkeley
and the Newbury in Chicago canceled their subscriptions.[6]

Regardless of Castañeda's amicable working relationship with Barker,
Benedict, and Winkler, tremors of prejudice and resentment rumbled with
greater frequency underneath the surface of apparent tranquillity. By mid-
January, 1933, stories about Carlos's "complications" radiated beyond the
confines of the Austin area. Although the precise nature of the "complications"
is unknown, in El Paso, Joseph I. Driscoll, lawyer and former state deputy of
the Texas Knights of Columbus, offered a prophetic comment: "Those other
exigencies which arise from vicious human nature, such as machinations to
overthrow someone through envy or jealousy and the like present other prob-

lems. Sometimes, . . . such plottings succeed, at least for the time; while in others, they effect their own downfall."[7]

At Saint Edward's University in south Austin, Rev. Dr. Paul J. Foik, chairman of the Texas Historical Commission for the State Council of the Knights of Columbus, empathized with Castañeda's position. Rather than suggesting defensive strategies, thereby aggravating the situation, Foik subtly turned Carlos's attention to an activity that both historians appreciated—examining primary materials in the Latin American Collection for answers to questions emanating from the Historical Commission's ongoing research project.[8] Sometime during this interval Foik recruited Carlos to write the second volume of what was then called "the Mission era." Surrounded in the library with photostatic copies of documents with which he was intimately familiar, in between routine duties Castañeda commenced the arduous task of ferreting out minute data from the records to construct the story of Spanish pioneers in late-seventeenth-century colonial Texas, not realizing that in accepting the challenge he took a decisive step in his seemingly troubled career.[9]

Preoccupied with his own problems, Castañeda discreetly avoided entanglements within the inner circles of the Texas Historical Commission. From an experience of the previous year he knew that a polite tension existed between Foik and Rev. Dr. Francis Borgia Steck, O.F.M., the historian contracted to write the first volume of the mission series. Under those circumstances Carlos preferred to remain on friendly terms with everyone, as demonstrated by the pleasant relationship he cultivated with Dr. Steck, who now resided with Franciscan confreres at Mission San José in San Antonio. Late in January, during a Sunday drive to visit his in-laws in San Antonio, Carlos went to San José to confer with Father Steck, no doubt to discuss a smooth topical transition from volume 1 to 2. Shortly afterward he told Foik: "I stopped in to see Steck for a few minutes. He seems to be happy and working hard. I enjoyed the visit." Apparently satisfied with the arrangement, Castañeda concentrated on documentary research that pertained to his assignment for the second volume.[10]

Unknown to Carlos at the time were discussions within leadership circles of the Texas Historical Commission that impinged upon his relationship with the renowned Franciscan scholar. Academic credentials aside, the personality trait that particularly disturbed Foik about Steck was the latter's tendency to be cerebrally aloof and incapable of receiving constructive criticism. In short, Steck gave the impression of being more of an intellectual maverick than a team player. Deeply grieved about the situation because it involved a brother priest, Foik asked trusted members of the commission for their counsel. The subject was so touchy that one respondent, a priest assigned to a parish in Sherman, Texas, "purposely waited 3 or 4 days" hoping to arrive at "a different opinion," without success. Finally, blunt, candid, and direct, Father Joseph G. O'Donohoe advised Foik: "If possible break with Dr. Steck and let Carlos Castañeda write the . . . other volumes of the Mission History. I fully see all the complications that might ensue and adverse criticism but it's going to be the same old mess with Dr. Steck with every volume and everything you want done. Is our contract so iron clad that you can't get [it] away from him without serious trouble? Our mistake was in even considering the Franciscans. Castañeda can do as good if not better [work] than Dr. Steck—of course the [Franciscan] Order will have to lose some merit but that's their own fault." [11]

Meanwhile, alarmed by reliable information that legislation banning foreign-born nationals from working in state colleges and universities had indeed been introduced, Castañeda promoted a new proposal that, if approved, would permit him to conduct research in major depositories in Spain, with documentary benefits accruing to the Latin American Collection and the Texas Historical Commission. Quite possibly the plan stemmed from a belief that if he were away from campus on an important assignment, hostile elements inside and outside the university would refrain from attacking a missing target. In the end the plan never materialized because overlapping bureaucratic layers failed to reach a consensus, but the fact that the administration even considered it was an affront to Carlos's detractors in the library system. It is not altogether clear whether internal resentment of Castañeda's latest proposal originated from professional jealousy, normal in an expanding operation, or from rabid hostility toward Catholicism, which in this instance ricocheted against the Knights of Columbus and the Texas Historical Commission, or from prejudice against highly gifted Mexican nationals occupying positions of visibility and prestige. [12] Father Foik, who was knowledgeable about the intricacies of monolithic institutions, suspected the Wrenn Library as the main source of Castañeda's problems. The curator of that library, Foik told a confidant, in February, "has been working to cross-purposes with some of the other women in the archives department [i.e., Winnie Allen]. Of course, I have nothing definite on which to base my suspicion other than to state that this is not the first time that these folk[s] have been implicated in some sort of conspiracy to remove Dr. Castañeda. He has been too successful for their comfort, and by contrast they have suffered." [13]

While Castañeda was refining his proposal for a research trip to Spain, he and Winnie Allen tried to wind up the affairs of the Mexican Photo Print Company. Before they could close their accounts they needed to pay off a loan to the American National Bank in Austin. To obtain the money to pay the bank Carlos delivered the final volumes of documents due to the library, after which he submitted a voucher for payment to President Benedict. Overwhelmed "with other University problems" possibly associated with the legislative session, Benedict requested a delay of "ten to fifteen days" to consider the invoice.[14]

President Benedict delayed much longer than the normal two-week grace period. A month later Castañeda beseeched the president's office for a decision: "I do not wish to inopportune you with this matter at a time when you have so many other pressing business . . . but I have been urged by the bank here and by other creditors to whom I owe money as a result of the activities of the Company to make as early a settlement as possible and it is for this reason that I am again calling your attention to this matter."[15] As other matters intervened forcing Castañeda to divide his energies in different directions, the voucher matter dragged on for another six weeks, with the president asking for infinitesimal clarifications about entries in Castañeda's exceedingly detailed report.[16] In early April, in the midst of a controversy surrounding Carlos that started in the library and spread to the legislative chambers, Benedict finally reached a favorable decision that allowed the Mexican Photo Print Company to end its business operations.[17]

During this time a new spate of criticism from opponents within the library culminated in a serious crisis for Castañeda. The trouble originated in a reorganizational plan that Winkler drafted in order to improve the management of the library and to suppress criticism of his loose rule and laid-back style. Foremost in Winkler's plan was combining the Latin American library with the "very considerable collection of Texana" under the sole custody of Carlos E. Castañeda. Administratively the plan was sound because of the thematic compatibility of the two collections. Unfortunately, Winkler, already embattled by "factional rivalry," failed to assess how the plan might conflict "with the ambitions of another member of the library staff." This individual was Mattie Austin Hatcher, university archivist and a member of the Daughters of the Republic of Texas (DRT), an influential society of women. Unable to block Winkler's design inside the university and highly agitated about "the impropriety of putting the Texas collection under the supervision of a native of Mexico," against whose forbears "the ancestors of these patriotic ladies" had fought at the Alamo and San Jacinto in 1836, a delegation of the DRT effectively lobbied key members of the House Appropriations Committee to intercede.[18]

Although the legislature had already adopted a bill banning foreign nationals from state government,[19] this act did not affect Carlos because of a provision excluding longtime residents. Unable to dislodge Castañeda on grounds of citizenship and not wishing to appear blankly racist, the DRT group, in tandem with discontented elements in the university library, sought to use a more sophisticated weapon—financial pressure. Earlier in the session, by mandating "a minimum cut of 25%" in faculty and staff salaries at the university,[20] the legislature had reduced Castañeda's salary from its six-year plateau of twenty-four hundred dollars to eighteen hundred dollars. Now, with further prompting from the DRT group and from its allies, the Texas legislature trimmed Carlos's salary even lower to fifteen hundred dollars, a move cleverly calculated to force the humiliated victim to resign rather than work at near-starvation wages.[21]

The reality of how his enemies had manipulated the Texas legislature against him shocked Castañeda. The news also dismayed his loyal friends. As before, Foik traced these latest machinations to the curator of the Wrenn Library in particular:

> Carlos has been so active that he has aroused jealousies in the library and archives departments. Miss Ratchford and some others have tried by every means to remove Dr. C. from his position, much to the worry and chagrin of the more important scholars and professors of the history department. . . . It is "getting somebody's goat" to see this Catholic and Mexican swing into prominence. Indirectly these persons do not seem to like the presence of a Roman collar in the archives and Garcia Library. They realize perhaps that we are likely to steal some of their thunder. Of course, I am not letting this worry me in the least. These evidences of bigotry and narrow-mindedness must be endured.[22]

Eugene C. Barker immediately offered moral support. Although not a Catholic himself, the elder professor was "very open-minded, and, as a whole, very sympathetic and understanding of the problems of Catholics in Texas." According to Carlos, who certainly was in a position to know, Mrs. Barker was "almost a Catholic." Such tolerance stemmed from the fact that the Barkers had reared their son David, adopted from a Catholic orphanage, in the Roman faith. All along Carlos revered Barker as "both a gentleman and a scholar" who stood by him in times of woe.[23]

For a few days Carlos's emotions fluctuated between outrage and acquiescence. Then, with calm resolve, he mounted a spirited offensive, not necessarily to overturn the decision, which was virtually impossible, but to contain the damage as much as was feasible. With deliberate caution Castañeda assessed the few options available to him. Resignation was one option he had definitely considered, but his friends—Barker, Hackett, and Winkler—strongly advised against it. A leave of absence, such as an extended research trip to Spain, was another distinct possibility. No doubt this is what Carlos had in mind when he remarked to Father Foik: "But as long as there is life there is hope!"[24]

In the midst of this uncertainty, in early May, Castañeda received distressful news that his elder brother Timoteo had been robbed and murdered in Freeport. Assuming responsibility, as he did whenever a major crisis hit the family, Carlos contacted "a good criminal lawyer to assist the District Attorney to bring the culprit or culprits to justice." Within a week he drove to Houston to confer with Clarence R. Wharton, an attorney who was also a competent avocational historian.[25] Owing to that fraternal connection, Wharton advised Carlos to hire an investigator in the town of Angleton to compile a dossier of the facts surrounding the homicide. Wharton reassured Castañeda that he would join another attorney, Robert Bassett of Richmond, Texas, as special counsel to prosecute the case if the grand jury indicted the accused. "I am very anxious," Wharton wrote Bassett, "to extend this courtesy on account of Castañeda, who is in every respect a worthwhile citizen."[26] Wharton went even further; he notified Sheriff Jim Martin of Brazoria County that he was "very interested in the recent assassination" that had occurred at Freeport. Describing the victim's brother as an "educated gentleman connected with the University of Texas" and a personal friend, the lawyer solicited the sheriff's cooperation in "any activity" that he might "be able to put forth in aid of the prosecution."[27] Aware of Castañeda's financial plight, Wharton informed the investigative attorney that he hoped he could "accept the employment at a compensation" Carlos could "afford to pay."[28]

In the middle of the third week in July the lawyers prosecuting the case telephoned the library to inform Castañeda that preliminaries would start within two days. Unable to attend because his assistant was on vacation, Carlos hoped Wharton would keep him apprised of developments.[29] Leaving nothing to chance, the attorney who had conducted the investigation, Floyd Enlow, sent Carlos a telegram urging his presence in the courtroom. Reluctantly Winkler granted permission. Believing the trial "would be a matter of a day or two," Carlos hurried to Angleton, county seat of Brazoria. Unexpectedly a summer storm and "other unforeseen circumstances" caused further delays. However, once the trial lawyers commenced proceedings, the outcome was seldom in doubt. Bassett, the "vigorous" prosecutor, obtained a jury "conviction and a severe sentence."[30]

While Castañeda dealt with this tragedy, Eugene C. Barker persuaded the senior faculty in the history department to recommend to the college dean, and ultimately to President Benedict, Carlos's appointment as adjunct professor for "the first term of the Summer Session" extending from early June to the middle of July. Upon his return to the Latin American Collection, Castañeda promptly accepted the offer, agreeing to teach two courses for "a compensation of $325.00, subject to the final action of the Board of Regents." Aware of the controversy that hovered above his name, he promised the president he would "try to fulfill the duties of my position to the best of my ability."[31]

Appreciative of the benevolent gesture but cognizant that it was only a temporary solution, Castañeda recalled more pleasant times he had enjoyed at the College of William and Mary in Virginia in the mid-1920s. Encouraged by having an earned doctorate to his credit, Carlos once again applied for "an opening" in the department of either Spanish or history at his "former salary of $2200." Although sympathetic with Castañeda's untenable situation in Austin, the college president, J. A. C. Chandler, disclosed that budgetary cutbacks had forced him to eliminate one faculty slot in "the Modern Language Department for the coming season."[32]

Naturally disappointed with the negative news from Williamsburg but not altogether disheartened, Carlos applied next at the University of New Mexico in Albuquerque. Unquestionably through the intercession of France V. Scholes, Carlos received a surprise offer "with a salary of $2,000.00," which, after weighing the disadvantages and advantages of moving to the Land of Enchantment, he turned down. Determined not to capitulate until he had exhausted all resources, Castañeda asked for an appointment with President Benedict. "I decided to take the bull by the horns and have it out with the administration," he reported to Foik. Just before the interview he received a windfall offer that uplifted his confidence and enabled him to negotiate from a position of strength—the superintendency of the San Felipe Public Schools, a district for students of Mexican descent in the barrio located on the eastern edge of Del Rio, with a salary twice the amount he would receive in Austin. In the meeting with Benedict the president focused attention on two main points: the salary issue and a continuing association with the Latin American Collection. Exercising administrative discretion, the president assured Carlos that he could make a slight adjustment in salary, that is, he would reduce the "cut from 40 to 30 percent," but such action required approval by the board of regents. Faced with a limited range of options, Castañeda asked Benedict for a year's leave of absence beginning September 1 so that he could accept the superintendency in Del Rio, a factor disclosed to Winkler. Before finalizing the agreement Carlos obtained additional concessions from Benedict and Winkler, both of whom desired to safeguard the prestige of the Latin American Collection. First, he received assurances that either his assistant, Richard Burrell, or Maureen Wilson of the catalog department would become ad interim curator in his absence. Next, he secured the privilege of returning "to Austin about once a month to take a look around and keep my eye on everything." Then, vital for the success of ongoing research for the Texas Historical Commission project, he received authorization from Winkler "to carry on the correspondence for international exchanges and in every way continue to be identified with the Collection." Finally, he received permission to use materials from the library during the leave of absence. Armed with these important concessions, Castañeda walked out of the presidential suite a proud man who had defended his honor and integrity under adverse conditions.[33]

Although he had negotiated his official leave without counsel of his close friends, Foik and Barker, who were away on vacation, Castañeda later welcomed the senior professor's approbation: "I think you were wise to accept the Del Rio place on leave from the University." [34] By early August, Carlos's decision to accept the San Felipe superintendency was a matter of public discussion. In a section devoted to professional news the editor of the *Hispanic American Historical Review* euphemistically explained the leave of absence as necessary "to make investigations in the history of the Catholic Church in Texas for the Knights of Columbus Historical Commission, as well as various researches for the University of Texas." [35]

Actually, there was much truth in the allusion to the Texas Historical Commission's research project. What had begun as a casual understanding between Foik and Castañeda now required formal agreement on the eve of his departure for Del Rio. Carlos suggested definite yet flexible guidelines to govern the working relationship between editor and historian.

> *And now we come to our private and tentative arrangement for the continuation of the History of the Church in Texas. As you will have noticed I made sure that I could use materials from the Collection with [a relevant] point in view. I expect to have considerable time, or at least plenty of time, to do a good deal of work on my own while at Del Rio. It will entail some difficulties, of course, but I think I can do the work if you are still of that mind. But the question of the remuneration or compensation which I would expect under the circumstances will have to be reconsidered in light of the circumstances.* [36]

The "circumstances" to which Carlos referred centered on recent developments within the Texas Historical Commission. Living in Austin, a city in which few secrets acquired immunity from discussion, Castañeda had become aware in the spring of an imminent shakeup in the structure of the Knights of Columbus project. Months before, when the Reverend Dr. Steck accepted the task of writing the first volume of the mission series, amid fanfare of a statewide convention apparently he never inquired about the extent of financial support the Knights of Columbus had allocated to the Texas Historical Commission. Steeped in the Franciscan tradition of placing complete trust in Almighty God for the temporal needs of the faithful, Steck generally ignored the business aspects of his contractual relationship with Foik until there was something specific that he needed. Idiosyncrasies aside, Steck was a gifted scholar and prolific writer who worked diligently, unconcerned about an emerging pile of manuscript papers in longhand. It was only when the mound became unmanageable, especially in comparing passages and references, that he asked

Foik for the services of a secretary. Flustered by the request, Foik invited Steck
for a consultation to acquaint him with the reality of how "the financial situation is at stake." [37] So eager was the chairman to reach an amicable accord
with the friar that twice within a month he traveled to San Antonio for consultations at Mission San José. No doubt with Foik's counsel, Castañeda, in San
Antonio for a speaking engagement at the home of attorney Henry Drought,
visited Dr. Steck at the mission friary to discuss their own progress in the project.[38] Unlike some commission members who expressed anger at Steck's im-
portunate attitude, Foik advised patience as opposed to terminating the contract. Endowed with a wider vision of the overall project, the chairman truly
respected the merit of Steck's scholarship. He told one member: "I appreciate
your rage, but I do not think that we would be serving our own interests by
dismissing him at this stage. I am sure that we will all admit, when the first volume appears, that it was best to tolerate his idiosyncrasies and to handle the
matter with diplomacy. He has read to me portions of certain chapters which
please me because of the scholarly research and the human interest contained
in them." Consequently, in the transitional days between winter and spring
Foik and Steck reached "a sort of compromise agreement" which the Holy
Cross priest proposed "in view of the depleted treasury." [39] For the next six
months extending into the autumn season, the "compromise agreement" with
Dr. Steck stood like a fragile edifice poised against a whirlwind.

Unquestionably an awareness of the problems that swirled around the
Franciscan scholar, coupled with an anxiety at having to leave Austin for Del
Rio, motivated Castañeda to clarify what he expected as compensation for his
contribution to the commission's project. Certainly the geographic separation
was a crucial factor that would infringe upon the flow of communication,
as he reiterated to Foik who was still on vacation in Indiana: "I would like to
make at least a monthly trip to Austin to get materials and to confer with you.
This will entail added expense. I will be glad to do the work under the terms
I roughly stipulated in the little memorandum I gave you, but I will expect
$50.00 a month as I will have additional expenses and I will in all probability
have to use a stenographer to do the typing." [40]

Preparatory to his departure from Austin, besides packing printed materials needed to pursue essential research and arranging to rent the family homestead, Carlos contacted an official in the State Department of Education (precursor of the Texas Education Agency) regarding the matter of a valid teacher's
certificate, an essential requirement for assuming the superintendency of the
San Felipe schools. One prominent stumbling block seemed to be his status as
a legal alien residing in Texas. His lengthy residency and previous teaching experience in Beaumont and San Antonio, however, reinforced by a signed declaration proclaiming his intention to become a naturalized citizen, satisfied

the authorities. Greatly relieved, Castañeda, to reassure his new employers he would remain on the job long enough to implement much-needed reforms, eagerly signed a two-year contract.[41]

In the latter part of August the Castañedas bid farewell to friends in Austin and drove south for a brief stopover in San Antonio. With a combination of sadness and gratitude for a new beginning, they followed a narrow two-lane highway to Del Rio. Upon arriving in the dusty border town they rented a white-framed house located at 109 East Second Street.[42]

Del Rio, county seat of Val Verde, was an important regional passageway into Mexico, being the junction of several highways and a stop terminal of the Southern Pacific Railroad from Louisiana to California. Initially named San Felipe by Spanish explorers who traversed the land on the feast day of Saint Philip, the town was officially designated Del Rio by United States postal authorities late in the nineteenth century to avoid confusion with the historic community of San Felipe in Austin County. Out of deference to tradition, however, the Hispanic barrio of Del Rio retained the original Spanish name. By the time Superintendent Castañeda arrived in 1933, the population of the entire community, which had totaled about fifty in 1880, exceeded ten thousand inhabitants.[43]

The barrio known as San Felipe embraced an area east of the city limits of Del Rio that roughly resembled an imperfect rectangle. On the south "a string of hills" called Subidas del Aguila (ascent of the eagle) formed a highly visible boundary. To the west the San Felipe Creek, from which landmark the barrio had derived its name, served as a natural line of demarcation. At the northern edge the course of the creek bed meandered eastward until it intersected the railroad track, which completed the fourth side of the rectangular configuration. In its humble origins San Felipe evolved from a gathering of Mexican immigrants, uprooted from their native homeland by civil strife and lack of opportunity, who found temporary shelter at Las Sapas (sod huts) or El Salto (natural spring), about a half-mile from where the creek formed a confluence with the Rio Grande. Eventually in the 1880s two enterprising sisters from south Texas (Paula and María del Refugio Losoya de Rivera) organized an extensive hacienda and absorbed many transient families into their labor force. Early in the twentieth century the presence of more Spanish-speaking immigrants, some of whom established small businesses, contributed to a sense of community. Among the institutions that survived the fledgling period of San Felipe were several churches—Methodist, Baptist, Catholic, and Presbyterian. Also notable were the pioneer enterprises, such as La Constancia (general store), *La Razón* (newspaper), El Hotel Plaza (hostelry), El Triúnfo (grocery store), El Casino (a popular theater for celluloid films and live entertainment), La Botica Hernández (apothecary shop), Bracamontes (dry goods store), and

Funeraria Díaz y Guerra (mortuary). A focal point of civic pride since 1908 was Plaza Brown, a gift of George Washington Brown, an aficionado of the Hispanic culture. To advance trading interests, business proprietors in San Felipe banded together as La Cámara de Comercio Mejicana (chamber of commerce). Aside from promoting business, the Cámara provided a catalyst for planning cultural and patriotic celebrations.

With the inauguration of residential mail service in 1929, postal and civil authorities determined that a systematic naming of streets and roads was imperative. Although some streets in San Felipe dated as far back as 1890, Castulo H. Gutiérrez, the first postal carrier appointed in the community, accepted the task of implementing a logical method. The system he introduced early in 1930 commemorated the surnames of the barrio's leading residents: Ignacio Andrade, Domingo Arteaga, Pedro Barrón, Francisco Cantú, James Chapoy, Darío Cuéllar, Guadalupe S. Díaz, Santos S. Garza, and José B. Rubio.

Vital to the growth of the community was a school system. Members of Commissioners' Court of Val Verde County created the San Felipe Common School District No. 2, which maintained a single school. Even with the construction of a second school in 1910 and an expansion of the initial structure in 1914 to accommodate increased enrollment, classroom facilities at San Felipe remained overcrowded. In 1928 the trustees of the neighboring Del Rio Independent School District, apparently seeking to increase its base of public revenue without consulting the area residents, petitioned the county school board for permission to annex San Felipe into its jurisdiction. A storm of protest by Santos S. Garza, an early founder of the community whose solemn words—"I am San Felipe!"—personified the opposition, resulted in a successful court battle to prevent annexation. Ultimately, in the summer of 1929, the county school board conducted a special hearing to consider a petition to convert San Felipe into an independent district. The outcome, overwhelmingly in favor of the proposition, led to the election of the first board of education of the San Felipe Independent School District. Promptly the new board approved two proposals: plans for the construction of a high school building and the hiring of M. R. Nelson as superintendent. For nearly three years Nelson guided the San Felipe schools through the formative stages of growth. In April, 1933, the board of trustees extended the superintendent's contract for another year. Four months later, anxious for the district to attain accreditation through vigorous fresh leadership, the board dismissed Nelson, thus creating the vacancy that brought Carlos E. Castañeda to Del Rio.[44]

With little time to prepare for the opening of the academic year, Castañeda devoted most of the Labor Day weekend to reviewing and revising plans bequeathed to him by his predecessor and by the local board of trustees. He also met with the trustees to discern a sense of support for whatever reforms needed to be introduced.[45] On the eve of the opening day, secure in the knowledge that he enjoyed the confidence of the board, Carlos confided to Father Foik: "Well, here I am ready to open schools tomorrow with everything in readiness. Believe me, I have been working during the last week getting all the details ready."[46]

As superintendent Castañeda possessed definite ideas about using the moral influence of his office to achieve change. Just before leaving Austin he shared with Winkler some of his thoughts about the situation in Del Rio: "The problems arising from the presence of Spanish speaking children in our public schools have long held my interest. During the last two or three years the question of Spanish speaking children has become more acute, particularly in the Del Rio area. I have watched with deep interest the attempt to solve the question by the establishment of separate schools." Rejecting the concept of "separate schools" as unacceptable, Castañeda obviously favored evaluating "local conditions" in Del Rio prior to proposing specific remedies for improving "the facilities of the schools" as well as "the character of the children, the preparation of the teachers, the home environment, and all the other aspects of this important and complicated problem facing our public school system."[47]

The opening-day euphoria that Castañeda enjoyed quickly dissipated when a deputy sheriff delivered to his office a citation directing him, along with Santos S. Garza (board president) and Guadalupe S. Díaz (secretary), to appear before the presiding judge of the 63rd District Court to give compelling reasons why a permanent restraining order should not be issued against the San Felipe Independent School District and its new superintendent. On Labor Day former superintendent Nelson had filed a formal complaint with Judge Brian Montague pleading that since he possessed a binding contract to perform the role of instructional leader, the board had acted improperly, if not illegally, in hiring Dr. Castañeda for the same administrative post. In response to the court's directive the lawyers representing the school district filed documentation, signed by Santos Garza and Castañeda, pointing out that revised statutes governing public education in Texas provided clear guidelines for submitting grievances to the state superintendent of public instruction and that Nelson had not exhausted that line of remedy. Satisfied with the defense attorneys' arguments, two weeks later Judge Montague dismissed the complaint and the temporary restraining order.[48] Nelson subsequently filed a "cross action suit" against the school district, apparently to regain his old job or to obtain a large money settlement. Late in February, 1934, Judge Montague ruled in favor of the plaintiff. Immediately the attorney representing the San Felipe schools, Robert M. Lyles, served notice of an appeal. After satisfying legal requirements of a bond set "at $3,000 to supersede the judgment," he petitioned the Fourth Court of Civil Appeals in San Antonio.[49]

The litigation dragged back and forth for several years, extending far beyond Castañeda's tenure as superintendent. Ultimately, when all options had been exhausted, Chief Justice Edward W. Smith upheld the decision of the lower court in favor of Nelson and instructed officials of San Felipe Independent School District to set aside revenue from delinquent and uncollected ad valorem taxes to satisfy the outstanding obligation to the first superintendent.[50]

Leaving legal proceedings to the school board and its attorney, Castañeda settled into the routine of public school administration. Soon he realized how demanding—and at times even frustrating—the job could be for a scholar accustomed to the tranquil seclusion of a university library. Still, he relished the excitement of occupying a position of instructional leadership. Since his office was located in the new high school, he frequently had occasion to greet the students and faculty. Naturally he visited the other schools to become acquainted with the overall educational program in the district. At the outset his foremost objective was to improve the quality of instruction so that the district could receive accreditation from the State Department of Education. Within a few days he concluded that raising the standards of teaching along with motivating the faculty and students to renew their commitment to education required almost constant supervision. For assistance Castañeda relied on the school principals, whom he encouraged to perform the role of instructional captains on their campuses. During the first two months of school the burden of the superintendency kept him extremely busy. Clearly he learned on the job that public school administration in a district that desperately wanted to meet state standards for accreditation exacted a heavy toll from the leader at the helm. Fortunately the job was custom-made for Castañeda. While he needed to heal a flagging spirit, the San Felipe schools benefited from his energetic leadership. To build wider community support for the schools Carlos spoke to several chapters of the association of parents and teachers as well as to the civic clubs in the area. During a quiet interlude before Thanksgiving he described to Foik the "new spirit" of the San Felipe schools that he led: "But all in all we are making splendid progress even if I say so myself. The schools are beginning to run like real schools and there is a distinctly new spirit among the students, the teachers, and the town towards the San Felipe schools and their superintendent. To enumerate a few of our recent achievements we put on a special Armistice parade that was a complete surprise. Over 800 children marched in perfect order and keeping step. A year ago you could not make fifty march in or out of step." For a finale on the evening of the Armistice holiday Carlos delivered a patriotic speech at a banquet hosted by the local American Legion, after which the audience "duly praised" him for his comments. Not inclined to lose momentum, the superintendent next encouraged the schools to sponsor a program "to raise funds for a health drive." Ignoring the woes of the Depression, the schools collected "$120.00 clear in one night." In yet another fund-raiser Castañeda integrated extracurricular activities with the goals of the American Red Cross. On this occasion the Parent-Teacher Association (PTA) chapter of the San Felipe High School "contributed three times as much" as any other campus. These successes, Castañeda observed, were "the result of hard and persistent work on my part." [51] While he had undertaken these patriotic activities in all sincerity, no doubt Castañeda also intended to prove to his detractors in Austin that Spanish-speaking Americans were just as loyal and dedicated as native-born citizens. The events also served to demonstrate to the local community that the board of trustees had made a sound decision in selecting him as educational leader.

As Castañeda found his footing as school superintendent, back in Austin, in a progress report mailed to all members of the Texas Historical Commission, Father Foik strongly recommended selecting Carlos as "a new historiographer to complete the Mission Era history." Admittedly, a contractual arrangement still existed with Dr. Steck for the initial volume of the series, but Foik was anxious to record the terms of Castañeda's relationship to the commission. The proposal from Carlos that Foik presented to the group contained minute details reflecting the economic squeeze caused by the Depression.

I will agree to undertake the history of the Mission Era for the Texas Knights of Columbus Historical Commission, beginning with the second volume and the year 1694, more or less, on the following terms: To begin work in September, 1933, provided I do not leave for Spain; to receive a compensation of fifty dollars ($50.00) a month for a period of nine months each year, subject to my continued employment by the University of Texas; to be allowed ten cents per page of final copy, when this is turned over to the Commission; to be furnished the necessary stationery and two typewriter ribbons a year; to appear as author of the volumes I may write, these to be published under the editorship of the Chairman of the Commission; to be helped by the Commission in the revision of the manuscript.

Undeniably an advocate in Castañeda's corner, Foik summarized the advantages of hiring a second researcher: "He is peculiarly suited for the Mission Era history, having pursued his doctorate work on Padre Morfi's *History of Texas,* which is richly annotated. Hence, the Chairman feels confident from the viewpoint of scholarship that he will fill the requirements. Dr. [Castañeda] thinks that he will have the second volume ready by June, 1934, and ... there is no doubt that the Mission Era history will be completed in time for the Centenary." [52]

In promoting Castañeda for the position of second historiographer Foik inadvertently rekindled the controversy of Dr. Steck's tenuous connection with the Historical Commission. One member who served as secretary, Father O'Donohoe, eager for the project to assume a definite form and direction, promptly responded: "I am not in favor of Dr. Steck completing even the first volume, preferring to have Dr. Castañeda to start the history from the very start, though he would have to use part of Dr. Steck's work. However, if the other members are willing that Dr. Steck complete Volume 1, then I'll stand with the majority." Not inclined to lose an advantage, O'Donohoe quickly added, "In case of Dr. Steck's removal, I heartily approve of Dr. Castañeda's substitution." [53] Another member, Joseph I. Driscoll, concluded, "much as we may regret such course, ... : we should sever our relations with Rev. Dr. Steck upon the completion of the first volume." With regard to Castañeda's selection, Driscoll deferred to Foik's "wise judgment." However, in view of the commission's impoverished budget, the lawyer questioned the wisdom of paying Carlos ten cents per typewritten page of "completed work" in addition to a monthly stipend of fifty dollars. Obviously embarrassed by the absence of precise guidelines for the Franciscan historian, Driscoll now wished to rectify that oversight: "Further, I think [Castañeda] ... should be compelled to satisfy the Commission at intervals, for example by the month, that he is working steadfastly at his task and should turn over installments of the work as completed in proof of his discharge of his engagement." [54]

While it may not have been Foik's intention to raise the issue of Steck's continued involvement in the project, the chairman learned he had the votes to terminate the Franciscan's contract whenever the timing was propitious. Late in September, 1933, in a letter to Adina de Zavala, a Hispanic member of the DRT whom he trusted, Foik indicated that the matter had been decided: "There is another matter that I am giving to you in confidence, for no announcement will be made formally as yet. I will merely intimate to you that it is the purpose to terminate the services of Rev. Dr. Steck when he completes the first volume. I will not go into detail regarding this contemplated change. I will tell you by word of mouth when I visit San Antonio. The substitution of Dr. Castañeda has already been effected. He is now working on the second volume. You will hear more about this when I see you." [55]

Toward the end of September, Castañeda drove to Austin for a whirlwind stop at the Latin American Collection and a quick consultation with Foik at

Saint Edward's University. Among the topics they discussed was the matter of fair compensation for research and writing. At issue was Driscoll's objection about an extra charge of ten cents a page, which Carlos agreed to reconsider when he returned to Del Rio.[56] Amid a myriad of daily appointments Superintendent Castañeda delayed giving Foik a response, preferring instead to keep school business separate from professional writing. Late one evening, after coming home from the office, he explained, "I have been as busy as a bee since my return and have had no time to write you." Then he proceeded to comment on a long list of outstanding topics, saving for last the question of adequate compensation. Deferring more to Foik than to Driscoll, Carlos declared: "I have thought the [business] matter over while working . . . my readings and notes and have come to the same conclusion that you have. I believe it will be satisfactory . . . to waive the matter of ten cents per page and the furnishing of sta[t]ionery, although I believe that you should at least furnish me a couple of reams of paper since I am going to pay for the typing." Accordingly the revised agreement, excluding the minor points, retained the main provisions of "$50.00 a month for nine months, payable either monthly or quarterly, (that is every 2½ months)." More critical was the schedule of work that Carlos projected: "I will try to have a chapter or two each month and give evidence that I am keeping at the job steadily. I hope to be able to have the second volume completed by June, but I do not bind myself to finish it, since it is difficult to tell now how many chapters it will include. However I agree to do a reasonable amount of work, more than enough to justify the expense or cost to the commission, and certainly more than six chapters in two years as my predecessor."[57] The unceremonious swipe at his "predecessor" emanated from the frustration of having to work twice as hard simply to keep pace with cost-of-living adjustments while Driscoll in El Paso monitored picayune details.

Meanwhile the rift that had lingered indefinitely between Foik and Steck by late October ruptured into unpleasant recriminations. From the national capital, where he had accepted a faculty appointment at Catholic University of America,[58] Steck alleged that Foik, in a report to the Texas Historical Commission, had tarnished his professional reputation. Specifically, the Franciscan declared that the chairman in a "disgustingly unfair" manner was "spreading" stories that the historian had fallen "down on the job." Throwing down the gauntlet, Steck demanded that Foik rectify an "erroneous impression" created among the general membership of the Knights of Columbus. In a letter to Castañeda, Steck vented his hurt and anger: "If . . . [Foik] fixes up the above two points in his report to the next meeting of the Commission on Thanksgiving, I shall finish the first volume which, he says, is the suggestion of the

Commission. Meanwhile others may write the rest of the volumes. And then Foik can put his name down as editor-in-chief." [59] In defense of his reputation the Franciscan fired a bristling salvo:

> *Of course, if I write the first volume, it won't be a gratis job by any means. The Commission will have to meet my conditions in the way of financing the work; and this financing will be higher than it was heretofore. My share in the enterprise will henceforth be on a strict business basis with money for secretarial help and for other expenses furnished in advance. So I'll wait till Thanksgiving until I see his report in the Minutes. If it is to my liking, all right. Then he and the Commission can have the work already done. If not, why it will be just too bad so far as they are concerned. . . . Perhaps he thinks I haven't done anything on the work all this while; well, let him think so. And if he thinks I won't have time here [in Washington] to write at least the first volume, well, he's mistaken. I will have time and I won't have to be surrounded with secretaries, either, to do my bidding and take dictation.* [60]

In this unfortunate dispute between two strong-willed clerics, each side mustered compelling reasons to justify courses of action. What both clergymen refused to admit was that the Texas Historical Commission, in its haste to launch its project of long gestation, had failed in its supervisory role by not providing the historiographer with guidelines and reporting deadlines. Unable to find a neutral space in which to reconcile their differences, the two men continued to exchange recriminations into the winter season.

In between noteworthy civic events and the burdensome administration of the public schools Castañeda found time, particularly in the early-morning hours, to devote to historical research and writing. By Thanksgiving week he surprised Foik with a solid progress report: "I have not entirely neglected the History of the Church in Texas. I have two chapters completed now and am having them copied so I can bring them together with my rough draft of the third when I come up there either the end of this month or the first week of December." Productivity aside, a problem that greatly troubled Carlos was the unresolved "Steck affair" that hung like a pall over the Texas Historical Commission. Unlike earlier years when he managed to remain aloof, Castañeda in 1933 found himself being pulled into the vortex of the controversy. Along with his progress report to Foik he enclosed a copy of Father Steck's letter of uncompromising demands and commented: "Read the letter and tell me just what you think of it and what you are going to do about it. . . . You can judge for yourself just what is the best policy to follow under the circumstances." Cognizant of the professional opportunity the commission was extending to him, Castañeda still struggled to maintain a sense of objectivity about the situation. With a clearer perspective on the matter than Foik currently enjoyed, he continued: "I am willing to go on with the work, but I wish we could settle the Steck affair in some way before proceeding very much further. There is no question that the Commission has a right to carry on the work in any way or form they see fit, but some sort of amicable arrangement with Father Steck should be reached to prevent a lot of undesirable publicity. I am making this statement with the frankness I am accustomed to talk with you always. Do not misunderstand me or think I am taking up for Father Steck. I only have at heart the best interest of the Commission and its work." [61]

The commission, indeed, needed positive publicity to offset possible negative repercussions stemming from its internal problems. In order to inform wider audiences about the current work in Texas, Foik persuaded the editor of the *Hispanic American Historical Review* to announce the availability of a series of published monographs under the rubric of Preliminary Studies of the Texas Catholic Historical Society. Initiated in 1930 to publicize the larger project of a comprehensive history of the Catholic Church in Texas, the Preliminary Studies gradually attracted the attention of prominent scholars in the wider academic community. [62]

Owing to a scarcity of travel funds, Foik canceled the meeting of the Historical Commission scheduled for the Thanksgiving holidays, but he kept the members informed about developments surrounding the work of the two historiographers. Growing impatient with the inordinate amount of time and energy dedicated to the issue, O'Donohoe, the secretary, bluntly informed Foik: "You will simply have to begin at the beginning with our history. The few immature chapters Dr. Steck has written are not worth their salt. Throw them out and let Dr. Castañeda do all of it. This is the sixth or seventh time I've offered this advice, and I'm telling you it's the only sensible and sane thing to do. Just forget Dr. Steck." [63]

Although he often denied it, Foik agonized over the festering problem. As a trained historian he appreciated the quality of Steck's scholarship, but the slow rate of progress still disturbed him, particularly because the state's centennial in 1936 was imminent. When he read the Franciscan's letter of ultimatum, Foik concluded that the situation was irreparable. With discernible pain, he confided to Castañeda: "Carlos, I have borne with the taunts and the insults of that man, and the time has come now to speak definitely my mind. I will not express much . . . except to put you at ease." After reviewing a lengthy catalog of dealings with Dr. Steck, Foik released his repressed emotions: "His rash judgments of the Chairman are figments of his own imagination, and can be borne by me without any loss of sleep, for my conscience is clear on the matter. I have kept a secrecy on all matters regarding the Commission, as you so well know. I have not confided even to you the misjudgments that have been pronounced by Dr. Steck. But when he attempts to use the Commission as a pawn, then I will no longer be silent because the interests of the Commission are greater than those of any of the individual members; and that applies to the Chairman more than anyone." Resolving to "put an end to all this wrangle," Foik reassured Castañeda that he was "not involved with the mix-up" and consequently had "no reason for any worry." [64]

Toward the end of the first week in December, Castañeda advised Foik that his trip to Austin would be delayed. He also expressed appreciation for "the first check" that the chairman had mailed. Although he received an increased salary as superintendent, the school district paid its employees in script, which was redeemable for goods and services but not convertible into currency. He wrote Foik: "I did not have one single cent of cash. The little check simply saved my life and I am duly grateful for its timely arrival. It certainly proved the truth of the old adage: a friend in need is a friend indeed! It came when I needed it most." With respect to the volume on which he was working, Carlos reported slower progress on account of the fact that he had almost exhausted the materials borrowed from the university library. The duties of the superintendency also contributed to a reduction in productivity: "I am also feeling the lack of time. A number of things have come up in the school that have taken more time than usual, but now I have everything settled again and I can get down to hard work. I hope to bring to you in final form at least three chapters and an outline for one or two more that we may discuss. . . . The thing reads well, . . . and I do believe it will arouse interest." [65]

A week later Castañeda pondered whether he had allowed too much space to historical background in some passages. "You will be able to judge for yourself," he wrote Foik, "when we go over what I have already written. I feel, however, that the political events and the forces behind the missionary movement are essential to an understanding of the work that was actually accomplished by the missionaries. They give the setting and show that in spite of the political turmoil and wrangles of the officials the missionaries accomplished wonders." Trying hard to maintain a balance between school administration and historical writing, as a sign of good faith Castañeda asked the Holy Cross priest not to send another check until he had delivered "something tangible" in the form of a sizable installment of the manuscript. He wrote, "I am putting all the time on it and I know that as soon as I get things going the way they should, which should be at the beginning of the next term in January, I . . . will make a great deal more progress than I am now making." [66]

After spending Christmas in San Antonio, Carlos drove to Austin, where he worked in the quiet, familiar surroundings of the Latin American Collection. Foik, for his part, used the lull between Christmas and New Year's Day to think and pray that an unpleasant decision he had to make was correct and just. Following a meeting with Carlos, and particularly after reading the chapters submitted, the chairman notified Dr. Steck in Washington that he was being "released from his agreement" to write the first volume.[67] Two weeks later the commission secretary, aware of the anguish that decision had caused Foik, gently probed the delicate subject: "I have been wondering just how much progress Mr. Castañeda has been making in the writing of our history, for I presume that the Steck incident is now only one of the past and is now a nearly forgotten episode in the existence of our commission."[68] From El Paso fastidious lawyer Joseph I. Driscoll counseled: "with regard to the action taken by you . . . against the historiographer in severing relations with him as such, I give my approval to the course you have followed. . . . and in view of all the circumstances as well as the attitude and ultimatum of Rev. Dr. Steck, I do not see what other course you could have followed." As an afterthought he added, "Your decision as to Dr. Castañeda as substitute for Dr. Steck is also approved."[69] Late in the spring the Franciscan historian, who had been at the center of the controversy, provided the final commentary. Writing from Washington, Steck told Foik that he hoped his letter would not be interpreted "as an expression of regret on my part over the action of the Commission" and that he trusted the chairman would extend to Castañeda, toward whom the Franciscan entertained "the kindest feelings" and sincere gestures of "justice and courtesy which you till now have denied his predecessor."[70]

For several years afterward the severance of Dr. Steck from the Texas missions project remained a sensitive point among professional historians and others who wondered how such an ambitious undertaking could become so entangled in bitter recriminations. While it is true that Steck was a difficult person with whom to work, the manner in which Foik and the commission treated him was patently unjust. Part of the difficulty stemmed from the fact that underneath the veneer of polite civility there lurked irreconcilable differences. Whereas Steck was a Franciscan with a sense of long historical tradition, Foik was a member of the Congregation of the Holy Cross, a latecomer on the North American scene. If both priests had been dedicated missionaries working in a foreign land, instead of historians engaged in a research project of great magnitude, this difference would not have mattered, but when these two clerical scholars operated in close proximity they generated friction. In his role as chairman Foik resented a talented outsider encroaching upon his intellectual domain. Steck, too, donated his share of kindling to the controversy. As a trained researcher the Franciscan preferred neat, concise "packages" of history to study and interpret, exemplified by his landmark publication on Père Jacques Marquette, the Jesuit explorer. When confronted by the scope of the Texas missions project, Steck simply "panicked"; he could not construct parameters for the subject matter. Although he was superb in deal-

ing with sixteenth-century colonial Mexico, his orderly mind was baffled by
seventeenth-century frontier Texas. Unfamiliar with the broad sweep of Spanish borderlands history, Steck consequently worked at an exceedingly slow
pace, which absolutely frustrated Foik the editor. In the end, confident because
he had Castañeda as a stand-in, Foik astutely manipulated the historical commission to get rid of the Franciscan historian.[71] There were no winners in this
sorry episode; there were only survivors with bruised sensibilities, Castañeda
included.

Back in Del Rio, Castañeda temporarily set aside historical writing to devote complete attention to the problems of the San Felipe schools. Among the
most challenging of these were the severe budgetary constraints that stemmed
from the relative poverty of his district and the scantiness of funds received
from the state. Out of a maximum apportionment of fourteen dollars per scholastic for the academic year, as late as mid-April the San Felipe district had received less than 50 percent of the state allotment. Receipt of some of those
funds in late March allowed Santos S. Garza, president of the school board,
to authorize the redemption of Series C deficiency warrants, which had been
issued to employees the previous November. Shortly thereafter receipt of another apportionment from Austin permitted the school board to retire Series
D warrants for December, with half of the payroll distributed in cash and the
balance in scrip.[72]

By January, 1934, student enrollment in the San Felipe schools had increased to 1,229. Faced with a shortage of teachers and limited classroom facilities, the administration split the lower grades into half-day sessions. At the
same time Castañeda searched for resources to address other basic needs
among his students and the wider community. Through a federal relief agency,
with supplemental funds provided by a local chapter of the Parent-Teacher Association, he introduced a free lunch program for undernourished pupils. He
also continued the health campaign he had begun in the fall, persuading the
city health authorities, again with the help of the PTA, to open a clinic in the
schools to inoculate students with diphtheria toxoid.[73] A few months later, together with the districtwide PTA and Dr. W. Rex McWilliams, a local physician, Castañeda lobbied the State Health Department to procure five hundred
units of typhoid antitoxin "at a very low cost." To explain to community residents the importance of "the immunization work," Carlos gave an illustrated
lecture in the school auditorium to a large audience of Spanish-speaking listeners. A survey in the schools revealed "that 874 youngsters needed the typhoid immunization," and Dr. McWilliams assured the parents that his inventory of five hundred adult units was sufficient to inoculate the students.[74]
In April, Castañeda organized a Latin American Health Week, which focused
on tuberculosis. Two physicians from the Texas Tuberculosis Association,

Dr. Manuel Urrutia and Dr. Simón Rodríguez, gave presentations at San Felipe to the students and their parents.[75] At most of these activities the superintendent was highly visible and vocal.

Not content with public-health initiatives, Castañeda also inaugurated an evening education program for adults. With tenuous support from the Civilian Works Administration (CWA), a federal emergency relief agency designed to assist public projects of short duration, the superintendent recruited volunteer teachers to organize the instruction. Adults who enrolled in the program from outside the boundaries of San Felipe paid a nominal fee which was returned if the district received CWA funds. Likewise, the teachers worked without compensation until such time as federal funds became available.[76]

In early May, Castañeda enjoyed the satisfaction of seeing San Felipe High School host its first "field day and track meet," with students invited from the neighboring communities of Bracketville, Comstock, and Langtry. Activities included a luncheon for all the participants, a baseball game between San Felipe and Comstock, "race events for boys and girls, high and broad jumping for junior and senior boys and girls," "indoor baseball for girls and other events."[77]

Over the course of the academic year, with consistent encouragement from the superintendent, the faculty and principals in San Felipe upgraded the level of instruction in several areas of the curriculum. In recognition of that achievement, the State Department of Education notified Castañeda in May that San Felipe High School had earned "14 affiliated credits" toward accreditation, signifying that the district had advanced beyond probationary status. J. W. O'Banion, director of supervision with the state agency, wrote: "Commendations are due the San Felipe Schools for: The many evidences of standard work being done on the part of teachers and pupils, the excellent physical education program being developed; the interest being shown in music; the . . . organization of the schools and the renewed interest shown by the school board and the town people in general in the San Felipe Schools."[78]

On May 25 Castañeda presided at the high school commencement exercises, where the students, all Hispanic in heritage, received their diplomas. To deliver the major commencement address Carlos had invited a member of the history faculty at Sul Ross Teachers' College in Alpine, Clifford B. Casey, to speak on the topic of leadership. Observing that Spanish-American pioneers, as well as their Anglo-American counterparts, "had succeeded because they had courage, daring, ambition, and vision," Casey urged the seniors to become leaders in a momentous endeavor: "The Latin-American youth of Texas has a great mission in our State. It is up to you to bring about a better understanding between the two great peoples of the two Americas: The Spanish Americans and the Anglo-Americans."[79]

Before he closed the schools for the summer Castañeda compiled a statistical analysis of student enrollment at San Felipe which he forwarded to Val Verde County superintendent Marie Gronde Adams. Comparing enrollment reports from the two districts in the county, Mrs. Adams declared that San Felipe's student population, totaling 1,988, exceeded the census of the Del Rio schools by sixty-seven pupils. Superintendent Castañeda failed to find great consolation in knowing that San Felipe's enrollment was higher than the adjacent district's. The statistics merely forecast problems for the upcoming year in serving a burgeoning student population in limited classroom facilities. Although increased enrollment would have ordinarily meant a slight increase in state assistance, that benefit was put in doubt by an anticipated change in the funding formula that would allocate revenue on the basis of "average attendance" rather than numerical registration.[80]

During the spring semester of 1934, working long hours every day, Castañeda resumed systematic writing on his assignment for the Texas Historical Commission. Toward the end of April he promised Foik that he would complete volume 2 by the end of the summer.[81] Over the Easter recess Carlos drove to Austin to confer with Foik and to obtain research materials from the Latin American Collection. During this interval he joined the Knights of Columbus, affiliating himself with Council 1017 in Austin.[82] In May he returned to Austin to present his report to the Texas Historical Commission. Leaving Del Rio on Tuesday, May 15, at the close of normal business hours and driving carefully to avoid "the usual accidents" that periodically broke "the monotony" of travel along the Austin highway, Carlos arrived at the Driskill Hotel shortly before two o'clock in the afternoon. Apart from the technical aspect of his report, which he handled with ease and authority, Castañeda emphasized to Foik and the other commission members that he would depend heavily on their monthly stipend to support his family through the summer months of writing in San Antonio.[83]

With Castañeda's salary in San Felipe being paid in scrip, financial concerns during this period weighed heavily on his mind. During his trip to Austin at Easter he had consulted with Eugene C. Barker about the prospect of teaching history in the summer session. Possibly because attitudes in some quarters of the university had not improved appreciably, Barker delayed responding to his inquiry.[84] In the end, after answering an invitation to interview at Our Lady of the Lake College, Castañeda spent the summer in San Antonio, where he taught "a one hour lecture course as a special feature" in the curriculum.[85]

Experiencing the economic crunch almost on a daily basis, Castañeda punctuated his letters to Foik with pleas for assistance. In late April, after traveling to Austin to discuss his progress on volume 2, Carlos implored Foik, "Please see if you can arrange for me to get at least my traveling expenses, that is gasoline and oil, for it is a hack [*sic*] of a long ways from here." Then, shifting in typical fashion to an offensive strategy, he asked, "Say, . . . what about getting an honorary LL.D. from your institution?" [86]

In early July, desperately in need of funds to pay expenses, he asked Foik (in Detroit on vacation), to intercede with the Knights of Columbus to send him "at least $100.00 this month as I need the money to live this summer." In justification of the request, Carlos described the work he had completed:

> *I believe, without boasting, that the manuscript reads smoothly and that I have cleared up a number of points, giving a considerable amount of information hitherto unknown. For example the founding of San Miguel and Dolores missions in East Texas had always been hazy and date undetermined. I have definitely fixed the date and have given details as to their founding. . . . But the best chapter is the third I have just finished on the establishment of the Mission of San Antonio de Valero and the first civ[i]l settlement in San Antonio. Up to now there are not five pages in print on the subject, and these were written by [Robert Carlton] Clark and are all incorrect. Morfi had little to say on the subject, but I have succeeded in getting the most minute details and have, by compressing the material I have found on the subject, written about fifty pages on this important episode.* [87]

At Our Lady of the Lake College in San Antonio, where Castañeda taught during the summer of 1934, the nuns of the Congregation of Divine Providence reserved for him an isolated corner of the library where he worked "from eight to nine hours a day, without interruptions." They even provided "a good fan" to alleviate the heat and extended a privilege of allowing him to eat in the dining hall whenever he did not "feel like going home for lunch." Sensitive to the need of cultivating good human relations, Carlos advised Foik, "I think the Commission should write a letter of acknowledgment and thanks to The Mother Superior here." [88]

Toward the end of July, dismayed that he had lost contact with Foik, who was no longer in Detroit, Castañeda struggled to finish another chapter. Addressing a letter to Foik at Notre Dame University, he complained: "I have completed over 175 pages of final text in the first three chapters. But I want to tell you it is a hard job to keep it up through all this heat." To attain that remarkable level of productivity Castañeda had hired a typist at "10 cents a page for one original and three carbons," which he assessed as "pretty cheap." Having exhausted his limited money resources and now living on credit, again he pleaded with Foik, "I wish you would send me some money as soon as possible to pay the typist, the baker, or the butcher, or the landlord." Highly in his favor, of course, was a steadily mounting manuscript, which might cease to grow, Castañeda warned, if sorely needed funds did not arrive in time to save "a starving historian." He told Foik: "Well, you better send me some money, or I will have to go and shine shoes . . . and let the history wait until I have more leisure for research. I can't keep on working without a few pennies to keep the wolf from the door. I think I have done well to turn out over 175 pages of final copy in a month and ten days. If I keep up the pace, I'll finish by the end of summer." [89] By stretching the small stipend he received for teaching at Our Lady of the Lake to pay for basic necessities, Castañeda weakly protected his dignity for a few days, but eventually circumstances forced him to borrow fifty dollars from Reverend Monsignor Mariano S. Garriga, a trusted member of the Historical Commission who resided in San Antonio. [90]

During the year that Castañeda had been gone from Austin the situation at the university had deteriorated instead of getting better, causing Carlos to comment in August: "I am keeping my eyes open for an opportunity somewhere else if possible for next year. It is a downright shame the way things are in Austin, but when the odds are against you the best policy is not to play your own hand." [91] One lead Castañeda pursued concerned a position in Albuquerque. On one of his visits to the Latin American Collection during the summer Carlos learned that the University of New Mexico had plans to develop an archival center and anticipated hiring someone to take charge of an innovative "program of historical research in the Spanish American field." With little hope of succeeding but frantically trying to escape the economic doldrums, he asked the eminent Herbert E. Bolton to mention his name "in case you are consulted and provided your conscience permits you." [92]

It was probably during this summer in San Antonio, while Castañeda worked on the second volume of the Catholic saga, that he wrote an essay, "Silent Years in Texas History," a study of early Spanish exploration, which his mentor Professor Barker published in the October, 1934, issue of *Southwestern Historical Quarterly*. [93] Castañeda continued working on the second volume for the Historical Commission until past the middle of August. Now definitely more experienced in public school administration, he pragmatically concluded that he needed at least two weeks to prepare for the opening of the new academic year. With Barker's help the previous spring he had applied for an extension of his leave of absence from the university "until September 1st, 1935," which would allow him to fulfill the second year of his contract in San Felipe. [94] Asking Foik to remember him in prayer, Carlos promised to finish the volume as soon as he had things "running smooth[l]y again." [95]

After the fall term began, Castañeda noted that enrollment for September, 1934, totaled 1,049 students, an increase of 129 over the same period the previous year. The current census did not include the children of migrant-worker families who would not return to Del Rio until after the fall harvest.

As they had done previously, the principals and teachers quickly determined how many half-day sessions would be required in the elementary grades while preserving a full-day curriculum for the high school. In spite of the severe constraints upon his schools Castañeda continually sought ways to broaden the students' educational experience. In addition to introducing departments of physical education and music, he energetically supported the organization of the high school's "Mustang band" and a pep squad.[96] Early in the fall of 1934, through contacts in Austin, the superintendent secured fifty books from the Texas State Library "for the little folks . . . to stimulate interest and encourage the young Latin-American citizens to read." The assortment included works by Irving Babbit, Will Durant, Hermann Hagedorn, Emerson Hough, and Percivil Christopher Wren. With a librarian's appreciation for books as sources of knowledge, Castañeda said that the volumes were "a choice collection for students of the primary, intermediate, and high school grades and relate to history, mechanics, philosophy, home furnishings, etc."[97]

Utilizing the classroom facilities of San Felipe High School, Castañeda again encouraged adults to register for the night program. Funded by the Texas Relief Commission to provide unemployed teachers with an opportunity to work, the fifteen-week term offered classes in English, civics, commercial geography, Spanish, commercial arithmetic, and health. To enable adult students to receive the benefit of individual attention, the superintendent recommended that the board hire eight teachers in order that the classes, which operated from seven o'clock to nine o'clock in the evenings, could remain small in enrollment.[98]

During the fall, 1934, semester Castañeda also directed his attention outward beyond his district. Some of his efforts were aimed at cultivating good relations with the state superintendent of public instruction in Austin.[99] For example, he spoke frequently to chapter meetings of the Parent-Teacher Association, usually on the topic of "racial and religious tolerance." Gradually his speaking commitments took him to regional PTA conferences, and in the fall he addressed the annual conclave of the Texas State Teachers Association.[100]

Undeniably there was in the young superintendent a reformer's streak that soared to the surface during his brief tenure with the San Felipe schools. Castañeda saw that the struggle to attain equality education for Hispanic students was the same everywhere in Texas, and he believed that a victory in one locale became a source of inspiration for all of those citizens carrying on the fight. To further the cause he accepted an invitation to address a large outdoor rally in San Antonio's west-side barrio on October 24, 1934. Organized by Eleuterio Escobar, a businessman and influential member of LULAC, the rally reportedly drew between ten thousand and thirteen thousand people. At issue were the deplorable condition of Mexican schools in San Antonio and the repeated failure of the local school board to consider meaningful improvements. On this occasion Castañeda shared the platform with a number of prominent speakers, including L. A. Woods, state superintendent of public instruction. The crusade in San Antonio for the upgrading of substandard schools in the west side led to the formation two months later of the Liga Pro-Defensa Escolar, which soon represented over fifty organizations. Although the league waged a vigorous campaign to prod the school board into action, significant progress in addressing the disparities between facilities for Anglo students and those for Mexican-American students did not begin until after World War II.[101]

With all the time he spent on educational matters in the fall of 1934 Castañeda also continued to work on volume 2 for the Historical Commission. Shortly before the school year began in September, finding a lull in the planning period and encouraged by receipt of a "belated check" from Foik, Carlos discovered a reservoir of latent optimism: "I have everything pretty well in hand and expect to get down to work on the history again by the end of next week."[102] True to his prediction, Castañeda resumed writing on the manuscript at home in the evenings. Comfortable with the thrust of the story line, he reported to Foik: "I started on the history work again . . . just like I did during the summer. I expect to finish the last part of the fourth chapter by the end of the week and before the end of the month I'll have the 5th and 6th done, I think." To achieve his goal he asked to borrow eleven volumes of the *Southwestern Historical Quarterly,* in addition to those requested a week and a half earlier, from the library of the Texas Historical Commission. Asking Foik to send the volumes "either by parcel post or Express Prepaid," he added, "The Commission should stand the expense of transportation, don't you think so?"[103]

As Castañeda labored with the schools during daylight hours and on historical note taking and writing in the evenings, Foik at Saint Edward's University meticulously edited the finished manuscript and compiled "a comprehensive index for the chapters already submitted." To motivate Carlos to accelerate the writing pace, Foik informed him that Herbert E. Bolton had "agreed to read the manuscript as soon as it is ready." Convinced that it would be more advantageous for Bolton to evaluate the first and second volumes in succession, the chairman, in an effort to expedite the project, decided to let Carlos consult six chapters of the unfinished manuscript written by Dr. Steck, "the erstwhile historiographer of Catholic Texas History." In a humorous aside, prompted perhaps by Castañeda's comment that the Historical Commission should pay for postage on the *Quarterly* volumes, Foik alluded to Carlos's habit of driving hurriedly at night in order to keep daytime appointments at distant locations and opined that "the Commission should not be responsible for accidents along the way, such as running into deer, etc."[104]

A month after the beginning of the school term Castañeda contemplated another brisk visit to Saint Edward's to confer with Foik on a host of details. With the aid of references gleaned from articles in the *Southwestern Historical Quarterly* he had managed to finish another chapter. Sensitive that Foik had criticized his motorist skills, the superintendent replied: "As to the accidental killing of deer and other game while traveling along the king's highway [an actual reference to place-name geography found in his research and writing], I have an insurance policy now to cover such emergencies and unexpected expenses so that the treasury of the Commission need not feel any uneasiness on this subject. The only real danger, and this cannot be eliminated, is the unexpected snuffing out of the weak flame of the historian, but the Lord will provide." Pleasantly surprised by the news of Foik's index-in-progress, Carlos reluctantly admitted that daytime distractions in the school office hindered his momentum in writing. Moreover, as he gradually advanced the writing of the second volume toward completion, the thought of having to track backward to an earlier chronological period depressed his spirit: "It is most unfortunate that I had to begin with the second. Were it not for this fact we would be in a position now [to] bring out one volume before next spring and [then the] other next fall."[105]

The Castañedas decided to spend the long Thanksgiving holiday with Elisa's relatives in San Antonio. During an interlude on the weekend, to test clarity of thought and expression, Carlos read a portion of his manuscript that dealt with the colonial origins of San Antonio to the Alumnae Association of Our Lady of the Lake College. Publicized in the local newspaper, the presentation attracted a sizable audience, including a few members of the Daughters of the Republic of Texas who listened attentively to his remarks. "Much interest," Carlos reported, "was shown in the new facts brought out by the study."[106]

With the Texas Historical Commission meeting in Austin the week after Thanksgiving, Castañeda dispatched his periodic report to Foik for presentation to the group. Attributing the slowdown in writing to "numerous and diverse causes," the historiographer narrowed the problem to an unsynchronized work schedule: "The difficulty of getting all the necessary sources has been great because of the distance and the fact that due to his other duties, it is not practical for him to make frequent trips to the archives of the University of Texas and those of the Historical Commission in the University of St. Edward's." Not wanting to end his report on a negative note, Carlos promised steadfast productivity but at a slower pace: "The historiographer has reluctantly come to the conclusion that during the remainder of the school year the work of composition will per force be slow, but he hopes that during the coming summer he will not only be able to complete the second volume but get a good part of the first volume in shape." [107]

Privately Castañeda's concern about his progress was greater than he revealed in his report. He had optimistically promised Foik a solid turnout of finished material by a self-imposed deadline and then, for unforeseen circumstances, had fallen behind schedule. Somehow, despite minor setbacks, he had managed to produce an impressive number of pages, especially during his writer's retreat at Our Lady of the Lake the previous summer. Still, the 1936 centennial loomed ahead, and the Historical Commission had pledged to contribute to the observance at least two volumes of a comprehensive history of the Catholic presence in Texas. There seemed to be no possible way, given his time-consuming schedule as superintendent, that he could finish the outstanding balance of writing before the deadline. At the end of November, not without intensive soul-searching, Carlos prepared another report to the Historical Commission in the form of a candid summary with a startling new proposal that he delivered to Foik: "Since September, 1934, to the present the work has stood stagnant because my other duties have not permitted me to do any concentrated work in composition. During this time I have been busy in taking notes and studying the sources I am using, but have not had the time necessary for composition. These facts have made me come to the realization that if the Commission wishes to have the work finished in time for publication in 1936, a new policy will have to be adopted." Essentially, what he proposed was to remain nominally as superintendent, without compensation but available for major decisions, and to work full-time on the contents of the two volumes, provided the Historical Commission would "raise the necessary funds" to pay the equivalent of his salary of two hundred dollars a month. Relieved of daily administrative duties, Carlos would have seven months, beginning in February, to produce "about 800 pages of final copy . . . which will assure the completion of Volumes I and II of the Mission Era by the end of the summer of 1935." Feeling a moral obligation to the students and teachers of his district, Castañeda reserved the month of May to attend to the business related to the San Felipe schools.[108] While waiting impatiently for Foik's answer and to uplift the family's morale in the event his proposal to the Historical Commission were rejected, Castañeda initiated discussions with a touring agency about the prospect of conducting an excursion to South America the next summer.[109]

Meanwhile, at Saint Edward's, Foik tabulated early responses from commission members. By mid-December he advised Carlos: "It has always been my experience that when a person wants to expedite something, there is always an obstacle. Dr. Driscoll is playing hide-and-seek, but I have no doubt that he will give . . . his approval. The State Deputy, who controls the treasury, has replied favorably by wire. Fathers Garriga, O'Donohoe, and [John S.] Murphy also favor the move; so we have sufficient affirmative decisions to act. I feel . . . there will not be a negative voice, though by negligence some may be silent." Foik explained that the commission would need "to go into a huddle" to work out details for "a financial arrangement" to satisfy Carlos's requirements. Then, knowing the hardships that continued to haunt Carlos and his family, the chairman conveyed a spiritual bouquet as a gift for the holidays: "I wish . . . to offer you my best wishes for a joyous Christmas and a Happy New Year. I will place a memento for you, your dear wife and baby in the Holy Sacrifice of the Mass on Christmas Day. May God bless you for the many sacrifices you are making for His honor and glory. I feel confident that a sublime satisfaction awaits you for the excellent cooperation you are giving the Commission and particularly its Chairman, who will always hold you in highest esteem and friendship." [110]

Disappointed that he had to abandon a "cherished trip to South America" but grateful for the chance to nurture his beloved vocation as historian, Carlos looked forward to returning home "to Austin in time to begin work the first week in February." For the time being he pondered when and how to notify the school board of his momentous decision. "I am hoping and praying," he told Foik, "that I can make them see it the way I do and that they will permit me to return to Austin without any hard feelings in the matter." [111] Just before Christmas the Historical Commission's consensus became complete when Driscoll, who had been away from his law office for nearly a month, removed a troublesome lingering doubt in Carlos's mind. The lawyer's vote of confidence in Castañeda, buried in an avalanche of stilted verbiage, was vital because he represented the laity, among whom were generous contributors to the treasury: "it seems to me there can be no serious objection to his proposal and of our adoption of the same, provided he has fulfilled his contract to date." [112]

Immediately after the Christmas holidays Castañeda advised the school board of his decision regarding the history project. Worried that he had taken an irreversible step in his career without the security of a written contract, Carlos nevertheless worked feverishly "winding up all school affairs" and drafting detailed guidelines for his successor, covering "all emergencies and mark[ing] out the general policy to be followed during the remainder of the year." [113] In mid-January, with legal assistance from Driscoll, Foik mailed a "draught" of an intimidating contract in triplicate addressing every conceivable problem in a working relationship between researcher-historian, editor, and sponsor. The chairman asked Carlos to amend the sections that needed refinement so that a permanent document could be typed. "You may rest assured that the business relation will be handled by us according to your wishes, and therefore you need have no misgivings on the matter as far as the Commission is concerned."[114] Likely recalling the fate of another historian, Castañeda carefully pored over the legal jargon that Driscoll had inserted to produce what lawyers cherish, an airtight covenant. In turn Carlos responded with "a few corrections in the original text" and introduced "two additional stipulations and agreements" that he insisted "must be made part of the contract." One item that needed revision and clarification pertained to authorship: "[Specifically] where the transfer and all my rights to the manuscript are stipulated, I insist, . . . that the right of authorship is not to be transferred. The way the contract reads the Commission could publish the whole under its own name without mentioning mine in any manner or merely as that of a clerk, a thing which I know they [meaning Driscoll] did not intend."[115]

Castañeda then turned to the problem of working out "satisfactory arrangements" with the school board. When the board hired Carlos in 1933 they needed a leader with sterling academic credentials to guide the schools through troublesome shoals in attaining full-fledged accreditation. Now, a year later, they still needed a spirited leader to remain at the helm while the school district battled in the courtroom against the claims of the first superintendent. Therefore, the trustees offered a compromise. They would grant released time for the superintendent to perform his contractual obligations to the Texas Historical Commission provided that for half salary he would retain an official presence with the San Felipe schools on public occasions, such as board meetings and special events. "The Board," Castañeda told Foik, "would not consent to my resigning, or giving up the job entirely. They insist that I must continue to be considered the Superintendent and that once a month I meet with the Board to discuss matters of general interest. This stipulation is just and fair and I agreed to it. It is for this reason that I amend the . . . third paragraph with regard to my severance of my relations [with the San Felipe schools] and my residence."[116]

Castañeda's response gave Foik plenty about which to worry. Proceeding on the assumption that Carlos would resign his position in San Felipe, the chairman had recommended acceptance of the historian's proposal to the commission. Now Carlos's intention to retain a tenuous connection with the district bothered his sense of propriety. Not knowing precisely how much of the historian's time would be tied up with school business particularly troubled him. Foik told Carlos: "That places me therefore in an awkward position, for there should be a time limit set up for these trips [Del Rio to Austin] so that there may be assurance on your part for the fulfillment of [the] contract according to the context of the entire instrument for agreement. I presume that we can arrive at a satisfactory understanding, however, when you present yourself to sign on the dotted line." Recalling the unfortunate misunderstanding with Dr. Steck, Foik declared: "You will realize that my caution in this matter is . . . the result of past experience on agreements that have been less formal. I am not referring to you personally, but even here [at Saint Edward's] arrangements have . . . broken down because of more pressing duties." Left with no other option but to continue friendly negotiations, Foik invited Castañeda to Saint Edward's to finalize "matters for this business agreement and any discussions related thereto." Carlos, in turn, tried to assuage the chairman's apprehension: "I feel that we can easily arrive at a satisfactory understanding and I have been working many extra hours since [the] new year making copious notes in order to lose no time in getting down to writing." [117] Satisfied with the assurance, Foik refrained from pressing Carlos for specific timetables: "Certain revisions according to your suggestion have been made in the contract which we will discuss at greater length, and at the same time you can lay before me your plans for the future." [118]

The next few months of work tested Castañeda's mettle as historian and administrator. Rather than uprooting his family from Del Rio, he had elected to drive periodically to Austin to consult with Foik and to select research materials. Initially he stayed in Austin for several days, but quickly he abandoned that schedule. "You were right," he told Father Paul; "I was homesick and wanted to be near the family again." In the comfort of home he devoted "from ten to twelve hours a day" on the final chapters of the manuscript to reach the quota of a hundred pages for the first month of full-time writing. Struggling hard to attain that goal caused him to comment, "There is one thing I am beginning to realize, and that is that to make 100 pages of final copy in a month is a real He-Man's Job." [119]

After meeting the first deadline Carlos continued outlining succeeding chapters and revising sections of the manuscript already written. To break the monotony of constant writing, in February he took the family for a long weekend to Monterrey. "It was a nice trip and afforded me a much needed relaxation," he reported later to Foik. A few days after returning refreshed to his task he mailed another installment and pledged to produce "slightly over one hundred pages for the 20th" of March. He told the priest: "I am glad you are revising the manuscript carefully, because, you know as well as I do, that composing under the conditions I am doing it, the manuscript is bound to suffer from the tremendous strain under which I have to write. If I had more time, the prose would need much less revision, but under the circumstances, it is not strange that there should be a slip here and there. . . . I sincerely appreciate your careful revision of the copy I turn over to you." Forecasting completion of the second volume by May, he observed, "If it is not finished, it won't be my fault, for I certainly am trying and will continue to do so." [120] By isolating himself from mundane school problems, in less than a week Castañeda produced another installment. Carlos admitted: "I know it can be improved, but the facts are all set down and the narrative does not read so badly. I think it is an interesting chapter and a real contribution, because many of the facts and details I have brought out have never been made known to the public before. I think it gives an excellent picture of life in Texas between 1722 and 1730 and will make a fine background for the next chapter on [Gen. Pedro de] Rivera's inspection." Working under the fearful pressure of the monthly deadlines, Carlos reminded Foik that it was "a real task to turn out this history in such a short time. I hope I can stand up under this strain." [121]

If the burden of writing were not enough for Carlos, Foik came up with a scheme for "a series of pageants to be sponsored by St. Edward's University" to promote the upcoming publications. Honestly believing that Castañeda could rapidly recall from memory scenarios depicting historical events in the Spanish colonial history of Texas, the editor asked:

> I wish, . . . that you would give the idea some consideration and perhaps there are episodes that you can summon by a little reflection that would have dramatic consequences principally to the Franciscan Era and to the Indian scenes that are narrated already in the history that has been [written] and will be taken up in the third and fourth volumes. For instance, I have a picture [in mind] of the Indian welcome to [Capt. Domingo] Ramón and the Padres, and the scene depicting the smoking of the pipe of peace. I thought . . . we could outline the action in a number of scenes that would supply material for this pageantry.

Possibly envisioning himself as drama coach, Foik sketched in detail what he thought would be required in the way of equipment and costumes to stage such pageants.[122] Enthusiastic about the installments Carlos had either mailed or delivered to Austin, he commented cheerily: "I hope that you have recovered from the drive of early March and that you are now deeply immersed in the concluding chapter of Volume II. As soon as this is all accomplished, we will celebrate, you may be sure." When not thinking of theatrical productions Foik added entries to the evolving index and tightened stylistically Castañeda's manuscript.[123]

As another springtime arrived in Del Rio, Carlos was indeed "deeply immersed," but not in what Foik preferred. Taking a break from the writing task, Superintendent Castañeda returned to the public arena to work "like fury" finalizing local arrangements for an Interscholastic League gathering. Then he drove out at night "in the middle of the worst storm" Del Rio resi-

dents had experienced "in fifty years" to keep an appointment the next morning in Alpine.[124] Traveling 225 miles along a narrow, twisting highway, he
arrived at the campus of Sul Ross State Teachers' College, situated on a prom-
ontory overlooking the small town and the beautiful Davis Mountains. Following customary salutations and time for a social cup of coffee, Carlos was
escorted by his hosts to the lecture hall for the opening session of the New
Mexico–West Texas International Relations Club Conference. After a casual
luncheon participants at Castañeda's round-table session examined the topic
of "The Present Situation in Mexico." Invigorated by an opportunity to perform again in a college setting but tempered by years of writing about Franciscan missionaries in Texas, Carlos emerged (just as Barker had predicted
earlier) as a champion defender of the Hispanic experience in the Americas. Bristling at irresponsible statements made at the round-table discussion,
Carlos waited until the panelists had finished reading their prepared essays before rising to offer an extemporaneous rebuttal.[125] As he reported later:

> *Let me tell you, they had a young fellow from El Paso who read the most*
> *virulent attack on the Church I have ever heard or read. He used as the*
> *mildest adjective the word "putrid" and all the other adjectives were con-*
> *centrated bombs of boundless hatred and unspeakable prejudice. The audi-*
> *ence was in sympathy with him. My position was indeed a ticklish one as*
> *leader of the round table, . . . but I gracefully descended from the chair and*
> *took the floor, and with tact, with veiled irony, with sly humor, with a*
> *telling blow here and there, in forty-five minutes so destroyed the impres-*
> *sion the other man made and riddled his venom-tipped thrusts, that he got*
> *up and . . . said, "When I came here I thought I had a good speech, but*
> *I have little or nothing left now." I tell you right now it took fast thinking*
> *and the utmost self control to keep cool and undo the harm done by the*
> *speaker . . . after I got through talking, the other speakers [academicians and*
> *laypersons] took the tip and tuned down their talks accordingly.*[126]

For the rest of the conference Castañeda relished the give-and-take of "oral
combat," after which, at the evening banquet, he thanked his college hosts (including President H. W. Morelock) for their courteous hospitality.[127]

Hurriedly descending the Trans-Pecos highlands, again in an intermittent
downpour, Carlos retraced the long route at night back to Del Rio. After only
a few hours of sleep Superintendent Castañeda with a burst of energy walked
into San Felipe High School the next day to preside at the Val Verde County
Interscholastic League competition. He reported: "My schools covered themselves with glory. We won out and are the all county champions. Since then
I put on a school exhibit of work done by children and it has been another

triumph. Naturally all these things keep me constantly on the go and in a tremendous nervous strain, but I am standing up fine. I feel fit and will continue to carry on." [128]

Toward the end of March, after this physical and emotional marathon, Carlos returned to the history project. "I have not done much more than a little bit of reading, mightily little at that," he admitted to Foik. However, he promised the chairman he would resume work "in earnest." He also enthusiastically endorsed Foik's proposal for a pageant: "Keep working on the idea. I think it is splendid and deserves to be pushed and carried into execution in spite of obstacles." [129]

Subsequently, unable to participate in another outdoor rally because of a cold, Carlos encouraged Eleuterio Escobar to pursue the struggle for an equitable distribution of funds to maintain the schools in the barrios of west-side San Antonio. He wrote: "I sincerely congratulate you on the splendid work you have done in the defense of the schools of West End and you know that I am with you 100 percent in all efforts to improve conditions there. You can always count on me as your sincere friend and warm admirer for your fearless leadership in defending the rights of the Mexican children of San Antonio." [130]

Meanwhile, with more than passing interest, Foik scanned the daily Austin newspaper for information about legislative action relating to "the status of educational appropriation for the University of Texas." Caught in the crunch of the upcoming centennial celebration, the editor keenly realized that successful publication of the volumes-in-progress hinged on Castañeda's renewed association with the Latin American Collection. Genuinely concerned that Carlos not be victimized by another legislative maneuver such as that in 1933, Foik offered sage advice: "I think that it is imperative that you bring influence to bear so that you may get an adjustment [of your salary] before the matter gets to the floor of either chamber. Is there anything that can be done at this end? I do not wish to interfere or get mixed up in a political tangle unless it is absolutely necessary. By this I mean that it may be possible for me to be of assistance but I believe that you should direct the movement so that you may not suffer as a result of our over-zeal for your welfare." [131] Heartened by Foik's message, Castañeda concurred with his suggestion: "I do not read the papers here regularly and to make things worse, the local paper carries little or no University news. . . . You are quite right. It will be necessary [to take action] as soon as possible. I am going to San Antonio . . . and from there will arrange to have one or two members of the [appropriations] committee worked upon. [132] If Castañeda initiated lobbying efforts on his behalf, the influence on the final outcome was minimal. In the university's new budget for the 1936–37 biennium the legislature raised the salary for the librarian of the Latin American Collection from the previous level of fifteen hundred dollars to eighteen hundred dollars, just slightly above the recommended 15 percent increase but on par with the allocation for the curator of the Wrenn Library.[133]

Naturally disappointed with the modest increment but relieved that the legislative wrangling was over, virtually paving the path for his reentry into the Latin American Collection, Carlos redoubled his concentration on research for the concluding chapters. Recognizing the need to acquire additional information, in mid-April he took Elisa and Consuelo with him on a semileisurely weekend drive to Austin. Apart from research, an ancillary objective for the trip was to coordinate a convenient date with J. Evetts Haley for vacating their rented home. Spending an entire morning looking "for one thing" and finding "half a dozen" other items, he compiled a tidy cache of material. However, the necessity of providing for the needs of a wife and child on the road slowed his pace. Unable to stay longer, Carlos decided to skip an afternoon appointment at Saint Edward's University and return to the border. In San Antonio, where he and his family stopped for an overnight rest, Elisa's relatives persuaded her and Consuelo to stay for the festive Battle of Flowers Parade later in the week. Agreeing to the plan, early in the morning Carlos continued the journey westward to Del Rio, arriving just in time to control a minor crisis in the superintendent's office. "As I suspected," he told Father Foik, "my presence was anxiously desired. There will be an important board meeting tonight and I will have my hands full preparing for it to-day." [134]

After the board meeting Castañeda secluded himself at home to devote long hours to writing. At Saint Edward's, meanwhile, Foik worried about several items on his agenda relating to the annual meeting of the Texas Knights of Columbus in May. To assist Carlos's work on volume 1 he dispatched a copy of Dr. Steck's manuscript by insured parcel post.[135] Chafed that Carlos had missed their scheduled appointment, the editor also sent him a mild reprimand: "I know you have been crowded with many activities, but I had hoped to get something on paper regarding the projects that are very important to the Catholics of Texas. It is true that these matters do not come within the scope of your contract, but I have been depending on your promises made in correspondence with me, but I have received no tangible results. You promised to select, with me, a program of pageantry which was to be presented to Father [Joseph] Maguire [president of Saint Edward's] for his consideration." [136] Before the missive reached the border Carlos returned one of his "promises," a critique of a manuscript entitled "Sketch of the History of Texas," by a friend of the chairman, that Foik had sent for evaluation.[137] In effect, the critique became an extra stress on an already creaking schedule.

Piqued by what he considered unjust criticism, Castañeda firmly pushed back, at least enough to clarify the issues. He wrote: "The difficulty is not that I am holding down two jobs. The real trouble is that through my good nature you have tried to saddle on me the responsibility for two or three additional honorary jobs. . . . But I have felt and still feel that my first duty is to the K. of C. Historical Commission in completing the second volume, and to the San Felipe Schools in administering them until the end of the school year. All other matters are secondary and I do not feel even a moral obligation in postponing them to accomplish the first two purposes." Turning to the research problem that had contributed to writer's block, for the first time in months of heavy correspondence Castañeda revealed the reason for the slack in productivity.

> The El Paso Chapter has proved a much more difficult task than any of those tackled in the second volume. The materials for a connected story of the gradual exploration of the vast region from San Juan Bautista to El Paso have not been collected. All I have found after a careful search of all the transcripts in the University of Texas, are a few disconnected and partial accounts of different expeditions at both ends of the line. I have voluminous notes on each of these separate efforts but I cannot bring myself to write a disconnected and checkered chapter which will detract from the unity of the rest of the volume. I am in a real quandary. It isn't that I am shirking my work, nor that I have not made an earnest effort to get the facts. The trouble is the material is not available. I have sent for one more document which I need from Austin. As soon as I get it, I will . . . write some sort of an account. . . . Were it not for the fact that the material at hand is so unsatisfactory, I would have written this chapter by now. I have put off writing it because I feel that I may find something else which may clear the situation. I wish I had not undertaken it. I realize that it should be done and that it will be a real contribution because there is nothing on the subject, but this very consideration makes it all the more difficult and impossible to turn it out in the finished form with the rapidity, the precision, and the coherence which characterize the rest of the book.

Quickly endeavoring to heal bruised feelings, Carlos offered an olive branch: "If you have other pressing things to do my advice is to do them and leave the rest of your time to check the last chapter. The Commission has much to be happy over in having at least one complete volume, thanks to my strenuous efforts and your Herculean cooperation." [138]

About ten days before closing the San Felipe schools Castañeda journeyed to Taylor, approximately twenty-five miles northeast of Austin, to report to the Historical Commission meeting jointly with the Knights of Columbus on his progress with the history. At that time he presented the first harvest of seeds sown nearly a decade before.

It is with pleasure and pardonable pride that the historiographer informs the Commission . . . that a whole volume, consisting of 543 typewritten pages of text, covering the period from 1694 to 1731, has been completed and is now ready to be turned over to the proofreaders. The accomplishment of this task has required constant application, but the historiographer has been animated in his efforts by the desire to see the concrete realization of a work planned ten years ago, as a fitting tribute to the faithful and zealous Franciscan Padres and other pioneers, who with love and unstinted heroism gave their lives to lay the foundations of this great State.

Carlos also reminded the commission of the project's wider scope: "But the historiographer is fully aware, . . . that the task is just begun. There remains a large portion to be done. He is at this time, already busily engaged in examining the voluminous materials that will enable him to write as fully the portion which remains to be covered in the subsequent three volumes. It is his purpose to work steadily, and with the same enthusiasm, in the hope that before the centennial year is over, he will have at least one more volume in the hands of the Commission in time for its publication before the close of 1936." [139]

With one book-length manuscript in the editor's possession, the Texas Historical Commission contemplated a course of action for its publication. Besides considering the option of contracting with a major publishing house, such as Macmillan, the members entertained an attractive proposal from Victor Pannell, a Knight of Columbus delegate and representative of Von Boeckmann-Jones, a small but reputable printing company in Austin. Von Boeckmann-Jones offered to invest a sizable amount of risk capital in the publication venture, leaving the Historical Commission altogether free of financial responsibility. What the Austin firm expected in return was an energetic promotional campaign by the constituent councils of the Knights of Columbus throughout the state. [140] Impressed with Pannell's presentation but not wishing to rush into a contract, the commission members deferred a decision until later. However, because they had a bulky manuscript on hand after years of waiting, they reopened discussion on the matter of a title for the history series. Contemplating this question the previous September, Foik had proposed as a working model *Texas: The Land of Sacred Shrines and Memories.* Soliciting Castañeda's reaction, the chairman explained the rationale for his choice: "It has been suggested that the binder's title be the word 'Texas' alone and that the secondary title appear on the general title page. Of course each volume may also have a special title representing the contents of that particular volume. I want you to give this matter considerable thought if you have any leisure moments at all. My reason for a properly chosen title is to protect ourselves against prejudice if the words 'Catholic Church' were used on either the binding or title page. In this matter I am upheld by certain bookmen whom I have consulted." [141] After some consideration Castañeda said he thought the title "good, but a little long yet." As an alternative he suggested *Texas: Unrecorded Triumphs of the Faith:*

> *This title suggests nothing of a church history, it is indefinite enough to arouse curiosity and to be mysterious and one may almost say romantic. It appeals to the imagination, and in the final analysis it is essentially correct for the triumphs of the missionaries and their work as such as remained unrecorded and they were triumphs of the Faith more than of the Sword. I will not argue in support of the title further. You read it over, close your eyes, think of a title page and the bold letters staring you in the face* TEXAS: UNRECORDED TRIUMPHS OF THE FAITH *and tell me with all sincerity if you do not feel a strong desire to turn the page and see what it is all about. That is the real test.*[142]

When the Texas Historical Commission assembled in late November, 1934, Father Foik proposed the succinct title *Our Texas Heritage,* after which, after considerable discussion, Monsignor Mariano Garriga offered *The History of the Catholic Church in Texas,* which the group adopted.[143] Garriga had not consulted with Castañeda, however, and the historian subsequently offered "some very forceful reasons" that persuaded the monsignor to concede that his "former opinion was not correct." At the Taylor meeting in May, 1935, Castañeda's suggested title *Our Texas Heritage: A Comprehensive Treatment of the Catholic Church in Texas* was discussed. The word *Catholic* and the length of the subtitle generated extended discussion, after which Monsignor Garriga moved to rescind the decision of 1934 and substituted *Our Catholic Heritage in Texas, 1519–1936* as a "modified title" for "the entire series of volumes." To preserve the integrity of the latest alternative Castañeda explained that the new title was not his concept, "but rather Dr. Foik's suggestion. We had quite a discussion this past year and finally compromised." Apprehensive about offending Jewish, Protestant, and other readers, some members advocated deleting the word *Catholic* altogether from the title. In the end, however, Garriga's new proposal carried the day, and *Our Catholic Heritage in Texas, 1519–1936* prevailed as the title of a landmark series of volumes that would become synonymous with Carlos Eduardo Castañeda.[144]

With a sense of having accomplished two formidable tasks—the superintendency of the San Felipe schools and the completion of volume 2 of *Our Catholic Heritage in Texas*—Castañeda returned to Del Rio to close out his tenure as administrator. Tidying up affairs in the office, Carlos announced to the press the redemption of two series of scrip, totaling forty-three hundred dollars, leaving outstanding only one issue to be retired. Next he invited two guest speakers to address the community at school graduation exercises. As a special favor to the superintendent Cleofas Calleros, prominent among Hispanic Americans as an El Paso civic leader, public speaker, and lay historian, spoke at a ceremony for the eighteen students promoted from grammar school to high school. At San Felipe High School on the second night, with Castañeda in his customary role as master of ceremonies, W. A. Stiegler of the State Department of Education appealed to the graduating class of seven to discover their inner talents and to perfect them through constant application.[145]

In the few remaining days in May, Castañeda carefully reviewed documents requiring his signature for deposit among the district's permanent records. Whenever feasible he personally thanked members of the board of trustees (particularly veterans such as Santos Garza, Guadalupe Díaz, and G. G. Velasco) for the staunch support they gave to his administration. Admittedly, in the last five months of his tenure Castañeda had stayed away from daily supervisory routine, but overall his energetic presence in San Felipe gave to the barrio residents a feeling of dignity and worth. With pride in what he and the faculty had accomplished through team effort, Carlos wistfully transferred the symbolic baton of leadership to Gilberto Cerda, his chosen successor, who earned the promotion through on-the-job training with the outgoing superintendent. At the end of the month the Castañeda family bid final farewell to Del Rio. As they approached the highway at the east end, crossing the bridge over San Felipe Creek, no doubt Carlos and Elisa reflected on how their lives had intertwined with the dreams and hopes of the people of the barrio—and especially of the students and teachers. Driving toward San Antonio, the former superintendent was grateful he had found summertime employment teaching history at Our Lady of the Lake College. Besides the opportunity to teach, he anxiously looked ahead to writing the first volume of the mission series.[146]

Return from the Border, 1935–38

After a hiatus of nearly two years in public school administration Carlos E. Castañeda returned home from the border. During the summer of 1935 the family remained in San Antonio while Carlos taught a history course at Our Lady of the Lake College and defined the scope and content of the first volume of *Our Catholic Heritage in Texas*. Having completed the second volume, highlighting Spanish colonial development from 1693 to 1731, Castañeda honestly confronted the challenge of reconciling the scope and content of another historian's manuscript with his own conceptual design of topics to include in the companion tome. After several weeks of wrestling with the problem of trying to salvage as much of the original work as possible, he admitted his frustration to the series editor, Rev. Dr. Paul J. Foik, C.S.C., of Saint Edward's University in Austin: "I have read critically through the entire portion done by [Rev. Dr. Francis Borgia] Steck. I do not even like the chapter divisions. His style and the way he has organized the materials he used are abominable. I am going to scrap the whole thing and regroup it and treat it after my own fashion. I would like, very much, however, to discuss the entire plan . . . with you. When I get started writing, it is going to go like wildfire." To maintain an amicable working relationship with the editor, as well as to procure library materials needed to write the new volume, Castañeda drove to Austin early in the summer to consult with Foik.[1]

Of even greater urgency, however, was finding long-term employment. Initially Castañeda considered reviving job discussions with the University of New Mexico, but he quickly abandoned that idea when the school failed to make a serious offer. In time for the Fourth of July celebration Carlos received confirmation from the University of Texas of his "official appointment as Latin American Librarian" carrying "full restoration" of his former salary. "I feel this was a commendable act of justice on the part of the administration," he told Foik, "and it shows that Dr. Benedict and the Board of Regents were sincere in their desire that I should return."[2] Although Castañeda gallantly absolved the university of all blame for the discrimination he had suffered, he manifested a skittish mood toward pockets of conflict that lurked inside and outside the library.

Notwithstanding the vow to accelerate his writing "like wildfire," the level of productivity remained dormant. To be sure, Castañeda consulted the books borrowed from the library and compiled "full notes," but somehow composition eluded him to the point that he was unable "to write a single line." While he attributed the lack of productivity to the demands of teaching, the real cause for his low energy level was the tremendous attention he had devoted to revising the Fray Juan Agustín Morfi manuscript, which had been his doctoral dissertation, to satisfy requirements of the editorial committee of the Quivira Society in Los Angeles. Eager to get another publication to his credit, Carlos had immersed himself in the revisions in order to finish ahead of schedule. "They can go over the corrected manuscript," he explained to Foik, "and send it to the press." Highly "elated over the prospect of getting Morfi out" as a book in autumn, Castañeda, comparing the subject matter of his contribution vis-à-vis an earlier Quivira Society monograph on Texas governor Martín de Alarcón, opined that his work stood "out like the sun against the moon." Genuinely concerned, however, about his obligations to the Texas Historical Commission of the Knights of Columbus, Carlos promised the editor that at the end of summer, when the family had resettled in Austin, he would be able to concentrate on writing. Certainly by the end of the year, if not by Thanksgiving, he expected to "have most of the first volume finished." [3]

Shortly before returning to Austin, Castañeda arranged with J. Evetts Haley, who had rented the family home (described by the occupant as "a right nice little house"), to vacate the premises at a convenient time for both tenant and landlord. In late August the Castañedas moved back into their modest residence at 301 West Thirty-seventh Street grateful to be in familiar surroundings again. Carlos's domain, of course, extended beyond the neighborhood to the Latin American Collection. He undoubtedly experienced a tinge of triumph as he walked "through those exotic, arched doors at the west end of the corridor on the third floor of the University Library" and surveyed the "atmosphere of hushed serenity" that pervaded everything. Clearly this was his secondary home. Looking down, he noticed the floor covering, "aged brown in color, yet efficiently springy" for comfortable "soft walking." Glancing around "the spacious room" in which he had worked long hours, he fondly approved of the decorations "in quiet yet deep color." All the trimmings were "smooth browns" with the exception of the ceiling beams, which reflected "broad areas of quiet blue." Stepping through a "leather-covered door" at the north end of the room, Carlos rediscovered the treasure of the Genaro García Collection—"two tiers of bookstacks in [a] one-ceilinged room, kept spic and span in the most modern manner." Occupying a sizable section of wall space, just as he had arranged them, several "built-in bookcases" displayed "shelf upon shelf" of old books behind glass that, were it not for the building's adequate ventilation system, surely would have emitted a "faint, acrid odor" of antiquity. What especially intrigued Castañeda about the Latin American Collection was "its workability." Under his curatorship the contents of the library, "arranged for use, not merely as a spectacle," included "many spectacular things below its quiet exterior."[4]

As Carlos occupied himself with library routine, interspersed with research and composition, Foik carefully reviewed basic expectations for negotiating with a reputable company to publish *Our Catholic Heritage in Texas*. The chairman admitted that Catholic publishing firms, even "the most prominent and successful," could not "be relied upon to fill the ticket." Proximity to both editor and historian was a factor that persuaded him to favor an Austin company, Von Boeckmann-Jones, especially because the owners were willing to invest twenty-five thousand dollars' "worth of capital" in the publication of the series. Having made up his mind, Foik expected nothing less than full support from the Texas Historical Commission. Foik told commission member Joseph O'Donohoe: "We cannot delay publication any longer seeking a firm that will take over the entire series. I will not go into the details of any contract at this time . . . that [decision] has been entrusted to . . . a committee composed of the Chairman, the State Deputy [of the Knights of Columbus], and the Past State Deputy [Joseph I. Driscoll], but I wish it to be known emphatically that on such an important consideration, I expect the cooperation of every active member of the Commission and that [shall be] *muy pronto.*[5]

Meanwhile Castañeda the historiographer (as the commission referred to him) searched for new opportunities to supplement his university salary. An unexpected windfall was an invitation to teach a graduate course on the Southwest at Our Lady of the Lake College under the auspices of the Southern Branch Summer Session sponsored by Catholic University of America. Castañeda was anxious to establish a visible connection with the fraternity of borderlands scholars when he accepted the part-time job at Our Lady of the Lake. To this purpose he finally persuaded the college dean, Sister M. Angelique Ayres (elevated to Mother Superior), to purchase for the library a photostatic set of the Saltillo Archives—consisting of approximately two thousand pages of documentary sources bound in fifty volumes—at a reduced price of $1,000, payable in annual installments of $250 beginning in January, 1936.[6]

In November, Castañeda happily notified Foik about his progress with the manuscript: "My Coronado chapter is coming along nicely. I know you are going to enjoy reading it."[7] Of immediate urgency for the chairman, however, was securing permission from the editor of *The Catholic World* in New York to reprint Carlos's 1932 essay, "The First American Play." To stimulate public interest in the upcoming volumes of *Our Catholic Heritage,* Foik reactivated the Preliminary Studies of the Texas Catholic Historical Society. In this instance the chairman envisioned a bilingual edition of a historical drama, "The Conversion and Baptism of the Last Four Kings of Tlascala in New Spain," preceded by the author's "constructive and valuable" introductory essay.[8]

Traveling to San Antonio late in November, Castañeda presented an overview of his accomplishments with the initial volume to the Texas Historical Commission, then meeting on the campus of Incarnate Word College: "Beginning with the earliest exploration of the Gulf coast by [Alonso Álvarez de] Pineda in 1519, the various expeditions, explorations, and attempted settlements that touched any part of the present State of Texas will be carefully studied in this volume to determine just what parts were visited. In this manner the discovery, exploration, and gradual extension of knowledge acquired concerning the State, its native population, and its physical characteristics will be presented in a connected narrative." Aware that most members of the commission were not professional historians, Castañeda embellished his report with interesting details as a preview of forthcoming attractions in the finished product. To remind them that the serious practice of history was time-consuming, he outlined a few outstanding problems: "Much remains to be done in the completion of the volume in hand, but steady application of the historiographer hopes to bring it to a close before the next meeting of the Historical Commission. The careful and critical examination of the sources and the findings of the leading scholars in this romantic and truly marvelous era of Texas history will reveal many details heretofore unsuspected and will disclose the earliest history of the State as vividly and as graphically as the later period."[9]

Like a miller separating grain from chaff during threshing, Castañeda applied a rigorous methodology of internal and external criticism to the documentary evidence. To an inquiry from a scholar who myopically preferred studying only the Spanish period of northern Tamaulipas (formerly Nuevo Santander), Carlos replied: "The documentary sources for the history of mission evidence in the lower Rio Grande Valley have not been studied yet, and this accounts for the great ignorance concerning this matter. The sources cited by Miss [Florence] Scott are taken from the document[s] relating to the work of [José de] Escandón and refer only to the original settlement and early development but not the [subsequent] events. When I get to this portion of the history I will be able to tell . . . more about it."[10] Casting off signs of lethargy that had plagued him in the summer, Castañeda examined the sources and explained to Foik the times and routes of two seventeenth-century frontiersmen named De León: "the statement that the first Spanish exploration party crossed the Río Grande in 1723[,] which [Hubert Howe] Bancroft's History cites[,] is entirely unfounded as you know, for Alonso de León, Sr. crossed the Río Grande as early as 1653 and his son crossed in the region of the lower Río Grande valley [in the 1680s]." [11]

Partly motivated by the imminent release of *History of Texas, 1673–1779, by Fray Juan Agustín Morfi, Missionary, Teacher, Historian* in an attractive two-volume edition, Carlos plunged into the task of drafting, revising, and finalizing chapters for the Knights of Columbus project. With family and friends he welcomed the Texas centennial year and the arrival of first copies of the new book. Unabashedly he tried to convince librarians to order the Morfi title. [12]

Five years had elapsed since that memorable day in Mexico City when he discovered the Morfi manuscript amid a pile of "rich and extensive" documents belonging to San Francisco el Grande convent, general depository of all Franciscan missionary records of colonial New Spain. With the publication of his annotated translation of Fray Morfi's chronicle, Castañeda took advantage of the opportunity to inform the public about his adventures in Mexican archives. J. Villasana Haggard, a graduate student in history, captured the essence of the 1930 event in Mexico City for a Dallas newspaper.

> Two weeks after his arrival, Dr. Castañeda came upon a manuscript of about 300 pages without a title or signature. Ordinarily he would have passed it up, but the particular handwriting attracted his attention. As he began to peruse it he discovered that it was a history of Texas. Being familiar with the handwriting of Fray Juan Agustín Morfi as found in other manuscripts of the prolific friar, it was not difficult for him to determine beyond a doubt that the manuscript was none other than the long lost "History of Texas." In 600 paragraphs of manuscript, numbered consecutively and occupying 337 pages, Father Morfi had summarized, in his characteristically clear and pointed style, the history of Texas from 1673 to 1779. In the finished draft . . . Father Morfi cut out all the nonessentials. Death, however, prevented him from putting the finishing touches to the monumental work. The manuscript contained numerous interlinear corrections and there were two small notebooks where they were to be inserted in the manuscript. [13]

Castañeda seldom missed an opportunity to expound on the Morfi book or related topics of Texas history. One evening in the spring, accompanied by a Catholic chaplain, he visited the camp of a Civilian Conservation Corps (CCC) facility in Pflugerville, a rural community in northeast Travis County. Following a weekly religious service camp administrators invited Castañeda and Father Lawrence A. Ferrero, O.M.I., to dinner, after which the guests toured the classrooms of the CCC's "educational program." At the invitation of a history instructor Carlos delivered an impromptu lecture to approximately one hundred "officers and enrolled personnel" of Company 3809 of the "tree army" in which he included fleeting comments about current research and composition. An appreciative group of CCC directors extended an invitation for Carlos to return for "another visit soon." [14]

By springtime the centennial observances planned by private groups and organizations complemented the official celebrations scheduled for the general public. Certainly the programs of the former did not compare to the scope of the latter, but they coincided with the commemoration of the independence of 1836 that culminated in the creation of the Republic of Texas. The Philosophical Society of Texas, a premier civic organization founded by Mirabeau B. Lamar, second president of the republic and its initial officer, included in its roster the names of prominent stalwarts of the nineteenth century, such as David G. Burnet, Anson Jones, David S. Kaufman, and Ashbel Smith. Reorganized in 1936 under another charter to celebrate the Lone Star centennial, the Philosophical Society of Texas recruited an illustrious band of scholars. Whereas the new membership contained the names of Eugene C. Barker, Herbert E. Bolton, Umphrey Lee, and Victor Schoffelmayer, a marked difference in the two lists, signifying a change in attitude and tolerance, was the induction of Carlos E. Castañeda. [15]

Similar to the Philosophical Society in its resolve to participate in the centennial, the Texas Historical Commission launched a publicity campaign to promote the forthcoming release of the initial volumes of *Our Catholic Heritage*. In an edition of *The Southern Messenger*, a biweekly newspaper that boasted numerous subscribers in all six Catholic dioceses in Texas (Amarillo, Corpus Christi, Dallas, El Paso, Galveston, and San Antonio), Father Foik and Von Boeckmann-Jones coordinated efforts to stimulate readers' interest in the new publication.

Volumes 1 and 2 of "Our Catholic Heritage in Texas" will be ready for delivery by June 1, 1936. This work is printed in Franklin Old Style type on 70-pound Clear Spring Text, Antique Finish.

Each volume will be illustrated in keeping with the era treated therein. There will be approximately 450 pages of reading matter to the volume. The histories will be bound in Blue Moorish Fabrikoid, embossed in Mission Gold.

The First Edition will be limited to 1,000 sets of seven volumes each. For those placing their order for the entire set by June 10, 1936, and sending with it a check for $10 to cover the cost of the first two volumes, we will *send two beautiful engraved etchings of the Alamo and Concepcion Missions of San Antonio of San Antonio. . . .*

The price of "Our Catholic Heritage in Texas," will be Five Dollars per volume post-paid.[16]

Encouraged by the widespread attention his scholarly endeavors had cultivated, Castañeda channeled his energies to the Latin American Collection during daylight hours and at night labored under pressure to meet the deadlines of *Our Catholic Heritage.* Meanwhile, at Saint Edward's University, Father Foik endeavored to expedite the work toward completion. One afternoon, for instance, three researchers of the Works Project Administration came by his office in search of historical information for an *American Guide Book.* In exchange for citing *Our Catholic Heritage in Texas* in their report Foik allowed them to read diligently "the page proof sheets of our history, soon to be published." [17] At home, writing under extremely rigorous late-hour or early-morning schedules, Castañeda finished the first volume by mid-May, a few weeks behind schedule because he had discovered "new materials that had to be incorporated in the closing chapters" to add dimension to the final product. Consequently, the delay embarrassed the printers at Von Boeckmann-Jones, who had promised "to release the first two volumes for circulation by June first." [18] Aware of the delay but not perturbed about it, Castañeda delivered what he thought would be his final report to the Texas Historical Commission. At the Hotel Buccaneer in Galveston he summarized the magnitude of the enterprise and the difficult constraints under which he had labored. Aside from minor details pertaining to seventeenth-century expeditions that penetrated the territory of Texas, obviously inserted to indicate depth and scope of scholarly research, Castañeda's report was essentially a lesson in historiography: "As a result of the careful examinations of the voluminous sources . . . the historiographer has been able to piece together the connected narrative of the history of Texas from 1519 to 1731, showing that incidents and events that happened to have little or no relation to the subsequent history of the state [actually] had direct bearing." He described how he had endeavored "to present the truth in light of the sources" at his disposal. In reconstructing "the glorious epic of the spiritual conquest" of Texas, he selected from "the voluminous materials" in the library only the documents that yielded "the most significant and human details." His report continued:

Errors there are, for it is impossible to escape them, but a conscientious effort to reduce these to a minimum has been constantly made. In the main the fundamental facts are vouched for; in every instance the source or sources for each statement have been indicated; and a full and detailed bib-

liography, with the place where the sources may be consulted, has been in-
cluded. For the convenience of the reader and those who may turn to the
pages of the two volumes now completed, a detailed alphabetical index has
been made for each volume by the chairman of the Commission.

He concluded by acknowledging Foik's "useful suggestions, kind encouragement, and constant guidance" during the research and writing phases of the
two volumes.[19]

Temporarily liberated from the burden of deadlines, Castañeda finalized an
unsettled matter in June, namely taking an oath as a naturalized citizen of the
United States. He was motivated in part by the centennial observance, which
was reinforced by the reality that he had lived in Texas for nearly thirty years
and the need to provide security for his family. In January, in response to an
application filed the previous month, he had received notification from the
office of Immigration and Naturalization Service (then under the Department
of Labor) that his Declaration of Intention to become an American citizen had
been issued. Whether he took the matter for granted or simply treated it as one
of several issues in a crowded schedule, it is truly mystifying why Castañeda
decided to be reticent about this important milestone in his life. Accordingly,
six months later on June 8, 1936, at the U.S. Court for the Western District of
Texas he officially became a citizen of his adopted country.[20]

Insulated at last from critics in the library, at least on the citizenship issue,
Castañeda devoted the rest of the month to discharging obligations in the
Latin American Collection. That summer he accompanied President Harry Y.
Benedict and Professor Charles W. Hackett, along with city, state, and church
dignitaries, to a luncheon at the Driskill Hotel in downtown Austin to pay
tribute to Father Paul J. Foik on the silver jubilee of his ordination as a priest.
During the program Carlos joined several speakers in praising the fifty-six-
year-old Foik for his work in chairing the Texas Historical Commission,
which was "sponsoring the Centennial history of the Church" in the Lone Star
State. Then Foik acknowledged the cooperation extended by the University of
Texas "from the president down" in granting permission to photocopy early
documents in the library's archives. In particular the chairman signaled out
Castañeda for his most recent contributions and especially "for his painstaking work in searching these documents, virtually all of them . . . in Spanish."[21]

Ever faithful to the principle of family unity, a few days after the luncheon
Castañeda tried to negotiate a mutual exchange with the dean of Our Lady of
the Lake College in San Antonio. For allowing his niece María Castañeda to
enroll at the school for the rest of the year, he offered to donate a set of sixty-
seven volumes of the Saltillo Archives to the library. "I want her to live at the
college and to take piano lessons, art work, and physical education," he in-

formed Mother Angelique. As events turned out, for reasons of delicate health María deferred enrolling at the college, but the inquiry allowed Uncle Carlos to renew contact with the sisters of the Congregation of Divine Providence.[22]

When long-range plans for teaching a summer course at Our Lady of the Lake failed to materialize, Castañeda promptly secured a short-term appointment in Albuquerque. From the University of New Mexico he promoted the upcoming release of the initial volumes of *Our Catholic Heritage in Texas*.[23] Notwithstanding his firm dedication to work, Carlos enjoyed sharing simple pleasures with his family. For that short stay in Albuquerque they rented a house in the city's northeast quadrant near Sandía Mountain, which dominated the horizon. Daughter Consuelo vividly recalled that experience in New Mexico: "And we had a beautiful, huge, I mean old-timey backyard . . . [and] back porch (screened-in porches, you know), and we used to rest, sit there in the back. And this huge mountain, not but a few hundred feet in front of us, would be in the background. And those most gorgeous sunsets, . . . [were] just beautiful. I've never forgotten that. And, we used to sit out there. . . . He used to smoke a pipe a lot or light a cigar, and just talk and watch the sunset, or go walking up the mountain as the sun was setting."[24]

Following that sojourn in New Mexico, Carlos and the family returned to Austin. Reinvigorated by the summertime pleasure of conversing almost on a daily basis with scholars such as George P. Hammond and France V. Scholes, Castañeda rumbled into the Latin American Collection weighed down by one or two overloaded briefcases. Helen Ardel Moore, a coworker in the cataloging department of the library, recalled Carlos's "long lope" as he darted from one section to another: "He never seemed in a hurry, but he covered a great deal of ground in a short time. In appearance he was neat, though his clothes were often faded, but nobody thought anything about it because we were all working because we needed to, during the Depression. . . . I made only twenty-five cents an hour, but, of course, his much more important work paid him a much higher wage."[25]

Meanwhile, ensconced in the hill-top campus of Saint Edward's, Father Foik pored over the galley sheets clarifying ambiguous passages in the narrative. Before proceeding to page proofs, if revisions became impractical and prohibitive the editor earnestly sought Carlos's help with respect to proper names and locations of Franciscan missionaries at La Junta de los Ríos, near the confluence of the Rio Conchos and the Rio Grande opposite the Big Bend of Texas.[26]

At this phase of the project interruptions became standard procedures in the Latin American Collection, as Carlos deftly moved from one inquiry to the next. Among the changes of which he ardently approved was the assignment of a work-study student under the auspices and funding of the National Youth

Administration. Jack Autrey Dabbs, Carlos's young assistant, described their initial encounter:

> *I first met Dr. Castañeda in the Fall of 1936. At the time I was a graduate student in Spanish at the University of Texas and on the N.Y.A. program. . . . When I reported to work with him, he sat down with me and explained what he wanted done. He had already started on the project of preparing a guide to the MSS [manuscripts] in the Latin American Library, but he had had little time to work on it. He explained to me how he wanted cards written with basic descriptions of each MS., and he showed me where the MSS were kept, mostly in the locked glass cases of the old Latin American Library on the third floor of the Main Library Building.*[27]

Generally satisfied with Dabbs's meticulous progress, Castañeda plunged into other activities related to his work. During the euphoria of the state's centennial the University of Texas received "a special grant" to purchase additional volumes for the library system. To compile an assessment of needs the university administration appointed an ad hoc committee (Carlos included) to draft a policy for the Latin American Collection. One autumn afternoon, while the committee deliberated behind closed doors, two ladies politely interrupted the discussion. Castañeda described the visitors: "One was past middle age, and the other was a young girl. They were the mother-in-law and the daughter of the late William B. Stephens of Mexico, of whom Demetrio García, a well-known Mexican book dealer and collector[,] said, 'His books and manuscripts relative to Spain's possessions in the Southwest make him an authority as a collector.'. . . They brought a small portfolio with a few selected items to find out if we were interested in the purchase of the entire collection." The book "samples" indeed aroused the interest of the committee members, particularly Castañeda, whose identify with the borderlands school of history was now firmly established. For the time being, however, all they could do as a group was to recommend to the administration that a serious evaluation of the Stephens collection be undertaken at the earliest opportunity.[28]

As the centennial year of 1936 advanced toward the end of autumn Castañeda merrily welcomed one accolade after another. Besides *Our Catholic Heritage,* which awaited critical review, a bit of news that boosted his morale was a decision of the Yanaguana Society to publish his master's thesis under the title *Report of the Spanish Archives in San Antonio.* Pledging cooperation to Frederick C. Chabot, leader of the society in San Antonio, Carlos responded: "I have consulted the University authorities and they have given their consent. The only stipulation is that the University Library be given ten copies when published. Personally I hope you can give me five. . . . Before it goes to press, I would like to run over a copy to correct a number of typographical errors. Furthermore, I will be glad to read galley and page proof[s] to insure as accurate a printing as possible." [29] While these publications represented occasions for celebration, Carlos had another reason for rejoicing. In November, among family and friends, he celebrated his fortieth birthday. In between work and celebration he joined Father Foik on a trip to the gulf coast to attend the installation of Monsignor Mariano S. Garriga, charter member of the Texas Historical Commission, as coadjutor bishop of Corpus Christi. In Garriga's elevation to the Catholic episcopacy the two historians gained access to an influential voice among the hierarchy in Texas for promoting scholarly projects.[30]

Unencumbered by immediate writing pressures, Castañeda accelerated his work schedule that also included counseling students who came by the library. Jack A. Dabbs recalled: "Frequently I had to go to him for help in making out the entry for one MS or another. My impression was that he was a very active person, combining duties as librarian of the Latin American Collection, helping students with library problems, and interspersed with all of this his interest in counselling Latin-American students—mostly Mexicanos but lots of Tejanos also—who came to him with personal problems." Devoting fifteen hours a week to the special project in the Latin American Collection, Dabbs acquired a unique perspective of how Castañeda operated. He wrote:

> I worked . . . at a carrel . . . or at one of the big tables near the glass cases at the side of his desk. . . . At this time the Texas Collection occupied the south end of this large room. . . . Thus I observed his activities nearly all of the 15 hours a week. I remember being impressed from the beginning by his energy, knowledge of Spanish and the Library, and his friendly and helpful attitude toward everybody. I do not remember anyone coming to him for help and being turned away. He always tried to offer some helpful suggestion, even when he could really do nothing. Of course this often meant breaking into a conference with one person to talk to a newcomer. When I ran into some difficult spot and needed help, he was always ready not only to answer my questions but to give me a short lecture on what [the manuscript] was all about and to add information.[31]

During the Christmas holidays Castañeda traveled west to El Paso to speak at a centennial marker dedication, hosted by two local councils of the Knights of Columbus, commemorating late-seventeenth-century Spanish colonial settlement at Mission San Antonio de la Ysleta. Ironically a celebration that began as a simple, straightforward program soon became entangled in a web of misunderstandings, miscues, and bruised egos. Compounding the situation were three factors: 1) the uncertainty of whether the engraving company (Rodríguez Brothers of San Antonio) would complete the job and deliver the marker in time for dedication on Sunday, December 6, 1936; 2) independent plans by another committee to honor the bishop of El Paso, Most Reverend Anthony J. Schuler, S.J., on his "Golden Jubilee celebration" at midmonth; and 3) Castañeda's complex schedule of speaking engagements, organized to reduce traveling expenses by stopping at prearranged locations from San Angelo to El Paso. Ultimately the granite marker arrived just before the rescheduled date of December 20, allowing Carlos to reshuffle his schedule of guest lectures. Gauging his pace of travel to arrive in El Paso on the weekend of the dedication, Castañeda thoroughly enjoyed the multiple festivities planned by his friend Cleofas Calleros, including a dinner party. Recalling the time Calleros had driven to Del Rio to speak at a commencement ceremony, Carlos gladly repaid the favor, publicizing at every turn the work of the Texas Historical Commission.[32] After the last event Calleros notified Foik, who was unable to attend: "During Carlos' stay in El Paso we made good use of his services. He certainly put the Knights of Columbus Historical Commission and our 'Catholic Heritage,' on the map[.] He did a great service to El Paso and this region, and to this we are indebted to the Commission and particularly to you."[33]

Castañeda returned home to celebrate the holidays with Elisa and Consuelo. Obviously he had much about which to be grateful. By denying himself the delight of ordinary social pleasures, he found the time to finish writing the first volume of *Our Catholic Heritage*. Combined with the completion of the second tome begun in Del Rio, he had fulfilled the promise of the Knights of Columbus to the Lone Star centennial. Equally fulfilling to Castañeda was the publication of Fray Morfi's *History of Texas*, reviewed by J. Villasana Haggard:

> A more appropriate person than Dr. Castañeda could hardly have been found to translate and edit this book. His bilingual aptitude has enabled him to make a flawless translation. The highest tribute that can be paid him is to state that the reader is not conscious the work is a translation. . . . by masterful research Dr. Castañeda has enriched Father Morfi's work with thorough and enlightening footnotes. The reader is compelled to ignore the mediocre style of the translator's introduction and his excessive use of pronouns with indefinite antecedents by the scholarship he displays in his presentation of the Franciscan's masterpiece.[34]

Shortly after New Year's Day, elated by early reviews of the Morfi book, Castañeda drove to San Antonio to speak to members of the Yanaguana Society at a Sunday afternoon meeting.[35] Society president Chabot, eager to advertise the group's publication of Castañeda's 1923 thesis, distributed advance copies of the book to Herbert E. Bolton at the renowned Bancroft Library in California. Quite proficient with archival inventories, Bolton acknowledged the gesture with a cogent observation: "Dr. Castañeda has done an admirable piece of work in preparing the Guide to the Spanish Archives in San Antonio and it reveals a surprising amount of important materials."[36] Mother Angelique, unable to attend Castañeda's presentation at the Yanaguana Society's "open house," relied upon a college alumna to convey a fairly accurate description of the proceedings. Disappointed that Castañeda had not visited the campus, the dean admitted hearing from secondhand sources that he had given "a very interesting lecture." Aware that Carlos had written several chapters of *Our Catholic Heritage* in the college library, Mother Angelique reassured the author: "We have your two volumes. I have not yet got to the reading of them, but I shall give myself that pleasure as soon as possible. They make a fine appearance, and I know the material is good."[37]

Following the appearance before the San Antonio group Castañeda gradually resumed work on a successive volume of *Our Catholic Heritage*. Admittedly exhausted by the rigorous demands to complete the initial volumes for release "during the centennial year of Texas Independence," Carlos relaxed by indulging in other types of stimulating deeds requiring high level of energy. Although he refrained from asking Foik about plans for future editions, he knew that the commission had projected several volumes to cover the entire colonial period of Texas and the modern era. For the time being he maintained discreet silence, which worked to his advantage. In the transition between Christmas and the new year Foik persuaded him to continue the series.[38] The decision to select Castañeda made sound business sense because no other mature scholar with intimate knowledge of the documentary sources was available. Unlike earlier years when he zealously wanted to be affiliated with this exciting enterprise, Carlos now waited for the offer to come to him. Apart from professional recognition, there was another factor that compelled him to accept without much hesitation. As librarian of the Latin American Collection his salary had not improved substantially; consequently he needed the stipend from the Knights of Columbus to supplement his income. Emotionally secure but just barely solvent, Castañeda happily accommodated the agreement with the commission into a heavy and untidy work schedule.[39]

Meanwhile the university administration, responding to the ad hoc committee's recommendation to evaluate the Stephens Collection, in February dispatched Carlos to Mexico to conduct a close-up "personal examination." Delighted by the assignment, he performed the necessary assessment with careful attention to detail. Not long afterward he recalled that experience: "It was not an extensive aggregation of books and manuscripts, but a very choice selection of bibliographical items of great value to the history of California, Arizona, New Mexico, and Texas. The manuscript section relates to the same area; namely, the northern provinces of Mexico, such as Durango, Sonora, and Chihuahua. The newspaper files were as valuable as the books and manuscripts. There were in all thirteen hundred printed items and twenty thousand pages of manuscript sources in round numbers." Returning to the library, Castañeda prepared a report recommending "the advisability of purchasing this collection," which the board of regents accepted "not only with favor but with enthusiasm" in granting its approval. Once negotiations commenced in earnest, advancing gradually toward a price agreement, it was only a matter of time before Castañeda became intimately involved with the W. D. Stephens Collection.[40] With so many commitments clamoring for attention, he turned to other challenges which, like the Knights of Columbus project, he handled with suspenseful aplomb.

Shortly afterward in the spring the university administration appointed a committee of scholars (Kenneth H. Aynsworth, Carlos E. Castañeda, and Charles W. Hackett) to travel by train to Los Angeles, California, to examine the contents of yet another collection assembled by Joaquín García Icazbalceta, celebrated Mexican linguist, essayist, and bibliophile. Castañeda reported:

> *During his life time he amassed the best and most extensive collection of Mexican imprints and original documents of the sixteenth century. Some of the latter he published in his various series of Documentos for the history of Mexico. At the time of his death in 1894, he was the recognized authority on sixteenth century Mexico. To his vast scholarship, he added a fastidious and discriminating taste. His library reflects the eye of the connoisseur and the erudition of the scholar. Through the political vicissitudes that have beset Mexico during the last thirty years, this precious collection was saved, hidden in cellars, packed in unsuspected secret recesses, or carted to the houses of loyal friends, only to be again brought together when the immediate danger [had] passed.*

During the turbulence of the last phases of the twentieth-century revolution and its aftermath somehow, as if by prior arrangement, item by item, "like matched pearls of a priceless string," virtually the entire García Icazbalceta collection, described as "the most valuable Mexican imprints of the sixteenth century," threaded their way northward to Los Angeles. Friends of the University of Texas in California promptly notified library officials in Austin about the availability of this significant collection. To prepare for the trip to the West Coast, Castañeda obtained a checklist of the items offered for sale, including

García Icazbalceta's "private catalogue" printed in 1927 by Federico Gómez de Orosco. When the trio of scholars arrived at Union Station near historic Olvera Street they hurried to the repository that temporarily accommodated the famous library. Working diligently "in the space of three hours" before closing time, they individually examined a multitude of priceless items including the "*Doctrina* of [Archbishop Juan de] Zumárraga of 1544, the *Doctrina* of [Fray Pedro de] Gante of 1553, the *Recognitio Sumularum* of Alfonso de la Veracruz of the same year, his *Physica Speculatio,* the *Provisiones, cédulas e instrucciones* of 1563, the *Dialogii* of [Francisco] Cervantes de Salazar of 1554, the *Constituciones* of the archbishop of Mexico of 1560 [Alfonso de Montúfar], and over two score of similar bibliographical treasures." Near the end of that initial survey Kenneth Aynesworth exclaimed: "Gentlemen, I am emotionally exhausted." Carlos concurred: "We were all tired, completely overcome by the emotional reaction at beholding such treasures." The next day they returned for a more leisurely assessment, examining in the process "an original letter of [Hernán] Cortés, a memorial written in his own hand by Bartolomé de las Casas, the original manuscript of Mendieta's *Historia Eclesiástica indiana,* a part of the *Residencia* of Viceroy Antonio de Mendoza, a letter of Gerónimo López, and hundreds of other invaluable original manuscripts of the sixteenth century." Upon concluding their evaluation the three scholars returned to Austin and promptly forwarded a proposal to the university administration recommending the acquisition of the Mexicana collection of Joaquín García Icazbalceta. Since the Texas legislature was then meeting in regular session, President Harry Y. Benedict, with the sanction of the board of regents, decided to appeal to the lawmakers for a special appropriation to consummate the purchase. Traveling the short distance from the campus to the capitol grounds, Benedict suffered a fatal heart attack. The legislature, either as a gesture to the fallen leader's memory or as a symbol of pride in excellence, appropriated the funds that entitled the university library to buy the García Icazbalceta Collection by autumn of that same year.[41]

In between long trips, book promotions, guest lectures, and library duties Castañeda labored with the subject matter for volume 3 of *Our Catholic Heritage.* Monsignor William H. Oberste, a respected church historian who later joined the enterprise in an editorial capacity, described that mental struggle: "Dr. Castañeda undertook this work as a part-time project. . . . at the University of Texas his principal work left little time for the stupendous research he had undertaken. Nevertheless, at every free moment, at all hours, for days, weeks, and stretching out into years, he devoted himself to the task of writing the series of *Our Catholic Heritage.* Taking into account all the labors involved, the first volumes of the series appeared in quick succession."[42] Meanwhile, largely through the networking of the editor, who was of French Canadian lineage, the Institute Historique et Heraldique of France—an organization that had been in existence for over fifty years—conferred upon Foik and Castañeda a decoration of merit and corresponding membership in recognition of their respective contributions that resulted in the publication of the first volumes of *Our Catholic Heritage*.[43] Castañeda humbly appreciated the gesture because now he had claimed a loose strand of his French ancestry from his mother's cultural heritage.

By early May, buoyed by the French accolade, Castañeda reported to the Texas Historical Commission in Mineral Wells that, having finished two-thirds of the story of the next volume, he "no longer had to find his way through uncharted seas." With help from "monographs and a few books" containing abundant information for the 1731–63 period of Spanish colonial history, especially Bolton's *Texas in the Middle Eighteenth Century,* he had not only enhanced the narrative but "enriched" the story line by bringing "out in full relief many events and incidents dimly outlined or hazily suggested by previous historians." Focusing on the core of the treatise, which reflected the excellence of his archival research in Mexico, Castañeda explained to the group the significance of the subtitle: "Very appropriately the third volume will be called the *Missions at Work*. It was during these years between 1731 and 1763 that the missions in Texas reached their maximum development. Although the expansive force that gathered such momentum in this period did not automatically cease in 1763, but continued to operate as late as 1794, the best examples of missionary endeavor are to be found in the course of this volume now almost completed."[44]

With another commission meeting behind, Castañeda returned to Austin and delved into his multifaceted work. Among the administrative changes he encountered in the library during this season the most challenging was adjusting to the management style of Donald Coney, who had succeeded Ernest W. Winkler as director. Comfortably attuned for several years to Winkler's loose style of direction, Castañeda faced a litany of prescriptive rules under Coney's regime which assuredly reminded him of a popular axiom in Mexico during the lengthy rule of Porfirio Díaz that proudly proclaimed *poca política pero mucha administración* (little room for politics but lots of administration). Actually the two librarians, respectful of each other's talents, worked harmoniously, but Coney seemingly thrived on finding picayune details to burden Castañeda's daily schedule. For example, not being familiar with Texas history, he referred to Carlos an inquiry "concerning the colors of the uniforms worn by Mexican soldiers during the attack on the Alamo" in 1836. Thoroughly versed on the perennial nature of the inquiry, Carlos replied that there was "little or no dependable information on the subject. To determine with accuracy the color and design on the uniforms will require many hours of painstaking research." Information pertaining to sources he happily provided; conducting research for an out-of-town petitioner was outside his normal realm of duty. Alert to extra employment for students, especially those from Latin American countries, Carlos extended a proposal to the patron who had inquired about the uniforms: "If you wish us to secure a student to do this work for you at your expense, please let us know. The sources of information on this subject are mostly in Spanish."[45]

Again indicative of Coney's watchful supervision, the director informed Castañeda that he had received a criticism from the librarian at the University of Houston to the effect that a Hispanic teacher at San Jacinto High School had bragged she could obtain books from the Latin American Collection in Austin that generally did not "circulate outside the Library." Although Coney dismissed the criticism as something that may have occurred before his arrival or perhaps entirely inaccurate since the information had "passed through a second party," nonetheless he used the occasion to remind Carlos of another directive on procedure: "I am sure I have spoken of the desirability of centralizing our extramural loans with the Loan Department at the Library Council meeting from time to time. It may be, however, that you were absent. No Staff Manual sheet, to the best of my recollection, has ever been issued on this point but I think it is apparent that it is the better part of wisdom for us to maintain uniform relations with our extramural borrowers. This can best be achieved by centralizing loans at the Loan Desk."[46]

More worrisome for Castañeda than the director's overly cautious approach to library control was the termination of Jack A. Dabbs's assistance with the manuscripts inventory under the National Youth Administration program. By then the working relationship between librarian and graduate student had deepened into genuine friendship. Unable to continue for lack of government funding, Dabbs applied for employment in nearby Lockhart as a classroom teacher of Spanish.[47] As the student prepared to launch a teaching career, promising to return for a visit in the fall, Castañeda finalized his own travel plans for the summer.

Foremost among his priorities, largely through the influence of Father Foik, was an invitation to address the Catholic Library Association. Relying upon firsthand knowledge and experience, Carlos quickly assembled a few pertinent thoughts gleaned from archival manuscripts into a cogent essay. Arriving in Kansas City, Missouri, with barely enough time for an overnight rest, he rushed to the podium to inform the delegates about "Materials for the History of the Church in Latin-America in the University of Texas."[48] Flushed with accolades of that presentation, Carlos hurried back to Austin to work on the remaining passages for the third volume of *Our Catholic Heritage*. In the solitude of office 2601 in the corner of the library tower, with a commanding southern view of the campus and the capitol complex in the distance, he drafted and revised the narrative of eighteenth-century Franciscan evangelization in Texas. Before the summer ended he delivered the completed manuscript to Foik and then enjoyed a quiet respite with his family before starting another round of activity in the fall.

To expedite the volume toward production at Von Boeckmann-Jones, sometimes Carlos drove along Congress Avenue to Saint Edward's University to deliver corrected galley sheets to Father Foik. Likewise, to reduce turn-around time, the priest picked up page proofs from the printer and carried them to Carlos's desk at the Latin American Collection. By these and other friendly gestures of cooperation the historian and editor submitted the final work on volume 3 to the printer before Carlos's dual celebrations in November. During the Thanksgiving holidays Jack Dabbs stopped by the Latin American Collection to check on the progress of the guide to manuscript holdings. Surrounded by familiar trappings at "the big desk" in the library, Castañeda happily welcomed his former assistant. In response to Dabbs's inquiry about the guide, Carlos admitted that "little or no progress" had been accomplished since the end of spring. In search of an honorable solution to a vexatious problem, Castañeda extended to Dabbs an enticing proposal: 1) To revive the project and work on weekends whenever he could come into Austin from Lockhart, for which Castañeda would pay out of his meager resources an hourly wage; or 2) to continue the work without salary but "on the basis of co-authorship." Genuinely intrigued with the offer, Dabbs recalled: "After a short consideration I accepted the second proposal, and we became co-workers from that moment." For the remainder of the school year Dabbs drove to Austin practically every weekend: "The routine was for me to drive over from Lockhart [on] Saturday morning and work until noon . . . when the L.A. Library closed, then I would take an armload of the MSS up the elevator to Dr. Castañeda's office in the corner of the Tower, Room 2601, where I had his typewriter available and could work Saturday afternoon and Sunday until either I finished with the armload or until it was time to leave for Lockhart in the afternoon."[49]

As the autumn season merged with winter, besides the return of Jack Dabbs, Castañeda found ample reasons about which to celebrate. First, he and Elisa enjoyed the gift of sound health. Next, their five-year-old daughter Consuelo filled their home with delight. Then, on the professional side, his book *A Report on the Spanish Archives in San Antonio, Texas,* in circulation for nearly eight months, received an excellent review from Ike Moore, a critic at Hillsboro Junior College, who acknowledged the work "of major significance in the study of local Texas history": "Dr. Castañeda's careful study includes these largely routine papers [land grants, deeds, and wills], but in addition reveals over a thousand documents, overlooked when the transfer was made [of the Béxar Archives to UT at Austin in 1899], which relate intimate details of governmental, business, and religious life. In thus giving unity to the collection, the compiler has performed a lasting service to all students of Texas history." [50] Finally, on the basis of his scholarship and with help behind the scenes from Father Foik and friends, Castañeda received a dual honor from the American Catholic Historical Association (ACHA): an invitation to present a formal paper at the organization's eighteenth annual meeting and a nomination as first vice president. Accompanied by Father Foik, Carlos traveled to Philadelphia two days after Christmas where at the end of the week he mesmerized the convention audience with his florid platform style and an essay entitled "The Beginning of University Life in America." [51] While visiting the City of Brotherly Love, Castañeda took advantage of the ACHA's concurrent meeting with the American Historical Association to commingle with delegates from other states and universities. In contrast to earlier conventions when he was an aspiring scholar, now his reputation as a practicing historian and librarian attracted the admiration and respect of younger people who sought his advice and counsel. In less than a week reports of his presentation radiated to the hinterland. Charles O. Hucker commented on Castañeda's essay in a manuscript for a future issue of *Library News*:

> Dr. Castañeda, who is particularly interested in the Spanish and Mexican influence on the history and institutions of the Southwest, made a detailed study of the early education in what was called New Spain in the Sixteenth Century. He drew a few comparisons between the early days of the University of Mexico, founded in 1553 [sic], and Harvard University, founded almost a century later in 1636. Students in the University of Mexico, he found, . . . lived a rather gay life, much more like that of the average student in the United States today than that at Harvard in . . . early times, where students lived a rather cloistered life. Harvard was a religious school at its founding. [52]

Highly pleased with his election as vice president of a prestigious national organization, Castañeda rushed home to begin the new year of 1939 with his family. On account of a growing number of commitments he rarely traveled to Brownsville as in previous years. Instead his sisters frequently visited him in Austin. Or, as a compromise to reduce travel on the highway, they all convened in San Antonio with Elisa's relatives. On such occasions he enlarged his appointment calendar to accommodate reunions with friends in the history fraternity. Ordinarily he preferred weekend visits to San Antonio, but at times circumstances forced him to opt for one-day excursions. In mid-January, for example, he held "a long talk" with Frederick Chabot, from whom he heard that a Dallas physician, William E. Howard, needed a permanent depository for his "excellent collection of manuscripts and books" relating to colonial Texas and Mexico. Personally acquainted with the physician and aware of his fondness for San Antonio, Carlos immediately suggested Our Lady of the Lake College as the depository. Although nothing definite resulted from the contact, owing to Dr. Howard's decision to consider the State Building in Dallas "as a museum for historical documents," Castañeda's initiative sustained his public image in the larger community of Texas.[53] On another occasion in the same month he hurriedly drove to San Antonio to introduce Irving A. Leonard, representative and resident scholar of the Rockefeller Foundation, to faculty members and librarians at Our Lady of the Lake. Upon learning later that Leonard had complained he had been spirited "around rather briskly," Carlos, who had a reputation as a fast automobile driver, apologized to the distinguished visitor: "I hope the ride to San Antonio was not the straw that broke the camel's back, for it was undertaken with the very best of intentions."[54]

One reason for Castañeda's propensity to move swiftly was related to the university administration's decision to send him on a whirlwind trip to Mexico "to bring the entire Collection" of W. B. Stephens to Austin. In this context Irving Leonard's recent visit to the Southwest was crucial because Castañeda envisioned asking the Rockefeller Foundation for a grant with which to purchase the segment of books pertaining to Texas and Mexico. However, since the executors of the Stephens estate preferred keeping the collection intact, Carlos recommended buying the entire inventory and then, to recover part of the expenditure, extending options to George P. Hammond of New Mexico and Herbert E. Bolton of California to purchase the sections that complemented the holdings of their respective libraries.[55]

Working within a flexible schedule that allowed ample time to inventory the Stephens Collection and to attend social functions in Mexico City, Castañeda spent about two and a half weeks on the special assignment. When he returned to the Latin American Collection he promptly informed Coney and friends in the history fraternity of the outcome of his sojourn in Mexico. In particular he shared candid impressions of the trip with Irving Leonard: "I returned from Mexico . . . and brought back with me the W. B. Stephens Collection. It is truly a wonderful collection, of which I will tell you more [later] . . . I saw several of your friends in Mexico City, among them Don Pablo Martínez del Río. They all send you regards. I wish you had been along with me. I had a wonderful time."[56] Castañeda's enthusiasm about the Stephens Collection fomented stereotypical remarks of Texan chauvinism in some parts of the Southwest. Hammond of New Mexico responded defensively to Castañeda's success:

> It seems to me that you and I must be perfectly frank and define our interests if we are going to get anywhere. If you are going to try to purchase part or all of the collection I should like to have you tell me frankly; if you do not intend to bid on it I shall leave no stone unturned to bring it to New Mexico, for it would give us a splendid though small beginning on a Mexican collection. If we should get it I would be glad to arrange an exchange with you for duplicate materials that you may have and I believe we could work out such a scheme. I am sure you will understand how I feel in regard to this matter and surely hope that our interests may not clash.[57]

Even under adverse conditions Castañeda's style was conciliatory. If Hammond's comments piqued his feelings, he kept silent counsel. On the other hand, with Bolton he initiated a candid discussion concerning the Stephens Collection. He told Bolton: "As you say . . . the New Mexico material may be pertinent either to Texas or to California. Personally, let me assure you that should you feel an interest in the New Mexico materials, and should Dr. Hammond be unable to make the necessary arrangements for their acquisition, I would be very glad for you to have them." Admitting that the collection had been released on consignment, Castañeda shared a few details with Bolton: "Fortunately, the materials have been placed in my hands, and I have very plainly explained to Miss Stephens that I will try to get her a fair price, but not an exorbitant price, such as private collectors might be willing to pay. In other words, you, the University of New Mexico, and this University will have an opportunity to offer what each considers a fair and equitable price for the portion of the collection in which each is interested. I have as yet made no estimate as to its worth, because I have not examined the manuscripts nor completed the calendar."[58]

As the exchange of views among historians continued, Carlos compiled two sets of correspondence pertaining to the Stephens Collection for Donald Coney's edification, pointing out that his plan of distribution followed the suggestion of the delegate from the Rockefeller Foundation to define "fields of interest of the various centers for Latin-American studies in this country."[59] As curator of the Latin American Collection, Castañeda later drafted a cogent memorandum in which he identified five state universities (California, New Mexico, North Carolina, Texas, and Tulane) that had "collections of relative importance for the teaching and the study of Latin or Spanish American culture and civilization." To be sure, while there were "other extensive and valuable collections" in private depositories such as the Huntington and Stanford libraries in California, the Newbury in Chicago, and the John Carter Brown in Rhode Island, it was essential, he cautioned, in view of budgetary restraints, for state universities committed to the Spanish-American field to define their special areas of endeavor. As an indication of how well informed he was on the subject, Castañeda outlined the parameters for each of the five universities.

Tulane University, he noted, had virtually limited its special field with the establishment of a Bureau of Middle American Research, confining its scope of work mainly to archaeology and anthropology in "that portion known as the Caribbean area including the southern part of Mexico and the South American republics." Thanks to the guide that he and Dabbs were compiling, Carlos declared that the University of Texas had "already established a priority in the field of Mexican history and literature as well as for all phases of Mexican culture." Moreover, under his curatorship the Latin American Collection had augmented its holdings not only in legal documents and government publications, including "literature of all Spanish America in general, but more particularly on Argentina, Chile, and Peru." With commensurate pride in his accomplishments, he recommended that Texas should be permitted to continue developing the broad field "of South American history and literature." Aware that South Carolina also coveted the same hemispheric field, which he said did "not equal" the Texas holdings, Castañeda suggested working toward a mutual agreement on certain countries or periods, "such as, early and colonial history and literature in one case, and modern history and literature in another." Narrowing the focus to the aspirations of George Peter Hammond in the Land of Enchantment, Castañeda observed that New Mexico not only had "started late" but had "been less fortunate in securing the necessary funds for development of a special collection." Its interest, he pointed out, was "more in the Spanish southwest," and, consequently, its curriculum leaned "toward the native civilization" of that region. Finally, with respect for Bolton's contribution to the library acquisitions at Berkeley, Carlos alluded to the stability of that depository: "California has a strong Mexican collection in the Bancroft Library. Its interest has been on the Spanish southwest and in the history of those sections within the United States which once belonged to Spain."[60]

While Castañeda's memorandum influenced his own university administrators more than library directors elsewhere, in recognizing the prominence of the Latin American Collection in comparison to other depositories, the experience of writing it gave its author a sense of pride in being associated with such invaluable holdings. Apart from demonstrating how well he understood the support role of a Latin American collection to the teaching missions of a major university, perhaps Castañeda desired to convey a subtle hint to Donald Coney. In any event, deeply immersed in dividing the Stephens Collection into regional content areas, Carlos kept Bolton apprised of the latest advancement: "I have . . . finished listing the W. B. Stephens Collection. . . . The owners want $40,000.00 for the entire collection. The two lists I am sending you represent about half. From the little I know about California bibliography, it seems to me that the manuscripts in this division are of unusual value and interest. But you are a better judge. I wish you would look them over." [61] Even when nothing concrete materialized with regard to splitting the Stephens Collection, the contact Carlos established with Bolton symbolized a rite of passage into the fraternity of borderlands historians. Earlier, through Hackett, Castañeda had claimed third-generational kinship with the senior historian; lately, with several publications to his credit, he truly considered himself an honorary member of Bolton's celebrated round table. From another perspective, the contact depicted Castañeda's emergence from under the shadow of Hackett's dominant wing into the bright light of center stage.

Secure with his station in life, Castañeda exchanged several letters with Bolton. In one piece of correspondence he inserted ancillary memorandums about his books: "By the way," he candidly asked Bolton, "did you ever find time to write that review you promised me on the first two volumes of *Our Catholic Heritage*?" Bolton promptly replied: "No, I am sorry to say I have not found time . . . I read the first volume and made notes, and then was turned aside by urgent duties and have not been able to get back to the job." Recognizing the quality of Carlos's scholarship, Bolton added: "Permit me at this time to congratulate you on an excellent piece of work about which I shall say more at a later time." As the seasons progressed from winter to spring Castañeda continued to remind Bolton about an unredeemed pledge: "You asked . . . once if I had a particular publication for which I wanted you to review them. There is nothing I would appreciate more than your reviewing them for the *American Historical Review*." [62]

During this interval Donald Coney seriously pondered what to do with the talented librarian-historian. On the one hand he valued Carlos's presence in the Latin American Collection because of the expertise and service he dispensed. On the other hand, he detected in his Latin American librarian a restless energy that constantly spilled over into numerous activities. Moreover, Coney correctly discerned that no matter how professional and courteous Carlos behaved in his relations with library colleagues there still festered a few petty jealousies and animosities left over from the previous administration. Finally, there was Carlos's predilection for teaching, which he nurtured sporadically during summers. Unless the University of Texas forthrightly declared its intentions toward his career, another institution (possibly New Mexico) might recruit him. Thus, for a combination of reasons, Coney submitted an attractive proposal to the historians recommending "that Dr. Castañeda's present salary of $2,400 be kept in the Library budget but that he give half of his time to the History Department in a teaching capacity, to be placed on a nine months basis, and receive any increase in salary out of the History budget." Milton R. Gutsch, successor chairman of the department, designated Eugene C. Barker as advocate of the proposal for a meeting of the senior historians who constituted the budget council. Barker, who had watched Castañeda's development from a promising undergraduate to a mature scholar, enumerated the advantages to be derived from such a lateral transfer by each constituency—the library, the department, the university, and the candidate himself. Convinced of the merits of the proposal, the historians "instructed" Barker to draft "a definite statement of the Council's understanding of the terms of the agreement and present it to Librarian Coney for consideration." Incisive in his transactions, Barker pared the issue down to its essential points: "1. Castañeda is to be put on a nine-months schedule. 2. He will give half-time to teaching. 3. The History budget will be charged with future additions to his salary." Satisfied with the historians' collective decision, Coney and Gutsch signed an agreement recommending to the university administration a change in Castañeda's status effective September 1, 1939, of the upcoming biennium.[63] Even as he waited, Carlos's career took a great leap.

Meanwhile, between excursions to assess book collections, Castañeda redoubled his efforts to complete the third volume of *Our Catholic Heritage* before the next regular meeting of the Texas Historical Commission. When the historical commission convened in May at the Plaza Hotel in Laredo, Foik conceded to him the privilege of reporting. Castañeda began: "Since the last meeting . . . a year ago, the third volume . . . entitled *The Missions at Work* has been completed. This volume which covers the period from 1731 to 1761 was turned over to the printer . . . and is now ready for distribution." Indisputably in command of the subject matter, Castañeda estimated termination of "the manuscript of the fourth volume by the end of the year." Grateful for Foik's support, he praised "the helpful and harmonious cooperation of the Chairman . . . whose constant encouragement and timely suggestions have proved invaluable." [64]

Resolving to hone his teaching skills, in tandem with conducting research for the continuing saga of *Our Catholic Heritage,* Castañeda negotiated another short-term appointment at the University of New Mexico. By mail he remained in contact with Father Foik, who had meandered north on vacation to Kansas City, South Bend, and Detroit.[65] Albuquerque's arid environment, accented by the fragrance of pine trees and piñón shrubs, exhilarated Carlos's sense of purpose. Instead of residing near Sandía Mountain, this time he rented a house close to the campus, which gave him an option of walking to work. For recreation he and the family indulged in sight-seeing tours.[66] Besides the normal activities associated with a working vacation, Castañeda reluctantly allowed duties with the Latin American Collection to invade his family's solitude. Through the intercession of a former student who had traveled to South America, Carlos received an interesting letter from Diego Muñoz, a professor at the University of Chile, offering to sell "his private library, consisting of some fifteen hundred printed items including the most complete set of books by or about José Toribio Medina outside of the National Library of Santiago."[67] Unable to accomplish much from Albuquerque, Castañeda recommended to Coney further inquiry to determine the extent of the collection.

When the summer term ended, Carlos thanked his hosts, primarily Scholes and Hammond, for the courtesies extended to him and commenced the long drive to Austin. To reduce the strain of long-distance travel he carefully planned the itinerary to include rest stops in towns where friends resided (El Paso, Alpine, Del Rio, and San Antonio). Back on familiar terrain by midsummer, Castañeda resumed work with Dabbs on their mutual project, reviewing and amending entries for a guide of manuscripts in the Latin American Collection. Jack Dabbs described the work routine of that summer:

> In the morning I went to classes. After lunch I came to our work place, the big table in front of the glass cases in the L.A. Library. Dr. Castañeda would show up after lunch also, and we would check and revise each card, comparing the entry with the MS. He now added what I had not done—the annotations about previous publications of the Documents. In many cases he would bring a published text and we would compare it with the MS to see whether they were the same. This was my first experience with such bibliographical study, and I was learning from scratch. Much of this work came out of his head, and therefore I was always far behind him.[68]

In the mornings, while Dabbs attended classes, Castañeda assisted researchers and, in between requests, worked on several projects, one of which was the possibility of acquiring the Muñoz Collection. Whenever the situation was propitious with university administrators he advanced the cause of this acquisition. Before long, with Castañeda's active involvement, the University of Texas purchased the Muñoz library. Carlos recalled later: "How extensive this is may be deduced from the fact that the list of Medina items adds to over two hundred. Here was a selected group of Chilean books, mostly history, with a complete file of the *Anuales* of the national university and all with standard reference works and sets of printed sources.[69]

Bowing to pressures of deadlines, Castañeda and Dabbs spent most of the afternoons collating, shifting, and organizing the cards before advancing to final typing of the manuscript. When they had almost terminated rechecking the cards, Castañeda consulted Coney to discuss "some arrangement for typing." After an extremely long session with the director that took up much of an afternoon, Carlos returned to the Latin American Collection quite agitated and in a rare angry mood. Sitting next to Dabbs, he stared in silence at the drawer of cards. Finally, after recovering his composure, he told the assistant they needed "to reorganize the whole thing." For practical reasons compatible with the actual arrangement of manuscripts in the glass cases, Carlos and Jack preferred a chronological sequence. However, in compliance with Coney's directive, first they divided the cards "into large geographical areas," then they alphabetized the entries, and, as the last step, they aligned them in chronological order. Dabbs remembered: "So we started separating the cards accordingly, making stacks of them and then making the arrangements that you see in the final copy of the published *Guide*. That took some time. I, of course, did not think it was a good idea, nor did he, but I must say we never argued or had a falling out—I was doing a job that was fascinating to me— I accepted his superior knowledge, and I was in an apprentice relationship to him, that is, a learning relationship, and right or wrong, I was learning things all the time."[70] To remain in close proximity to the project Dabbs accepted a teaching appointment as adjunct professor of Spanish at nearby Saint Edward's University. The flexibility of his schedule allowed him to conduct classes, attend graduate courses, and assist Castañeda in the afternoons and on Saturdays. Aware of an imminent deadline, Dabbs diligently worked "several weeks" on the final manuscript, pounding away on Castañeda's "old Underwood typewriter." Although the two collaborators "proofread" the last copy of the manuscript, the process was neither as exact nor as rigorous as the proofreading of some of "the other books" that they had written together. Still, they labored under heavy "pressure because the editors kept writing inquiries about when they were to get the typescript out."[71]

In the meantime, mainly through Father Foik's foresight and persuasion, the State Council of the Knights of Columbus agreed to dispatch two sets of the first three volumes of *Our Catholic Heritage* to the Vatican. His Holiness Pope Pius XI received a deluxe edition "bound in the finest grade of white Morocco kid," valued at $450. To publicize the gift and gesture Castañeda exhibited the books for a short period at the university library "on the main floor near the lower desk." The campus newspaper described the display: "Each beautiful volume of the presentation copy has hand-illumined dedication pages on parchment, drawn and colored by the head of the art class of Saint Mary's in Austin. The books, hand-tooled, gold leaf inlaid, with end papers of heavy silk, are representative of the finest type of American bookbindery." The books eventually arrived at the Vatican. Attendants promptly displayed the leather-bound volumes in the Vatican Museum and deposited the regular set in the library.[72]

Just before the Christmas holidays Castañeda and Dabbs cautiously assembled their manuscript for personal delivery to the editor, Lewis Hanke, then a faculty member at Harvard University affiliated with the Hispanic Foundation of the Library of Congress. Carlos hand carried the packet to Chicago, where he met Hanke at the meetings of the American Historical Association. After discussing the manuscript and related matters with the editor, Castañeda happily sauntered into the plenary session of the American Catholic Historical Association. His crowning moment occurred when Rev. Francis S. Betten, S.J., chairman of the nominations committee, formally recommended to the assembly the name of Carlos E. Castañeda for president.[73]

As he rode the train home from Chicago, assuredly Castañeda reflected on the highlights of his accomplishments since his return from the border. First, he had resolved an insurmountable problem of writing in reverse order the first two volumes of *Our Catholic Heritage*. Next, in comparison with previous work, he had rapidly completed the writing of the third volume. Then, thanks to the timely intercession of Donald Coney and Eugene C. Barker, he secured a partial transfer to the history department of the University of Texas. Finally, at the age of forty-two, he had ascended to the presidency of the American Catholic Historical Association. Of one thing he was certain: he intended to deliver a dynamic presidential address.

The Glory of Knighthood, 1939–42

Inspired by the accolades and courtesies that accompanied election to the presidency of the American Catholic Historical Association, Carlos E. Castañeda returned home to enjoy the few remaining holidays of the Yuletide season. Across the Colorado River in Austin, at the hilltop campus of Saint Edward's University, Father Paul J. Foik, chairman of the Texas Historical Commission of the Knights of Columbus, thanked Monsignor Peter Guilday, secretary of the American Catholic Historical Association (ACHA), for the honors the group had conferred upon his friend Don Carlos. Alluding to Castañeda's contribution to the current writing and publication of *Our Catholic Heritage in Texas,* Dr. Foik declared: "The project is progressing favorably because of his scholarship. We have every reason to feel proud of his work. I know that you are in a position to measure his success in the historical field which . . . will now furnish a pattern of example for all the other states of the union." [1]

Unquestionably the widespread publicity surrounding *Our Catholic Heritage,* conjoined with the prestige of the ACHA presidency, was gaining for Don Carlos, as Father J. Elliot Ross had predicted two decades before, an ever widening constituency. On the first day in February, Castañeda dashed off by automobile in the middle of the week to deliver a speech in Dallas. To a meeting of the Federal Reserve Club, assembled in the Dallas Power and Light Company auditorium, he spoke with vigorous authority based on his latest research and writing on the topic of "Economic Aspects of Spanish and French Rivalry in Texas." [2] Don Carlos's disposition for accepting out-of-town speaking engagements caused library director Donald Coney to realize, however slowly, the value of his presence in the Latin American Collection. Invariably, whenever Carlos was absent on official business, visitors with more than a passing interest in Latin American history and culture would come by the library and ask specifically for him. As a stopgap measure Coney proposed creating a display "of the more exhibitable Latin-American items." Conceding that neither he nor his assistant, Alexander Moffit, was sufficiently conversant on the subject, the director casually suggested to Carlos the merits of the show-case: "It occurs to me it would be a good idea for you to select and segregate in a special case exhibitable items so that Mr. Moffit and I could get them out and show them to people. It would also be a good idea for you to write some notes on these [articles] so that he and I could be informed and would thus not need to display our ignorance so fully as might otherwise be the case." [3] Since Coney had not phrased the suggestion in the form of a mandate, Casta-ñeda, preoccupied with other issues, temporarily disregarded the hint.

Of more immediate priority to him was planning another trip—this time by automobile—to Washington, D.C., with Father Foik. Not only was Casta-ñeda to be one of the main speakers at the convention of the Catholic Library Association, but his talk, delivered partly in Spanish and partly in English, was to be broadcast internationally. Leaving Austin the day after Easter, Carlos and his companion arrived in the nation's capital in the middle of the week. For three days they endured a hectic round of formal and impromptu meet-ings. Castañeda obviously relished the attention he received as the current ACHA president. He used the medium of his broadcast address, on the four hundredth anniversary of the introduction of printing in America, "to spread the truth about his chosen field—Mexico, his native land, and Texas." In be-tween the broadcast and other activities Castañeda took advantage of the proximity to Catholic University of America, where he negotiated a contract to teach in the summer session. He looked forward to an opportunity of con-ducting research for ongoing projects in the Library of Congress as well as teaching.[4]

After their return from the convention Foik concentrated on editing a siz-able segment of manuscript for volume 4 of *Our Catholic Heritage* and then delivering it to the printers for transformation into galley sheets. Carlos, work-ing at a feverish pace, tried to catch up on a backlog of commitments, includ-ing a progress report to the Texas Historical Commission. When the Knights of Columbus gathered at the Raleigh Hotel in Waco for their annual conven-tion in May, Castañeda apologized for the "series of circumstances" that had rendered impossible completion of the fourth volume which he had subtitled *The Passing of the Missions*. Nevertheless, he reported that only one chap-ter remained to be written, and he expected to finish it before the end of the month. To reassure listeners who worried about coordinating sales campaigns with actual delivery of books, Carlos revealed a plan that Father Foik had worked out with Von Boeckmann-Jones Company: "With the cooperation of the printers, who have already set the type for the portion completed, it is rea-sonable to expect the fourth volume to come off the press before the end of the summer." The phase of the report that appealed most to him, because it constituted the core of the document, pertained to the main thrust of the narrative. Avowing that he had labored diligently to maintain the "same standard" of scholarship as in the previous volumes, Carlos explained: "Care has been taken to present impartially the facts, weaving into the narrative the human elements in order to present, not merely the record of accomplishments but a living picture of life in Texas in the eventful years that mark not the failure but the passing of that remarkable Christian institution that was the chief force in the spread of civilization in our State, the Spanish mission. Their work was done and like other pioneer institutions they passed into the realm of history, leaving us the blessings of a rich heritage." [5]

As summer approached and prior to leaving town for Catholic University of America, Carlos redoubled his efforts to fulfill outstanding obligations, most of which related to publication deadlines. Meanwhile Coney, seeking to learn more about Castañeda's unit, asked Ernest W. Winkler about the history and holdings of the Latin American Collection. Winkler promptly summarized his inventory of the Genaro García library in 1921, prior to Castañeda's arrival, and informed Coney exactly where he would find three bound volumes describing the contents and for each title a corresponding "shelf number." [6] Why Coney chose to ask Winkler instead of Castañeda, who with the help of Jack Autrey Dabbs had recently compiled a comprehensive guide to the manuscript holdings in the Latin American Collection, is difficult to understand, unless it pivoted on the unresolved matter of the showcase exhibit.

After receiving Winkler's response, Coney reminded Carlos about the need to arrange an exhibit of Latin American materials. Unlike his previous suggestion, this time the library director was firm and curt, signifying that he had consulted the catalogs: "Before you leave for the summer, please set up an exhibit for display during your absence that will contain, among other things, a papal bull, a Mexican codex or two, and other items which are popular display materials. One or two Icazbalceta items might be included to illustrate this collection. I imagine the Cortez manuscript and the Zumarraga Doctrine [sic] Breve, including some manuscript material with descriptive notes if possible." [7]

Reacting like a doting parent shielding his children from potential harm, Castañeda politely informed Coney that lack of a temperature-controlled environment would severely jeopardize the collection's priceless holdings. He wrote: "Before following your suggestion in regard to the display of a papal bull, some codices, the Cortés Ms. and the *Doctrina Breve*, . . . I ought to call your attention to the serious deterioration that will be suffered by these valuable materials if they are placed on display for the whole summer under the conditions and with the [inadequate] facilities available in the Latin-American Room." Specifically, Carlos warned about possible discoloration and fading, insecurity of existing cases, and the physical location of the Latin American Collection on the west side of the building with exposure to the relentless summer sun. He informed Coney, "We are not prepared . . . to display valuable and rare books and documents whose very age makes them frail and whose rarity and value demand more adequate protection against the effect of the elements upon them." All the same, not inclined to be insubordinate, he conceded: "If, however, in your opinion, it is better that we display the objects you enumerate, I shall be glad to get them out and make the corresponding descriptive cards for them."[8] Confronted by reality, Coney modified his position appreciably, explaining that the typist had inadvertently omitted an entire "paragraph and part of a sentence" from his directive:

> *Where I said, "I imagine the Cortez manuscript and the Zumarraga Doctrina Breve" I continued not as indicated in the note but by saying that these were probably too valuable to be displayed for as long a period of time as suggested. I then went on to ask that you bring together a shelf of books which could be used for showing interested visitors through the room by those who will be in charge during your absence this summer. The conclusion of the last sentence in the first paragraph [i.e., the paragraph quoted above] related to this sentiment and not to the exhibit materials. As for my suggestion about the display of the Mexican codex, I had in mind, of course, not an original but one of the more startling facsimiles.[9]*

During this exchange over the display of documents Castañeda hit the road for yet another public function, this time in Normangee, in Madison County, about 120 miles northeast of Austin. Accompanied by coparticipants Father Foik and Professor Barker, he gracefully circulated among the crowd that gathered at Norwell Park on Thursday, May 25, to commemorate the 248th anniversary of the blazing of El Camino Real, the Spanish king's historic highway, with the dedication of a twelve-foot monument erected by the State Centennial Commission. At eleven o'clock in the morning the program commenced with four bands providing the music for a "colorful parade" that included Normangee students dressed in costumes of early frontier days. As a member of the Centennial Commission's advisory board of Texas historians, Father Foik spoke briefly about the cultural significance of the celebration; he was followed by Castañeda, who traced the route and history of the royal road from the Rio Grande to the Trinity River and "the mission in East Texas." Then the two listened attentively to Barker, who discussed highlights in the life of Stephen F. Austin.[10]

For six weeks in the summer (extending from June 4 through August 12, 1939) Castañeda indulged in a working vacation at Catholic University of

America. Every afternoon during the week he conducted three classes in succession: the ABC powers (Argentina, Brazil, and Chile), Mexico since independence, and Spain's colonial empire.[11] On off-duty time in the mornings the experience of browsing through the Division of Latin American, Portuguese, and Spanish of the Library of Congress was like a busman's holiday. Often at the university campus he readily availed himself of every chance to engage in lively conversation with faculty members such as Monsignor Peter Guilday, with whom he assuredly discussed ideas for his presidential address at the annual meeting of the American Catholic Historical Association in December.

However, Castañeda missed by several weeks greeting the Reverend Dr. Francis Borgia Steck, the Franciscan he had known since the formative years of the project that resulted in *Our Catholic Heritage*. Even though the two scholars had not met in several seasons, their professional paths intersected at different intervals. About a month before Carlos's arrival at Catholic University, John Tate Lanning, interim editor of the *Hispanic American Historical Review* following the sudden death of William Spence Robertson, invited Father Steck to appraise a submission from Castañeda. Titled "Beginnings of Printing in America," the manuscript evolved from the speech Carlos had presented recently at a conference of the Catholic Library Association. "If it is worth publishing just as it is," counseled Lanning, "we can proceed; but, if you think that it could be improved by certain modifications, indicate that also before you suggest turning it down completely." Although "swamped with work" and in poor health in need of medical "attention," Steck returned a favorable verdict: "I think the article by Dr. Castañeda [is] a nice piece of work, and would publish it if I had anything to say." As with any scholarly enterprise, the Franciscan offered helpful suggestions for improving the flow of the narrative. He advised Lanning, "You will notice that I went over it rather carefully and made a few corrections here and there. Of course, you are at liberty to ignore these, though I think some of the corrections improve the working of the title." Shortly thereafter, as Castañeda was en route to Washington, Steck took off for Mexico on a two-month sojourn that included visiting historic places and conducting "some studying in the archives."[12] Steck's commentary on Carlos's article was important on a personal level because it demonstrated that his friendship with Castañeda had survived the trauma of earlier years when the Franciscan had haplessly collided with the leadership of the Texas Historical Commission.

Fresh from a rewarding instructional experience, as soon as Carlos returned to Austin he looked forward with great anticipation to his transfer, albeit on a part-time basis, to the history department. The previous March a special committee of senior faculty, including Charles W. Hackett, had approved an "advanced course" to be offered exclusively "by Mr. Castañeda in the next

Long Session" in September. After consulting briefly with Carlos the committee recommended this course description: "27D. History of Spain and Portugal. Moorish domination, Christian reconquest, growth of political unity;
beginnings of Portugal; establishment of Habsburg absolutism; Spanish and
Portuguese discoveries, exploration, and colonial empires; loss of Spanish and
Portuguese colonies; the nineteenth century; the Spanish Republic of 1932.
Emphasis on institutional and cultural development." [13]

Raymond Estep, then a graduate student, recalled a few details of this milestone event in Carlos's life:

> I got to know Castañeda during that first year [1938], but I was a student
> of Hackett, and of Barker, and the other History Department members, and
> Castañeda was librarian. But by my second year, they (by they, I mean
> the History Department) let Carlos teach a course in Spain and Portugal—
> not in Latin America, but Spain and Portugal. Now he had been teach-
> ing [during the] summers in the Latin American areas—Hackett's courses
> when Hackett would take off, you know they had two terms of summer
> school. . . . And, actually Hackett had in that period of time only two
> courses—Spanish South America and Spanish North America—and then his
> seminar and his theses work. So that was the Latin American history pro-
> gram in the pre–World War Two period. And so, they just didn't have a
> place for Castañeda. The History people thought of Castañeda as librarian,
> and . . . as he began to move into the History Department the library staff
> began to think of him as a historian. . . . I always had the feeling that he was
> really just between two stools; it hurt him in promotions, in salaries.[14]

Cognizant of the liabilities inherent in half-time assignment with the history department, Castañeda focused more on the positive aspects than the
negative ones. For him it was far better to have one foot firmly planted with
the historians than to bask indefinitely in the glory of the library without any
prospect for advancement. Prominent among the first generation of students
to enroll in the course on the history of Spain and Portugal, Estep provided a
cogent recollection of Castañeda's pedagogic style:

> I had the experience of having him . . . the first time he had ever taught this
> course. . . . And it was a rather detailed course. I think it dealt a little too
> much with genealogical detail, chronological detail. This is my viewpoint of
> it now. But your sources that you had to work from in that period of time
> were rather difficult. Castañeda was working like a dog to stay ahead of
> us. . . . He had just been assigned to it . . . a few weeks or months before he
> taught it. And so, you . . . just had to work to stay a lesson or a week ahead

of the students. And I knew he was doing this, because I'd seen him at his desk working hours at a time preparing his notes before he'd go to class. And I'm sure that [years later] ... he had a much greater grasp of the course and probably was able to put things in greater perspective.[15]

Valdemar Rodríguez, who later became a junior-college instructor, reminisced about those pre–World War II years at the Austin campus:

I found his lectures interesting; his notes were not even typed—they were handwritten and he had bad handwriting to read. And he always lectured looking down, just as if he were reading his notes, but he wasn't reading.... All that he needed to do was just [to take] one glance. I do not know whether he went over his notes or not. But when I started with him ... he was standing up, but after that he conducted his lectures sitting down. He never got excited lecturing; it wasn't that monotonous type of voice either. He was sort of interesting, just like any other instructor bringing in jokes, sometimes repeating them over and over.[16]

Another graduate student of that generation, Joe B. Frantz, shared this perspective:

I took a course under him, History of Spain and Portugal, which was largely, of course, Carlos Castañeda. He had it all highly interesting. He was a very literate sort of man, always terribly energized. In those days he was getting up at four every morning and running until midnight, and always [with] a big black cigar in his mouth. He was determined he was going to get that Catholic Heritage through before he died. He was doubling as Latin American librarian and as a professor of history.[17]

Insofar as teaching, research, and writing were complementary elements of professional commitment, the fact that Castañeda's ongoing contributions to *Our Catholic Heritage* continued to command favorable reviews unequivocally counted among historians in assessing his progress and development as an academician. George Peter Hammond, after reading the third volume in the series, signaled out Castañeda's gift of written expression: "The author writes with enthusiasm and tireless zeal. His style is almost conversational and gives evidence of the fact that he has digested his sources well. He has presented an informative and readable narrative, and any student who wishes further information on this period [1731–61] will find a wealth of contemporary source material in the bibliography."[18] W. Eugene Shiels, a Jesuit scholar at Loyola University in Chicago who had trained under Herbert E. Bolton at

Berkeley, meticulously scrutinized the contents of the same volume. Not without its share of lumps and laurels, Father Shiels's review pricked the skin in a few passages:

> *The historical work of Dr. Castañeda leaves little to be desired. Frankly showing his dependence on others who cultivated part of the field before him, his own contribution nevertheless demands wide recognition. The book is well-knit as a composition. The documentation is full, the bibliography adequate. The story is made intelligible by placing the achievements of the Querétaro college in the foreground. Good maps are wanting; the large plate of Texas lacks an addition to show the ground about Los Adaes and Natchitoches. Mention of the law requiring missionaries to teach Spanish to their charges needs qualification in order to make the action of other [religious] orders understandable. It should be stated that the mission system far antedated the Texas story, though the author deserves commendation for his large and clear sketch of the working of that system. . . . Some proofreading might have eliminated a few weak word uses. Withal, there is no significant episode passed over, and an air of finality pervades the book in spite of the unassuming modesty of the style. The final volume in the colonial story will be waited with interest and a hearty welcome.*[19]

Jerome V. Jacobsen, another Jesuit historian and a Boltonian like Shiels, examined Castañeda's contribution in a wider perspective:

> *The half-way mark in the progress of a great project is approached with the completion of the present publication. This, the third of the seven-volume work, carries the story of the development of the area of Texas, as it was known in the colonial times, down to the year 1761, thirty years beyond the stopping point of its predecessor. Dr. Castañeda maintains the even and interesting style of his previous books, and the publishers continue to set up his narrative in pleasing form. The three books on the shelf now loom as a satisfying achievement. It is quite a pity that the sponsors of this notable enterprise have not quite met with the whole-hearted response they deserve, in particular with a ready and large sale. . . . Persons who purchase this set on Texas history have no reason to suppose themselves in some fashion, donors to a cause; they are not; the volumes are worth the price; they were written to be read and they are readily written.*[20]

Elated by such reviews, and at the same time generous in thanksgiving, Castañeda completed the manuscript for the fourth volume in the fall of 1938, which Foik subjected to critical editing and then hand carried to Von

Boeckmann-Jones for printing. With minimum delay Carlos commenced work on volume 5. Shortly after returning from his summer in Washington he had welcomed the assistance of another work-study student. Recommended by relatives and friends, José Rubén Moreno, a pharmacy student from Browns- ville, arrived in late summer at Castañeda's desk in the Latin American Collec- tion in search of a typing job. What the librarian-professor desperately needed at the time was someone to perform all-around secretarial duties. During his absence in Washington, for instance, a mound of correspondence had accu- mulated. Consequently, whenever he was in the library Carlos in quick ca- dence dictated responses to Moreno, who frantically tried to keep pace in long- hand. "Usually," recalled Moreno, "Dr. Castañeda dictated from pencil notes written on half-sheets of yellow paper folded in the middle." The student as- sistant admired his mentor's ability to compose literary passages for *Our Cath- olic Heritage* from those folded half sheets. If the student interrupted him to clarify a point of dictation, Castañeda became highly annoyed because the de- lay broke the momentum of his creative thinking. One concession that the stu- dent appreciated was that he could type the manuscripts and letters in the soli- tude of Castañeda's office on the twenty-sixth floor of the library tower. Since José's schedule was so flexible, Carlos periodically invited him home to con- tinue the dictation. At the end of rare all-night work sessions, the student cooked breakfast while Castañeda rushed through the house looking for mis- placed items that, when found, he impatiently thrust into a well-worn leather briefcase.[21]

Coincidental with Carlos's traditional celebrations of his birthday and saint's day in November, the publishers delivered to the Texas Knights of Co- lumbus multiple copies of the fourth volume, which bore the subtitle *The Pass- ing of the Missions, 1762–1782.*[22] As autumn transformed the color of the landscape in the hill country around Austin, Castañeda shifted attention from one priority to another. Uppermost in his mind was the presidential address for the upcoming convention of the American Catholic Historical Association scheduled for the last week in December. Meanwhile, among a stack of com- mitments, he entertained plans for a reunion with Father Steck at the Decem- ber conference.[23]

By mid-December events began to move rapidly with the long-awaited release by Harvard University Press of "a gigantic compilation," namely *A Guide to the Latin-American Manuscripts in the University of Texas Library,* for which Castañeda and Dabbs had performed yeoman duty. No doubt Dabbs, who was adjunct professor of Spanish at Saint Edward's University, came over for the celebration with Father Foik. A university announcement described the achievement: "A complete list of the manuscripts, the guide rep- resents the accumulation of more than 1,000,000 pages of original manuscripts, transcripts, typescripts, typed copies and photostats gathered during the past 40 years." The photostats included, of course, the vast collection compiled under Castañeda's direction in various Mexican archives.[24]

In December, Castañeda and Foik, along with Dabbs and Estep, finalized plans for traveling to Washington, D.C., to attend conventions later in the month. In the afternoon of Christmas Day, following the usual custom of attending mass, opening gifts, and then enjoying a home-cooked dinner, Don Carlos and party climbed into the family Studebaker to begin the long drive to Washington, D.C. Late in the afternoon, approaching Little Rock, they encountered a heavy rainstorm that reduced their rate of progress. Determined to reach Memphis that night yet fatigued by tedious driving, Castañeda asked Raymond Estep to relieve him at the wheel. Estep reported:

> *I had never driven an automobile with free-wheeling [mechanism]. I was always accustomed when you took the foot off the gas [pedal], then the engine engaged and it acted to slow down the car. . . . Well, I had been driving for years. . . . I got in behind the wheel of this Studebaker, and the first time I took my foot off . . . the gas—instead of the car slowing down with the engine it just free-wheeled! I jammed down on the brake, . . . I just wasn't prepared for this kind of driving. I guess I drove fifteen or twenty minutes, and Carlos got exasperated with me. He said, "I'd rather drive myself. Let me over there!" And he drove the rest of the way . . . he had tremendous physical stamina in those days. He was a top-notch driver, . . . really a first-rate driver. . . . he could have been a race driver if he had tried.[25]*

Unable to find lodging in Memphis, they proceeded for another seventy-miles into Jackson. Arriving just before midnight, as Dabbs recalled, they ate dinner and arranged to sleep "in a private home—a tourist home—but a very nice place in my estimation."[26] The following morning after breakfast the travelers continued their journey through a moderate snowstorm for the entire length of Tennessee, stopping for the night at Bristol on the Virginia state line. When they emerged from their tourist cabins in the morning Carlos and his companions discovered a ten-inch blanket of snow on the ground. Undaunted by the weather, they warmed up the Studebaker and then headed toward Roanoke, with Carlos as "chief driver." Several miles down the highway, with snow flurries impeding their vision, the Studebaker either slid off the surface or "Carlos dropped a wheel off the shoulder." Regardless of what caused the mishap, Estep vividly remembered how Castañeda expertly controlled the vehicle through that frightful experience: "As we did a 180 [degree spin], just off the shoulder, making about thirty-five or forty-miles-an-hour right in the middle of that highway, and we were headed back the way we were coming. Well, we all caught our breath and Carlos got us straightened around. And we proceeded at a little more leisurely pace on snow and ice the rest of the way to Washington. But he handled that car beautifully even in that snowstorm." [27] On the last leg of the trip into Washington the passengers "took turns driving through Virginia." Jack Dabbs, who was scheduled to attend a foreign language convention in Philadelphia, cheerfully accepted his round of duty. He later recalled: "There was a lot of snow, and I recall one time I was driving when I met another car, and the brakes would not hold, and we slid off to the left of the road into a snow bank—no damage, and we got off [the drift] all right. Then the radiator froze, and we put some cardboard in front of the radiator so the wind would not blow on it so hard, and then it warmed up. Finally, we made it into Washington." Familiar with the layout of the streets in the District of Columbia from previous visits, Castañeda drove straight to the railroad station to drop off Jack "with instructions to meet them at the Mayflower Hotel in four days." [28]

In consort with the American Historical Association the leadership of the American Catholic Historical Association convened its twentieth annual meeting at the Mayflower beginning on Thursday afternoon, December 28. As individuals casually meandered into the meeting hall, they cautiously stepped over cables or walked around a bank of microphones that work crews of the National Broadcasting Company had installed for the main event of the program. At four o'clock Professor Herbert M. Coulson of Saint Louis University called the general session to order. Following customary greetings, latest announcements, and perfunctory remarks the chairman, on cue from the broadcast director, formally introduced President Carlos Eduardo Castañeda. Grateful for the honor, Carlos rose energetically from his seat, smiled to the audience, and approached the podium with a sheaf of papers. Aware that his presidential address would be broadcast live (or recorded for later transmission throughout the hemisphere), he had judiciously selected the title "Our Latin American Neighbors." [29] Cognizant that the radio audience was more numerous than that gathered in the hall, he plunged immediately into his prepared speech. In the initial passage he sketched the Pan-American movement from the postindependence congress to the more recent Lima Conference of 1938:

> The profound influence of the announcement of the "good neighbor" policy made by President Roosevelt is truly remarkable. It struck a fundamental chord and found immediate response throughout the twenty republics south of the Río Grande because of its sincerity and the spontaneous translation into positive acts. The Buenos Aires Conference in 1936 marked the dawn of a new era for the countries of the western hemisphere. The work

begun there was furthered by the Conference of Lima in 1938. In Septem-
ber of this year there met in Panamá, where [Simón] Bolívar led the first Pan
American Congress in 1826, the ministers of foreign affairs of the twenty-
one American republics in accord with the provisions of the Treaty for the
Maintenance, Preservation, and Reestablishment of Peace. This was the first
application of inter-American relations of the procedure of consultation. It
was a forward step of the greatest significance in international cooperation
in the western hemisphere.

Pivoting skillfully, Castañeda launched into a reaffirmation of Bolton's Greater
America hypothesis:

A wave of interest, of sincere desire to learn more about our Latin Ameri-
can neighbors is sweeping the country. Every public spirited citizen, every
organization and club throughout the land is seeking information about
our southern neighbors. A new conception of what has rightly been called
"Greater America" is spreading, and an explanation is being demanded of
those differences which characterize the two prominent civilizations in the
New World, which but yesterday aroused either contempt or idle wonder.
The history of Latin America is being diligently and intelligently studied in
an earnest effort to understand Spanish civilization in the western hemi-
sphere. Americans are approaching the subject with an open and sympa-
thetic mind.

Sensitive to other historians' contributions to the field, Don Carlos praised
Edward Gaylord Bourne, John Franklin Jameson, and Herbert Eugene Bolton,
whose scholarship had blazed channels for understanding Latin American culture. While extolling the virtues of Catholic historians endowed with the gift
of insight, he sensed that because of their northern European ethnic and religious background most listeners in the audience, though certainly not everyone, lacked the discernment to appreciate the nuances of Hispanic American
civilization with the assurance born of his own experience as a researcher.
Now with a sizable captive audience before him, Carlos informed the historical fraternity that a Hispanic Catholic scholar could probe deeper in search
of truth and perspective relating to Latin America:

If there is one fundamental element that characterizes and differentiates
the history and the philosophy of life of Spanish America, it is the role
played by the Church. Next to the racial element contributed by Spain, the
teachings of the Church formed, molded, and created the spirit of the new
race. Spanish American civilization cannot, therefore, be understood or ad-

equately appreciated without a correct evaluation and interpretation of the religious factor that underlies it. Just as the spirit of the Middle Ages left its imperishable imprint on Gothic Architecture, so did the fervent faith of the missionary leave its imprint upon the spirit of the races of Spanish America. This fundamental fact cannot be wholly grasped by the non-Catholic historian, but it is the key to the understanding of many of the differences that otherwise appear unexplainable. Next to the language handicap, a lack of knowledge of the philosophy and the organization of the Church and its influence upon the resultant civilization is the greatest obstacle to an understanding of our southern neighbors.[30]

Following the presidential address everything else at the conference was anticlimactic for Carlos. For the next two days as he, Foik, and Estep maneuvered through the Mayflower's convention facilities the scholar from Brownsville discovered he had become a minor celebrity owing to the positive reception accorded *Our Catholic Heritage* by professional historians. "Dr. Castañeda liked to receive honors, he enjoyed the ceremonies," recalled Moreno, his quasi-secretary, "but he would quickly forget them and return to work on whatever project he had suspended."[31] Perhaps inspired by the accolades or possibly encouraged by Professor Barker, Carlos resolved to play an active role in the affairs of the newly created Latin American Institute at the university. The institute had been established the previous summer with Charles W. Hackett as director.[32] Although few had bothered at the time to consider what role Castañeda might play in the program, Don Carlos knew that as librarian of the Latin American Collection he was in a natural position to contribute effectively. At this juncture the librarian received an invitation to participate. Two weeks after returning from Washington, Castañeda took off for Dallas to promote upcoming activities of the institute via the network facilities of the Mutual Broadcasting Company. By now Carlos was familiar with radio microphones and announcers. Beginning at 8:15 P.M. on Thursday, January 18, 1940, he spoke for a quarter of an hour on the subject of "The Origins of Culture in the Americas." Designed to introduce the Latin American Institute's summer program, his talk was transmitted by the Mutual network to Mexico and Central and South America. Listeners in the Austin area heard Carlos's speech through the local Mutual outlet, station KNOW. Castañeda announced that the institute's summer program would include "a series of six weekly half-hour broadcasts," likewise over the Mutual system, to foster "Pan-American friendship and understanding."[33]

Through the medium of radio, albeit sporadically, the name of Carlos Eduardo Castañeda became known to scholars throughout the Americas. In the immediate future inestimable benefits would accrue to both Castañeda and the Latin American Collection, the one gaining an ever-widening reputation and the other, important book acquisitions. For the time being the librarian-historian indulged in his usual fare of multiple activities. From an earlier radio broadcast on the subject of printing in the Western Hemisphere, which resulted in a major journal publication, Carlos retained a sufficient amount of unused material to support another essay with a slightly different perspective, which he submitted to *Publisher's Weekly*.[34] Ernest W. Winkler, in typical direct fashion, promptly informed Donald Coney that Carlos had produced a worthwhile contribution: "Dr. Castañeda's article in P.W. is better than the title: 'The First Printing Press in Mexico.' That title fits the first paragraph only, as the rest of the article clearly shows. It is a good article, intended to be readable rather than learned."[35]

Castañeda's dual reputation as librarian and historian allowed him to move with ease back and forth from the academic community to the public sector. In October, 1939, when the City Council of San Antonio, then led by dynamic mayor Maury Maverick, Sr., approved a proposal "to re-create almost in the heart of the business district a part of an old Spanish village," it turned to the University of Texas for assistance. Confronted with "a lack of adequate information about the early history" of colonial San Antonio, the mayor invited a trio of scholars—historians Hackett and Castañeda and folklorist J. Frank Dobie—to help the city with documentation. Of the trio Castañeda, on account of his intricate knowledge of materials in the Latin American Collection, furnished the most substantive data about the settlement known as La Villita. Don Carlos commented on the appropriateness of the San Antonio project: "No better monument to the Spanish pioneer in the Southwest could be erected. . . . The adobe house, the machete, and the wooden yoke of the original builders of La Villita are symbols of Spain's pioneers in the Southwest—just as the log cabin, the Bowie knife, and the muzzle loader have become symbols of the Anglo-American trail blazer."[36]

In the springtime of 1940 Castañeda and Dabbs became reunited in another project of mutual interest with the arrival of several crates of books and manuscripts from Paraguay. The university's negotiations for the acquisition of the library of Manuel E. Gondra, former president of Paraguay and onetime diplomatic minister in Washington, had begun in 1939. However, because of delays and the certitude that the materials would not arrive before publication deadline, the collaborators decided not to include reference to the Gondra Collection in their *Guide to the Latin-American Manuscripts in the University of Texas Library*. The library consisted of "approximately nine thousand volumes and over twenty thousand pages of manuscript sources, originals and copies made in South America and Seville" related to the history of Paraguay. Besides books and manuscripts, the collection included about 190 maps, prints, and original drawings.[37]

To reimburse Dabbs for routine expenses Castañeda petitioned the University Research Council for a grant-in-aid of fifty dollars "to get the work started." Dabbs reported: "*Don* Carlos and I got keys to the entrance [of the central area] and someone provided a couple of chairs and a working table, and the lighting was adequate. Now the center of operations shifted to this room. I moved my typewriter in [a rebuilt Underwood, with the same keyboard as Castañeda's typewriter], got a supply of 3x5 cards and a ruler, and I was ready. The box of books remained intact until much later—at least until after I left in November." Setting aside the box of books for later inventory, Dabbs and Castañeda removed the manuscript material for preliminary review. Then, realizing that most of the manuscripts were reproductions of nineteenth-century documents from the Archivo General de Indias in Spain, "but valuable none the less," they opted to compile a separate list for later reference. Dabbs recalled:

> *This detailed work on the Gondra Collection began in the late spring, and my routine meant less contact with Don Carlos. I spent most of my afternoons in the dungeon-like central room in the Tower. Although [Castañeda's] office 2601 was only a few steps away, I rarely went in any more. . . .*
>
> *The rest of the spring of 1940 and the summer went along as I have described. I saw less of Don Carlos in the afternoon—mostly when he dropped in to see how I was progressing.*[38]

Finally, on the basis of a preliminary evaluation, Castañeda wrote a general description of the manuscripts, "pointing out some items of special interest." Although he was the sole author of this essay, published in the 1940 edition of *Handbook of Latin America,* Carlos submitted the piece as a joint enterprise, thus showing his gratitude to Dabbs, who by then had reported for active duty with his National Guard unit, the 141st Infantry Regiment of the 36th Division.[39]

In mid-May, 1940, Castañeda joined Foik and other friends at the Plaza Hotel in Corpus Christi for the twenty-fourth regular meeting of the Texas Knights of Columbus Historical Commission. Summarizing his activities as chairman, Father Foik noted the editing and distribution of 750 copies of two issues of *Preliminary Studies* of the Texas Catholic Historical Society; Jack A. Dabbs's translation of "The Texas Missions in 1795," originally published in *Mid-America;* and Castañeda's reprint edition of "The Beginnings of Printing in America," which first appeared in the *Hispanic American Historical*

Review. The Holy Cross priest singled out for special comment the editorial work, proofreading, and conferences with the author and publisher relating to volume 5 of *Our Catholic Heritage*.⁴⁰ Foik's report seemingly indicated that the fifth volume, like the fourth, was being typeset as sections were completed. In his own report Castañeda presented a thematic overview explaining that the years covered in the present volume were "a period of transition, during which the mission as a frontier institution disappear[ed], the presidio cease[d] to be the center of social life, and the civil settlement [grew] in importance, and the impact of the Anglo-American advance [was] felt in all its force." Whether through overt optimism or subtle impatience, Carlos told the commission that the volume would "cover the period from 1780 to 1836," assuring them that these years were "replete with significant details essential to the understanding of the modern era." In his pragmatic conclusion Castañeda observed: "The historiographer has completed about half of the manuscript, but expects to have all of it in the hands of the editor early this summer. It is safe to assume, therefore, that the volume will come out in the fall at about the same time as its predecessor last year. Accuracy had not been sacrificed for vividness and the same standard set in the previous volumes has been maintained throughout."⁴¹ Little did Carlos realize that this volume would be the most difficult to finish because of unforeseen setbacks that thwarted his progress.

Refreshed by his quick trip to the gulf coast, Castañeda hurried to Austin to revise lecture notes for teaching the course on the history of Spain and Portugal, 1500–1821 in tandem with the Latin American Institute's summer program. With support from the Rockefeller Foundation and the Social Science Research Council of Learned Societies, the University of Texas hosted a special Latin-American Studies Institute during the first summer session of 1940 to construct a solid foundation of respectability for the academic-research program inaugurated by Hackett and his colleagues. Throughout the six-week period Castañeda was quite visible and interacted with everyone whom he encountered—students, guests, faculty, and visitors. Besides classroom instruction, the schedule included outdoor public lectures each Monday evening, eight radio discourses via the Texas State Network, and as a finale, a conference on international relations in the Western Hemisphere featuring discussions by scholars and journalists from the United States and Latin America. Carefully structured to coincide with the aims of the Roosevelt administration's Good Neighbor Policy, the institute attained its broad objective of promoting cultural relations between the Americas.⁴²

Castañeda took advantage of the euphoria of the special institute to propose to the history department a new seminar on sixteenth-century Spanish institutions. After serious consideration the faculty "voted not to offer this course next year but listed for Castañeda instead, in addition to Spain and Portugal, a section on western civilization,[43] which he stoically tolerated as obligatory duty until he could move more securely into the Latin American field. With one class listed for Monday, Wednesday, and Friday at eight in the morning and the other for Tuesday and Thursday at the same hour, the assignment seemed tailored to accommodate Castañeda's schedule for the remainder of the day. The budget council of the history department also recommended a supplemental salary for Carlos of $202.50 for his participation in the summer program and for supervising the thesis work of graduate students.[44]

Undaunted by the rejection of his proposed class, Carlos turned his attention to a quite different matter. Evidently acting on the suggestion of Father Foik (assuredly endorsed by Most Reverend Mariano S. Garriga of the Texas Historical Commission), the bishop of Galveston, Christopher E. Byrne, through a myriad of ecclesiastical channels nominated Castañeda for a prestigious papal honor—knighthood in the Equestrian Order of the Holy Sepulchre of Jerusalem. Needing assistance in obtaining requisite church certificates, Castañeda sought help from his younger sister Josefina in Brownsville, who contacted the pastor of Immaculate Conception Church in Rio Grande City for a copy of Carlos's baptismal record.[45] On the merit of his volumes of *Our Catholic Heritage*, Carlos now stood on the threshold of papal recognition. However, as he knew with certitude from the study of medieval history, matters at the Vatican progressed with deliberate absence of urgency.

At the conclusion of the summer institute Don Carlos embarked on a new project related to the manuscript he was writing for *Our Catholic Heritage*. Although the Matamoros Archives represented the first copying challenge that he had undertaken nearly a decade earlier, owing to the fact that most of the nineteenth-century documents pertained to a later period in Texas history, he had intentionally delayed the compilation of a reference calendar until the need became apparent. Now that there was such a need, the documents, stored at Saint Edward's University, required rearrangement in a chronological or topical sequence before such a calendar could be compiled. Acting on a moment's whim, Carlos hired a graduate student, Joe B. Frantz, for that critical job. Frantz recalled:

> One Sunday morning, sleep-in time, when I was a beginning graduate student, my doorbell rang and there stood a postman with a special delivery letter. I signed, wondering what was so all-fired important. The letter was from Carlos Eduardo Castañeda, whose office was three blocks from my apartment, and it directed—no, commanded—me to be at his office in the Tower at 0900 on Monday. I showed up on time; he said, "Good," pushed

me out of his office, down the Tower elevator, and into his car and drove
like a Río taxi driver across town, singing at the top of his voice a current
radio jingle about how Mentholatum cures it all. As we crossed the South
Congress bridge and headed toward the lower city limits, I wondered where
on earth we were going. Finally we hit the campus parking lot of Saint Ed-
ward's University, spraying gravel halfway to Buda as we pulled up a half-
inch from St. Ed's noble main building.

After introducing Frantz to Father James P. Gibbons and some other priests
and brothers, Carlos spread out the work that he wanted the graduate student
to do, which was "to calendar papers." Frantz remembered, "Somewhere towards the end of laying it out and telling me what he'd pay me and so on (why,
it was 50¢ an hour), and I'd set my own hours, but he expected me to work
four hours a day." After the verbal agreement had been reached, Castañeda
asked Frantz, "By the way, you're Catholic, aren't you?" Frantz, of course, denied the religious affiliation, which prompted Castañeda to ask several follow-
up questions in rapid-fire cadence: "What were you doing at St. Austin's
Church on Sunday? That's why I decided to name you to this job. I wonder
who it was?" Perplexed by the situation, Castañeda stared at the ceiling,
grinned, and said: "Oh, hell, you can have the job anyhow." Frantz, who
maintained a friendship with Don Carlos for almost two decades, recalled his
particular contribution to *Our Catholic Heritage:* "So, that's how I went to
work and spent the summer working at St. Edward's University with the
Knights of Columbus who were actually paying for the project. And from that
time forward, anything I did [professionally] Castañeda would always say, 'I
discovered him. I just picked him out of the crowd!' A bit of joking; and we
had a lot of fun with it over the years." [46] Satisfied with Frantz's progress with
the sequential arrangement of the Matamoros documents, Castañeda then
counseled the graduate student to proceed to the time-consuming task of typing the calendar. Meanwhile library director Coney proposed a modest exchange agreement: "It seems to me that the simplest way for us to handle the
acquisition of a carbon copy of the Matamoros Archives you are having transcribed [i.e., calendared] for your own use would be for us to pay your typist
directly for the part of his labor chargeable to this carbon copy. The Library
could also supply you for transmittal to your typist a sufficient quantity of paper to make the carbon copy on." [47]

     Between multiple commitments in the lecture hall and in the Latin Ameri-
can Collection, Carlos retreated to his work office on the twenty-sixth floor of
the tower. Raymond Estep, who periodically met with Carlos in that office, described the interior:

in the period that I knew him, . . . what I recall of being in his office in the
Tower . . . were all these folders with his manuscripts (I guess it was his
sources or copies of source material) that he had there where he was work-
ing, putting together these different volumes of the Heritage. *A lot of his lec-*
ture notes he prepared on the desk that he had in the Latin American Col-
lection. . . . And he would spend an hour or two . . . a day working behind
his desk in there, and then maybe in the afternoon he might be altogether
[in a different place]. . . . But in Carlos' office there were tremendous num-
bers of piles of manila folders with material that he was using in writing one
of the volumes of Our Catholic Heritage in Texas.[48]

Jack Dabbs, who worked on a regular basis on that floor, provided additional
graphic details about Carlos's office:

The furniture other than a typing chair and a swivel chair, consisted of two
blue leather chairs from the Latin American Library—one of them was usu-
ally piled high with books, papers, and odds and ends, when he had two vis-
itors he had to clear one of the chairs off. He had a couple of pictures on
the wall—one I believe [was] his diploma and a fancy eagle or bird made of
horn. At least one other chair, usually piled high with papers, stood by the
door to the closet on the left end of the room from the door. This was al-
ways stuffed with papers, old drafts of books and articles, some books, and
boxes.[49]

With natural aplomb Castañeda labored under the stress of part-time
teaching, research, writing, public speaking, and librarianship. Despite his determination to finish the fifth volume of *Our Catholic Heritage,* the variance
of topics began to frustrate him. Essentially the difficulty was striking a balance in the material relating to different independence movements—Mexican
insurgency against Spain and Texas' separation from Mexico. Eventually he
resolved the problem by terminating the volume in 1810, with the twilight of
Spanish rule, but for the moment he wrestled with the knotty question. Compounding the problem was the fact that Father Foik, debilitated by illness,
prudently curtailed his work schedule, which meant that Carlos's manuscript
remained unedited for long stretches of time.

Hopefully optimistic that his friend's health would improve, in the autumn
Castañeda reduced his pace of activity. Then, too, he needed to catch up on
neglected correspondence. Among those with whom he stayed in contact, if
only sporadically, was Frederick C. Chabot of San Antonio. Feeling a twinge
of guilt for not attending reunions of the Yanaguana Society, Carlos, in grati-

tude for elevation to the status of "honorary" member, volunteered to review the group's recent publications in major journals.[50] In the final months of 1940 he accepted two other honors, largely in recognition of his work with *Our Catholic Heritage*. Following the accolade from the Yanaguana Society he received notification of his election as "corresponding member" of the Mexican Antheneum of Arts and Sciences. Not obligated to be present for a ceremony, and unable to attend in any event on account of limited funding, Carlos simply promised to cooperate with this "semi-official" association, which was composed of Mexico's outstanding scholars, in "promoting and stimulating interest in scientific and artistic development.[51] Just before Christmas, Don Carlos received another announcement—this time from New York—that the Hispanic Society of America, founded in 1904 to promote "the advancement of Spanish and Portuguese culture" in countries where those languages were spoken, had conferred upon him corresponding membership.[52] Carlos graciously accepted the honor because, like a beautiful ribbon, the membership could be symbolically tied to the lance of a knight-errant. Around Thanksgiving, Carlos welcomed the news that the budget council of the history department had selected him "and 7 others" to teach in the second term of "the 1941 Summer Session."[53] While Castañeda's half-time salary as librarian remained static, it was the summer teaching that generated modest increments to his annual income, along with periodic stipends from the Knights of Columbus. Still, Carlos constantly battled to provide his family with elemental necessities.

As the old year neared its end Castañeda remembered the swirling activities of the previous December when he and Father Foik, accompanied by Dabbs and Estep, had driven to the nation's capital for the historical conventions. Now, a year later, his level of productivity with *Our Catholic Heritage*, although moderately satisfactory, was sluggish. This was partly owing to Father Foik's rapidly declining health; his illness had been diagnosed as a "diabetic infection" that necessitated prolonged care at Seton Hospital in Austin. While obviously worried about his friend's condition, Carlos derived a reason for rejoicing from the news that his wife Elisa was pregnant again.[54]

Shortly after the new year of 1941 commenced Castañeda got involved in the intriguing challenge of determining the origins and authenticity of several pieces of eighteenth-century art, one of which was a portrait of Fray Antonio Margil de Jesús, frontier missionary and founder of historic San José y San Miguel de Aguayo. His lack of experience in evaluating colonial Mexican art in no way deterred Carlos from advancing into the center of a lively discussion at a local historical society meeting in Arlington, midway between Dallas and Fort Worth. Believed to be "some of the oldest cultural art pieces in the United States," two paintings and three religious statues found at the old Franciscan missions in San Antonio eventually brought Castañeda into contact with Charles Muskavitch, member of the Russian nobility and conservator affiliated with galleries and museums in Dallas and Sacramento. Carlos's contribution, aside from discovering the existence of these art pieces at the missions, came in the form of research. During one of his trips to Mexico City he had encountered references to art inventories "in an ancient, hand-written manuscript" housed in the Biblioteca Nacional. From that source he quoted "exact descriptions of the work—size, color, and figure." Frustrated by an inability to distinguish original pieces from copies, he called for assistance from Muskavitch and the latter's wife Gail Northe, Texas radio commentator. After culling for several days through countless fragmentary references in archival records, Muskavitch and his wife concluded that five pieces—four at Mission San José and the fifth "high above the stage" at downtown San Fernando School—were "authentic Spanish colonial art." [55]

In March, Castañeda's life momentarily turned upside down when his intimate friend and editor, Father Paul J. Foik, died unexpectedly at Seton Hospital. To be sure, Foik was a victim of "a long and lingering illness," but since the Holy Cross priest had stoically endured that malady for years no one, least of all Carlos, suspected the end was imminent. Foik's death cast the Texas Historical Commission into a tailspin. [56]

On Tuesday morning, March 4, 1941, Castañeda entered a crowded "black-draped chapel" at Saint Edward's University to join "Church dignitaries and lay friends" in paying final respects to Father Foik. Prominently seated in pews reserved for the clergy were two bishops, eight monsignors, and "more than seventy priests." At the conclusion of a solemn requiem mass the Very Reverend Stanislaus F. Lisewki, C.S.C., president of Saint Edward's, escorted the sealed coffin to the depot for conveyance by train to Notre Dame University for burial. [57] That afternoon Castañeda paid personal tribute to his deceased friend in a radio broadcast over station KNOW. Reviewing the life of the Canadian-born cleric, Carlos filled in gaps in the obituary "with his own opinion" as he traced Foik's career as historian, educator, librarian, and "sincere and faithful servant of Christ." [58]

Coinciding with the memorial service for Father Foik, the executive committee of the Texas Historical Commission, led by Mariano S. Garriga, coadjutor bishop of Corpus Christi, conducted an emergency meeting at Saint Edward's University to select a successor chairman. Most members of the commission agreed that Father Peter P. Forrestal, who, like Foik, belonged to the Congregation of the Holy Cross, was a logical choice as interim chairman. Castañeda's opinion carried considerable weight: "I had rather work under him than anyone else I know. He thoroughly understands our work; he has intimate knowledge of the Archives of Spain, has translated several of our preliminary studies and loves Texas dearly." Unanimity about Forrestal notwithstanding, a vexing problem that momentarily confronted the commissioners was the fact that the priest was currently teaching at Notre Dame University in Indiana. Consequently they realized it would be imprudent, if not an imposition on the religious order, to demand pulling him away from the classroom "in mid-term." With regard to the status of *Our Catholic Heritage*, the commissioners were gratified that the fifth volume was "practically ready for the press." In the months before Foik's death Castañeda had produced sufficient pages for the editor to read and amend "up to page 308," leaving a balance of "about 200 pages more to be finished and the index to be revised and corrected." However, the geographic separation between South Bend, Indiana, and Austin, Texas, was a factor the commissioners could not ignore. Sensing an impasse, but careful not to disturb the consensus, Castañeda summarized the importance of having access to an editor close at hand:

> *The real value of a permanent chairman to me is to be able to discuss with him personally from time to time the plans and outlines of each chapter, what point to stress, what material to leave out as irrelevant. The stimulus of this contact with Dr. Foik, these weekly conversations of several hours' length were of the greatest value to me. The reaction from all this was invaluable to me. This constant personal contact with the permanent chairman is the finest encouragement to me and absolutely necessary. Besides there is a great deal of proof reading, technical corrections and catching of mistakes that I need a chairman to advise [consult] with [on a regular basis].*

Aware of Castañeda's concerns, Bishop Garriga recommended the immediate appointment of an interim chairman to provide the commission a semblance of continuity. In the meantime the prelate recommended appealing to the religious superior of the Congregation of the Holy Cross to "give us one of your Fathers to succeed Dr. Foik" as permanent "Chairman of our Commission." To reinforce their position the members of the executive committee unanimously approved the choice of Dr. Forrestal for permanent chairman.[59]

With the question of the chairmanship still up in the air, Castañeda focused attention on staking out a piece of curricular territory in the history department. Extremely careful not to encroach upon Hackett's domain, Carlos proposed the creation of a seminar on Iberian institutions. To win the approval of his colleagues Castañeda explained that the "New Scheme" actually provided flexibility "so that Latin-American students could get course work" in this field whenever Hackett was not offering a seminar. At a follow-up meeting in early April the historians clarified the issue of Castañeda's new course, to be listed in the next biennial catalog, by appending several prerequisites and a succinct description: "Spain's political and governmental developments and the administration of its colonial empire."[60] With the "Adoption of a New Scheme" Castañeda cautiously continued the gradual transition from the library to the history department.

Meanwhile the Latin American Collection, preempting half of his university time, indirectly rewarded him with another accolade. In recognition of Carlos's work on Paraguayan maps and the Gondra Collection, the American Geographical Society of New York conferred on him the designation of fellow. In announcing the selection the society emphasized that its criteria for choosing "persons as fellows" rested solely on the basis "of their outstanding work in the field of geography and maps."[61]

Less than a month after the emergency meeting of its executive committee the Texas Historical Commission faced the necessity of appointing an on-site leader to guide the affairs of the organization. With Dr. Forrestal indefinitely committed to Notre Dame University, the commissioners scheduled an extraordinary convocation at the Gunter Hotel in San Antonio (coinciding with the courtly installation of Robert E. Lucey as archbishop of San Antonio) to brief the Reverend James P. Gibbons, C.S.C., of Saint Edward's University, who had courageously accepted the arduous position of interim chairman. As such, he had agreed to monitor the completion of the "monumental," seven-volume history of the church in Texas. Finding himself overwhelmed with work on campus, and with his wife pregnant, Castañeda skipped the meeting. In a letter to Father Gibbons, which the acting chairman read at the meeting, Carlos described the problems that blocked completion of the fifth volume of *Our Catholic Heritage:*

> *This volume presents many more difficulties than the four that have preceded it. The period covered has been approached from many different angles by different historians and there are numerous monographic studies on the various incidents to be portrayed. In order to keep the same standard of scholarship and to justify the work, it is essential that all the findings by other historians be incorporated and in a sense integrated into [a] connected narrative. But the task does not end here. If the volume were to include nothing else, it would be only a compilation. It is necessary to coordinate the various studies and add the new information which sources hitherto unused reveal. Herein lies the real contribution.[62]*

With the finished sections of the volume he expressed genuine satisfaction:

> *In the six chapters that have been completed there is much new information that will be hailed as a distinct contribution, such as the establish-*

ment of new lines of communication between the distant outposts of [the] northern frontier, the economic basis for the secularization of the mission, the secularization in detail, the establishment of new Indian policies as a result of the changed conditions of the frontier, and the beginning of colonization as a means of defense against encroachments. These subjects have been treated in the chapters already finished, but there are many others yet to be worked out.[63]

In the first weeks of spring Castañeda was clearly showing signs of physical and mental exhaustion. Privately he still mourned the death of his longtime friend and editor. No matter how much cooperation he had pledged to the new leadership of the Texas Historical Commission, a smooth transition eluded him. In the months to come he would vacillate between commitments. In his letter to Gibbons, Carlos admitted that he plainly lacked the motivating drive of prior seasons: "The strain of eight years of exhausting work on the first four volumes; the increase of work at the University as a result of my teaching activities, which have been added to my library duties; and the inescapable effects of prolonged and sustained effort have combined to slow me down. In spite of my willingness to work, I find that I am unable to accomplish as much as I used to and this in itself has tended to discourage me. In short, I find that I need a rest." Admittedly the work at the university was a contractual matter; on the other hand, he pursued the writing of *Our Catholic Heritage* as a way to earn extra income. Still, the latter obligation, a commitment he had willingly accepted because of his friendship with Father Foik, was progressing slowly with frequent halts and fewer starts. As an author with considerable experience behind him Carlos offered a persuasive argument for delaying publication of the latest tome. "I have come to the conclusion," he continued to Gibbons,

that in regard to the fifth volume there is little use to hurry the work. If I were to finish it between now and the first of June, the publishers would probably proceed to bring it out in the summer. It is a well known and established fact that books published in the summer pass unnoticed, because most of the men interested in serious studies are enjoying a vacation at that time. The best time for publication of a book is in the fall. Under the circumstances, I am going to do everything I can to finish by June, but I would suggest to the Commission to persuade the publisher to postpone the actual release of the book until fall.[64]

In fact, it was the experience of writing four volumes of *Our Catholic Heritage* plus another hefty tome advancing toward completion that prompted Carlos to give earnest consideration not only to his future career but also to his role with the Texas Historical Commission. He counseled the interim chairman:

> It may be well for the Commission to give serious thought to this matter and to look about for possible authors. I feel that I cannot undertake to write the last two volumes immediately. Upon the completion of the present volume, I need to get a rest for a year at least. There is no sense, however, to suspend the work. The original plan was to have different men write each volume. Why not return to that plan? The Commission can find one or more men to begin work even now on the last two volumes. The work of assembling the materials, and the beginning of the writing can go on concurrently. There is no need to wait even for the completion of the fifth volume.

Lacking the energetic, charging, jovial style of even a year before, Castañeda complained of sheer exhaustion. He explained: "I would like to make it clear to the Commission that I am willing and ready to complete the fifth volume; that after[wards] . . . I must have a rest; and that if after a year or so, I can be of help in cooperating with the writing of the last two volumes I will be glad to render whatever service I can. But I feel that I owe it to myself to stop as soon as I finish the present volume for the sake of my health, which is seriously endangered. Frankly, I am conscious that the strain is beginning to tell on me." [65]

Indicative that by the early 1940s Castañeda was growing weary of the tremendous load he had imposed on himself was Joe Frantz's recollection of two divergent schools of opinion around the university campus. One group of Carlos's colleagues "liked him" tremendously while an opposing faction "couldn't stand him." Owing to the pressures under which he labored, gradually he acquired traits of crankiness. Frantz recalled:

> He had an explosive temper and was a gut fighter. And he could just chew somebody unmercifully. I know Father Gibbons told me one time that summer: "He comes in here and kicks me around. And three minutes later he'd get his arm around my shoulder and treat me like I was his old buddy. He may forget that soon, but I don't forget that soon. I can't get kicked in the face and humiliated . . . and get over it. It takes me a while." And there were a number of people around here that Castañeda just landed on their faces with both feet. And they were not about to recover and you'd sympathize with them.[66]

Even in the quiet solitude of the Latin American Collection, Carlos occasionally flared up when an inquiry annoyed him. Library director Coney, at the request of a New York patron, asked Carlos to evaluate a manuscript on the Franciscan missions of New Mexico. Not knowing anything about the author or the audience to which the narrative was aimed, Castañeda postponed reading the manuscript until after Easter and then drafted a caustic critique of the work.

> *I have looked over the manuscript of Mr. [Arthur] Train. After reading it, I find it is impossible to offer any constructive criticism. It is neither literature nor history. It is a nice jumble of facts and fiction which would not even pass as folklore. Just one example or two: On page 4, in referring to the missions of New Mexico, he says they were the smallest and most primitive, which is perfectly absurd. The ruins there are still amazing. On page 19, his description of a Franciscan is ridiculous and derogatory. On page 31, his description of the milking of a cow is equally absurd.*[67]

His ego bruised, if not battered, Train promptly replied to Coney: "The description of milking a cow is taken from Bancroft; the unfortunate lapse about the New Mexico missions is due to the fact that I visited most of them several years ago, and the California missions more recently and had formed an apparently inaccurate impression of their relative importance. The description of a tonsure seems to be loosely phrased."[68] In a letter of the same date to Castañeda, a recognized expert on the subject of Latin American culture, Train selected his words carefully: "I should have explained that the book in question is intended as a children's book. . . . This does not excuse errors, of course, but the type of book and space limitations make it practically impossible to do justice to Latin American culture and the whole Spanish era." Clarifying that the manuscript had been sent to Coney at the suggestion of the director of the New York Public Library, Train concluded: "I suppose it is not reasonable to assume that the three errors you were kind enough to point out are the only major blunders in the chapter. I only regret that you did not extend your valuable criticisms to other parts of the manuscript."[69]

Another facet to Castañeda's ratings on the popularity chart emanated from smoldering animosities dating from the early 1930s that periodically surfaced. Unknown to Carlos, the hierarchy of the Catholic Church in Texas discreetly monitored the trajectory of his career vis-à-vis merit pay increases and cordial human relations in the workplace. In Austin a trusted confidant of Archbishop Robert E. Lucey of San Antonio observed in July, 1941: "Dr. Castañeda is of inestimable value to the Church and Texas university." The prelate's correspondent labeled a high-ranking administrator as "a bit bigoted" and remarked that "some of the other history professors resent Dr. Castañeda whom they refer to as Mexican." To redress the situation the hierarchy contemplated finding outside employment for Carlos, possibly a government appointment, that not only would strengthen his academic standing but also would accrue to him "international recognition." [70] Although nothing resulted immediately, the discussion signified that there were individuals outside of the academy who, notwithstanding his feisty nature, looked out for Castañeda's interests. At the conclusion of the spring semester the president of Saint Edward's University notified Castañeda that in recognition of his exemplary scholarship he would receive an honorary doctorate at the fifty-sixth commencement exercises. Shortly before the appointed time of four o'clock in the afternoon of Sunday, June 1, 1941, Carlos arrived at the administration building of the Catholic university for robing and assuming his place in the academic procession. Promptly on the hour the commencement marshal led the procession toward Abbey Theater "for the conferring of degrees" and citations of honor. For once in his adult life Castañeda sat through an entire ceremony without delivering a major speech. Following the principal address by Very Reverend Walter F. Goltaka, S.M., president of Saint Mary's University of San Antonio, Father Lisewki conferred the honorary degree of doctor of laws on three recipients: the commencement speaker; Castañeda; and in absentia, B. Dudley Tarlton of Corpus Christi.[71]

If the Saint Edward's commencement lacked the high drama that he appreciated, with the advent of summer Carlos's morale soared after receiving notification from the Vatican through normal ecclesiastical channels that Pope Pius XII in recognition of ongoing scholarship had conferred on him knighthood in the ancient Equestrian Order of the Holy Sepulchre of Jerusalem, the highest honor that the Catholic Church bestowed on the laity and clergy. To allow ample time to plan an appropriate investiture on the campus of the University of Texas, Carlos selected Sunday, October 12, for the ceremony, to coincide with the anniversary of Columbus's encounter with America.[72]

In the meantime Castañeda remained close to his family, awaiting the birth of the new baby. Not content with the schedule of nature and the attending obstetrician, on the Fourth of July he took Elisa and their daughter Consuelo on a short drive to Bastrop, east of Austin, in the hope that the mild strain of the automobile ride would induce labor, thus giving to the child the gift of birth on a historic national holiday, comparable to his own Armistice Day birthday. Later in the afternoon three tired Castañedas returned home without incident. The next day, minus festive celebration or fanfare, Elisa gave birth to a second daughter whom they named Rosemary.[73]

Relieved of anxiety and overjoyed with the presence of another daughter, Castañeda, while not overlooking his promise to finish the current volume of *Our Catholic Heritage,* welcomed the opportunity to earn supplemental income by teaching two sections of a class on the history of Spain and Portugal, with an aggregate enrollment of twenty-six students, in the second session of summer school.[74] To assist Carlos with routine clerical duties the history department assigned to him a female student, with funding from the National Youth Administration, for twenty hours of work a month.[75] With the beginning of the long term in September, Castañeda resumed his fluctuating schedule of part-time instruction (western civilization and Spain and Portugal) and the curatorship of the Latin American Collection.[76]

As autumn embraced the hill country, gently dabbing the trees with blotches of golden hues, Castañeda and his friends looked forward with great expectation to his investiture "in the white mantle" of a knight of the Holy Sepulchre. Beginning in late September the student newspaper carried informative articles about the "colorful scene from Medieval ages" that would unfold on campus. Focusing on the fraternal union in which Carlos would be inducted, *The Daily Texan* reported: "The oldest Catholic religious order in existence, its historical beginnings can be traced to Godfrey, Duke of Buillon [Bouillion], by whom it was instituted in 1099 in commemoration of the recapture of Jerusalem by the crusaders. Antedating such Catholic religious orders as that of Saint John of Jerusalem and the Knights Templar it is purely honorary and confers knighthood for merit, devotion, service and loyalty."[77] Behind the scenes Castañeda worked feverishly to involve different constituencies in the celebration. Donald Coney in the library directorate and Milton R. Gutsch in the history department jointly dispatched an invitation to university colleagues asking them to support the unprecedented gala event:

> On October 12, one of our colleagues will receive a singular recognition of a scholarly contribution in the field of Spanish-American history. Dr. Carlos E. Castañeda will be made a knight of the Holy Sepulchre in a very colorful ceremony to be held in Gregory Gymnasium at 10:30 in the morning. You are cordially invited to attend.
>
> At one o'clock on the same date, a testimonial dinner will be given in his honor at the Stephen F. Austin Hotel in the Capital Ballroom. The guest speakers will be President Homer P. Rainey, Archbishop Lucey of San Antonio, and Bishop Byrne of Galveston. You are invited to attend. The dinner will be informal, and the price per plate will be $1.00. If you plan to attend the dinner, please indicate that intention . . . to Miss Florence Escott, Garrison Hall 109.[78]

Focusing on the fact that Castañeda was to be "the eighth man in the history of Texas to be proclaimed a knight" in the prestigious order, a student journalist on the staff of the campus newspaper wrote an insightful commentary for the Saturday edition that placed the celebration in a broader context:

Dr. Castañeda's honor is even more significant because of the long road
he has come, having started out as a humble Mexican boy.

Recognition by the Catholic Church and initiation into the oldest and
highest-ranking Catholic order open to laymen came to Dr. Castañeda
largely because of his work in his church.

The eminent scholar has made a name for himself locally and nation-
ally ... through his research work in Latin-American history and through
his development of the University's Latin-American Library into one of pre-
eminence in this field. His efforts have made the University second only to
Mexico City as a center for research.

Acknowledging that the investiture of the next day would redound favorably
upon the candidate for knighthood, the editorial writer concluded:

But it will also focus attention upon the University as the home of this
honored person. Dr. Castañeda's achievement will help to put the Univer-
sity even further forward as a center of religious as well as educational
advancement.

So, it's congratulations and thanks to Dr. Carlos E. Castañeda.[79]

On Sunday morning, Columbus Day—celebrated throughout Latin America as Día de la Raza (day of the people)—a delegation of fourth-degree
Knights of Columbus, attired in "full regalia" of plumed hats, capes, and
swords, greeted the arriving guests at the entrance of Gregory Gymnasium. As
the guests filled the bleachers in the cavernous facility they gazed at the colorful decorations that conjured up a "flavor of the crusades, remembrances of
bits of Chaucer, the life of St. Thomas Becket, and the other dim retrospec-
tions into the realm of long ago" that obviously reflected the aesthetic values
of the Equestrian Order of the Holy Sepulchre.[80] To one side, but conspicu-
ously in view of the audience, Rev. James D'Autremont, C.S.C., directed the
choir of Saint Edward's University, "augmented" by cantors from Seton Hospital. On cue from the master of ceremonies, Rev. Vincent F. Holden, C.S.P.,
of Saint Austin's Church, a magnificent procession entered the great hall, led
by local and visiting clergy and followed by dignitaries of church and state and
their knight escorts of honor. Then a squire, walking slowly, carried a white
cape adorned with a scarlet cross of Jerusalem, spurs, a sword, and a plumed
hat. Finally, bringing up the end of the procession and flanked by two pages,
Castañeda, dressed in an elegant black tuxedo with swallowtails and white tie,
walked down a center aisle between two rows of high-ranking escorts from the
Knights of Columbus and stopped at the foot of an altar erected especially for

the occasion.[81] Joe B. Frantz, who sat in the audience that approximated four thousand, shared a glimpse of that resplendent ceremony. Frantz reported: "He was, of course, . . . naturally proud of his knighthood by the Church. . . . the first such ceremony [that] took place in Gregory Gym. It brought out all the ermine in the Church—practically. . . . It was a real Roman spectacle and also a command performance, if you knew Castañeda, because presumedly [sic] he was counting the house to see if you were there and making a list of who wasn't." [82]

From his unobstructed vantage point on the floor, waiting for the choir to conclude its processional hymn, Castañeda surveyed the full house. Nodding reverently, he acknowledged the presence of the venerable clergy at the altar: Most Reverend Francis C. Kelley, bishop of Oklahoma City and Tulsa and, simultaneously, prior of the Western American Lieutenancy of the Equestrian Order of the Holy Sepulchre; Most Reverend Christopher E. Byrne, bishop of Galveston; his longtime friend the Most Reverend Mariano S. Garriga of Corpus Christi; and Most Reverend Laurence J. FitzSimon, bishop-designate of Amarillo. Looking at the section reserved for special guests, he smiled at Elisa and Consuelo, next to whom were his sisters from Brownsville, María and Josefina Castañeda, accompanied by their "only living aunt" on the maternal side of the family, Ella Leroux Fredelier of San Antonio. He also noted the attendance of several dignitaries of the Texas State Council of the Knights of Columbus with whom he was acquainted because of their support of *Our Catholic Heritage*. Facing forward, Carlos admired the altar, "draped with lace cloth embroidered in gold," which pleased his sense of propriety.[83]

Except for a random cough or murmur, a solemn silence permeated the hall as the master of ceremonies introduced Right Reverend Monsignor Michael H. Abraham D'Assemani, of Michigan City, Indiana. As personal representative of the Patriarch of Jerusalem, Most Reverend Aloysius Barlissina, Monsignor D'Assemani read a Latin proclamation, with a brief English translation, designating Carlos Eduardo Castañeda a Knight of the Holy Sepulchre. Empowered by authority of the proclamation, Bishop Kelley, aided by Father Holden, summoned Castañeda to kneel in front of the presider's chair. "What asketh thou?" intoned the prior. The candidate, with a microphone at his left, slowly replied in a clear voice so that all in the auditorium could hear: "I ask to be received as a Knight into the Equestrian Order of the Holy Sepulchre of Jerusalem." The bishop then inquired: "Dost thy condition enable thee to live honorably and keep up the dignity of this Sacred Order?" Confidently yet humbly the candidate answered: "By the grace of God, I am able to uphold the condition and dignity of this Equestrian Order of Knighthood." There followed a ritual of more questions and responses, after which Castañeda clasped his hands and placed them between the knees of the prior, signifying not only a position of helplessness but also complete surrender and confidence in God the Lord. At this point in the investiture Carlos avowed "to serve and defend loyally his Lord until death." Accepting the sword from the squire, the presiding prelate gently struck the candidate three times upon the back, declaring after the third tap, "I dub thee Knight. Arise, Sir Knight." The bishop then awarded to Carlos the "emblem of knighthood"—a pair of spurs, a cloak which the attending knights placed on the honoree, and a plumed hat. Thoroughly enjoying the high drama, Castañeda retired to a side near the altar where he joined "other vested knights" of the same order, and he stayed there throughout the remainder of the ceremony, which included a Pontifical Mass.[84] Another student who witnessed the investiture, Joe W. Neal, remembered that not even the rising temperature in the gymnasium stifled the dignity of the proceedings: "I had never seen as much pomp and ceremony and costume as marked that occasion. It was a magnificent spectacle and well deserved." [85]

Against the background of liturgical music the principal celebrant, Bishop Byrne, robed in vestments worn at the memorial field mass held at San Jacinto Battleground on the occasion of the Texas centennial five years earlier and using a chalice presented to him at that historic assembly, invited the other prelates and assisting clergy to join him around the altar.[86] After the Gospel reading Bishop Kelley, renowned as a "brilliant" ecclesiastic of the modern church, delivered a stirring homily in which he addressed ancient traditions and contemporary events,[87] particularly reports of naked aggression spreading across Europe and Asia. He commenced with an overview of the origins of Catholic knighthood: "The military orders of knights, . . . came out of the hospitals. They can with some authority be called the founders of hospitals. . . . These warrior monks . . . saved and sent the tradition of honor and love down the centuries to our own day. The Knights of St. John called themselves Hospitallers. The Knights of St. Lazarus were both lepers and nurses of lepers." Next the bishop informed the audience of the legacy bequeathed by tradition to knights of the Holy Sepulchre. Notwithstanding the intervention of nine centuries, the sterling values of knighthood remained timeless in their application:

> The Order of the Holy Sepulchre is at least as old as that of the Hospitallers. Its duty was to guard the tomb of Christ. Its early Grand Masters were Popes. Its Grand Master even today is the reigning Pontiff. It is by his authority that its Rector, the Patriarch of Jerusalem, creates new knights. It is royal too in its founder, the Crusader Knight of Jerusalem. It still guards the Holy Sepulchre by its alms and its devotion. But, above all, in a modern world into which it does not seem to fit, the Order of the Holy Sepul-

chre remains, as does that of the Hospitallers, to keep alive the memory of days of greatness when, against the evils of barbarism, the cross was set; when honor and devotion gathered true men for the saving of Christian civilization.

Then, alluding to war clouds casting ominous shadows across the landscape of Europe and the Orient, Bishop Kelley reminded the audience that stout-hearted men of honor were still in demand if the spread of aggression were to be deterred:

Fifty years ago a man wrote: "Causes which gave rise in those days to deeds of romance will never come again. The lawlessness and disorder which began the chivalric spirit have vanished before the advance of civilization. . . . We must henceforth regard the mailed knight and his deeds of chivalry . . . as never again to be repeated." But fifty years have passed and the undying ideal has not passed with them. Again the hordes are on the march. Again lust for conquest fills the hearts of men. We may not now call for the mailed men of the past, but we do still call for iron men, knights, who carry in their souls the chivalry that is born of honor.

Finally, the Canadian-born homilist recognized the intellectual and individual virtues of the most recent knight: "This is the lesson of today's ceremony. In the person of a man of honor, honor is again being exalted and crowned. It is good that he is found in a fortress not of military might but of learning. The occasion as well as the ceremony is symbolized, for the seeds of chivalry blossom into all that a university truly should represent." [88]

At the conclusion of the Pontifical Mass, with the bishops' arching miters and flowing vestments in clear view and with knight escorts performing assigned duties amid the inspirational singing of the choir and cantors, the recessional march truly captivated the audience. Moving along with the crowd toward the exit, Castañeda smiled and waved to friends and acquaintances, thoroughly enjoying every nuance of the celebration. Outside the gymnasium he stopped at the sidewalk to receive felicitations from hundreds of persons who had traveled to Austin to share his special day. As the clock in the university library tower sounded the chimes of half-past noon Castañeda and his family, church and university dignitaries, and others in the throng boarded automobiles for a short drive south of the capitol complex to the Stephen F. Austin Hotel on Congress Avenue. Still the celebrity of the day, Castañeda, accompanied by an entourage of well-wishers, strolled into the spacious ballroom. With aplomb an honor guard from the Knights of Columbus escorted Carlos and Elisa to their reserved seats at the head table. A prominent Houston attorney, Robert H. Kelley, also a Knight of the Holy Sepulchre, presided at the luncheon "as toastmaster." To commence the banquet Kelley invited Bishop Garriga to pronounce a blessing. The toastmaster then introduced four speakers, each of whom paid tribute to Castañeda—Gus P. Strauss, state deputy of the Knights of Columbus; Dr. Homer Price Rainey, president of the University of Texas; Bishop Kelley; and Bishop Byrne. Indicative of the public awareness Castañeda's investiture had attracted, Kelley read congratulatory messages from Archbishop Robert E. Lucey of San Antonio; Archbishop John J. Cantwell of Los Angeles; Mary Q. Garthar of Houston, president of the Galveston Diocesan Council affiliated with the National Council of Catholic Women; Gov. Coke R. Stevenson; and Mayor Tom Miller of Austin. The toastmaster also presented Elisa R. Castañeda, wearing an elegant black hat, "to the large assembly." [89] Three decades later Doña Elisa remembered a few highlights of that grand event.

> it took place at Gregory Gym. And it was full of people. It was a procession of many of the bishops . . . from the state here and from out-of-state, who came for the occasion. . . . Homer Rainey made a talk and many of the faculty people were present, all of our friends. . . . It was a very important affair in our lives. And after that we had a big luncheon. . . . It was a very impressive event. . . . They don't do so much about it now. I noticed when others have received [knighthood] they haven't made as much commotion as they did at the time [of Carlos's investiture]. There were so few [knights] at the time.[90]

Elisa also clarified the circumstances surrounding Carlos's selection for the signal honor: "I will say this: Most of the ones who are made Knights of the Holy Sepulchre are very wealthy people who can contribute to the . . . Church and can contribute financially a great deal to the Order. But in certain cases like in my [husband's] we were poor, more so than your name [O. Wayne Poorman, the interviewer]. And he was selected because of his work [and] not because of his financial status . . . because of his monumental work in [writing] the history of Texas, *Our Catholic Heritage*.[91]

Gratified by the gestures of friendship and goodwill, Castañeda rose from his chair to acknowledge individuals who had guided his career. Noticeably absent from the gathering was Father John Elliot Ross, C.S.P., former chaplain of the Newman Club at the University of Texas. "It was Father Ross," Carlos informed the audience, "who first persuaded me to leave civil engineering to enter the field of history. Today, he is unable to be here—he is disabled by paralysis and lies in a hospital bed in Charlottesville, Virginia." Next he expressed "words of homage" to Eugene C. Barker, the professor who, along with Father Ross, had profoundly influenced his decision to be-come a historian. Exhilarated by his induction into the ranks of the knights of the Holy Sepulchre, Carlos thanked Bishops Byrne and Kelley for their support in the nomination process, and his new fraternal brother, Robert H. Kelley. To the Knights of Columbus he extended special gratitude "for the success" he had achieved in borderlands history. "It was an outlay of sixty thousand dollars made by the Knights of Columbus in Texas over the last ten years that helped to write the Catholic history of this state." He also thanked the fourth degree Knights of Columbus, numbering nearly thirty, who performed escort duty, all of whom were from out of town—from Houston, Galveston, El Paso, Port Neches, Groves, Nederland, and Taylor. Ever mind-ful of his family, Castañeda presented to the audience his aunt from San Antonio and his two sisters, whom he described as "teachers in Brownsville." To close the festive banquet Monsignor D'Assemani intoned a prayer of thanksgiving.[92]

Within a few weeks after the investiture Castañeda ordered a "traditional" white uniform decorated "with black and gold braid" and a personal saber for use on special occasions. Regulations of the order prescribed that he wear his "white, ankle-length cape" with its red Jerusalem cross (a large cross surrounded by four smaller ones) on top of the formal uniform.[93] In view of Carlos's stringent financial situation, the decision to order a custom-made uni-form likely originated with suggestions and donations from friends and ad-mirers. Reports of Castañeda's investiture spread rapidly to editorial offices of professional organizations with which he was associated.[94] The editor of *Commonweal* opined: "That the Holy See should have selected him for so sig-nal an honor is most gratifying to serious students of Latin American affairs. He is the sort of scholar who, in these days of somewhat hectic interest, is needed to guide Americans safely and sanely amid delicate problems. A loyal citizen of his adopted country and a fervent Catholic, he is a most useful leader in Pan American affairs. . . . Now the Pope himself has set on his labors a seal of approval."[95]

Undoubtedly Castañeda basked in the afterglow of the investiture well past his forty-fifth birthday and the observance of his saint's day in November. Just before Thanksgiving the budget council of the history department assigned to him office 116 in Garrison Hall, a subtle gesture that connoted another firm step in the transition from librarian to historian. Moreover the depart-ment recommended an expenditure of $405 as Carlos's supplemental salary for teaching in the 1942 summer program.[96] Greatly motivated by the recog-nition he had received, Castañeda "resumed in earnest" the challenge of writ-ing the last chapters of volume 5 of *Our Catholic Heritage*. Periodically he submitted sheaves of manuscript to Father Gibbons at Saint Edward's University for final editing. On some occasions the priest-editor conferred with Carlos in the solitude of the Latin American Collection. Gradually the two scholars worked through their "period of adjustment," and the project moved closer to completion.[97]

As an indication of how much Castañeda had grown in stature and acceptance in professional circles, upon the death of Charles E. Chapman at the University of California two senior historians at Austin (Barker and Hackett) confidentially recommended him for a faculty appointment at the Berkeley campus. Unable to write in detail on account of a tight travel schedule, Hackett advised his contact in California on December 1, 1941: "Professor Barker and I are in thorough accord on the matter of a recommendation to you of a man for the position made vacant by Professor Chapman's death." Left with the responsibility of compiling a lengthy evaluation of his former protégé's development as a historian, Barker conceded to Frederick L. Paxson on December 3: "We don't want to get rid of Castañeda. I feel, however, that California offers him greater opportunities for advancement than we can soon promise him here; and I am confident that he could give you thoroughly excellent service. You may wish to know about his salary. I think he receives about $3500 a year, distributed in the bookkeeping department between the history department and the library. Bolton knows Castañeda." Lest there be any doubt about where Carlos's loyalty rested in the midst of mounting international tension, Barker added: "Castañeda is a citizen of this country."[98] Carlos never went to California, however, not even for an interview, because the outbreak of World War II altered the lives of Americans everywhere.

Right after the new year Carlos made plans for attending a convention in Washington, D.C., of the Inter-American Bibliographical and Library Association. In the third week of February he departed for the national capital to participate in a round of discussions on "Archival needs in Latin America, Latin-American bibliographical problems, and Inter-American library activities" with such luminaries in the field as Samuel Flagg Bemis. Plunging into an exchange of views regarding "the preparation of comprehensive guides," Carlos, speaking from practical experience, urgently recommended that "work in archives and libraries of the United States be done by scholars of the various Latin-American states concerned." In particular, he counseled: "Some of those states might publish their own guides as official documents." Agreeing with Dr. Miron Burgin, who initiated discussion on bibliographical problems, that circumstances had transformed the bibliographer from "a mere recorder of publications" into "a consultant and or assistant" to researchers, Castañeda reported on the existence of a great assortment of newspapers and magazines in the Latin American Library of the University of Texas, which, like the Gondra Collection, were, "unfortunately, still in storage, uncatalogued, and unavailable for use." [99]

While in Washington, Castañeda never failed to make courtesy calls on historians at Catholic University of America. During this trip he reserved part of a Saturday morning for visiting with an old friend, Rev. Dr. Francis Borgia Steck. Later he expressed surprise at finding the campus virtually deserted: "I tried to call on several other friends, but everyone was out on Saturday morning. It seems you are the only one who works on that day. I wasted all morning and returned to Washington in time for lunch." [100]

Whether as librarian or historian, Carlos commanded respect at these professional meetings for his intimate knowledge of the Latin American Collection that he shepherded. Not unmindful of his multiple contributions, in March, 1942, the budget council recommended to the university administration a merit salary increase of $250 for him, "half charged against the history department and the balance against the library, for the upcoming year." [101]

By springtime Father Gibbons finished editing Castañeda's final chapters and delivered the manuscript to the publishers. Later, when the Texas Historical Commission assembled at the Blackstone Hotel in Fort Worth for its twenty-sixth regular meeting, Castañeda, with energy fully recharged, attended the conclave to give his report and to answer questions with respect to future volumes. Undeniably his investiture as a knight of the Holy Sepulchre had infused him with renewed self-confidence. The fifth volume, subtitled *Texas in Transition,* shed light on many aspects of the state's history that had "generally been neglected" by other scholars: "With the exception of the excellent study by Mrs. Mattie Austin Hatcher, *The Opening of Texas to Foreign Immigration,* long since out of print, there is nothing written concerning the fundamental changes which the colonial policies of Spain underwent during this transcendental era. In the years 1790 to 1810 events took place in Texas and along the frontier which profoundly affected the subsequent history of the State and which in a large measure prepared the way for the coming of the Anglo-American pioneers." Citing the inclusion of numerous events and personalities from American history (such as Aaron Burr, the Louisiana Purchase, the Neutral Ground Agreement, Philip Nolan, James Wilkinson, and Zebulon Montgomery Pike), Carlos concluded that section of his report and moved to the next challenge:

> The historiographer is pleased to report that he has started to organize the materials available to him in preparation for Volume VI, which he hopes to complete in much less time. Within the compass of the succeeding volume

will be included the complete disintegration and end of the Spanish admin-
istration of the Church in Texas and the uncertain beginnings of the Anglo-
American Hierarchy. Up to the present time, no historian has discussed the
development and administration of the Church during these trying years
that saw the political sovereignty of the State pass from Spain to Mexico and
from Mexico to the Anglo-American settlers of Texas. He will need more
than ever the help and guidance of each and every member of the Commis-
sion. More and more reliance will be placed henceforth on the sources of
the various religious orders and institutions. With their cooperation and
blessings, the historiographer ardently hopes to be able to finish the heavy
task before him in less time than it took him to complete the preceding
volume.[102]

Cognizant of the tribulations under which Carlos had struggled to finish the
fifth volume, his friend Bishop Garriga moved that the historiographer's report "be accepted with feelings of great relief at the promises that he makes."
As a reciprocal sign of his commitment to the project, Castañeda presented
to the commission a collection of manuscripts he had "gathered in the last
few years for the history of the Catholic Church in Texas, some of which have
already been used." To emphasize the significance of the miscellany, he explained that the documents were "from various archives, public registries, and
also from private collections," and that the contribution was "invaluable for
the Catholic history of Texas." In the discussion that ensued Carlos informed
the commission of some specific manuscripts in the collection:

Some of them should be published as separate monographs. One in partic-
ular by Dr. [Herbert E.] Bolton deserve[s] publication—a report of mission
life day by day; the duties, the trials, the experiences of the missionaries in
Texas; also a report on mission life in El Paso and New Mexico, which is in
the Diocese of El Paso, and other documents also of great interest to the his-
tory of Catholicity in Texas. Some day these documents should be translated
into English and published by the Commission after completion of the pri-
mary task of publishing the general history of Catholicity in Texas.[103]

Documents, resolutions, appropriations, and reports—all were vital to the
work of the Texas Historical Commission, but not one item on the agenda at
the Fort Worth meeting attracted more attention than the publisher's audit
with its comprehensive sales summary of *Our Catholic Heritage in Texas.*
V. H. Pannell of Von Boeckmann-Jones Company reported that up to May 5,
1941, the firm had sold sixty-nine volumes of the series, for which the com-

mission was entitled to a "check in the amount of $34.50 as royalty of 50¢ per volume" on the sales to date. Pannell also provided a numerical breakdown of sales for each volume since initial publication in 1936.

Volume I 550
Volume II 518
Volume III 473
Volume IV 435

. 1,976

Sent out for review   80

. 2,056

For the fifth volume in production Pannell estimated completion in "approximately ninety (90) more days." [104]

In June, Castañeda and Father Gibbons made a hurried trip to Monterrey, Nuevo León, in search of documentary materials in the cathedral archives. With "gracious courtesies" extended by Archbishop Guillermo Tritschler y Córdoba and especially by the reverend rector of the cathedral, the two researchers conducted "as expeditiously as possible the work of investigation." Carefully they examined and microfilmed relevant documents in the cathedral archives. Castañeda reported later: "Among these was a valuable collection of letters of Joaquín Arredondo, the commandant general of the Interior Provinces with headquarters in Monterrey from 1812 to 1821. These letters throw much light on the relation of the Church to the movement for independence of Mexico and the filibustering activities of various bands of adventurers in Texas, such as Gutiérrez-Magee, Mina, Toledo, Aury, Lafitte, and Long. Similarly interesting were the Minutes of the Cathedral Cabildo and other related documents." From Monterrey the pair journeyed southwestward to Durango, where they surveyed "the city, State and Church archives." As in Monterrey so, too, in Durango; thanks to Carlos's elevated status as a knight of the Holy Sepulchre, they gained the confidence and "full cooperation" of Archbishop José María González Valencia, who allowed them "to work at any and all hours and to have free and unhampered access to all the records in the Cathedral." Recalling prior experiences in archival depositories, Castañeda observed that these ecclesiastical records were "the fullest and most complete" that he had "seen in any Church in Mexico during the last fifteen years of investigation." With respect to Texas alone, their discoveries staggered the imagination: "There is no richer archive in Mexico today for the economic history of the Church in colonial days. It contains over 100,000 pages of detailed

records giving intimate and minute accounts of inestimable value for a better understanding of the work of the Church as an economic institution; the
sources of its revenues and the extent of the sums collected; the manner in
which they were spent to relieve the poor and the sick, to impart instruction,
to spread the faith and to civilize the Indians." Although in the municipal depository they failed to discover anything of interest, in the state archives they
found a cache of "much valuable material," which, unfortunately, they could
not survey fully because Castañeda became unexpectedly ill (probably caused
by an intestinal viral disorder).[105]

Beyond the success of archival research, the automobile trip to Monterrey
and Durango gave Carlos and Gibbons an opportunity to become better acquainted. The priest-editor observed firsthand how animated and industrious
Castañeda became amid ancient documents. Also he learned to appreciate the
diplomatic finesse with which Carlos entered the Mexican chanceries to gain
access to private collections. Whereas Father Foik had accompanied Carlos to
numerous conventions, the two friends never journeyed into Mexico on an
archival expedition. Although Castañeda's association with Father Gibbons
hardly approximated the friendship level he had enjoyed with Foik, the trip to
Mexico served to cement an amicable working relationship.

Upon returning to Austin, Castañeda grasped the reality of how the global
conflict had affected life on the campus. He sadly comprehended how many
of his graduate students had abruptly left the university for active duty with
the armed forces. Raymond Estep, who had written a dissertation on Lorenzo
de Zavala, secured dispensation only to fulfill oral examinations for the doctorate before reporting for induction into the army. Estep told Carlos: "I've
been working in the orderly room for two weeks taking dictation, etc. I'm not
very efficient so don't expect to be here long. College men certainly take a
brow beating from non-coms who've only been through the 6th or 8th grade.
They don't dare give us an even break or a kind word and they expect us to
know the rule book after two weeks." [106] Another of Castañeda's friends who
got drafted into the army air corps was Dick M. Burrell, his former student
assistant in the Latin American Collection. Learning that Burrell had not
qualified for cadet training, Carlos offered a bit of consolation: "You will have
to keep them flying like 'hell' on tierra firme. I do not doubt that your vocab-
ulary could be greatly enlarged with words much more expressive than those
found in dictionaries." Remembering that Estep had been assigned to the
same military installation, Sheppard Field near Witchita Falls, but to a different squadron, Carlos urged: "Look up a friend of mine in the 407th T.S.
Squadron; his name is Pvt. Raymond Estep. . . . He got a Dr.'s degree just before he was called to the service, and . . . [is] now a buck private like you. You
will find him a fine young fellow." [107]

It is doubtful that Castañeda entertained, however remotely, notions of serving in the armed forces. Still, some faculty members assuredly discussed possibilities of contributing in some measure to the war effort. In response to a professor's inquiry, the board of regents late in the summer "adopted a policy of granting leaves of absence to members of the University Faculty only for service with the armed forces, except in those instances which the President and the Board consider to be absolutely essential to the war effort." [108] It is likely that Castañeda learned of this policy as soon as it became a matter of public record. For the time being, however, he remained closely tied to his university responsibilities.

Wartime conditions notwithstanding, Carlos and Elisa continued to enjoy social gatherings with friends and colleagues. Although by choice Elisa remained in the background, devoting attention to the needs of their daughters, she kept pace with social affairs at the university. Eugene C. Barker, who was fond of the Castañedas, commented that Elisa was "a graceful, socially pleasant young woman with a good deal of experience in [the] faculty environment." [109] Whenever possible Carlos and Elisa attended reunions with friends and acquaintances at Cafe Monterrey on Sixth Street in downtown Austin. Without any agenda on hand Mexican American physicians, lawyers, students, a few LULACs, and their spouses congregated at this restaurant where waiters hurriedly rearranged tables to accommodate such spontaneous gatherings. George I. Sánchez, a professor of education, and Castañeda frequently attended these luncheon meetings, sometimes arriving ahead of their spouses. On one occasion when a group of wives arrived late at the café, Castañeda, renowned for his gallant salutations complete with polite bows, graciously greeted each of the ladies including Elisa, whom he absentmindedly yet formally addressed: "How do you do, Mrs. Castañeda?" Afterward still wondering why Elisa was miffed at him, he continued socializing and enjoying the fellowship of pleasant company. [110]

Toward the end of 1942 Castañeda assisted President Rainey in finalizing a proposal for a reciprocal exchange program with the Autonomous University of Michoacán. [111] In early December, Carlos drove to San Antonio to deliver a lecture sponsored by the local chapter of Phi Beta Kappa. At Alamo Hall on the grounds of the historic former mission Castañeda, basing his talk on knowledge gleaned from recent scholarship, spoke on the topic of "San Antonio in the early 1800s." [112] With that public address he closed the year and, with the understandable uneasiness that affected many citizens, waited to see what the new season would introduce.

From Academician to Wartime Public Servant, 1943-44

The impact of World War II altered the lives of numerous individuals at the University of Texas. As did many others, Carlos E. Castañeda pondered the type of contribution he could make during the national emergency besides buying war bonds and defense stamps. At forty-six, with a wife and two young daughters to support, the possibility of active military service seemed unrealistic. For the time being he devoted attention to his duties in the Latin American Collection and the history department.

Stemming in part from genuine patriotism created by the global conflict, the faculty of his department adopted a "new requirement" for students to enroll in several courses in American history. Encouraged by this development, which would necessitate hiring "additional teachers," Castañeda applied to Milton R. Gutsch, departmental chairman, for a full-time appointment as associate professor. "For years I have worked in the library," he reminded Gutsch, "but this is not my real interest, nor have I had any special training or technical instruction in library science." In January, 1943, favorably inclined to consider Carlos's request, the faculty on the budget council noted that his strength was "largely in the Latin-American field." Accordingly Charles Wilson Hackett proposed a tentative schedule whereby he and Castañeda "each year" would offer alternating courses in Latin American history. The proposed plan would not take effect, however, until increased enrollment justified a change (which probably would not occur until the 1944-45 academic year). In the meantime the historians directed Gutsch to inform Carlos that their recommendation, although conditional, would acknowledge that "his contacts and his scholarship" constituted "a distinct asset to the Department."[1]

Following the meeting of the budget council Carlos shifted his attention south to Our Lady of the Lake College in San Antonio, where a decade earlier the sisters of the Congregation of Divine Providence had offered their hospitality while he struggled with the writing challenge of the initial volume of *Our*

Catholic Heritage in Texas. Desiring to promote Pan Americanism in the area, Carlos sought to find an academic forum to accommodate Manuel Toussaint, Mexico's outstanding art historian and critic. Aware that Toussaint's itinerary included San Antonio as well as Austin, Castañeda immediately thought of Our Lady of the Lake. To the college dean, Mother Angelique Ayres, he wrote: "I have always felt a deep interest in the welfare of your college because of its fine scholarly reputation which reflects the church and our faith. For this reason, I have always tried to help in my own modest way to enhance its good reputation. This was the motive that impelled me to suggest that Mr. Toussaint should speak first at your college to your student body." [2]

Another reason San Antonio attracted Carlos's attention was the recent death of his longtime friend and associate Frederick C. Chabot, founder of the Yanaguana Society. An active member of the society, Louis Lenz, contacted Carlos about an appropriate memorial for Chabot. Responding to some members' concern that Chabot's death meant "the end of the Yanaguana Society," Carlos reassured them that they were "all mistaken." Even so, the concern of Lenz and others stemmed from the knowledge that not a few civic-minded leaders advocated merging the Yanaguana Society with the larger and newer San Antonio Historical Association. "Personally," Castañeda wrote, "I hope that we can find somebody to carry on the splendid work that was being done by our friend." Realistically, however, he cautioned: "It is going to be difficult to find anyone who will give as much of his time and effort to it as he did." [3] Ultimately, notwithstanding Lenz's efforts and Carlos's encouragement, the Yanaguana Society dissolved in 1947. [4]

Meanwhile wartime pressures compelled university administrators to reform the class schedule with the onetime instruction of "The 1943 Intersession," projected for the entire month of June, to permit degree candidates "to finish their work." Castañeda volunteered to participate in the innovative schedule by offering an accelerated graduate seminar on the economic problems in the colonial history of England and Spain in North America, 1500–1750, which focused on "the land system, the labor supply, the utilization of natural resources, trade and its administration, the beginning of industries, and the growth of towns." [5] For the late "Unit" of the summer session he agreed to teach his course on Iberian institutions and to supervise graduate students in thesis work. [6]

In April, as a temporary diversion, Castañeda drove to Houston to deliver "the principal speech" on the anniversary of the 1836 battle of San Jacinto. A naturalized American citizen since 1936, yet proud of being "Mexican-born," Carlos proclaimed to the vast audience on the plain of San Jacinto that they had assembled "to do honor to the men that made Texas free." [7] Mindful of the discrimination he had experienced more than a decade before, when cir-

cumstances forced him to seek temporary employment in Del Rio, Castañeda's tempo undoubtedly quickened as he interpreted the significance of the
events that culminated in the battle of San Jacinto, when Texan defenders commanded by Sam Houston, ably assisted by native Tejanos recruited by Juan N.
Seguín, defeated the vanguard of Centralist forces led by Gen. Antonio López
de Santa Anna. Complementing the irony of the moment, Carlos assuredly reflected on his most recent accolade—appointment to the board of editors of
the prestigious *Hispanic American Historical Review.*[8]

Three weeks later Castañeda returned to the coastlands, first to Houston to
promote interest in "character-building" at a youth rally sponsored by the
League of United Latin American Citizens and held at City Auditorium,[9] and
then to Galveston for the regular meeting of the Texas Historical Commission
of the Knights of Columbus. Once again convening at the Buccaneer Hotel
near the waterfront, the commissioners began their deliberations at midafternoon on Monday, May 10, 1943. Rev. Dr. James P. Gibbons, C.S.C., the chairman, reported on the successful outcome of an archival survey he and Castañeda had conducted in Monterrey and Durango the previous summer. With
regard to Carlos's work on the sixth volume Father Gibbons expressed a general desire that it be finished in time for publication in 1945, the centennial
year of Texan annexation to the United States of America. Scheduled on the
agenda as the last important item of business, Castañeda's report was a blend
of tidings and disappointment. With five volumes to his credit, no one dared
question his ability to perform under pressure, either with reference to level of
productivity or editorial deadlines. Nonetheless, Carlos felt obligated to explain that although he had commenced using the documents "gathered" in
Mexico and had begun to consult "other sources at his command" in anticipation of writing the sixth volume, his total output approximated "little
more" than a few research notes. "Various circumstances," he confessed, had
melded "to keep him from writing during the year just ended," foremost of
which were "lack of time and peace of mind, both indispensable to the work
of composition." He conceded that besides his teaching duties and the half-
time curatorship of the Latin American Collection, there were also "the frequent and unavoidable invitations to speak to groups interested in learning
more about our southern neighbors and the preparation of monographic studies for publication" that drained his reservoir of energy. Reflecting the insecurity that gripped society on account of the war, Castañeda's formal report contained elements of confidence, hesitancy, and vagueness:

> No one, . . . realizes more poignantly than the Historiographer the urgent
> need for completing this history so generously and enthusiastically spon-
> sored, promoted and supported for more than twenty years by the Knights

of Columbus of Texas and its worthy Commission with which it has been his privilege and pleasure to work since 1925. But the uncertainty and unrest of a work shaken to its very foundations have not spared the Historiographer, who has not had the necessary peace of mine for his arduous task. His determination to complete the work, nevertheless has not wavered. He is as anxious as the members of the Commission and the publishers themselves to complete the work as soon as possible. Before the summer is over he expects to begin the actual writing, which after the research is completed, is relatively an easy task. How much he can accomplish during the year is impossible to determine in advance, but it will depend largely on the time he will be able to dedicate to writing and research. The various factors which will determine the amount of work completed are, in a measure, within the control of the Commission.

In essence what Carlos proposed was that he would apply for a partial leave of absence from the university on the condition that the Knights of Columbus pick up his salary and commit an additional "fifty to sixty dollars a month for clerical assistance." [10] Pragmatic as the proposal appeared, neither the Texas Historical Commission nor Castañeda possessed sufficient latitude, given the exigency of wartime conditions, to enter into serious negotiation. As a practical alternative, however, the commissioners appointed Father Raymond J. Clancy, C.S.C., of Saint Mary's Church in Austin, as backup historiographer for the seventh volume of *Our Catholic Heritage,* effective July 1, 1943. "The major portion of his work," explained Chairman Gibbons, would be "writing the history of Texas and of the Catholic Church . . . from 1845 to 1936; stressing the history of Roman Catholicism, . . . [including] economic, political, and social movements in their relation to the Church." [11] Preoccupied with other matters, Castañeda acquiesced.

Even before the conclusion of the short term in June, Carlos became affiliated with plans for a Cooperative Field School in Mexico City, an enterprise involving faculties and students from several universities with special interest in Latin American issues. On the last weekend in June, right after the intersession terminated, with expense money drawn from his departmental salary he left Austin by train for the border. [12]

In the relative comfort of a passenger train, with ample time to reflect on personal and professional goals, Castañeda reviewed essential points of a "telephone conversation" of June 25, 1943, with Rev. Dr. Francis J. Haas, chairman of the Fair Employment Practice Committee (FEPC), a federal agency within the executive department. Charged with monitoring complaints of job discrimination by ethnic minority workers in businesses holding defense

contracts, the FEPC endeavored to resolve disputes through mediation between representatives of labor and management. As a result of the June conversation Haas had invited Carlos to Washington, D.C., "as soon as possible"
in July "for an interview and consultation." Haas later reiterated in writing:
"It is expressly understood that these arrangements [for an interview] do not
constitute an offer of employment and that the only expense to the Government in connection with your visit shall be transportation and $6.00 per day
subsistence allowance during the period of this service."[13]

Exactly when Castañeda became interested in the work of the Committee on Fair Employment Practice cannot be determined. Obviously radio and
newspaper reports about the agency, created by Executive Order 8809 on
June 25, 1941, to neutralize threats of public demonstrations by black civil
rights activists and workers led by Asa Philip Randolph and Walter White,[14]
must have stimulated discussion among faculty members at the University
of Texas. Professor George I. Sánchez of the Department of Education, for instance, a year after the FEPC had been organized contacted the agency's executive secretary, Lawrence W. Cramer, to offer "interesting and instructive"
commentaries on contemporary social issues. In turn, Cramer, seeking to build
widespread public support, outlined the agency's plans for expanding operations into the western half of the country. He also discussed civilian wartime
appointments in public service.

> *The President's Committee on Fair Employment Practice, and I espe-*
> *cially, feel that it does not have a sufficient background to settle out of hand*
> *all of the problems which are raised in the racial relationships between per-*
> *sons of Spanish-American and Anglo-American origin in the southwestern*
> *area. The Committee is now seeking personnel who might work in this field*
> *for it. It plans to establish regional offices, one of them in San Francisco, one*
> *in Denver, and one in Dallas. These officers will be under the jurisdiction of*
> *a Director, and will have two or three field investigators working out of*
> *them. If you know of any persons who have special knowledge in this field*
> *and who might be interested in accepting appointment with the Commit-*
> *tee, I shall be glad to have recommendations from you. Entrance salaries of*
> *Field Investigators will run from $2,600 to $3,800 per annum. The Direc-*
> *tors of field offices in smaller cities will be* PAID *$4,600 per annum and in*
> *larger cities $5,600 per annum.*[15]

Highly encouraged by the response, Sánchez, a native of New Mexico with a
lengthy tenure in Texas, eagerly recommended friends and acquaintances in
both states but, ironically, excluded Castañeda.[16] Articulate and outspoken,

like Castañeda, Sánchez enjoyed the respect and confidence of a sizable number of faculty members on the Austin campus. Likely it was through these sources that Carlos learned about the work of the FEPC.

During his sojourn in Mexico City with the Escuela de Verano, Carlos conducted negotiations relative to an FEPC appointment. As soon as an offer seemed certain, he initiated petitions for a leave of absence from the University of Texas. "This Committee," he informed President Homer P. Rainey, "has formally offered to me the appointment of Associate Director of the Regional Office which will be established shortly in Dallas to deal with all cases of discrimination on account of race, creed, color, or national origin in all war industries in the Southwest." To expedite the decision-making process Carlos deftly phrased his petition in the form of a gentle reminder: "I have explained to the Committee that my acceptance of the proffered appointment is dependent upon my securing an extended leave of absence from the University for the duration [of the war] in accord with the policy adopted by the Board of Regents." [17] Meanwhile his colleagues in the history department, not at all surprised by recent developments, endorsed his application "for a leave of absence for the duration." [18]

Proceeding on the assumption that permission for a leave of absence was a routine matter, Castañeda dispatched a lengthy letter to Washington with numerous questions that Chairman Haas passed on to top administrators William Maslow and Malcolm Ross. Haas assured Carlos: "Your coming into the service of the FEPC is part of a larger plan of the Committee to work out, so far as it can, an equitable and humane solution of the evils to which Spanish Americans are compelled to submit. I feel sure that you will be a very important factor in helping the Committee to achieve this result." [19]

Notwithstanding delays in mail service, events advanced rapidly at the University of Texas. Aware that a regental meeting would not occur until late in September, President Rainey consulted the library director and the chairman of the history department to inquire if they could "make satisfactory arrangements" to cover Castañeda's absence from campus. Assured by both administrators that Carlos's duties would be handled internally, Rainey approved the request. He informed Castañeda in Mexico: "We all recommend to the Board of Regents that you be granted such leave beginning September 1, 1943 and continue through June 30, 1944. It is not possible, you know, to grant a leave beyond the contract period of appointment though such leave might be continued upon additional application. We assume this leave will not affect your serving in the Exchange Field School in Mexico City although you did not indicate a definite date of your assuming your new duties." [20]

Accustomed to the vicissitudes of university administration, where initiative alternated with delay, Castañeda soon encountered the lethargic nature of the federal bureaucracy. Eager to commence public service at the end of the Cooperative Field School, Carlos asked Chairman Haas for "official confirmation" of his appointment and "travel authorization." Late in July an administrative officer of the FEPC acknowledged a few of Castañeda's questions directed earlier to Haas. With consummate finesse Theodore A. Jones deflected the thrust of Carlos's inquiry regarding an effective date of employment: "As soon as the Bureau of the Budget provides the funds for field operations, your appointment will be submitted to the Civil Service Commission for approval." Jones counseled that following receipt of such funds, possibly at the end of July, "a few days will be required . . . to obtain the final formal Civil Service appointment." [21]

In view of the fact that Castañeda had hurried off to Mexico at the end of June following the close of the 1943 intersession and actively participated in the Escuela de Verano for at least six weeks, it is conceivable that he did not journey to Washington until August, if he made the trip at all. In any event, in the exchange of correspondence he seemed to enjoy a congenial relationship with the FEPC chairman, whom he addressed on occasion as "Rev. Dr." or "Father Haas," which suggests that the two men may have met before, perhaps on the campus of Catholic University of America in Washington, D.C., where the cleric served as dean of the School of Social Science.[22] Even without an interview, it is likely that Castañeda's solid professional reputation weighed heavily in the negotiations, augmented by letters of recommendation from trusted friends and the prestige of his knighthood. Not knowing Carlos's exact whereabouts, Jones in early August dispatched a terse telegram to Mexico City and Austin: "PROOF OF CITIZENSHIP REQUIRED BEFORE APPOINTMENT WILL CLEAR STOP PHOTOSTATIC COPY OR ORIGINAL STOP." [23] Jones's telegram signified that confirmation of Carlos's appointment was imminent. By mid-August, Castañeda reluctantly bade farewell to his family and rushed to Dallas, where he rented a small apartment. On Monday, August 23, in the presence of Theodore Jones, Castañeda officially took the oath as an employee of the FEPC with an initial title of senior examiner. Since the Dallas regional office was at an incipient stage of development, Jones empowered Carlos to commence operation by interviewing prospective candidates for subordinate staff positions. During the few days Jones was in town he and Carlos "discussed plans for office space, equipment and other details" of the unit which would have jurisdiction over Texas, Louisiana, New Mexico, and Arizona, the states constituting Region X. Through orientation briefings the new examiner concluded that the success of the FEPC would depend on an amicable working relationship with the War Manpower Commission (WMC). Accordingly, in consultation with Henry Le Blanc, deputy director of the latter agency, Castañeda decided to lease temporary office space in the Allen

Building, "across the street from the Mercantile Bank," where the WMC occupied "all of the sixth floor." [24]

Before the month ended, Castañeda proudly informed Haas "that the regional office is now fully set up." [25] Utilizing the pragmatic leadership skills he
had acquired years before as school superintendent in Del Rio, Carlos scheduled a press conference for August 27 to inaugurate the FEPC office and to explain its mission. As complaints were filed, he explained to the press, he would
reserve for himself the "Latin American cases," while another official, as yet
unidentified, would "handle the negro cases." Clarifying the goal of the FEPC
office, he commented further: "We will attempt to correct only economic discrimination and will take no action in social affairs." "Our purpose," he told
the press, "is that every man in the same type of work, whether it be in a war
plant or digging ditches will regardless of race be paid the same sum and that
there will be the same opportunities for promotion." [26]

As interim leader of the FEPC office in Dallas, Carlos waited impatiently
for the permanent director to arrive so that he could "get out and make a rapid
survey of actual conditions in the more important industrial areas both in
Texas and New Mexico, in which Latin American labor is used." [27] While he
waited, even prior to the agency's formal opening, he scheduled appointments
with principal administrators of the War Manpower Commission who, because of their past experience, were knowledgeable about "problems involving Latin Americans" in the Southwest. The interviews he conducted with
Glenn O. McGuire, regional chief of training for WMC, and J. B. Wear, chief
of placement, were extremely helpful as he forged out of the comfort of academic life into the arena of public administration. Undaunted, Carlos moved
freely in the Dallas community, talking with Latin American leaders to obtain
general impressions of the city and with the Mexican consul "to acquaint
[him] with the objectives" of the FEPC and to demonstrate "our desire to cooperate in the case of complaints coming to him." From these contacts and
other sources he found that "the situation of the Latin American in the city"
regarding gainful employment was "satisfactory in the main." In between
community visits and discussions with WMC personnel, Carlos interviewed
applicants for employment as examiners and submitted his first progress report to Washington.[28]

As reward for his diligence William Maslow, director of field operations in
Washington, recommended to Chairman Haas that Carlos be elevated in rank,
even if only for a short period, to acting regional director. Maslow advised
Castañeda: "You will serve as such until the Regional Director is appointed
which may not take place for a month or so. All your correspondence and public contacts, therefore, should be made as Acting Regional Director. When the
Regional Director is appointed you will then become Associate Director with

a Civil Service title of Senior Fair [Employment] Practice Examiner." Maslow also advised Castañeda on proper reporting procedures: "I suggest that all your communications about the regional office should be addressed to me. I will route them to Msgr. [Monsignor] Haas or any other staff members who may be interested." [29]

Anxious to charge into the public arena, Castañeda had, before receiving Maslow's directive, drafted an ambitious "Plan for Survey of Territory" that he sent to Haas for review. His spirit uplifted by the anticipated arrival of a prospective colleague from Amarillo, Carlos concluded with a set of recommendations that reflected an unbridled vitality for his work:

> It will be highly advisable for the work of this regional office to have three or four Field Examiners appointed in the more important districts within the regional area. I believe we should have a man in San Antonio, one in Houston, one in El Paso, one in Albuquerque, and one in New Orleans who could look into all questions arising in these important centers and who could keep in close touch with local developments. I do not know whether this suggestion is proper, or in order, but I feel it should be brought to your attention. During my survey in the field I will look up and interview possible candidates [for employment] without making any promises, or even letting them know of our intended plans. Upon my return, I will be in a position to suggest names and give the qualifications of my proposed candidates for appointment in the various districts indicated. [30]

Not wanting to stifle Castañeda's initiative but still wishing to bring him into harmony with procedural guidelines, Haas replied that he had "carefully noted" the substance of Carlos's recent report and then advised him: "For the sake of economy, kindly report the activities of your office to Mr. Will Maslow. I shall receive from him summaries of what you are doing and you can be sure that I will follow your work with great interest." [31] Whereas Monsignor Haas tended to be diplomatic, Maslow was blunt and direct: "CANNOT APPROVE PROPOSED TRIP THROUGH REGION AT THIS TIME. NECESSARY FOR YOU FIRST TO ESTABLISH OFFICE ON WELL ORGANIZED BASIS." No doubt to emphasize where authority resided in the federal bureaucracy, Maslow intimated that he might ask Castañeda to conduct an investigation in New Mexico. [32]

Since Carlos lacked authorization to visit metropolitan centers in his jurisdiction, he remained close to the office. On the eve of the commemorative celebration of Mexican independence—El Diez y Seis de Septiembre—he arrived at Pike Park to deliver "the principal address." Shortly after 8:30 P.M. the chancellor of the local Mexican consulate opened the ceremonies. Squeezed into the program between "numerous typical and patriotic" songs and dances, which were highlighted by a performance of the Fifth Ferrying Group Band from Sheppard Field, Carlos spoke to a large crowd that responded emotionally as he recalled events of 1810 that culminated in Mexico's bid for independence. Promptly at midnight Consul Luis Pérez-Abreu rang a bell, symbolic of Father Miguel Hidalgo's action in 1810, and recited *El Grito de Dolores*, the priest's battle cry urging Mexicans "to fight for liberty."[33] Aside from the civic importance of the event, Castañeda's presence at Pike Park cemented cordial relations between his office and the Mexican consulate.

Meanwhile Maslow kept inundating Carlos with teletyped directives, one of which reminded him not to leave Dallas until he had the office "running smoothly." Gradually the director of field operations manifested more and more confidence in Carlos's ability as an administrator. He told Castañeda: "Originally you were told that you were to specialize in Mexican cases. In view, however, of your appointment as Acting Director, you are responsible for processing all types of cases within the area assigned."[34]

As Castañeda attended to a multitude of duties associated with the work of the FEPC, he periodically cast fleeting glances at matters pertaining to borderlands history at the University of Texas. For instance, when Rev. Gabriel Tous, T.O.R., asked for assistance in locating a rare source, Carlos sent an intercessory letter to Winnie Allen, his longtime colleague at the university archives. Carlos also mentioned to Allen that while the FEPC work "made it impossible" to begin drafting chapters for the sixth volume of *Our Catholic Heritage*, whenever practical he was using "every opportunity to gather data" on the subject.[35] Coincidental with his transition from academia to wartime service with the FEPC, the government of Peru, in recognition of his extensive association with the Latin American Collection, bestowed on Castañeda membership in the Society of Friends of the National Library of Lima. This particular accolade tremendously pleased Carlos because the same tribute went to Herbert E. Bolton of the widely renowned Bancroft Library at Berkeley, whom he greatly admired.[36] Several months later the budget council of the history department recommended an increase in Carlos's part-time teaching salary "to $1,700 on the basis of scholarship and general service to the University." Subsequently the historians approved the recommendation so that, if sanctioned by the administration, his salary would be thirty seven hundred dollars, an amount to be equitably charged against the respective budgets of the department and the library.[37]

After Castañeda had been with the FEPC for about six weeks, Maslow softened his hard-nosed bureaucratic attitude toward the acting regional director. In response to another of Carlos's weekly reports, besides commending the director's vigorous attack on the problem of discrimination, Maslow shared some observations that were "not intended as criticism but as advice from one with perhaps more experience in government service." Maslow cautioned: "Be careful to take no official action or even to express an opinion about matters not within our jurisdiction. While you should always try to be helpful to all complainants, remember that our jurisdiction is limited to discriminatory *employment* practices. If you can refer a complainant to an appropriate agency that has jurisdiction, by all means do, but do not express an opinion either to the complainant or the other agency about the merits of the complaint." Finally, since Castañeda's weekly summaries were official public documents available upon request to other government agencies, Maslow counseled his director not to express opinions about socio-economic questions except "when necessary to our understanding of a particular case." [38]

Castañeda's weekly reports indicated a flurry of activity in processing complaints of discrimination in various employment situations, ranging from aircraft construction companies and training centers to railroads and theaters. The number of complaints received by the Dallas office increased so rapidly that Maslow took time to counsel Carlos on practical accounting procedures for handling the flow of paper in his regional unit.[39] To expedite matters the Washington director of field operations encouraged Carlos to make "a special effort" to terminate cases that had "been pending more than six months." As Carlos's office had not been in business six months, the implication of Maslow's letter was that minority workers had filed complaints of job discrimination earlier with other federal agencies and some of these cases now fell within the purview of Region X.[40]

To align the work of the Dallas office with that of other FEPC units, as well as to give Castañeda's staff the benefit of counsel, Maslow dispatched his associate director of field operations and a prominent black American, Clarence Mitchell, "by plane" to Texas.[41] At the time of Mitchell's visit in mid-October, Castañeda's staff consisted of two field examiners (Clay L. Cochran and L. Virgil Williams, the latter of whom still had not been sworn in) and two clerk-stenographers. In evaluating the office's "present work" load and "probable future development," Mitchell conceded, pending availability of funds, that another stenographer was essential. At Castañeda's insistence Mitchell reviewed routine procedures, especially "various field instructions," to ensure that everyone had "a clearer understanding of the subject." In addition to these lengthy discussions Mitchell gave tentative approval to Carlos's plans for sending Williams to Louisiana and Cochran to Houston, Galveston, Freeport, and San Antonio. On these extended "field tour[s]" the examiners would interview complainants, cultivate contacts "with minority group leaders and union organizations," and compile data on existing conditions in industrial centers. There then remained nothing else to occupy Mitchell's time except to watch as Castañeda energetically supervised the transfer of personnel and equipment to a suite of offices located on the tenth floor of the Mercantile Bank Building. As planned, the move brought the FEPC within even closer proximity to the War Manpower Commission.[42]

Around the time of Mitchell's visit Castañeda, mindful of the need to promote community relations, accepted invitations to speak at a few civic functions. At the inauguration of the Pan-American Theater, for example, he delivered "a brief talk" on the "work and scope" of the FEPC "to a large audience of Latin Americans." Next, on Columbus Day, he addressed the guests at a Pan-American Round Table luncheon at the Adolphus Hotel. Taking advantage of the occasion, he explained to "this influential women's organization" the overarching goals of the FEPC, clarifying that its "jurisdiction was strictly confined to economic discrimination in war and defense industries." Finally, on the weekend after Mitchell's departure for Washington, Carlos drove to Fort Worth to attend a convention of the Texas Mid-Continent Oil and Gas Association as an interested "observer." Attracted by one of the sessions, "Forum on Wage and Salary Stabilization," moderated by Floyd McGowan, chairman of the regional office of the National War Labor Board, Carlos assured Maslow: "I took no part in the discussion but I took full notes and during the meeting met some of the representatives of the various oil companies in attendance." [43]

Whether he realized it or not, in assuming the directorship, even on an interim basis, Carlos truly became a modern knight without armor. Without grandstanding, he viewed his job with the FEPC as a mandate to correct injustices perpetrated against minority workers in the Southwest. Anticipating friction because of ambiguities in federal guidelines, Maslow cautioned Carlos not to proceed too fast: "The Committee has for some time been considering the general question of whether regional directors should make investigations of what they believe to be discriminatory employment practices in the absences of filed complaints. The problem is a complicated one because [the War Manpower Commission] feels that such work is properly within its jurisdiction. Accordingly, for the time being do not proceed in the above case. I expect to get some clarification of the entire problem within the next two weeks." [44]

Long before the civil rights movement became a main current in American society Castañeda, Maslow, Cochran, Williams, and others of their generation, through the medium of the FEPC, stood in the vanguard of social reform. In Region X, confined by guidelines to monitoring industries holding government contracts for either goods or services, the FEPC attempted to break the yoke of segregation in training centers in Louisiana. Maslow explained: "The Committee's position, of course, is that as long as one Negro is denied admittance into a training school for whites, separate but equal facilities must be provided. If the training school objects to the expense of having a duplicate facility for a small number of Negroes you can point out to them that if they wish they can admit Negroes into the school for whites."[45] By late October, with numerous complaints on file, Castañeda showed signs of restlessness. Processing complaints in proper order, with correct cross-reference codes and notations of "final disposition," was an adequate beginning; what he desperately wanted to do next was to charge into the arena of investigative hearings, exposing for public scrutiny the injustices of some employers in paying substandard wages to ethnic minority workers or else denying to them opportunities for advancement. Castañeda bombarded Washington superiors with detailed weekly summaries advocating corrective action because Maslow finally conceded in the matter of hearings: "The staff is now analyzing the complaints involving Latinos with the thought that a hearing should be held in your area as quickly as possible."[46] A week later, still withholding authorization for full-fledged public hearings, the director of field operations commended Carlos's leadership: "Although we have not yet been able to pass upon all the questions raised by your weekly report of October 25, I cannot forbear to compliment you now upon an excellent and interesting job."[47]

The delay in authorizing Castañeda to conduct hearings stemmed not so much from a lack of resolve in Washington as from a normal slowdown created by a change in leadership. Before the month of October ended, Malcolm Ross succeeded Francis J. Haas as FEPC chairman. Following a realignment of priorities and responsibilities, Maslow notified Castañeda to dismiss "all cases against motion picture theaters for lack of jurisdiction."[48] At the same time the director of field operations, now functioning under the FEPC's Office of Emergency Management, gave Carlos tentative approval to proceed with preliminary planning for an investigative hearing. Meanwhile Carlos proposed a regional conference, a suggestion that prompted Maslow to respond affirmatively lest his Region X director lose interest altogether. Maslow said: "We think the regional conference idea is a good one but that the conference should be conducted by Mr. Ross, the Chairman. We also agree with you that a hearing is necessary and believe it extremely likely that one will be held. In the meantime, therefore, proceed to investigate specific complaints, building up your files in preparation for a hearing; that is, take affidavits of witnesses, etc. If you need help we may send you an attorney. Keep us advised of developments."[49]

As the regional staff gathered evidential materials in anticipation of a hearing, another prominent Negro leader from Washington—Dr. Robert C. Weaver, chief of the WMC's Minority Groups Services—paid a courtesy visit in the fall to the FEPC office in Dallas. Forewarned by Maslow, Carlos knew of Weaver's noteworthy contribution to drafting "the national WMC policy on discrimination." Accordingly, in mid-November, since a cooperative liaison existed between the two agencies and in view of the fact that both he and the distinguished visitor possessed earned doctorates, Castañeda determined that he could "be completely frank with [Weaver] in discussing problems." [50]

Shortly after Weaver's visit Castañeda and Cochran made an authorized journey to Corpus Christi to conduct a series of interviews, one with management and two with labor unions. In all three instances—with representatives of American Smelting and Refining Company, with officers of Zinc Workers' Federal Labor Union (Local 23245, American Federation of Labor), and with Alkali Workers' Industrial Union, an affiliate of United Gas, Coke, Chemical and Allied Workers (Local 153, Congress of Industrial Organizations)—the FEPC examiners politely but firmly asked precise questions to ascertain the veracity of the complainants' allegations about discrimination through dual salary schedules, denial of promotion, and restrictions in job training. While Castañeda, as presiding officer, conducted the hearings on an evenhanded basis to obtain perspectives from management and labor unions, Cochran, although not a prosecutor, jabbed and parried with his sharp questions. In the third interview, with officers of the CIO local, the FEPC examiners uncovered damaging testimony about the existence of gentlemen's agreements and two-tiered entry levels, one that routed Anglo workers into salaried positions and another that consigned Hispanic laborers to jobs at minimum wages. For two days Castañeda and Cochran conducted their interviews, visited plants and facilities, and afterward whenever possible talked informally with workers and supervisors, all in the interest of trying to reconcile inequities for the sake of the national war effort. [51]

Emboldened by the finesse with which he had carried out the Corpus Christi assignment, the interim regional director now advocated buttressing the FEPC's moral resolve in future hearings by publicizing them in advance in order to draw attention to the workers' grievances, a suggestion that greatly alarmed Maslow in Washington. Acting to curb Castañeda's runaway enthusiasm, the director of field operations swiftly dispatched a teletyped message: "WHILE WE ADMIRE YOUR INGENUITY AND RESOURCEFULNESS THE PROCEDURE AND PARTICULARLY THE IDEA OF ADVANCE PUBLICITY IS DANGEROUS." For a periodic assessment of the situation in Dallas, in late November, 1943, Maslow again sent his associate director, Clarence Mitchell. [52]

Mitchell's visit gave Castañeda an opportunity to isolate a pattern of complaints of discrimination by Negro workers in defense industries. Among numerous complaints, Carlos and staff flagged a Fort Worth firm, Consolidated-Vultee Aircraft Corporation, for close scrutiny. Even before his arrival

Mitchell had asked Castañeda to solicit the cooperation of the Army Air Corps representative at the company, Col. Roy Ludick, for assistance in eliminating barriers to black laborers' advancement in pay grade. Keenly aware of Mitchell's position in the executive branch of government, the colonel promptly reported "that 100 Negroes had been upgraded, that 75 additional colored workers were needed immediately for the janitorial pool; and that as soon as the 75 . . . workers were secured, 25 more would be upgraded." Satisfied with that modest progress, Mitchell, Williams, and Castañeda went to nearby Fort Worth to inform leaders of the Negro Welfare Council about the FEPC's efforts to achieve "more adequate utilization" of black laborers at Consolidated-Vultee.[53] Guardedly optimistic, council leaders expressed reservations about management's sincerity, based on its poor performance in the past in providing statistical data as required by WMC guidelines. Even so, the FEPC officials readily welcomed every breakthrough, no matter how minimal, in their difficult mission.

As priorities such as these beset his interim directorship, Carlos dealt with the question of the budget as a perfunctory duty. Unaccustomed to federal haggling in matters of fiscal planning, his proposals for the next six months, although not extravagant, exceeded normal anticipated increases for staff, equipment, and services. Under the current level of funding Castañeda had not depleted authorized allotments, but because of his inexperience as a member of the government bureaucracy, Theodore Jones determined that the acting director in Dallas needed a little guidance. Writing on November 30, he advised Castañeda: "Your estimate of budgetary requirements recently submitted requested more positions than now allocated to your region. Nominal staff increases are provided in our budget and probably will be made available January 1, 1944 by the device of raising our ceiling on personnel (See Public Law 49—78th Congress). Major staff increases cannot be expected, however, until additional experience is gained in field or decentralized operations." Extending a modicum of hope to a noncareerist in government service, Jones explained the process by which Region X would qualify for additional personnel: "Standards of performance must be determined for each region and actual work and case load activity compared with these standards. A time study will be made within the next few weeks as one of the steps toward obtaining the personnel you believe necessary to carry out your functions as Regional Director."[54]

A few weeks later, in mid-December, just as Castañeda's small staff was acquiring momentum as a team, the armed forces inducted Clay Cochran.[55] Meanwhile a spontaneous campaign on Castañeda's behalf—in the form of letters, telephone calls, and impromptu talks—had originated at various points in the Southwest and gravitated toward Washington, D.C. A strong supporter of Castañeda for the directorship of Region X was Congressman Antonio M. Fernández of New Mexico, who personally appealed to Chairman Ross to make the appointment. Impressed by the groundswell of support for Castañeda, the chairman cautiously evaluated the merits of the matter before reaching even a tentative decision. Following a two-week trip to the West Coast, shortly after Thanksgiving, Ross wrote a lengthy memorandum to Carlos: "We have the highest regard for your sincerity and diligence. I, personally, was very proud to discover how many people whose judgment we must respect also entertain that high regard for you. All this is to be weighed in arriving at a judgment on whether, as the many letters request, you should be made permanent director. There are other considerations which also must be weighed in arriving at that judgment." What perplexed Ross was not Castañeda's competence for the job, a qualification that the acting director had ably demonstrated, but rather determining in what capacity he could perform most effectively in advancing the goals of the FEPC. As the committee's resident "specialist on Spanish-American and Mexican-American" affairs, approximately three million people would "directly and inferentially" come under his jurisdiction. Moreover, recognizing that Carlos's "special interests" transcended "regional boundaries" in the greater Southwest, even north to Colorado and Wyoming, Ross correctly concluded that the current situation stretched "very thin the good which one man can do." Accordingly Ross reduced his conclusion to a succinct verdict: "We need all your energy and wisdom on the one specific problem." [56]

For the time being, Ross remained discreet with regard to the selection of regional leadership. In strictest confidence, however, possibly to boost morale in the Dallas office, he informed Carlos that the FEPC might "hold hearings in its mining cases some time in February or March, and perhaps at Phoenix." Although quite tentative, the plan meant that Castañeda's involvement with the hearings "would be very intense." Ross then offered a hint of how he intended to use Carlos's talents: "The entire issue of eliminating discrimination against Mexicans depends on how wisely and well we conduct ourselves during the next few months. It might be tragic to miss that opportunity because of a need to divert your attention constantly to the administrative job and to the problems of the Negroes in your region." [57]

In December, Castañeda attended, as a special guest, an extraordinary convocation of the Dallas Bar Association, at which one of the attorneys read a paper entitled "Pan-Americanism and the Lawyer." Carlos later reported to Maslow that at least in Dallas members of the legal profession manifested genuine interest in transforming President Roosevelt's Good Neighbor Policy into an effective instrument for eradicating discrimination in the workforce, a goal that had "both a national and inter-national bearing." [58]

Coincidental with the presidential initiative the Texas legislature, at the request of Gov. Coke Stevenson, had authorized in 1943 the establishment of a Good Neighbor Commission to foster improved relations with Mexico. Under the leadership of its executive secretary, Pauline R. Kibbe, the Good Neighbor Commission invited the Inter-American Relations Committee of the University of Texas to cosponsor a meeting "to promote good will for the United States and Mexico." Meanwhile, in Washington, Ross finally decided to relieve Castañeda of the drudgery of routine administration by elevating his assignment with the FEPC to special assistant to the chairman with responsibility for Latin American issues. Anxious for the appointment to be made official at the conference, in the presence of all the consuls from Mexico serving in Texas, Carlos asked Mitchell to persuade Ross to release the announcement on December 17, during the meeting, for the encouragement of "the many Latin-Americans who have problems" in Region X.[59] Pleased to cooperate, Ross sent an expeditious verification of the promotion, hoping it would reach Castañeda before his scheduled departure for Austin: "THIS WILL CONFIRM YOUR APPOINTMENT AS SPECIAL ASSISTANT TO THE CHAIRMAN FOR LATIN AMERICAN PROBLEMS. YOUR JURISDICTION COVERS ALL FEPC REGIONS WHERE SUCH PROBLEMS ARISE. HEADQUARTERS AT DALLAS. LETTER FROM MASLOW EXPLAINING ADMINISTRATIVE RELATIONSHIPS FOLLOWS. PLEASE ANNOUNCE THIS TOMORROW. HEARTY CONGRATULATIONS."[60]

Eager to see his family, whom he had infrequently visited since August, Castañeda hurried to Austin before receiving the chairman's message, instructing the staff to transmit the anticipated notification to him in care of the Good Neighbor Commission. Once in Austin, Carlos contacted old friends at the Latin American Collection and at Saint Edward's University, home of the Texas Historical Commission of the Knights of Columbus. Before the conference convened, he kept a prearranged appointment at Samuel Huston College, an African-American school deep in the east side of the city, where he spoke to the student body "on the nature and scope" of the FEPC and particularly on "the extent to which non-whites" were being hired by companies performing work for the government. Then he got involved in a spirited discussion with students who earnestly asked him "pertinent questions" concerning realistic opportunities "for the integration of non-whites in war industries." Following his appearance at the college Carlos proceeded to the conference at the Stephen F. Austin Hotel, where he introduced himself to consular officials, guests, and other participants. Since the program listed his presentation for the next day, Castañeda listened attentively to the lead-off speakers, one of whom was Rafael De La Colina of the Mexican Embassy in Washington. Later, during intermissions, he exchanged comments with people in the audience. If the public had previously viewed him as a historian and librarian at the University of Texas, on this occasion Carlos symbolically hoisted the banner of President Roosevelt's Committee on Fair Employment Practice. At a banquet that Friday evening Dr. Homer P. Rainey presided at the head table from where, with an impeccable sense of timing, he proudly announced Carlos's appointment as special assistant to the FEPC chairman.[61] Area newspapers picked up the announcement as a major story.

Following the conference in Austin, Castañeda moved his family to Dallas and settled into a basic but comfortable apartment within reasonable distance of his office. His daughter Consuelo later recalled that his frequent absences from home now stemmed from the need to promote "equal opportunity, which today is *the* thing, but at the time it was more equal opportunity for the Mexican American." In this context she perceived her father as "a pioneer." Concerning those absences from the family, Consuelo remembered: "So, we moved to Dallas, because Daddy would be home maybe one week out of a month, and in order to see him, five days out [of] a month; the rest of the time he was out flying around to Washington, to Georgia, . . . seeing about the Mexican American, speaking about job opportunities. He always had time to sit down and hear a person's problems out. Many times he used to complain that he did not have time for the family because he'd spend his time seeing about getting this poor person a job." [62]

Seemingly more concerned about the plight of other people, Castañeda ignored his own state of health. Although cognizant of the frequency of heart disease among his blood relatives in Brownsville, he maintained a hectic schedule of activity. "He wouldn't stop doing things," recalled Elisa, "he wanted to continue with his work *full force*." Unknown to the family for two years, Carlos suffered his first, early-warning heart attack in Dallas, a fact he suppressed until he underwent a routine medical examination in Austin.[63]

Monsignor Anton J. Frank of Houston, who later worked closely with Carlos on the last volume of *Our Catholic Heritage,* recalled that historical research and composition receded into the background during the war years. "There was nothing else he did but work for the United States Government. He was considered *the man, a key man,* and didn't think he had a choice about it. He felt his loyalty to his country had to come first. All of us felt it was justifiable, the whole thing." [64]

During the transitional period in December, Castañeda endeavored to review and terminate some of the outstanding cases, such as the Corpus Christi investigation. Indicative of an attitude he would encounter while examining complaints throughout the Southwest was the comment of an employment recruiter who avowed "that Mexicans, although not being paid the same wages as Anglos in the various industries, had no reason to complain because they were, in fact, getting more than they had ever earned before."[65]

Aware of the selection of a permanent director for the Tenth Region, Carlos waited in Dallas for the arrival of his successor, Leonard M. Brin, who had delayed his departure from Washington for a week in order to undergo special training. To facilitate a congenial transition, Maslow assured Carlos that Brin, a native Texan with a doctorate in the humanities, could read, speak, and write Spanish fluently; moreover, he had accumulated several years of experience in government work, first as a field examiner for the National Labor Relations Board and only recently as an employee of the Office of Strategic Services. Always concerned about FEPC goals, Maslow commented: "I am sure you two will like each other and will work together smoothly." Sensitive to how transitions in management affect human relations, Maslow noted that plans had been initiated to enlarge the facilities of the Texas headquarters "so that you will have an office for yourself whenever you are in Dallas."[66]

Before the year ended, Carlos expressed concern about reporting channels. If, as his new title indicated, he was special assistant to FEPC Chairman Malcolm Ross, was it not logical that he should communicate directly with his ultimate superior in Washington? He soon learned that with government bureaucracy the form of a straight line is often curved. "My function," Maslow explained," is to act as liaison between you and [Ross] and to see that you get prompt cooperation." At the same time Maslow conceded to Carlos the prerogative of determining his own schedule "without advance clearance" for short-distance travel related to "emergency situations," though he preferred that Castañeda "synchronize" his itinerary with Washington's "overall planning for the various regions" in which he would "operate." Maslow assured Castañeda that there was "no disposition" on his part "to curb" Carlos's mobility, allowing him wide latitude to conduct "a great deal of travel over the entire" southwestern region from Texas to Arizona. Since Castañeda had performed dual duty as interim director and as senior examiner, Maslow endorsed his proposal for "a salary increase or reclassification to a base pay of $5600 per annum." However, because the agency had exceeded its budgetary allowance, he recommended waiting for an opportune time to petition the Budget Bureau, "either this Spring or perhaps even earlier," to discuss Castañeda's claim to a salary increment.[67] Informed of Carlos's concerns over questions regarding travel and reporting procedures, Ross intervened to describe his hectic work schedule as FEPC chairman and to extend personal reassurance. He wrote Carlos: "I cannot give you an adequate idea of the demands on my time in Washington, not to mention the preparation of speeches and travel which I now have to undergo. Please take my word for it that what you are doing is of the greatest possible interest to me, but that it will save my time immensely if you follow the suggestion of reporting through the Director of Field Operations. I am sure that you and Mr. Maslow can work out any minor questions that arise." [68]

In a year-end summary of "Important Unadjusted Cases" for the region, shared with Clarence Mitchell, Castañeda compared the record of progress in eradicating economic discrimination against Mexican American workers and African Americans. During December, Don Carlos had conducted conferences with management officials of three of the major oil companies in Houston—Humble Oil, Sinclair Refinery, and Shell Oil. The representatives of management and labor for one company, who told Castañeda "that no changes would be made in [the] discriminatory upgrading program now in effect," reflected the stubborn resistance of the industry. A subordinate official at Shell also admitted to an FEPC examiner that the company paid "Latin-Americans and Negroes a lower wage than whites." Justifiably angered, Carlos concluded that the employment program, if left unmodified, "deadends all Latin-Americans at the level of janitor and gard[e]ner." Gradually, perhaps reluctantly, the labor union yielded, but it waited for management to amend its hiring and promotion policy. Resorting to delaying tactics, Shell officials explained that sudden shifts in policy would produce unpredictable, far-reaching consequences that, in turn, "would have such detrimental results" that the company did "not see any reason for change." With Clay Cochran's help, at the start of the new year Castañeda and the FEPC achieved modest gains, persuading Humble Oil, Sinclair Refining, and finally Shell Oil to lessen the degree of discrimination in their employment and advancement policies.[69]

Although the FEPC's chronicle on behalf of Hispanics in Texas was encouraging, its record concerning black workers was woefully bleak. In Fort Worth, for instance, after almost twenty months of negotiations Consolidated-Vultee Aircraft Corporation refused "to upgrade Negroes on a basis comparable to white employees." In New Orleans, Delta Shipyard adhered to a similar policy. Another company, Todd Johnson Dry Docks, conducting business in Louisiana and Texas, hired Negro workers at low-entry levels and then neglected to advance them to higher wage brackets.[70]

After a week of intensive orientation regarding FEPC policies, guidelines, and objectives, Leonard M. Brin assumed duty as Region X director. Appropriate to his position, he occupied the office that Castañeda had vacated; but he did not provide adequate facilities for his predecessor. Annoyed by the oversight, Carlos tolerated the inconvenience for several weeks as he briefed his successor about routine office operations and future plans for investigating complaints of job discrimination in the field. Before long, with two strong-willed personalities working in close proximity, the situation on the tenth floor of the Mercantile Bank Building became explosive. Carlos, via telephone, asked Maslow to clarify lines of accountability and responsibility. "I realize," acknowledged Maslow, "that we may perhaps unfortunately have placed you in a difficult position with Dr. Brin, but I hope that both of you will be patient with each other and with me and will work out an amicable adjustment." [71] Unable to wait for a resolution, and taking advantage of an opportunity to travel to Washington in the first week of February, 1944, Castañeda scheduled an appointment with Will Maslow. [72] In the course of serious discussions pertaining to the situation in the Dallas office, both men expressed concern and offered suggestions for remedying the work environment. Ultimately they worked out a satisfactory settlement. To appease Carlos, who had performed yeoman service in the office for six months before Brin's arrival, the director of field operations reiterated in a memorandum the cardinal points of the agreement: "Ample space should be provided for you in Dallas. This should mean an office of approximately 250 square feet. If this space can be obtained in the Mercantile Bank Building, it should be adjacent to the regional office with a separate entrance, if possible, for your use. Also, appropriate designation [of Castañeda's name and title] should be made in any directory and on the door." The agreement also allowed Castañeda, whenever he returned to Dallas from investigative work in the field, to request clerical assistance of his choice from regional director Brin. [73]

Even more precise was the second memorandum, in which Maslow, addressing ambiguities in Carlos's job description, eliminated vexing points of conduct between Brin and Castañeda. In matters pertaining to "adjustment of complaints made [by] or involving Latin-Americans," the initiative "for action, docket and process" resided with Director Brin, who, if necessary, could request Carlos's assistance. Dr. Brin's sphere of jurisdiction covered only the states of Texas, Louisiana, New Mexico, and Arizona, however, whereas Castañeda's authority embraced more territory. In his new role with the FEPC, Carlos's "major responsibility" regarding Latin American workers who filed complaints had become more specialized. Besides assisting in the preparation of conferences or interviews, Castañeda's "main function" now obligated him to monitor "active cases involving Spanish or Mexican-Americans and [to] offer suggestions as to action to be taken and then personally to take over for adjustment such cases as the respective regional directors [felt] he should handle either initially or at later stages." What the federal verbiage signified was that Carlos was to be the chairman's troubleshooter in addressing issues raised by Mexican American workers. The final paragraph in Maslow's memorandum concluded: "The Special Assistant shall make contact and establish close relations with the various organizations and governmental agencies interested in the problems of minority groups in general and of Latin-Americans in particular by acquainting them with the nature and scope of the work of the Committee and pointing out how we can cooperate mutually for the attainment of a common goal."[74]

Relieved of routine duties and grateful for the clarification of responsibility, Castañeda focused on plans for an extended tour to west Texas, New Mexico, Colorado, and Arizona. Although his investigation would not be the first federal survey of labor conditions in the Southwest, unique to this visit was the prestige and ethnicity of the examiner. In each region he scheduled "meetings with different Latin-American groups" to gain insights about "conditions in the area" and, hopefully, to establish contacts with leaders among the workers in the mining industry. Carlos promised Maslow that during this tour he would not reveal privileged information about the possibility of FEPC hearings, which might jeopardize their investigation. To prepare for this assignment he compiled a thick portfolio of outstanding unadjusted cases, most of which he had initiated and processed, to have on hand for Brin's perfunctory review.[75] Receiving an invitation to speak to an important gathering of Hispanic leaders in Denver, Castañeda eagerly advanced the date of his "planned trip" so as to be in Colorado by the middle of February. At a meeting of the Pan American Club, which had a sizable membership "of both Anglo and Latin-Americans," he greeted business and professional men as well as "employees of the various Federal Agencies, and social leaders in the community." He estimated that "about 300 persons" attended the meeting. Following an address by Victor Borella, a labor leader, the master of ceremonies introduced Carlos, who spoke in detail about the "work, purposes, and aims" of the FEPC. "Considerable interest," he informed Maslow, "has been aroused as the result of the address made at the meeting." Castañeda stayed three days in Denver contacting leaders in the Hispanic and Negro communities, including the Mexican consul, a minority groups officer of the War Manpower Commission, and "various Catholic leaders, and representatives of organized labor." The situation Castañeda observed in Denver pleased his sense of fair play. Out of an aggregate population of 400,000 inhabitants, the Mexican Americans comprised "approximately 25,000 or 30,000" and, surprisingly, experienced "little or no social discrimination." The two main industries—Gates Rubber Company and Remington Arms Company—employed a combined workforce of 10,000 men and women. Prior to the war these two companies had denied employment to Latin Americans and Negroes, but by the time of Castañeda's visit management no longer practiced a policy of absolute exclusion. Castañeda noted, however, "a more marked tendency" to block the employment of Negroes than Latin Americans. Another outstanding problem that annoyed him, one identified through various interviews, pertained to "discrimination in upgrading," with management restricting Latin American and Negro workers "to certain unskilled or semi-skilled positions" in the labor force. Since the visit to Denver was exploratory rather than investigative, Castañeda refrained from deliberately soliciting formal complaints. However, he distributed "complaint blanks" to some of the leaders he had met. Elated by the outcome of his discussions in Colorado, Castañeda drove south into New Mexico and proceeded to Silver City, in the southwestern corner of the state, where he had arranged to interview complainants with the American Smelting and Refining Company, Kennecott Copper Corporation, and "other mining companies" in the region.[76]

The civility of the urban Denver experience hardly prepared Carlos for the shocking confrontation with rural New Mexico. Arriving on a weekend in rustic Silver City, which had a population of fifteen thousand inhabitants, he checked into a hotel where, in his usual jovial manner, he struck up a conversation with one of the maids. Obviously impressed with his polished demeanor and fluency in English, and certainly not knowing the purpose of his visit to the vicinity, the maid launched into her choice prejudice. She said: "The Mexican and Negroes in this area are getting too numerous. The Negroes ought to be sent back to the South where they belong and the Mexicans should be sent across the river. If we don't do something about the immigration laws there is not going to be enough room in this country for the Americans." So prejudiced was the maid toward minorities that she refused to allow her son to attend school in Silver City, where he would be compelled "to mingle with Negroes, Mexicans, Chinese, Indians, etc." Her only alternative was to pay for instruction by "a private teacher." Admittedly "an extreme case," the views of the maid served as "a good index" of how "certain sectors of the population" actually felt about "minority groups in this area."[77]

In three days Carlos acquainted himself with "the principal mines and refineries" located within a twenty-five-mile radius of Silver City: American Smelting and Refining Company (Vanadium, Ground Hog, and Hanover); Azarko Mining Company (Vanadium); Black Hawk Mining Company (Hanover); Empire Zinc Mining Company (Hanover); Kennecott Copper Corporation (Chino, Hurley, and Santa Rita); Peru Mining Company (Hanover and Kearney Shaft); and U.S. Smelter and Mining Company (Vanadium). At six of the companies the Congress of Industrial Organizations (CIO) represented the workers' interests. The seventh enterprise, Kennecott Copper, eroded its workers' benefits by allowing three unions—American Federation of Labor, CIO, and the Brotherhood of Railway Trainmen—to negotiate separate contracts. In search of information, Castañeda talked with company officials and union stewards during regular business hours; in the evenings, after work, he interviewed complainants to update his files. Initially union representatives manifested skepticism at Carlos's presence in the area, owing to a prior "field investigation" conducted by FEPC officials who had raised the expectations of workmen and then created disappointment by not implementing corrective measures. To restore the credibility of the FEPC, Carlos attended a meeting at a workers' "clubhouse" in Santa Rita, where he spoke in Spanish to an audience of approximately "150 Latin American employees" about the "nature and purpose of the federal agency he represented.

Castañeda's visits to the job sites revealed that over 80 percent of the total number of workers employed by the seven mining companies were "of Mexican extraction." A recent social phenomenon, the steady influx into the workforce of Indians from surrounding reservations, further complicated labor relations at the mines. In the course of his investigation Carlos discerned the practice of three types of discrimination: 1) improper classification of workers; 2) management's refusal to promote employees to positions of higher skill and responsibility; and 3) maintenance of a wage-differential scale whereby minority group laborers consistently received lower salaries than white employees. Upon minute inspection of ancillary complaints, which reminded him of conditions in some communities he knew in south and west Texas, Castañeda concluded that an integral to the "subtle" economic discrimination was the imposition of social barriers throughout the region:

> Mexicans are not allowed to sit in the same place with Anglos in the picture shows; certain public establishments, such as barber shops and restaurants, either refuse to serve Mexicans, or serve them in a separate table or compartment; in the schools the children, while allowed to sit in the same rooms, . . . are separated in aisles and . . . are not allowed to go out for recess at the same time as the Anglos, so that they cannot play together. These are only a few of the concrete evidences of social discrimination which is strongly reflected in the treatment accorded Mexican labor in the mines and refineries in this area.[78]

Satisfied with the mechanics of his visit to Silver City, if not with the plight of minority workers, Carlos returned to Colorado, this time to Pueblo, where he had agreed to speak at a labor rally held by the United Steel Workers of America, a CIO affiliate. Responding to the "wide publicity" generated for the meeting, more than three hundred persons, of whom over half were Mexican Americans, entered the CIO hall on February 22, the traditional holiday commemorating George Washington's birthday. The remainder of the audience included "a goodly number of Negroes," augmented by delegates from "Jewish, Slovak, Roman Catholic, and Polish organizations." In fact, so effective was the publicity that the executive committee of the Democratic Party in Pueblo had postponed its meeting to enable its members to attend the rally. From his vantage point on the platform Carlos assessed the crowd as being representative "of workmen, civil officials, and interested parties." Speaking first in English, he explained the nature and scope of the FEPC, after which he elaborated on the essential points in Spanish "for the benefit of the Latin-American workers" who had remained in the hall at the conclusion of the meeting. While his speech was designed more to uplift morale than to solicit formal complaints, Castañeda afterward interviewed "many of the workers," asking them to mail their formal petitions to him "with full details in the near future." As he had discovered elsewhere, the "chief type of discrimination" emanated from management's "refusal to upgrade Latin-Americans to skilled job positions": although the steel mills used minority workers in "skilled operations," they classified them as common or semiskilled laborers.[79]

Following the conclusion of the Pueblo rally Castañeda drove south across the entire length of New Mexico to El Paso. Arriving at his destination on Friday, February 25, he plunged immediately into a round of introductory meetings. With the help of Modesto Gómez, president general of the League of United Latin American Citizens (LULAC), Carlos had secured appointments to meet with "various Latin-American leaders, representatives of local unions, and workmen in the American Smelting and Refining Company and in the Phelps-Dodge Copper Corporation." Owing to the brevity of his visit to the border city, he promptly conferred with Jess Nichols, of the International Union of Mine, Mill, and Smelter Workers, and J. S. Chávez, president of Local 541 at Phelps-Dodge. Altogether, leaders of three CIO locals in El Paso gave assurances of their genuine commitment to eliminating discrimination. On Sunday, February 27, when labor leaders could guarantee a sizable turnout of members for a rally, Castañeda not only spoke to the workmen about the FEPC but also solicited numerous complaints "from among those present." To expedite the paperwork, Carlos transmitted by air mail "docket cards for all these cases" to Maslow in Washington, D.C. In his report to Maslow he recounted the usual pattern of economic discrimination, particularly at the two smelters, where the wage scale was "from 15¢ to $1.50" lower than that for comparable jobs at Silver City. Carlos also obtained from Chávez of Local 501 a statement about selective practices at Phelps-Dodge Copper Corporation:

Not a single Latin-American is employed in a supervisory capacity. It is the set policy of the company to employ only Anglos in supervisory positions. Many Latin-American employees with long years of experience in the various departments who could efficiently perform the duties of supervisors, are refused an opportunity and are not even given a trial. Anglo-Americans without experience are frequently appointed to supervisory positions. In the

Mill Department recently, the appointment of inexperienced Anglos has
lowered the production of that department 40%, as shown by the company
records.[80]

Back at his Dallas office in early March, 1944, Carlos compiled detailed reports of his visits to the western cities and cast tentative plans for another excursion. Based on recent experiences, he advised Maslow that public hearings
were essential, provided they were conducted near the complainants' homes.
Although Maslow had suggested Tucson or Phoenix as "probable" sites for
such hearings, Castañeda expressed concerns of a practical nature. "Are complainants and witnesses to appear at their own expense," he asked, "or is there
provision made to defray their expenses?" Meanwhile, as FEPC senior officials in Washington decided on a course of action for the hearings, Castañeda
journeyed south to San Antonio "to check on some cases with the Censorship
Department at the Post Office, where new evidence of discrimination against
Latin-Americans" had been reported. From San Antonio he proceeded to Arizona to survey labor relations in the mining district surrounding the communities of Bixby, Globe, Inspiration, and Miami.[81]

During a sojourn of five days in Arizona, Carlos established a base in Phoenix, where he consulted with representatives of the War Manpower Commission and the Mexican Consulate. Owing to a large number of Mexican nationals working in the mines, the consulate had become a friendly conduit
through which Spanish-speaking laborers lodged complaints. An editor of an
influential Spanish-language weekly newspaper, J. Franco, whom Carlos described as "a man with wide connections and of dynamic character," verified
assertions of Mexican community leaders that WMC personnel had extended
"wholehearted cooperation" in trying to resolve a few of the major problems
affecting minority workers. Judicious in time allocation, Carlos spent two
days in Miami, sixty-eight miles east of Phoenix, and in the nearby hamlet of
Inspiration, both in the heart of the mining district. Miami Copper, the company that controlled the economic life of the former settlement, employed a
labor force of approximately 1,400, 10 percent of whom were Latin Americans. Of the nearly 240 Hispanics, about 60 percent worked underground,
while the remaining 40 percent performed "surface jobs." Owing to the vigi-
lance of the leadership in CIO Local 586 in strongly defending the rights
and dignity of labor, few complaints emerged during interviews conducted
with union members. On the other hand, unpleasant conditions at Inspiration
Consolidated Copper Corporation spawned a thick folder of grievances. Em-
ploying about 1,500 men, of whom one-third were Latin Americans, the company operated a leaching plant to which most minority workers had been relegated. With such a concentration of Spanish-speaking laborers at one facility,

Carlos instinctively knew he would encounter "rank discrimination" being practiced against Latin Americans. Not surprisingly, after the interviews he found "twelve good, clear-cut cases of discrimination" based on national origin. Carefully soliciting "full and detailed statements" for each complaint, Carlos noted that each case was "well-defined, and different." Because Arizona now fell within the jurisdiction of the FEPC regional office in Los Angeles, he forwarded all pertinent records to California for transmittal to Maslow in Washington. In the remaining days, not having access to an automobile, Castañeda tapped his sources in Phoenix for general information about conditions in other mining areas and the companies "operating therein," which he summarized in a succinct report for Maslow's perusal.

During his time in the field Castañeda had deduced certain pragmatic truths about his government role that he also conveyed to Washington:

> In securing information as to conditions, and interviewing the individual workmen, the ability to speak Spanish is of the greatest importance. It is true that more than one-half of the Latin-American workers speak English, most of them . . . very brokenly. They know the terminology of the mines, they understand instructions, and orders in connection with their work, but they are unable to explain in English the conditions against which they wish to complain. I also have found in my experience in Silver City, El Paso, and in my recent visit to Arizona, that they tell their troubles much more freely to me because I am of their own race than they do to an Anglo examiner. They feel innate distrust because they have been betrayed so frequently by men who have posed as their friends, and who have sold them out stock and barrel.[82]

Before he returned to Arizona to conduct "a more thorough survey" of living and working conditions in the mining district, Carlos advised his superiors in Washington that it was "essential" that they carefully plan strategy together, and that they know what other public agencies interested in related facets of the problem (such as the National War Labor Board and the Non-ferrous Metals Commission in Denver) intended to achieve, so as to "determine the manner" in which the FEPC should proceed toward its own objectives.[83]

Eager to sustain the momentum for the FEPC, Carlos traveled to Washington early in April to consult with the director of field operations and his staff. Not inclined to waste time after arriving at the national capital, on a Sunday afternoon he drafted a detailed memorandum outlining specific tasks for a proposed public hearing regarding "discriminatory practices in the Mining Industry in New Mexico, Arizona and West Texas." Summarizing talking points for the meeting with Maslow's staff the following day, Carlos's

memorandum included the names and assignments of two women—Dr. Ruth
Landes, an academician in government service; and Mrs. Willetta Gutleben, a
career employee—who would assist him in a fact-finding sweep in the Southwest. Concerning Mrs. Gutleben, who normally helped him with clerical work
in Dallas, Castañeda suggested: "She could be transferred to Phoenix for the
period necessary for the preparation of all the materials for the Hearing. Her
previous experience, her thoroughness, and her sense of responsibility would
make her the ideal person for the job. The regional office can get along very
well without her services." [84] Unable to finalize all details in one meeting but
satisfied with the acceptance of his overall proposal, Carlos returned to Texas
for a few days of work and relaxation.

Interspersed with a family reunion in Dallas and preparation for another
investigative tour of the mining industry, Carlos indulged in a bit of therapeutic cerebral activity—writing a speech on the topic of "Franciscan History"
for delivery at an appropriate occasion. Undoubtedly the location of his new
office on the ninth floor of the Irwin-Keasler Building, a block away from the
offices of Region X, provided a sanctuary from the beehive environment at the
Mercantile Bank complex. [85]

In mid-April, 1944, Castañeda flew to Washington to confer with Malcolm
Ross, Will Maslow, and others prior to conducting a comprehensive inquiry
into labor conditions in the southwestern mines. By then practically everyone concerned with the mission had endorsed Carlos's plan for dispatching
Dr. Landes and Mrs. Gutleben ahead to El Paso to handle preliminary tasks.
Following three days of intensive discussions Castañeda arranged a brief lay-
over in Dallas to see his wife and daughters. Then, anxious to join his colleagues in the field, he drove all night with as few rest stops as possible so as
to arrive in El Paso on the morning of Friday, April 21. [86] Owing to the expansive nature of the industrywide investigation, coupled with the gravity of
most of the situations he had previously assessed, Castañeda realized he would
work in the field for an extended period of several months. Beginning in El
Paso, where he reviewed the meticulous work of Landes and Gutleben, he
crisscrossed the states of New Mexico and Arizona, ferreting out details concerning prior complaints and gathering data on new grievances. At virtually
every locality complaints fell into one of three categories with which Carlos
had become intimately familiar: dual-track wage scales, inappropriate job
classification, and management's reluctance to promote minority personnel.
For inquiries in the field he usually took Mrs. Gutleben along to maintain efficient record-keeping of the visits. Dr. Landes, only moderately fluent in
Spanish, stayed behind to conduct follow-up interviews that would buttress
earlier petitions.

From El Paso in the last week of April, Carlos forged ahead into Arizona, sustaining two tire blowouts en route to Miami. Assigning Landes to reinterview complainants, Castañeda drove with Gutleben to Ray-Sonora, "a typical mining town" where Kennecott Copper directed a large operation with an aggregate workforce of "between 1500 and 1800 men of whom the bulk" were Latin Americans. Unlike miners in other areas, who had mostly joined CIO locals, the workers in this hamlet had elected to be represented by the American Federation of Labor (AFL). The harsh reality that quickly riveted the attention of the FEPC visitors to this remote vicinity was the segregation of living quarters. Appalled by the discovery, Castañeda later informed Maslow that Hispanics resided in their own community "located one mile from Ray," the latter being "the place where the Anglo workers and most of the administrative staff live." Sonora, the Spanish-dominant hamlet situated above a canyon, accommodated "a population of 2200" and resembled "a Mexican town in any area" south of the border. "Spanish is practically the official language," Carlos reported.

Apart from the social segregation, which he could not address, Castañeda confronted the problem of proving economic discrimination. On account of the manpower needs of American armed forces on the battle fronts, most Anglo workers at Ray had patriotically reported to induction centers. As a consequence, management had promptly discarded its dual-salary system and adopted the lower wage scale for the remaining workers.[87] Probing around for at least two days, mainly through the assistance of Arturo Bustamante, local union secretary, Castañeda gathered twelve complaints against the company. The Spanish-surnamed laborers, who constituted "from 70 to 80 percent" of a total workforce of nearly eight hundred men, complained that while management assigned them to "unskilled, semi-skilled and skilled jobs," it barred them from working in the electrical department, which paid higher wages. Even more devious, although company officials promised open employment and promotion opportunities, behind the scenes they practiced "misclassification." In effect, management classified all workmen either as "miners or timbermen." Within the labyrinth of a large mining enterprise the workers actually operated "drills, locomotives, tipping or dumping machinery, and all other kinds of machines." After closely analyzing the problem Carlos noted that "miners and timbermen" also performed the "duties of pipe fitters, repair helpers in the mechanic shop and in the locomotive shop, act[ed] as brakemen, trackmen, and every other conceivable job even to that of assayers." Worse yet, when Kennecott began operations at Ray-Sonora, the Arizona state legislature had authorized the corporation to pay substandard salary "rates . . . based on the percentage production per men employed" because the company anticipated extracting only low-grade copper ore. Subsequently the miners discovered new copper veins of a higher quality "mineral content." Ignoring this windfall, Kennecott officials took advantage "of the original privilege" conceded by the legislature and continued to maintain a lower salary structure. "The discovery of richer ore," implored Castañeda, "and the fact that the production of the mine has been maintained even with a working force reduced by almost 50 percent, should be the strongest argument in insisting that the present state of affairs be changed, and that the prevailing wages of the industry be paid the workmen here." He also advocated reclassification of the workers in accordance with the actual duties they performed.[88]

In light of the "primitive" environment of the "mining centers" at Ray-Sonora, Castañeda determined that it was inadvisable either for Dr. Landes to attempt "a follow-up" or for Mrs. Gutleben to accompany him to the next destination, Hayden-Winkleman, twenty-two miles to the south "in the mountains over very rough roads." Despite the remoteness of this operation, Castañeda felt compelled to investigate it so as not "to slight" any employment location in the industry.[89]

The area of Hayden-Winkleman consisted of two towns separated by a distance of four miles. Constructed on company property, Hayden represented the business center where both American Smelting and Refining and Phelps-Dodge Corporation had located their offices. Looking at the terrain, Carlos quickly noted a smelter, managed by the former enterprise, and a mill, operated by the latter. He also observed that while most "Anglo officials and workmen" resided in Hayden, the Latin American families lived across a canyon in a small community called San Pedro, also on company property. The deplorable situation Castañeda encountered at Hayden and its satellite community of San Pedro made previous stops seem humane by comparison. He was incensed to find that the company enforced "strict segregation within its property." In contrast, Winkleman, outside of company control, functioned without segregation, resulting in relatively harmonious relations between Anglo and Hispanic workers and their families, a fact he emphasized to Maslow. In Hayden the company's policy of coerced segregation applied not only to the town's single "moving picture theatre" but also to the school and "all public establishments" in the locality. Not surprisingly, the gross "pattern of discrimination" spread over into "the wage scheme, the upgrading practice, and the classification of workmen in force." With the help of a friendly atmosphere provided by the AFL local at Phelps-Dodge, Castañeda discerned that that company practiced more deliberate discrimination at the mill than American Smelting and Refining at its smelter. Notwithstanding the presence of an AFL local, the contract between labor and management at Phelps-Dodge contained a debilitating clause that virtually nullified seniority provisions and other forms of job security: "Employees may be disciplined, demoted, transferred from one occupation to another, suspended or discharged by the company's supervisory employees authorized so to do." Carlos "docketed" ten complaints in the region (four against Kennecott Copper and six against American Smelting and Refining), which, combined with another fourteen cases compiled at Ray-Sonora, constituted a hefty packet for the western FEPC office in Los Angeles.[90]

With zeal tempered by courtesy to both management and labor, Castañeda drove back and forth across the Arizona landscape collecting data for an area-wide hearing on the mining industry. Although the particulars varied, the overall pattern of discrimination stretched endlessly without any immediate solution. After leaving Hayden-Winkleman, Carlos retraced his route north-ward and then approached the Clifton-Morenci area near the state boundary with New Mexico. Complicating the issue of discrimination in Clifton, located in a canyon seven miles below the town of Morenci, was an acrimonious ri-valry between the CIO local and its AFL counterpart. Previously the dominant bargaining agency for labor, the AFL component had retained the loyalty of "old members," most of whom were Anglos, while the upstart CIO local had gained the support of the Indians and the Latin Americans. The CIO's pledge to eliminate discriminatory practices for its membership intensified the ani-mosity in the open-pit mine, mill, and smelter operated by Phelps-Dodge Cop-per Corporation. Adding another dimension to the economic discrimination at Clifton was the company's decision, owing to a shortage of male workers, to hire Anglo but not Hispanic women. These women, initially assigned to "clean-up jobs," mainly "janitorial positions," gradually received advance-ment into higher-paying responsibilities "as mill operators, operator helpers, in the power plant department, blower pump operations and helpers, com-pressor operators and helpers, and in the electrical department." The employ-ment level for women fluctuated from 200 to 300, but at the time of Casta-ñeda's visit the number had dropped to "about 150."[91]

Confronted by the facts and filed complaints, management acknowledged that its "policy was discriminatory" but insisted this was unintentional. Even if job vacancies occurred, plant manager C. G. Davis explained, Hispanic women could not be hired "because there was only one dressing room and one shower room available, and . . . frankly, there existed a strong prejudice on the part of the Anglo women which would result in trouble." Firmly yet diplo-matically Castañeda informed Davis that employment practices in Clifton were in "direct violation of Executive Order 9346." Embarrassed, perhaps even chafed, that a labor advocate from the executive department had pene-trated the remoteness of the region, Davis offered a catalog of explanations for the situation at Clifton, all of which Carlos politely brushed aside as inadequate. Finally the manager conceded that "there was a remote probability" of hiring additional female workers and that the company would extend "equal opportunities for employment to Latin-American applicants." [92]

Treated even worse by management than the Hispanic workers were the Indian laborers. Castañeda's investigation disclosed that because of a labor shortage "since the beginning of the war," the company had resorted to hiring "common" workers from "the Indian Reservations." At the time of his visit Phelps-Dodge employed "as many as 300 Indians," mostly from the Navajo tribe, as unskilled laborers. Taking advantage of the Indians' tendency to return "to their reservation to work on their individual farms" for a few days at a time, combined with the fact that many of them "had little schooling" or could not speak English, management glossed over the evidence that some of their Native American laborers had attained "high school and college training" in order to justify paying all of them low wages. Castañeda labeled the corporation's policy toward these workers "irresponsible" because it attempted to replicate the disadvantages inherent in "the pattern of the Indian Reservation." He found even more deplorable the conditions of the camp in which the Native Americans lived, which was located "at the old site" of the town of Metcalf:

> A tract of land is provided by the company for them to reside in. This is located down in a deep canyon directly below the open-pit above Morenci. It is a sort of Indian Reservation with a Deputy Sheriff under the employ of the company serving as General Manager for the Indian Camp. Although it is a scant three miles . . . below the open-pit mine, down a steep incline of more than 1500 feet, and across the canyon to the Indian Camp, the distance by the highway around the precipitous cliff on which the mine is perched, is 14 miles. In the morning the Indian workers are picked up at the camp and driven to work in trucks. But in the evening when the work is over, they have to go back on foot over a steep down-grade called the Indian trail, which is so steep down the side of the cliff that the men literally slide in a hunched position for a distance of more than a 1000 feet. The trail is so precipitous that frequently the men suffer a fractured leg . . . I personally saw the trail, and it is more steep than any ski or toboggan slide. [93]

The Indians complained to Carlos about the company's ingenious device to coerce them into staying at the camp by controlling their payroll deductions. Phelps-Dodge, Castañeda reported, charged the Indians "an exorbitant rent for their living quarters," which was "deducted from their pay each two-week period." Starting at $3.00 for single men twice a month, the fee structure escalated "to $5.50 for married men, and $7.50 for men with children." Castañeda reported: "The company tries to force all Indian workers to stay at the Indian camp. Some of the older Indians protest they cannot go down the steep incline in the evening, and they frequently secure quarters in Morenci. The company tries to make them go to the Indian Camp by continuing to deduct rent for quarters from their pay. We have a complaint filed of this nature." [94] Wielding only the moral force of his office and a veiled threat of exposure by an industrywide public hearing, Castañeda accomplished little on this visit except to acquaint leaders among Latin American workers and union officials "with the provisions of Executive Order 9346 and the nature and scope of the work of the Committee." [95]

Altogether, from El Paso to Clifton-Morenci, Carlos and his assistants assembled a portfolio of eighty cases involving workers "in all departments" of the industry, ranging "from common labor to skilled job positions." In view of the extraordinary circumstances, Castañeda seized upon a concession he had undoubtedly secured during his Washington visits and communicated directly with Chairman Ross. His investigation, he reported, had exposed a variety of forms of economic discrimination against minority workers. Besides such common abuses as the refusal to upgrade workers and the incorrect job descriptions for some employees, he and his staff had uncovered even more clever practices in the guise of "wage differential scales under the pretext of artificial or arbitrary classification and discriminatory work assignments." The expansive scope of their investigation revealed

> a marked and wide-spread variation in wage scales for the same types of work or jobs in the different mining centers in Texas, New Mexico, and Arizona, so that two smelters, located 20 or 30 miles apart, pay wages for the same type of work that sometimes [differ] as much as $1.00 a day. This particular condition results in a strong desire of men to move from the smelter paying lower wages to that paying the higher scale. The stabilization program [initiated to encourage high productivity during wartime] enables the companies to refuse to grant release to their men, which intensifies the discontent among the workers who feel that they are being frozen in their jobs in order that the companies may maintain a low wage scale. [96]

With nearly a year of hands-on experience in field examination, accented by "close contact" with discontented workers complaining about discrimination in employment, Castañeda concluded that the FEPC was simply applying Band-Aids to a social illness that required radical surgery. Feeling a bit frustrated because high-ranking officials in the U.S. Department of State, worried about how diplomats from Latin American nations might interpret labor unrest in the Southwest, had pressured the FEPC to reconsider the likelihood of conducting hearings in El Paso that could result in undesirable, possibly controversial, publicity with regard to charges of discrimination, Carlos borrowed a medical analogy to illustrate the serious nature of the problem. He asked Ross:

> *Now, then, do you want me to hold conferences with management in Arizona and New Mexico? If such conferences are held by me, and I take up with the companies the individual cases already docketed, the companies will either correct the individual grievance or explain it away. I seriously doubt that in a private conference we will be able to obtain from companies a correction of their discriminatory practices. The individual cases docketed are symptomatic. Like the pulse and temperature of a patient they merely indicate a serious organic disorder. Specific drugs can lower the heartbeat and the temperature without curing the patient or permanently removing the cause for the sym[p]toms observed. The settlement of individual cases may be made to give the appearance of a correction of discriminatory practices without in fact curing the illness.*[97]

Typical of his work habits, Castañeda had planned to leave the Clifton-Morenci area and proceed south to Bisbee, Arizona, near the international border, but an urgent telephone call from a labor leader in Silver City, New Mexico, convinced him to alter his itinerary.[98] The short drive to Grant County, New Mexico, broke the monotony of the field investigation. At the Santa Rita Mines, Castañeda ferreted out the essential facts in an ironic case of discrimination perpetuated against an Anglo worker. J. Kimball, a shovel operator with a year and a half on the job, returned to work following a month of convalescence to recover from pneumonia. To Kimball's surprise, a mine supervisor assigned him to duties as an oiler. Naturally the worker balked at what he considered a demotion in job and salary. The shovel foreman and an assistant mine superintendent insisted that Kimball should gratefully perform the "oiling" tasks because if they were to reassign him to his previous job, management would be compelled "to use Mexicans as oilers," which was an alternative "the company did not want" to consider. Generally annoyed about his own demotion and the company's refusal to hire Hispanics as oilers, Kimball assured Castañeda that not only was he "willing to testify to the veracity" of his statement, but he could "produce several witnesses who overheard the remark." Castañeda promptly secured an appointment with William Goodrich, manager of the Santa Rita Division of Kennecott Copper Corporation, to resolve Kimball's complaint and to extract from management a clarification of the "company's policy" as it affected "the employment of Spanish-Americans as oilers." Using his title of assistant to the chairman as a persuasive lever, Castañeda offered Goodrich a friendly reminder about the prohibition against discrimination in the war industries.[99]

For over two months, as an arid summer followed a pleasant spring, Castañeda remained in the Southwest crisscrossing the Arizona–New Mexico state line and carrying out the mission of the President's Committee on Fair Employment Practice. Carlos frequently drove at night from one location to the next in order to devote daylight hours to the work of the committee. He interviewed mine workers, labor leaders, plant managers, and even military officials. While he enjoyed the company and assistance of his female associates in compiling documentation to support the investigations and conferences, normally he worked alone while on the road. Living out of a suitcase in less than first-rate hotels, Castañeda stayed in continual contact by mail and telephone with Dallas and Washington, D.C., advising superiors of his accomplishments, setbacks, and future plans. Week by week he maintained a relentless pace investigating a litany of complaints, constantly hearing a familiar refrain from workers alleging unfair treatment in regard to salary or in exclusion from job training and promotion. No matter how trivial, he thoroughly examined each specific complaint, a process that demanded tremendous energy and commitment. Obviously longing to see his family, but thankful he did not have to subject them to numerous inconveniences on the road, Carlos resembled a circuit rider as he traveled through Ajo, Bisbee, Cottonwood, Douglas, Globe, Hayden, Inspiration, Jerome, Miami, Phoenix, Ray, Sonora, and Winkleman. After zigzagging along highways and unpaved back roads, by the end of June he had returned through Clifton and Morenci to Silver City, where he contacted Will Maslow in Washington for further instructions.[100]

On June 23 Maslow telegraphed a curt directive to Carlos at the Murray Hotel in Silver City: "PROCEED WITH EL PASO CONFERENCES. AVOID PUBLIC CONTROVERSY OR THREATS OF HEARINGS."[101] Anxious to conclude his investigative work and be reunited with his family, Castañeda rushed down to El Paso and registered at the Hotel Del Norte. On the morning of June 26 his meeting with executives and labor leaders at American Smelting and Refining Company progressed amicably. In the afternoon he encountered stiff resistance from a lawyer representing Phelps-Dodge Refining Company, who haughtily questioned the presidential committee's authority on grounds that his clients' contract with the CIO local included a nondiscrimination clause. Accordingly, the lawyer argued, complaints filed with the FEPC should be resolved by the union's grievance committee. Thwarted by that setback, Castañeda stayed in El Paso another day to send a report of his field work in Morenci, Arizona, and then returned to Dallas with a portfolio of unfinished business.[102]

During Castañeda's sojourn in the Southwest, the President's Committee on Fair Employment Practice had come under heavy criticism from southern conservative members of Congress who disapproved of gains for African American workers. In early June, 1944, Maslow explained to Carlos that the agency was in the midst of "a crucial struggle for survival." Although the House of Representatives had approved the FEPC budget appropriation by a margin of four votes, the committee anticipated "an equally close shave in the Senate." Irrespective of exemplary records achieved in other FEPC regions, Castañeda's work in the Southwest became the agency's showpiece.[103] In the third week in June, following the Senate's approval of the appropriation measure, Clarence Mitchell congratulated Castañeda for his indirect contribution to the successful outcome. During a heated debate on the merits and limitations of the FEPC, Sen. Dennis Chávez, chairman of the Committee on Labor and Education, had energetically defended the agency, citing Castañeda's efforts in eradicating discriminatory practices in his home state. "No doubt you will be gratified to know," Mitchell told Carlos, "that Senator Dennis Chávez of New Mexico mentioned some of your accomplishments in a speech defending [the] FEPC on Monday, June 19."[104] Chávez's fortuitous remarks actually stemmed from Carlos's earlier visit in February to New Mexico, Colorado, and Arizona, when he counseled members of labor unions to be vigilant against unfair tactics in the workplace, rather than from Castañeda's ongoing investigation. As Carlos knew from years of diligent service in the academy, recognition and reward evolve slowly from the value of past accomplishments and not from contemporary activity, no matter how laudable. Back in Dallas, Carlos enjoyed a few days at home with the family. On the Fourth of July, Castañeda worked in his office at the Irwin-Keasler Building on a summary report covering the eleven companies he had visited in the Southwest. Altogether the number of complaints totaled one hundred, with those in the upgrading and misclassification categories accounting for "62% of the cases filed and docketed." Regarding the attitudes of the companies, Carlos wrote:

> In every instance, with the exception of the Phelps-Dodge Refining Company in El Paso, which is not to be confused with the Phelps-Dodge Copper Corporation in Arizona, every company agreed to and did discuss with considerable frankness the various complaints presented, pointing out which [ones] had already been handled either through grievance committee machinery, or through arbitration by the National War Labor Board. Furthermore, they discussed frankly other points as indicated in the various individual reports sent to . . . [Washington, D.C.] on the conferences held.[105]

Relying on his firsthand observations and discussions, Carlos reflected on the investigation's main accomplishments: "Lastly, in about 40% of the cases pre-

sented the companies agreed to remedy the condition that gave rise to the
complaint, or proved to some extent that the refusal to upgrade or transfer a
complainant was due to other factors than his or her race or national origin.
From this point of view, it may be said that the conferences held with management were successful in correcting about 40% of the individual cases and
in bringing management around to a more serious consideration of the problem of discrimination and in convincing them of the importance of eliminating it." [106]

Castañeda also sketched the relative strength of the various labor organizations and the degree of their support for Latin American workers:

> There are four different labor organizations that control in varying degrees
> bargaining [relations] with management in the various mine, mills and
> smelters visited. These are the affiliates of AFL, CIO, United Mine Workers,
> and the Brotherhood of Railway Trainmen. Until the last three years the
> AFL had more or less been the bargaining agency in most of the mining
> centers in Arizona. Since 1941 the CIO has organized locals and through
> regular procedure held elections and has become the bargaining agency in
> most of the mining centers. Of the 18,000 or more men employed . . . in
> Southwest Texas, New Mexico, and Arizona, it may be said that on an aver-
> age the Latin-Americans constitute from 40 to 50%. In certain areas the
> percentage of Latin-Americans is as high as 80, or even 90%, particularly
> if . . . departments in which unskilled or semi-skilled labor is required are
> considered.[107]

Castañeda noted that leaders of the CIO locals were "still living up to their
promise" of actually "securing higher wages and new avenues of promotion
for Latin-Americans," but as "skilled job positions" became available their
fervor waned. On the other hand, the AFL, threatened by the rival union's
inroads into the ranks of Hispanic labor, had become "much more liberal
in its attitude towards Latin-Americans" and constantly gave assurances to
minority members that the locals would defend "their rights for promotion"
in tandem with "their ability and seniority." Both labor unions, in fact, willingly cooperated with the FEPC and provided ample "information on general
conditions." Two other unions—the Brotherhood of Railway Trainmen and
the United Mine Workers—competed for the support of labor in the Southwest. Castañeda dismissed the United Mine Workers with a pithy observation:
"They are attempting to organize in various places throughout Arizona, but
as yet have not obtained sufficient membership to request an election." As for
the Brotherhood of Railway Trainmen, it had confronted the FEPC investigation with a recalcitrant attitude. Instead of a long list of complaints, Carlos

cited just one example to fortify his report: "The Brotherhood of Railway Trainmen in their contract with Kennecott Copper . . . at Silver City state that seniority for trackmen and car droppers do not entitle them to promotion to switchmen, switchenders, motormen, etc. This bars the promotion of Latin-Americans to the jobs indicated." [108] Altogether the experience of visiting work sites, listening attentively to workers' grievances, and discussing problems with management provided Castañeda with numerous forums in which to argue the goals of the FEPC. Moreover, the pain of discrimination he had suffered in his own career made him all the more determined to eradicate it as a social evil, particularly at a time when Americans of varied ethnic backgrounds were fighting a war to uphold democratic ideals around the world.

In mid-July, Castañeda went to Washington to render an accounting of his field investigation to FEPC superiors. The visit gave him an opportunity to confer directly with Maslow, Mitchell, and Ross, and to clarify possible ambiguities in his frequent reports from the Southwest. At the conclusion of the meetings, after allowing time for hasty telephone calls to friends in the history fraternity, Carlos returned to Dallas with firm plans to conduct follow-up conferences with union officials and company managers prior to scheduling area-wide hearings on the mining industry. The purpose of such conferences was to allow labor and management to adjust outstanding cases of discrimination themselves rather than have the President's Committee on Fair Employment Practice or the National War Labor Board intervene. Afterward, based on the number of "unadjusted" cases, the Dallas FEPC team could proceed with public hearings. Not lacking courage but desiring to win by persuasion rather than confrontation, Carlos offered suggestions to Maslow concerning preparation for the hearings, from the best type of testimony to the number of witnesses who could address "the broader issues of discrimination in the mining industry." He also included the matter of "expert" witnesses within the scope of his recommendation.[109]

Before proceeding further with plans for a public hearing, Carlos resumed communications with Phelps-Dodge Refining in El Paso. Armed with a hefty dossier that FEPC staff had compiled on the refinery's extremely slow progress in resolving its labor disputes, Castañeda wired a succinct message to the company's manager, William Knowles: "INVESTIGATION INTO ELEVEN CASES ON WHICH CONFERENCE WITH YOU [WAS] REFUSED[,] ALLEGEDLY ON [THE GROUNDS OF] PREVIOUS SETTLEMENT THROUGH GRIEVANCE COMMITTEE[,] REVEALS TEN WERE PRESENTED TO UNION CONTRACT WITHOUT SATISFACTORY ADJUSTMENT. THE OTHER HAS NOT BEEN HANDLED BY GRIEVANCE COMMITTEE. NONE HAS BEEN REFERRED TO NWLB. REQUEST CONFERENCE WITH YOU SATURDAY, AUGUST 12, TEN AM. LETTER FOLLOWS."[110]

Embarrassed, no doubt, by the information the FEPC had compiled through its interagency network, the refinery officials requested a week's delay to conduct an internal review of personnel actions. Meeting finally in the office of the company's legal counsel, J. F. Hulse, who initially had refused to cooperate with the FEPC, Castañeda conferred with the attorney, Knowles, and the latter's assistant, E. W. Donohue. Conducting discussions from a position of strength, Carlos "took up each of the complaints individually." Unable to mount an obstinate defense as before, Hulse declared that Phelps-Dodge Refinery did not support a "discriminatory policy," and that his clients, "anxious" to resolve complaints satisfactorily, preferred not "having to go over the details again and again with representatives of different Federal agencies."[111]

Although Phelps-Dodge Refinery ultimately, if somewhat reluctantly, conferred with FEPC officials, not all episodes resulted in similar endings. Castañeda knew that large corporations frequently hid their unfair practices by playing one federal agency against one or two others. On several occasions after joining government service Carlos learned of incidents in which corporations, vulnerable to charges of selective discrimination, had maneuvered between the Non-ferrous Metals Commission and the National War Labor Board for discretionary review of their activities to avoid confronting the FEPC and possible exposure.[112] They thus gained time to maximize profits, and since they furnished a vital resource, copper, for the war effort, they were able to spread a mantle of patriotism over their operations.

Even more frustrating to Castañeda than facing opposition lawyers was having to defer to legal consultants recruited by the FEPC to assist the Dallas regional office in preparing for a public hearing in Phoenix, Arizona. Starting late in September legal preparations advanced at an exasperatingly slow pace.[113] Two and a half months later, just before Christmas, an Arizona examiner advised Carlos that local arrangements were "progressing satisfactorily" in regard to the Phoenix Mining Hearing. The prime cause for the delay stemmed from the torturously cautious approach of Frank D. Reeves, an attorney in the Office of Emergency Management. Not only did the lawyer minutely scrutinize every memorandum Castañeda had sent from the Southwest, but he also interviewed director of field operations Maslow and briefed A. Bruce Hunt, director of Region VII, whose jurisdiction encompassed Arizona and California. Reeves's motive for delaying the date of a public hearing stemmed from a strategy of designating two sites—one in southern Arizona and another in western New Mexico—to capitalize upon publicity that would redound favorably to the FEPC if U.S. senator Chávez were to testify at Silver City. Unlike Castañeda, who confronted executives on their own turf, Reeves, the wary lawyer, wanted to be certain that documented testimony, expert witnesses, and selection of a prime geographic location for a hearing would mesh to produce a favorable outcome. In short, Reeves, as a bureaucratic perfectionist, wanted the FEPC to win without taking calculated risks.[114]

For his part Castañeda performed like a loyal field captain. Besides sharing candid observations and reactions to Reeves's analyses and recommendations, he provided Hunt in Tucson, Arizona, with detailed assessments of docketed cases.[115] Throughout most of the autumn, waiting for a decision on the hearing, Carlos carefully reviewed data on old cases in Texas (Austin, Biggs Field at El Paso, Houston, Kelly Field in San Antonio, and Newgulf) and New Mexico (Santa Rita Mines) for evidence of improvement in minority workers' relations with management.[116] Before the year ended, Castañeda invited Hunt to join him in Houston to observe how he conducted conferences with company executives and union leaders at Shell Oil Refinery, as well as to discuss the merits and limitations of prospective witnesses for the Phoenix Mining Hearing. Carlos's prior affiliation with the Inter-American Relations Committee at the University of Texas, especially his role as secretary, rewarded him with a knowledge of potential witnesses (diplomats, economists, educators, historians, and sociologists). In fact, he enthusiastically recommended a colleague in the education department at the Austin campus: "I understand that George Sánchez, one of the outstanding Latin-American authorities in the Southwest, who is highly respected and who has been sick for some time in Washington, has just returned to New Mexico and is now in Albuquerque. He was the Director of the Inter-American Relations Committee of the University of Texas. Although he is convalescing at Albuquerque, I feel confident that he would be glad to appear at the Hearing if we desire his cooperation." [117]

After almost a year and a half with the FEPC, Carlos E. Castañeda at the end of 1944 approached another milestone with public hearings on the mining industry looming, he hoped, in the near future. He fervently wanted his investigation to bear fruitful results for the workers who looked to him for constructive change. Still, he knew that the delaying tactics of government lawyers were greatly eroding minority workers' confidence in the FEPC.

Superintendent Castañeda at outdoor rally at Sidney Lanier High School, San
Antonio, 1934. The School Improvement League, founded by Eleuterio Escobár
(far right), sponsored the rally. *Courtesy Eleuterio Escobár Collection,
Institute of Texan Cultures, University of Texas at San Antonio, #71-125.*

Most Rev. Mariano S. Garriga, Auxiliary Bishop of Corpus Christi. *Courtesy Catholic Archives of Texas.*

Milton R. Gutsch, chairman, Department of History, University of Texas at Austin. *Courtesy Prints and Photographs Collection, The Center for American History, The University of Texas at Austin, CN 07249.*

Carlos and Elisa with baby daughter Rosemary. *Courtesy of Rosemary C. Folks and Consuelo C. Artaza, Houston.*

Donald Coney, Director of Libraries, University of Texas at Austin.
Courtesy Prints and Photographs Collection, The Center for American History,
The University of Texas at Austin, CN 06249.

Castañeda with Rev. James P. Gibbons, C.S.C., successor chairman of the
Texas Knights of Columbus Historical Commission.
Courtesy Rosemary C. Folks and Consuelo C. Artaza, Houston.

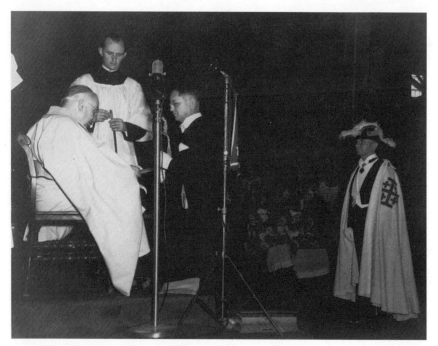

Castañeda's investiture as Knight of the Equestrian Order of the Holy Sepulchre of Jerusalem, October 12, 1941, Gregory Gymnasium, University of Texas at Austin. *Left to right:* Most Rev. Francis C. Kelley, Rev. Vincent F. Holden, C.S.P., Castañeda, and Sir Knight Robert C. Kelley.
Courtesy of Rosemary C. Folks and Consuelo C. Artaza, Houston.

Castañeda in procession behind honor guard of 4th Degree Knights of Columbus, followed by Bishop Mariano S. Garriga, Corpus Christi, ca. 1949.
Courtesy Catholic Archives of Texas.

Homer Price Rainey, president of the University of Texas at Austin, 1939–44.
Courtesy Prints and Photographs Collection, The Center for American History,
The University of Texas at Austin, CN 07250.

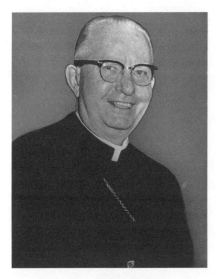

Most Rev. Robert E. Lucey,
Archbishop of San Antonio.
Courtesy Catholic Archives of Texas.

Castañeda speaking at San Jacinto
Monument, Houston. *Courtesy Elisa R.*
Castañeda/O. Wayne Poorman.

Rev. Monsignor Francis J. Haas, first
chairman, President's Committee on
Fair Employment Practice and later
bishop of Grand Rapids, Mich.
*Courtesy George G. Higgins Collection,
Archives of the Catholic University
of America.*

Rev. Monsignor Patrick J. McCormick,
president of Catholic University of
America. *Courtesy General
Photographic Collection,
Archives of the Catholic
University of America.*

Most Rev. Laurence J. FitzSimon, Bishop of Amarillo, and
Cleofas Calleros, El Paso. The book shows the progress
of the research and publication of *Our Catholic Heritage
in Texas* from 1936 to 1949. *Courtesy Catholic
Archives of Texas, Diocese of Austin Chancery.*

Aerial view of Catholic University of America campus (looking north).
Caldwell Hall, McMahon Hall, and the university gymnasium appear in the
top half of the photo. *Courtesy General Photographic Collection,
Archives of the Catholic University of America.*

Most Rev. Louis J. Reicher, Bishop
of Austin. *Courtesy Catholic
Archives of Texas.*

SCANNING THE PAGES of one of Carlos E. Castaneda's seven volumes on "Our Catholic Heritage in Texas" are these representatives of the Texas Knights of Columbus Historical Commission, which held its annual meeting here Wednesday. Left to right, seated, are Rt. Rev. Joseph G. O'Donohoe of the diocese of Dallas; Most Rev. M. S. Garriga, bishop of Corpus Christi, and Most Rev. Laurence J. FitzSimon, bishop of Amarillo. Left to right, standing, are Rev. Anton J. Frank, pastor of Annunciation Church, and Mr. Castaneda.

Members of the Texas Knights of Columbus Historical Commission examine Castañeda's sixth volume of *Our Catholic Heritage in Texas* in Houston, 1949. *Seated, left to right:* Right Rev. Monsignor Joseph G. O'Donohoe, Most Rev. Mariano S. Garriga, and Most Rev. Laurence J. FitzSimon; *standing, left to right:* Right Rev. Monsignor Anton J. Frank and Castañeda. *From the* Houston Chronicle.

Carlos with daughter Rosemary and sister Josefina Ella, by side entrance of Bexar County Courthouse, San Antonio. *Courtesy Rosemary C. Folks and Consuelo C. Artaza, Houston.*

Presentation of the Junípero Serra of the Americas Award, 1951,
Washington, D.C. *Left to right:* Very Rev. Mathias Faust, O.F.M.,
Ex-Procurator General of the Franciscan Order; Castañeda;
Most Rev. Amleto G. Ciocognani, Apostolic Delegate to the United States; and
Most Rev. Sigebald B. Kurz, O.F.M., Prefect Apostolic of Yungchow, China.
Courtesy Academy of American Franciscan History, Berkeley, California.

Backyard family photo: Consuelo and husband Hugo P. Artaza, Rosemary, and Carlos and Elisa (seated).
Courtesy Rosemary C. Folks and Consuelo C. Artaza, Houston.

Castañeda in Caracas, Venezuela, greeted by U.S. Ambassador Fletcher Warren.
Courtesy Elisa R. Castañeda/ O. Wayne Poorman.

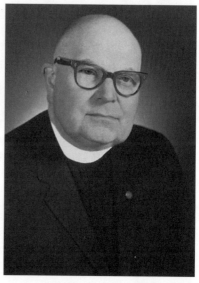

Rev. Monsignor Anton J. Frank.
Courtesy Archives, Diocese of Galveston-Houston.

Castañeda in Venezuela with Rev. Monsignor Nicolás E. Navarro,
rector of the Academia Nacional de la Historia, Caracas.
Courtesy Rosemary C. Folks and Consuelo C. Artaza, Houston.

Rev. Monsignor William H. Oberste.
*Courtesy Corpus Christi Diocesan
Archives, Corpus Christi.*

Castañeda's sister, Josefina E. Castañeda,
and his widow, Elisa R. Castañeda, at the
dedication of the Perry-Castañeda Library
at the University of Texas at Austin,
November 19, 1977. *Courtesy News
and Information Service, The University
of Texas at Austin, Negative File #5995.*

The Perry-Castañeda Library, University of Texas at Austin.
*Courtesy News and Information Service, The University of Texas
at Austin, Negative File #5995.*

Portrait of Castañeda by José Cisneros

From Regional Director to Full-Time Historian,
1945-47

On New Year's Day, 1945, Carlos E. Castañeda and his secretary Mrs. Willetta Gutleben reported for work at the regional FEPC office in Dallas. The possibility of salvaging something useful out of a public hearing, aimed at eradicating discrimination against Hispanics, Indians, and Negroes in the mining industry, weighed heavily on his mind.[1] A factor that irritated him more than misguided favoritism by some employers was the lack of concerted resolve within the FEPC. Nearly everyone agreed that discriminatory practices existed in the Southwest, but some FEPC officials dawdled so much over the form and procedure of a hearing that minority workers began to lose faith in the agency. A representative of the Mine, Mill and Smelter Workers Union, Orville Larson, had met with Castañeda to discuss a labor problem in Laredo. Informed about the FEPC's intent to hold a hearing in Phoenix, Larson replied, "I'll believe it when I see it." Castañeda, on the verge of returning to the field to restore workers' confidence, on January 2 recommended postponing "the hearing two or three weeks."[2]

Castañeda's willingness to delay the hearing probably stemmed from privileged information concerning his "imminent appointment" as director of Region X and the consequent need to devote some time to the transition. In addition to this sudden development, Will Maslow, director of field operations, proposed changing the boundaries of Region X by adding Arizona and Colorado and removing the lower gulf coast from Brownsville, Texas, to New Orleans. Since "a re-arrangement of some kind" hinged on securing approval of the Executive Department's Budget Bureau, a procedure that involved endless haggling, Castañeda sidestepped that issue for the time being. He may have also perceived that the ultimate decision would be favorable to his family's needs and wished, therefore, to avoid jeopardizing the outcome.[3]

On the first weekend in January, Carlos left Dallas for another round of visits in New Mexico. He stopped in El Paso, where he spent the weekend "checking some details" in complaints against the local American Smelting and Phelps-Dodge refineries. On Monday, upon arriving in Silver City, New Mexico, he learned that "unfavorable weather conditions" had delayed the arrival of two FEPC lawyers—A. Bruce Hunt and Frank Reeves—from Tucson, Arizona. Undeterred, Carlos worked alone for two days reinvestigating complaints against Kennecott Copper until the legal team from Arizona came to his assistance. Together the three FEPC officials interviewed complainants and then conferred with Verne Curtis, representative of the Congress of Industrial Organizations in the Silver City–Santa Rita region. To expedite the reporting process Hunt dispatched a telegram to George M. Johnson, deputy FEPC chairman in Washington, summarizing the "substance" of the trio's inquiry. He noted that seven complainants had either joined the armed forces or left the area, that complainants in two cases had been promoted to their "desired jobs," that "two cases require[d] further investigation," and that "six cases [were] without merit." He reported: "CIO REQUESTS TIME TO FILE COMPLAINTS IN WHAT IT REGARDS AS MERITORIOUS CASES. WILL ADVISE YOU OF DEVELOPMENTS IN MORENCI, HAYDEN AND RAY, ARIZONA, DURING NEXT TWO WEEKS. . . . REEVES AND CASTAÑEDA FULLY APPROVE OF THIS TELEGRAM. LEAVING HERE SUNDAY."[4] Disappointed with the meager results of their work in Silver City, Castañeda expressed his frustration in a candid letter to Maslow. His criticism ranged from the condescending attitude of FEPC lawyers to the repeated failure of the committee to effect substantial change in the workplace:

> Not being a lawyer, I cannot speak with authority on the legal merits of the cases dismissed as not [being] meritorious. But regardless of the merit or lack of merit of the complaints reinvestigated, the fact remains that discrimination is evident on every hand; that the [working] men have grown increasingly dissatisfied with our efforts in their behalf and seriously doubt our sincerity; and that the union itself looks with askance upon the supersilious [sic] approach of our legal representatives. . . .
>
> The indefinite postponement of the hearing, which now seems inevitable, is going to be a severe blow to the prestige of the Committee in the Southwest. Both the [labor] unions and the companies, as well as the working men themselves, know that since 1942, when Mr. [Daniel] Donovan and Mr. [James] Fleming first investigated . . . the mining industry, the Committee had periodically promised to eliminate discrimination, [it] has sent from time to time representatives supposedly to bring the matter to a head, and that each time it has turned out to be a fizzle.[5]

Convinced that "the standards adopted" for determining "the validity" of various complaints would not contribute to an exemplary hearing, Carlos abruptly terminated his fieldwork and returned to Dallas by a circuitous route through Amarillo and San Antonio, where he had "urgent cases" that required his "immediate attention."[6]

Meanwhile, in Washington, FEPC chairman Malcolm Ross successfully guided the agency through its negotiating "session" with the Budget Bureau. In late January he dispatched a rare "note" to Carlos expressing regret that the Southwest hearing had "become so indefinite." Alluding to an upcoming reorganization of regional offices, the chairman also cited the necessity of traveling to Texas to "hold conferences with interested people both in Dallas and San Antonio.[7]

After returning to the Dallas office from his field trip, Castañeda indulged in a bit of relaxation by escorting his wife, Elisa, to a dinner of the Texas Philosophical Society. Gratified by an opportunity to get away from wartime-related problems, Carlos thoroughly enjoyed renewing acquaintances in the academic community. The only stressful moment in the evening was when Winnie Allen, a longtime colleague at the University of Texas Library, acted "so cussedly independent" at dinner that her "cold stare" unnerved Carlos and Elisa. This tiny rift in collegiality emanated from Castañeda's failure to reply promptly to Allen's earlier inquiry about an 1834 diary of a trip through Texas compiled by Mexican colonel Juan N. Almonte, a translation of which became one of Carlos's first publications in the *Southwestern Historical Quarterly*. Injured by the snub, Castañeda later explained that his fieldwork had precluded answering personal mail. "I do not have a copy," he advised Allen, "nor do I know where it may be secured, other than from your *dear* friend, Mr. [Earl] Vandale, who, as you say, bought the original [manuscript]." Obviously missing the interaction of campus life, Carlos conveyed conciliatory New Year's greetings to Allen, promising that they would "soon have a real powwow" in the sanctuary of "your archives."[8]

In early February a telegram from Malcolm Ross confirmed Castañeda's promotion at the FEPC: "YOU ARE HEREBY APPOINTED REGIONAL DIRECTOR [OF] NEW REGION X. HOLD ALL PUBLICITY UNTIL WE PREPARE ANNOUNCEMENT FOR NATIONAL AND LOCAL RELEASE. YOU WILL FUNCTION FROM DALLAS OFFICE UNTIL SAN ANTONIO OFFICE [BECOMES] AVAILABLE."[9] On a whirlwind trip to San Antonio, Castañeda stopped in Austin to confer with Milton R. Gutsch, chairman of the history department at the University of Texas. Shortly thereafter Carlos formalized the gist of their impromptu discussion by requesting an extension of his "leave of absence for the remainder of the academic year 1944–1945." Although he "had intended to return" to the Austin campus at the end of February, his appointment as regional director required that he continue his work with "the President's Committee" for the duration of the war. Gutsch forwarded the petition with his approval to the university administration, which routinely granted the extension "without pay during the spring semester, March 1– June 30, 1945."[10] Essentially, the history department handled Castañeda's leave of absence on a semester-by-semester basis. Next, although occupancy would not become effective until June 1, he rented living quarters for the family in San Antonio at 88 Lewis Street. Even more remarkable, given wartime rationing, he applied for residential telephone service.[11]

Leaving Elisa and their daughters in Dallas (to allow Consuelo to finish the school term in May), at the end of February, Carlos leased office space on the third floor of the New Moore Building at 106 Broadway in downtown San Antonio, a block west of Alamo Plaza. Amid the turmoil of moving into Suite 323 the new director planned a tentative itinerary for Chairman Malcolm Ross, who accepted his suggestion "of taking a night train from Dallas on the 26th, arriving in San Antonio on the 27th." Allowing Carlos flexibility with the schedule, Ross wrote: "I will be in your hands and pleased to follow whatever program you want."[12]

One of Castañeda's greatest concerns was having an "adequate staff" to accomplish the mission assigned to his newly realigned region. Given the geographic expanse of Regions X (Arizona, New Mexico, and Texas) and XI (Louisiana), he promptly notified the FEPC Central Office in Washington that it was virtually impossible to investigate the increased volume of complaints with just one field examiner. Sensitive to Castañeda's situation, Will Maslow explained the budgetary constraints: "we realize that your staff is woefully inadequate. Our difficulty, however, is we have only thirty-seven field examiners throughout the entire country and no vacancies anywhere. The only way we could give you another man would be to take one from another region. I have hopes, however, that Congress will give us enough money next year for more personnel."[13] Castañeda's pressure evidently had an effect, however, because Eugene Davidson, who assisted Maslow in field operations, swiftly solved the problem. He wrote: "We understand clearly that your office as well as all other offices in the country are under-staffed and that no perfect job can be done with such limited staff. However, . . . we do not have any vacancies anywhere . . . and . . . we have reached our employment ceiling. In order to assign to you an examiner for the San Antonio office we were forced to reduce the number of examiners in the New York office which has . . . made that office less effective. The policy of doing the best we can under our budgetary limitations is not short-sighted but results from necessity."[14] Clarence M. Mitchell, also in field operations, wondered if Castañeda's administrative process might be expedited by "having some of our official documents translated into Spanish." Specifically, the associate director identified "the complaint form which will be used by individuals filing charges with the Committee." Mitchell refrained from discussing the suggestion "with anyone in the Central Office" until he had received Carlos's "opinion."[15]

The messages from Washington gave Castañeda an idea for discussing the concerns of the FEPC, particularly those problems relating to Spanish-speaking workers, in a national forum. During a Regional Directors' Conference in Washington, with permission from FEPC superiors, on March 14, 1945, he appeared before the Senate Committee on Labor and Education, chaired by U.S. senator Dennis Chávez of New Mexico.[16] Sensing a friendly atmosphere, Carlos, after customary introductions, launched into a scathing summary of the plight of minority workers in the Southwest, beginning with the oil industry and the railroads.

> *Eighteen months of investigation in connection with complaints filed with the President's Committee on Fair Employment Practice involving Mexican-Americans in Texas, New Mexico, Colorado, Arizona, and California, shows that in spite of the constantly increasing demand for manpower for the successful prosecution of the war, the Mexican-American reservoir of available labor has been neither exhausted nor fully utilized at the highest skill of the individual worker.*
>
> *In the oil industry, basic and essential to the war effort, Mexican-Americans have been refused employment in other than common labor, yardman, and janitor classifications regardless of qualifications or training in higher skills. The practice is so firmly entrenched that it has been reduced to the blueprint stage. Employment charts in general use throughout the oil industry restrict the employment of Mexican-Americans to the three positions mentioned.*
>
> *The railroads and the brotherhoods and the railway unions have likewise generally restricted the utilization of available Mexican labor supply. By Mexican, no distinction is made between Mexican national and American citizens of Mexican extraction, who are restricted in general to common labor, trackmen, general maintenance labor, and car droppers, regardless of previous training, time of service, or other qualifications.*[17]

Castañeda turned next to the mining industry, in which he had experienced the most frustration, largely through some lawyers' lack of fortitude: "The mining industry in the Southwest with very few exceptions employs Mexicans only in common labor and semiskilled jobs. In many instances they are restricted from underground work, where wages are higher and the danger is less. Mexicans can be oil-helpers, crane operators helpers, and helpers to most skilled jobs and positions and machine operators, but they never can be employed or classed as master craftsmen or machine operators."[18] Speaking with confidence in his research data, Carlos chastised the military and the utility companies for their lackluster efforts in hiring minorities:

> *In military installations throughout the Southwest, where large numbers of civilians are employed, Mexicans are hired but not always on a level of equality, be they of American citizenship or not. Frequently they are found in jobs that do not utilize their highest skill. They have been promoted slowly and with evident reluctance.*
>
> *Public utility companies and telephone and telegraph companies through- out the Southwest have failed to utilize the available Mexican labor supply in other than common-labor jobs, with ra[r]e exceptions here and there.*[19]

Castañeda then praised three closely related industries for their evenhanded policies on employment and promotion. He said: "The aircraft and shipbuild- ing industries, be it said in all justice, have given the Mexican worker practi- cally equal opportunities to develop his various skills and to attain promotion in accord with his qualifications. This is true of munition and arms factories. But since these are essentially war industries that on VE- and VJ-day will not be readily reconverted to civilian goods productions, their workers will be the first to seek employment in the newly acquired industrial skills."[20]

Asked by Senator Chávez if he had personally observed "the so-called Mexican-Texan, and the Mexican national," Carlos digressed from his pre- pared text. Responding with emotion and conviction, he tapped into the well- spring of personal experience: "In connection with the work of the commit- tee, and also in the years previous to the establishment of the committee, I have been interested in the condition of the Mexican-American, or the Latin American, in the State of Texas. There are in Texas approximately 1,000,000 persons of Mexican extraction, of which more than 60 percent are American citizens. In employment practices there is no difference made whatsoever be- tween a Mexican national and an American citizen of Mexican extraction. If a worker's name is a Spanish one, he is considered as Mexican and treated as such."[21] Undoubtedly recalling his brief tenure as superintendent of the San Felipe Schools in Del Rio, he described the plight of some Spanish-surnamed families in the early 1930s: "During the days of relief, the various agents who distributed relief [products], allowed much less to Mexican families . . . [i.e., 'anybody with a Spanish name'] than to Anglo-American families, . . . and they did it on the assumption that a Mexican does not have to eat so much, that he is not used to eating butter and bacon and other rich foods, and that if they gave it to them it might make them sick."[22]

Senator Chávez then shifted the line of questioning to current events in the Western Hemisphere. Citing the Chapultepec Charter, an accord signed two weeks earlier in Mexico City in which the Latin American republics planned their role in the United Nations organization soon to be created,[23] he asked the witness to comment on the ideal versus reality in domestic affairs. Chávez asked, "How much do you think that charter, or our lip service, or our so-called feeling of good-will, will have on the average man south of the border when he knows that the conditions that you have described to the committee exist in Texas?"[24] Fearful of compromising the FEPC, Castañeda courteously responded that he "would rather leave the answer to the question" to someone else. Chávez deftly parried with a different question: "But from your experience as a member of the F.E.P.C. agency, you know that those conditions that you have described exist not only in Texas but throughout the entire Southwest, wherever Americans of Mexican or Spanish extraction live?" Cornered, unable to evade the issue any longer, Carlos replied: "In speaking before Clubs interested in Pan-Americanism, this question has been asked, 'Do the people south of the Rio Grande feel kindly toward this country?' And I have had to say that there are many people . . . who seriously doubt the protestations of friendship made, when the ways in which the Mexican-Americans and Mexican nationals are treated in the Southwest are reported in Mexican newspapers."[25] Senator Chávez next asked Castañeda to comment on initiatives by the U.S. government and "the great State of Texas" to improve human relations in the workforce. The witness replied: "Yes, I think there is a sincere effort being made. We have been trying [to attain] that [goal] for many years and at present there are even greater efforts being made through persuasion, but the roots of prejudice are so deep-seated in the Southwest that it is going to take something more than persuasion to bring about a change of conditions."[26] Toward the end of lengthy questioning Senator Chávez tried to extract from Castañeda a closing statement on pending legislation to eradicate discrimination in American society. As an employee of the government and the FEPC, Carlos tried to exempt himself from answering, but the committee chairman kept pressing for a response. "Well, suppose we were to abolish that agency, and its personnel," asked Chávez; "would you still be for a Fair Employment Practice Committee?" Castañeda replied: "Yes. I would say that we in Texas—and I am speaking now not as an employee of the F.E.P.C., but as one of those who has worked for many years in trying to eradicate discrimination against Mexican-Americans—I would say that we in Texas are convinced that the solution to the problem is legislation, . . . that can be effectively enforced so as to restrain that small minority, but very aggressive minority, that, because of ignorance, perhaps, practice[s] discrimination that brings shame upon our American democracy."[27]

As he had often done following his participation in an academic event, Carlos returned home with a sense of triumph. Immediately he released two statements to *La Prensa,* an influential Spanish-language newspaper published daily in San Antonio. The first statement summarized the essence of his testimony before the Senate Committee on Labor and Education. The second declaration constituted a stinging denunciation of the Texas Good Neighbor Commission for opposing legislation, sponsored by state senator Franklin J. Spears, to eliminate overt discrimination in the employment arena.[28]

Unconcerned for the moment about what misconceptions his statements might engender, Carlos temporarily enjoyed the attention created by the newspaper articles, copies of which he proudly shared with Malcolm Ross.[29] Chairman Ross exercised remarkable restraint in counseling Castañeda to consider the interests of the agency ahead of personal predilections. For instance, the article in *La Prensa* that criticized the Texas Good Neighbor Commission was indiscreet. Instead of antagonizing potential allies, Ross preferred "to make the best use of people with authority in the field." Rather than reprimanding the director, he offered words of friendly caution:

> *I have no doubt that Mexican-American sentiment in the Southwest approved your views, and if you had been really a private citizen you should have expressed exactly how you felt about it. But complete abandon of opinion, publicly expressed, is one of those things which public servants must do. I am constantly under that limitation, the more so that FEPC is in a hot, controversial field. Further, I could not drop the title "Chairman" and say things with impunity which I could not do under my official title. You are in the same boat. Plain "Carlos Castañeda" is just as well known as Regional Director Castañeda. Certainly R. E. Smith would not distinguish between you as a citizen and you as an FEPC official.*

In clarifying the scope of prudent conduct in public affairs, Ross encouraged Castañeda to speak on issues pertaining to the FEPC but to avoid the temptation of partisan slip: "The only safe rule is not to make any public statements which criticize other agencies or which take sides on legislative matters. Does that mean that you cannot continue to explain to the public the work of the Committee? Certainly not. Do so by all means. Our purposes and how we operate offer a wide platform which you have usefully utilized on many occasions. Keep it up—but keep out of the political field!"[30]

Hampered by limited resources, including office personnel, but determined to investigate outrageous incidents of racial discrimination, Carlos selectively assigned his new field examiner, Wilbert Doerfler, to interview complainants and to compile basic information on reported cases. A notorious example of discrimination against Negro workers occurred in Kingsville, Texas, where the Brotherhood of Locomotive Firemen and Enginemen and the Missouri-

Pacific Railroad practiced flagrant forms of exclusion. The investigation focused on two issues: the company's refusal to promote African American workers and to increase their salaries, and the union's adamant policy of ignoring minority members during wage negotiations, based on the flimsy excuse that the Brotherhood did not have a Negro auxiliary. Castañeda informed the FEPC Central Office about the labor problem in Kingsville, a ranching community in south Texas: "Negro Hostler Helpers accumulate no seniority for promotion to Hostlers, who are appointed from Firemen with the required seniority. Hostler Helpers get four cents [an hour] less than Firemen when performing the duties of Hostler Helpers and colored Hostler Helpers are paid straight time for overtime while others are paid time and one-half." [31]

Castañeda and Doerfler then visited the Naval Air Station near Corpus Christi to discuss with the personnel relations officer, Lt. Comdr. A. B. Miller, complaints filed by Negro workers. After interviewing all complainants they met privately with Dr. H. Boyd Hall, president of the area chapter of the National Association for the Advancement of Colored People, regarding the "general situation" at the base. Ranking naval officers "emphatically stated their desire to eliminate all discrimination." In the presence of the FEPC officials the navy team summoned "various foremen and supervisors" to the headquarters building to inform them "that discrimination must cease." Before their departure Castañeda and Doerfler thoroughly investigated and settled each case. [32]

Closer to the regional office in San Antonio the two FEPC officials advised the military how to resolve a touchy problem at Kelly Field. The command headquarters had demonstrated its commitment to the principle of nondiscrimination by promoting a Hispanic, Ernesto Herrera, as unit chief of the clothing and hardware branch in the supply division. Maj. Alec Chesser, personnel relations officer, notified Doerfler that twelve Anglo women "in the department immediately protested their unwillingness to work under a Mexican and threatened to resign." The Army Air Corps officers promptly countered the ploy by advising the women that "it was their privilege to resign if they so desired" but that in their written termination documents they would be compelled to disclose "their refusal to work under a Mexican foreman." Blocked by the officers' "firm stand" on the issue, the women abandoned their protest and returned to work. [33] At Brooke General Hospital, located at Fort Sam Houston, the FEPC officials encountered only minor incidents of discrimination, which they amicably resolved. Prior to their intervention, hiring tradition had customarily relegated Negro workers "to classified labor and custodial jobs." Castañeda proudly reported to Washington: "This pattern has been broken and a precedent established." Even within the regional office Carlos advocated promotion for meritorious employees. In the case of his own secretary, he asked Maslow: "What action has been taken . . . for reclassification of Mrs. Willetta Gutleben to CAF-5?"[34]

Castañeda's residency in San Antonio gave him an opportunity to indulge in matters related to Latin American history. In May the program director of the San Antonio Historical Association invited him to speak at one of its "interesting, well-attended meetings." Carlos enthusiastically agreed to present a paper entitled "The San Antonio River through the Ages."[35] Such occasions genuinely bolstered his morale.

As regional director, Castañeda never allowed the exigencies of financial management to dampen his outlook or disturb his sense of mission. In early June, with a month still remaining in the current fiscal year, Maslow and Theodore A. Jones apprised Carlos that his operating-funds balance had dropped to $133.[36] Of more immediate concern to Castañeda, however, was the survival of the agency in congressional budgetary maneuvers. In San Antonio, Carlos attended a joint meeting of the local Mexican Chamber of Commerce and the League of United Latin American Citizens, involving "50 or 60 representative leaders," to explain the Fair Employment Practice Committee's scope of work and "what it had been able to do in this area to give equal economic opportunities to members of minority groups." The two organizations appointed "a special committee" to monitor "recent development[s]" in the struggle for the FEPC in "the War Agencies Appropriation Bill."[37]

At the end of June, in a clever game of weekend parliamentary jousting, southern Democrats in the House of Representatives blocked an appropriation of $771,000 for the war agencies. FEPC supporters in the U.S. Senate, led by James M. Mead of New York, pledged support from "additional funds" contained in legislation labeled "deficiency bills." Senate Democratic Leader Alben W. Barkley worked out a compromise through an amendment to the multiple "deficiency bills" sponsored by Sen. Dennis Chávez of New Mexico to award the FEPC emergency funding of $466,000.[38] A week later the FEPC's "Southern foes" in the House scored another blow with a devious ploy, a measure that would keep the agency "alive" with a "token" appropriation of "perhaps as much as $200,000 to continue operation." Compared with the agency's original request of $599,000 for the new fiscal year, the "token" action forecast the end of the FEPC.[39] In conference committee, where the budget for war agencies was hammered out, the FEPC received $250,000, which consisted of "just half" of the projected amount needed to operate "in the 12 months beginning July 1."[40]

The cutback in funding immediately precipitated drastic reorganization at regional levels. In the ensuing consolidation the termination of the New Orleans office resulted in the transfer of all "docket cards and cases, active and closed," to Castañeda, whose region now included Louisiana as well as Texas,

New Mexico, Arizona, and Colorado.[41] Speaking in August with the *Daily Texan*, student newspaper at the University of Texas, Castañeda explained that the regional FEPC center in San Antonio would continue functioning "as a governmental reconversion agency," as directed by national headquarters, to ease the transition from wartime to peacetime conditions.[42]

Meanwhile, in July, Eugene C. Barker had recommended to the board of regents a half-time salary for Castañeda of sixteen hundred dollars as associate professor for the academic year 1945–46. Barker's intervention secured a safety net for Carlos in the event his government employment were to be terminated in the middle of the academic year.[43]

During the summer Castañeda honored a request by the former administrator of the defunct New Orleans office to attend a meeting in Fort Worth hosted by the "colored" Young Men's Christian Association. Carlos went to the meeting specifically to confer with leaders of the National Association for the Advancement of Colored People and the Urban League of New Orleans, as well as delegates of the "NAACP of Fort Worth and Dallas, and representatives of the other colored groups interested in minority problems from Temple to San Antonio." He quickly formed a coalition of broad support for the FEPC by organizing the participants "into an advisory committee" to his regional office. Seeking further support, participants invited representatives unable to attend the meeting, such as a delegation from Houston, to join "the Committee soon." [44]

No sooner had he returned from Fort Worth than news of an Allied victory over Japan in the Pacific prompted "minority groups in San Antonio" to wonder how "the end of the war" would affect the FECP. On Thursday, August 16, 1945, Castañeda welcomed to his office a large delegation of "colored" leaders representing the Progressive Voters League, San Antonio Negro Chamber of Commerce, NAACP, Local Council for a Permanent FEPC, Negro Press, Brotherhood of Sleeping Car Porters, National Negro Congress, Peoples Educational Press, and National Alliance for Postal Employees. Castañeda explained to them that the Fair Employment Practice Committee "still had jurisdiction in some instances and would continue to operate until the order [that had created the agency] was suspended." Next he conferred with Hispanic leaders representing the League of United Latin American Citizens, the Mexican Chamber of Commerce, Committee of One Hundred, the Federation for Industrial Education and Protection, the Latin-American Optimist Club, and the League of Loyal American Citizens. These leaders endorsed the principle that the FEPC "should be continued as an essential agency" with adequate funding by Congress.[45]

For Clarence Mitchell, who had succeeded Will Maslow as director of field operations, Carlos drafted a revised scope of work for the FEPC that reflected budget and personnel reduction and the possibility of permanent status. Recent developments, he admitted, required innovative "methods" to conduct the work of the FEPC "efficiently and effectively" under the provisions of Executive Order 9346. His plan advocated "greater cooperation" between intergovernmental agencies, minority group organizations, labor unions, and religious and civic liaisons. Aware of the vital role performed by secretarial staff, he included a section that addressed problems and solutions.

> The secretaries of various regional offices will have to do a much greater and much more important job than heretofore. Much of the routine case correspondence will have to be delegated to the secretary. Office interviews will have, likewise, to be conducted by them in the absence of the regional director. They should be made more thoroughly acquainted with case handling and the writing of Final Disposition Reports. It should be added that because of the greater responsibility that inevitably will fall upon them under the set up made necessary by circumstances, they should be classed as Senior-Clerk-Stenographers, CAF-5. The difference in cost represented by the reclassification of such regional secretaries as are not already CAF-5, is about $15.00 a month, a sum which is far below the actual amount of additional work which they will have to perform and the added responsibility which they must per force assume.[46]

The reduction of FEPC funding forced Castañeda to conduct inquiries about alleged discrimination by mail. In August and September he reviewed grievances against Southwestern Bell Telephone (San Antonio) and the Naval Air Base (Corpus Christi). In New Orleans he dealt with complaints against Higgins Aircraft Company and Todd-Johnson Dry Docks. Among the cases transferred to San Antonio he evaluated the status of complaints filed against Magnolia Petroleum Company and Beaumont Iron Works (Texas) and Colmar Steamship Corporation (Louisiana).[47]

Publicly Castañeda displayed a gallant outlook, planning a visit to New Orleans to discuss the merits of outstanding cases with labor and management officials, and making a whirlwind fact-finding trip to Corpus Christi. Privately, however, he prepared for an imminent transition in career by renewing contacts with civic and professional organizations. On Columbus Day (October 12) he presented "an elaborate program" about the FEPC at a convocation of the Pan-American Optimist Club of San Antonio. A few days later he addressed the Bexar County Teachers Association "at their first annual meeting on October 16."[48]

By the end of October neither Malcolm Ross nor Clarence Mitchell bothered to deny that the FEPC was in steep decline. Nonetheless, they sent Castañeda guidelines for reporting the "best information" available on labor-related issues: "OBVIOUSLY COMPLETE DATA IMPOSSIBLE WITHIN TIME LIMIT BUT [WE] ASSURE YOU PROJECT VALUABLE. BE SURE TO INCLUDE PERTINENT ANECDOTAL MATERIAL."[49] By this time, however, Castañeda knew the difference between useful reporting and busywork. Sadly, in mid-November he announced the closing of the San Antonio office on December 15 "due to lack of funds."[50]

Phasing out the regional office demanded most of his time, but still he managed to accelerate contacts with professional historians. In a letter to a Franciscan scholar affiliated with *The Americas* in Washington, D.C., he relayed his tentative plans "to stay in San Antonio until February 1st and then return to the University."[51] Meanwhile, aware that Castañeda would definitely return to the Austin campus, Milton R. Gutsch reminded interim president Theophilus S. Painter that the history department had recommended an increase in salary for Carlos "from 3200 per nine months to $3400." The new library director, Alexander Moffit, concurred with the arrangements related to Carlos's split appointment, "beginning March 1."[52] Following instructions from FEPC headquarters, at the end of work on December 15 Castañeda and Mrs. Gutleben picked up their few personal belongings, locked the door of the FEPC office on the third floor for the last time, and rode the elevator to the lobby of the New Moore Building from where they walked separately to their parked automobiles. Just prior to closing, a fiscal officer in Washington promised to mail to Castañeda a complete report of taxable income earned during the year."[53] The FEPC, a wartime agency of the Executive Branch of government that tried to protect the dignity of ethnic minority workers, suffered an inglorious demise in peacetime at the hands of opponents in Congress. From the first day to the last, Carlos E. Castañeda served his country honorably as an official of the FECP.

In an essay entitled "Our Personal Relations with Mexicans" Malcolm Ross praised Castañeda's involvement with the President's Committee on Fair Employment Practice:

The FEPC Regional Director for Texas, Dr. Carlos E. Castañeda, came on loan from the University of Texas to whose faculty he has now returned. He is a naturalized citizen, born in Mexico. In the college and capitol town of Austin he walks the streets as free from insults as any man. His complexion happens to be fair. He travels anywhere in the southwest without embarrassment but many of his friends of Spanish descent—lawyers, business men, Mexican consuls have been turned away from public doors. They do not like it. They get mad, write letters, form committees. With one accord they came to its support when Dr. Castañeda opened an FEPC office in Texas.[54]

Just as induction into public service was not without its share of disloca-
tions, returning to the academic community required a settling-down period.
Staying in San Antonio until February soon lost appeal for Castañeda. Shortly
after the new year he returned to the Latin American Collection, without salary, where he gradually retrieved research projects left unfinished because of
the war.[55] One project pertained to the sixth volume of *Our Catholic Heritage
in Texas,* which, although started, had not advanced beyond initial research.
Formally he could not embrace the project until the Texas Historical Commission of the Knights of Columbus reactivated the contract, but he knew this
technicality would eventually be satisfied.

Aware that the Texas Historical Commission had not convened since 1944,
when he had mailed his last progress report, and uncertain about the group's
postwar plans, Carlos undertook to renew old friendships with the Catholic
hierarchy. With the Most Reverend Laurence J. FitzSimon, bishop of Amarillo,
he discovered an affinity in their mutual appreciation of rare history books. To
reinforce his friendship with FitzSimon, Castañeda took advantage of his mid-
week teaching schedule and planned a weekend visit to Amarillo in early May.
Accompanied by Elisa and their daughter Rosemary (age four and a half and
affectionately called Rosita), Carlos arranged his itinerary to arrive in the Panhandle late on a Sunday afternoon. He reserved part of Monday to discuss
books with Bishop FitzSimon. In the course of their visit the topic of the Texas
Historical Commission naturally entered into the discussion. On Monday evening Carlos spoke to the Amarillo Garden Club. The following morning the
Castañeda family left the Panhandle and motored back to Austin.[56] Carlos's
relations with the Catholic hierarchy soon yielded dividends, as revealed in an
enthusiastic message to Bishop FitzSimon: "Thanks for the boost with Archbishop [Edwin V.] Byrne [of Santa Fe]. I am really interested in doing at least
three volumes on the history of the missions in New Mexico and as soon as I
finish the sixth volume of OUR CATHOLIC HERITAGE, I am going to start on
the other job, but I will need financial help and I appreciate . . . your [assis-
tance in] preparing the ground." [57]

That spring Castañeda, reinvigorated by his return to academic life, behaved like a supreme knight commander coordinating battle plans on several
fronts of the North American continent. In early March he decided to decline
the summer school course that Milton Gutsch had reserved for him and accepted instead an appointment with the university's Institute of Latin American Studies to teach at the Cooperative School in Mexico City.[58] With that
situation revolved, and with the matter of the sixth volume firmly appended
to the agenda of the Texas Historical Commission, Carlos launched an overt
campaign to secure a senior-level faculty appointment at Catholic University
of America in Washington, D.C., a position made vacant by the resignation of

Rev. Dr. Francis Borgia Steck, O.F.M. Over the years Castañeda had maintained excellent contacts, personally and professionally, with faculty members at Catholic University, but in this instance the historian who suggested Carlos for the job was Lewis Ulysses Hanke, then director simultaneously of the Hispanic Foundation and the Library of Congress. To Martin R. P. McGuire, dean of the Graduate School of Arts and Sciences at Catholic University, Carlos described his long-range plans: "Naturally, should I move at this time I would want to make a . . . [change] that will be as permanent as it is possible for human beings to be. One of the reasons why I would consider moving to Washington is that I feel it is one of the few places in this country where I would find the type of source material I need to continue my productive work in the history of the Southwest." [59]

As the employment scenario in Washington unfolded, Carlos worked with E. C. Delaney on a children's textbook, *The Lands of Middle America*, an upcoming publication from the Macmillan Company. Writing in a "conversational style," the authors incorporated "the customs, habits, and geography of Mexico and Central America" into a slender volume for primary-school students. Convinced that "the best way to establish better relations with neighboring countries" was to teach children "simple facts" about the people and lands of the region, Carlos included descriptions of Latin American schools and pupils while not overlooking "farm products, eating habits, Indians, and other topics of interest" to small readers. [60]

Liberated from the restraints of government service, Castañeda also sought to promote understanding of Latin America in a May interview with a reporter of the *Daily Texan*. In response to a question of how the "spread of communism" in Latin America posed a threat to U.S. policy "toward those countries," he pointed without hesitation to the exploitation of "materials and labor" by American investors and their payment of "very low prices and wages there." He explained, "It is all right to develop resources of the Latin-American countries, but give them a square deal." Otherwise, he cautioned, wanton exploitation would lead to an escalation of tension, because "a hungry man listens with an open mind to communist propaganda." His perceptions honed by years of study, Castañeda assessed U.S. policy in the hemisphere: "Latin-America has been too weak to be anything but a good neighbor to the United States. The people feel that the Inter-American Policy of the United States is going to be used as a screen for economic imperialism, under the guise of a good neighbor, to exploit their resources and laboring capital." [61]

Seemingly in one season Castañeda overcompensated for what he had neglected during wartime. In *Texas Geographic Magazine* he published an article "concerning little-known attempts to colonize the Lower Rio Grande Valley." His essay focused on initiatives by Francisco de Garay, governor of Jamaica and a contemporary of Hernán Cortés, to establish a community at the mouth of the Rio Grande. If Garay had succeeded, Carlos avowed, it would have become "the oldest permanent settlement in the United States."[62]

In June, Castañeda traveled to San Antonio for the first meeting in two years of the Texas Historical Commission.[63] The chairman, Reverend James P. Gibbons, C.S.C., opened the session with an introduction of the membership, including two newcomers—Monsignors Anton J. Frank of Houston and William H. Oberste of the Diocese of Corpus Christi—who subsequently played vital roles in editing for publication the final volumes of *Our Catholic Heritage*. After calling for and listening to a number of detailed reports that took up most of the morning, the chairman finally recognized the historiographers, Castañeda and Father Raymond Clancy, C.S.C. Coincidental with Castañeda's entry into government work, the commission had hired Reverend Clancy to write the seventh and concluding volume. Carlos, who spoke first, delivered an uncharacteristically brief report. He advised the group: "I have no written report with me. At the present time I would say that since 1943 I have been unable to do much work on the sixth volume. I have done a considerable amount of [collateral] reading. I have more time now that I'm through with my [government] assignment. I have outlined the volume and already completed the third chapter and have all the materials to complete the work by the end of this year. The volume is called 'The Struggle for Freedom.' "[64] Next Father Clancy delivered a lengthy, at times ecclesiastically technical, report describing his volume's chronological and geographical scope, as he envisioned it. The cleric shocked longtime members of the Historical Commission with his disclosure that he had compiled more "than sufficient" research data for his single volume "to be concluded with the year 1897." Since Knights of Columbus councils all over Texas would be expected to support the project, as they had loyally done in the past, the prospect of underwriting more than two additional volumes greatly disturbed veteran members of the advisory group. In related matters, besides deciding to preserve at Saint Edward's University the research materials Castañeda and others had compiled since the early 1930s, the group agreed to name the collection the Catholic Archives of Texas.[65]

Chairman Gibbons informed the commission that Castañeda, "in view of the rising costs of living," had requested an increase in compensation for work on the sixth volume "from $2.00 to $2.50 per page" from number 100 to the end of the volume. After minimum discussion the members approved the request.[66]

Meanwhile, at Catholic University of America, Monsignor Patrick Joseph McCormick, rector of the school, conferred with Dean McGuire and Rev.

Dr. Aloysius K. Ziegler, head of the history department, on the substance of an offer to make to Castañeda. "I am pleased," wrote McCormick on June 20, "to offer you an appointment in the Department of History with the rank of Full Professor, effective at the beginning of the scholastic year 1946–1947." While the generous offer included a salary of forty-five hundred dollars for nine months, the rector candidly informed Castañeda that final approval rested with the university's board of trustees, who would not convene until November. Therefore, if Carlos accepted the tentative offer, he would begin as associate professor at forty-five hundred dollars, until the faculty senate formally recommended to the board of trustees his advancement to the rank of professor. To eliminate any doubt in Castañeda's mind about the sincerity of the offer, the monsignor reassured him that "from inquiries I have made, . . . the Senate will vote its approval of your appointment." [67]

On the verge of leaving for Mexico, Castañeda mulled over the tantalizing offer for nearly a week. To be sure, he discussed the matter with Elisa and possibly Eugene C. Barker. Entering into his deliberations was the fact that Father Clancy had resigned from the *Catholic Heritage* project. After devoting three years to the task of "gathering materials, translating many of these records from French, German, Czech, Polish, and Latin, and comparing secondary sources with the originals," declining health and other circumstances forced the priest to accept the reality that he was incapable of condensing the data into a single volume. Thus, Castañeda faced the prospect of writing the seventh volume, which Archbishop Robert E. Lucey, as the senior prelate of the Historical Commission, viewed as the concluding tome.[68] These commitments, the upcoming trip to Mexico, and the job offer from Washington presented Castañeda with a dilemma. Wanting neither to reject nor accept "a tentative offer" and inclined to complete his current obligations, Carlos suggested postponing the reporting date until February of the following year. He explained to McCormick the rationale for his request: "I would not like to disregard the obligation I have contracted with the hierarchy of Texas and the K of C Historical Commission in connection with this work. Were it possible to give me the appointment offered effective as of February 1st, I will be pleased and honored to accept." [69] Aside from creating a comfortable breathing space, the delay gave Castañeda a bargaining chip to use in future negotiations.

In the meantime the Mexico City project, with its various American components, proceeded on schedule. On July 1 the University of Texas delegation joined James B. Griffin (University of Michigan) and James F. King and Herbert E. Bolton (University of California at Berkeley) in the collaborative enterprise advertised as Summer School for Foreign Students, in affiliation with the National Autonomous University of Mexico. The program extended from July 1 until August 14, 1946,[70] and drew an enrollment of 1,063 students, some Mexican and "the great majority" from the United States. Among the courses offered, Bolton taught his mainstay attractions (history of the Americas and a seminar on the northward expansion of New Spain), while Charles W. Hackett reserved for his domain a course on South America since independence and a seminar on modern Latin America. Carlos developed two new courses dealing with the foreign policy of the United States in Latin America.[71]

Midway through the session Monsignor McCormick's response finally reached Castañeda, advising him it was "agreeable" to the administration of Catholic University to make the "appointment effective as of February 1, 1947."[72] Delighted with the news, Carlos informed Hackett, who in turn assuredly notified senior members of the history department at the University of Texas. For the time being there was nothing either professor could do but to wait for further developments. During this time Castañeda evaluated several collections of rare books for the Latin American library or any other institution interested in acquiring them, claiming afterward that he had been "busier than a bee in mid summer." One library that he assessed belonged to Basave Negrete del Castillo, an octogenarian bibliophile who was willing and anxious to sell. Hoping to find a buyer for "the old man," Castañeda contacted Father Roderick Wheeler, director of the Academy of American Franciscan History, now located in Potomac, Maryland, near Washington, D.C. Indicative of the extent of the collection, he offered to microfilm for Wheeler the two-volume catalog (over eight hundred single-spaced pages) for a nominal sum of "about 20 or 25 dollars." Looking ahead to teaching at Catholic University, he told the Franciscan that he would leave his family in Austin until he could rent living quarters in Washington. Cautious about expenses, Carlos sounded out Wheeler: "I am counting on your hospitality to house me while I am looking around for a place."[73]

While not teaching classes, evaluating collections, or participating in extracurricular activities with students and colleagues, Castañeda delighted in the fact that Elisa and his daughters had accompanied him to Mexico. In addition, Raymond Estep, a graduate student who had returned to the University of Texas to complete doctoral studies, had enrolled in the summer institute, and occasionally he and his bride joined the Castañedas for dinner. Older than most of the other students in the program, Estep enjoyed a special relationship with Don Carlos that predated the war years.[74]

Not surprisingly, Castañeda took advantage of this time in Mexico to maintain a rigorous schedule in the archives. According to Estep: "every time you'd see him he was just charging . . . he drove that way, he walked that way; he was just a man perpetually in motion except when he was sitting down working. But he was a tremendously fast worker, and I suspect . . . [he was]

one of the few people in that period who could have handled all of the manuscript material as well as he did because he was so at-home in the language.
Anyway, it takes a while to get acquainted with manuscript Spanish 400 years
old, [or even] 300 years old." [75]

Before the session ended, the University of Texas, pressured by a real possibility of losing Castañeda, countered with "a similar appointment" and comparable salary.[76] Elated with the decision, Carlos hurriedly informed Bolton
"that he had been approved as a full professor at the University." The eminent
historian looked him directly in the eye and said: "They should have done it
a long time ago." [77] Carlos revealed a glimpse of the fraternal bond that developed that summer when he expressed gratitude shortly after for "anything
you can do in the way of saying a good word for your adopted 'boy,' who has
always regretted not being one of your boys by rights." Castañeda also re-
affirmed the boost in morale he had derived from Bolton's presence at the summer school: "It was certainly a real pleasure and an inspiration to have worked
with you . . . in Mexico." [78]

After the summer session ended, Castañeda stayed in Mexico for at least
another week to rummage through dusty *librerías* in search of rare books and
documents for Bishop FitzSimon. Homeward-bound, he stopped in Laredo to
discuss career moves with a longtime friend, Bishop Mariano Garriga. Back
in Austin, Carlos considered the benefits and disadvantages of his decision to
remain at the University of Texas. An obvious drawback was that the salary
adjustment was three hundred dollars "less than at Washington." However,
owning a modest home on West Thirty-seventh Street outweighed "the high
cost of living in Washington and the housing situation," which, by some standards, seemed "worse" than in Austin.[79] Then, too, the recent promotion to
professor signified that the board of regents had finally recognized his value to
the campus community. On Labor Day he dispatched an apologetic letter to
Monsignor McCormick: "I had been hesitant to accept your generous offer
outright because of the high cost of living in Washington, particularly as regards rents. In view of the changed conditions, the fact that I own my home
in Austin, and that it will be much more convenient for the writing of the
last two volumes of OUR CATHOLIC HERITAGE IN TEXAS to remain here, I
thank you for the honor so kindly done [to] me and with deep regret find myself unable to accept it." [80]

At the start of the new academic year in September, Castañeda performed
a few housekeeping chores on campus. First, he moved out of the Latin American Library, satisfied that Nettie Lee Benson, his "assistant since 1942," had
been appointed to succeed him.[81] Next, as a full-time member of the history
faculty but unable to relocate in Garrison Hall for lack of space, he reluctantly
accepted the library director's assignment of Office 2501 (instead of his old

2601) in the Tower. Jack A. Dabbs, who was familiar with the facilities, described Castañeda's transfer: "He had moved back most of the same furnishings that he had had years before, the pictures, horn-bird, books, typing table, and the closet of odds and ends. For all practical purposes it was the same office."[82] Before the end of September, Carlos received the sad news from New York concerning the death of a longtime friend, Rev. J. Elliot Ross, C.S.P.[83] No doubt the obituary caused him to reflect pensively on the number of times Father Ross's presence—in Austin, San Antonio, and Williamsburg—had enriched his own life. Freed from the burdens of the library, Carlos in November joyfully celebrated his patron saint's feast day and his own half-centennial milestone.[84]

Fully enjoying the privileges of professorship, Carlos began the new year by planning a specialized course on "the Spanish colonial system."[85] For mundane tasks such as typing rough drafts of manuscripts, compiling bibliographic lists for courses, and other clerical work he welcomed the assistance of Fritz K. Knust, a graduate student who received a stipend of $153.60 for the spring semester.[86] In between classes Carlos reviewed materials for an April lecture tour in Louisiana organized by Ursuline College in observation of Pan American Week. Under the general theme of "The Culture of Spanish America," he planned ten lectures, most of which he extracted from his essays published as Preliminary Studies of the Texas Catholic Historical Society.[87] The series began on Sunday, April 13, "with a radio broadcast from New Orleans." Castañeda contributed his share to the success of the conference. On Monday he traveled northwest to speak at Louisiana State at Baton Rouge. The next day he retraced his route to deliver an evening lecture at Ursuline College in New Orleans. On Wednesday he returned to Baton Rouge to address an audience at the Catholic Youth Center. Finally, he concluded his marathon on Thursday at Xavier University in New Orleans.[88]

During the spring Castañeda finally found a buyer for an unsold set of sixty-seven volumes of the Matamoros Archives that he had photocopied in 1928. Bishop FitzSimon of Amarillo offered to acquire the set of documents, made even more valuable after nearly twenty years by the fact that "a severe rainstorm" in 1932 had irreparably damaged the originals. The prelate mailed Carlos a down payment of two hundred dollars and agreed to pay the balance of eight hundred dollars in installments spread out over a five-year period. Since FitzSimon did not have a climate-controlled depository in which to store the collection, Castañeda arranged with the academic dean of Our Lady of the Lake College in San Antonio for the library to continue holding the set until another repository became available.[89] The dean, Mother Angelique Ayres, confirmed the essence of the curatorship: "Since we could not buy the Matamoros photostats, I am very happy that you are going to Bishop Fitz-

Simon. I understand that he is specializing in Texas History and very much hope he will be able to get back to the State the splendid collection that Father [Paul J.] Foik made and sent to Notre Dame. We are happy to house the material as long as His Excellency wishes us to do so. We shall have [a] fire proof room for it in the new library." [90]

Bishop FitzSimon's acquisition of Texana materials stemmed from a deep personal interest in the subject. What the prelate envisioned was a future research center built around the bulk of the Catholic Archives of Texas. He also reactivated the Texas Catholic Historical Society, which received incorporated status by the Texas bishops in April, 1947. Castañeda met periodically with FitzSimon in Austin and San Antonio to discuss drafts of the constitution and bylaws for the group and to offer "such suggestions as may occur to me." [91]

Comfortably ensconced in the university community as a full professor, enjoying the company of scholars and Latin American historians, Castañeda never deceived himself into believing that secular evils in national life were not his responsibility. When Robert K. Carr, executive secretary of President Truman's Committee on Civil Rights, asked him in late April to submit "a *confidential* statement on the subject," [92] Carlos responded promptly with a lengthy commentary that combined reason, passion, purpose, and resolution. His cover letter succinctly summarized the issue:

> More than twenty years of work in behalf of the Latin American in the Southwest has convinced me that at the base of the various forms of discrimination suffered by them in the political, social, economic, and educational fields, lies the economic. This is, in my humble opinion, the real root of the evil.
>
> Refusal to give the Latin American citizen equal opportunities for employment and advancement, and the denial of the same wage for the same type of work to members of this group have condemned this segment of our population to a substandard level of living that forms the basis for all other forms of discrimination by which the economic exploitation itself is justified.
>
> Briefly, the Mexican, be [he] an American citizen or not, is generally refused employment except in certain types [of] undesirable unskilled jobs. Furthermore once employed, he is refused advancement, . . . regardless of his ability. Thus his income is restricted and held below that of the average citizen. As a result, he and his family are forced to live in homes that lack every comfort and sanitary devices, they are ill dressed, ill cared for, and ill fed. They are unable to keep their children in school. Consequently their physical appearance and their education are substandard. The community concluded that in a country of equal opportunities a group that remains in

this condition is considered inferior, and, consequently, an inferior wage and inferior field of advancement are justified.[93]

Castañeda used the FEPC as a model for eliminating artificial economic barriers. His remarks on the plight of farm workers in his native Lower Rio Grande Valley, however, led to the introduction of a completely new concept, a remedy never before discussed by the FEPC. He began with a reference to the controversial Bracero program, a binational arrangement inaugurated in 1942 during the administrations of Franklin D. Roosevelt and Manuel Ávila Camacho, which permitted the entry of Mexican farm laborers into the United States to work in agricultural fields in the Southwest. When the global conflict ended in 1945, the Bracero program continued. Postwar Mexican laborers began to migrate far north from the Lower Rio Grande Valley and other border regions to harvest crops in the states of Indiana, Michigan, Minnesota, and Wisconsin.[94]

Castañeda identified the flaw in the current situation: "There is no federal or state law setting a minimum agricultural wage."[95] Carlos condemned the effect that low-wage practices had imposed upon society in the absence of such legislation.

The Mexican American in Texas is now taking to the roads in dilapidated cars, going to California, to Michigan, to Colorado as migrant labor[ers] to secure temporary relief and earn a decent wage. But at the same time he is increasing the housing, the school, the feeding problems of the areas into which he is forced to live in search of a living wage. When winter comes and seasonal employment is over, many of them will return to their former homes with little or nothing left; while many others will remain in the fields to become public charges of the communities [that] lured them by a wage which in itself is low, but which compared to Texas wages appears a princely one.[96]

Extolling the patriotism of Mexican Americans, Castañeda argued their right to just and equitable treatment.

When it is recalled that over three-quarters of a million young men from the Southwest fought and bled, suffered and died for the maintenance of democracy in the recent holocaust just past, [that] in proportion to the number of men in the armed forces there were more Latin Americans who received the Congressional Medal of Honor, and that these people have a deep and abiding faith in democracy, the situation becomes tragic, a real travesty on de-

*mocracy. These citizens, like all others, have an inalienable right to the en-
joyment of equal rights and opportunities to improve their standard of living and to better enjoy life.*[97]

In May, Castañeda traveled to San Antonio for another session of the Texas
Historical Commission, convened on the beautiful campus of Incarnate Word
College. No one who scanned the lengthy agenda speculated on the possibility of a short meeting. The senior members, led by Bishop FitzSimon, devoted
ample discussion to the sensitive issue of separating the Texas Catholic Historical Society, a creation of the Knights of Columbus Texas Historical Commission, from the parent organization. Another topic that consumed a considerable amount of time pertained to clarifying ambiguities in an old formal
agreement between the Historical Commission and Saint Edward's University
regarding the disposition of the Catholic Archives of Texas. Once again, with
clarifications, the members retained the current arrangement with Saint Edward's as a temporary expedient. They also entertained plans for an aggressive marketing campaign outlined by Von Boeckmann-Jones, the publisher, to
sell current inventories of the five volumes of *Our Catholic Heritage* to university and public libraries but deferred action on a recommendation to print
a condensed edition for secondary schools.[98]

In between other issues Castañeda presented a straightforward progress
report on his work with the sixth volume: "The historiographer is glad . . .
that considerable progress has been made. Up to the present time seven chapters have been completed, turned over to the Chairman [Father Gibbons], approved and put in final form ready for the printer. It is hoped that by the end
of the summer the remaining third of the volume will be completed and that
it can be turned over to the publishers. Frequent conferences have been held
with the Chairman and with other persons in regard to the general organization and the presentation of the many subjects discussed."[99] The report signified that nearly eighteen months after returning to the academy Castañeda
had finally rediscovered the elements of a harmonious working relationship
with Father Gibbons. Looking ahead with trepidation to the final volume,
owing to the complexity of the format and a slight concern about Gibbons's
health, Castañeda cautiously informed the group of his preparations for the
next challenge: "While working on this volume, the historiographer has spent
some time examining and arranging the materials turned over to him for the
seventh volume. This preliminary examination has revealed that there is a considerable amount of data which needs to be assembled before writing can be
started. In the fall the historiographer will call on the different diocesan historians for help. It is to be expected that they will give their generous cooperation, which will be of vital importance to the completion of the last volume

of this history." [100] A week after the meeting Castañeda evaluated the results: "Much was accomplished in an atmosphere that was far different from that . . . meeting last year." Part of the success derived from the ambiance of a college campus (as opposed to an archiepiscopal chancery), but most of the productivity stemmed from two important decisions and the cooperative manner in which they emerged: uncoupling the Texas Catholic Historical Society from the apparatus of the administrative unit, and defining a "satisfactory arrangement" for the preservation of the Catholic Archives of Texas. From Castañeda's perspective the latter decision was critical: "Until the seventh volume is completed, . . . it would be best to keep the archives at St. Edward's." [101]

Out of the sessions of the Texas Historical Commission, Bishop FitzSimon and Castañeda forged a strong friendship reminiscent of an earlier relationship between the historian and the group's first chairman, Father Foik. Carlos derived great personal satisfaction in assisting the prelate assemble a worthwhile Texana library. He wrote to FitzSimon: "I take a certain amount of pride and I am happy to know that I have helped you secure a few choice items for your collection. That is exactly the way I feel about the matter. Your deep and sincere interest in the history of Texas, a field to which I have dedicated so many years of my life, finds a vibrant cord in my heart." [102]

Castañeda devoted the first part of the summer to drafting and revising passages for the sixth volume of *Our Catholic Heritage*. After the Fourth of July holiday the writing decelerated because he found himself "definitely tied down until the end of August with my teaching in the second term." In between classes, whenever he struggled with writing, the heat and humidity absolutely drained his creative energy. "The heat has been no worse than in the past," he told Bishop FitzSimon, "but it is no laughing matter. To speak of it makes perspiration trickle down my warm brow." [103]

Occasionally Carlos fantasized about an elusive dream, a long summer vacation with the family in a temperate climate. Whatever "spare time" he found, however, he invested in "the sixth volume," which he desperately wanted "to finish as soon as possible." As he admitted to the bishop of Amarillo, the task that loomed behind the sixth volume fairly nauseated him: "The thought of having to start at once on the seventh [volume] is positively sickening. Maybe when the weather gets cooler in the fall I may feel better about it. There are so many other things I want to do, which I have had to put off year after year, that it will be the greatest relief to get the job completed. Here is hoping that all my pep will not be gone by that time." [104]

In mid-August, although far from finished with volume 6, Castañeda found solace in an invitation from Vito Alessio Robles to participate in a history conference in September amid the lofty, arid atmosphere of Chihuahua. The theme of his original essay for the eighth "annual meeting of the Mexican Congress of History" focused "on the Court of Inquiry instituted by order of the Secretary of War [William L. Marcy] of the United States in regard to the use of secret service money for the Purchase of Peace" in association with the military operations of Gen. Winfield Scott "and his march from Puebla to Mexico City." [105] President Painter "designated" Carlos as the university's official representative at the conference.[106]

With all arrangements for the Chihuahua meeting finalized before the end of August, Castañeda left Austin right after summer school for a fast-paced Labor Day vacation with his sisters in Brownsville. When he returned home he hastily inserted a few cosmetic revisions in his essay, the scope of which he refined to "the relations of Scott and Santa Anna" prior to the capture of Mexico City. Completing such revisions meant that Carlos had to reshuffle his work schedule. Candidly he admitted that the sixth volume had "been sort of trailing water during the summer." To some extent Father Gibbons's serious illness with stomach ulcers also contributed to the delay. However, as Castañeda promised Bishop FitzSimon, his champion with the Texas Historical Commission, he would "get to work on [the volume] and really get it finished" as soon as he returned "from Mexico the last week" in September.[107]

After his trip to Chihuahua, Castañeda devoted the remainder of the year to tidying up unfinished tasks. A senior member of the history faculty, he continued to work at an exhausting pace. And although his two outstanding commitments for completing *Our Catholic Heritage in Texas* began to feel like millstones around his neck, still he persevered magnificently.

Aɹcendancy to the Summit, 1948–50

In the spring of 1948 Carlos received an invitation, tangentially related to his scholarship, to participate in an episcopal installation of great significance to the region in which he lived and worked.[1] The year before, in response to re-peated recommendations from the Catholic hierarchy in Texas, the Vatican had formally erected the Diocese of Austin, an area of 22,180 square miles that embraced the territory of twenty-five counties, most of which were located north of the Colorado River. Following this decision the Holy See announced the appointment of the Most Reverend Louis J. Reicher as the first bishop of Austin.[2] As details of the consecration ceremony were finalized, the local arrangements committee invited Carlos E. Castañeda of Austin, Robert H. Kelley of Houston, and John Baca of Granger to serve as honor guards to the bishop-designate. In Galveston's historic, century-old Saint Mary's Cathe-dral on Monday, April 14, Castañeda and his fraternal friends, attired in dash-ing regalia as knights of the Equestrian Order of the Holy Sepulchre of Jeru-salem, solemnly escorted the new prelate to the main altar for the consecration rites. Given his busy schedule, Carlos likely skipped the public reception at the Gálvez Hotel in order to return to his classes in Austin.[3]

The following month the Catholic clergy around Austin executed plans for an elaborate installation ceremony for Bishop Reicher.[4] On Thursday, May 13, dressed again in his elegant regalia, Carlos joined three other papal knights in a "colorful and liturgical procession" at the recently designated Saint Mary's Cathedral of Austin.[5]

Bishop Reicher's consecration and installation served as pleasant interludes in a whirl of professional activity. In April, Castañeda hurriedly drove south to San Antonio to the campus of Our Lady of the Lake College to receive, among several honorees, a citation recognizing his contributions to Texas and Latin American history. This tribute may have helped offset the disappointment of missing the annual meeting of the Mississippi Valley Historical Association, where Castañeda had been asked to preside over the newly restored session on

Latin America. Although Carlos had already made plans to attend, in the end the pressure of campus responsibilities prevented both him and Charles W. Hackett from making the trip.[6] Castañeda soon immersed himself in a new task related to the *Catholic Heritage* project. Until a more permanent depository could be secured, Bishop Laurence A. FitzSimon of Amarillo had agreed to serve as curator of the research material collected for the study. Before shipping the collection to Amarillo, Castañeda prepared an inventory of the photostatic documents and other material. To assist in compiling the inventory he secured the clerical services of Margaret Stoner McLean, wife of a former student, Malcolm D. McLean. Highly pleased with the quality of Mrs. McLean's work, Carlos apprised Bishop FitzSimon that she had "considerable experience in bibliography" and was "a fast, intelligent, and thorough worker."[7] By early June, sometimes in stifling heat, he and Margaret McLean had meticulously arranged a multitude of inventory cards for microfilming as a backup reference. When every conceivable detail had been ironed out, Carlos advised Bishop FitzSimon to anticipate delivery of several storage boxes of archival materials.[8]

Castañeda's normal round of duties and projects stopped abruptly in late May when he received a distressing telephone call from Brownsville advising him that his brother Fernando in Matamoros "was very sick." In typical fashion he drove frantically to Brownsville to console family members about Fernando's declining condition. Across the river in Matamoros the patient gallantly lingered for three days before "his heart finally gave way and he died" on Thursday, May 27.[9] Right after the funeral Carlos returned to Austin, where a heavy schedule at the university numbed his grief.

During June and July, Castañeda finished the last chapters of the sixth volume of *Our Catholic Heritage*. After the Fourth of July he began teaching in the second summer session. In early August he drove down to San Antonio for a whirlwind visit with Bishop FitzSimon to discuss conceptual approaches for the last volume of the series. Back in Austin he conferred with Rev. James P. Gibbons, chairman of the Texas Historical Commission of the Knights of Columbus, about the work completed and the projected seventh volume. With Gibbons about to depart on vacation, Carlos made his own plans for a two-week excursion with the family to Amarillo, where he could link pleasure with work in the bishop's private library. Accordingly, he asked his friend the prelate to reserve "a small cottage, or cabin, or something for myself and family (wife and two daughters, one 15 and one 7) for two weeks around August 28 or 29 to September 13 or 14."[10]

As the end of summer school neared, Castañeda juggled his itinerary to accommodate a side trip to visit his sisters in Brownsville. Hence, he wrote FitzSimon not to expect their arrival until the first or second day in September.[11]

Meanwhile, in San Antonio longtime friends associated with La Liga Pro Defensa Escolar (The School Improvement League), primarily Eleuterio Escobar, invited Castañeda to be master of ceremonies at an evening rally on the last day of August to protest substandard classroom facilities in the barrios of the west side of the city. Aware that Escobar's colleagues needed his presence to enhance the prominence of the rally, Carlos agreed to speak but declined the role of master of ceremonies.[12] Using the medium of La Prensa, an influential Spanish-language newspaper, the league's leaders publicized Castañeda's upcoming participation and invited the public to attend the rally in "the patios" of Sidney Lanier High School on the evening of Tuesday, August 31.[13]

When Castañeda and his family arrived on the school campus, the size of the neighborhood audience, estimated at "more than 3,000 West Side residents," simultaneously surprised him and inspired his oratorical talents. Casting aside formalities, he began with a ringing denunciation of the condition of "Latin-American schools throughout Texas" and praised the School Improvement League's efforts in waging "a battle for better classroom facilities in the West Side." Encouraged by the emotional response of the crowd, which had come to hear a fighting speech, Carlos lambasted administrators who had allowed the inferiority of the west-side facilities to continue in "violation of the state school law." Reminding the audience that fifteen years earlier he had assisted Eleuterio Escobar in conducting a survey of the San Antonio schools, he concluded that "West Side school conditions are as bad today as they were then, if not worse." Castañeda also questioned delays in implementing improvements for the west-side schools when "new projects" had recently been approved and initiated "in three other sections of the city where classrooms" had been maintained "up to the standard."[14]

Castañeda's fiery speech unleashed a storm of criticism against the leadership of the San Antonio Independent School District. The president of the board of trustees, Harry H. Rogers, immediately "rapped" Castañeda's comments as "unreasonable and unfair," avowing that the facts proved the administration's equitable treatment of schools throughout the district: "I have headed the school board for only two years, but I am certain conditions are not as bad as they were 15 years ago. . . . Dr. Castañeda did not have factual information. He probably received his information from hearsay."[15] Rogers's defense of school policy convinced only the partisans of the board's majority. A local newspaper assessed Carlos's attack as "a sharp, well-founded indictment" of the entire public school system of Texas while focusing on "the San Antonio situation." Delving into the specific charges Carlos had leveled, the newspaper investigated conditions at some of the schools, after which it released a list of categories where improvement was desperately needed. Besides buildings, the most obvious item, the list included "equipment, lighting, sanitation, playgrounds, fire proofing, and fire-escapes." Noting that educational facilities in 1948 carried "a far heavier pupil-load" than in 1933, the paper conceded that "because of depression and war" the school district had fallen "some 15 years behind" with its construction program. In a lengthy editorial the newspaper endorsed Castañeda's arguments and counseled the school district to eliminate virtual "fire-traps" in the west-side neighborhoods.[16] Since he had started on his vacation trip to the Panhandle right after the rally, Castañeda remained unaware for a time of the impact his speech had achieved.[17] Two years later San Antonio taxpayers approved a $9.3 million bond issue for school construction.[18]

After spending at least ten days in the temperate climate of the plains around Amarillo, Carlos and his family returned to Austin for the beginning of the fall term. Anxious to complete *Our Catholic Heritage,* he persuaded Father Gibbons not to teach courses for personnel at Seton Hospital in order to have "more time" to work with him on the seventh volume and to guide "the sixth through the press."[19]

Since the topics of the seventh volume were not themes with which he was intimately familiar, Castañeda opted for new approaches to gather the data he needed, which partly explained his frequent consultations with the bishop of Amarillo. To cope with the additional research demands Castañeda sought the assistance of a graduate student. The history department assigned Valdemar Rodríguez, who had earlier applied for a teaching fellowship. Unhappy with the research assignment, which he found "sort of dull," Rodríguez was nevertheless willing to perform the required tasks to Carlos's satisfaction.[20] Notwithstanding Rodríguez's contributions to the research enterprise, publication of the sixth volume stalled in the autumn due, in part, to the death of Father Gibbons's sister in Chicago. The chairman's absence from Austin delayed the editing process indefinitely. Even so, Carlos maintained an optimistic outlook on the situation. "The sixth volume is finished," he wrote FitzSimon, "and will finally go to press as soon as he returns."[21] In the interim, to assist Castañeda in refining the conceptual design of the final volume, Bishop FitzSimon invited him "to come to San Antonio" during the Columbus Day observance, when the prelate would be making another brisk visit to Incarnate Word College.[22]

During the fall Castañeda cultivated a friendship with a promising artist in El Paso, José Cisneros, whose exquisite pen-and-ink drawings of southwestern life he genuinely appreciated. Carlos agreed with Carl Hertzog, eminent printer and book designer at Texas Western College in El Paso, that Cisneros was a "talented" artist who would achieve great merit. When the opportunity arose, he persuaded the artist to provide illustrations for the sixth volume of *Our Catholic Heritage in Texas.*[23] No matter how heavy his work schedule, Carlos in the prime of life seldom missed an opportune moment for salutary diversion. Among the speaking invitations he accepted was one to lecture in November in Monterrey, Nuevo León. Temporarily hampered by his automobile not being in good operating condition, he invited a student who owned a heavy "car that could negotiate the highway" to accompany him. Early the next morning Castañeda and Joe W. Neal left Austin and journeyed toward Laredo, where they crossed into Mexico. In midafternoon they arrived at Hotel Monterrey, where Carlos telephoned his "contact" to get information about the program. That evening they attended a reception in Carlos's honor at the home of Dr. Roberto Guajardo, president of the Instituto Tecnológico de Estudios Superiores de Monterrey. Years later Neal rated the social event as "one of the finest parties" he had attended "in Mexico before or since." The Instituto Tecnológico, he surmised, had pulled "out the red carpet for Don Carlos." The next evening Castañeda delivered his lecture there before "an audience of 30 people." Although he gave a sterling performance, commensurate with his reputation, privately "he felt he had wasted his time in coming so far for such a small group." Neal described the celebration that occurred later in a fashionable café: "After the lecture, we were taken to the north [section] of town for *cabrito* [roasted goat meat]. We were treated with all shapes and forms of *cabrito* by a man who had been to the lecture. The evening, along with *cerveza* [beer] went on until about midnight. We had made it clear that we were driving home that night but they insisted on providing more refreshment and entertainment." [24] In the early-morning hours, as they drove toward the border, Neal asked Castañeda who their gracious host had been, to which Carlos candidly replied: "I haven't the slightest idea." The response momentarily startled the student, who recalled that Don Carlos and the host "had acted like the best of friends for the entire evening." Much later, in thoughtful reflection, Neal offered an insightful observation: "This is an illustration of how he never met a stranger and was affable to everyone." [25]

Looking ahead to the next year, Castañeda asked Gutsch, the department chairman, to consider him for a teaching assignment in the 1949 summer school. Gutsch obliged by submitting a proposal to the budget council that included $850 for Carlos, a figure that represented about 16.5 percent of his regular salary of $5,000. [26]

Castañeda began the new year as he had concluded the old one, with a parcel of unfinished tasks. Although sometime during the years of government service he had discerned at least an early warning of possible heart trouble, he discarded caution and continued with his frenetic work schedule. In February, 1949, he experienced a sudden discomfort that temporarily stunned him. Attributing the episode to probable indigestion, Carlos refused to discuss the medical flare-up with anyone outside the immediate family except the Reverend Dr. Francis B. Steck, O.F.M., now at Quincy College in Illinois. He told

Steck: "I got a bit careless the last two weeks and walked like a hurricane and ate a bit more than I should and yesterday I got a slight attack, that is a severe sharp pain that almost knocked me out. Felt uncomfortable most of the afternoon, but I am feeling fine again today. Just cut out eating and walked a little slower. I have to be careful about heavy meals, definitely; and I must not rush like a whirlwind when I start down the street." [27] Quietly concerned about his health but unwilling to introduce major changes in his lifestyle, Carlos asked a simple favor of his Franciscan friend: "Say a prayer for me now and then that the Lord . . . [will allow] me a little longer to finish two or three things I have on hand right now." [28] Not surprisingly, his "two or three things" covered a wide range of commitments. Archbishop Robert E. Lucey, for example, invited him to write "a brief sketch" to be included in a "Jubilee publication" being planned by the Archdiocese of San Antonio. Without the slightest hesitation he "agreed to do it." Next he began drafting the first chapter of volume 7 of *Our Catholic Heritage,* which he assessed as "coming along fine." In between tasks he dabbled in sales and exchanges of rare history books, an avocation that he hoped would result in modest supplemental income for the family. During this time he also compiled a curriculum profile listing his "works, honors, etc.," which he dispatched to Bishop FitzSimon to use with discretion for a possible "appointment to the Vatican Academy of Rome." [29] At the moment his plans did not include research in the Vatican Archives, but undoubtedly he calculated that such an appointment would be helpful intellectually and recreationally. Keenly aware of the pressures impinging upon his spare time, Carlos turned to his episcopal friend in Amarillo for sympathetic understanding: "If I can just keep up with the various and sundry activities in which I am engaged and live through it, I'll be able to breathe easier by the time fall comes." His calendar of "sundry activities" now included an essay for the inaugural of an Augustinian college near Philadelphia and preparations for "a special international congress in Argentina," tentatively scheduled to take place between March 30 and April 10.[30]

Now a scholar of international renown, Castañeda received in February, 1949, from the University of Cuyo in Mendoza, in western Argentina near the Andes, an invitation to attend the First National Congress in Philosophy as the "official delegate" of the University of Texas. Carlos notified Bishop Fitz-Simon that the sponsors of the congress would "pay all expenses, and I will have to fly both ways." A week later he wrote, "If you have any friends in Argentina you wish to be remembered to, let me know." [31]

In the meantime the Vatican announced the appointment of the Most Reverend Mariano S. Garriga as successor bishop of Corpus Christi. Castañeda and Father Gibbons hastily made plans to attend the episcopal installation. Although such events were no longer a novelty for him, Carlos especially enjoyed the "enthronement" ceremony, mainly because his friendship with Bishop Garriga paralleled his association with *Our Catholic Heritage in Texas.*[32] Upon his return from Corpus Christi, José Cisneros surprised him with a delicately drawn illustration depicting "the martyrdom" of Fray Antonio Díaz de León, the last Franciscan missionary to serve in Texas, for inclusion in the sixth volume of the series. "It is perfectly executed," Carlos told the artist, "and I thoroughly like the entire composition."[33]

Spiritually renewed by the rapidly moving events of springtime, Castañeda redoubled his efforts and completed his essay for the "Jubilee" publication of the Archdiocese of San Antonio. The result, "Pioneers of the Church in Texas," greatly pleased the archbishop, who compensated Carlos with "a check as a token of his appreciation."[34]

At the end of March, carrying an introductory letter signed by President Painter, Castañeda boarded a commercial aircraft for his excursion to South America. His itinerary listed stops in Mexico City, Central America, Lima, Santiago, and finally Mendoza. As his flight soared above the snow-capped Andes he surely reflected on the remarkable feat of Gen. José de San Martín, whose army in 1814 scaled the majestic cordillera and liberated Chile and Peru from Spanish rule.[35]

As the aircraft slowly taxied to the terminal in Mendoza, Castañeda observed signs welcoming visitors to the heartland of the wine country. Disembarking in the Southern Hemisphere, he encountered autumn in April. As he rode into town escorted by a welcoming committee, he marveled at the tall *plátanos falsos* (sycamore maples with green and silver leaves) that were irrigated by acequias conveying water from the highlands and that shaded the broad sidewalks and crossways on both sides of the street. At the University of Cuyo, located in foothills that, except for extensive vineyards everywhere, resembled the arid terrain of Albuquerque, Castañeda met a small delegation from the United States—Harold E. Davis of The American University, Arthur L. Campa of Denver, and John Engelkirk of Tulane University.[36] In the course of the week-long conference Carlos mingled with delegates from Canada, England, France, Germany, Italy, Spain, "and all of Latin America."[37] Responding to the elegance of South American hospitality, Castañeda quickly forgot his resolution about moderate eating. Happily he indulged in long, animated lunches and even longer and livelier dinners. Participating in sight-seeing tours around Mendoza, he shared with José Cisneros a running commentary on the places he visited through the medium of souvenir postcards.[38] At the end of the congress, in recognition of his contributions to inter-American relations, Carlos received membership in the Centro de Estudios de Argentina.[39]

Back in Austin, "safe and sound after a wonderful trip to South America," Castañeda eagerly resumed work on *Our Catholic Heritage,* about which he sent a progress report to Bishop FitzSimon: "Don't think that I have neglected my work on the seventh volume. The first chapter is finished and copied in final form and the second is almost complete. I expect before the end of the next two weeks to have another chapter finished, which will make a total of . . . [nearly] two hundred pages in final form, with the whole month of May still ahead to concentrate on the work." [40]

Castañeda's sporadic progress with the seventh volume stemmed partly from the nontraditional sources diocesan archivists throughout Texas were providing and the need to travel to Amarillo, where these records were being collected, to select the materials he needed for his work.[41] In May unforeseen events in quick succession forced him to postpone a trip to the Panhandle indefinitely. First, on the advice of physicians in Amarillo, Bishop FitzSimon checked into a hospital for rest and medical observation. Next, Father Gibbons, whose editorial supervision was vital to the project, informed Carlos that he would undergo surgery "in the very near future." Worried but not demoralized, Castañeda found solace in the news of Bishop FitzSimon's release from the hospital and in the fact that Von Boeckmann-Jones had received corrected page proofs for the sixth volume, which was now "complete in every detail except running it through the press." [42] Publication of the volume had been delayed because Von Boeckmann-Jones had won a printing contract from the Texas legislature and consequently virtually suspended other projects in order to print the multitude of bills and proceedings when the legislature convened in regular session of January, 1949.[43] With adjournment of the biennial session in sight, Carlos was hopeful that the company would publish the book within a reasonable period. It was, he remarked, "without boasting, the best volume yet." [44]

Concerned about the unusual delays surrounding this particular tome but fairly satisfied with the current rate of research and composition, Castañeda pensively reviewed the span of his association with *Our Catholic Heritage in Texas:* "It has been a long and trying task. But it is rapidly coming to its end. The hours of research, writing and rewriting, and of checking it has taken over a period of seventeen years [which] is incalculable, but all that is behind us now. Just a little while, a few more hours of pending toil and it will be finished." Taking stock of his investment of time and intellect, Carlos weighed the trade-offs his commitment to the project had encompassed:

> *During all this time I have had to carry my full teaching load, along with a bit of extra writing and book reviewing, and lecturing here and there, but many other things have had to wait. When I do finish entirely with the seventh volume, the things I have put off will be mountain high and I will have to continue on the same strain as before. Well, for one thing, I have enjoyed*

the work, and I thank the Lord for having given me something to keep one busy through the years, which will in a very modest way, be useful to others in understanding the cost of love and sacrifice which the establishment and spread of the Faith in Texas has entailed.[45]

At the conclusion of the spring term Castañeda drove alone to Amarillo to discuss major themes for volume 7 with Bishop FitzSimon. Among the research materials he borrowed to take home were primary documents "of great value" and microfilmed editions of *The Southern Messenger,* a biweekly church-related newspaper owned and operated by the Menger family of San Antonio, which he considered an "indispensable" source. Since the bishop would be away from his diocese on a mandatory *ad limina* visit to Rome, a journey required of all prelates to give an accounting of their stewardship to the pontiff who had appointed them, Carlos resolved "to work steadily" during the summer on the remaining sections of the final volume.[46]

In between summer school classes Castañeda worked with his sources from the Catholic Archives. Although the draft of half the volume was finished, the results fell short of his rigorous expectations. What annoyed him was the unevenness of development. "The first three chapters are naturally much more detailed than the rest of the volume will, because of its general nature, have to be." Nonetheless, he expressed optimism that the final product would be "a creditable piece of work."[47] Aside from the stifling summer heat, one factor that may have contributed to Carlos's sluggish productivity was the inordinate amount of time he devoted to ferreting out minute details in the Latin American Collection for Father Steck's ongoing translation of Fray Toribio de Motolinía's *Epístola Proeemial,* a rare sixteenth-century manuscript. Aware of occasional fierce competition among scholars to publish annotated translations of informative colonial documents ahead of potential rivals, Carlos reassured the Franciscan that he would not "divulge [his] confidence." Still, he jibed the friar in a friendly manner because Steck "had a secretary." Ever conscious of his own work pile, Carlos would have dearly loved to have such help: "Wish I had one as good as I had in government employment with [the] FEPC. But I do have [a] student aide."[48]

A week before the fall term began, Castañeda reveled in yet another international conference. From noon on September 4 until the evening of September 9, 1949, the First Congress of Historians of Mexico and the United States convened in Monterrey, Nuevo León. Sponsored by the Academia de Ciencias Históricas de Monterrey, the American Historical Association, and the Instituto Nacional de Antropología e Historia, the conference attracted the participation of sixty-seven delegates from Mexico representing thirty-four universities and learned societies, and seventy-four delegates from the United States representing fifty-five universities and scholarly institutions. Among the fifteen formal sessions was one devoted to "archival problems," which occupied an entire morning. As a result of a lively exchange of views and comments, Julio Jiménez Rueda, chairman of the archival session, appointed a binational commission on resolutions. Castañeda agreed to serve as president of the commission, assisted by Clarence H. Haring, France V. Scholes, Virgilio Garza, and Jiménez Rueda.[49]

Castañeda's international excursions rejuvenated him, and he returned to Austin eager to begin the academic year. In between classroom lectures he spent long hours writing.[50] Unable to work out the logistics of a trip to Amarillo, Carlos and Father Gibbons decided to wait until later in the autumn when they could confer with the leading prelates on the Texas Historical Commission in either Goliad or Corpus Christi.[51] Conceivably the decision to postpone their travel coincided with Castañeda's private resolution to moderate his lifestyle. With Reverend Dr. Steck he again shared candid views about his medical problems: "Do remember me in your prayers. My old ticker has been doing all right as long as I take things slowly, particularly in walking. I also have to watch my eating. If I over eat I immediately feel the effect. I do not have to keep any special diet, just have to eat moderately and avoid fats within reason."[52] Steck's humorous advice confirmed the gravity of the situation: "Now, my dear Carlos, take care of your ticker. Walk more slowly and take your regular rests. . . . But so it is, . . . your and my *bandy-rooster* days are over. We'll just have to begin acting like sedate old men, sitting back a little and letting the 'much wilder' younger generation do their part and show their stuff. In short, we'll have to slow down now and pack up our things for the 'big journey' home."[53]

Although initially Carlos denied to himself and others the serious nature of his illness, knowledge of his condition spread. Joe W. Neal recalled that "his 'heart attacks' were legendary on campus. He used to park where he wished and would become very irate at getting tickets on his car. One time, after an accumulation of tickets, he appeared before the parking and traffic committee and had a slight heart attack during the process of presenting his argument. Needless to say, the Committee gave him a disabled sticker and from then on he had no trouble parking where he pleased."[54] Jack A. Dabbs, who as a graduate student had become a close friend while working on calendars of special collections, offered another recollection:

> When he returned to his office, he said the doctor [had] told him to keep a bottle of whiskey handy and to take a swig when he felt signs of any trouble with his heart. Several times when we were checking things together, he stopped and went to the closet where he kept the . . . whiskey and drank a

jigger of it. He also carried some pills which he was supposed to take in case of a recurrence of the pains, but I don't recall his taking any when I was present. He did tell me that when he was in the worst of the second attack, the doctors told him to stay quiet and not to talk. But he kept on talking and said to me later that there was no use in telling him not to talk, because as long as he was alive he was going to keep talking, and that if he couldn't talk he would just as soon be dead.[55]

Joe B. Frantz remembered a later development related to Carlos's struggle with his heart problem: "He used to have [posted] on his office door up in the Main Building the usual thing that most professors have (his was a little larger than most things)—[a card indicating] what office hours are. It said something like: CASTAÑEDA. M. W. F.—9 to 10. And then [the] F was scratched out, and it was M. W.—9 to 10. And below that [the W] was scratched out, leaving just Monday—9 to 10. Then that [day] was scratched out [leaving] By Appointment Only. You'd see his progression as he got faster and less patient."[56]

Much to his physicians' consternation, Carlos may have reduced his walking gait, but he continued to pile up additional commitments. In mid-October, 1949, he delivered a guest lecture, "Destiny and the New World," at Incarnate Word College in San Antonio.[57] Constantly searching for sources of supplemental income—especially to pay medical bills—Castañeda volunteered to teach in both sessions of summer school in 1950, for which the history department budgeted $1,766 (which constituted about 17 percent of his annual salary).[58] In December, Carlos left Austin by train for an annual assembly of the Academy of American Franciscan History. The convocation began traditionally with a solemn mass to commemorate the feast of Our Lady of Guadalupe. On Monday evening, December 12, Carlos energetically chaired the academic session, held in the auditorium of McMahon Hall at Catholic University of America. At the conclusion of the program, which included formal papers by three "noted historians" who examined "various aspects of the life of Fray Junípero Serra," the academy paid "homage to Dr. Herbert E. Bolton, recipient of The Americas Award for 1949."[59] Castañeda and the audience roared at the anecdotes the honoree inserted into his brief yet hilarious acceptance speech, "The Confession of a Wayward Professor."[60] An event of this magnitude easily lulled Carlos into celebrating life and forgetting his problems. Not surprising, during his absence from campus his work accumulated. Avowing that his "trip to Washington" had been "most enjoyable," he conceded that every week it seemed like he got "more and more behind and [had] more and more work to do."[61]

During the holidays between Christmas and the first week of the new year Castañeda journeyed to Amarillo to consult with Bishop FitzSimon and to procure documents that he hoped would clarify certain research questions. Even so, the historical "circumstances" that resulted in the establishment of the Dioceses of Amarillo, Dallas, and El Paso still eluded him. However, at Saint Edward's University his inquiry about some reference works ended in frustration when he learned that they had been shipped to Amarillo. Highly irritated by these reversals, he lamented an earlier decision to the prelate: "Winding up the seventh volume has become exceedingly irksome. I wish with all my heart that Father [Raymond] Clancy had finished it. I would gladly refund the Commission what they have paid me if they could find somebody else to finish it. Perhaps I am just worn out. It has been a long and exacting period. Pray that the Lord gives me the strength and light to finish this last volume for good." [62]

Through the early months of 1950 Castañeda struggled with the skimpy sources pertaining to the various Catholic dioceses in the state. Bishop Fitz-Simon remained a loyal confidant during his ordeal. [63] Just as Carlos was on the brink of solving the knotty problem of the dioceses, he hit upon another question that bedeviled him for weeks. The difficulty this time related to the Extension Society, which had provided considerable funding to the Catholic Church in postindependence Texas. [64] Restless and impatient, Castañeda took advantage of a brief interlude in April at the funeral of Bishop Christopher Byrne in Galveston to confer with FitzSimon. Immediately after the service he asked the prelate for more assistance: "I regret to have to bother you, my dear bishop, with all these details, but you were so kind in offering to help when I saw you yesterday, reaffirming your good intentions of cooperating, that I [have] been encouraged to make this call on your kindness." [65]

By early springtime Castañeda reluctantly reined in his tendency to accept more projects than he could reasonably discharge. In April he sought Bishop FitzSimon's advice about a research project that, for once, he preferred to avoid. Since the specific undertaking pertained to a history of the Knights of Columbus in Texas, his concern was finding a discreet way to remove himself from serious consideration without offending the sponsors of *Our Catholic Heritage*. [66]

That spring Castañeda had a joyous occasion to celebrate when his eldest daughter, Consuelo Dolores, graduated from Austin High School. Elisa and Carlos hosted an elegant, formal dinner in the graduate's honor at Green Pastures, a popular family restaurant in south Austin. [67] Reinvigorated by his daughter's success, Carlos rushed to Houston to speak at an annual convention of Serra International, an organization dedicated to recruiting candidates for the priesthood. Then he headed to northeastern Kansas to deliver a commencement address at Saint Mary College, a small liberal arts school for women located in Xavier, a suburb of Leavenworth. [68] At the "graduation exercises" Castañeda spoke on the issue of "The Bounds of Church and State in Education." He concluded his remarks with a moving rendition of a poem by Douglas Mullock entitled "The West." So stirring was his delivery that afterward students in the audience requested copies of the poem "to keep" as mementos of the ceremony. Castañeda later described his enjoyable visit to Kansas to Bishop FitzSimon, with whom he shared a copy of the commencement speech: "I put considerable time on it and believe I have brought out some basic facts in a short and convenient form." [69]

In the summer Castañeda shouldered a full teaching load, made to feel heavier by theses and dissertations he had to supervise. Compounding matters, Father Gibbons underwent surgery for the removal of "about three-fourths of his stomach." Although the priest's recovery progressed satisfactorily, his hospitalization delayed secretarial and editorial work on the manuscript for the seventh volume of *Our Catholic Heritage.*[70] During a lull between summer sessions Carlos and Ted Deming, a student assistant, traveled to Amarillo to conduct research in the Catholic Archives. The Christian Brothers provided Carlos with "a room in the dormitory," accommodations which permitted him "to attend Mass and start early every morning [and] . . . work until late in the evening." With Deming's help, within a week he had compiled "copious notes" on such topics as "the various religious orders, communities, societies, etc., the circumstances under which they came, hospitals, Catholic welfare, and other subjects for the last chapters," which he had "been unable to put in final form because of lack of materials." [71]

Notwithstanding his productivity in the Panhandle, when Castañeda returned to Austin his morale sagged. Father Gibbons's surgery and slow convalescence, combined with Von Boeckmann-Jones's failure to publish the sixth volume of *Our Catholic Heritage* in a timely fashion after receiving corrected page proofs, obviously weighed on his spirit. Still, he managed to keep things in proper perspective, especially the unflinching support of friends such as FitzSimon. He wrote: "My dear Bishop, let me say in all frankness that it is the genuine sympathy and interest which you have taken in this work that has been a sustaining incentive, for even my old friend Bishop Garriga has lost faith in the work ever being finished. However, it will be finished early this fall. The matter will then rest with the publishers and I will at long last have peace of mind." [72]

Unexpectedly, in late summer Castañeda's spirits soared. Marc Simmons, an undergraduate student who had been in Europe, returned to the United States conveying official greetings to Don Carlos from the Spanish government. Simmons also carried a beautiful medallion designating the recipient a knight commander of the Order of Isabel la Católica, an honor created in 1815 by Ferdinand VII to recognize meritorious contributions to Spanish American culture. Simmons delivered the gifts (medallion and scroll) to the Castañeda residence, where the surprised honoree, confined to bed for prescribed rest, received the courier with handshakes and *abrazos* (hugs).[73]

Castañeda's receipt of the award marked the first time that membership in the order had been conferred on a resident of Texas.[74] To highlight the honor students and staff of the Newman Club planned a full program for his investiture in mid-October. The local arrangements committee invited Pablo Merry del Val, cultural attaché of the Spanish Embassy in Washington and nephew of the late Rafael Cardinal Merry del Val, to preside at the investiture ceremony. The program began at midmorning, October 19, with a pontifical mass celebrated by Bishop Louis J. Reicher at Saint Mary's Cathedral in downtown Austin. Monsignor William H. Oberste, who had studied the Spanish missions of Refugio, delivered the sermon. Next the Capital City Council of the Knights of Columbus hosted a luncheon in Castañeda's honor.[75] Hoping until the last minute that Herbert E. Bolton would be the "main speaker of the evening," the Newman Club had reserved the ballroom of the Texas Union Building for the investiture and reception. Promptly at eight o'clock the ceremony, "very imposing and . . . carried out with due dignity," commenced.[76] Rev. Gerald E. Maguire, C.S.P., director of the Newman Center, welcomed the public and special guests to the solemn occasion. Following the invocation Professor Charles Wilson Hackett of the Latin American Studies Institute praised Castañeda's *Our Catholic Heritage* as "the best Texas history that has ever been written." Then Señor Pablo Merry del Val, speaking "in impeccable British English," gracefully invited Castañeda to step forward. Attired in the formal regalia of a Knight Grand Cross of the Equestrian Order of the Holy Sepulchre of Jerusalem, replete with sword and scabbard, the candidate knelt in front of the attaché. Together they recited the oath: "I do swear to live and die in the Roman Apostolic Catholic Faith; to defend the mystery of the Immaculate Conception, to sustain the Spanish tradition of culture in the Americas, to protect the poor, the sick, and the helpless, and to be loyal to all members of the Order." Señor Merry then took Castañeda's sword and with it made the sign of the cross above his head. Gently he tapped the candidate on the back and bid him to rise. Carlos received the sword, kissed the handle, and returned it to the scabbard. Last, Señor Merry pinned the insignia of the Order of Isabel the Catholic on the left breast of Carlos's uniform and then bowed.[77] Later Castañeda wrote Bolton: "You will never know how much we missed you at the ceremony. A million thanks for your warm congratulations and . . . regrets . . . [for] not having been able to come. We hoped and waited until the last minute and were deeply disappointed at your absence. We understand, of course, the circumstances."[78]

Castañeda's energy had been recharged in late summer when he learned of his newest honor. First he finished an introduction, "The Irresistible Challenge of the Pueblos," for a book entitled *Jesuit Beginnings in New Mexico*, edited by Sister Lilliana Owens, S.L.[79] Subsequently, unable to achieve much headway with the last manuscript for *Our Catholic Heritage*, Carlos turned to a collaborative effort he and Jack A. Dabbs had begun earlier, a compilation of a calendar for the Manuel Gondra Collection.[80] In the fall of 1950 Castañeda arranged for the publication of the calendar, sponsored by the Institute of Latin American Studies, with Editorial Jus in Mexico City. In turn, the institute agreed to purchase "500 copies at a predetermined price." As soon as Castañeda and Dabbs sent the typescript of the Gondra calendar to the publisher, they searched for another project of mutual interest.[81]

After his investiture, his motivation fortified by news from Von Boeckmann-Jones that the sixth volume would be ready as soon as they could "get the covers," Castañeda resumed work on the final tome. A year after consulting the microfilmed edition of *The Southern Messenger,* he discovered that his research notes had "grown cold," which necessitated another perusal of the newspaper "for the years 1900–1908." On the positive side, he reported to FitzSimon that "Father Gibbons is now giving full time to the work of the history." Incurably optimistic, Carlos predicted that by "working together" and invoking "God's grace," they would "finish the 7th volume by the end of the year."[82] Relieved of "all teaching duties" at Saint Edward's University until the following spring, Father Gibbons assisted Carlos by searching through the microfilm "for materials on the early history of the K. of C. in Texas in particular."[83]

During the Christmas season, totally unknown to Carlos, the bishop of Oklahoma City and Tulsa, Most Reverend Eugene J. McGuinness, seized upon an idea he considered meritorious and contacted the auxiliary bishop of Washington, D.C., John P. McCormick, who also served as rector of Catholic University of America. Acting on behalf of the Texas hierarchy, Bishop McGuinnes informed the venerable rector that the episcopal leadership was "very pleased with the distinction" Carlos E. Castañeda had "brought to the Church because of his learning and sincere Catholicity," and they thus recommended that he be considered "for a possible honorary degree" from Catholic University. Presenting Castañeda's cause, Bishop McGuinnes continued:

> The sixth volume of his History of Texas is now in the hands of the printer, page proofs having been corrected and returned. Although sponsored by the Knights of Columbus and called Our Catholic Heritage in Texas, *it is the first real complete history of Texas written by an historian and based on original sources that has ever been attempted. He is a past President of the American Catholic Historical Society [sic] and was recently asked to preside*

at a . . . [special] celebration which the Franciscans had in Washington. . . .
He has been, moreover, honored by the Holy See and is a Knight . . . Grand
Cross of the Order of the Holy Sepulchre. If you can do anything for this
learned and distinguished Catholic, I know that it would be looked upon
with great favor throughout this section of the country. I wish you would
let me know the possibility of any such honor.[84]

Fully aware of the slow nature of ecclesiastical matters, the Oklahoma prelate
derived satisfaction from knowing he had started a process that would ultimately reach fruition. For Carlos E. Castañeda, however, the immediate goal
of completing the last volume of the series remained elusive. That agenda, foremost among his scholarly projects, carried over to the next year.

At the Summit, 1951–53

In the early 1950s Carlos E. Castañeda ascribed priority to finishing the seventh volume of *Our Catholic Heritage in Texas,* although he continued to pursue other scholarly projects as well. And he accrued still more honors for his work, even as he hoped for recognition at his own university. With a firm commitment to Catholic social action, he also contributed his efforts on behalf of several groups that sought to improve conditions for Hispanics in the Southwest.

In February, 1951, Castañeda launched a personal drive among friends in the Academy of American Franciscan History to promote the sixth volume of *Our Catholic Heritage.* The gaping time lag between the publication of the fifth volume years ago and the release of the sixth tome in early February especially rankled him. Castañeda suggested "that an early review . . . of the long waited" title, delayed by the war, would "be of interest to Catholic historians."[1] The friars in Washington promptly accommodated Carlos's wishes by assigning the new volume to J. Manuel Espinosa, a career employee of the U.S. Department of State, for analysis. "Heartiest congratulations upon the appearance of this volume," wrote Father Alexander Wyse, director of the academy. "May you do many more good things like this for the Church and for scholarship."[2]

Castañeda usually performed a mutually beneficial service before asking for special favors. In this instance he had agreed to translate a manuscript about Spanish colonial art written by Fray Benjamín Gento Sanz, resident scholar at the academy, which he began with relative ease. In his letter requesting a review of volume 6 Carlos told Wyse that the piece was "almost finished," although it had taken "longer to translate" than he had expected. "The work in the original Spanish is exuberant in the extreme," Castañeda wrote, "and the use of so many unusual architectural and art terms has contributed to the difficulties of making a smooth translation."[3] Wyse concurred with Carlos's assessment: "As you say, his style is very florid, and will justify a little trimming here and there." Nonetheless, he assured Carlos that the translation would be published "as soon as possible."[4] Despite Castañeda's resolve to finish the job quickly, the work dragged on until finally, two years later, he admitted defeat. "In view of the circumstances," he wrote Wyse in February, 1953, "and with my most humble apologies to the Academy and to Father Benjamín, I am returning the original text in Spanish and the portion I attempted to translate, that it may help whomever [sic] decides to undertake the task again."[5]

In all likelihood Castañeda was originally thrown offtrack by a tragedy in the history department. Upsetting in itself, the event precipitated developments that Castañeda found bitterly galling. On February 26, 1951, in a despondent mood following "a serious operation" for the removal of a kidney stone, Charles Wilson Hackett committed suicide.[6] A week after the funeral Milton R. Gutsch, department chairman, convened a meeting of the history faculty to distribute Hackett's workload. Since Castañeda already carried a full load of four courses, Gutsch temporarily assigned Hackett's Mexican history class to Dr. Frank R. Knapp, a junior member of the department. Next he "combined" Hackett's graduate seminar with Castañeda's and permitted doctoral candidates working on dissertations to choose their directors. Castañeda thus inherited five of Hackett's graduate students: Joseph Carl McElhannon, Thomas Fonso Walker, David Martell Vigness, Michael O. Lancaster, and John H. McNelly.[7] Whereas the sudden acquisition of so many talented candidates surely bolstered Carlos's ego, some of the other arrangements infuriated him. With respect to the issue of assigning Knapp, who had only "one year's experience" since receiving the doctorate "to teach the ranking course" in Mexican history, Carlos's strong objections forced the department to declare in writing that it was "a temporary arrangement for the remainder" of the spring semester. The department further conceded that in September, Castañeda would "take over all work in the field of Mexico and Central American history," which he had staked out as his field.[8]

In his struggle to assert his seniority Carlos won the first skirmish, but he experienced bitter frustration when he tried to succeed Hackett as director of the Latin American Studies Institute. His unsuccessful quest for the directorship created rifts in some quarters of the university and fomented a rancorous feud with the incoming successor. Castañeda felt that some university administrators showed gross insensitivity in not recognizing his contributions to the institute. He also believed that his growing prominence as the author of *Our Catholic Heritage in Texas* likely damaged him in the eyes of a few influential administrators who preferred to hire an outsider with a more secular outlook on Latin America. Carlos shared his perceptions with trusted friends at the Franciscan Academy: "Behind all these tortuous maneuvers is [the fact] that I am a Catholic who has made no bones about the matter, but has proudly let it be known that [he] was one. It is a little late in life for me now to undertake to make a [job] change. I have tenure and . . . [am] sure they won't discharge me, but they can make me continue to take a second place. We are trying to work out a more satisfactory agreement and have hopes of success. Do say an extra prayer for me." [9]

In the aftermath of Hackett's death Castañeda volunteered to write an appropriate memorial for *The Americas,* even though, he told Wyse, "I still continue to overload myself." [10] Theophilus S. Painter, president of the university, also appointed Castañeda to serve on the committee charged with drawing up a memorial resolution in Hackett's honor. [11]

Buoyed by incremental gains in the history department, Castañeda's morale received a further boost by Eugene C. Barker's assessment of the sixth volume of *Our Catholic Heritage* as "a definitive history of Texas for that period." Carlos told Father Wyse, "The Lord in His kindness tempers the storm to the shorn lamb." Still, he lamented that after working "hard and faithfully for so many years to attain recognition in order to secure well deserved advancement," it was utterly frustrating to discover there was "nothing at the end of the trail but further exercise of humility." [12] Castañeda was later even more pleased when J. Manuel Espinosa's evaluation of the same volume, although written from a different perspective, essentially agreed with Barker's appraisal. Espinosa's positive remarks moved Carlos to declare, "It is things like this that make me reconciled to minor slights." [13]

When Lewis Ulysses Hanke, a Harvard graduate and director of the Hispanic Foundation of the Library of Congress, arrived in Austin for a round of interviews, university administrators proffered him not only the directorship of the institute but also the title of Distinguished Professor of History. After conferring with the candidate and observing the reaction of colleagues, Carlos bowed to the inevitable. "He is a good man," he informed Father Wyse, "the best we could have secured for the purpose and one with . . . [whom] the others here in the field, as well as myself, can work." Still, he found it extremely difficult to reconcile himself to being relegated "permanently to a second place" because it was unlikely that the board of regents would ever sanction "two distinguished professors in the same field." To his friend at the Franciscan Academy, Carlos confided that being "a Catholic and a Mexican" effectively blocked his chances of becoming a distinguished professor. Noting the "two strikes against him," Carlos conceded to the friars that there was "little to do but to pray that the Lord gives us resignation and fortitude to bear our Cross." [14]

By mid-April, Castañeda's cloud of gloom began to dissipate. Contributing to his spiritual renewal was a decision by the board of trustees of Catholic University of America to confer upon him an honorary doctorate. [15] The award, first suggested by Bishop Eugene J. McGuiness of the Diocese of Oklahoma City and Tulsa and endorsed by Bishop Louis J. Reicher of Austin, had won the approval of the university rector (now auxiliary bishop), Most Reverend Patrick Joseph McCormick.[16] The rector officially notified Carlos of the decision, advising him that the degree would be presented at commencement on June 6. Castañeda's acknowledgment manifested a keen appreciation, avowing that "it will henceforth be my endeavor to prove myself worthy of this high honor bestowed upon me by the ranking Catholic institution in the United States through your kind recommendation and that of the honorable Academic Senate of the University."[17] Elated by the announcement, Castañeda shared "the good news" with friends at the Franciscan Academy. He told Father Wyse that he looked "forward to the occasion with much anticipation," particularly because the decision had come "as a much needed salve to my hurt ego, sadly trampled upon recently, as you know."[18]

Reinvigorated by the honor, Castañeda bolted into action. Aware that Lewis Hanke's acceptance of the position at the University of Texas meant he would give up the directorship of the Hispanic Foundation of the Library of Congress, Carlos, encouraged by friends in Austin, launched a campaign to succeed him. Although he personally knew the librarian, Luther H. Evans, a fellow Texan whom he had met in Monterrey, Castañeda considered it awkward to pursue a direct approach. The strategy he favored was for others to contact the librarian on his behalf. He even enlisted "a couple of very close friends" of then senator Lyndon B. Johnson "to get him to make the suggestion to Evans," something Johnson did within a month. Not a bit reticent, Castañeda asked the Franciscans to seek a recommendation for him from His Eminence, Francis Cardinal Spellman, archbishop of New York, who served as honorary grand prior of the Equestrian Order of the Holy Sepulchre of Jerusalem in the United States. Covering as many angles as possible, Carlos suggested to the friars that they should clear the matter "with His Excellency the Apostolic Delegate," a diplomat who represented the Vatican in Washington, "before presenting it to the Cardinal."[19] In a postscript he added: "Let me make it clear that my position here, while not pleasant now, is secure. . . . I am merely trying to leave voluntarily under more favorable circumstances. If the Library of Congress deal, or any similar one, could be worked out, it would solve my problem with dignity and make the powers that be realize their injustice in my case."[20] The Franciscans pledged their support in promoting his "appointment as Director of the Hispanic Foundation" and quietly exercised their contacts with influential members of the Catholic hierarchy. Father Wyse told Carlos: "I would not want to pretend that we have any great influence, but what[ever] associations we have we will gladly use. . . . It so happens that I expect to have an appointment with the Apostolic Delegate within the next few weeks, and on May 16 I am to attend a function at which I may be able to get a few moments of private conversation with Cardinal Spellman. I will take advantage of those providential occasions to discuss the matter with them. . . . I will be glad to take some more direct steps in the near future."[21] Among the "more direct steps" was the Franciscan Academy's decision to bestow the Serra Award of the Americas for 1951 upon Castañeda. The friars' decision caught Carlos by surprise. "I have no words," he told Wyse, "to thank you, the Academy and the Minister General of the Franciscan Order for the high award it has been agreed to bestow [on] me. I feel truly unworthy of so high an honor and feel grateful from the bottom of my heart for such generosity." Evidently the notification about the award he would receive in Washington calmed his spirit, which had been troubled over temporal affairs that "poor, blind mortals often . . . do not understand and fret unnecessarily about." The friars tentatively scheduled the event for October 4, "the feast of St. Francis," which Carlos considered "most appropriate," since he had "always been an ardent devotee of . . . the gentlest of Saints."[22] While the spring semester slowly wound down, the Alba Club, a campus organization established in 1946 to recognize the contributions of "outstanding" Latin Americans in Texas, elected to honor Castañeda. In presenting the award to Don Carlos at the annual banquet, held on May 5, 1951, the club acknowledged the longevity of his presence at the University of Texas, ranging from his three-year stint as a student of engineering to his latest contributions to the history of Texas and the Spanish borderlands.[23]

In mid-May, Castañeda traveled to Galveston to deliver a lengthy progress report to the Texas Historical Commission of the Knights of Columbus. Describing his sacrifices and tribulations of nearly eighteen years with *Our Catholic Heritage*, Carlos summarized his achievement as he eagerly looked forward to the end of the project:

> The work which is about to be completed is not a history of the Church in Texas, nor a history of the missions. It is that and much more; it is the complete economic, social, politico-military, and cultural history of the state to 1836, and the development of the Catholic Church in Texas since independence, the latter being the specific subject of the seventh volume. What Stewart McGregor, the author of the "Texas Almanac," said in his review of the sixth volume is applicable to the whole series. One may say, pardon my lack of modesty, that "this is history—good history—with the Church included."[24]

Returning to Austin, Castañeda finalized plans for the journey to Washington, where he would receive his honorary doctorate. Carlos had decided to include Elisa and their "two little girls," who he admitted were "not so little any-more," and to make the Washington trip a family vacation.[25] Since the price of four train tickets would wreck their budget, they opted to travel by automobile.[26] Near Bethesda, Maryland, they checked into "a very nice tourist home" close to the academy, whose friars volunteered to drive Carlos wherever he "needed to go."[27]

At ten o'clock in the morning of Wednesday, June 6, attired in his academic regalia "but without a hood," Carlos promptly reported "at the main corridor of Caldwell Hall," where he found his place in the processional lineup behind "the faculties, and before the Chancellor and the Rector." At 10:30 the procession began, slowly moving toward the university gymnasium. Shortly before noon the master of ceremonies intoned Castañeda's name and a litany of his achievements, after which the rector, Bishop McCormick, placed a purple hood over the recipient's shoulders.[28] The master of ceremonies then read the text of the citation the rector had presented to the honoree.

Carlos Eduardo Castañeda, Professor of History in the University of Texas, by his indefatigable scholarly labors has made the glorious Catholic past of Texas and the adjacent regions live again in the pages of his many books and articles. His scholarship truly exemplifies the happy union of sound critical method and warm devotion to the Catholic faith. He has long been equally distinguished also as a courageous leader in Catholic Action, and especially in promoting the rights and welfare of his fellow citizens of Mexican descent.

The Catholic University of America, therefore, in recognition of the outstanding achievements of Carlos Eduardo Castañeda, illustrious Catholic scholar and public leader, Knight of the Holy Sepulchre, takes pleasure in conferring upon him the Degree of Doctor of Laws, honoris causa.[29]

Following the commencement ceremony and customary receptions, Castañeda and his family spent time sight-seeing in the nation's capital, zealously filling each day with tours of museums, monuments, and galleries.[30] Before departing for Texas they bade farewell to the friars who had received them with so much affection. Father Wyse later wrote Carlos: "We were delighted to see you again, and to have the privilege of meeting Mrs. Castañeda and the girls. The honor which the University paid to you was one in which we too rejoiced and we were happy to see . . . just tribute being paid to your important work for the history of the Church."[31] On the homeward trip the Castañedas traveled a scenic route along the coast, from Virginia to Florida, before turning west through the Deep South. In New Orleans they paused for an extra day of sight-seeing, which Carlos acclaimed as "very enjoyable."[32]

Since teaching duties in the summer program would not begin until the second term, Carlos renewed his collaboration with Jack A. Dabbs, a member of the faculty of foreign languages at Texas A&M College. The project they mutually selected was the Juan E. Hernández collection of manuscripts that the University of Texas had purchased. To entice Dabbs to reside in Austin during the summer of 1951 and 1952, Carlos obtained "some small funds" from the Institute of Latin American Studies.[33]

About this time Castañeda encountered another rebuff from the university administration. Upon reviewing "the List of Standing Committees for 1951–1952," he discovered that President Painter had not appointed him to the library committee as he thought had been arranged. Carlos quickly dispatched a mild protest to the executive suite: "Early in the spring in a conversation with you in your office concerning the matter you made a brief memorandum and told me I would be placed on this committee. The omission is due, perhaps, to an error in typing." [34]

Castañeda's failure to lodge a stronger complaint may be explained partly by the host of duties that he shouldered within the history department. At the doctoral level he headed two supervisory committees, with additional service on two others. He also participated as a member of five committees administering qualifying examinations to students seeking advancement to the final stage of graduate study. In addition, he chaired the examination committees of four candidates defending their dissertations and served as a member of one other. Finally, he led a supervisory committee at the master's level. All of this required endless hours reading and revising candidates' manuscripts, followed by frequent appointments for individual counseling. Besides the foregoing labors, Castañeda consistently promoted the work of his graduate students. In the summer of 1951, for example, he sent an essay by Malcolm D. McLean about a nineteenth-century Mexican historian to *The Americas*. The following year he dispatched an article by E. Victor Niemeyer to the same journal and assisted Raymond Estep in getting his dissertation on Lorenzo de Zavala published by Librería Porrúa Hermanos y Cía in Mexico City.[35]

In June, Castañeda was "agreeably surprised" to receive "a personal note of congratulations" from the apostolic delegate in Washington. The message motivated him to redouble his campaign for the directorship of the Hispanic Foundation. Evidently the Catholic hierarchy along the New York–Washington corridor was genuinely interested in his professional career, because Monsignor Bruno Vittori, the apostolic delegate's counselor, asked Carlos "to suggest just how His Excellency can help in the matter." Sensitive to the separation of church and state in American politics, Castañeda suggested an oblique approach through Attorney General J. Howard McGrath, who, as a member of the Equestrian Order of the Holy Sepulchre, could delicately "take up the subject" on behalf of a brother knight with Dr. Evans at the Library of Congress.[36] Throughout the hot summer Wyse and Castañeda maintained contact regarding the vacancy. Late in July the Franciscan wrote: "We have heard nothing as yet as to the Library of Congress, but will . . . inform you when any news reaches us." From Austin, Carlos advised the friar, "I have a lot of powerful political friends pushing the matter . . . down here and I am still holding my fingers crossed."[37]

Early in August the quest ended. Through his contacts Castañeda learned that Dr. Evans had selected James Ferguson King, of the University of California and former managing editor of the *Hispanic American Historical Review,* as Hanke's successor. More relieved than disappointed about the outcome, Carlos avowed that while King was "a good man," the Californian failed to match at least "half the qualifications" he possessed. Castañeda believed Evans had based his choice "largely on age," wanting a director not older than "his middle forties." On the threshold of his fifty-fifth birthday, Carlos stoically accepted the verdict: "Well, it was a good fight and I was delighted to find I had as many friends as [those who] did not back me for the job."[38]

At the start of the 1951–52 academic year, Lewis Hanke assumed the directorship of the Latin American Studies Institute. Although Castañeda earnestly resolved to work harmoniously with the new administrator, before long a combination of personality clashes, petty jealousies, and honest differences of opinion virtually destroyed their professional relationship. Individuals who were close to Castañeda remembered the bristly nature of this ugly, divisive feud. Jack Dabbs recalled that Castañeda generally "favored" Hanke as an applicant for the position, but after the appointment was announced he became "disenchanted" with the director and expressed "many unpleasant things" about him.[39] Philip J. Sheridan, a doctoral student at the time, believed the conflict "was a liberal and conservative [polarization] in one sense. Two completely opposite extremes. It was a shame, a sad thing." The scholarly differences between Castañeda and Hanke hinged essentially on their interpretation of Spanish American history. As a natural outgrowth of his study of the role of crown and cross in the exploration, occupation, and settlement of the Spanish borderlands, Castañeda had become a champion of the church. Hanke, on the other hand, had built his academic reputation on his study of one sixteenth-century personality, Fray Bartolomé de las Casas, bishop of Chiapas, who defended the cause of the Indians against the crown and, by extension, the institutional church.[40] Whereas neither Castañeda nor Hanke identified his work in ideological terms as being either liberal or conservative, Hanke lauded Las Casas and condemned certain policies of church and state, while Castañeda defended the Spanish presence in colonial America as a positive experience. The tension between their two positions had been evident to

Sheridan: "And then you could never convince or prove anything about Hanke being a religious bigot, but we [graduate students] often felt that . . . Hanke had adopted Las Casas because . . . [he] was a liberal Dominican priest in the 1500s. . . . And if that was true or not, I don't know, but that was his forte, . . . this struggle for justice. And as for Carlos, he would actually commend [Hernán] Cortés for destroying the idols [of native Americans]. And as for the anthropologists and Hanke they would have condemned Cortés."[41] Valdemar Rodríguez, who typed correspondence and manuscripts for Don Carlos, witnessed Castañeda's emotional outbursts after meetings of the Institute of Latin American Studies.

If Hanke would do something just a little bit out of the ordinary, [Castañeda] would write a letter to the president. That's how much he disliked him. Likewise whenever they would have [Institute] Council meetings (and I know because I used to write those letters) . . . [afterwards he would write] to the president or to the dean . . . telling him of some of the things [that irritated him] and some of the letters [were] even written to Hanke [pointing out] . . . where he was wrong. And I thought in writing those letters [he harmed himself] . . . I remember exactly what I told [him]. I said, "Dr. Castañeda, I am not going to mail this letter to see if you'll reconsider it tomorrow, because I don't think that you should send it." . . . he got so mad, I said, "This is going to cost you another heart attack."[42]

Elisa Castañeda, who was considerably removed from daily campus affairs, recalled relations between Hanke and her husband in measured terms: "[Hanke] was a very happy person, very nice. We liked him, but toward the end there was not a very close friendship with my husband—something to do with their work. And they [the Hankes] were here and then left [in 1961] and went to Washington. I heard from them several times."[43]

With all the stress at the university, coupled with the pressure of research, composition, lectures, seminars, and meetings, Castañeda probably welcomed as therapeutic relief the chance to work again with the School Improvement League in San Antonio. For more than two decades the league, founded by Eleuterio Escobar, had conducted outdoor rallies to protest the blighted condition of schools in west-side barrios. In past years on two separate occasions Don Carlos had appeared on the platform as keynote speaker, lending his prestige to the goals of his San Antonio friends. By the decade of the 1950s the league's leaders had modified their strategy, abandoning school-yard rallies but continuing to lobby school-district officials. In early October, Maury Maverick, Sr., former mayor of San Antonio and onetime member of Congress, sought an appointment on behalf of the league with Harry Rogers, president of the school board, for the purpose of presenting and discussing a petition. Maverick informed Rogers that the league's delegation would include "Dr. Carlos Castañeda of the University of Texas, Mr. Eleuterio Escobar, Mr. Alonso S. Perales, Rev. Issac S. Lugo and others. Inasmuch as Dr. Castañeda is one of the foremost authorities on education in the United States, it is requested that you give us a sufficient allocation of time."[44] The group scheduled an appointment for Wednesday, October 10. To defray Castañeda's traveling expenses Escobar sent him a check for forty dollars, which Castañeda returned since he had not planned to stay overnight.[45] As author of the petition the group would present, Castañeda suggested that they convene an hour beforehand in Alonso Perales's law office for a strategy session. Don Carlos strongly recommended a simple presentation of the petition without argumentation. In the event that school officials should ask questions stemming from the contents of the petition, which concerned an equitable distribution of maintenance funds and the construction of new schools, he counseled giving candid responses without confrontation: "If they need time to study the propositions," he advised, "we will reply matter-of-factly that we are favorably disposed and are keenly interested in their ultimate decision." As a practical measure, Castañeda suggested waiting a month before planning another meeting with the school administrators. In the meantime the league publicized its goals in the *San Antonio Evening News* and *La Prensa*.[46]

A month later Castañeda returned to San Antonio for a follow-up meeting in Rogers's office. During the discussion Rogers frequently cited a report that showed "specific expenditures for buildings in the entire system." Aware of the Korean War's impact upon stockpiles of vital materials, Carlos cautioned his associates after the meeting to soften their demands "for new school buildings because there is a lack of construction steel." He continued: "This does not mean that we should give up all efforts for the remainder of the school year. I believe that if we concentrate on a single objective we can get tangible results. We should present to the school board a new report and request, showing specific figures, for a concrete improvement." Accordingly, he asked Escobar to obtain from the school board a copy of the expenditures report that Rogers had used in their last meeting. Castañeda then analyzed the data, comparing expenditures on the basis of student population in the neighborhoods adjacent to each school. The results, he told Escobar, showed that expenditures were proportionally "much higher in sections other than the west side." Armed with statistical evidence, the league leadership could plan a course of action to address "one project, one school, one specific thing" that needed "immediate attention."[47]

While the league continued to press for reforms, Castañeda suspended his work with the group by late November in order to return to academic obligations. In December the *Bulletin of the Business Historical Society* (later changed to *Business History Review*), sponsored by the Harvard Business School, published his essay on the establishment and operation of the Banco Nacional de Texas.[48]

That same month Carlos traveled to Washington for the convocation of the Academy of American Franciscan History, rescheduled from October. On the way he stopped in Gainesville, Florida, where he represented the university as a delegate of the Institute of Latin American Studies in the second Annual Conference on the Caribbean, December 6–8. From Gainesville he proceeded to Washington to receive the Serra Award of the Franciscan Academy, which made him proud and at the same time overwhelmed him because "previous honorees were very prominent people."[49]

The eighth annual convocation of the academy began on Sunday, December 9, 1951, with a "Solemn Pontifical Mass in honor of Our Lady of Guadalupe," celebrated by the apostolic delegate to the United States, Most Reverend Amleto G. Cigognani, at the Monastery of Mount Saint Sepulchre in Washington. A contingent of knights of the Holy Sepulchre, acting as an honor guard, escorted Castañeda into the sanctuary. Rev. Dr. John Tracy Ellis, of the history faculty at Catholic University of America, delivered the homily, in which he emphasized "the educational and cultural achievement of the Franciscans in Central America in the last four and a half centuries." The congregation included members of the diplomatic corps, mainly from Latin America.[50]

The next evening an impressive assembly of diplomats, prelates, professors, scholars, and representatives "of various historical groups, cultural institutes, and learned societies" convened in the auditorium of McMahon Hall at Catholic University of America for the public session of the convocation. The Most Reverend Sigebald B. Kurz, O.F.M., prefect apostolic of Yungchow, China, presided at the session. Dr. Robert C. Smith, art historian at the University of Pennsylvania, addressed the assembly and introduced the principal speaker, France V. Scholes, dean of the Graduate School of Arts and Sciences at the University of New Mexico, who presented an original essay, "Franciscan Missionary Scholars of Colonial Central America."[51] The academic sessions then culminated in the presentation of the Serra Award of the Americas for 1951. Rev. Roderick Wheeler, O.F.M., vice director of the academy and editor of *The Americas,* summarized "the great difficulties and personal privations" the honoree had "encountered in bringing to fruition his great projects of research." Then Father Wyse, director of the academy, paid the next tribute:

> *Gifted by nature with an admirable diligence and industry, accompanied by good fortune in his painstaking research for the fragments of the past, bring-*

ing to the interpretation of history a solid scholarship coupled with an impartial devotion to Truth, Carlos Eduardo Castañeda occupies a place of eminence among American historians. His publications, marked alike by an engaging originality and an unquestionable profundity, have enriched forever the cultural life of our nation and reach out, like a mighty ocean of good-will, to embrace the whole expanse of the Americas. In his noble profession of educator he has had the quality of inspiring his students, and they, enkindled by the fire of his enthusiasm, form a generation of young scholars whose growing reputations in various Universities of the country reflect vicarious glory on the master himself. His public and private virtues as a broad-visioned and self-sacrificing citizen, a devoted father of a Christian family, a dedicated communicant and faithful son of the Catholic Church, shower further distinction on a career already notable for scholarly attainments.[52]

On behalf of the Academy of American Franciscan History and the minister general of the Order of Friars Minor, Bishop Kurz presented to Castañeda a beautiful "hand-illuminated parchment diploma."[53] Attired in his uniform as knight grand cross of the Equestrian Order of the Holy Sepulchre, Carlos then delivered an acceptance oration titled "Why I Chose History." Reviewing salient events of his career, he extended a challenge to emerging scholars:

To the young men and young women of today who desire a comfortable living, I do not recommend history as a career. There is no money in it, not if you write serious history. There is much work, much self-satisfaction, some recognition, some honor, but no money. However, if they are interested in helping to present objectively the truth as gleaned from the actions of men through the ages, if they are disposed to sacrifice personal comfort and personal pleasures for long hours of tedious and confining work in the scrutiny of old records and books, trying to find out what happened, when, how and why; if they feel that they can find self-expression in this thankless task, then let them follow the charming and beguiling Clio, the gentle, contemplative muse that on Olympus tried to keep the record straight.[54]

He closed on a personal note: "The high honor conferred on me tonight by the Academy . . . is one that I deeply appreciate and humbly accept, conscious of my numerous shortcomings. I pray, with a grateful heart, that it may serve to keep me ever constant in the search for historical truth as I expectantly continue to explore the long corridors of time."[55]

On the heels of this lofty honor Castañeda accepted a local accolade. In mid-January, 1952, he attended the awards ceremony of the Newman Club in Austin to act as guest speaker and to receive a special testimonial. Carlos had been involved with this campus organization for Catholic students since his undergraduate days, when, with the encouragement of Father John Elliot Ross, he had served as one of the first presidents of the Newman Club. Accordingly, "in grateful tribute for more than 25 years of faithful service" to the club, the students presented to Carlos a distinctive "key of the John Henry Newman Honor Society." [56]

Within the department, in a rare moment of collegial cooperation, Lewis Hanke and Castañeda set aside personal differences to present a detailed plan of course revisions and spheres of responsibility. With the approval of the department, Carlos received a fairly equitable distribution of the offerings in his field. He took charge of three new courses—Iberian background of Latin American history, the Mexican Revolution, and the Caribbean since 1810— in addition to Spanish North America to 1810 (and since 1810) and a seminar on the history of Spanish North America, with selected topics in the colonial period (with a counteroffering in alternate years on selected topics in the national period). [57]

As spring approached, Castañeda did more traveling. In San Antonio he participated in an evening ceremony at Our Lady of the Lake College honoring his friend Alonso S. Perales, a civil rights lawyer. Seated among the dignitaries on the stage of Thiry Auditorium, Carlos presided at the session in which Consul Antonio Elías of Galveston bestowed "the rank of commander in the Spanish Order of Civil Merit" on Perales. Later in the program the honoree, reviewing "his past and present labors against racial discrimination," expressed "profound appreciation" to Castañeda, whom he described as a "learned and brilliant exponent of Latin-American culture in the Americas." [58] Next he attended a week-long seminar in San Antonio, sponsored by The Brookings Institution of Washington, D.C., and the Cooperative Southern University Conference, on "Problems of United States Foreign Policy." Held the first week in April at the Plaza Hotel, the seminar was restricted to "only 100 invited participants" from colleges and universities in Arkansas, Louisiana, New Mexico, Oklahoma, and Texas. [59]

In late April, Castañeda's commitment to social action caused him to juggle his teaching schedule so as to "be among the speakers" at a three-day Catholic Conference for the Spanish-Speaking People of Texas in Austin. Supported by the Catholic hierarchy of Texas, the conference attracted clergy and laity from the southwestern United States "to participate in discussions of the affairs and problems of the parishes and missions in this area." Also speaking at the conference at the Commodore Perry Hotel were Neville G. Penrose of the Good Neighbor Commission; Ernesto Galarza of the National Farm Labor Union; Thomas Sutherland of the Human Relations Council of Texas; William

Rogers of the U.S. Department of Labor; and Rev. John M. Hayes of Incarnate Word College, chairman of the Priests' Social Action Committee. Robert E. Lucey, archbishop of San Antonio and chairman of the Bishops' Committee for the Spanish-Speaking, presided at the session in which Castañeda delivered a provocative talk entitled "What Price Migratory Labor!"[60] During an interlude in the proceedings, Alonso Perales asked Carlos to transmit to Bishop FitzSimon of Amarillo a petition drafted by "a group of Latin-Americans" from Slaton, a town located southeast of Lubbock. Castañeda assigned "the manuscript copy" to a student assistant, who typed it exactly "as the original, without correcting the spelling or the grammar." Afterward Carlos sent the material to his friend the prelate.[61]

Next on Castañeda's calendar was the spring banquet of the Alba Club, where on May 3 he joined four other "previous recipients" in cheering Alonso Perales, the 1952 honoree.[62] Taking advantage of the weekend, Carlos drove to Alice, a trip of approximately two hundred miles, to confer with civic leaders from south Texas who were concerned with the issue of civil rights and human relations. The meeting gave Carlos an opportunity to greet old friends and acquaintances, such as José T. Canales, a lawyer from Brownsville and former state representative; Professor Luz Sáenz of McAllen; Dr. Exiquio González; and other participants "from Alice, San Antonio, the Valley and other places." Disappointed that other civil rights groups, such as the American G.I. Forum and the League of United Latin American Citizens, continued to do little to advance the cause of the Spanish-speaking, the assembly at Alice on May 4, 1952, formed the Texas Good Relations Association (TGRA). Organized to attract the support of Latin American citizens of Texas as well as immigrants from Mexico, the TGRA appointed Adela S. Vento of Edinburg and Professor Sáenz as coleaders of a membership drive. In order to fund scholarships for needy high school graduates wishing to attend college, the organizers created three levels of membership: regular (five dollars), sustaining (twelve dollars), and life or honorary (one hundred dollars).[63] Generous with his time, ideas, and counsel, Castañeda undoubtedly contributed more in prestige and encouragement than he did in monetary support.

A week later Castañeda and James P. Nash, K.S.G., served as papal knights at an outdoor mass in Austin's Woodridge Park, a service that opened the forty-eighth annual State Council of the Knights of Columbus.[64] During the meeting Rev. James P. Gibbons, chairman of the Texas Historical Commission, recommended that the general convention set "aside $750.00 for salary and other expenses" for Father Stanley Crocchiola, a priest and historian from the Diocese of Amarillo on loan to the Knights of Columbus project. As Castañeda's research assistant on volume 7, Father Crocchiola resided for several months in Austin "collecting and compiling" information for the final tome.

Incurably optimistic, Carlos confidently informed Bishop FitzSimon that "under this arrangement" he would be able to compose the seventh volume "in final form in two or three months."[65] By mid-July he reported that Father Crocchiola had "applied himself diligently to the task" Carlos had assigned to him and needed to consult "three other items in the Jesuit archives" in El Paso. Castañeda expected that work to be finished by the end of the month.[66]

That same summer Castañeda and Jack Dabbs resumed work on their calendar of the Manuel Gondra Collection, which they had begun in 1939. Their guide, containing "467 pages and a 100-page index," was finally published in December, 1952. The collaborators enhanced the value of the publication by rendering the titles of the manuscript in Spanish and the "descriptions and contents" in English. The Institute of Latin American Studies ordered more than 250 copies of the Calendar "for foreign distribution," leaving the balance of the inventory with the publisher in Mexico City for private sales.[67]

In early 1953 Castañeda received the sad news of Herbert E. Bolton's death in California.[68] A month later, inundated with commitments, he returned Father Benjamín Gento Sanz's manuscript to the Franciscan Academy along with his unfinished translation.[69] Although he made slow headway with volume 7 of Our Catholic Heritage, he completed an essay on social and political developments in Spain and Latin America, which was published in late 1953 in an anthology, Church and Society, edited by Joseph N. Moody, S.J., of Fordham University.[70]

Within the campus community Castañeda continued to encounter both sociability and departmental politics. He evidently enjoyed the monthly luncheons the department began holding in the spring of 1953, for in the fall he and a colleague, Robert C. Cotner, proposed continuing the new tradition.[71] However pleasant these social gatherings might have been, the departmental meetings frequently descended into endless discussion. Such was the case when Castañeda, as chairman of a "special committee" that had studied the prospect of offering a curricular minor in history, presented a recommendation that an undergraduate adviser be appointed. The historians quickly divided themselves into opposing camps over the issue. Finally, with an amendment allowing students to consult the chairman or "his designate" as adviser, the faculty approved the reform.[72]

However, endless discussion was hardly reserved for questions of academic policy. When Castañeda requested in April, 1953, that the department install a telephone in his office in the Tower, the faculty hashed the matter over, after which someone "suggested that the Institute of Latin-American Studies be asked to pay half the cost of such phone," with the balance to be charged to the history budget's maintenance and equipment account. Unable to resolve the issue, the faculty "voted to leave the matter open until the next meeting."[73]

Evidently as late as 1953 an office telephone constituted an amenity that not every senior professor merited at the University of Texas.

Counterpoised against such aggravations were the honors that Carlos continued to reap. In mid-April the Texas state senate unanimously adopted a resolution paying tribute to Castañeda, a "fine gentleman and distinguished scholar[,] for his many achievements and contributions in the field of higher education, for his outstanding abilities and tireless efforts in Pan-American friendship, and for the honor that he has brought to the State of Texas and to the University of Texas." [74]

Moreover, the Texas legislature invited Castañeda to address a joint session on Pan American Day, April 14. [75] Although the observance of this day had become traditional in Washington, D.C., the celebration in Austin marked the first time that any of the states had accorded Pan American Day official recognition. [76] The idea for Castañeda's address originated with Neville G. Penrose, chairman of the state's Good Neighbor Commission, whom Carlos had met the year before at the Bishops' Conference for the Spanish-Speaking. [77] No matter how many presentations Castañeda had made in the past, this one truly challenged him. As a Hispanic professor speaking before the Texas legislature, he wanted to give a virtuoso performance. Several days before his speech Carlos shared a copy of the text with the university's new president, Logan Wilson, who responded with felicitations for his "splendid presentation." [78]

At eleven o'clock in the morning of April 14, Lt. Gov. Ben Ramsey declared the senate adjourned and led his colleagues into the house chamber. A welcoming committee, composed of five members from each legislative house, then greeted the "distinguished guests" and escorted them to prearranged seating. First to enter was a large delegation of consuls "stationed in Texas" who represented Argentina, Brazil, Chile, Colombia, Costa Rica, the Dominican Republic, Ecuador, El Salvador, Guatemala, Mexico, Panama, Paraguay, Peru, and Venezuela. Castañeda and his family arrived amid a throng of invited guests representing Pan American Round Tables of Texas and the United States and a variety of other organizations, including the National Catholic Welfare Conference, San Antonio Chamber of Commerce, League of United Latin American Citizens, and American G.I. Forum. Lawyers, educators, ministers, radio station executives, and honorary consuls completed the entourage. Present to record the event were the Voice of America and Austin radio station KTXN. [79]

House speaker Reuben E. Senterfitt then presented Sen. Rogers Kelley, president pro tempore of the senate, "to the Joint Session." In turn, Senator Kelley introduced Neville G. Penrose, chairman of the Good Neighbor Commission of Texas. Penrose acknowledged the other dignitaries in attendance and then introduced Carlos Paniagua, a cellist and exchange scholar at the

University of Texas from Guatemala, who played "Preludio" by Johann Sebastian Bach.[80] As the cellist concluded his performance, Penrose approached the microphone to introduce Castañeda: "In preparing the program for today's joint session, the name of a man came to mind almost immediately as the ideal choice for a speaker. He is a man who is eminently qualified in the field of Latin American relations—historian, author and expert. He has written widely on the subject of Latin American affairs and is one of the most highly respected men in this field today. I am pleased indeed to present to you Dr. Carlos E. Castañeda of the University of Texas."[81]

At the microphone, basking in the generous applause, Castañeda began his address on "Pan Americanism and World Peace." First acknowledging Simón Bolívar's dream of hemispheric unity in the nineteenth century, he provided a historical overview of regional meetings, beginning with the Inter-American Conference of 1890 in Washington, D.C., where delegates forged the concept of a Pan American Union, and culminating with "the provisions of Article 51 of the United Nations Charter," which facilitated the creation of the Organization of American States. Placing his topic within the broad framework of contemporary global events, he counseled the audience: "We in Texas, the gateway to and the link with all the rest of Latin America, fully agree that we cannot and must not, neglect our southern neighbors in the midst of the all-absorbing situation in Korea, Berlin, and Malaya. On the contrary, we firmly believe that in proportion as the world situation in Europe, Asia, and Africa darkens, we should strengthen the bonds of unity that bind the people of the Western Hemisphere as the greatest guarantee of security and the preservation of world peace itself."[82] Today, he noted, "modern aviation, improved weapons, and atomic power" could easily breach a country's borders. Castañeda advocated, therefore, that security for the Americas be based "on hemispheric solidarity." This solidarity, he argued, "rests largely not on military prowess, but on the individual strength of each . . . of the twenty-one nations that constitute the Organization of American States and on their determination to resist any and all aggressions. This strength and this determination are inevitably dependent upon the respective development of the economic potential, the individual ability to resist aggression whether it be economic, social, cultural, or military and the enrichment of their cultural heritages."[83] Castañeda presented a catalog of specific recommendations on how the United States could render assistance to Latin America. At least a decade before the Alliance for Progress became a cornerstone of American foreign policy, he declared that a concerned citizenry would no longer tolerate "the continuance of backward areas, where social insecurity and epidemic diseases are prevalent, where malnutrition is widespread and unchecked, [where] soil erosion threatens to convert fertile areas into sterile deserts." These evils, he warned, "hamper the

collective progress of the American nations, weaken the sum total of the effec-
tiveness of hemispheric solidarity, and seriously menace the future programs
and prosperity of all." Returning to his introductory theme, he concluded to
rousing applause, "Let us help to make the dream of Simón Bolívar, who first
envisioned a united New World of independent nations living in friendship as
good neighbors, become a reality." [84] After the program, as the audience filed
out of the house chamber, Castañeda stayed behind to accommodate radio
technicians who requested a "ten-minute condensation" of his speech in Spanish for rebroadcast later by the Voice of America.[85]

A month later, on May 11, the Texas Historical Commission assembled in
Fort Worth for its thirty-fifth annual meeting. Discussion of commission business had taken place in several gatherings just prior to the formal meeting.
On May 7, in Refugio, where Castañeda and Father Gibbons were attending
"the Silver Jubilee" of Monsignor William Oberste's sacerdotal vows, the
commission had convened informally in the priest's study. The next day at
the Adolphus Hotel in Dallas some members of the church hierarchy had
discussed their expectations of the final volume of *Our Catholic Heritage in
Texas*. When the commission convened three days later those attending,
instead of making policy decisions as in prior years, listened attentively as
Father Gibbons and Castañeda explained the delays in concluding the last volume. Two Knights of Columbus officials, Supreme Director R. Conroy Scoggins and State Deputy Reynaldo Garza, whose approval was required before
additional funds could be committed to the project, had initially expressed
their opposition. After hearing Castañeda describe the impossibility of mesh-
ing disparate topics, some of which had to be deleted, they withdrew their objections. Sensing an opportunity, Carlos proposed that he be authorized to recruit an assistant "of his own choosing, some graduate student or other person
trained in historical research." Saying that "he had no one specifically in
mind," Carlos assured the group, especially Garza and Scoggins, that "he
would obtain a qualified person at $100.00 or $125.00 a month in return
for working five afternoons a week for three months." The Texas Historical
Commission "unanimously" accepted his recommendation and authorized
the expenditure.[86]

Castañeda returned to Austin "entirely" satisfied with the results of the
Fort Worth meeting. To secure approval for a research assistant, he had not
broached the issue of an "honorarium or compensation" for himself. Instead
he had suggested the new arrangement to avoid requesting "any additional expense" for his services until he completed the volume. Ironically, just as one
problem was addressed, another arose to jeopardize the project. When Father
Gibbons returned to Saint Edward's University, he received a peremptory order from his religious superior at South Bend, Indiana, "to report at the Pro-

vincial House as early in June as possible" because the Congregation of the
Holy Cross had not received "remuneration" for his services to the Texas Historical Commission. Accordingly, the reverend provincial had decided not to
allow Father Gibbons "to remain any longer in Austin." Confronted with the
possibility of having to leave the project, Gibbons promptly notified the State
Council of the Knights of Columbus. To correct an embarrassing oversight,
the State Council offered to underwrite two scholarships—one in memory of
Rev. Dr. Paul J. Foik, the founding chairman of the Texas Historical Commission, and another in honor of Father Gibbons—pledging to Saint Edward's
University an endowment of $5,000 "for each." Ultimately the reverend pro-
vincial allowed Father Gibbons to remain at Saint Edward's. In the meantime,
however, concerned about the unsettled situation in Austin, Castañeda abandoned plans to spend the last week in June as a "house guest" of Bishop Fitz-
Simon in Amarillo.[87]

Unable to indulge in a bit of work and relaxation in the Panhandle, Carlos
took advantage of another offer that required less strenuous driving. Oddly,
for the first time in their long friendship Bishop Garriga invited him to his residence in Corpus Christi. Besides the house, which the guest described as "a
lovely place," Castañeda was impressed by "the fine boat" that the bishop
owned.[88] His visit to the coast may have prompted Carlos's decision to consider buying a boat as therapy for his health problems.

As Castañeda ordered his priorities for the summer, he received an enticing
offer from an American oil company operating in Venezuela. Aware of his stature as an internationally renowned scholar, the Creole Petroleum Company,
as a philanthropic gesture, donated nineteen hundred dollars to the Institute
of Latin American Studies to cover Carlos's expenses (transportation, lodging,
meals, and incidentals) during an extended excursion of "45 to 60 days in Venezuela" when he would confer with "leading historians" and acquaint himself
with the country's libraries and archival collections. Fascinated by the proposal, Castañeda wrestled with his conscience for the rest of the summer as
he contemplated a variety of optional schedules, all of which proved unsatisfactory. In view of his commitment to the Knights of Columbus and his obligations to his graduate students, together with the imminent release of two of
his publications under the auspices of the Latin American Studies Institute,
Carlos reluctantly postponed the trip hoping to reschedule later since the grant
did not include a disqualifying deadline.[89]

Although he could not take off for an extended tour of Venezuela, Castañeda grabbed an invitation in mid-July to present a paper, "God's Work in the
Southwest," at a three-day regional symposium of the Catholic Conference for
the Spanish-Speaking in Albuquerque, New Mexico. The essay was so well
received that *El Universal,* a leading newspaper in Mexico City, included a

translation in its Sunday supplement. At the suggestion of His Eminence Samuel Cardinal Stritch, archbishop of Chicago, Castañeda sent the manuscript to *Extension Magazine,* where it appeared in November.[90] While at the conference Carlos "reminded" Archbishop Edwin V. Byrne of Santa Fe that he hoped someday "to write the history of the missions of New Mexico." Reflecting on the remark later, he confided to Bishop FitzSimon: "Here I am about to get out from [under] a twenty-year stretch writing the history of the missions in Texas and I am already trying to get another cross to bear."[91]

While struggling with the final volume of *Our Catholic Heritage* Castañeda continued to accept new projects. These tasks impeded his progress on the book and contributed even further to his emotional turmoil. One such undertaking was assumed at the behest of a Cuban sociologist, Carlos A. Echánove Trujillo, who asked him to translate into English a treatise that had already been published by the University of Havana. Since the book, *Sociology and Social Thought in Latin America,* was in another discipline, Castañeda invited a former student, Dr. George B. Martin-Vegue, at Florida State University to draft the initial translation. Carlos then had to wait for months before he received "the rough translation" and could proceed with revisions.[92]

In June, as the translation problem was being resolved, the governor's office called on the university with an urgent request. Desiring to enhance friendly relations between the state of Texas and the Republic of Mexico, Gov. Allan Shivers informed President Wilson that he would like for Castañeda to select an appropriate number of historical manuscripts in the Latin American Collection to be copied and conveyed as a gift to President Adolfo Ruiz Cortines. Advised by Ruiz Cortines that 1953 coincided with "the Second Centennial of the birth of Don Miguel Hidalgo y Costilla," father of Mexican independence, Governor Shivers envisioned sending a delegation that would include Castañeda, Sen. Rogers Kelley, and members of the Texas Good Neighbor Commission to deliver the documents "in person in the interest of adding to our common historical knowledge" and in appreciation of Mexico's "historic benefactor."[93] Informed by the president of the governor's request after his trip to Albuquerque, Carlos replied: "I fully agree with you that the Governor had an excellent inspiration when he thought of it. This is the sort of thing that furthers the best goodwill between Texas and Mexico."[94]

Taking time from other projects, Carlos pored through catalogs he and Jack Dabbs had compiled in search of "documents relative to the life of Miguel Hidalgo," after which he prepared an inventory of "about thirty-five items" for the president's approval. Cognizant that two photostatic copies of each document were desired—one for President Ruiz Cortines and the other for the Museum of Mexican History at Chapultepec—Castañeda suggested that the sets be bound in leather, "in keeping with the spirit of good neighborliness" that had inspired the gift. He also offered to supervise "the copying and bind-ing of the documents" and then asked Wilson to "indicate if the work is to be done at the expense of the University or the Governor's Office, or the Good Neighbor Commission." Picking up the cue, Wilson forwarded Castañeda's inquiry to the governor's office.[95]

Requests for Castañeda's help arrived in his office from all directions. In the fall he received an appeal from a newly formed group, the Texas Old Missions and Forts Restoration Association. Sympathetic to their goals, he was unable to offer more than moral support. The restoration of the missions was "a must," he wrote back. "I just wish I had more time." [96]

Following the Albuquerque conference in July, Carlos anxiously resumed work on the seventh volume of *Our Catholic Heritage*, revising and retyping drafts of previously written chapters. Describing his method to Bishop Fitz-Simon, he explained that he wrote "everything long hand first. I can't com-pose on the typewriter, nor can I dictate. I have tried the Dictaphone and the typewriter. I simply cannot write except with a pen in hand. Then a week or two later, when the manuscript is typed, I read it, and by then it is cold and I can tell more about it in an objective manner." Whenever possible, FitzSimon then clarified "points in the finished manuscript" that Carlos "had left pend-ing." Impatient with his rate of progress, Castañeda resolved once again to bring the project to a conclusion: "I have made [up] my mind to . . . grind away, like an enormous tractor, down the field, letting nothing turn me away from the main purpose." In spite of his resolve, however, the scattered nature of the sources and Castañeda's dependence on others for information contin-ued to slow things down. Writing ground to a halt, for example, whenever he exhausted his latest batch of material from FitzSimon. When the bishop sug-gested that he make another research trip to Amarillo, Carlos replied: "you are perfectly right about the advantages of 'diggings' in the archives, but let me say that I really gave the whole . . . [collection] a good spading when I was there for almost two weeks, working eight and ten hours a day. I took . . . good, full notes, which I am finding very useful. I have a pretty good idea of what is in the archives on the modern period and unless you have made some great additions of late, I do not think there is much more than what I got two summers ago." And, indeed, the bishop failed to uncover "additional material." [97]

With the holdings of the Catholic Archives helpful but not wholly ade-quate, Castañeda cast a wide net in an effort to make up the deficiencies. One individual who rendered valuable assistance was Rev. Bernard Doyon, O.M.I. While conducting research on his own project, a study of the Missionary Soci-ety of the Oblate Fathers in Texas, Father Doyon gathered material for Carlos in European archives.[98]

Needing to give an account of religious orders and lay organizations in Texas, Castañeda distributed "over 160 questionnaires" to selected groups in order to obtain "information about their establishment and work." [99] It had also been decided that the last volume should include biographical cameos of all the incumbent bishops in Texas. While a few chanceries had responded immediately with "satisfactory" sketches, "some of them," Carlos observed, "most of them rather, did not even answer the request." [100] Not even repeated entreaties had secured the requisite information from the diocesan historians. [101]

Another topic on which work had stalled concerned the participation of the Catholic Church in the Texas centennial observance in 1936. Castañeda lamented to FitzSimon that the section would "not look very good" if it were "based on only one newspaper account." To remedy the problem he reluctantly accepted the necessity of consulting "the files of the principal newspapers in Texas," such as the *Dallas Morning News,* the *Houston Chronicle,* the *San Antonio Express,* and the *El Paso Times.* "You see, my dear Bishop," he complained to FitzSimon in October, "it is this sort of thing that has delayed [indefinitely the completion] of volume seven." Annoyed and frustrated, he blamed the situation on "various members" of the Texas Historical Commission who had neglected to arrange the materials "together in folders or volumes," which would have expedited the task of composition. [102]

As if these difficulties were not enough, a rumor circulated in some quarters that Castañeda was prolonging the work intentionally. Frustrated with his lack of control over the volume, Carlos took umbrage at even the most unintentional oversight. In late July, shortly after Father Gibbons distributed a summary of the proceedings of the last meeting of the Texas Historical Commission, Carlos dispatched a lengthy protest challenging several points in the document. One complaint pertained to a historical overview of the project dating back to 1923. In this section Chairman Gibbons, unfamiliar with the early years, had inadvertently glossed over crucial information that explained why the project had taken so long to complete. "It pains me to have to recapitulate all the facts," Carlos asserted, "but I feel that since [from the formative years] of the first Commission there remain today only Bishop Garriga and Monsignor Donohoe, I [am] duty bound to put them down for the record." He reassured the chairman: "We have worked together too long and have a mutual high regard for each other which does not permit me to attribute the remarks to intentional malice, but I have become sensitive because after twelve years of unselfish dedication to this work, I have become aware lately of charges that I have prolonged the work for personal gain." [103]

On November 14, 1953, Castañeda suffered another heart attack. Besides medication and diet the physicians prescribed "about two months of complete rest." [104] For a few days the patient meekly surrendered to the orders of the doctors, to "the good care" of his wife and daughters, and to "the Lord's will." [105] As soon as the crisis subsided, Carlos summoned his graduate assistant Valdemar Rodríguez to bring books from the library so that he could continue research for a paper to be read at the annual meeting of the American Historical Association in Chicago over the Christmas holidays. In the morning, in between catnaps, Castañeda read the books piled all over his bed. Then in the afternoon he dictated passages to Rodríguez for typing. The student disliked making these home visits because Elisa, acutely aware of her husband's serious heart condition, "did not want him to be writing that paper but he insisted." Every time Rodríguez visited Castañeda, Elisa sternly warned him: "You're going to come in, but you're just going to work one hour or two hours." [106]

Unable to attend the Chicago meeting, Carlos sent one of his graduate students, Cecil E. Johnson, as his surrogate. At the session on colonial Latin America, chaired by Lewis Hanke, Johnson dutifully read Castañeda's essay, "Spanish Medieval Institutions in Overseas Administration." [107] Joe B. Frantz, who attended the convention and was quite familiar with Castañeda's unique "dramatic style," recalled the performance. "I never felt much sorrier" for Johnson, Frantz said. "[He] pronounced all the words, but the trouble is the thing was set up for Castañeda's particular brand of arm-waving dramatics, you know, full of great charges and sail-ons and that kind of thing." Johnson, as "an ordinary person" standing at the podium, "reading soberly looked absolutely ridiculous." Castañeda, if he had been present, "would have been in character, but not the student." [108]

In his essay, later published in *The Americas,* Carlos avowed that the medieval "heritage could be fully understood only by examining the customs and laws of the Spanish monarchy from the reconquest to the discovery of the New World." Moreover, once transplanted in the American mainland, the development and shortcomings of the Spanish institutions required close examination in "light of certain basic, medieval concepts such as the dignity of man and the missionary obligations of the monarchs." In the author's interpretation, "These Christian ideals of the Middle Ages" portended an "unending struggle of the crown and the church to convert and civilize the Indians." [109]

The critics on the panel vigorously jumped on Castañeda's thesis, which Cecil Johnson hesitated to defend against the professionals. Charles J. Bishko, of the University of Virginia, questioned the author's propensity for using "the term 'medieval'" as virtually synonymous with "spiritual, idealistic, and even Christian." Acknowledging that Spanish monarchs regarded the conversion and protection of the aborigines as "their Christian duty," Bishko conceded that the method used to attain this goal "was by no means clear."

Bailey W. Diffie, of City College of New York, criticized the essay's "restricted" scope, which failed to include "discussion of the political, economic, fiscal, commercial, technical, social, and cultural institutions in Spanish expansion overseas." [110]

During December, Castañeda caught up on his correspondence with the aid of a dictaphone.[111] On December 12, "sitting up by his bedside," he dispatched a congratulatory message to the friars at the Academy of American Franciscan History for having selected Clarence H. Haring as the recipient of the Serra Award. Grateful for the gift of life, he summed up his situation: "I wish I were not confined to the house. . . . The worst is over, I am getting along fine but slowly, thanks be to God. I am now allowed to sit up, read and write for three hours a day. Everyday I am regaining my strength and, if no mishap, I [shall] resume my work after the first [of the year]." [112]

The Twilight Years, 1954–58

Obviously not in prime health, yet thankful for a gradual recovery, Carlos E. Castañeda, fifty-seven years old, constantly invited visitors to his modest residence on West Thirty-fourth Street. Besides a legion of graduate students and university colleagues, the list included a prelate of the Roman Catholic Church. After the new year, when Elisa was more tolerant of her husband's extended conversations, the Most Reverend Laurence J. FitzSimon, bishop of Amarillo, paid a courtesy call. Eventually Castañeda's physician allowed him to perform modified service on campus, limited to "one hour of class daily, then back to bed the rest of the morning till lunch time, then to bed until 3:30." From late afternoon to nine o'clock in the evening Carlos alternated his schedule between sitting, reading, writing (letters or manuscripts), and receiving visitors. As his strength improved, the physician promised to consider permitting him "to do much more" work by February. Meanwhile, for the first time in his life, he admitted needing "to be careful" in avoiding "all exertions and emotional upsets."[1]

Throughout the spring Castañeda made a steady recovery. Although he refrained from accepting new commitments, he selectively targeted old projects for a degree of advancement. One of these was the essay he had written for the 1953 meeting of the American Historical Association. He first offered the piece as his contribution to a special volume honoring the Reverend Dr. Francis Borgia Steck, O.F.M. Realizing, however, that the essay's focus might not fit the thematic scope of the volume, he shifted strategy and submitted the manuscript to *The Americas*. "I feel that it ought to be published," he wrote Alexander Wyse, a senior editor, "judging from the heated protest" the paper generated during the discussion period at the conference.[2] In the interim another essay on Spanish exploration and evangelization, initially published in *Extension Magazine*, appeared as a translated reprint in *Obsservatore Romano*.[3] From his convalescent bed Castañeda also adroitly promoted a publication of Francisco Cervantes de Salazar's *Diálogos*, a translation by Minnie

Lee Barrett Shepard for which he had written a lengthy introduction. The University of Texas Press distributed the work "as a memorial" to the four hundredth anniversary of the Royal and Pontifical University of Mexico (renamed in the twentieth century Universidad Nacional Autónoma de México).[4]

As the spring semester came to a close, Castañeda's work schedule picked up momentum. "I am feeling much better," he told the friars at the Academy of American Franciscan History: "[I] have continued to improve and [am] almost back to normal, but I have to rest a number of hours during the day, avoid all physical exercise and exertions, and lastly lead a calmer life." He conceded that the new regimen was hard for him, but he was "learning to do things in a lazy way, which seems to be what I will have to do . . . if I want to stay around a while." [5]

In the summer of 1954, as Castañeda indulged in a restful ten-day vacation at the southern tip of Texas in Brownsville, the Academy of American Franciscan History underwent a change of leadership.[6] Father Alexander Wyse entrusted the directorship to his chosen successor, Rev. Dr. Antonine S. Tibesar, O.F.M., who promptly sought Carlos's advice on sensitive issues involving the conduct of an exalted member of the historical fraternity.[7]

Confined to light duty in the summer months but anxious to contribute meaningfully to the profession, Carlos assisted Thomas E. Cotner as coeditor of a series of essays honoring the memory of Charles Wilson Hackett, founding director of the Institute of Latin American Studies.[8] In the fall Castañeda explored the possibility of securing a visiting faculty appointment for the summer of 1955 in Albuquerque. Capitalizing upon his experience writing *Our Catholic Heritage in Texas,* he contemplated expanding the scope of his research to include "the early history of the New Mexico Missions." As he had done on other occasions, Carlos envisioned combining teaching and research with a family vacation in the "Land of Enchantment." Not about to initiate anything that even remotely resembled the magnitude of *Our Catholic Heritage,* Castañeda outlined his plan to a friend, France V. Scholes, academic vice president at the University of New Mexico: "My idea is to write something on a popular vein, a matter of 'divulgarization' of New Mexico's rich and fascinating past. If I could teach in your Summer School it would give me an opportunity to use many sources I need to consult both in your Library and at Santa Fe." [9] Scholes kept Castañeda waiting for several months before informing him that he had arranged for a nephew to teach in New Mexico's summer program. Not resentful that the teaching venture in New Mexico had failed to materialize, Carlos offered Scholes friendly counsel: "I hope your health improves and that you take care of yourself as I have been doing since my heart attack a year ago." He also asked Scholes what inducement would be required to bring him to the University of Texas for a guest lecture. With Lewis Hanke away in Spain for most of the year, Castañeda suggested a springtime visit for which he would request from the Institute of Latin American Studies an honorarium of "$75.00, at least, maybe more." [10] Ultimately, administrative pressures at the Albuquerque campus related to "work on the annual budget" prevented Scholes from accepting Castañeda's invitation.[11] Meanwhile, the new director of the Academy of American Franciscan History solicited Carlos's advice on a complex plan for expanding the facilities of the research center. Father Tibesar proposed selling the academy's property in Washington for fifty thousand dollars and relocating the headquarters in the countryside near Potomac, Maryland. Cognizant of the high cost of land in the District of Columbia, Carlos told the friar he had underestimated "the real value of [the] present location." By way of concrete example, he described a local project in which he had been peripherally associated: "We bought two small fifty-four foot lots in Austin, opposite the University for the Newman Club for $100,000. But whatever you may be able to get for the . . . [present] location, it is an undisputed fact that it would never be sufficient to pay for the new plant you have envisioned." [12] Although he could not influence the real estate negotiations from Austin, Castañeda remained interested in "the general architectural plan for the proposed home of the combined Franciscan research center" [13] in Potomac, which eventually became a reality.

About this time Castañeda suspended most of his projects to master the skill of boating as a form of relaxation. Joe B. Frantz described the boat episodes on Austin and Travis Lakes "as typical Castañeda": "Most of the graduate students spent about half their time out there, caulking it, painting it, and the thing never would work, . . . he was no hand at machinery and it was always breaking down, and he was always getting four feet off shore and having to be rescued. He worked like a dog on the boat . . . and his tension flared over the boat as much as it ever had over anything else; so it was just a transference of tension and not a pleasure or recreation at all." [14]

Over time Castañeda invested in better equipment and better boats. About a year after acquiring his first craft, Carlos wrote a friend: "Next time you come and we go boat-riding we will have no trouble getting the engine started. I have a new quiet Johnson 25 motor with self-starter. All you . . . do is press the button and the boat is off." [15] Raymond Wheat, a faculty member at Sul Ross State College in Alpine, who had earlier gravitated toward Castañeda as a teacher and mentor, provided another glimpse of this new pastime: "His chief hobby in the 1950s . . . was his motor boat. He would take me and my two sons—then aged 12 and 9—on exciting tours of Lake Austin. He handled the boat somewhat as he did an automobile—or perhaps as a Spanish Don handled a spirited horse." [16] In his determined quest for prescribed relaxation

Castañeda progressed through several boats, beginning with a "13-foot" brown craft equipped with an "outboard motor," advancing to "a lighter, fiber-glass" model, and finally splurging on "a small cabin cruiser." Daughter Consuelo vividly recalled those outings with friends and family: "He did not care for fishing, but he just liked to ride out in the lakes. . . . He would ask fellow students to come along, to spend Saturday afternoon or Sunday afternoon and [to] bring their wives or just friends along. We would go with the family and just . . . spend an evening . . . [admiring] the sunset. . . . The young people would go swimming and my dad would just sit on the boat, smoke his pipe or cigar and enjoy talking with everybody." [17]

In the autumn of 1954 Castañeda cut back on his boating to help Elisa plan Consuelo's upcoming marriage to Hugo P. Artaza, an exchange student from Paraguay. Carlos scored a triumph when Bishop Louis J. Reicher accepted his invitation to witness "the exchange of marriage vows as official representative" of the Diocese of Austin, assisted by one of the graduate students, Rev. Charles E. Ronan, S.J., who agreed to celebrate the nuptial liturgy. As Father Ronan later recalled: "The Bishop wished to do this to show his regard and respect for Doctor Castañeda[,] who had done so much for the Church in Texas and who had been so highly honored by the Holy See." [18] Since the betrothed couple were university students, they chose the date of Saturday, December 18, for the wedding, two days after classes recessed for the Christmas vacation. At midmorning on the wedding day, which turned out to be "cold but sunny," the throngs of guests, many of whom were university students from out of town, arrived at Saint Austin's Church. In the vestibule of the church the wedding party lined up for the procession. On cue from the concelebrating clergy the procession began, with Castañeda more excited than the bride, only to be stopped and sent back to the vestibule. The nervous bridegroom caused the delay when he discovered he did not have the marriage license in his possession. The officiating clergy granted a fifteen-minute delay while he retrieved the document from the glove compartment of the car in which he had ridden to the church. Finally the procession resumed in earnest. As the bride and her father approached the altar, Carlos tripped, causing some guests in the congregation to wonder if the mishap was a warning of another heart attack. Throughout the ceremony, concerned about her father, Consuelo frequently glanced back to see that he was all right. After the service and the wedding photographs, the Castañeda-Artaza party gathered for a brunch reception at Green Pastures, a popular restaurant in south Austin. The newlyweds then left on a honeymoon trip to Mexico City, where they observed the celebration of Las Fiestas Navideñas. A week later they hurriedly drove to Brownsville for a family reunion on New Year's Day. Much to their disappointment, the newlyweds learned that Carlos and Elisa had canceled their trip to the valley for the holidays when their other daughter, Rosemary, became seriously ill with pneumonia.[19]

As the new year began, Castañeda resolved to assist Jack Autrey Dabbs in finishing the guide to the Juan Hernández y Dávalos Collection. After Dabbs finished writing entries for the guide on index cards, he and Carlos would collect a stack of original documents and go over the descriptions together. Dabbs recalled that whenever Castañeda

> came to anything that did not sound right, we would stop and check the manuscript. He caught several items in this way that I had done wrong or had missed. Sometimes we would have to change the spelling of a name, or he would question whether an action could have taken place as described. His detailed knowledge of Mexican history was of great value to us, and he handled just about every document in the collection in this fashion. He had little to do with the index or with the search to determine whether a given document had been published. But with my experience with the Guide and then with the Gondra calendar, I felt pretty secure with what I was doing.[20]

Through these efforts they finished the manuscript in the spring. Subsequently they proposed to the Institute of Latin American Studies a similar project for the Mariano Riva Palacio Archives. Their application was ultimately approved, and Dabbs began work on the guide sometime around August.[21]

In the summer Castañeda abandoned plans for a vacation in order "to stay right here and carry on in a futile effort" to finish "the many things" he had on his agenda.[22] In early June he delivered the principal luncheon address at the inaugural Southwest Writers Conference, sponsored by the newly formed South Texas Historical Association and the Corpus Christi Byliners. For his topic he suggested "a paper on José de Escandón," the first successful founder of the area now served by the new historical society.[23] The guide to the Riva Palacio Archives constituted another project, while a third task involved a promotional brochure on Fray Antonio Margil de Jesús and the Texas missions that Carlos had promised to draft for Henrietta Henry of Waco. Henry, who was seeking a state charter for the Texas Old Missions and Forts Restoration Association, also appealed to Castañeda for suggestions on how to obtain an endorsement from the Catholic hierarchy for a fund-raising campaign. "I think our cause is right," he reassured her, "and [it] is for the good of both the Church and the State."[24]

Cautiously increasing his workload, Castañeda petitioned the university administration for "a Research Assignment for the Spring Semester 1955–1956," which was granted. That designation, combined with a "leave of absence for the term stipulated," meant that Carlos could at last take advantage of the offer by the Creole Petroleum Company to finance a research trip to Venezuela.[25] His authorized leave permitted the history department to transfer his "unused salary" of $3,950 to a discretionary account called "Honoraria for Visiting Consultants."[26]

In autumn Carlos found ample reason to rejoice. On November 19 his daughter Consuelo gave birth to a son whom the parents named Hugo. Overcome with emotion, Castañeda neglected correspondence and other projects, blaming "an uproar" in the household created by the arrival of his "new grandson." He characterized himself as "a dazed grandfather and absent-minded professor" who had allowed projects to drift.[27]

By early December, Carlos had regained full control of his work schedule. Grateful for the spiritual guidance he had received as an undergraduate, he volunteered to serve on a fund-raising campaign for a modern Newman Club Center. "I don't know why," he told Henrietta Henry, "but I seem to have a [k]nack of getting involved into more things than any other human being I know." Specifically, he had accepted the charge of sending a personal appeal "to Papal Knights mostly." He said, "We have a dozen or more Papal knights who are filthy with money and who could, if they wanted, easily contribute a quarter of a million dollars to put up a building." Henry's new organization advocating the restoration of Spanish colonial monuments also needed funds to attain its goals, but Carlos emphasized to her the difficulty of getting Papal Knights to respond to an appeal: "I am beginning to doubt if there is a lance sharp enough and stout to penetrate their armor or a battle axe so sharp as to reach their frozen brains when it comes to turning loose money for a cause worthwhile. Time will tell."[28] Besides the final volume of *Our Catholic Heritage*, Castañeda's writing commitments included "an address for a historical meeting in Louisiana" to be delivered in January, an article for *Catholic Encyclopedia* "now being revised," and a "brochure on the Texas missions" to insert in an upcoming publication from the Academy of American Franciscan History, *Life of Fray Antonio Margil, O.F.M.*, by Eduardo Enríque Ríos.[29]

During the holidays Castañeda practiced moderation by not imbibing "too much cheer but just enough to be cheerful." Two days into the new year he resumed work on a number of pending projects. First he reviewed the application papers for a charter for the Texas Old Missions and Forts Restoration Association, which he found "entirely satisfactory" and without need for any revisions. Next he telephoned the Chancery of Austin for an appointment with Bishop Reicher to discuss the goals of the new organization.[30] A week later, after conferring with the prelate, Carlos summarized for Henrietta the outcome of their discussion: "He pointed out that since our project is intended to mark and reconstruct, if possible, the location of all the Spanish missions in Texas, this would affect the jurisdiction of all the Bishops; that in order to avoid future difficulties and conflict he would suggest that before the charter is obtained, the approval of Archbishop [Robert E.] Lucey and all the various Bishops in Texas be obtained and that they be invited to subscribe to the charter and asked to suggest a layman from each of the Dioceses respectively [to serve on an advisory board]." [31] Deeming the prelate's suggestion a "sound" one, he continued: "We certainly do not want to start out full of hope and find ourselves in a pickle over jurisdictional matters from the start." In observance of ecclesiastical protocol, he dispatched a letter to Archbishop Lucey, within whose archdiocese were located most of the monuments of the Spanish colonial era, hoping to win his endorsement before contacting other prelates in Texas. Still, as he cautioned Henrietta, the prompt receipt of the necessary responses from "the entire hierarchy" would be tantamount to a small "miracle." [32]

In mid-January, Castañeda set aside his preparations for the trip to South America to discharge another outstanding commitment—delivering the keynote address at a meeting of the North Louisiana Historical Association at Shreveport. His paper, "The Caddos: Their Customs, Traditions and Land," focused on the main group of natives who had inhabited the territory "on the Red River, just above where the Sabine River joins it" and thus asserted claim as "chiefs of all tribes in the vicinity." [33]

News of Castañeda's upcoming trip to Venezuela traveled far, spread by a network of friends and former students. Learning of his visit, the Texas Ex-Students Association of Lima, Peru, invited him to speak to the alumni in that Andean city on March 2, Texas Independence Day. "Barring unforeseen circumstances," he informed University president Logan Wilson, "I will fly from Caracas to Lima for that purpose during my stay in Venezuela." Acutely aware of the rules of protocol in Spanish-speaking countries, especially in academic circles, Castañeda recommended to the president that he be commissioned to convey official and "friendly greetings" from the Austin campus "to the Rectors of universities and colleges in Venezuela and Perú." Recalling earlier successes in Mexico, he reminded the president to attach "the official seal and ribbons" to each document of greeting. [34] Wilson accepted Carlos's suggestion and asked him to compile a list of the rectors' full names, their proper titles, and addresses of institutions. [35] Castañeda also enlisted the endorsement of the Good Neighbor Commission of Texas and Gov. Allan Shivers to enhance the status of his personal diplomacy. [36]

As Castañeda finalized plans in Austin, his hosts in Venezuela prepared a full itinerary, complete with a VIP reception at the airport. On February 9, 1956, the aircraft that he and Elisa had boarded in Texas landed at Maiquetia International Airport, named in honor of the nearest village and located forty-five minutes' driving distance from Caracas. Outside the terminal near the runway U.S. ambassador Fletcher Warren, another 1921 graduate of the University of Texas, joined Vicente Cupello, of Creole Petroleum's public relations department, in welcoming the distinguished scholar. Delighted by the surprise reunion with a fellow classmate, Castañeda escorted Elisa as they exchanged greetings with other members of the welcoming delegation.[37] Waiting for their luggage to be unloaded, Carlos gave Ambassador Warren a summary of his itinerary, including the side trip to Lima. As "an enthusiastic and loyal" alumnus, the envoy quickly persuaded his friend to remain in Venezuela instead while the embassy staged on March 2 "the first Texas Exes rally in Caracas." Warren explained that "over 4,000 Texans" resided in Venezuela, of whom more than a thousand were graduates of the University of Texas. If Castañeda agreed to stay in Caracas for the event, the ambassador promised to attend the rally as honorary chairman "of the meeting of Texas-Exes." Overwhelmed by the social swirl, Carlos quickly sent an air-mail report to Logan Wilson advising him of the change of schedule.[38]

In his first round of activity in Caracas, Castañeda visited the Central University of Venezuela and the National Academy of Languages. At "a special program" commemorating the centennial of the birth of Juan Manuel Cagagal, founder of the School of Engineering and the Academy of Mathematical Sciences, he enjoyed being recognized as the official representative of the University of Texas.[39] Besides the academic communities, Carlos also toured the installations of Creole Petroleum at Langunillas, Tía Juana, and La Salina, all located directly west of the capital city. At a luncheon hosted by the company at Tía Juana Country Club, Castañeda informed journalists that the "main purpose of his visit" was to use the scholarship awarded to him to study Venezuela's history and to consult ecclesiastical archives "concerning the colonial times." Trying to anticipate their needs on the road, Vicente Cupello accompanied the Castañedas to every event.[40] Typical of these visits was Carlos's sojourn in southwestern Venezuela, where he personally delivered President Wilson's greetings to Dr. Joaquín Mármol Luzardo, rector of the Universidad de Los Andes in the town of Mérida, situated on the eastern spur of the cordillera approximately 350 miles from Caracas. Following customary formalities, the rector guided the guest from Texas to "the archives and the old books." In the auditorium of the law school library Carlos addressed an assembly of faculty and students about the University of Texas, describing its establishment and operation. In closing he expressed a "desire" to promote cultural exchanges "among institutions of higher learning all over the Americas." Dr. Mármol Luzardo subsequently advised President Wilson: "We are all in favor of this idea, as it will make much easier the tasks our universities are engaged in."[41]

From Mérida near the Andes, Carlos's small entourage traveled north to the coastal region of Lake Maracaibo, where he delivered greetings and a lecture at the Universidad Nacional de Zulia. Highly pleased with the outcome of his speaking tour, he especially relished being "lionized and treated as a king everywhere." At the end of three weeks he recorded his impressions of Venezuela and Caracas, whose burgeoning population had expanded in the last decade from two hundred thousand inhabitants to nearly a million: "This is a wonderful country and Caracas has an ideal climate. People live here to 80 and 100 as a general thing. . . . It is amazing. Talking about the prophecy of tremendous development in this part of the world, Venezuela is a shining example of it." Lamentably, he observed, unprecedented development also fomented unbridled inflation: "The dollar here shrinks into insignificance and the U.S. tourist finds that his dollar buys just a third of what it does in the good old U.S.A. When I get back, . . . I'll still kick about high taxes, but not prices. No hotel here, even the lowest, has a room for less than $5.00 a day, and the type of hotel called first class charges $15.00 a day for single, $20.00 U.S. for double. Meals are something out of this world. You can't get a breakfast for less than $1.25 and a noon day meal for less than $3.00. If you want a good meal, it runs [from] $8.00 to $10.00." Notwithstanding the effects of inflation, Carlos appreciated the opportunity of traveling through the vast expanse of a country that had produced national heroes of the stature of Francisco de Miranda and Simón de Bolívar. Mindful of his less than robust health, he attended mass on a daily basis.[42]

Meanwhile, the American Embassy staff proceeded with plans for the alumni rally in Caracas on March 2. Castañeda, having decided to remain at the capital, asked his former graduate student E. Victor Niemeyer, director of the Cultural American-Peruvian Center in Lima, to act as his surrogate in conveying President Wilson's greetings and his own "regrets to the Texas Exes" in the Andean highlands.[43] A few days before the scheduled rally in Caracas, a communication from Austin arrived at the American Embassy. In addition to sending a message for Castañeda to read on March 2, Logan Wilson commended Fletcher Warren for his initiative: "I trust that the occasion will not only be one for the formation and renewal of associations and ties among our own former students, but also between the people of Venezuela and those of this country."[44]

On Friday evening, March 2, 1956, Carlos and Elisa went to the American Embassy to attend the rally. Ambassador Warren circulated easily among the guests, as did Castañeda, who hardly needed coaching on the art of greeting people.[45] During the program the ambassador formally introduced his fellow classmate, who read the message from the president of the University of Texas addressed to the alumni "in Caracas and all Venezuela": "I am delighted to learn that our Professor Carlos E. Castañeda is meeting with you on this important occasion. . . . It is gratifying . . . that we have in Venezuela more than 1,000 graduates of the University of Texas. We are greatly honored by having included among our former students there the distinguished Ambassador from the United States, Mr. Fletcher Warren, a graduate of the Class of 1921, and a classmate of Dr. Castañeda." In conclusion President Wilson expressed the hope that the March 2 gathering in Caracas would become an annual event.[46] Castañeda then gave "a splendid talk" that resulted in the organization of a Venezuelan alumni chapter, whose application for a charter he offered to hand carry to Austin. Pleased with the rally and its result, Fletcher Warren predicted: "We are now squared away for a real celebration on March 2, 1957."[47]

Toward the end of the rally, as guests mingled before leaving, an alumnus of the class of 1936 named Brinsdale casually informed Castañeda that he had acquired "a complete set of the *Caracas Gazette,* a very rare and valuable" local newspaper, as well as numerous "other books," mostly about Venezuela. Brinsdale asked Carlos if the Latin American Library at the Austin campus "would be interested in receiving his Venezuelan collection as a gift." Recognizing a windfall, Castañeda accepted the offer and then discussed details with the donor about "its shipment through the Embassy."[48]

In the last two weeks of his sojourn in Caracas, Carlos accepted an invitation to present a formal talk at the Academia Nacional de la Historia. Attired in a dark suit accented by a black bow tie, he delivered his remarks to a large audience without the benefit of a podium. Afterward Monsignor Nicolás E. Navarro, the rector who had accompanied him on the platform, committed the academy to an exchange program with the University of Texas, "which is so similar to our traditions and our history."[49] Amid his last courtesy calls in the capital Castañeda returned to the campus of the Universidad Central de Venezuela, with which he had "become quite familiar," to examine archival collections.[50] On March 21, having expressed farewells to their hosts, Carlos and Elisa boarded an aircraft for the flight to Texas. Castañeda's efforts in Venezuela had earned a letter of appreciation from President Wilson, who praised especially "the meeting at the Embassy and the fine public relations work you are incidentally accomplishing for the University."[51]

In Austin once again, Castañeda basked in the afterglow of his adventure in South America. Undoubtedly at Elisa's insistence he rested for a few days before resuming work on unfinished tasks. One completed project from which he derived much satisfaction was the release, after years of hard toil, of *Independent Mexico in Documents: Independence, Empire, and Republic,* a work that he and Jack Dabbs considered a culminating footnote "to the story of the Hernández y Dávalos collection." George Peter Hammond of the University of California at Berkeley conferred unstinting praise: "This book, representing an inestimable amount of labor, could only have been done by someone with a knowledge of the problems of the researcher. Scholarship is immeasurably enriched by tools of this nature." [52]

As the spring days became fairly pleasant and predictable, Carlos took his family and student friends for boat rides on the nearby lakes. On May 8, 1956, without warning, he sustained another "coronary attack" that required intensive care at Seton Hospital. During "the first 36 hours" the attending physician described Carlos's prognosis as "a tossup" and advised the family to call a priest to anoint the patient. When his condition stabilized, the medical staff moved him to a regular ward where for a whole month he continued recovering. Following his release from the hospital Carlos stayed home for long-term convalescence. Within a few days the constraint of not being allowed to do anything caused brief spells of boredom. Although for years he had resisted the temptation, his fear that boredom might progress to depression motivated Carlos to convince Elisa they should purchase a television set. That summer, while he stayed "at home all the time" without doing "much of anything" other than sitting and writing a few letters for "a couple of hours" at a stretch, television provided a distraction for the restless patient. Later in the summer he avowed that this new medium of communication was an excellent way "to while away the time and to see . . . baseball, boxing, and football this winter." Not surprisingly, the traumatic ordeal had left him "somewhat shaky ever since." With a tinge of melancholy humor, Castañeda reflected on the irony that he, who "years ago" had been compared to a "Spanish tornado," was "now hardly a gentle breeze." [53] "Everybody from the doctor on down" advised him to relax, and so he guarded against overexertion.

Writing in August to Henrietta Henry, he expressed enthusiasm for her manuscript article "Spanish Missions in Texas" and disquietude over his own project, the seventh volume of *Our Catholic Heritage*. At times in mild desperation, he expressed the wish that the volume would come out before he died. One thought that especially troubled him was the fact that of the members of the Texas Historical Commission who had begun the work in 1932, only a trio remained—Bishops Mariano S. Garriga and Lawrence J. FitzSimon and himself.[54]

In the fall of 1956, almost completely recovered, Castañeda returned to the classroom on a part-time basis. On weekends when the weather was warm or mild he indulged in his boat rides, habitually insisting on the presence of two or more graduate students for companionship and, more importantly, for assistance in an emergency. One of these students, Valdemar Rodríguez, remembered that Castañeda had procured "a beautiful boat" toward the end of his life. Concerned for their professor's health, the students usually performed all tasks that required physical stamina. Reminiscing about these outings, Rodríguez described an idyllic scene: "And we would go out there and camp; he liked sardines and onions and crackers. . . . We never fished or anything like that, we just rode the boat." [55]

Although he had curtailed his work schedule, students who consulted Castañeda about a variety of problems found his capacity for engagement undiminished. One whom he advised was Robert Kelly Acosta, a student of bicultural lineage. Acosta had applied for a room in Moore-Hill Hall, then one of the newest dormitories on campus. Acosta's ancestry, combined with the fact that he was the first Tejano allowed to live in the dormitory, irritated some of the other residents, notably students from east Texas. Unable to oust him through acts of snobbery, some in the dormitory resorted to "mean" pranks. On the verge of quitting the residence hall, Acosta sought out Castañeda "for consolation and support." After hearing the student's story and checking out his record of superior grades, Don Carlos shared this advice: "Integration, indeed, is important. Stay at Moore Hall. The problem you describe is not yours but theirs. Acculturation works both ways. You need them and they need you. Stick to the matter and do not run away. Soon they will recognize that it is not the color of the skin that makes a difference. You certainly are equipped to prove this thesis." Greatly encouraged by the advice but heartened even more because a distinguished professor had taken time to listen to his problem, Acosta remained in the dormitory. Gradually, when the other students discovered his scholastic record of "many A's," they stopped their harassment and began consulting him as a tutor.[56] Similarly another student, William Soza, visited Castañeda in his Tower office in the fall of 1956 to discuss an issue related to the Alba Club, its membership, and scholastic achievement. He emerged from the meeting with tremendous respect and admiration for this historian: "I recall vividly the intensity of [Castañeda's] competitiveness and intellectual powers. He was most pleased that day. He said, 'We really got them this time. We got three of our Mexicanos [inducted in]to Phi Beta Kappa—two of them in the third year.' After that we went into discussing the Alba Club and its current and future activities." [57]

Off and on during the year, squeezed between international trips, hospitalization, convalescence, teaching, and counseling sessions, Castañeda finally concluded the seventh volume of *Our Catholic Heritage*. Immensely relieved, he sent the manuscript to Father James P. Gibbons at Saint Edward's University for editorial review. Oddly, for several months the editor postponed reading the final draft, distracted by the possibility of a reassignment to aid his slow convalescence. Piqued by the priest's dilatory behavior, but more because no one offered a workable solution to the impasse, Carlos mailed a lengthy complaint: "Personally I am fed up and feel that with only a few more years of life left, I need to turn my energies to something more concrete and of more advantage to me. I'll be glad to serve in an advisory capacity, or as editor, or anything else, but not as the old battle ax or war horse that I have been." [58] Late in the fall, shortly before his sixtieth birthday, Castañeda discussed the delay with Robert H. Kelley of Houston, a fellow knight in the Equestrian Order of the Holy Sepulchre, who agreed to "put the pressure on dear Father Gibbons" in an effort to see if the editor could expedite the manuscript. Ultimately the leadership of the Knights of Columbus resolved the deadlock by virtue of oblique maneuvers. The chief knight politely but firmly asked Father Gibbons to "turn over the completed manuscript to the State Council," which would then convey it to Reverend Monsignor William H. Oberste in Refugio "for final editing." An exasperated Castañeda appealed to the monsignor: "Lord, how I do hope we can get it to the printer soon. I shall be glad to help and cooperate with illustrations, the bibliography, the indexing, and proofreading. Ever since Father Foik's days proofs have been read jointly always by the editor and myself." [59]

Satisfied that the State Council had taken charge of guiding the manuscript to publication, Carlos paused in November to enjoy his patron saint's feast day and his sexagenarian celebration. Consuelo, the eldest daughter, described his exuberant conduct on such special occasions: "Whenever we would give him something—for his birthday or for Christmas, well, he'd take it right out and put it on—whatever it was . . . shoes or a tie or socks. Well, he was like a kid about Christmas and birthdays, and he anticipated with eagerness to see what he was going to receive. And no matter how big or how small the present was, he just made a big to-do over it." [60]

Renewed by the November observances that meant much to him, Castañeda extended his exuberance into the Christmas season with the purchase of a "1957 Dodge, 2-door sedan" to augment the family's transportation. Modest investments in the stock market and a tidy savings account had at last given Carlos a modicum of middle-class security. [61]

During the holidays Carlos confronted another long delay in publishing the seventh volume of *Our Catholic Heritage*. Father Gibbons, reassigned to Holy Cross Seminary in Indiana, had departed and taken with him all the materials related to the unfinished volume. Three months into the new year, after rummaging through his personal papers, the former editor mailed two bundles containing remnants of Castañeda's last manuscript—one to the publisher and another to Monsignor Oberste. Upon receiving his packet in Refugio, Oberste promptly notified Archbishop Lucey (who was instrumental in his appointment as the new editor) that he would travel to Austin to consult with Don Carlos "about the steps to be taken . . . to get out this final volume without [further] delay." Charitable to a fault, the monsignor absolved his predecessor of intentional procrastination. He wrote, "I think Father Gibbons is now glad that the matter has been taken out of his hands." [62]

Meanwhile Von Boeckmann-Jones set the material it had received into type and then sent the manuscript and galley proofs to Edwin D. Gunter, executive secretary of the Texas State Council in Austin. In turn, Gunter personally delivered the materials to Castañeda, who was shocked by the mutilated condition of his manuscript and by the consequent "mess" in the galleys. "I suppose," he wrote Oberste, "the printers will just have to start again from scratch. Really the long manuscript corrections should be refused by the ordinary printer. I still wonder where the rest of the materials are. Mr. Gunter assured me he had received nothing and he is under the impression that Father Gibbons probably will send the rest of the materials to you." [63] Remembering the difficulties he had had assembling sufficient data to compose the manuscript, Castañeda described to his new editor the amount of reconstructive work that would be necessary to salvage his scholarship: "Frankly I am dismayed at the mess in which my original manuscript is and I am afraid a lot of it is going to have to be retyped. I'll try to go over what Mr. Gunter [re]turned to me and I hope the rest of the material will come to you in whatever form . . . before you come . . . to Austin and we can discuss the whole matter, decide on a plan of action and then I will be able to go ahead once I know what we are to do. Mr. Gunter offered the services of his office for recopying." Finally, Castañeda expressed the hope that "the Lord give you the patience of Job and the strength of Hercules for the task is no less than that of the classical [Augean] stables." [64]

In facing the latest challenge associated with the seventh volume, Castañeda altered his work habits. Although he had resumed full-time teaching at the university, he adjusted his schedule to include more writing and resting time at home. Taking advantage of the new Dodge sedan, occasionally he and Elisa indulged in weekend excursions to Houston to visit their married daughter and her family and, whenever time permitted, to stop by the library of Incarnate Word Academy for discussions about travel in Mexico with Sister M. Agatha Sheehan, whose graduate study he had supervised. [65]

Fortunately for Castañeda and the editorial process, Monsignor Oberste enjoyed the support of "a very fine Assistant Priest" to whom he delegated many routine duties around the parish. With his schedule lightened, the editor applied himself to the task "of getting out his volume as soon as possible." After carefully reading galley sheets against manuscript pages, Oberste checked the corrections that Father Gibbons had made in Castañeda's typescript. Acknowledging that some of the former editor's alterations were "quite apropos," the monsignor refrained from changing Castañeda's writing style, except for revising a "few sentence structures" and substituting "some words" to clarify obscure passages. Otherwise, he told Carlos: "Your writing runs quite smoothly with a clear continuity." To relieve the author of the monotony of revisions, the priest asked him to mail "carbon copies" of chapters in his personal archive for reference in rechecking comparisons and marking "down my own suggestions." Oberste assured Castañeda, "You can then review the corrected copies, and revise them according to your own judgment, for after all you *are* the author." [66]

Highly impressed with the monsignor's gracious style of editing, Castañeda conducted a "terrific search among mountains of materials" at home and at the office for the chapter carbons to expedite the revisions. Promising to devote regular time to the enterprise after the end of the spring term, Carlos declared he was "holding up pretty well" with his "classes, committee meetings, [and] dissertations to supervise," as well as a manuscript for a textbook and "a few odds and ends." [67]

Among those odds and ends was Castañeda's commitment to read a paper in Lincoln, Nebraska, at the fiftieth annual meeting of the Mississippi Valley Historical Association, May 2–4, 1957. Unable to attend the conference because of his heart problem, Carlos asked Joe B. Frantz to read his essay "on Spain's reaction to French incursions on the Mississippi" at the Spanish Southwest session, chaired by John A. Hawgood of Birmingham, England. Castañeda's essay spanned a century of intercolonial rivalry in the gulf region, extending from La Salle's encroachment in east Texas to the Peace of Paris of 1763, which expelled France as a power in North America.[68] His friend's assistance in reading the paper allowed Carlos to clear his own campus calendar by the end of the semester.

In June, Castañeda met with Monsignor Oberste in Austin to assess the work that had been completed and to identify outstanding issues. Following their meeting Oberste apprised Archbishop Lucey about the progress they had accomplished: "I have read the entire manuscript, suggested some revisions, and now Dr. Castañeda will have made his own revisions within the next few days so that the manuscript will be ready for the printers by the beginning of August. There remains, of course, the reading of the galley and page proofs, and also the writing of a proper index." Thinking of marketing angles, Castañeda and Oberste recommended to the prelate including a photograph of Pope Pius XII "as the frontispiece" and also incorporating a letter from His Holiness commending the Knights of Columbus "for their outstanding work in publishing the history of the Church in Texas." The archbishop, they wrote, could decide how to route the matter "through proper channels." [69]

As he grappled with revisions during the summer Castañeda contemplated a way of enhancing the aesthetic quality of the last volume. Remembering a prior collaboration with José Cisneros, he discussed with the artist in El Paso the possibility of creating a "symbolic page" depicting the Knights of Columbus. Once again in firm control of the rewriting, he confidently estimated a realistic deadline of July 31, after which he would assemble "the entire manu-script complete and ready to turn over to Von Boeckmann the first week in August, maps, illustrations, etc., all in final form." The "last task" that Carlos and Oberste faced was the work of arranging alphabetically "a condensed bi-ography of the hierarchy of Texas," which they anticipated finishing in "a couple of days" in September.[70]

Meanwhile José Cisneros prepared "a rough sketch" for the full-page illus-tration Carlos and the monsignor wanted to insert opposite a drawing of Mis-sion Concepción. Sharing the sketch with Oberste, Carlos explained that the artist preferred to include the state seal, which was more complementary in design, rather than the outline of Texas behind the shield of the Knights of Co-lumbus. Taking the initiative, Carlos authorized Cisneros "to go ahead with the final drawing," but to reduce the size of a knight's helmet, which seemed to be "a little out of proportion."[71]

After the Fourth of July and just before the start of the second summer ses-sion, Castañeda traveled to Brownsville for a week's vacation.[72] Anxious to confer with Oberste, he detoured through Refugio, near Corpus Christi, where the two scholars discussed small technical problems that needed to be resolved. Upon returning to Austin, Carlos met with Edwin Gunter, from whom he learned that the State Council had arranged with Von Boeckmann-Jones to take all remaining copies of the first six volumes and "to dispose" of them as "complete sets" among the various Knights of Columbus councils throughout Texas. By liquidating the company's inventory of unsold books, the State Council hoped to encourage the publisher to show "greater interest" in pro-moting the seventh volume. As soon as Castañeda received Cisneros's "fin-ished pen picture" of the Knights of Columbus emblem, he showed it to Gun-ter, who "liked it very much." Eager to conclude another facet of the project, Carlos sent the drawing to Oberste for his approval, at the same time asking the editor to nudge the State Council to compensate the artist for his work "in the amount of $50.00." With "two more jobs" yet remaining—compiling a bibliography and "an appendix with an alphabetical list of the hierarchy of Texas"—Castañeda proclaimed with "great feeling" that this labor of love would "be finally completed in every detail" a quarter of a century after he first "began to work on it."[73]

Castañeda and Oberste fulfilled their responsibilities in connection with the last volume of *Our Catholic Heritage* a few days before their self-imposed deadline. With time left for last-minute editorial cosmetics, Oberste hinted to Carlos that to give the closing paragraph in the preface a bit "more of an 'umph,'" he should expand it. He continued, "What your book will mean for the future generations, made possible through the funding of the Knights, might be worthwhile stressing."[74] Carlos readily accepted the suggestion and revised the preface to give proper recognition to the Knights of Columbus. For typing the appendix and bibliography, both of which were supplemental tasks, he asked Oberste to secure a modest additional stipend from the State Council.[75]

Castañeda's recommendations seemed reasonable to Oberste, who wrote Gunter that fifty dollars for Cisneros's rendering of "the escutcheon of the Texas State Council" was justified "for so distinguished a drawing." As to the supplemental writing that Castañeda had "been called upon" to perform, the editor recommended "a payment of $150.00 for this extra work," which the State Council approved.[76]

At midmorning on August 6, 1957, Carlos Eduardo Castañeda toted a hefty bundle as he strolled into the offices of the Texas State Council in south Austin. With an infectious grin on his face, he delivered the finished manuscript to Edwin Gunter. That afternoon Gunter conveyed the packet to Von Boeckmann-Jones. "I suppose everything is now up to the printer," Carlos later wrote Oberste. "Praised be the Lord!" In a generous mood, Carlos suggested spreading the credit around by asking Oberste to recommend to Archbishop Lucey the appointment of Reverend Monsignor Anton J. Frank, pastor of Annunciation Church in Houston, as *censor deputatus* to confer the "Nihil Obstat or imprimatur," verification that the contents of the manuscript conformed to ecclesiastical standards.[77] When Lucey acceded to the request, Castañeda was delighted: "He will appreciate the honor, the job is not onerous, and it is a small distinction that he has earned for the long years in the Commission and his deep interest in the history of the Church in Texas."[78]

Two days after delivering his manuscript to the State Council, Castañeda exulted to Oberste: "I feel like a new man now that I do not have that . . . [burden] on my shoulders that has weighed down on me for a quarter of a century. It is a delightful relief, I am here to tell you."[79] Looking ahead to the end of the summer session on August 27, Carlos contemplated relaxing for "a day or two" at Monsignor Oberste's "seaside cottage." The cleric, who had developed a cordial relationship with Castañeda, expressed great pleasure with the idea and advised: "My little cottage at the bay should be ready after August 27 following a complete renovation, and I shall certainly be disappointed if you will not come down for several days [of] rest."[80]

Castañeda's fantasy of a brief vacation vanished quickly, however. Grading papers and supervising dissertations "crowded" his schedule, as did helping his daughter Rosemary get ready for school. "I am afraid I am not going . . . to get out for the rest in your little cottage by the Gulf," he lamented to Oberste at the end of August.[81] Concerned about his friend's health, the monsignor extended an alternative invitation for "the Thanksgiving or Christmas holidays." In the meantime he shared with Carlos a copy of a letter from Archbishop Lucey praising them for their mutual foresight in soliciting an endorsement from the Vatican for the last volume of *Our Catholic Heritage*.[82] The letter read: "The cordial communication from His Holiness Pope Pius XII will . . . be a source of satisfaction to our . . . Knights of Columbus as well as to the Most Reverend Ordinaries of Texas, the Historical Commission . . . and in a particular way to our good friend Dr. Carlos Castañeda. Congratulations . . . for your thoughtfulness in obtaining this letter as an introduction to the final volume of this excellent series. Greetings."[83] Pleased with the latest developments, Castañeda suggested that in late September or early October he and Oberste should "pay the publisher a visit" to deliver the illustrations for the volume and to pick up galley proofs, if they were ready.[84]

With volume 7 in press Castañeda now focused his energy on affairs at the university. One matter that engaged his attention related to the publication of a dissertation he had directed, "Francisco Zarco, Spokesman of Liberalism in Mexico," by Raymond C. Wheat. A grateful author later acknowledged the assistance rendered by his mentor: "Perhaps the outstanding thing that comes to mind was the way Dr. Castañeda taught me how to write. I had earned my MA Degree at Sul Ross State University; but my thesis, a translation of a book by Nellie Campobello, was not an outstanding piece of work. Dr. Castañeda spent hours revising the manuscript of my dissertation; I think I wrote Chapter I about five times."[85] Eager to induct Wheat into the realm of established authors, Castañeda had sent the Zarco manuscript to Librería Porrúa Hermanos y Cía in Mexico City for publication in Spanish. His endorsement alone, according to Wheat, sealed the editorial board's decision: "They published it—naturally it was acceptable if Dr. Castañeda [had] sent it. What a fortunate person I was to have been his student!"[86] Convinced of the merit of the work, Castañeda had also, however, offered the publisher a judicious incentive. Earlier in the year he had persuaded the executive committee of the Latin American Studies Institute to authorize an expenditure, not to exceed a thousand dollars, for the purchase of 250 copies of the Francisco Zarco title. Subsequent to that decision the committee adopted "a uniform policy" to govern such expenditures by requiring an external evaluation of "any manuscript being contemplated for publication under similar terms." In principle Carlos agreed to the new policy, but when the executive committee attempted to enforce the rule retroactively, he stubbornly resisted because a prolonged delay would sabotage the Zarco project. Appealing the matter to President Logan Wilson, he succeeded in getting the decision overturned. Carlos justified the manner in which he had promoted the project by arguing that the book's timely publication would identify "the University of Texas with the observance of the first centennial of the liberal Constitution of 1857 which remained in force until 1917." Proud of Wheat's research, Castañeda explained that "until this study was made under my direction," virtually nothing had been initiated either in Mexico or the United States in the form of a critical assessment of Francisco Zarco.[87]

Castañeda's solicitude also extended to incoming graduate students. José Roberto Juárez, an alumnus of Saint Edward's University, typified the new generation of scholars. Married and with a growing family, Juárez enrolled at the University of Texas in the fall of 1957 as a Woodrow Wilson Fellow. Shortly after arriving on campus he went by Castañeda's office to introduce himself. The student remembered:

> He received me as he always did subsequently, with a big smile and body language that told you he was there to help even though he was buried in piles of paper. . . . He got to the personal level right away as a means of making . . . [me] feel at home. . . . He was delighted to find out I was from Laredo and that I was fluent in Spanish. Immediately we shifted to our mother tongue. He advised me . . . what courses to take, suggested I earn as many Spanish credits as possible through challenge exams, and started me on my way to a Master's Degree in Latin American Studies with a major in History and minors in Anthropology and Literature.[88]

Castañeda remained constantly alert for opportunities to foster cultural exchanges with Mexico under the auspices of the Institute of Latin American Studies. Late in the fall Dr. Antonio Castro Leal, director of the summer school and extension programs at the Universidad Nacional Autónoma de México (UNAM), paid a visit to Carlos's office in the library Tower. Wanting to encourage "closer cooperation" between UNAM and the University of Texas, the director asked Carlos to act as an intermediary with Logan Wilson in designating two faculty members, "with or without students," to participate in the summer program in Mexico. Specifically, Dr. Castro Leal needed a historian who could "give five public lectures" on United States history, "tracing briefly its [developments] to 1900" and then examining in detail modern trends in the twentieth century. He wanted a second instructor to offer parallel lectures in American literature. President Wilson responded "with interest" to the UNAM proposal.[89]

Castro Leal, through Castañeda, also informed Wilson that "for 13 years" the UNAM extension courses had been offered in San Antonio. He invited the UT president, or his representative, to attend the inaugural ceremony for the new session on January 12, 1958, at the downtown campus of San Antonio College. Finally, the director inquired if he and his staff could meet with Wilson "to discuss matters concerning mutual interchange and cooperation between the two universities that may be of interest to the United States and Mexico." [90]

Earlier Castañeda would have leaped at the opportunity to serve the University of Texas in an exchange program with UNAM. Late in life, however, two factors weighed against such a commitment, namely his health and a paternal instinct to be with his married daughter's family as she awaited delivery of another child. During the Christmas break Carlos, Elisa, and Rosemary rushed to Houston to spend part of the holidays with Consuelo and Hugo Artaza. While there, Castañeda sent a message to Logan Wilson urging him to appoint someone to represent the University of Texas "at the inauguration" of UNAM's extension courses in San Antonio on January 12.[91]

After Christmas, believing that Consuelo would not give birth for another week, Carlos, Elisa, and Rosemary leisurely drove south to Brownsville, a distance of 352 miles, to welcome the new year among the Castañeda clan. Their happy reunion was interrupted on January 1, the day after their arrival, when they received "an urgent telephone call" from their son-in-law informing them that Consuelo had gone into labor. Racing against the clock, they stopped in Refugio long enough to refuel the Dodge and to retrieve an overnight case Elisa had left behind at a Humble gasoline station on a previous visit. Continuing the journey in a gallant "effort to beat the stork," the weary travelers ran into an unseasonable snowstorm that retarded their progress. They finally arrived in Houston late in the evening. Disappointed that the stork had flown faster than they, the three Castañedas welcomed the news that Consuelo and Hugo "had a fine baby boy" whom they intended "to christen Carlos Policarpo." [92] Obviously the choice for the child's first name greatly pleased the doting grandfather.

Upon returning to Austin the first weekend in January, Castañeda casually reviewed his calendar of activities. First he inquired at Von Boeckmann-Jones about the status of page proofs, which had been delayed by the demands of a special session of the Texas legislature. Rather than continuing to call personally, he asked Edwin Gunter to telephone Werner Jessen at Von Boeckmann-Jones and pressure him "to hurry up the work." Next he wrote to his longtime friend Bishop FitzSimon, who had suffered a stroke, to wish him a speedy recovery. Through the *West Texas Register,* a diocesan newspaper in Amarillo, he had learned that the prelate was "again able to walk with a little help." [93] Then he proudly sent to Logan Wilson an advance copy of Raymond Wheat's *Francisco Zarco,* attaching to it blurbs from book reviews published in Mexican newspapers that completely justified his early support of the project. The critic for *La Prensa* had written: "Of facile reading, interesting, and beautifully simple as the life of Francisco Zarco. . . . It is up to the present the most important biography we have of the man. . . . It will occupy a place of honor on our bookcases and libraries." *Excelsior* acclaimed the work of Porrúa, pointing out that the publisher "leaves nothing to be desired. . . . The University of Texas has given us a fundamental book in *Francisco Zarco: Spokesman of Liberalism and Reform.*"[94]

In recognition of the exemplary role Castañeda played in promoting the Institute of Latin American Studies, the university administration designated him to represent President Wilson at UNAM's "inauguration" of the extension division in San Antonio on January 12.[95] Carlos probably relished the assignment because the drive to San Antonio was neither strenuous nor long and Elisa would have an opportunity to visit relatives.

In late January he renewed contact with Bishop FitzSimon, who had "fully recovered" and expected to return to work at his chancery. Disappointed that Von Boeckmann-Jones had still not provided page proofs for review and correction, he shared with the prelate a copy of the latest issue of *The Age of Mary,* dedicated to *Sor* María de Agreda, a seventeenth-century Spanish nun, to which he had "contributed the episode of the Woman in Blue."[96]

Shortly after the adjournment of the special session, Von Boeckmann-Jones resumed work on the last volume of *Our Catholic Heritage.* In mid-February the publisher sent two sets of page proofs to William H. Oberste. Castañeda recommended that the monsignor in Refugio and Father Frank in Houston proofread the pages first, after which he would scan their corrections and forward everything to Von Boeckmann-Jones. Carlos suggested to the publisher that to "save time" in the future they run off three sets of revised page proofs so that he, Oberste, and Frank could read the printed matter simultaneously and "catch all the typographical errors." Rather forlornly Carlos expressed the sincere hope and ardent prayer "that somehow the book will be finished in time" for the upcoming state convention of the Knights of Columbus.[97]

As soon as he received the initial page proofs, Monsignor Oberste briefed Father Frank on his "first responsibility" as censor deputatus, which was to ensure that Castañeda had "not written anything against Faith and Morals." Frank was also to assist them in correcting "any printing errors" he might find. With regard to the publication schedule, Oberste wrote: "We are now pushing the publisher with might and main to get the book out by next May. This work has been delayed because they have had the completed manuscript since August. Von Boeckmann-Jones are the official printers of the Texas Legislature, and since this is their bread and butter we cannot blame them for giving the preference to the demands of the State—after all we kep[t] the printers dangling for years and years, and so we do have to be patient, and see what happens."[98] Late in February, Castañeda and Oberste met in Austin for the last time. During their appointment with Werner Jessen at Von Boeckmann-Jones they returned corrected page proofs and discussed illustrations for the book and printing schedules for the remaining chapters. Delighted with the results of their meeting, Oberste promised his colleagues to return "when things get rolling along," at which time they would together "check the progress being made." [99]

In the subtle transition from winter to spring in central Texas, amid a multitude of ongoing projects, Castañeda contracted "a slight attack" of influenza that drained his energy and seriously "affected" his heart. Confined to bed for two weeks, he reluctantly advised the history department either to dismiss his classes or to secure a substitute lecturer. His physician, M. E. Kreisle, firmly prescribed that he curtail "all extra activities," including "trips out-of-town." This restriction upset his plans to attend Oberste's fiftieth anniversary in the priesthood. Carlos wrote to his friend, "It breaks my heart into more pieces than it is already broken not to be able to come to your Silver Jubilee." Keeping in touch with Jessen by telephone, he received last-minute progress reports on the seventh volume, which he mailed to Oberste. On April 1, 1958, against Elisa's protests, Carlos drove to the campus to conduct his classes. Later in the afternoon he complained to the monsignor: "It is hard . . . to do nothing but meet my classes and stay home in bed the rest of the spring, but that is the price I am going . . . to pay for forgetting myself and attempting to do as much as I used to before I busted the heart block in my internal engine." [100]

Valdemar Rodríguez, then teaching at University Junior High School while finishing his dissertation, regularly looked in on Castañeda during this period. The week of Easter vacation Rodríguez visited with him for a few minutes on Monday afternoon and on Tuesday telephoned to inquire "how he was getting along." The next day after school the student went home to Kingsville, confident that he would see Don Carlos the following week.[101] That Wednesday morning Castañeda trudged to campus. Joe B. Frantz saw him and was shocked by his friend's appearance:

A call came in from his wife saying that it looked like he was through this time. Why, he had a nine o'clock, and those of us who had got up there early heard the word and we made arrangements to dismiss the class, tell them to come back next time, [that] we'd know more about it, . . . certainly no class today, and we'd try to find out what we'd do the rest of the semester. Lo and behold, who should come in, looking drawn and pale as death but Castañeda! "Carlos, what on earth? We thought you were sick?" "I am sick, [he said] I am about to die. But here it is . . . two months to go to the end of the semester, and I haven't made any plans for the class . . . and I figure I had

to dismiss them." So he struggled off the death bed in effect. As I recall
he had another attack when he got home. But it was a typical Castañeda
maneuver.[102]

After dismissing his class Castañeda decided to go to his office in the Tower to
collect materials with which to work at his leisure. Evidently the stress of so
much activity aggravated his heart ailment, because someone "found him in
the office, gasping for breath." Apprised of the emergency, the library staff
summoned an ambulance, which rapidly shuttled him to Seton Hospital.[103] In
the emergency room medical personnel stabilized his condition and assigned
him to a regular hospital bed. All through the night and into the morning
of Holy Thursday the nurses monitored the patient's vital signs. His daughter Rosemary remained constantly at his bedside. In the afternoon, preparing
himself for the inevitable, Carlos asked a hospital chaplain to bring holy com-
munion to his room. After sundown his condition suddenly plummeted. Fifteen minutes before midnight Castañeda died of an "acute myocardial infarc-
tion" at the age of sixty-one years, four months, and twenty-three days.[104]

In the shock, grief, and confusion following his death someone mistakenly
reported that Don Carlos had died on Good Friday, April 4, 1958. Undoubtedly his affiliation with the Equestrian Order of the Holy Sepulchre of Jerusalem perpetuated the erroneous impression. The family gave the responsibility for arranging the last rites to Weed-Corley Funeral Home. Owing to the
intervention of Holy Week observances, the mortuary directors scheduled
the funeral rosary, a traditional service among Roman Catholic families, for
the evening of Easter Sunday, to be officiated by Rev. Robert J. Murphy.[105]

On Good Friday the news of Castañeda's death reverberated across the university campus and throughout the far reaches of the state. Don Carlos's demise affected people who knew him in a variety of ways. José Roberto Juárez,
a graduate student, was in Laredo for the Easter break. He said, "I remember
the shock of the news and crying and then saying a prayer for the repose of his
soul. . . . Although I had known him for only seven or eight months, he had
touched my life profoundly." [106] Joe B. Frantz informed Valdemar Rodríguez
in Kingsville, who found it "very hard to believe" because he had seen Carlos
earlier in the week.[107] Another student, E. Victor Niemeyer, who pursued a career in the foreign service in Latin America because of Castañeda's influence,
remembered him fondly as someone who "deserved the title of Defender of the
Faith far more . . . than Henry VIII." [108]

Over the weekend Monsignor Oberste accompanied two prelates—Bishops Garriga and Reicher—to the Castañeda residence to express personal con-
dolences to "the bereaved family." [109] On Monday morning, April 7, the Catholic hierarchy of central Texas, with the concelebrating clergy, stood at the

entrance of Saint Austin's Church to welcome the mourners. Outside, positioned between the hearse and the vestibule of the church, an honor guard of fourth-degree Knights of Columbus flanked the six pallbearers who carried the casket, draped in white linen, to the catafalque. Seventeen members of the faculty, serving as honorary pallbearers, walked behind the casket into the nave of the church. From the sanctuary, facing an immense throng of mourners, the principal celebrant, Rev. William Blakeslee, C.S.P., who had worked with Castañeda in the Newman Club movement, approached the catafalque. In the celebration of the Solemn Requiem Mass, Father Blakeslee officiated; Bishop Louis J. Reicher of Austin presided; Bishop Mariano S. Garriga of Corpus Christi preached the funeral sermon; Reverends John J. Stanley and Robert J. Murphy, both of the Congregation of the Holy Cross, served as deacon and subdeacon, respectively; and Monsignor William H. Oberste, vicar general of the Corpus Christi Diocese, assisted in the liturgy as a gesture of solidarity in the work he had shared with the deceased scholar. After the church service the funeral cortege slowly curled around the university to Mount Calvary Cemetery, across the interstate highway east of the campus. At a grave site near the gate marked by a plain granite headstone, the pallbearers gently lowered the casket.[110] A humble inscription commemorated the interment of a once-dynamic knight without armor: Carlos Eduardo Castañeda, 1896–1958.

Farewell to a Project

Bulletins announcing the death of Carlos Eduardo Castañeda quickly reached the editorial offices of newspapers and journals. Within the state of Texas two leading dailies acknowledged the magnitude of his contributions. The *Fort Worth Star-Telegram* praised his commitment to scholarship: "Dr. Castañeda was influential in the development of the University of Texas' Institute of Latin American Studies and had guided much research in the Latin American field. His contribution to the standing of the University is reflected in the many acts of recognition that have been accorded him. It is through the presence of such scholars as he that the stature of institutions of higher learning is principally measured. Replacing Dr. Castañeda will be no easy undertaking, for he was born to the environment of his scholarly interest."[1] In a similar vein, the *Dallas Morning News* lauded the inspiration and support he had imparted to others: "Southwestern history suffered a serious loss in the passing of Dr. Carlos E. Castañeda. Through his work as a librarian and teacher at The University of Texas, he implanted interest in Latin American history on many students, some of whom are now teachers. For those and others he helped to make accessible source materials that [cast] much light on the early development of Texas. His good influence will last long into the years ahead."[2] The *Austin American-Statesman* merely reprinted the *Star-Telegram*'s editorial but preceded it by a brief introduction: "In his lifetime, Dr. Carlos E. Castañeda gained international renown for himself and, in his field, for the University of Texas."[3] The newspaper of the Diocese of Austin, the *Lone Star Catholic*, acknowledged Castañeda as "a prolific author and authority concerning the Texas Revolution . . . [who had produced] a massive history of all affairs pertaining to the Spanish-American and Catholic culture of the Southwest."[4] *La Prensa,* a Spanish-language weekly published in San Antonio, lamented Dr. Castañeda's death as an "irreparable loss for Hispanicism in Texas." *La Prensa* continued, "Neither the State of Texas, nor the University of Texas, nor our Holy Roman Catholic and Apostolic Church, nor the Hispanic community in the United States of America can replace Dr. Castañeda, an outstanding citizen, who, through his cultural background and civic virtues, epitomized the honor and glory of the region to the Nation, to our Religion and to the ethnic group of which he was a part." [5]

Writing in the *Hispanic American Historical Review,* J. Lloyd Mecham, a colleague in the Latin American Studies Institute, succinctly summarized the scope of Castañeda's scholarship:

> *The passing . . . of Carlos E. Castañeda . . . terminated the career of one of our most distinguished and productive scholars and teachers in the field of Latin American history. Although his knowledge and competence in the whole area of Latin America was remarkable, it is in the history of Mexico, colonial and republican, that Dr. Castañeda revealed his exceptional talents in historical research and in graduate instruction. His influence will long continue, both through the medium of his voluminous publications and through the activities of his many graduate students who were privileged to share his dedicated enthusiasm for his subject.* [6]

As one who had had a working relationship with Castañeda, Mecham described what the loss meant to his colleagues at the university:

> *it will be the members of the Institute of Latin American Studies at the University of Texas who were Dr. Castañeda's intimate co-workers over the years who will be most aware of his absence. They are in the best position to appreciate, despite occasional differences of opinion, his fine qualities as a scholar, teacher, and affable colleague, and know how important he was to the progress of the Institute. The stimulation of his boundless enthusiasm and energy, and the profitable employment of his extensive acquaintance with Latin American scholars, will be greatly missed.* [7]

The American Catholic Historical Association, of which Castañeda had served as president before World War II, paid tribute to his accomplishments across the decades: "Dr. Castañeda's scholarly competence, genial and kindly personality, and devoted service to the profession brought him many honors. . . . Professor Castañeda's death will be mourned among a wide circle of former students, colleagues, and friends, a circle that steadily widened during the more than thirty years that he was actively engaged in teaching, historical research, and publication." [8] On behalf of the Academy of American Franciscan History, with which Castañeda had developed a lengthy professional relationship, Mathias C. Kiemen wrote in *The Americas:* "On April 5 we . . . received the sad news of the death of Dr. Carlos E. Castañeda. He had been ailing for some years, but recently had become more active again, so that his friends hoped for many more years of life for him. The Master of life and death thought differently. 'Don Carlos,' as his friends called him, had a full life." [9] Saddened by the death announcement, H. Bailey Carroll, director of the Texas State Historical Association, paid tribute to Castañeda as "the indefatigable sponsor and producer of a large amount of work in Latin American and Texas history." Although "classroom, religious, and civic functions" constituted "vital facets" of Castañeda's "dynamic career," the achievement that impressed Carroll most was Don Carlos's "prodigious bibliography of scholarly historical writings" that numbered "some seventy-eight" essays. "For his many distinguished contributions in the fields of education, writing, and history," Carroll concluded, "Dr. Castañeda received wide recognition and well-deserved honors." [10]

As the accolades mounted, Elisa, Consuelo, and Rosemary struggled to cope with the pain of their loss. No matter how much they might desire privacy, the demands of creditors had to be confronted. Complicating matters was the fact that Don Carlos had neglected to write a last will and testament, which delayed settlement of the estate. Hard-pressed to find the money to pay medical and funeral expenses, Elisa disposed of Castañeda's library for an undisclosed amount. [11] When news of the transaction became public knowledge, Monsignor William H. Oberste wrote to Bishop Laurence J. FitzSimon: "I know you will be interested in knowing that the personal library and collection of Dr. Castañeda was sold to Texas Tech by Mrs. Castañeda immediately upon the death of her husband. She stated that she needed the money desperately, and I understand that Dr. did not leave a Will. I know that Dr. Castañeda was in straightened circumstances, and for that reason he had to keep on teaching when he should have been in bed. I have no idea of the value of Dr. Castañeda's collection and accumulations, but I regret that it was not added to Your Excellency's collection." [12] Oberste lamented to Bishop Louis J. Reicher of Austin, "It is deplorable that Mrs. Castañeda so quickly sold the personal collection of Texana." [13]

The impact of Castañeda's death weighed heavily upon the history department and the Texas Historical Commission. Owing to the dependency of students on their major professor, Carlos's demise especially affected his doctoral candidates. James Presley, of Texarkana, described a catastrophe that befell a student at the orals examination:

> The year Don Carlos died, a friend of mine faced his orals a short time after the funeral. I thought he was well prepared. He knew Mexico from having lived there. He was extremely knowledgeable when he talked about any aspect of Latin America, and I know personally that he spent more [time]

*than the average student in the Latin American Library. I expected him
to sail through his orals. He didn't. When he came out I was waiting in the
Latin American Library and congratulated him. "I did not pass," he said,
tensely. Surprised, I asked why not. He told of having very difficult detail[ed] questions fired staccato-like at him. He was a straight-forward honest person. When he didn't know, he said so, and he told the committee this
when he really didn't know an answer.... A few minutes later he wistfully
said, "I certainly missed Don Carlos today." A moment or so later he added,
"He was the student's friend."* [14]

Another student, Valdemar Rodríguez, farther advanced in the graduate program, collided with unexpected delays when his new supervising professor
challenged his dissertation. He reported: "I was caught in the undercurrent
of all this because my dissertation was being read at this time. And when he
died they changed chairmen on me, and instead of . . . Dr. Castañeda it was
Dr. [Lewis] Hanke now. . . . I had written for a very conservative [director] or
had it written from a very conservative point of view to please Castañeda because he was sort of conservative. And then Hanke said, 'No, you will have
to change it, change a little bit'—after I had written four hundred and some
odd pages." [15]

While arrangements were made for Castañeda's graduate students, his un-
dergraduates also needed attention. Chairman Archibald R. Lewis announced
that Castañeda's two history classes would "resume at the regular time Thursday," following a week of official mourning. [16] With less than two months remaining in the spring semester, instead of hiring a temporary substitute, the
department covered Castañeda's classes by assigning its own personnel. Marc
Simmons, a student in one of the courses, recalled that Lewis Hanke "came in
and took over the history class I was in and made a nice speech about CEC's
contribution." [17] Chairman Lewis transferred the stipend of fifteen hundred
dollars reserved for Castañeda's supplemental salary in the first summer session to an active teaching slot, to which he assigned himself. [18]

Meanwhile the Knights of Columbus of Texas faced their own set of problems. Shortly after Castañeda's death Edwin D. Gunter, executive assistant
to the Texas Council, notified Reverend Monsignor Oberste in Refugio that
he had been appointed to chair "a special committee" charged with the responsibility of drafting a memorial resolution. [19] For Oberste the task was relatively simple compared to the challenge of completing the remaining work on
the seventh volume of *Our Catholic Heritage.* "It is certainly sad," he wrote
Gunter on April 10, "that Dr. Castañeda is no longer in the land of the living.
He got so much joy out of reading and correcting the first four chapters."
Wanting to resume work on the project as soon as possible, the editor sug-

gested a tactful strategy: "If you should have the opportunity please mention to Mrs. Castañeda that Doctor was working on the bibliography, and to check [for] this among his belongings. . . . Perhaps by this time the family is beginning to put the effects of Dr. Castañeda in order." [20]

In trying to reconcile the goals of the Texas Historical Commission with the need of the Castañeda family for privacy in their time of sorrow, Oberste welcomed the support of his fellow priest, Anton J. Frank, censor deputatus for the volume, who offered to help in any way he could.[21] Before the end of April, Oberste and Frank accepted the fact that the project would not be finished in time for the state convention of the Knights of Columbus in May. "Now that the good Doctor has been called to his reward," Oberste wrote Frank, "a delay here and . . . there will not make too much difference to the rank and file. He was indeed full of yearning to see the book finally finished." [22] Oberste then turned to writing a memorial tribute, anticipating that the State Council of the Knights of Columbus would decide to dedicate the volume to the memory of its author. "It is only appropriate that it [do] so," he told Gunter. "If you should judge the tribute inadequate," he continued, "please let me know and I shall try for new wording." [23]

In the last week of April, Edwin Gunter scheduled an appointment with Elisa Castañeda, from whom he obtained permission for Oberste to consult Don Carlos's materials. The papers were conveniently located "in one place" at his home whenever they were "needed." Doña Elisa, "extremely happy about the dedication of the seventh volume," also promised to furnish a photograph of her late husband for the editor's consideration.[24] Pleased with the breakthrough, the monsignor determined that he and Frank would not need the materials in Mrs. Castañeda's possession until they had "the complete book in page-proof." [25] Several weeks later Oberste visited the Castañeda home "to obtain a part of the manuscript" that the author had in his possession at the time of his death. The visit, unfortunately, was stressful for both parties. Oberste later wrote FitzSimon that Mrs. Castañeda "seemed put out that we had asked the Doctor to write Volume Seven." [26]

As the tedious process of proofreading continued, Father Frank noted that "much space" had been allocated to the Catholic Church Extension Society, so that not a single member "of the Hierarchy" in Texas would have cause to "be displeased" at the coverage given to the topic "by good Dr. Castañeda." [27] In the midst of proofreading Oberste concluded his draft of the memorial and mailed it to Gunter for review and revision by other members "of the Resolutions Committee." [28]

At the annual convention of the Knights of Columbus, held at the Hilton Hotel in San Antonio, May 18–20, 1958, Oberste, in the absence of a chairman or historiographer, presented the last official report of the Texas Historical Commission. The editor informed the convention that this tome was "now entirely set in type, in the form of page-proof, and that at long last, within a matter of months, this final volume will appear, and will be ready for distribution to all those interested in reading the history of the Catholic Church in Texas." Then Oberste paid tribute to his friend, "our esteemed and celebrated author." Describing Castañeda's quarter-century of work on the project, the monsignor noted his steadfast commitment to the enterprise even in the twilight months of his life:

> Fortunately he had completed the writing of the entire manuscript, and thus he is in fact the sole author of the entire series of Our Catholic Heritage in Texas. He lived with the ardent hope to see the actual completion of the task he had set out to do twenty-five years ago. He looked forward to seeing the seventh volume in print, bound, and in the hands of readers, but that pleasure and joy, in the Wisdom and Providence of God, was denied him. I do know, however, because of the number of conferences I held with him, and particularly our meeting just a week before his sudden death, that it was his delight to know that the day was not far off which would mark the publication of his complete work from Volume One to Volume Seven. In tribute to his prodigious labors, his perseverance in spite of many obstacles and delays, and in recognition of the greatness of his contribution, the State Council has most appropriately dedicated his Volume Seven to his memory.[29]

Applauding Castañeda's work, the delegates adopted the tribute proposed by the resolutions committee:

> WHEREAS, Dr. Castañeda most particularly gained renown in writing his immortal series of seven volumes . . . of Our Catholic Heritage in Texas under the auspices of the Knights of Columbus of Texas;
> WHEREAS, our esteemed Brother Knight, Dr. Carlos E. Castañeda, well merited the recognition of scholars and honor Societies of Learning, not only in our State but also nationally and internationally;
> BE IT RESOLVED that in mourning the loss of our Brother we are comforted by our Savior's Promise of salvation to all those who love Him; and that we shall always be mindful of him in our prayers, calling to mind the holy injunction of Sacred Scripture: "It is a holy and wholesome thought to pray for the dead";
> BE IT FURTHER RESOLVED that a copy of these Resolutions be engrossed, and presented to the bereaved family of the deceased; . . . on behalf of all the Knights of Columbus of Texas, with sentiments of sympathy and esteem.[30]

Confident that the seventh volume would soon be published, Oberste suggested to FitzSimon in early June the necessity of conducting "a final meeting" of the Texas Historical Commission, not only to sing "a great Amen" but among other matters "to dispose of a fund of $2,074.89," presently in the custody "of Father Frank, the Treasurer." This money, collected "in dribs and drabs" by the Knights of Columbus since 1928, constituted the balance of the commission's operating fund.[31]

A month later Bishop FitzSimon died in Amarillo.[32] With his passing, the Texas Historical Commission was reduced to a trio of truly dedicated partisans—William H. Oberste, Anton J. Frank, and Mariano S. Garriga. By the end of 1958 this group witnessed at last the publication of the final volume of *Our Catholic Heritage in Texas*. Subtitled *The Church in Texas Since Independence,* the volume covered "the period from 1836 to 1950."[33]

At the spring, 1959, convocation of the Knights of Columbus, Monsignor Oberste announced to the State Council that the work of the Texas Historical Commission "was finished" and recommended "that it [the commission] be dissolved." He also suggested that the commission's "Special Fund" of nearly $1,600 "be donated to The Texas Catholic Historical Society, Inc." Following the adoption of his recommendation Oberste "led the Convention in a prayer for Dr. Castañeda, through whose efforts the Knights had been able to complete, at a cost of $130,000, the tremendous project begun by them" more than a quarter-century before.[34]

Public acclaim for the completed series emanated from diverse quarters. *The Alamo Messenger,* a privately owned newspaper dedicated to reporting ecclesiastical events in Texas, observed that while "this great work" was "a tribute to the Knights of Columbus," simultaneously it was "a fitting memorial" to deceased members of the Texas Historical Commission, especially two scholars whose names stood "out in bold relief": Rev. Dr. Paul J. Foik, C.S.C., of Saint Edward's University; and Dr. Carlos E. Castañeda, K.G.C.H.S., of the University of Texas.[35] The editors of the *Catholic Historical Review* in Washington, D.C., agreed that Castañeda's work was "widely considered the best general history of Texas during the Spanish period, although its title might easily lead one to believe that it pertained only to ecclesiastical history."[36] By then another review, published in the *West Texas Register,* diocesan newspaper of Amarillo, had praised the series as "the most comprehensive history of Catholicism in the Southwest."[37] Late in the year Archbishop Lucey sent "a specially bound" copy of the last volume to Pope John XXIII at the Vatican.[38] At an annual meeting of the Texas Philosophical Society of Texas the archbishop remembered Castañeda in a solemn tribute: "Dr. Castañeda's presence will be long missed. He was a man without ostentation, with an ever-ready smile, humble and always the Christian courtly gentleman."[39]

Sam Liberto, Sr., a fourth-degree Knight of Columbus in San Antonio, who consistently endorsed the project at the annual conventions, assessed the outcome of Castañeda's work with sincere amazement: "I don't see how he finished it. The only thing I can say is the good Lord was with him all the way, because you can find few men who can do what he did. Tremendous lot of work. You know, he'd have to write and re-rewrite to get certain information. It took a lot of patience. He had it."[40]

Joe B. Frantz, who served as an honorary pallbearer at Castañeda's funeral, summarized his friend's multifaceted contributions to scholarship as "a record that most full-time historians would view with pride." Specifically, he singled out three titles that have become synonymous with Castañeda: *The Mexican Side of the Texan Revolution, Our Catholic Heritage in Texas,* and the annotated translation of Fray Juan Agustín Morfi's *History of Texas.*[41] Concerning the dedication of the Perry-Castañeda Library, Frantz declared: "Lord, how he would have gloried in having a major library co-named for him! For that act, I say to the administration: *¡Salud!*"[42] As a historian who began his work as a librarian, Castañeda would surely have enjoyed the irony of the celebration.

The board of regents of the University of Texas system created a myth etched in stone about the new library. In their haste to approve signage for the structure, the regents voted to inscribe Dr. Ervin S. Perry's surname ahead of the name Castañeda, ignoring altogether the fact that the historian had preceded the engineer on the campus by at least three decades. Shortly after the dedication, alumni from the 1940s and 1950s visiting the university incredulously stared at the library's nomenclature. "Oh, yes, I remember Dr. Castañeda," a former student remarked, "but I did not know his first name was Perry!"[43] Unquestionably, Castañeda would have smiled at the bizarre faux pas in the building's identification, gladly accepting the gift of half a library's name as being preferable to none.

President Lorene Rogers assessed the contributions of the two honorees as "pacesetters" of their respective generations. "Both marked the diversity in a lasting way, breaking as they did ethnic and racial barriers so that succeeding generations might find with greater ease the opportunities and responsibilities afforded by education."[44]

Carlos Eduardo Castañeda etched his "mark" beyond the labyrinth of the library building. From adolescence to adulthood he viewed education as a corridor to professional and civic success. In his unwavering commitment to the standard of work, scholarship, and service Don Carlos constantly struggled to attain the promise of the American dream. For a brief period Castañeda pursued the study of engineering as a lifetime career, but under the influence of Father J. Elliot Ross and Professor Eugene C. Barker he switched to history, the field in which he made his hallmark contributions. During Carlos's tenure as a librarian of the Latin American Collection, the enormous scope of the records he discovered and copied in Mexican depositories enabled him to blaze a pathway for his development as a historian. Through the meticulous process of analyzing the historical documents he not only acquired knowledge of their content but, equally important, he gained perception of the cultural environment in which they were initially produced.

Castañeda's reputation as a historian stemmed from the depth and breadth of his experience with the documents he consulted to compose the manuscripts that later became books and articles. His remarkable ability to comment extemporaneously on documentary materials and related themes, reinforced by an extensive publication record, distinguished Don Carlos as a scholar of first rank. In the style of Herbert Eugene Bolton, whom he greatly admired, Castañeda plowed a vast virgin field in the Spanish colonial history of Texas. Later scholars, in search of overlooked topics, cultivated smaller patches and produced noteworthy monographs, but not one has matched Castañeda's record of accomplishment. In retrospect, the anomalous Perry-Castañeda Library is a befitting capstone to his scholarly productivity.

Abbreviations

AAFH/FST/BC	Academy of American Franciscan History, Franciscan School of Theology, Berkeley, Calif.
ACWM	Archives College of William and Mary, Earl Gregg Swem Library, Williamsburg, Va.
AFPSH/SLM	Archives of the Franciscan Province of the Sacred Heart, St. Louis, Mo.
ALOMLB	Arnulfo L. Oliveira Memorial Library, Brownsville, Tex.
BLAC	Nettie Lee Benson Latin American Collection, University of Texas at Austin
BTHC	Eugene C. Barker Texas History Center (renamed Center for the Study of American History; original name used), University of Texas at Austin
CASA	Catholic Archives at San Antonio, Chancery of San Antonio, San Antonio, Tex.
CBF	Castañeda Biographical File, Barker Texas History Center, University of Texas at Austin
CDL	Collections Deposit Library, University of Texas at Austin
CECP	Carlos E. Castañeda Papers, Benson Latin American Collection, University of Texas at Austin
ECBP	Eugene C. Barker Papers, Barker Texas History Center, University of Texas at Austin
EEP	Eleuterio Escobar Papers
FBSP/QCBL	Francis Borgia Steck Papers, Quincy College Brenner Library, Quincy, Ill.
FVSP/CSWR/SC/UNMGL	France V. Scholes Papers, Center for Southwest Research, Special Collections/University of New Mexico General Library, Albuquerque, N.M.
HAHR	*Hispanic American Historical Review*
HEBP/BL/UCB	Herbert E. Bolton Papers, Bancroft Library, University of California at Berkeley
IWCL	Incarnate Word College Library
KCCF/CAT	Knights of Columbus Correspondence File, Catholic Archives of Texas, Chancery of Austin

LF/OAD/OLLU/SAT   Letter File, Office of the Academic Dean, Our Lady of the Lake University, San Antonio, Tex.

LRL/AT   Legislative Reference Library, The Capitol, Austin, Tex.

ODC/VVC   Office of the District Clerk, Val Verde Courthouse, Del Rio, Tex.

OLLU/SAT   Our Lady of the Lake University, San Antonio, Tex.

RDBAM,CF:RXWR   Records of the Division of Budget and Administrative Management, Central Files: Region X Weekly Reports

RDBAM,USG—ADM(M)   Records of the Division of Budget and Administrative Management, United States Government—Aliens in Defense, Mexicans (Miscellaneous)

RFEPC   Records of the Committee on Fair Employment Practice

RLD/RRH:SWH   Records of the Legal Division/Records Relating to Hearings: Southwestern Hearings

ROC,FS/DAM,CUA   Rector's Office Correspondence (1928–69), Faculty Series, Department of Archives and Manuscripts, The Catholic University of America

ROC:OC/CRF:CEC   Records of the Office of the Chairman: Outgoing Correspondence/Cross Reference File: Carlos E. Castañeda

TOMFRA/HHP   Texas Old Missions and Forts Restoration Association/Henrietta Henry Papers, Waco, Tex.

UTA   University of Texas at Austin

UTPOR:HD   University of Texas President's Office Papers: History Department, Barker Texas History Center

YSP/DRTL   Yanaguana Society Papers, Daughters of the Republic of Texas Library at the Alamo

Notes

Chapter 1

1. Dedication Program, Perry-Castañeda Library, UT News Release, Nov. 11, Dec. 5, 1977; News and Information Service, UTA. Located at Twenty-first Street and Speedway, the Perry-Castañeda Library, constructed at a cost of $21,700,000, initially opened in late summer, 1977. Dr. Lorene L. Rogers, president of UTA, unveiled portraits of the deceased honorees. UT historian Lewis L. Gould spoke on the relationship of "The Library and the Academic Community."

2. Josefina E. Castañeda, interview with Diana Gómez, tape recording, Brownsville, Tex., Dec. 15, 1970; Joseph William Schmitz, *The Society of Mary in Texas* (San Antonio: Naylor Company, 1951), p. 87; Entry No. 1364, Marriage Books of San Fernando, Microfilm Reel 46, CASA.

3. Elsie Upton, "Knight of Goodwill," *St. Joseph Magazine* 44 (June, 1943): 12, CBF; Certificate of Baptism No. 1, January 2, 1897, Baptismal Register, Book 3: 271, Immaculate Conception Church, Rio Grande City, Tex. Rev. Evaristo Repiso was born in 1845 in the town of Quantanilla in the Diocese of Placencia, Spain. He died in San Antonio in 1915 (Father Evaristo Repiso File, Archives of the Southern Province of the Missionary Oblates of Mary Immaculate, San Antonio, Tex.).

4. Josefina E. Castañeda interview; Upton, "Knight of Goodwill," p. 12.

5. [Ernesto González Salinas], "El Colegio de San Juan: Remembranzas," in *Secundaria Federal Lic. y General Juan José de la Garza,* by Anuario de la Escuela (Matamoros, Tamaulipas, Mex., n.p., 1966), p. 12, ALOMLB; Josefina E. Castañeda interview.

6. W. H. Chatfield (comp.), *The Twin Cities of the Border: Brownsville, Texas, Matamoros, Mexico, and the Country of the Lower Rio Grande,* pp. 2–3, 31–35; Stephen Fox, "The Border Brick Style in Twin Cities of the Río Grande: Brownsville and Matamoros," *Texas Highways* 45 (Jan., 1998): 38.

7. David Montejano, *Anglos and Mexicans in the Making of Texas, 1836–1986* (Austin: University of Texas Press, 1987), pp. 18—20, 96—99.

8. *Brownsville City Directory, 1913–1914,* p. 272, ALOMLB. The newspapers included *Adelante,* Hilario Borjas, editor; *Brownsville Herald,* M. J. Slattery, editor; *Cowboy,* Enríque E. Betancourt, editor; *Diario de la Frontera,* Dámaso Lerma, editor; *Demócrata,* Romaldo Treviño, editor; *Daily Sentinel,* H. H. Cummins, editor; and *El Provenir,* P. S. Preciado, editor.

9. Carlos E. Castañeda, Declaration of Intention [to apply for U.S. citizenship], Number 647205, May 28, 1919, Immigration and Naturalization Service, United States Department of Justice, Washington, D.C.; Josefina E. Castañeda interview; Upton, "Knight of Goodwill," p. 12.

10. Chatfield, *Twin Cities of the Border,* pp. 2–3.

11. Chula T. Griffin and Sam S. Griffin (comps.), *Record of Internments in the City Cemetery of Brownsville, Texas,* vol. 5 (1907–1912), p. 7, ALOMLB; Timoteo Castañeda, Standard Certificate of Death Registered No. 21111, Oct. 3, 1911, Texas Department of Health, Bureau of Vital Statistics, Austin, Tex.

12. Josefina E. Castañeda interview.

13. Ibid.

14. Ibid.

15. *Daily Texan* (student newspaper, UTA), Apr. 16, 1940, CBF; Alfonso F. Sapia-Bosch, "The Role of General Lucio Blanco in the Mexican Revolution, 1913–1922" (Ph.D. diss., Georgetown University, 1977), pp. 27–37.

16. Elisa R. Castañeda, interview with O. Wayne Poorman, tape recording, Austin, Tex., May 29, 1972.

17. Ibid.

18. Carlos Castañeda, Student's High School Record Card, 1912–1916, Archives of the Brownsville Public Schools, Brownsville, Tex.

19. Mrs. Thomas J. (Pat) Renaghan to the author, Mar. 26, 1981, Seguin, Tex., Almaráz Papers. The members of the graduating class of 1916 were Lambert B. Cain; Carlos E. Castañeda; Kathleen Craig; Burt E. Hinkley, Jr.; William B. Moler, Jr.; Louise K. Putegnat; B. Girard Thayer; Ruth Vertrees; and Maude B. White (Program, Baccalaureate Services, Brownsville High School, Class of 1916, May 21, 1916), CECP.

20. Tom Bowman Brewer, "A History of the Department of History of the University of Texas, 1883–1951" (M.A. thesis, UTA, 1957), p. 116; Elisa R. Castañeda interview.

21. Carlos E. Castañeda to Lillian Berlin, Mar. 4, 1927, CECP.

22. Josefina E. Castañeda interview; *Southern Messenger,* Oct. 2, 1941, OLLU/SAT; *Dallas News,* Oct. 14, 1941, CBF.

23. *Austin City Directory, 1918,* Austin–Travis County Collection, Austin Public Library.

24. David F. Prindle, "Oil and the Permanent University Fund: The Early Years," *Southwestern Historical Quarterly* 86 (Oct., 1982): 278–80.

25. For a detailed account of the power struggle between the executive mansion and the university community, consult Lewis L. Gould, "The University Becomes Politicized: The War with Jim Ferguson, 1915–1918," *Southwestern Historical Quarterly* 86 (Oct., 1982): 255–76.

26. *Southern Messenger,* Oct. 2, 1941, OLLU/SAT; *Austin Statesman,* Oct. 8, 1953, Austin–Travis County Collection, Austin, Public Library.

27. Philip J. Sheridan, interview with Félix D. Almaráz, Jr., tape recording, San Antonio, Tex., Jan. 26, 1973.

28. Vera Struve Lamm to the author, Nov. 15, 1992, San Antonio, Tex., Almaráz Papers.

29. Carlos Eduardo Castañeda, Official Transcript, UTA, July 28, 1972, Office of the Registrar (hereinafter cited as Castañeda Transcript).

30. *Daily Texan,* Apr. 11, 1943, CBF.

31. *Southern Messenger,* Oct. 2, 1941, OLLU/SAT.

32. Upton, "Knight of Goodwill," p. 12.

33. *Southern Messenger,* Oct. 2, 1941.

34. Edward H. Peters, C.S.P., self-interview, tape recording, Columbus, Ohio, 1972.

35. *Daily Texan,* Nov. 18, 1945; Upton, "Knight of Goodwill," p. 12; Walter P. Webb and H. Bailey Carroll, eds., *The Handbook of Texas,* vol. 1, p. 282.

36. Josefina E. Castañeda interview.

37. Castañeda Transcript.

38. Carlos E. Castañeda, "Why I Chose History," *The Americas* 8 (Apr., 1952): 476.

39. Joe B. Frantz, interview with O. Wayne Poorman, tape recording, Austin, Tex., May 23, 1972.

40. Frantz interview. Within two decades Castañeda's second in command rapidly advanced in his engineering career. Among other projects, he supervised construction of the Hoover Dam near Las Vegas. Years later, during a business trip to California, Castañeda drove out to Hoover Dam to view the facility. Looking closely at the dedication plaque, Carlos philosophically reflected on the Hillsboro-to-Fort Worth highway project: "I taught him everything he knew. I must be responsible for this marvelous structure!" (Joe B. Frantz, *The Forty-Acre Follies: An Opinionated History of the University of Texas,* p. 288).

41. *Ranger,* Mar., 1938, CBF.

42. Josefina E. Castañeda interview; Elisa R. Castañeda interview.

43. John Francis Bannon, *Herbert Eugene Bolton: The Historian and the Man, 1870–1953,* pp. 32, 35–36, 101, 110.

44. Carlos E. Castañeda, "In Memoriam: Charles W. Hackett, 1888–1951," *The Americas* 8 (July, 1951): 83.

45. Castañeda to Eugene C. Barker, Aug. 10, 1920, ECBP.

46. Upton, "Knight of Goodwill," p. 12; Castañeda Transcript; Brewer, "History of the Department of History," p. 116. Among Carlos's friends of the class of 1921 was Fletcher Warren, who later became U.S. ambassador to Venezuela and welcomed the historian on his visit in 1957 to northern South America (Logan Wilson to Ex-Students of The University of Texas in Caracas and all Venezuela, Feb. 24, 1956, UTPOR:HD).

47. Castañeda to F. O. Adam, Oct. 25, 1927, CECP.

48. *Beaumont City Directory, 1921,* p. 253; Castañeda to Barker, Oct. 15, 1921, ECBP.

49. Castañeda to Barker, Oct. 15, 1921.

50. Ibid.

51. Carlos E. Castañeda, "Why I Chose History," p. 477.

52. Castañeda to Eugene C. Barker, Nov. 16, 1921, ECBP.

53. Ibid.

54. Barker to Castañeda, Nov. 22, 1921, ECBP.

55. Marriage License No. 62762 (Carlos E. Castañeda and Elisa G. Ríos), *Marriage Records* 61: 222, Office of the County Clerk, Bexar County Courthouse, San Antonio, Tex.

56. Elisa R. Castañeda interview; Reverend Monsignor Anton J. Frank, interview with O. Wayne Poorman, tape recording, Houston, Tex., Dec. 29, 1972.

57. Elisa R. Castañeda interview.

58. Barker to Castañeda, Mar. 18, 1922, ECBP.

59. Castañeda to Barker, Apr. 24, 1922, ECBP.

60. Elisa R. Castañeda interview.

61. Ibid.

62. Teachers Salary and Service Records, Directory of San Antonio City Schools for the Year Ending May 31, 1923, Administrative Offices, San Antonio Independent School District, San Antonio, Tex.

63. Castañeda Transcript.

64. Castañeda to Barker, Sept. 30, 1922, ECBP.

65. Castañeda to J. Randolph, 1932, CECP.

66. Castañeda to Barker, Sept. 30, 1922, ECBP.

67. Certificate of Birth No. C-239-4132, Office of Vital Statistics, Public Health Department, San Antonio, Tex.

68. Castañeda to Barker, May 28, 1923, ECBP.

69. Entry No. 889, Baptismal Book 23 (Oct. 22, 1922–May 1, 1924), p. 127, Microfilm Reel VS41, CASA.

70. Castañeda to Barker, July 19, 1923, ECBP.

71. Ibid.

72. Ibid.

73. Castañeda to Barker, Aug. 10, 1923, ECBP.

74. Castañeda to Barker, Aug. 12, 1923, ECBP.

75. Carlos E. Castañeda, "A Report on the Spanish Archives of San Antonio" (M.A. thesis, UTA, 1923). In addition to Eugene C. Barker as supervising professor, the faculty committee included E. T. Miller and Charles W. Ramsdell, Sr.

Chapter 2

1. *Vital Facts: A Chronology of the College of William and Mary* (Williamsburg, Va.: College of William and Mary Library, 1975), p. 3; *Flat Hat,* Jan. 14, 1927, ACWM; Upton, "Knight of Goodwill," p. 13, CBF; Castañeda to H. L. Childs, May 28, 1929, CECP.

2. A. G. Williams to Castañeda, Feb. 13, 1927, CECP.

3. Frank L. Crone to Castañeda, Feb. 20, 1927, CECP.

4. Castañeda to William F. Blakeslee, Oct. 28, 1926, CECP; *Southern Messenger,* Oct. 2, 1941, J. D. Ashe Collection, Fort Worth, Tex.; *Webster's Biographical Dictionary,* p. 592; *The Official Catholic Directory Anno Domini 1988,* p. 753.

5. Upton, "Knight of Goodwill," p. 13.

6. *The Colonial Echo [1924],* p. 261, ACWM.

7. Castañeda to Barker, Oct. 29, 1923, ECBP.

8. Barker to Castañeda, Nov. 17, 1923, ECBP.

9. Castañeda to Barker, Nov. 23, 1923, ECBP.

10. Upton, "Knight of Goodwill," p. 13.

11. Castañeda to Barker, Jan. 4, 1924, ECBP.

12. Castañeda to Barker, Feb. 15, 1924, ECBP.

13. *Flat Hat,* Feb. 22, 1924, ACWM.

14. *Flat Hat,* Feb. 29, 1924, ACWM.

15. *Flat Hat,* Mar. 14, 1924, ACWM.

16. Castañeda to Barker, Feb. 15, 1924, ECBP.

17. Off and on for about two years, while residing in Virginia, Castañeda worked on a textbook. As late as 1926 he promised an editor at D. C. Heath and Company that he would have a manuscript "ready for your inspection in the near future." During World

War II he finally completed this project of long duration (Castañeda to Alexander Green, Oct. 4, 1926, CECP).

18. Castañeda to Barker, Apr. 21, 1924, ECBP.

19. Ibid. One of Castañeda's articles—"Can Anyone Learn Spanish?"—appeared in the March, 1924, issue of *Catholic School Interest,* a magazine that specialized in "education in general in the United States," and received favorable reviews. Another essay— "Did You Ever Stop To Think?"—came out in America, while *Missionary* accepted an article on Father Antonio Margil de Jesús. President J. A. C. Chandler complimented his efforts: "I am glad to see you are writing these articles, and I am sure that they will mean a great deal to those who read them" (*Flat Hat,* Apr. 25, 1924; Castañeda to Chandler, June 24, 1924; Chandler to Castañeda, Oct. 3, 1924; J. A. C. Chandler Files 1982.45— Box 6, C. E. Castañeda File (Sept. 1, 1924–July 1, 1925) (hereinafter cited as CF/C), ACWM,

20. Barker to Castañeda, May 10, 1924, ECBP.

21. Castañeda to Barker, Sept. 10, 1924, ECBP; Record Book, Board of Visitors, College of William and Mary (July 1, 1919–Apr. 2, 1934), Meeting of June 9, 1924, p. 82.

22. Castañeda to Barker, Sept. 10, 1924, ECBP.

23. C. E. Castañeda, "The Educational Revolution in Mexico," *Educational Review* 68 (Oct., 1924): 123.

24. *Flat Hat,* Oct. 3, 1924; Chandler to Castañeda, Oct. [1], 1924, CF/C, ACWM.

25. *Flat Hat,* Nov. 7, 1924, ACWM.

26. Castañeda to Chandler, Nov. 10 and Dec. 16, 1924, CF/C, ACWM.

27. *Flat Hat,* Nov. 14, 1924, ACWM.

28. *Flat Hat,* Dec. 12, 1924, ACWM.

29. "The Meeting of the American Historical Association at Richmond," *American Historical Review* 30 (Apr., 1925): 453.

30. *Flat Hat,* Nov. 7, 1924, and Jan. 9, 1925, ACWM; "Meeting of American Historical Association," p. 453.

31. Carlos E. Castañeda (trans. and ed.), "Statistical Report on Texas by Juan N. Almonte, 1835," *Southwestern Historical Quarterly* 28 (Jan., 1925): 177–222; Castañeda to Barker, Feb. 10, 1925, ECBP; *Flat Hat,* Feb. 13, 1925, ACWM.

32. Castañeda to Barker, Feb. 10, 1925, ECBP.

33. Barker to Castañeda, Feb. 19, 1925, ECBP.

34. Carlos E. Castañeda, "Modern Language Instruction in American Colleges, 1779–1800," *Catholic Educational Review* 23 (Jan.–Feb., 1925): 3–9, 92–106; *Flat Hat,* Jan. 30, 1925, ACWM.

35. Castañeda to Chandler, Feb. 22, 1925, CF/C, ACWM; Castañeda to Barker, Feb. 10, 1925, ECBP.

36. C. E. Castañeda, "Latin America's First Great Educator," *Current History* 22 (May, 1925): 223–25.

37. Chandler to Castañeda, May 11, 1925; Castañeda to Chandler, May 4 and 14, 1925, CF/C, ACWM.

38. Mexican Tour Expense Account, in Castañeda to Chandler, Nov. 14, 1924; Chandler to Castañeda, Nov. 24, 1924; Castañeda to Chandler, Dec. 5, 1924, CF/C, ACWM.

39. Castañeda to Barker, Feb. 10, 1925, ECBP.

40. Castañeda to Chandler, Oct. 6, 1924, Jan. 28, 1925, CF/C, ACWM.

41. Chandler to Castañeda, Mar. 12 and Apr. 2, 1925; Castañeda to Chandler, Apr. 9 and May 9, 1925, CF/C, ACWM.

42. Report, Summer School in Mexico, in Castañeda to Chandler, Sept. 7, 1925, CF/C (hereinafter cited as Report of 1925 Summer School in Mexico), ACWM.

43. C. E. Castañeda, "Is Mexico Turning Bolshevik?," *Catholic World* 123 (June, 1926): 366; Ramón Eduardo Ruiz, *The Great Rebellion: Mexico, 1905-1924* (New York: W. W. Norton & Company, 1980), p. 377.

44. *Flat Hat*, Sept. 25, 1925; *[National University of Mexico] Summer School News,* Feb., 1926, CF/C, ACWM.

45. Report of 1925 Summer School in Mexico, ACWM.

46. *Flat Hat,* May 23, 1925; Bulletin of the College of William and Mary in Virginia, Announcements of the Summer School in Mexico (hereinafter cited as College of William and Mary Bulletin: Summer School in Mexico), CF/C, ACWM.

47. E. W. Winkler to Castañeda, Mar. 9, 1926, CECP.

48. *Flat Hat,* Sept. 25, 1925; *Summer School News,* Feb., 1926; Report of 1925 Summer School in Mexico, ACWM.

49. Report of 1925 Summer School in Mexico, ACWM.

50. Castañeda to Chandler, Sept. 7, 1925, CF/C, ACWM.

51. Chandler to Castañeda, Sept. 17, 1925, CF/C, ACWM.

52. Castañeda to Chandler, Oct. 21, 1925; Chandler to Castañeda, Oct. 24, 1925, CF/C, ACWM.

53. Chandler to Castañeda, Nov. 6, 1925, CF/C, ACWM.

54. Castañeda to Chandler, Nov. 12, 1925, CF/C, ACWM.

55. Castañeda to Chandler, Nov. 16, 1925; Chandler to Castañeda, Nov. 18, 1925, CF/C, ACWM.

56. Chandler to Castañeda, Nov. 18, 1929, CF/C, ACWM.

57. Castañeda to Chandler, Nov. 19, 1925; Chandler to Castañeda, Nov. 30, 1925, CF/C, ACWM.

58. Castañeda to Rev. William F. Blakeslee, C.S.P., Oct. 28, 1926; Castañeda to Rev. James M. Gillis, C.S.P., Dec. 20, 1926, CECP. Following the celebration of the field mass, the Gibbons Club as a gesture of gratitude offered to donate "a portion of the wall around the campus" at William and Mary, agreeing to make full payment for the construction at the end of the calendar year. An appreciative president notified Castañeda: "This is a very gracious act on the part of the Club, and the college will be very grateful for the gift" (Chandler to Castañeda, June 2, 1926, CF/C, ACWM).

59. Castañeda to Chandler, Apr. 23, 1926; Chandler to Castañeda, May 5, 1926, CF/C, ACWM; Carlos E. Castañeda (trans. and ed.), "A Trip to Texas in 1828: José María Sánchez," *Southwestern Historical Quarterly* 29 (Apr., 1926): 249-88.

60. Castañeda, "Is Mexico Turning Bolshevik?," pp. 366-72.

61. Ibid. For a balanced survey of the power struggle, see David C. Bailey, *¡Viva Cristo Rey! The Cristero Rebellion and the Church-State Conflict in Mexico* (Austin: University of Texas Press, 1974).

62. Williams to Castañeda, July 2, 1926, CECP; Charles Phillips, "The Trouble in Mexico: A Reply to the Foregoing Article," *Catholic World* 123 (June, 1926): 372-80. In 1919, to promote and protect church interests in the Western Hemisphere, the American hierarchy established the National Catholic Welfare Conference, with headquarters in Washington, D.C. In 1925 the administrative committee of the NCWC dispatched Phillips, a former journalist and editor, to Mexico to assess the situation for the church. Shocked by eyewitness accounts and scenes he personally observed, Phillips formed a

hard-line philosophical stance on the issue of church versus state in Mexico (Douglas Slawson, "The National Catholic Conference and the Church-State Conflict in Mexico, 1925–1929," *The Americas* 47 [July, 1990]: 55–59).

63. Castañeda to F. R. Addington, Dec. 29, 1927, CECP.

64. Castañeda to Capt. Thomas P. Walsh, Nov. 10, 1927, CECP.

65. Winkler to Castañeda, Mar. 9, 1926, CECP. By the time Winkler extended his of-fer to Castañeda, the university's acquisition of the García Collection constituted an in-teresting chronicle of personal and institutional negotiations. In Jan., 1920, a diplomatic mission representing the Mexican government arrived in Austin to attend the inaugura-tion of Pat M. Neff as governor of Texas. As a reciprocal courtesy in December of the same year, Governor Neff appointed an official delegation—comprising Dr. Charles W. Hackett and two members of the board of regents, Henry Jacob Lutcher Stark and Joseph Alexander Kemp—to represent Texas at the presidential inaugural of Alvaro Obregón. During an interlude in the festivities, upon learning of the death of Genaro García, renowned Mexican historian and bibliophile, Hackett visited the family to express con-dolences. In the course of the visit the widow García informed him that the Mexican gov-ernment had declined to purchase for the national library the extensive collection of books and manuscripts her deceased husband had accumulated. Consequently, in dire need of money to support herself and her ten children, Señora García inquired about pro-spective buyers in the United States. Hackett hurriedly advised Stark and Kemp of the windfall opportunity to acquire the "finest and most extensive historical and literary col-lection" in Mexico. Before returning to Texas the two regents and Hackett agreed to se-cure an option to permit "a more careful" evaluation later of the contents of the García library. Within a month Ernest W. Winkler, then reference librarian at the University of Texas, journeyed to Mexico City to conduct an inventory and appraisal.

The García Collection, Castañeda recalled, consisted of twenty-five thousand printed items, "including numberless bibliographical treasures, important files of newspapers, fundamental sets of documentary sources, and rare editions." Among three hundred thousand pages of manuscripts were the personal archives of outstanding personalities in Mexican history, such as Antonio López de Santa Anna, Vicente Guerrero, Valentín Gómez-Farías, Ignacio Comonfort, Lucas Alamán, Mariano and Vicente Riva Palacio, and Teodosio Lares. After receiving Winkler's favorable report, the board of regents, re-sponding to Kemp's advocacy, resolved to acquire the Genaro García Collection. Follow-ing legal and financial transactions, the University of Texas assigned a library employee to accompany two members of the García family aboard a special train that transported "the precious shipment" from the high central plateau to the lowlands of the Rio Grande at Laredo. Just before World War II the board of regents adopted stringent rules to pre-vent their successors from acting with "the necessary" dispatch in the event "a similar opportunity" were to occur (Carlos E. Castañeda, "The Human Side of a Great Collec-tion," *Books Abroad* 14 [1940]: 116–17).

66. Félix D. Almaráz, Jr., "The Making of a Boltonian: Carlos E. Castañeda of Texas—The Early Years," *Red River Valley Historical Review* 1 (Winter, 1974): 331; *In-terim Knight* [Jan., 1970], J. D. Ashe Collection, Fort Worth, Tex.

67. Castañeda to Chandler, Mar. 16, 1926; Chandler to Castañeda, Mar. 19, 1926, CF/C, ACWM.

68. Castañeda to Chandler, Mar. 11, 1926; Chandler to Castañeda, Mar. 19, 1926, CF/C, ACWM.

69. College of William and Mary Bulletin: Summer School in Mexico, CF/C, ACWM.

70. Castañeda to Chandler, June 7 and 14, 1926; Chandler to Montaño and Pruneda, June 9, 1926, CF/C, ACWM.

71. Rev. W. A. R. Goodwin to the Honorable Alexander W. Weddell, June 9, 1926, CECP.

72. Castañeda to Chandler, June 7 and 14, 1926, CF/C, ACWM.

73. *Flat Hat,* Apr. 16, 1926, ACWM.

74. Castañeda to Joseph I. Driscoll, June 12, 1926, KCCF/CAT.

75. Ibid.

76. Ibid.

77. Chandler to Castañeda, June 15, 1926, CF/C, ACWM.

78. Castañeda to Luis Castañeda, Nov. 2, 1926; Castañeda to Daniel Cosío Villegas, Nov. 2, 1926, CECP.

79. Driscoll to Castañeda, June 22, 1926, KCCF/CAT. The Historical Commission of the State Council expanded its membership in 1926 to include Rev. Dr. Paul J. Foik, C.S.C., of Saint Edward's University, Austin, permanent chairman; Rev. W. Frank O'Brien of Texarkana; Rev. Joseph G. O'Donohoe, Waxahachie; Rev. Dr. Peter Guilday of Catholic University of America, Washington, D.C.; and two lawyers from El Paso, Joe G. Bennis and Joseph I. Driscoll, the latter state deputy of the Knights of Columbus.

80. Castañeda to F. O. Adam, Nov. 5, 1926; Castañeda to Charles W. Hackett, Sept. 10, 1926, CECP.

81. José Gutiérrez Castillas, *Historia de la Iglesia en México* (Mexico City: Editorial Porrúa, S.A., 1974), pp. 397-403; Bailey, *¡Viva Cristo Rey!,* pp. 82-93.

82. Castañeda to Luis Castañeda, Sept. 24, 1926, CECP; College of William and Mary Bulletin: Summer School in Mexico, CF/C, ACWM.

83. Castañeda to Hackett, Sept. 10, 1926, CECP.

84. Castañeda to Winkler, Sept. 13, 1926, CECP. In citing a topmost amount to Winkler, Castañeda included "a special bonus for extension work" that increased his salary "to about $2700" (Castañeda to Barker, Sept. 13, 1926, CECP).

85. Castañeda to Winkler, Sept. 13, 1926, CECP.

86. Castañeda to Barker, Sept. 13, 1926, CECP.

87. Barker to Castañeda, Sept. 18, 1926, CECP.

88. Castañeda to Barker, Sept. 23, 1926, CECP. Actually, Castañeda received one job offer for a teaching position at University Junior College in San Antonio, where a member of the history department took a leave of absence. The administration of the college sent Carlos a telegram offering an instructorship at a salary of $2,500. "Under the circumstances," Carlos explained to Barker, "I refused their offer." Barker subsequently revealed that he had recommended Castañeda for the faculty slot, adding, "It would probably have been permanent" (Barker to Castañeda, Oct. 14, 1926, CECP).

89. Barker to Castañeda, Sept. 24, 1926, CECP.

90. Winkler to W. M. W. Splawn, Oct. 5, 1926, CECP.

91. Winkler to Castañeda, Oct. 13, 1926, CECP.

92. Barker to Castañeda, Oct. 14, 1926, CECP.

93. Castañeda to Winkler, Oct. 16, 1926, CECP.

94. Castañeda to Barker, Oct. 18, 1926, CECP.

95. Castañeda to Havila Babcock, Oct. 28, 1926, CECP.

96. Castañeda to Crone, Feb. 9, 1927, CECP.

97. Castañeda to Adam, Nov. 17, 1926, CECP.

98. Winkler to Castañeda, Oct. 29, 1926; Castañeda to Winkler, Nov. 1, 1926; Winkler to Castañeda, Nov. 5, 1926, CECP.

99. Castañeda to Adam, Nov. 5, 1926, CECP.

100. Paul J. Foik to Castañeda, Oct. 28, 1926; Castañeda to Foik, Nov. 5, 1926, KCCF/CAT.

101. Castañeda to Hackett, Nov. 10, 1926, CECP.

102. Carlos E. Castañeda, "A Helping Hand to Mexico," *Commonweal* 5 (Nov. 17, 1926): 37-38.

103. Castañeda to Henry Goddard Leach, Dec. 13, 1926; Blakeslee to Castañeda, Dec. 15, 1926; Castañeda to Herbert Croly [?], Dec. 18, 1926, CECP.

104. Castañeda to Crone, Nov. 12, 1926, and Jan. 10, 1927, CECP; *Flat Hat,* Jan. 14, 1927, ACWM.

105. Castañeda to James M. Gillis, C.S.P., Dec. 20, 1926; Gillis to Castañeda, Dec. 31, 1926; Castañeda to Gillis, Jan. 3, 1927; Castañeda to Blakeslee, Oct. 28, 1926, CECP. Castañeda's enthusiastic support of student activities, especially his work with the Gibbons Club, impressed the college administration to such an extent that President Chandler "insisted that his successor be of the Catholic Faith" (*Southern Messenger,* Oct. 2, 1941).

106. Carlos E. Castañeda, "Why I Chose History," p. 478; Upton, "Knight of Goodwill," p. 13; Carlos E. Castañeda, "Modern Language Instruction in American Colleges," pp. 3-9, 92-106.

107. *Flat Hat,* Jan. 7, 1927, ACWM.

108. Castañeda to W. C. Stynor, Jan. 11, 1927; Castañeda to Babcock, Jan. 11, 1927, CECP.

109. *Flat Hat,* Jan. 14, 1927, ACWM.

110. Chandler to Castañeda, Jan. 24, 1927, CECP.

111. Castañeda to Crone, Jan. 10, 1927, CECP.

112. Castañeda to Adam, Nov. 17, 1926, CECP.

113. Castañeda to J. J. Stigstein, Dec. 3, 1926; Castañeda to Harry J. Schneider, Dec. 28, 1927, CECP.

Chapter 3

1. Castañeda to American National Insurance Co., Apr. 29, 1927, CECP.

2. Castañeda to Frank L. Crone, Feb. 9, 1927, CECP.

3. Louis C. Moloney, "A History of the University Library at the University of Texas, 1883-1934" (Ph.D. diss., Columbia University, 1970), p. 245. The sending of the Texas delegation was a reciprocal courtesy stemming from a diplomatic mission in Jan., 1920, that had attended the inauguration of Pat M. Neff as governor of Texas. Castañeda had observed the ceremony at the state capitol shortly before leaving for a job in the oil fields of Tampico (Carlos E. Castañeda, "Human Side of a Great Collection," p. 116).

4. Carlos E. Castañeda, "Human Side of a Great Collection," pp. 116-17; Moloney, "History of the University Library," pp. 239, 245.

The price of the collection and "related costs" totaled nearly $105,000, which exceeded the funds appropriated "for regular library expenditures." To make up the difference the regents obtained funds from other university sources (Moloney, "History of the University Library," p. 139). The widow García received $100,000 for her husband's library; an additional amount of $4,537.06 probably reflected expenditures for packing, transporting, special handling, insurance, railway fare, and incidentals for attendants (Moloney, "History of the University Library," pp. 239, 245).

Just before World War II the board of regents adopted stringent rules to prevent anyone, including its own membership, from acting with "the necessary dispatch" in the event an opportunity similar to that involving the García Collection were to occur (Carlos E. Castañeda, "Human Side of a Great Collection," pp. 116–17).

5. E. W. Winkler to E. C. Barker, Feb. 7, 1921, Library, 1919–20, Presidential Records, Archives, BTHC, quoted in Moloney, "History of the University Library," p. 245.

6. Castañeda to Havila Babcock, Feb. 9, 1928, CECP.

7. Castañeda to Frank L. Crone, Feb. 9, 1927, CECP.

8. Castañeda to F. O. Adam, Feb. 19, 1927, CECP.

9. Castañeda Transcript.

10. Castañeda to Lillian Berlin, Mar. 4, 1927, CECP.

11. Castañeda to A. G. Williams, Apr. 29, 1927, CECP.

12. Castañeda to Berlin, Mar. 4, 1927, CECP.

13. Castañeda to Herbert L. Ganter, Aug. 23, 1927, CECP.

14. Castañeda to Berlin, Mar. 4, 1927, CECP.

15. Typescript, El Club Mexicano; Receipt, Gregorio C. Camacho to Castañeda, Feb. 12, 1927, CECP.

16. Castañeda to Mana Licha (his sister Elisa), Dec. 7, 1929, CECP.

17. Castañeda to William Blakeslee, Jan. 23, 1928, CECP.

18. Castañeda to Sister Agatha, Sept. 24, 1929, CECP.

19. Agnes Charlton to Castañeda, Aug. 13, 1927, CECP.

20. Llerena B. Friend to Félix D. Almaráz, Jr., Mar. 17, 1973, Almaráz Papers.

21. Castañeda to Winkler, Apr. 1, 1927, CECP.

22. Castañeda to H. W. Childs, May 31, 1927, CECP.

23. Castañeda to Ganter, May 16, 1927, CECP.

24. Castañeda to Childs, May 31, 1927; Castañeda to Babcock, June 17, 1927, CECP; Paul J. Foik to Castañeda, Nov. 2, 1927, KCCF/CAT.

25. Castañeda to Babcock, June 17, 1927; Foik to Castañeda, Nov. 2, 1927, CECP.

26. "Affairs of the Association," *Southwestern Historical Quarterly* 31 (July, 1927): 86.

27. Castañeda to Babcock, June 17, 1927; Castañeda to Manas (Hermanas, his sisters in Brownsville), May 2, 1927, CECP.

28. Castañeda to Manas, May 2, 1927, CECP.

29. Castañeda to R. D. Calkins, June 18, 1927, CECP.

30. Castañeda to Crone, June 24, 1927, CECP.

31. Ibid.

32. Ibid.

33. Castañeda to Earl G. Swem, Aug. 9, 1927; Castañeda to Crone, Aug. 2, 1927, CECP.

34. Castañeda to Manas, May 2, 1927, CECP. Castañeda periodically commented to friends on Gloria's progress with Spanish. "I hope," he said to a Virginia friend, "that I can succeed in bringing her up speaking Spanish and English with equal ease" (Castañeda to Williams, Nov. 30, 1927, CECP). The following spring he reported: "Gloria is such a big girl you would hardly know her. She is very tall now and she speaks a sort of

broken Spanish. . . . [We try] not to push her as she has lots of time to learn. She has picked up a lot of things though" (Castañeda to Calkins, Apr. 18, 1928, CECP).

35. Winkler to Castañeda, July 23, 1927, CECP.

36. Castañeda to Winkler, Aug. 11, 1927, CECP.

37. Castañeda to Crone, Aug. 2, 1927, CECP.

38. Castañeda to Winkler, Aug. 11, 1927, CECP.

39. Ibid.

40. Ibid.

41. Castañeda to Swem, Aug. 9, 1927, CECP.

42. Castañeda to Babcock, June 17, 1927, CECP.

43. Castañeda to Ganter, Aug. 23, 1927, CECP.

44. Castañeda to Williams, Aug. 30, 1927; Castañeda to Babcock, Oct. 13, 1927, CECP. The courses were on governments of Latin America, inter-American relations, and the Spanish Southwest (Castañeda Transcript).

45. Castañeda to Mariano Cuevas, Oct. 20 and 29, 1927, CECP; *Diccionario Porrúa de Historia, Biografía y Geografía de México,* vol. 2, p. 1541.

46. Castañeda to Manas, Oct. 22, 1927, CECP.

47. Frantz interview.

48. Castañeda to Timoteo Castañeda, Oct. 22, 1927, CECP.

49. Castañeda to Capt. Thomas Walsh, Nov. 30, 1927; Castañeda to Williams, Nov. 30, 1927, CECP.

50. Castañeda to Manas, Dec. 28, 1927; Castañeda to Justice of the Peace Harry J. Schneider, Dec. 28, 1927, CECP.

51. Castañeda to K. R. Addington, Dec. 29, 1927, CECP.

52. Frantz interview.

53. Castañeda to Winkler, Jan. 19, 1928, CECP.

54. Castañeda to Winkler, Feb. 15, 1928, CECP.

55. Castañeda to Opal Gilstrap, Jan. 7, 1928, CECP.

56. Castañeda to Babcock, Jan. 19, 1928, CECP.

57. Castañeda to Mary E. Hudspeth, Feb. 3, 1928, CECP.

58. Castañeda to Babcock, Feb. 9, 1928, CECP. While the university administrators' decision to deny permission for Castañeda to lead the tour may have stemmed from an inflexibility normally found in large public institutions, as opposed to private corporations like William and Mary, there is also a distinct possibility that smoldering resentment in intralibrary management spilled into channels of communication, causing some authorities to question Carlos's priorities to the Latin American Collection. In any case, no sooner was this episode over when Castañeda conceived another educational tour plan, this time to the Caribbean. To Babcock in South Carolina he declared: "Well, I am ready to sail to Panama!" Ultimately, as Castañeda redirected his energies toward a more challenging venture in Mexico related to the library, the Caribbean excursion never materialized (Castañeda to Babcock, Apr. 3, 1928; Castañeda to Mrs. [Esther Pérez] Carvajal, Apr. 4, 1928, CECP).

59. Castañeda to Babcock, Apr. 3, 1928; Castañeda to Carvajal, Apr. 4, 1928, CECP.

60. Castañeda to Manas, Mar. 14, 1928, CECP.

61. "Affairs of the Association," *Southwestern Historical Quarterly* 31 (July, 1927): 384; "Affairs of the Association," *Southwestern Historical Quarterly* 32 (July, 1928): 100.

62. J. A. C. Chandler to Castañeda, Apr. 11, 1928, CECP.

63. Castañeda to Walsh, Apr. 17, 1928, CECP.

64. Castañeda to Foik, Apr. 11, 1928, CECP. To initiate research and composition on selected topics of early colonial Texas history, the leadership of the Knights of Columbus Historical Commission created a Texas Catholic Historical Society. This was the "association" to which Castañeda alluded in his letter to Foik (William H. Dunn, *Knights of Columbus in Texas: 1902–1977,* p. 8; see also "Texas Catholic Historical Society," in *The New Handbook of Texas,* vol. 6, p. 297).

65. Castañeda to Foik, Apr. 11, 1928, CECP. Although Vosper had elevated the standards of the School of Architecture at the University of Texas, the administration in 1928 fired him "for hiring a nude model." Afterward he served with distinction as chief designer with the College Architect's Office at Texas A&M College (later University) and worked on numerous projects in South Texas ("Samuel Charles Phelps Vosper," in *New Handbook of Texas,* vol. 6, p. 773).

66. Castañeda to Joseph I. Driscoll, May 3, 1928, KCCF/CAT.

67. Castañeda to Sister M. Angelique [Ayres], Apr. 25 and May 1, 1928; Sister Angelique to Castañeda, Apr. 30, 1928, CECP.

68. Castañeda to Winnie Allen, June 12, 1928, CBF; Castañeda to Sister Angelique, Mar. 19, 1929, LF/OAD/OLLU/SAT. For a summary of Winnie Allen's achievements in the Archives Department, consult Malcolm D. McLean, "Winnie Allen: The 'Mother of Texas History,'" *Texas Libraries* 50 (Winter, 1989–90): 124–29.

69. Castañeda to Manas, May 9, 1928; Castañeda to Baldomero Chacón, May 11, 1928; H. G. Holden, Photostat Corporation of America, to Castañeda, May 26, 1928, CBF.

70. Castañeda to H. H. Leonard, American Vice Consul, Matamoros, Tamaulipas, June 2, 1928, CBF.

71. Instrucciones Que Debe Seguir Fernando A. Castañeda en el Trabajo de Copiar de Documentos para la Universidad de Texas (undated typescript), CBF.

72. Allen to Castañeda, June 11, 1928, CECP.

73. *Southern Messenger,* May 24, 1928, CECP.

74. Elisa R. Castañeda interview.

75. Western Union Telegram, Fernando A. Castañeda to Castañeda, June 8, 1928, CECP.

76. Castañeda to Allen, June 12, 1928, CBF.

77. Castañeda to Sister Angelique, June 12, 1928, LF/OAD/OLLU/SAT.

78. Castañeda to Allen, June 12, 1928, CBF.

79. Ibid.

80. Ibid.

81. Castañeda to Fernando A. Castañeda, June 12, 1928, CBF.

82. Castañeda to Allen, June 15, 1928, CBF.

83. Ibid.

84. Western Union Telegram, Fernando A. Castañeda to Castañeda, June 16, 1928, CECP.

85. Castañeda to Fernando A. Castañeda, June 18, 1928, CBF.

86. Castañeda to Allen, June 18, 1928, CBF.

87. Allen to Castañeda, June 21, 1928, CECP.

88. *Southern Messenger,* June 28, 1928, Texas Collection, Incarnate Word College, San Antonio, Tex.

89. Castañeda to Cuevas, June 28, 1928, CECP.

90. Castañeda to Manas, June 28, 1928, CBF.

91. Castañeda to Allen, July 2, 1928, CBF.

92. Castañeda to Fernando A. Castañeda, July 2, 1928, CBF.

93. Castañeda to Maureen Wilson, July 6, 1928, CBF; Carlos E. Castañeda, "Why I Chose History," p. 479.

94. Castañeda to Peter P. Forrestal [undated, circa July 10, 1928], CBF.

95. Review Questions [for Spanish literature class taught at Our Lady of the Lake College], July 13, 1928, CBF.

96. Castañeda to Williams, Apr. 29, 1927, CECP.

97. Sister Angelique to Castañeda, July 31, 1928, CECP.

98. Castañeda to Cuevas, Aug. 1, 1928, CECP.

99. Castañeda to Ganter, May 16, 1927, CECP.

100. C. L. Sonnichsen, *Pass of the North: Four Centuries on the Río Grande*, vol. 1, p. 234; Castañeda to Cuevas, Aug. 1, 1928, CECP; Mariano Cuevas, *Historia de la Iglesia de México*).

101. Frederick C. Chabot to Castañeda [undated, circa Aug., 1928]; Castañeda to Chabot, Aug. 17 and 19, and Sept. 12, 1928, CECP.

102. Western Union Telegram, Cuevas to Castañeda, Oct. 4, 1928, CECP.

103. Castañeda to Chabot, Oct., 1928; Castañeda to Sister M. Angela Fitzmorris, Oct. 9, 1928, CECP.

104. Castañeda to Chabot, Oct. 1928; Castañeda to Jovita González, Oct. 8, 1928, CECP.

105. Castañeda to Fitzmorris, Oct. 9, 1928, CECP.

106. Castañeda to Chabot, Oct. 23, 1928, CECP.

107. Castañeda to Isabel Fineau, Oct. 31, 1928, CECP.

108. Castañeda to Cuevas, Dec. 11, 1928, CECP.

109. Castañeda to Cuevas, Jan. 9, 1929, CECP.

110. Cuevas to Castañeda, [undated, circa Jan., 1929], CECP.

111. An outstanding example of the religious and civil unrest from which Mariano Cuevas had escaped was the execution of fellow Jesuit Miguel Agustín Pro Juárez. Born in the town of Guadalupe in Zacatecas in 1891, Miguel Pro joined the Society of Jesus in 1911. The instability of the Mexican Revolution forced him to continue his education in the United States and Spain. Following a brief teaching appointment in Nicaragua, Pro went back to Europe to begin theological studies in Barcelona, which culminated in his ordination to the priesthood in Belgium. For reasons of delicate health, Father Pro returned to Mexico, focusing his ministry among the poor and less fortunate in society. On Nov. 13, 1927, in the midst of the Cristero Rebellion, an armed protest by traditional Catholics against the anticlerical government of Plutarco Elías Calles, four members of the National League in Defense of Religious Liberty reportedly tossed a bomb at an automobile transporting Gen. Alvaro Obregón on a political campaign tour of Mexico City. The police promptly arrested three suspects, not one of whom had any association with Father Miguel A. Pro, S.J. However, because the vehicle involved in the assassination plot had been registered in the name of one of Father Pro's brothers, police officials rushed to judgment. On Nov. 23, 1927, purely on circumstantial evidence, a military firing squad summarily executed Father Pro and his brother Humberto. Public outrage, manifested in an enormous funeral procession, intensified the conflict of the Cristero Rebellion (*Diccionario Porrúa de Historia, Biografía y Geografía*, vol. 2, p. 1678;

also consult Antonio Dragón, *Miguel Agustín Pro of the Society of Jesus, Martyr of Christ the King,* ed. Lawrence Drummond [Montreal: Messenger Press, 1930]).

112. Castañeda to Cuevas, Jan. 17, 1929, CECP.

113. Castañeda to Cuevas, Jan. 18, 1929, CECP.

114. Castañeda to Cuevas, Jan. 28, 1929; Castañeda to Cuevas, Jan. 9, 1919; Castañeda to Fineau, Jan. 9, 1929, CECP.

115. Cuevas to Castañeda, Jan. 24, 1929, CECP.

116. Castañeda to Cuevas, Jan. 28, 1929; Castañeda to Cuevas, Jan. 17, 1929, CECP.

117. Castañeda to Benjamín Garza, Feb. 28, 1929, CECP.

118. Castañeda to Winkler, Mar. 15, 1929, CECP.

119. Castañeda to H. W. Harper, Oct. 16 and 18, 1929, CECP.

120. Cuevas to Castañeda, [undated, circa Jan., 1929], CECP.

121. Castañeda to Babcock, Jan. 22, 1929, CECP.

122. Julio [?] to Castañeda, Feb. 10, 1929, CECP.

123. Josefina C. Castañeda, interview with Diana Guerra, Dec. 15, 1970, tape recording, Brownsville, Tex. With the consent of their father, Jesús Villarreal, the children moved into the Castañeda household. Years later, after graduating from the University of Texas at Austin, Elisa C. Villarreal married Alfredo Vásquez; in the 1970s she became professor of social work at the Worden School of Social Service, Our Lady of the Lake University, in San Antonio. Her younger brother, Carlos Castañeda Villarreal, the first Spanish-surnamed graduate of the U.S. Naval Academy, served as administrator of Urban Mass Transportation during the presidency of Richard M. Nixon (Verónica Salazar, "Dedication Rewarded," *San Antonio Star,* June 25, 1978; *San Antonio Express,* Nov. 7, 1972).

124. Juan Cárdenas, "Equality of Races Foremost Goal to Ben Garza," *Corpus Christi Caller,* Jan. 23, 1983, p. 21; Henry Santiestévan, "A Perspective on Mexican-American Organizations," in *Mexican-Americans Tomorrow: Educational and Economic Perspectives,* ed. Gus Tyler (Albuquerque: University of New Mexico Press, 1975), 177–79.

125. Castañeda to J. T. Canales, Feb. 17, 1929, CECP.

126. Ben Garza to Castañeda, Feb. 26, 1929, CECP.

127. Castañeda to Garza, Feb. 28, 1929, CECP.

128. Ibid.

129. Castañeda to Chabot, Feb. 20, 1929, CECP.

130. Castañeda to Winkler, Mar. 15, 1929, CECP.

131. Castañeda to Cuevas, Mar. 22, 1929, CECP.

132. Castañeda to Childs, May 28, 1929, CECP.

133. Castañeda to Winkler, May 30, 1929, CECP.

134. Castañeda to Cuevas, June 5, 1929, CECP.

135. Castañeda to Chabot, May 8, 1929; receipt from Mariano Cuevas, May 9, 1929, CECP.

Financial woes notwithstanding, Castañeda and Chabot collaborated in a high-risk speculative venture to publish a volume of "handsome photographs," limited to fifty copies, now considered rare and very expensive. The publication sold haltingly during the constraints of the Great Depression (Carlos E. Castañeda and Frederick C. Chabot, *Early Texas Album: Fifty Illustrations with Notes;* Castañeda to Herbert E. Bolton, Feb. 3, 1931, CECP).

136. Castañeda to France V. Scholes, June 9, 1929; Castañeda to Cuevas, July 20,

1929, CECP. In the summer of 1910 Herbert E. Bolton completed a manuscript that became an indispensable tool for serious researchers, *Guide to Materials for the History of the United States in the Principal Archives of Mexico.* At the beginning of the twentieth century, after the death of Col. Guy M. Bryan, grandson of Moses Austin and nephew of Stephen Fuller Austin, the University of Texas acquired "the vast collection" of the Austin Papers. Eugene C. Barker's contributions to the history of Western America should include his stellar work *The Life of Stephen F. Austin, Founder of Texas, 1793–1836: A Chapter in the Westward Movement of the Anglo-American People,* initially published in 1925 by the Texas State Historical Association (Bannon, *Herbert Eugene Bolton,* p. 80; William C. Pool, *Eugene C. Barker: Historian,* p. 145).

137. Castañeda to Allen, July 8, 1929, CECP.

138. Castañeda to Peter P. Forrestal, Aug. 20, 1929; Castañeda to Mrs. R. D. Calkins, Aug. 21, 1929; Castañeda to Chabot, Aug. 2, 1920, CECP; Elisa R. Castañeda interview, May 29, 1972; Burial certificate 8369, Book 35319, p. 25, Bureau of Vital Statistics, Brownsville, Tex.

139. Castañeda to Chabot, Aug. 2 and 28, 1929; Castañeda to W. T. Couch, Aug. 3, 1929, CECP.

140. Allen to Castañeda, [undated, circa Aug., 1929], CECP.

141. Castañeda to Cuevas, Aug. 20, 1929; Cuevas to Castañeda, July 30, 1929, CECP.

142. *General Laws of Texas,* 41st Legislature, Second and Third Called Sessions, 1929, p. 330, LRL/AT.

143. Castañeda to Forrestal, Aug. 20, 1929, CECP.

144. Castañeda to Cuevas, Aug. 20, 1929, CECP.

145. Ibid.

146. Cuevas to Castañeda, Sept. 11, 1929, CECP.

147. Cuevas to Castañeda, Oct. 8, 1929, CECP.

148. Castañeda to Cuevas, Sept. 18 and Oct. 15, 1929; Receipt, Castañeda to Cuevas, Nov. 27, 1929; Cuevas to Castañeda, Oct. 8, 1929; Castañeda to Forrestal, Nov. 30, 1929, CECP.

149. Castañeda to Chabot, Oct. 8, 1929, CECP.

150. Castañeda to *Southwest Press,* Jan. 8, 21, and 22, 1929; Irene Davenport, *Southwest Press,* to Castañeda, Jan. 16, 1929, CECP.

151. James A. Robertson to Castañeda, Oct. 12, 1929, CECP.

152. Ibid.

153. Castañeda to Sister Angelique, Sept. 5, 1929, LF/OAD/OLLU/SAT; Castañeda to Peter Guilday, Oct. 21 and Nov. 6, 1929, CECP.

154. Castañeda to Sister Angelique, Sept. 5, 1929, CECP.

155. Castañeda to Barker, Sept. 30, 1929, CECP.

156. Castañeda to Williams, Sept. 23, 1929, CECP.

157. Castañeda to Barker, Sept. 30, 1929, CECP.

158. Guilday to Castañeda, Oct. 16, 1929; Castañeda to Guilday, Oct. 21, Nov. 6 and 30, 1929, CECP; *Southern Messenger,* Dec. 5, 1929, OLLU/SAT.

159. Castañeda to Foik, Dec. 24, 1929, KCCF/CAT.

160. Deed Records, County of Travis, 445: 512–14 and 480: 78, County Clerk's Office, Travis County Courthouse, Austin, Tex.

161. Castañeda to Chabot, Nov. 30, 1929, CECP.

162. Castañeda to Chabot, Dec. 31, 1929, CECP.

Chapter 4

1. Castañeda to Peter P. Forrestal, Jan. 9, 1930, CECP.

2. Castañeda to Sister M. Angelique Ayres, Feb. 1, 1930, CECP.

3. Castañeda to Forrestal, Feb. 1, 1930, CECP.

4. Castañeda to Dorothy Schons, Jan. 24, 1930, CECP.

5. J. T. Canales to Castañeda, Jan. 11, 1930, CECP.

6. Castañeda to Forrestal, Jan. 9, 1930, CECP.

7. Roberto R. Treviño, "Prensa y Patria: The Spanish-Language Press and the Biculturalism of the Tejano Middle Class, 1920–1940," *Western Historical Quarterly* 22 (Nov., 1991): 455.

8. Castañeda to Mariano Cuevas, Jan. 15, 1930, CECP.

9. Castañeda to E. W. Winkler, Jan. 20, 1930, CECP.

10. Castañeda to Cuevas, Feb. 15, 1930, CECP.

11. Castañeda to H. E. Bolton, Mar. 22, 1930, CECP.

12. Castañeda to Peter Guilday, Mar. 26, 1930, CECP.

13. Castañeda to Sister M. Adriana, Apr. 15, 1930; Sister Adriana to Castañeda, Apr. 23, 1930, CECP.

14. Cuevas to Castañeda, Jan. 25, 1930; Castañeda to Cuevas, Feb. 1, 1930, CECP.

15. Cuevas to Castañeda, Feb. 19, 1930; Castañeda to Cuevas, Feb. 25, 1930, CECP. For his essay Castañeda initially proposed the title of "Manuel Doblado y su Actuación en la Guerra de Reforma." Later, in response to Father Cuevas's suggestion that he switch to another topic, Carlos decided to focus on Spanish colonial Texas as reflected in an assortment of maps in the Latin American Collection. Accordingly, he submitted a revised title of "Notas para la cartografía completa de la Provincia de Texas durante el período Colonial, 1520 a 1830" (Castañeda to Enríque C. Creel, Mar. 11, 1930; Castañeda to Cuevas, Mar. 18, 1930, CECP).

16. Castañeda to Edith Stow Haworth, Mar. 14, 1930; editors of *Catholic Historical Review* to Castañeda, Feb. 26, 1930; Peter Guilday to Castañeda, Mar. 10, 1930, CECP; Carlos E. Castañeda, Review of *Mexico and Texas, 1821–1836*, by Eugene C. Barker, *Catholic Historical Review* 17 (Apr., 1931): 490–92.

17. Canales to Castañeda, Feb. 19, 1930, CECP.

18. Ibid.

19. Castañeda to Canales, Feb. 26 and Mar. 5, 1930; Canales to Castañeda, Feb. 29 and Mar. 11, 1930, CECP.

20. Castañeda to Canales, Feb. 26, 1930, CECP. *La Prensa*'s editorial criticism of the Mexican government's policies, regardless of the revolutionary leader who occupied the presidential office, influenced the attitudes of middle-class exiles residing in the United States.

21. Castañeda to Barnhart Brothers and Spindler, Feb. 25, 1930, CECP.

22. Castañeda to Fred Dye, Mar. 11, 1930, CECP.

23. Castañeda to Canales, Mar. 30, 1930, CECP.

24. Castañeda to H. Y. Benedict, Feb. 20, 1930, CECP; Malcolm D. McLean, "E. D. Farmer International Fellowships," in *Papers Concerning Robertson's Colony in Texas, Introductory Volume: Robert Leftwich's Mexico Diary and Letterbook, 1822–1824* (Arlington: University of Texas Press/University of Texas at Arlington, 1986), p. 15.

25. Castañeda to Frederick C. Chabot, Mar. 7 and 11, 1930; Chabot to Castañeda, Mar. 9, 1930; Castañeda to Cuevas, Mar. 14, 1930, CECP.

26. Castañeda to Schons, Mar. 31, 1930, CECP.

27. Guilday to Castañeda, Mar. 27, 1930, CECP.

28. Castañeda to Guilday, Apr. 1, 1930, CECP.

29. Castañeda to Guilday, May 11, 1930, CECP.

30. Castañeda to Guilday, Sept. 27, 1930, CECP.

31. *El Universitario,* tabloid of *Club Latino-Americano* of UTA, Apr. 1930; Castañeda to Schons, Mar. 31, 1930, CECP.

32. Castañeda to Forrestal, Apr. 10, 1930, CECP.

33. "Notes and Comments," *HAHR* 10 (May, 1930): 246; Castañeda to Forrestal, Apr. 10, 1930; Castañeda to Cuevas, Apr. 11, 1930; Castañeda to Frank L. Crone, May 11, 1930; Castañeda to James A. Bardin, May 12, 1930; Castañeda to Fred D. Wells, June 17, 1930, CECP; *Diccionario Porrúa de Historia, Biografía y Geografía de México,* vol. 1, p. 903.

34. Castañeda to Guilday, May 11, 1930, CECP.

35. Frederick Eby to Castañeda, May 13, 1930; Castañeda to Eby, May 14, 1930; C. W. Hackett to Castañeda, May 7 and 26, 1930; Castañeda to A. G. Williams, June 3, 1930, CECP.

36. Castañeda to Williams, June 3, 1930, CECP.

37. *El Universitario,* Apr. 1930; Castañeda to Williams, June 3, 1930, CECP.

38. Castañeda to Crone, June 3, 1930, CECP.

39. Castañeda to Chabot, July 9, 1930.

40. Ibid.

41. Carlos E. Castañeda, with Early Martin, Jr., *Three Manuscript Maps of Texas by Stephen F. Austin* (Austin: Privately printed, 1930); Castañeda to Bolton, Feb. 3, 1931; Castañeda to Alfred B. Thomas, Feb. 9, 1931, CECP.

42. Crone to Castañeda, July 10, 1930; Castañeda to J. A. C. Chandler, July 12, 1930; Castañeda to Crone, July 14, 1930; Castañeda to E. G. Swem, July 14, 1930, CECP.

43. Castañeda to Chandler, July 12, 1930; Castañeda to Crone, July 14, 1930; Chandler to Castañeda, July 12 and 17, 1930, CECP.

44. Castañeda to Crone, Apr. 11, 1930, CECP.

45. Castañeda to Benedict, July 24, 1930, CECP.

46. Castañeda to Leonides González, July 25, 1930, CECP.

47. Charles Stephenson to Castañeda, Aug. 16, 1930; Castañeda to González, July 25, 1930, CECP.

48. Castañeda to Rhea [?], Aug. 21, 1930; Castañeda to Winkler, Aug. 18, 1930; Castañeda to Cuevas, Sept. 6, 1930, CECP; Upton, "Knight of Goodwill," p. 14, CBF.

49. *San Antonio Express,* Aug. 15, 1930.

50. Castañeda to Rhea [?], Aug. 21, 1930, CECP.

51. Winkler to Castañeda, Aug. 16, 1930, CECP.

52. Castañeda to Cuevas, Sept. 6, 1930, CECP.

53. Castañeda to Winkler, Aug. 18, 1930, CECP. As an ambulatory convalescent, Castañeda soon became restless. "I can't keep idle much longer," he confided to Frank L. Crone in Virginia. Foremost on his wish list was a trip to Washington, D.C., and in a whimsical mood he invited Crone to a weekend reunion in the nation's capital. "On the way [to Washington] we should be able to do a lot of talking and gossiping," he told his friend (Castañeda to Crone, Aug. 18, 1930, CECP).

54. Allen to the Castañedas, Aug. 18, 1930, CECP.

55. Castañeda to Gilbert J. Garraghan, Aug. 21, 1930, CECP.

56. Garraghan to Castañeda, Aug. 20, 1930, CECP.

57. Castañeda to Allen, Sept. 10, 1930, CECP.

58. Castañeda to France V. Scholes, Sept. 26, 1930, CECP.

59. Scholes to Castañeda, Oct. 25, 1930, CECP.

60. Castañeda to Scholes, Oct. 28 and 19, 1930, CECP.

61. Scholes to Castañeda, Nov. 8, 1930, CECP.

62. Guilday to Castañeda, Nov. 4, 1930, CECP.

63. Castañeda to Guilday, Nov. 12, 1930, CECP.

64. Castañeda to Chabot, Nov. 24, 1930, CECP.

65. Castañeda to Scholes, Dec. 4, 1930, CECP.

66. Castañeda to Guilday, Dec. 5, 1930, CECP. Castañeda's essay finally appeared in the Oct. issue (*Catholic Historical Review* 17 [Oct., 1931]: 257–95).

67. Telegram, Paul J. Foik to Joseph I. Driscoll, Nov. 30, 1930, KCCF/CAT.

68. Telegram, Driscoll to Foik, Dec. 1, 1930, KCCF/CAT.

69. Castañeda to Scholes, Dec. 4, 1930, KCCF/CAT.

70. Carlos E. Castañeda, "Why I Chose History," pp. 479–80; Castañeda Collection of Documents for the History of Texas, undated typescript, p. 5, CBF.

71. Castañeda to Foik, Dec. 9, 1930, KCCF/CAT.

72. Castañeda to Foik, Dec. 12, 1930, KCCF/CAT. Colegio Grande and Convento Grande were interchangeable terms in the Spanish colonial epoch.

73. France Scholes, "Problems in the Early Ecclesiastical History of New Mexico," *New Mexico Historical Review* 1 (Jan., 1932): 32–33.

74. Carlos E. Castañeda, "Why I Chose History," p. 480; "Juan Agustín Morfi," in *New Handbook of Texas,* vol. 4, p. 833.

75. Castañeda to Foik, Dec. 12, 1930, KCCF/CAT.

76. Carlos E. Castañeda, "Why I Chose History," p. 480.

77. Sheridan interview.

78. Castañeda to Foik, Dec. 9, 1930, CECP.

79. Foik to Driscoll, Dec. 12, 1930, KCCF/CAT.

80. Foik to Castañeda, Dec. 13, 1930, KCCF/CAT.

81. Ibid.

82. Foik to Driscoll, Dec. 15, 1930, KCCF/CAT.

83. [Foik] to Castañeda, Dec. 16, 1930, KCCF/CAT.

84. Foik to Nan Dougherty; Driscoll to Foik; Driscoll to Castañeda, Dec. 17, 1930; Castañeda to Foik, Dec. 18, 1930, KCCF/CAT.

85. Castañeda to Foik, Dec. 27, 1930; Castañeda Report to the Knights of Columbus Historical Commission, Jan. 20, 1931, KCCF/CAT; José Bravo Ugarte, *Diócesis y Obispos de la Iglesia Mexicana (1519–1965)* (Mexico: Editorial Jus, 1965), p. 55.

86. Castañeda to Foik, Dec. 27, 1930, KCCF/CAT.

87. Ibid.

88. Castañeda to Foik, Jan. 8, 1931, KCCF/CAT.

89. Castañeda Report to the Texas Historical Commission.

90. Castañeda to Foik, Jan. 8, 1931. KCCF/CAT.

91. Foik to Driscoll, Jan. 13, 1931, KCCF/CAT. An irritating occurrence associated with the Mexican research trip involved a registered letter from Driscoll that became lost in the mail. Taking advantage of Carlos's presence in Mexico City, Father Foik asked him to purchase copies of rare books from a reputable dealer. Anticipating reimbursement within a reasonable period, Castañeda paid $90 dollars for part of a book order. Mean-

NOTES TO PAGES 95–100

while, aware of Carlos's limited resources, Driscoll air-mailed a draft on a New York bank in the amount of $180 to cover the initial expenditure plus additional purchases. Unfortunately, Carlos did not receive the letter until six weeks later. In the meantime, inquiries about the lost letter took up an inordinate slice of time that Castañeda could have devoted to his dissertation (Foik to Driscoll, Jan. 13, 1931; Félix González, Administración de Correos, to Castañeda, Jan. 22, 1931; Castañeda to Driscoll and to H. C. Kramp, Jan. 29, 1931; Postmaster Kramp to Driscoll, Jan. 31, 1931; Driscoll to the State National Bank of El Paso, Feb. 6, 1931; Driscoll to William P. Gallighan, Feb. 6, 1931, KCCF/CAT).

92. Castañeda to James Fred Rippy, Jan. 17, 1931, CECP.

93. Carlos E. Castañeda, "Human Side of a Great Collection," p. 118.

94. *General Laws of Texas,* 42nd Legislature, Regular Session, 1931, p. 576, LRL/AT.

95. Moloney, "History of the University Library," pp. 184–285.

96. Carlos E. Castañeda, "Customs and Legends of Texas Indians," *Mid-America* 3 (July, 1931): 48–56.

97. Castañeda to Alfred B. Thomas, Mar. 3, 1931, CECP.

98. Benedict to Special Committee, Apr. 3, 1931, CECP.

99. Program, Texas Folk-Lore Society, San Antonio, Tex., Apr. 17–18, 1931, CECP.

100. Foik to Castañeda, May 26, 1931, KCCF/CAT.

101. Castañeda to Thomas, July 31, 1931, CECP.

102. Castañeda to Chabot, May 28, 1931, YSP/DRTL.

103. Chabot to Mrs. Lane Taylor, June 5, 1931, YSP/DRTL. Chabot and his supporters organized the Yanaguana Society in 1930 but delayed filing papers of incorporation until 1933.

104. Castañeda to J. Elliot Ross, June 9, 1931, CECP.

105. Castañeda to Frank C. Patten, Sept. 26, 1931; Castañeda to Frances Louise Reast, Oct. 15, 1931, CECP.

106. Castañeda to William Ekin Birch, Nov. 30, 1931, CECP.

107. Castañeda to R. M. Tryon, Nov. 10 and Dec. 4, 1931; Tryon to Castañeda, Dec. 11, 1931, and Jan. 9, 1932; Castañeda to Thomas, July 31, 1931; Castañeda to Samuel F. Bemis, Dec. 19, 1931, CECP. Through the efforts of a faculty member in history and education at the University of Chicago who arranged for the initial invitation to the Minneapolis meeting, Castañeda's essay appeared in print a year later (Tryon to Castañeda, Jan. 9, 1932; Castañeda to Tryon, Jan. 26, 1932, CECP; Carlos E. Castañeda, "The Teaching of History in the Secondary Schools of Mexico," *Historical Outlook* 24 [May, 1933]: 246–52).

108. Castañeda to James A. Robertson, Nov. 21, 1931, and Mar. 9, 1932; Thomas to Castañeda, Dec. 4, 1931; Castañeda to Thomas, Dec. 7, 1931, CECP.

109. Castañeda to C. A. True, Nov. 12, 1932, CECP.

110. Castañeda to Foik, Jan. 8, 1932, KCCF/CAT.

111. Castañeda to Foik, Jan. 8 and Mar. 29, 1932; Driscoll to Foik, Jan. 29, Mar. 5, Apr. 29, May 16, Aug. 4, and Sept. 26, 1932; Foik to Castañeda, Mar. 9, 1932, KCCF/ CAT; Benedict to Barker, Apr. 11, 1932; Benedict to Castañeda, Jan. 19, 1932; Castañeda to Benedict, Jan. 25, 1932, CECP.

112. Thomas to Castañeda, Jan. 12, 1932; Castañeda to Thomas, Jan. 14, 1932, CECP.

113. Thomas to Castañeda, Jan. 18, 1932, CECP.

114. Thomas to Castañeda, Feb. 9, 1932, CECP.

115. Castañeda to Thomas, Feb. 15, 1932, CECP.

116. T. P. Walsh to Castañeda, Mar. 4, 1932, CECP.

117. Castañeda to Walsh, Mar. 22, 1932, CECP.

118. Foik to Joseph G. O'Donohoe, May 3, 1932, KCCF/CAT.

119. *Alamo Messenger*, Dec. 15, 1932, OLLU/SAT.

120. Driscoll to Foik, Apr. 29, 1932, KCCF/CAT.

121. Carlos Eduardo Castañeda, "Morfi's History of Texas: A Critical, Chronological Account of the Early Exploration, Attempts at Colonization, and the Final Occupation of Texas by the Spaniards, by Fr. Juan Agustín Morfi, O.F.M., Missionary, Teacher and Historian of the Order, 1673–1779" (Ph.D., diss., UTA, 1932).

122. Upton, "Knight of Goodwill," p. 14, CBF; Castañeda Transcript.

123. Castañeda to Benedict, Jan. 25, 1932; Benedict to Winkler, Mar. 15, 1932, CECP.

124. Castañeda to Donald Mackenzie Brown, June 24, 1932, CECP. Latin American intellectuals challenged the theory of the superiority of the Caucasian race with a "nativist movement called indigenísmo," or Indianism. By exalting the role of the Indian in Latin American society, the intellectuals argued that the European culture was a continuation of Indianism, a conclusion that gave prominence to the mestizo element that combined the two legacies as manifested in the gains of the Mexican Revolution (Ernest E. Rossi and Jack C. Plano, *Latin America: A Political Dictionary*, p. 16).

Ramón Beteta (1901–1965), born in Mexico City, attended the National Preparatory School. In 1920 he interrupted his education to join the administration of President Venustiano Carranza. That year he received a scholarship to the University of Texas. In 1923 he received a bachelor's degree in economics; he returned to Mexico City to enroll in the National Autonomous University from where, in 1926, he received a law degree. For several years he offered courses in law and economics at Universidad Nacional Autónoma de México (UNAM). For nearly twenty years Beteta discharged numerous government assignments at home and abroad. In his last appointment (1953) he served as Mexican ambassador to Italy. In his career in politics and economics he delivered numerous lectures at international conferences and contributed extensively to scholarly publications (*Diccionario Porrúa de Historia, Biografía y Geografía de México*, vol. 1, pp. 259–60).

Herbert Ingram Priestley was born in Michigan in 1875. He attended the University of Southern California; after graduation he accepted a teaching position in Luzón in the Philippine Islands. Three years later he enrolled in USC's graduate program in history. In 1907, after receiving his master's degree, he continued teaching in the California public schools. In 1912 Priestley entered the doctoral program at the University of California at Berkeley as a student of Herbert E. Bolton. At the same time he worked as assistant curator of the Bancroft Library. As Bolton's sixth student to complete the program, Priestley received the doctorate in 1916, after which he promptly accepted an invitation to become a member of the history faculty. Priestley solidified his position by publishing his dissertation, *José de Gálvez: Visitor General of New Spain (1765–1771)*, within a year after joining the faculty. He also worked in various capacities associated with the Bancroft Library. Upon Bolton's initial retirement in 1940, Priestley succeeded his mentor as director of the Bancroft. Meanwhile, he shifted the focus of his scholarship to the Mexican Republic but later broadened the scope to include a comparative study of French colonization overseas. In 1941 Priestley suffered a debilitating stroke that virtually ended his career in history. He died on Feb. 9, 1944 ("Historical News and Comments," *Missis-sippi Valley Historical Review* 31 [June, 1944]: 177–78).

125. Reast to Castañeda, Aug. 2, 1932; Castañeda to Reast, Aug. 3, 1932, CECP.

126. Castañeda to Williams, July 29, 1932, CECP.

127. Castañeda to Benedict, Jan. 10, 1933, CECP.

128. Castañeda to Margaret Roy, Sept. 21, 1932, CECP.

129. Williams to Castañeda, Oct. 17, 1932, CECP.

130. Castañeda to Crone, Oct. 22, 1932, CECP.

131. Driscoll to Castañeda, Oct. 29, 1932, KCCF/CAT.

132. Félix D. Almaráz, Jr., "The Return of the Franciscans to Texas, 1891–1931," *Catholic Southwest* 7 (1996): 91–114.

133. *Southern Messenger,* Oct. 27, 1932, OLLU/SAT.

134. House Chronicle of San José Mission (1931–47), Oct. 12, 1932, p. 43, AFPSH/ SLM.

135. Castañeda to Bardin, Oct. 15, 1932, CECP.

136. Bardin to Castañeda, Oct. 20, 1932, CECP.

137. Castañeda to Sister M. Borromeo, Nov. 5, 1932, CECP; Michael Walsh, ed., *But-ler's Lives of the Saints,* p. 361; "Affairs of the Association," *Southwestern Historical Quarterly* 31 (Apr., 1928): 384; "Affairs of the Association," *Southwestern Historical Quarterly* 32 (July, 1928): 100.

138. Castañeda to Robertson, Dec. 24, 1932, CECP; C. E. Castañeda, review of *Cul-ture Conflicts in Texas, 1821–1836,* by Samuel Harman Lowrie, *HAHR* (Nov., 1933): 482–84.

Chapter 5

1. Donald Wayne Whisenhunt, "Texas in the Depression, 1929–1933: A Study of Public Reaction" (Ph.D. diss., Texas Tech University, 1966), p. 140.

2. Brewer, "History of the Department of History," p. 117.

3. Moloney, "History of the University Library," p. 278; "Fannie Elizabeth Ratch-ford," in *New Handbook of Texas,* vol. 5, p. 449.

4. H. Y. Benedict to Eugene C. Barker et al., Jan. 4, 1933, CECP.

5. Barker to Benedict, Jan. 6, 1933, ECBP.

6. Castañeda to Benedict, Jan. 10, 1933, CECP.

7. J. I. Driscoll to Paul J. Foik, Jan. 17, 1933, KCCF/CAT.

8. Castañeda to Foik, Jan. 23, 1933, KCCF/CAT.

9. Sister M. Claude Lane, "Catholic Archives of Texas: History and Preliminary In-ventory" (M.S. thesis, UTA, 1961), p. 25.

10. Castañeda to Foik, Feb. 1, 1933, KCCF/CAT.

11. Joseph G. O'Donohoe to Foik, Jan. 31, 1933, KCCF/CAT.

12. Don E. Carleton and Katherine J. Adams, "'A Work Peculiarly Our Own'": Ori-gins of the Barker Texas History Center, 1883–1950," *Southwestern Historical Quar-terly* 86 (Oct., 1982): 217–18.

13. Foik to O'Donohoe, Feb. 24, 1933, KCCF/CAT.

14. Castañeda to Benedict, Jan. 24, 1933; Benedict to Castañeda, Jan. 25, 1933, CECP.

15. Castañeda to Benedict, Feb. 25, 1933, CECP.

16. Benedict to Castañeda, Mar. 29, 1933; Castañeda to Benedict, Mar. 3, 1933; [Ernest W. Winkler], "The Objects and Operations of the Mexican Photoprint Company and the University Library's dealings with same, . . ." [undated, attached to Castañeda to Benedict, Mar. 31, 1933], CECP.

17. Benedict to Castañeda, Apr. 4, 1933, CECP.

18. Barker to Thomas M. Knapp, May 24, 1934, ECBP.

19. *General Laws of Texas,* 43rd Legislature, Regular Session, 1933, p. 681, LRL/AT; Barker to Knapp, May 24, 1934.

20. Barker to Knapp, May 24, 1934.

21. *General Laws of Texas,* 43rd Legislature, 1933.

22. Foik to Adina de Zavala, Sept. 28, 1933, Adina de Zavala Papers, Texas Collection, Incarnate Word College, San Antonio, Tex.

23. Castañeda to Sister M. Agatha Sheehan, May 16, 1941, Mary Agatha Sheehan Letter Folder, Academy of the Incarnate Word, Houston, Tex.

24. Castañeda to Foik, Mar. 4, 1933, KCCF/CAT.

25. Castañeda to C. R. Wharton, May 15, 1933, CECP.

26. [Wharton] to Bob Bassett, May 18, 1933, CECP.

27. [Wharton] to Jim Martin, May 18, 1933, CECP.

28. [Wharton] to Floyd Enlow, May 18, 1933, CECP.

29. Castañeda to Wharton, July 18, 1933, CECP.

30. Castañeda to Wharton and Bassett, Aug. 3, 1933, CECP.

31. Benedict to Castañeda, May 31, 1933; Castañeda to Benedict, June 2, 1933, CECP.

32. Castañeda to J. A. C. Chandler, June 6, 1933; Chandler to Castañeda, June 13, 1933, CECP.

33. Castañeda to Foik, July 18, 1933, KCCF/CAT; Castañeda to Barker, Aug. 3, 1933, CECP.

34. Barker to Castañeda, [undated, circa Aug. 1, 1933], CECP.

35. Castañeda to Barker, Aug. 3, 1933, CECP; "Notes and Comment," *HAHR* 13 (May, 1933): 236.

36. Castañeda to Foik, July 18, 1933, KCCF/CAT.

37. Foik to O'Donohoe, Feb. 24, 1933, KCCF/CAT.

38. House Chronicle of San José Mission (1931–47), Jan. 1 and Feb. 21, 1933, pp. 54, 62–63, AFPSH/SLM.

39. Foik to O'Donohoe, Feb. 24, 1933.

40. Castañeda to Foik, July 18, 1933, KCCF/CAT.

41. Castañeda to W. E. James, assistant superintendent of schools, State Department of Education (Austin), Aug. 10, 1933, CECP.

42. Castañeda to Foik, Aug. 18 and Sept. 4, 1933, KCCF/CAT.

43. Walter Prescott Webb and H. Bailey Carroll, eds., *The Handbook of Texas,* 2 vols. (Austin: Texas State Historical Association, 1952), 1: 485–86.

44. A. E. Gutiérrez, comp., *A History of San Felipe: San Felipe High School in the 1930s,* pp. 16–30; J. B. Peña, "A History of the San Felipe Independent School District and Its Influence on the Community, 1929–1951" (M.A. Thesis, Sul Ross State College, 1951), 37; *M. R. Nelson v. San Felipe Independent School District, et al.,* Cause 3924, ODC/VVC.

45. The board of education of San Felipe included Santos G. Garza (president); Andrés

Cortinas, Sr.; Pablo G. Flores; Castulo H. Gutiérrez; Rodolfo H. Gutiérrez (secretary); Adolfo Maldonado; and Víctor Vásquez, Jr. (Gutiérrez, *History of San Felipe*, p. 29).

46. Castañeda to Foik, Sept. 4, 1933, KCCF/CAT.

47. Castañeda to Winkler, Aug. 10, 1933, CECP.

48. *M. R. Nelson v. San Felipe Independent School District, et al.,* Cause 3924, ODC/VVC.

49. Answer to Plaintiff and Cross Defendants to Petition of Mandamus and Injunction, *M. R. Nelson v. San Felipe Independent School District et al.,* Cause 4014, ODC/VVC; *Del Rio Evening News,* Feb. 21, 1934.

50. Final Judgment, *M. R. Nelson v. San Felipe Independent School District et al.,* Cause 4014, ODC/VVC; Cause 9704, Court of Civil Appeals, Fourth Judicial District of Texas, ODC/VVC.

51. Castañeda to Foik, Nov. 21, 1933, KCCF/CAT.

52. Foik to Active Members of the Texas Knights of Columbus Historical Commission, Sept. 14, 1933, KCCF/CAT.

53. O'Donohoe to Foik, Sept. 19, 1933, KCCF/CAT.

54. Driscoll to Foik, Sept. 27, 1933, KCCF/CAT.

55. Foik to Zavala, Sept. 28, 1933, Adina de Zavala Papers, Texas Collection, Incarnate Word College, San Antonio, Tex.

56. Foik to Castañeda, Oct. 4, 1933, KCCF/CAT.

57. Castañeda to Foik, Oct. 9, 1933, KCCF/CAT.

58. House Chronicle of San José Mission, Apr. 1, 1933, p. 67, and June 8, 1933, p. 74.

59. Francis Borgia Steck to Castañeda, Oct. 22, 1933, KCCF/CAT.

60. Ibid.

61. Ibid.

62. "Notes," *HAHR* 13 (Nov., 1933): 545. Actually, the Preliminary Studies of the Texas Catholic Historical Society commenced in Jan. of 1929 with the monograph *The Martyrs of the Southwest* by Foik and continued the following year with four contributions (*Early Catholic Explorers of the Southwest* by Castañeda; *The Espinosa-Olivares-Aguirre Expedition of 1709 and Ramón Expedition: Espinosa's Diary of 1716* by Gabriel Tous; and *Fray Juan de Padilla* by Foik). In 1931 the society reduced the number of essays to three (*The Solis Diary of 1767* by Peter P. Forrestal; *Icazbalceta: Education in Mexico City during the Sixteenth Century* by Walter J. O'Donnell; and *Earliest Catholic Activities in Texas* by Castañeda). For 1932 the number of contributions remained unchanged (*The Expedition of Don Domingo Terán de los Ríos in Texas* by Mattie Austin Hatcher; *The Venerable Padre Fray Antonio Margil de Jesús* by Forrestal; and *Forerunners of Captain De León's Expedition to Texas, 1670–1675* by Francis Borgia Steck). Finally, up to the time that Castañeda began his superintendency in Del Rio, the society published only two monographs (*The Six Flags of Texas* by Castañeda and *Captain Don Domingo Ramón's Diary of his Expedition into Texas* by Foik [William H. Oberste, *Knights of Columbus in Texas, 1902–1952,* pp. 184–85; Michael E. Zilligen, archivist, Catholic Archives of Texas, to Félix D. Almaráz, Jr., Feb. 22 and 25, 1989]).

63. O'Donohoe to Foik, Nov. 2, 1933, KCCF/CAT.

64. Foik to Castañeda, Nov. 28, 1933, KCCF/CAT.

65. Castañeda to Foik, Dec. 8, 1933, KCCF/CAT.

66. Castañeda to Foik, Dec. 15, 1933, KCCF/CAT.

67. Lane, "Catholic Archives of Texas," p. 51.

68. O'Donohoe to Foik, Jan. 15, 1934, KCCF/CAT.

69. Driscoll to Foik, Feb. 28, 1934, KCCF/CAT.

70. Steck to Foik, June 1, 1934, KCCF/CAT.

71. Barnabas Diekemper, O.F.M., to Félix D. Almaráz, Jr., Sept. 16, 1989; Antonine S. Tibesar, O.F.M., interview with Félix D. Almaráz, Jr., San Antonio, Tex., Sept. 23, 1989.

Francis Borgia Steck began his distinguished career as writer and historian at Saint Joseph's College in Teutopolis, Illinois, where he worked from 1913 to 1919, after which he collaborated for several years with the renowned scholar Zephyrin Englehardt, O.F.M., on the history of Franciscan missions in California. Subsequent to earning a doctorate in history at Catholic University of America in 1927, Steck joined the faculty of Quincy College at Quincy, Illinois. Later in the midst of his unpleasant experience with the Texas missions project, he accepted a prestigious appointment as professor of Hispanic-American history at his alma mater, Catholic University of America. Prior to his retirement in 1946 Steck achieved an impressive publication record with such works as *The Joliet-Marquette Expedition, 1673, The Franciscans and the Protestant Revolution in England, A Tentative Guide to Historical Materials on the Spanish Borderlands,* and *El Primer Colegio de América: Santa Cruz de Tlaltelolco.* In the postretirement years he continued scholarly research as an associate of the Academy of American Franciscan History in Potomac, Maryland (Francis Borgia Steck, ed. and trans., *Motolonía's History of the Indians of New Spain,* dust jacket).

72. *Del Rio Evening News,* Mar. 22 and Apr. 16, 1934.

73. *Del Rio Evening News,* Feb. 13 and 21, 1934.

74. *Del Rio Evening News,* Mar. 26, 1934.

75. *Del Rio Evening News,* Mar. 29, 1934.

76. *Del Rio Evening News,* Apr. 5, 1934.

77. *Del Rio Evening News,* May 3, 1934.

78. *Del Rio Evening News,* May 18, 1934.

79. *Del Rio Evening News,* May 26, 1934.

80. Castañeda to Foik, May 22, 1934, KCCF/CAT; *Del Rio Evening News,* May 29, 1934.

81. Castañeda to Foik, Apr. 26, 1934, KCCF/CAT.

82. Ibid.

83. *Del Rio Evening News,* May 16, 1934; Foik to Castañeda, May 5, 1934, KCCF/CAT.

84. Castañeda to Foik, Apr. 26, 1934, KCCF/CAT.

85. Ibid.

86. Ibid.

87. Robert Carlton Clark wrote a short thesis in 1901 on early Spanish exploration and missionization in east Texas. Entitled "The Beginnings of Texas: Fort Saint Louis and Mission San Francisco de los Texas," Clark's contribution subsequently appeared in the *Southwestern Historical Quarterly* 5 (Jan., 1902): 171–205 (H. Bailey Carroll and Milton R. Gutsch, comps., *Texas History Theses: A Check List of the Theses and Dissertations Relating to Texas History Accepted at the University of Texas, 1893–1951,* p. 29). Castañeda to Foik, July 5, 1934, KCCF/CAT.

88. Castañeda to Foik, July 5, 1934, KCCF/CAT.

89. Castañeda to Foik, July 28, 1934, KCCF/CAT.

90. Foik to Castañeda, Feb. 2, 1935, KCCF/CAT.

91. Castañeda to Foik, Aug. 30, 1934, KCCF/CAT.

92. Castañeda to Herbert E. Bolton, Aug. 10, 1934, HEBP/BL/UCB.

93. Carlos E. Castañeda, "Silent Years in Texas History," *Southwestern Historical Quarterly* 38 (Oct., 1934): 122–34. Foik immediately selected the essay for reprinting under the rubric of Preliminary Studies of the Texas Catholic Historical Society for 1935 ("Notes: Bibliographical Section," *HAHR* 15 [Aug., 1935]: 419).

94. Castañeda to Foik, May 9, 1934, KCCF/CAT.

95. Castañeda to Foik, Aug. 18, 1934, KCCF/CAT.

96. Peña, "History of the San Felipe Independent School District," p. 37.

97. *Del Rio Evening News,* Oct. 6, 1934.

98. *Del Rio Evening News,* Sept. 18, 1934.

99. Peña, "History of the San Felipe Independent School District," p. 37.

100. Upton, "Knight of Goodwill," p. 13, CBF.

101. *La Prensa* [San Antonio, Tex.], Oct. 23 and 24, 1934, San Antonio College Library; Castañeda to Escobar, Mar. 27, 1935, EEP, BLAC; "Eleuterio Escobar, Jr.," in *New Handbook of Texas,* vol. 6, p. 890; Mario T. García, *Mexican Americans: Leadership, Ideology & Identify, 1930–1960* (New Haven, Conn.: Yale University Press, 1989), pp. 70–72, 82–83.

102. Castañeda to Foik, Aug. 30, 1934, KCCF/CAT.

103. Castañeda to Foik, Sept. 11, 1934, KCCF/CAT.

104. Foik to Castañeda, Sept. 18, 1934, KCCF/CAT.

105. Castañeda to Foik, Oct. 1, 1934, KCCF/CAT.

106. Carlos E. Castañeda, Report of the Historiographer of the Mission Era of Texas History, Minutes of the 17th Regular Meeting of the Texas Knights of Columbus Historical Commission, St. Edward's University, Austin, Tex., Nov. 27, 1934, KCCF/CAT; Castañeda to Chabot, Dec. 10, 1934, YSP/DRTL.

107. Carlos E. Castañeda, Report of the Historiographer of the Mission Era of Texas History, Minutes of the 17th Regular Meeting of the Texas Knights of Columbus Historical Commission, St. Edward's University, Austin, Tex., Nov. 27, 1934, KCCF/CAT.

108. Private Report to the Members of the Knights of Columbus Historical Commission of Texas, Nov. 30, 1934, KCCF/CAT; Castañeda to Chabot, Dec. 10, 1934, YSP/DRTL.

109. Castañeda to Foik, Dec. 10, 1934, KCCF/CAT.

110. Foik to Castañeda, Dec. 13, 1934, KCCF/CAT.

111. Castañeda to Foik, Dec. 16, 1934, KCCF/CAT.

112. Driscoll to Foik, Dec. 22, 1934, KCCF/CAT.

113. Castañeda to Foik, Jan. 12, 1935, KCCF/CAT.

114. Driscoll to Foik, Jan. 14, 1935; Contract between Carlos E. Castañeda & Paul J. Foik; Foik to Castañeda, Jan. 15, 1935, KCCF/CAT.

115. Castañeda to Foik, Jan. 20, 1935, KCCF/CAT.

116. Ibid.

117. Foik to Castañeda, Jan. 22, 1935; Castañeda to Foik, Jan. 28, 1935, KCCF/CAT.

118. Foik to Castañeda, Jan. 29, 1935, KCCF/CAT.

119. Castañeda to Foik, Feb. 14, 1935, KCCF/CAT.

120. Castañeda to Foik, Mar. 1, 1935, KCCF/CAT.

121. Castañeda to Foik, Mar. 4, 1935, KCCF/CAT.

122. Foik to Castañeda, Mar. 21, 1935, KCCF/CAT.

123. Foik to Castañeda, Mar. 23, 1935, KCCF/CAT.

124. Castañeda to Foik, Mar. 27, 1935, KCCF/CAT.

125. *Sul Ross Skyline,* Mar. 13, 1935, Archives of the Big Bend, Bryan Wildenthal Library, Sul Ross State University, Alpine, Tex.

126. Castañeda to Foik, Mar. 27, 1935, KCCF/CAT.

127. Ibid.

128. Ibid.

129. Ibid.

130. Castañeda to Escobar, Mar. 27, 1935, EEP, BLAC.

131. Foik to Castañeda, Mar. 27, 1935, KCCF/CAT.

132. Castañeda to Foik, Mar. 29, 1935, KCCF/CAT.

133. *General and Special Laws of Texas,* 44th Legislature, Regular Session, 1935, p. 974, LRL/AT.

134. Castañeda to Foik, Apr. 23, 1935, KCCF/CAT.

135. Castañeda to Foik, Apr. 30, 1935, KCCF/CAT.

136. Foik to Castañeda, Apr. 30, 1935, KCCF/CAT.

137. Castañeda to Foik, Apr. 30, 1935, KCCF/CAT.

138. Ibid.

139. The Report of the Historiographer, Minutes of the 18th Regular Meeting of the Texas Knights of Columbus Historical Commission, Taylor, Tex., May 20, 1935, KCCF/CAT.

140. Minutes of the Texas Knights of Columbus Historical Commission, Taylor, Tex., May 20, 1935, KCCF/CAT.

141. Foik to Castañeda, Sept. 18, 1934, KCCF/CAT.

142. Castañeda to Foik, Oct. 1, 1934, KCCF/CAT.

143. Minutes of the 17th Regular Meeting of the Texas Knights of Columbus Historical Commission, Austin, Tex., Nov. 27, 1934, KCCF/CAT.

144. Minutes of the 18th Regular Meeting of the Texas Knights of Columbus Historical Commission, Taylor, Tex., May 20, 1935.

145. *Del Rio Evening News,* May 22 and 25, 1935.

146. *Del Rio Evening News,* Apr. 8 and May 25, 1935; Gilberto Cerda, "Las Escuelas de San Felipe," *El Mundo,* undated, ca. 1936, copy in possession of Mr. and Mrs. Eulalio Calderón, Jr., Del Rio, Tex.

Chapter 6

1. Castañeda to Paul J. Foik, June 10, 1935, KCCF/CAT.

2. Castañeda to Foik, July 3, 1935, KCCF/CAT.

3. Ibid.

4. [Truman Pouncy], undated manuscript, Library Records 1936–1937 (hereinafter cited as LR [date]), CDL.

5. Foik to Joseph G. O'Donohoe, Oct. 28, 1935, KCCF/CAT.

6. Memorandum, Castañeda to Mother Angelique Ayres, Oct. 28, 1935; Mother Angelique to Castañeda, Nov. 1, 1935; Castañeda to Mother Angelique, Nov. 5, 1935, and Jan. 7, 1936, LF/OAD/OLLU/SAT.

7. Castañeda to Foik, Nov. 7, 1935, KCCF/CAT.

8. Castañeda to James M. Gillis, Nov. 7, 1935; Gillis to Castañeda, Nov. 12, 1935, KCCF/CAT.

Traditionally most scholars attributed authorship of the drama, written in "simple dialogue," to Cristóbal Gutiérrez de Luna. Castañeda declared that the actual playwright was Toribio de Motolinía, sixteenth-century Franciscan missionary, whereas Gutiérrez de Luna had merely copied the manuscript ("Bibliographical Section," *HAHR* 18 [Aug., 1937]: 366).

9. Report of the Historiographer, Minutes of the 19th Regular Meeting of the Texas Knights of Columbus Historical Commission, San Antonio, Tex., Nov. 26, 1935, KCCF/CAT.

10. Castañeda to Foik, Dec. 11, 1935, KCCF/CAT.

11. Ibid.

12. Castañeda to Mother Angelique, Jan. 7, 1936, LF/OAD/OLLU/SAT; Castañeda to [name obliterated], Feb. 12, 1936, Fred White, Sr. Collection, Santa Fe, N.M. (copy in possession of author).

13. J. [Villásana] Haggard, "Lost History of Texas Found," *Dallas Morning News,* Apr. 12, 1936, CBF.

14. *Pflugerville Press,* Apr. 9, 1936, CBF.

15. *Huntsville Item,* Aug. 22, 1940, CBF.

16. *Southern Messenger,* Apr. 16, 1936, OLLU/SAT.

17. Foik to Castañeda, May 8, 1936, KCCF/CAT.

18. Report of the Historiographer, Minutes of the 20th Regular Meeting of the Texas Knights of Columbus Historical Commission, Galveston, Texas, May 18, 1936, KCCF/CAT.

19. Ibid.

20. Application for a New Naturalization Paper in Lieu of One Lost, Mutilated, or Destroyed, Number 17-B-202, Dec. 12, 1935; Duplicate Declaration of Intention, Number 845, Jan. 8, 1936; Certificate of Citizenship Number 3852566, Petition Number 756, June 8, 1936; Immigration and Naturalization Service, U.S. Department of Justice, Washington, D.C.

Castañeda's actual quest for American citizenship meandered for nearly seventeen years. Shortly after his release from a brief hitch with the armed forces during World War I, he filed a Declaration of Intention stating that he had crossed from Matamoros to Brownsville "on the Santa Cruz Ferry Boat" on or about June 30, 1906. Then, owing to the vicissitudes in his career, extending from Texas to Virginia and back, he neglected to act within the prescribed deadline, and the declaration's validity expired. Next, following his difficulties with legislative cutbacks in 1933, prior to leaving for Del Rio, Castañeda filed both a new Declaration of Intention and a Petition for Naturalization. Two years later, in the course of packing personal belongings for the move back to Austin, either he or Elisa inadvertently misplaced the documents. Finally, the frustration of not finding the missing papers motivated Don Carlos to file another application in earnest in December 1935 (Declaration of Intention, Number 647205, May 28, 1919; Declaration of Intention, Number 79182, July 27, 1933; Petition for Naturalization, Number 95279, July 17, 1933; Application for a New Naturalization Paper, Number 17-B-202, Dec. 12, 1935; Immigration and Naturalization Service, United States Department of Justice, Washington, D.C.).

21. *Southern Messenger,* June 25, 1936, OLLU/SAT.

22. Castañeda to Mother Angelique, June 29 and Aug. 13, 1936, LF/OAD/OLLU/SAT.

23. Castañeda to Foik, July 5, 1936, KCCF/CAT; Castañeda to Mother Angelique, June 29, 1936, LF/OAD/OLLU/SAT.

24. Consuelo Castañeda de Artaza, interview with O. Wayne Poorman, Sept. 19, 1971, tape recording, Houston, Tex.

25. Helen Ardel Moore to Félix D. Almaráz, Jr., May 9, 1991, Victoria, Tex., Almaráz Papers.

26. Castañeda to Foik, Oct. 7, 1936, KCCF/CAT.

27. Recollections of Jack Autrey Dabbs, Nov. 15, 1973, College Station, Tex. Handwritten (copy in possession of the author; hereinafter cited as Dabbs Recollections, date).

28. Carlos E. Castañeda, "Human Side of a Great Collection," pp. 119-10.

29. Frederick C. Chabot to Castañeda, Oct. 30, 1936; Castañeda to Chabot, Nov. 2, 1936, YSP/DRTL.

30. Joseph I. Driscoll to Castañeda, Nov. 6, 1936, KCCF/CAT.

31. Dabbs Recollections, Nov. 15, 1973.

32. Foik to Cleofas Calleros, Dec. 3, 1936; Calleros to Foik, Dec. 20, 1936, KCCF/CAT.

33. Calleros to Foik, Dec. 20, 1936, KCCF/CAT.

34. Review of *Morfi's History of Texas* by J. Villasana Haggard, *Southwest Review* 21 (Winter, 1936): 232.

35. Castañeda to Chabot, Dec. 18, 1936, YSP/DRTL.

36. Herbert E. Bolton to Chabot, Feb. 25, 1937, YSP/DRTL.

37. Mother Angelique to Castañeda, [circa Jan., 1937], LF/OAD/OLLU/SAT.

38. Report of the Historiographer, Minutes of the 21st Regular Meeting of the Texas Knights of Columbus Historical Commission, Mineral Wells, Tex., May 10, 1937, KCCF/CAT.

39. As late as the spring semester of 1938, Castañeda's library salary remained frozen at the original entry of $2,400 (Minutes of the History Department Council, UTA, Apr. 8, 1938, UTPOR:HD).

40. Carlos E. Castañeda, "Human Side of a Great Collection," *Books Abroad* 14 (1940): 120.

41. Ibid., pp. 118-19.

42. Oberste, *Knights of Columbus in Texas,* p. 194.

43. *Daily Texan,* May 15, 1938, and Nov. 18, 1945, CBF.

44. Report of the Historiographer, Minutes of the 21st Regular Meeting of the Texas Knights of Columbus Historical Commission, Mineral Wells, Tex., May 10, 1937, KCCF/CAT.

45. Castañeda to H. T. Pohl, Mar. 17, 1937, LR 1936-37, CDL.

46. Librarian [Coney] to Castañeda, May 13, 1937, LR 1936-37, CDL.

47. Dabbs Recollections, Nov. 15, 1973.

48. "Dr. Carlos Eduardo Castañeda," *Catholic Library World* 9 (Sept.-Dec., 1937): 132.

49. Dabbs Recollections, Nov. 15, 1973.

50. Review by Ike Moore of Castañeda's *A Report of the Spanish Archives in San Antonio, Texas,* in *Southwestern Historical Quarterly* 41 (Oct., 1937): 186.

51. Foik later reprinted the essay in the Preliminary Studies of the Texas Catholic Historical Society ("Bibliographical Section," *HAHR* 18 [Nov., 1938]: 605; "Historical Notes," *Southwestern Historical Quarterly* 41 [Jan., 1938]: 249-50).

52. Charles O. Hucker, Library News (typescript), Jan. 5, 1938, LR 1937-38, CDL.

53. Castañeda to Mother Angelique, Jan. 21, 1938, LF/OAD/OLLU/SAT; Castañeda

to Irving A. Leonard, Feb. 18, 1938, and Castañeda to Coney, Feb. 21, 1938, LR 1940–41, CDL.

54. Castañeda to Leonard, Feb. 18, 1938, LR 1940–41, CDL.

55. Castañeda to George P. Hammond, Jan. 21, 1938, LR 1940–41, CDL; Castañeda to Bolton, Jan. 21, 1938, HEBP/BL/UCB.

56. Castañeda to Leonard, Feb. 18, 1938, LR 1940–41, CDL.

57. Hammond to Castañeda, Feb. 17, 1938, LR 1940–41, CDL.

58. Castañeda to Bolton, Feb. 18, 1938, HEBP/BL/UCB.

59. Castañeda to Coney, Feb. 21, 1938, LR 1940–41, CDL.

60. Castañeda, Memorandum, Apr. 22, 1938, LR 1938–39, CDL.

61. Castañeda to Bolton, Apr. 20, 1938, HEBP/BL/UCB.

62. Castañeda to Bolton, Jan. 21, 1938; Bolton to Castañeda, Feb. 1, 1938, LR 1940–41, CDL; Castañeda to Bolton, Apr. 20, 1938, HEBP/BL/UCB.

63. Agreement Between the Library and the History Department on Division of Castañeda's time and salary, Apr. 13, 1938, Addendum to the Minutes of the History Budget Council, Meeting of the History Department Council, UTA, Apr. 8, 1938, p. 321, UTPOR:HD.

64. Report of the Historiographer, Minutes of the 22nd Regular Meeting of the Texas Knights of Columbus Historical Commission, Laredo, Tex., May 10, 1938, KCCF/CAT.

65. "Historical Notes," *Southwestern Historical Quarterly* 41 (Jan., 1938): 250; Foik to Castañeda, June 10, 1938, KCCF/CAT.

66. Artaza interview.

67. Carlos E. Castañeda, "Human Side of a Great Collection," p. 120.

68. Dabbs Recollections, Nov. 15, 1973.

69. Carlos E. Castañeda, "Human Side of a Great Collection," p. 120.

70. Dabbs Recollections, Nov. 15, 1973.

71. Ibid.

72. *Daily Texan,* Oct. 1, 1938, CBF.

73. Dabbs Recollections, Nov. 15, 1973; "Nineteenth Annual Meeting of the American Catholic Historical Association, . . . Dec. 28–30, 1938," *Catholic Historical Review* 25 (Apr., 1939): 64.

Chapter 7

1. Paul J. Foik to Peter Guilday, Jan. 12, 1939, KCCF/CAT.

2. *Southern Messenger,* Feb. 2, 1939, OLLU/SAT.

3. Donald Coney to Castañeda, Mar. 17, 1939, LR, CDL.

4. Upton, "Knight of Goodwill," pp. 13–14, CBF; Report of the Historiographer, Minutes of the 23rd Regular Meeting, Texas Knights of Columbus Historical Commission, Waco, Tex., May 8, 1939, KCCF/CAT; [Foik] to William Doheny, Mar. 20, 1939; Doheny to Foik, Mar. 24, 1939, KCCF/CAT; *Southern Messenger,* Apr. 6, 1939, OLLU/SAT.

5. Report of the Historiographer, Minutes of the 23rd Regular Meeting, Texas Knights of Columbus Historical Commission, Waco, Tex., May 8, 1939, KCCF/CAT.

6. [Winkler] to Coney, May 15, 1939, LR, CDL. Associated with his inquiry, which illustrated Coney's propensity for trivial details, was Winkler's candid acknowledgment that the "original cards of García's Catalog" had been removed from "their cabinet" and

were "now tied in bundles and piled in a corner" of the Latin American Library. For in-explicable reasons Coney waited five months to confront Castañeda about the cards on the floor: "It seems to me that it would be a good thing to have these at least stored in cardboard boxes for preservation" ([Winkler] to Coney, May 15, 1939; [Coney] to Cas-tañeda, Oct. 19, 1939, LR, CDL); Upton, "Knight of Goodwill," pp. 3–14, CBF; Report of Historiographer, Minutes of 23rd Regular Meeting, Texas Knights of Columbus His-torical Commission, Waco, Tex., May 8, 1939, KCCF/CAT.

7. Coney to Castañeda, May 24, 1939, LR, CDL.
8. Castañeda to Coney, May 27, 1939, LR, CDL.
9. Coney to Castañeda, May 29, 1939, LR, CDL.
10. *Southern Messenger,* June 1, 1939, OLLU/SAT.
11. The Catholic University of America: Announcements, Summer Session (June 30–Aug. 12, 1939), p. 49, DAM/ML, CUA.
12. John Tate Lanning to Francis Borgia Steck, May 11, 1939; Steck to Lanning, May 22, 1939, FBSP/QCBL.
13. Report of the Special Committee on an Advanced Course for Castañeda, Adden-dum to Minutes of the History Department, with Minutes, Feb. 15, 1939, UTPOR:HD.
14. Raymond Estep, interview with Félix D. Almaráz, Jr., tape recording, Washing-ton, D.C., Mar. 1, 1974.
15. Ibid.
16. Valdemar Rodríguez, interview with Félix D. Almaráz, Jr., tape recording, San Antonio, Tex., Jan. 24, 1974.
17. Joe B. Frantz, interview with O. Wayne Poorman, tape recording, Austin, Tex., May 23, 1972.
18. George P. Hammond, review of *The Mission Era: The Missions at Work, 1731–1761* by Carlos E. Castañeda, *Pacific Historical Review* 8 (Mar., 1939): 124.
19. W. Eugene Shiels, review of *Our Catholic Heritage in Texas, 1519–1936,* Vol. 3: *The Mission Era, 1731–1761* by Carlos E. Castañeda, *Catholic Historical Review* 25 (Oct., 1939): 344–45.
20. Jerome V. Jacobsen, review of *Our Catholic Heritage in Texas, 1519–1936,* Vol. 3: *The Mission Era, 1731–1761* by Carlos E. Castañeda, *Mid-America* 20 [New Se-ries, Vol. 9] (Oct., 1938): 293–94.
21. José Rubén Moreno, interview with Félix D. Almaráz, Jr., tape recording, San An-tonio, Tex., June 26, 1990.
22. Report of the Historiographer, Minutes of the 24th Regular Meeting of the Texas Knights of Columbus Historical Commission, Corpus Christi, Tex., May 13, 1940, KCCF/CAT.
23. Steck to Castañeda, Oct. 8, 1939, FBSP/QCBL.
24. *Austin Statesman,* Dec. 14 and 15, 1939, CBF; *Southern Messenger,* Dec. 21, 1939, OLLU/SAT; Memorandum No. 3, Final Pre-Conference Report, Conference on Bibliography and Research Materials in the Field of Latin American Studies, July 14, 1939, LR, CDL.
25. Estep interview, Mar. 1, 1974.
26. Dabbs Recollections, Feb. 24, 1974.
27. Estep interview, Mar. 1, 1974.
28. Dabbs Recollections, Feb. 24, 1974.
29. "The Twentieth Annual Meeting of the American Catholic Historical Asso-

ciation," *Catholic Historical Review* 4 (Apr., 1940): 78–79, 91; *Daily Texan,* Dec. 21, 1939, CBF.

30. Carlos E. Castañeda, "Our Latin American Neighbors," *Catholic Historical Review* 24 (Jan., 1940): 421–23.

In December, 1932, as president of the American Historical Association (AHA), Herbert E. Bolton delivered an address, "The Epic of Greater America," from which later emerged an inspiration for his broad approach to the study of the colonial experience in the Western Hemisphere. Just as the Spanish borderlands in North America needed to be studied in perspective to a larger framework of the Spanish Empire in America, Bolton advocated a broader examination of colonial life in the other Americas. Although he never postulated a so-called "Bolton thesis," the persuasive arguments in the AHA address fostered the evolution of a loosely knit "Greater America hypothesis" (John Francis Bannon, "The 'Other' Bolton," in *Bolton and the Spanish Borderlands,* ed. John Francis Bannon [Norman: University of Oklahoma Press, 1964], p. 301).

31. Moreno interview.

32. *Summer Texan,* July 16, 1939, LR, CDL.

33. *Daily Texan,* Jan. 4 and 18, 1940, CBF.

34. Carlos E. Castañeda, "The First Printing Press in Mexico," *Publisher's Weekly* 137 (Jan. 6, 1940): 50–52, LR, CDL.

35. [Winkler] to Coney, Jan. 14, 1940, LR, CDL.

36. *Daily Texan,* Jan. 4 and 18, 1940, CBF.

37. Dabbs Recollections, Feb. 24, 1974.

38. Carlos E. Castañeda, "Human Side of a Great Collection," *Books Abroad* (1940): 120; Dabbs Recollections, Feb. 24, 1974.

39. Dabbs Recollections, Feb. 24. 1974.

40. Paul J. Foik, Chairman's Memoranda of Activities, Minutes of the 24th Regular Meeting of the Texas Knights of Columbus Historical Commission, May 13, 1940, KCCF/CAT.

41. Report of the Historiographer, Minutes of 24th Regular Meeting of the Texas Knights of Columbus Historical Commission, Corpus Christi, May 13, 1940, KCCF/CAT.

42. Charles W. Hackett, "Notes and Comments: The Special Institute of Latin-American Studies at the University of Texas in the Summer of 1940," *HAHR* 29 (Nov., 1940): 650–54. The curriculum cross-listed courses in anthropology, business administration, economics, fine arts, geography, government, history, and foreign languages (Spanish and Portuguese). In addition to Hackett and Castañeda the history faculty included Daniel Samper Ortega of the Colombian Embassy, Arthur S. Aiton of the University of Michigan, and John L. Waller of Texas College of Mines at El Paso.

43. Minutes of the Budget Council of the History Department, UTA, June 13, 1940, p. 542, UTPOR:HD.

44. Definite Budget Recommendations of the History Department for the Summer Session of 1940, Addendum to the Minutes of the Budget Council of the History Department, Dec. 13, 1940; Revised Curriculum, Schedule and Staff, Summer Session, 1940, pp. 519–20, UTPOR:HD.

45. Rev. M. Fuente to Josephine E. Castañeda, June 14, 1940, CECP.

46. Frantz interview.

47. Coney to Castañeda, July 29, 1940, LR, CDL.

48. Estep interview, Mar. 1, 1974.

49. Dabbs Recollections, Feb. 26, 1974.

50. Castañeda to Chabot, Oct. 7, 1940, YSP/DRTL.

51. *Daily Texan,* Oct. 11, 1940, CBF.

52. *Daily Texan,* Dec. 19, 1940, CBF.

53. Minutes of the Budget Council, Nov. 19, 1940, p. 589, UTPOR:HD.

54. *Southern Messenger,* Jan. 9 and Mar. 6, 1941, OLLU/SAT; Rosemary Castañeda de Folks and Consuelo Castañeda de Artaza, telephone interview with Félix D. Almaráz, Jr., Houston and San Antonio, Tex., Sept. 3, 1990.

55. *San Antonio Express,* Jan. 19, 1941; *Austin Tribune,* [no date], 1941, CBF.

56. Oberste, *Knights of Columbus in Texas, 1902–1952,* p. 198.

Seemingly recovered, after being hospitalized for five months, Father Foik returned to Saint Edward's University in January, 1941, for convalescence. Late in February he suffered a serious relapse. The priest asked to be taken back to Seton Hospital. Despite prompt medical attention, Foik's condition "steadily" weakened. Early on Saturday morning, Mar. 1, 1941, he died peacefully (*Southern Messenger,* Mar. 6, 1941, OLLU/ SAT).

57. *Southern Messenger,* Mar. 6, 1941. The superior general of the Congregation of the Holy Cross, Very Reverend Albert Cousineau, celebrated the requiem mass, assisted by Very Reverend Walter F. Golatka, S.M., president of Saint Mary's University in San Antonio, and Reverend James J. O'Brien, C.S.C., pastor of Saint Mary's Church in Austin.

58. Unidentified newspaper, Mar. 5, 1941, CBF.

59. Minutes of Executive Committee of the Knights of Columbus Historical Commission, St. Edward's University, Austin, Tex., Mar. 3, 1941, KCCF/CAT.

60. [Minutes of] Meeting of the History Department, UTA, Mar. 6, 1941, p. 725; Apr. 1, 1941, p. 786, UTPOR:HD.

61. *Daily Texan,* Mar. 14, 1941, CBF.

62. Castañeda to James P. Gibbons, Minutes of Special Meeting of the Texas Knights of Columbus Texas Historical Commission, Mar. 27, 1941, KCCF/CAT. In addition to succeeding Foik as "head of the history department," Father Gibbons accepted responsibility as dean of the College of Arts and Letters at Saint Edward's University. As "temporary chairman" of the Texas Historical Commission, he agreed to monitor the completion of the "monumental" *Our Catholic Heritage in Texas,* five volumes of which Father Foik had edited before his death (*Southern Messenger,* Mar. 20, 1941, OLLU/ SAT).

63. Castañeda to Gibbons, Minutes of Special Meeting of the Texas Knights of Columbus Historical Commission, Mar. 27, 1941, KCCF/CAT.

64. Ibid.

65. Ibid.

66. Frantz interview, May 23, 1972.

67. Castañeda to Coney, May 1, 1941, LR, CDL.

68. Arthur Train, Jr., to Coney, May 12, 1941, LR, CDL.

69. Train to Castañeda, May 12, 1941, LR, CDL.

70. Father Pat Duffy to Archbishop Robert E. Lucey, July 28, 1941, Robert E. Lucey Papers, CASA.

71. *Southern Messenger,* May 29 and June 12, 1941, OLLU/SAT.

72. *Southern Messenger,* June 4, 1941.

73. Folks and Artaza interview.

74. Course Enrollment, Summer 1941, Addendum to Minutes of the History Department, with Minutes of July 17, 1941, p. 817, UTPOR:HD.

75. N.Y.A. Work and Workers, Addendum to Minutes of the History Department, with Minutes of July 17, 1941, p. 803.

76. Statistics on General University Enrollment, Sept. 30, 1941, Addendum to Minutes of the History Department, July 17, 1941, pp. 799–800.

77. *Daily Texan,* Sept. 26, 1941, CBF.

78. Coney and Gutsch to Colleagues, Oct. 1, 1941, UTPOR:HD.

79. *Daily Texan,* Oct. 11, 1941, CBF.

80. *Daily Texan,* Sept. 30, 1941, CBF.

81. *Southern Messenger,* Oct. 16, 1941, OLLU/SAT; *Daily Texan,* Sept. 30, 1941, CBF. Jack Roach and Leo Hogan served as pages to Castañeda, and John C. Kinana performed duties as squire.

82. Frantz interview, May 23, 1972.

83. *Southern Messenger,* Oct. 16, 1941; *Dallas News,* Oct. 14, 1941, CBF.

84. *Daily Texan,* Sept. 30, 1941, CBF; *Southern Messenger,* Sept. 25 and Oct. 16, 1941, OLLU/SAT; Michael H. Abraham D'Assemani, *The Cross on the Sword: A History of the Equestrian Order of the Holy Sepulchre of Jerusalem,* p. 94.

85. Joe W. Neal to Félix D. Almaráz, Jr., Austin, Tex., Feb. 3, 1975, Almaráz Papers.

86. *Southern Messenger,* Oct. 9, 1941, OLLU/SAT.

87. *Dallas News,* Oct. 10, 1941, CBF.

88. Francis C. Kelley, "Chivalry and Honor," sermon preached at the Investiture of Carlos Eduardo Castañeda as Knight of the Holy Sepulchre, Oct. 12, 1941, pp. 6–7, CBF.

89. *Southern Messenger,* Oct. 16, 1941.

90. Elisa R. Castañeda interview, May 29, 1972.

91. Ibid.

92. *Southern Messenger,* Oct. 16, 1941.

93. By 1948 the Equestrian Order of the Holy Sepulchre amended its regulations to allow knights to substitute a "full dress suit for the white uniform" but retained the cape as part of the formal attire (*Austin American,* May 12, 1948, CBF).

94. "Honors to Dr. Castañeda," *Catholic Library World* 13 (Dec., 1941): 85–86; "Notes and Comments," *Catholic Historical Review* 27 (Jan., 1942): 506.

95. "A New Knight," *Commonweal* 35 (Oct. 24, 1941): 4.

96. History Curriculum, Schedule, and Staff, Summer Session, 1942; Addendum to the Minutes of the Budget Council of the History Department, with Minutes of Nov. 18, 1941, pp. 852–54, UTPOR:HD.

97. Carlos E. Castañeda, Report of the Historiographer, Minutes of the 26th Regular Meeting of the Texas Knights of Columbus Historical Commission, Fort Worth, Tex., May 11, 1942, KCCF/CAT.

98. Charles W. Hackett to Frederick L. Paxon, Dec. 1, 1941; Eugene C. Barker to Paxon, Dec. 3, 1941, ECBP.

99. T. P. Martin, "Notes and Comments: The Fifth Convention of the Inter-American Bibliographical and Library Association," *HAHR* 22 (May, 1942): 416.

100. Castañeda to Francis Borgia Steck, Mar. 3, 1942, FBSP/QCBL.

101. Meeting of the Budget Council of the History Department, UTA, Mar. 20, 1942, pp. 903–904, UTPOR:HD.

102. Report of the Historiographer, Minutes of the 26th Regular Meeting of the Texas

Knights of Columbus Historical Commission, Fort Worth, Tex., May 11, 1942, KCCF/CAT.

103. Ibid.

104. Ibid.

105. Report of the Historiographer, Minutes of the 27th Regular Meeting of the Texas Knights of Columbus Historical Commission, Galveston, Tex., May 10, 1943, KCCF/CAT; José Bravo Ugarte, *Diócesis y Obispos de la Iglesia Mexicana (1519–1965)* (Mexico City: Editorial Jus, 1965), pp. 49–50, 67.

106. Raymond [Estep] to Castañeda, July 21, 1942, CECP.

107. Castañeda to Dick M. Burrell, Aug. 3, 1942, CECP.

108. Leo C. Haynes, secretary to the board of regents, to Holden Furber, Aug. 1, 1942, UTPOR:HD.

Castañeda witnessed other changes in September, 1942. The chaplain of the Newman Club, Rev. Dr. Vincent Holden, who had served as master of ceremonies at his investiture in Gregory Gymnasium, left the ministry at Saint Austin's for an assignment in New York City. Father A. J. McDonnell, C.S.P., assumed the ministry of the Newman Club at Saint Austin's and the University of Texas. Next Carlos learned that his longtime friend Bishop Mariano S. Garriga would be leaving Corpus Christi for new "residential quarters" in the rectory of Saint Peter the Apostle Church in Laredo. That change occurred because the former pastor had resigned in order to serve "in the United States Army as chaplain with the rank of major" (*Southern Messenger,* Sept. 3 and 17, 1942, OLLU/SAT).

109. Barker to Paxson, Dec. 3, 1941, ECBP.

110. Moreno interview.

111. Castañeda to Rainey, Nov. 18, 1942; Rainey to Castañeda, Nov. 25, 1942, UTPOR:HD.

112. *Southern Messenger,* Dec. 3, 1942, OLLU/SAT.

Chapter 8

1. Meeting of the Budget Council of the History Department, UTA, Jan. 11, 1943, UTPOR:HD.

2. Castañeda to Mother Angelique Ayres, Jan. 29, 1943, LF/OAD/OLLU/SAT.

3. Castañeda to Louis Lenz, Feb. 10, 1943, YSP/DRTL.

4. *New Handbook of Texas,* vol. 6, p. 1108.

5. Minutes of the History Department, UTA, Apr. 6, 1943, p. 1139, UTPOR:HD.

6. Summer Session, Sept.–Oct. Unit, Addendum to Minutes of the History Department, UTA, Apr. 16, 1943, p. 1150, UTPOR:HD.

7. *Dallas Morning News,* Apr. 22, 1943, CBF.

8. "Notes and Comments," *Catholic Historical Review* 29 (Apr., 1943): 125.

9. *Southern Messenger,* May 20, 1943, OLLU/SAT.

10. Minutes of the 27th Regular Meeting of the Texas Knights of Columbus Historical Commission, Galveston, Tex., May 10, 1943, KCCF/CAT.

11. *Southern Messenger,* June 24, 1943, OLLU/SAT.

12. Castañeda to President Homer P. Rainey, June 22, 1943; Vice President J. Alton Burdine to Castañeda, June 22, 1943, UTPOR:HD.

13. Francis J. Haas to Castañeda, June 28, 1943; RG 228, RFEPC, ROC:OC/CRF:CEC,

National Archives. All citations for the Records of the Fair Employment Practice Committee in this chapter, although from different subsections, originated in Record Group 228 in the National Archives of the United States. Accordingly, for economy of space, references to RG 228 and the National Archives will be deleted in subsequent citations.

14. Harvard Sitkoff, *A New Deal for Blacks: The Emergence of Civil Rights as a National Issue—The Depression Decade*, pp. 173–75, 319–32.

15. Lawrence W. Cramer to George I. Sánchez, July 25, 1941, RFEPC, Division of Field Operations, Office Files of Ernest G. Trimbel/Unarranged Correspondence.

16. Sánchez promoted his own "availability for employment" in Cramer's office. Included in his list of recommendations for regional directorships were Manuel C. Gonzales, a lawyer in San Antonio associated with the League of United Latin American Citizens (LULAC) and the Mexican Consulate; Dr. Herschel T. Manuel, professor of educational psychology; Dr. Rex D. Hopper, professor of sociology; Dr. Reginald Reindorp; Alfredo Vásquez of the censorship office in El Paso; Dr. Arthur L. Campa, ethno-folklorist at the University of New Mexico; and Antonio M. Fernández, another lawyer and candidate for Congress in New Mexico (Sánchez to Cramer, July 31, 1943, RFEPC, Division of Field Operations, Office Files of Ernest G. Trimbel/Unarranged Correspondence).

17. Castañeda to Rainey, July 14, 1943, UTPOR:HD.

18. Milton R. Gutsch to Rainey, July 16, 1943, UTPOR:HD.

19. Haas to Castañeda, July 17, 1943, RFEPC, ROC:OC/CRF:CEC.

20. Rainey to Castañeda, July 20, 1943, UTPOR:HD.

21. Theodore A. Jones to Castañeda, July 26, 1943, RFEPC, ROC:OC/CRF:CEC.

22. Castañeda to Haas, Aug. 27 and Sept. 2, 1943, RFEPC, RDBAM,USG—ADM(M). At the time of his appointment as FEPC Chairman the Reverend Francis J. Haas was dean of the School of Social Service at the Catholic University of America (CUA). At the height of the New Deal in the 1930s, Monsignor Haas enhanced his reputation as "a top-flight authority in labor mediation." He earned a doctorate in 1922 from CUA and from 1931 to 1935 served as director of the National Catholic School of Social Service. On Sept. 26, 1943, the Vatican appointed Monsignor Haas as bishop of Grand Rapids, Michigan (Typescript, "The Bishop Haas Papers," May 19, 1970, Archives, Manuscripts & Museum Collections, Catholic University of America, Washington, D.C.).

23. Jones to Castañeda, Aug. 2, 1943, RFEPC, ROC:OC/CRF:CEC.

24. Castañeda to Haas, Sept. 2, 1943, RFEPC, RDBAM,USG—ADM(M). Castañeda's position with the FEPC and his Civil Service title were separate issues. Although at the beginning of his government employment he functioned as associate director, his Civil Service classification was that of senior examiner.

25. Castañeda to Haas, Aug. 27, 1943, RFEPC, RDBAM,USG—ADM(M).

26. *Dallas News,* Aug. 28, 1943, CBF.

27. Castañeda to Haas, Aug. 27, 1943, RFEPC, RDBAM,USG—ADM(M).

28. Castañeda to Haas, Sept. 2, 1943, RFEPC, RDBAM,USG—ADM(M).

29. William Maslow to Castañeda, Sept. 3, 1943, RFEPC, ROC:OC/CRF:CEC.

30. Castañeda to Haas, Sept. 3, 1943, RFEPC, RDBAM,USG—ADM(M).

31. Haas to Castañeda, Sept. 6, 1943, RFEPC, ROC:OC/CRF:CEC.

32. Maslow to Castañeda, Sept. 7, 1943, RFEPC, ROC:OC/CRF:CEC.

33. *Dallas News,* Sept. 14, 1943, CBF.

34. Maslow to Castañeda, Sept. 13 and 17, 1943, RFEPC, ROC:OC/CRF:CEC.

35. Castañeda to Winnie Allen, Oct. 7, 1943, CBF; Lane, "Catholic Archives of Texas," pp. 58–59.

36. "Notes and Comments: Sociedad de Amigos de la Biblioteca de Lima," *HAHR* 23 (Aug., 1943): 547–48. Other recipients of the honor at the University of Texas included Charles W. Hackett, J. Lloyd Mecham, and Jefferson R. Spell.

37. Minutes of the Budget Council of the History Department, UTA, Feb. 11, 1944, UTPOR:HD.

38. Maslow to Castañeda, Oct. 6, 1943, RFEPC, ROC:OC/CRF:CEC.

39. Maslow to Castañeda, Oct. 12, 1943, RFEPC, ROC:OC/CRF:CEC.

40. Maslow to Castañeda, Oct. 13, 1943; Eugene Davidson to Castañeda, Oct. 15, 1943, RFEPC, ROC:OC/CRF:CEC.

41. Maslow to Castañeda, Oct. 7, 1943, RFEPC, ROC:OC/CRF:CEC.

42. Castañeda to Maslow, Oct. 18, 1943, RFEPC, RDBAM,CF:RXWR; Maslow to Castañeda, Oct. 7, 1943, RFEPC, ROC:OC/CRF:CEC.

43. Castañeda to Maslow, Oct. 18, 1943, RFEPC, RDBAM,CF:RXWR.

44. Maslow to Castañeda, Oct. 16, 1943, RFEPC, ROC:OC/CRF:CEC.

45. Ibid.

46. Maslow to Castañeda, Oct. 22, 1943, RFEPC, ROC:OC/CRF:CEC.

47. Maslow to Castañeda, Oct. 28, 1943, RFEPC, ROC:OC/CRF:CEC.

48. Maslow to Castañeda, Oct. 29, 1943; RFEPC, ROC:OC/CRF:CEC.

49. Maslow to Castañeda, Oct. 30, 1943, RFEPC, ROC:OC/CRF:CEC.

50. Maslow to Castañeda, Oct. 27, 1943, RFEPC, ROC:OC/CRF:CEC.

51. Investigation Conducted by Dr. Carlos E. Castañeda, Acting Regional Director, and Mr. Clay L. Cochran, Examiner of the Tenth Regional District of the President's Committee on Fair Employment Practice of Alleged Complaints against the American Smelting and Refining Company at Corpus Christi, Texas, November 18, 1943; Investigation Conducted . . . against the Zinc Workers' Federal Labor Union, Local 23245, A.F.L., November 18, 1943; Investigation Conducted . . . against Alkali Workers' Industrial Union, Local 153, C.I.O., November 19, 1943, RFEPC, RLD/RRH:SWH.

52. Maslow to Castañeda, Nov. 25, 1943, RFEPC, ROC:OC/CRF:CEC.

53. Castañeda to Maslow, Dec. 11, 1943, RFEPC, RDBAM,CF:RXWR.

54. Jones to Castañeda, Nov. 30, 1943, RFEPC, ROC:OC/CRF:CEC.

55. Castañeda to Maslow, Dec. 11, 1943.

56. Ross to Castañeda, Nov. 27, 1943, RFEPC, ROC:OC/CRF:CEC.

57. Ibid.

58. Castañeda to Maslow, Dec. 11, 1943.

59. Clarence M. Mitchell to Malcolm Ross, Dec. 14, 1943, RFEPC, ROC:OC/CRF:CEC.

60. Ross to Castañeda, Dec. 16, 1943, RFEPC, ROC:OC/CRF:CEC.

61. Castañeda to Maslow, Dec. 20, 1943, RFEPC, RDBAM,CF:RXWR; Mitchell to Ross, Dec. 14, 1943, RFEPC, ROC:OC/CRF:CEC.

62. Artaza interview.

63. Elisa R. Castañeda interview.

64. Frank interview.

65. Castañeda to Maslow, Dec. 27, 1943, RFEPC, RDBAM,CF:RXWR.

66. Maslow to Castañeda, Dec. [26], 1943, RFEPC, ROC:OC/CRF:CEC.

67. Maslow to Castañeda, Dec. 28, 1943, RFEPC, ROC:OC/CRF:CEC. Evidently Castañeda received the equity adjustment, because the subject never reappeared in the voluminous FEPC records.

68. Ross to Castañeda, Dec. 29, 1943, RFEPC, ROC:OC/CRF:CEC.

69. Mitchell to Maslow, Jan. 25, 1944, RFEPC, RDBAM,USG—ADM(M).

70. Ibid.

71. Maslow to Castañeda, Jan. 26, 1944, RFEPC, ROC:OC/CRF:CEC.

72. Castañeda to Maslow, Mar. 3, 1944, RFEPC, RDBAM,USG—ADM(M).

73. Maslow to Castañeda, Feb. 1, 1944, RFEPC, ROC:OC/CRF:CEC.

74. Maslow to Castañeda [different memorandum, same date as previous citation], Feb. 1, 1944, RFEPC, ROC:OC/CRF:CEC.

75. Castañeda to Maslow, Feb. 9, 1944, RFEPC, RDBAM,USG—ADM(M).

76. Castañeda to Maslow, Feb. 17, 1944, RFEPC, RDBAM,USG—ADM(M).

77. Castañeda to Maslow, Mar. 3, 1944, RFEPC, RDBAM,USG—ADM(M).

78. Castañeda to Maslow, Report of Field Trip to Silver City, [N.M.], Mar. 3, 1944, RFEPC, RDBAM,USG—ADM(M).

79. Castañeda to Maslow, Report of Field Trip to Pueblo, [Colo.], Mar. 3, 1944, RFEPC, RDBAM,USG—ADM(M).

80. Castañeda to Maslow, Report of Field Trip to El Paso, [Tex.], Mar. 3, 1944, RFEPC, RDBAM,USG—ADM(M).

81. Castañeda to Maslow, Mar. 13, 1944, RFEPC, RDBAM,USG—ADM(M).

82. Castañeda to Maslow, Report of Arizona Field Trip, Mar. 25, 1944, RFEPC, RDBAM,USG—ADM(M).

83. Ibid.

84. Castañeda to Maslow, Apr. 2, 1944, RFEPC, RLD/RRH:SWH.

85. Eugene Davidson, Assistant Director for Field Operations, to Castañeda, Apr. 13, 1944, RFEPC, ROC:OC/CRF:CEC.

86. Castañeda to Maslow, Apr. 22, 1944; Castañeda to Ross, May 4, 1944, RFEPC, RLD/RRH:SWH.

87. Castañeda to Maslow, Apr. 26, 1944, RFEPC, RLD/RRH:SWH.

88. Castañeda to Maslow, Apr. 28, 1944, RFEPC, RLD/RRH:SWH.

89. Ibid.

90. Castañeda to Maslow, Progress Report on Mining Industry Investigation, Hayden-Winkleman Area, May 4, 1944, RFEPC, RLD/RRH:SWH.

91. Castañeda to Ross, May 4, 1944, RFEPC, RLD/RRH:SWH.

92. Ibid.

93. Ibid.

94. Ibid.

95. Ibid.

96. Ibid.

97. Ibid.

98. Ibid.; Castañeda to Maslow, Conference with Kennecott Copper Corporation at Silver City, New Mexico, on J. Kimball Case, May 11, 1944, RFEPC, RLD/RRH:SWH.

99. Castañeda to William Goodrich, May 11, 1944, RFEPC, RLD/RRH:SWH.

100. Castañeda to Maslow, Summary Report of Area-Wide Mining Industry Investigation, July 4, 1944, RFEPC, RLD/RRH:SWH.

101. Maslow to Castañeda, June 23, 1944, RFEPC, ROC:OC/CRF:CEC.

102. Castañeda to Maslow, June 26 and 27, 1944, RFEPC, RLD/RRH:SWH.

103. Maslow to Castañeda, June 3, 1944, RFEPC, ROC:OC/CRF:CEC.

104. Mitchell to Castañeda, June 26, 1944, RFEPC, ROC:OC/CRF:CEC.

105. Castañeda to Maslow, July 4, 1944, RFEPC, RLD/RRH:SWH.

106. Ibid.

107. Ibid.

108. Ibid.

109. Castañeda to Maslow, July 29, 1944, RFEPC, RLD/RRH:SWH.

110. Castañeda to William Knowles, Aug. 5, 1944, RFEPC, RLD/RRH:SWH.

111. Castañeda to Maslow, Aug. 26, 1944, RFEPC, RLD/RRH:SWH.

112. Castañeda to Maslow, Sept. 1, 1944, RFEPC, RLD/RRH:SWH.

113. Castañeda to Maslow, Sept. 29, 1944, RFEPC, RLD/RRH:SWH.

114. Frank D. Reeves to A. Bruce Hunt, Oct. 13, 1944, RFEPC, RLD/RRH:SWH.

115. Castañeda to Reeves, Nov. 20, 1944; Castañeda to Hunt, Nov. 21, 1944, RFEPC, RLD/RRH:SWH.

116. Castañeda to Maslow, Nov. 24, 1944, RFEPC, RDBAM,CF:RXWR.

117. Castañeda to Hunt, Dec. 20, 1944, RFEPC, RLD/RRH:SWH.

Chapter 9

1. Castañeda to A. Bruce Hunt, Jan. 1, 1945, RFEPC, RLD/RRH:SWH.

2. Castañeda to Will[iam] Maslow, Jan. 2, 1945, RFEPC, RLD/RRH:SWH.

3. Maslow to Castañeda, Jan. 15, 1945, RFEPC, ROC:OC/CRF:CEC.

4. Castañeda to Maslow, Jan. 23, 1945, RFEPC, RLD/RRH:SWH.

5. Castañeda to Maslow, Jan. 23, 1945; Clete Daniel, *Chicano Workers and the Politics of Fairness: The FEPC in the Southwest,* p. 58.

6. Castañeda to Maslow, Jan. 23, 1945.

7. Malcolm Ross to Castañeda, Jan. 24, 1945, RFEPC, ROC:OC/CRF:CEC.

8. Castañeda to Winnie Allen, Jan. 25, 1945, CBF.

9. Ross to Castañeda, Feb. 5, 1945, RFEPC, ROC:OC/CRF:CEC.

10. Castañeda to Milton R. Gutsch, Feb. 13, 1945; H. T. Parlin to Acting President Theophilus S. Painter, Feb. 19, 1945, UTPOR:HD.

11. Castañeda to Maslow, Bi-Weekly Report for Period May 1–15, 1945, May 16, 1945, RFEPC, RDBAM,CF:RXWR. Southwestern Bell Telephone assigned to the Castañeda household a number that was easy to remember: GArfield 3396.

12. Ross to Castañeda, Feb. 16, 1945, RFEPC, ROC:OC/CRF:CEC.

13. Maslow to Castañeda, Feb. 26, 1945; Eugene Davidson to Castañeda, Aug. 6, 1945, RFEPC, ROC:OC/CRF:CEC.

14. Davidson to Castañeda, Feb. 27, 1945, RFEPC, ROC:OC/CRF:CEC.

15. Clarence M. Mitchell to Castañeda, Mar. 3, 1945, RFEPC, ROC:OC/CRF:CEC.

16. "Declaración del Doctor Carlos E. Castañeda," *La Prensa* (San Antonio, Tex.), Mar. 25, 1945, San Antonio College Library (hereinafter cited as SACL).

17. Testimony of Dr. Carlos E. Castañeda, Regional Director, F.E.P.C., Region 10, in Alonso S. Perales, ed., *Are We Good Neighbors?*, p. 99.

18. Ibid.

19. Ibid.

20. Ibid.

21. For a comprehensive overview of the plight of Mexican laborers, see Emilio Zamora, *The World of the Mexican Worker in Texas* (College Station: Texas A&M University Press, 1993).

22. Testimony of Dr. Carlos E. Castañeda, in Perales, *Are We Good Neighbors?*, p. 99.

23. Delegates at the Chapultepec Conference (officially named Inter-American Con-

ference) convened at the famous castle in Mexico City from Feb. 21 through Mar. 8, 1945. Among the topics of discussion were the impact of World War II upon the hemispheric nations and their expectations of the upcoming peace. Only El Salvador, which had severed diplomatic relations with Mexico, and Argentina, which the participating members of the Pan American Union refused to invite because of the Perón government's friendliness toward the Axis powers during the war, failed to attend (*Diccionario Porrúa de Historia, Biografía y Geografía de México,* vol. 1, pp. 588–89; John Edwin Flagg, *Latin America: A General History* [Toronto: Macmillan Company, 1969], p. 704).

24. Perales, *Are We Good Neighbors?,* p. 102.
25. Ibid.
26. Ibid.
27. Ibid.
28. *La Prensa,* Mar. 24 and 25, 1945, SACL.
29. Ross to Castañeda, May 15, 1945, RFEPC, ROC:OC/CRF:CEC.
30. Ibid.
31. Castañeda to Maslow, Bi-Weekly Report for the Period May 1–15, May 16, 1945, RFEPC, RDBAM,CF:RXWR.
32. Ibid.
33. Ibid.
34. Ibid.
35. "Texas Collection," *Southwestern Historical Quarterly* 49 (Jan., 1946): 433–34.
36. Maslow and Jones to Castañeda, June 1, 1945, RFEPC, ROC:OC/CRF:CEC.
37. Castañeda to Maslow, Bi-Weekly Report for June 1–15, 1945, RFEPC, RDBAM, CF:RXWR. The "War Agencies" were emergency administrative activities conducted within the Executive Department.
38. *San Antonio Express,* July 1, 1945.
39. *San Antonio Express,* July 8, 1945.
40. *Pittsburgh Post-Gazette,* July 13, 1945, Box 469, RFEPC.
41. Davidson to Castañeda, July 27, 1945, RFEPC, ROC:OC/CRF:CEC.
42. *Daily Texan,* Aug., 6, 1945, CBF; Davidson to Castañeda, Aug. 6, 1945, RFEPC, ROC:OC/CRF:CEC.
43. Florence H. Reiboldt, acting secretary, board of regents of The University of Texas, to Eugene C. Barker, July 23, 1945, ECBP.
44. Castañeda to Mitchell, Monthly Report for July 15–Aug. 15, 1945, RFEPC, RDBAM, CF:RXWR.
45. Ibid.
46. Ibid.
47. Castañeda to Mitchell, Monthly Report for Aug. 15–Sept. 15, 1945, RFEPC, RDBAM, CF:RXWR.
48. Castañeda to Mitchell, Monthly Report for Sept. 15–Oct. 15, 1945, RFEPC, RDBAM, CF:RXWR.
49. Ross and Mitchell to Castañeda, Oct. 29, 1945, RFEPC, ROC:OC/CRF:CEC.
50. *Austin American,* Nov. 15, 1945, CBF.
51. Castañeda to Michael B. McCloskey, Nov. 21, 1945, AAFH/FST/BC.
52. Gutsch to Painter, Dec. 15, 1945, UTPOR:HD.
53. Sinclair V. Jeter to Castañeda, Dec. 12, 1945, RFEPC, ROC:OC/CRF:CEC.
54. Malcolm Ross, "Our Personal Relations with Mexicans," in Perales, *Are We Good Neighbors?,* pp. 64, 72.

55. Castañeda to Rodrigo A. Molina, Jan. 9, 1945 [1946], AAFH/FST/BC; "Inter-American Notes: Dr. Castañeda Returns to the University of Texas," *The Americas* 2 (Jan., 1946): 377.

56. Castañeda to Most Reverend Laurence J. FitzSimon, May 7, 1946, KCCF/CAT.

57. Ibid. During his tenure with the Fair Employment Practice Committee, Castañeda lost regular contact with the Texas Historical Commission and the leading prelates affiliated with it.

58. Castañeda to Gutsch, Mar. 11, 1946, UTPOR:HD.

59. Castañeda to Martin R. P. McGuire, May 7, 1946, ROC,FS/DAM,CUA.

60. *Daily Texan,* May 17, 1946, CBF. In addition to *Lands of Middle America* (1948), the Macmillan Company had also published *A History of Latin America for Schools* (1944), co-authored by Castañeda and Samuel Guy Inman, as part of its Inter-American Series edited by George I. Sánchez. Later the United States Armed Forces Institute adopted *A History of Latin America* for its instructional program.

61. *Daily Texan,* May 10, 1946, CBF.

62. Carlos E. Castañeda, "First European Settlement on the Rio Grande," *Texas Geographic* 9 (Aug., 1945): 28–31; *Daily Texan,* May 17, 1946, CBF.

63. *Southern Messenger,* June 13, 1946, OLLU/SAT.

64. Report of the Historiographer of Volume VI, Minutes of the 29th Regular Meeting of the Texas Knights of Columbus Historical Commission, San Antonio, Tex., June 18, 1946, KCCF/CAT.

65. Minutes of the 29th Regular Meeting, KCCF/CAT.

66. Ibid.

67. Monsignor Patrick John McCormick to Castañeda, June 20, 1946, ROC,FS/DAM,CUA.

68. Lane, "Catholic Archives of Texas," p. 60.

69. Castañeda to McCormick, June 26, 1946, ROC,FS/DAM,CUA.

70. The Texas delegation included Charles W. Hackett, Fred Mason Bullard, George Charles Marius Engerrand, Rex Devern Hopper, Jefferson Rea Spell, Enrich Walter Zimmerman, and Castañeda ("Professional Notes: Personal News," *HAHR* 26 [May, 1946]: 271).

71. "Professional Notes: Summer School, National University of Mexico, with the Cooperation of the Universities of California, Michigan, and Texas and the Spanish Language Institute," *HAHR* 26 (Aug., 1946): 441–42.

72. McCormick to Castañeda, July 1, 1946, ROC,FS/DAM,CUA.

73. Castañeda to Roderick Wheeler, July 24, 1946, AAFH/FST/BC.

74. "Professional Notes: Summer School, National University of Mexico, with the Cooperation of the Universities of California, Michigan, and Texas and the Spanish Language Institute," *HAHR* 26 (Aug., 1946): 443; Estep interview.

75. Estep interview.

76. Castañeda to McCormick, Sept. 2, 1946, ROC,FS/DAM,CUA.

77. Joe W. Neal to Félix D. Almaráz, Jr., Feb. 3, 1975, Almaráz Papers.

78. Castañeda to Herbert E. Bolton, Oct. 11, 1946, HEBP/BL/UCB. Administrators of the twenty-sixth annual summer school program established headquarters at La Casa de los Mascarones on Calle Ribera de San Cosme 71 ("Professional Notes: Summer School, National University of Mexico, with the Cooperation of the Universities of California, Michigan, and Texas and the Spanish Language Institute," *HAHR* 26 (Aug., 1946): 443).

79. Castañeda to FitzSimon, Aug. 30, 1946, KCCF/CAT.

80. Castañeda to McCormick, Sept. 2, 1946, ROC,FS/DAM,CUA.

81. "Professional Notes: Personal News," *HAHR* 26 (Nov., 1946): 633.

82. Dabbs Recollections, Feb. 24, 1974.

83. *Southern Messenger*, Sept. 26, 1946, OLLU/SAT.

84. Castañeda to Gutsch, Dec. 16, 1946; Gutsch to Parlin, Dec. 16, 1946, UTPOR:HD.

85. Brewer, "History of the Department of History," pp. 172–73.

86. Gutsch to Parlin, Feb. 13, 1947, UTPOR:HD.

87. Castañeda to Gutsch, Dec. 16, 1946, UTPOR:HD. Castañeda's contributions to the Preliminary Studies of the Texas Catholic Historical Society, published between 1931 and 1940 and distributed under the auspices of the Texas Knights of Columbus Historical Commission, included: *Earliest Catholic Activities in Texas, The Six Flags of Texas, Silent Years in Texas History, The First American Play, Pioneers in Sackcloth,* and *Beginnings of Printing in America.*

88. *Dallas Morning News,* Apr. 13, 1947, CBF; Castañeda to Gutsch, Dec. 16, 1946, UTPOR:HD. The conference, organized by Ursuline College, garnered the support of several corporate sponsors: Louisiana State University, Loyola University, Tulane University, Southwestern Louisiana Institute at Lafayette, the Archdiocese of New Orleans, and two "business firms interested in Latin American trade," United Fruit Company and Marine Forwarding and Shipping Company (Castañeda to Gutsch, Dec. 16, 1946).

89. Castañeda to FitzSimon, Apr. 29, 1947, KCCF/CAT.

90. Mother M. Angelique to Castañeda, May 3, 1947, KCCF/CAT. During his long-term residency at Saint Edward's University, Father Foik began collecting rare books on the subject of Texas and the Catholic Church. As his private collection expanded, periodically he shipped packets of books to Notre Dame University Library, an institution that he considered the mother house of the priests and religious brothers of the Congregation of the Holy Cross working in Texas.

91. Castañeda to FitzSimon, May 9, 1947, KCCF/CAT.

92. Robert K. Carr to Castañeda, Apr. 29, 1947, in Perales, *Are We Good Neighbors?,* pp. 57–58.

93. Castañeda to Carr, May 9, 1947, in Perales, *Are We Good Neighbors?,* pp. 58–59.

94. Matt S. Meier and Feliciano Rivera, *Dictionary of Mexican American History* (Westport, Conn.: Greenwood Press, 1981), pp. 55–56; Carlos E. Castañeda, "Statement on Discrimination Against Mexican-Americans in Employment," May 9, 1947, in Perales, *Are We Good Neighbors?,* p. 61.

95. Carlos E. Castañeda, "Discrimination Against Mexican Americans in Employment," in Perales, *Are We Good Neighbors?,* p. 61.

96. Ibid., p. 62.

97. Ibid.

98. Minutes of the 30th Regular Meeting of the Texas Knights of Columbus Historical Commission, San Antonio, Tex., May 31, 1947, KCCF/CAT.

99. Report of Historiographer Carlos Castañeda, in Minutes of the 30th Regular Meeting of the Texas Knights of Columbus Historical Commission, San Antonio, Tex., May 21, 1947.

100. Ibid.

101. Castañeda to FitzSimon, May 28, 1947, KCCF/CAT.

102. Ibid.

103. Castañeda to FitzSimon, July 24, 1947, KCCF/CAT.

104. Ibid.

105. Castañeda to Gutsch, Aug. 11, 1947, UTPOR:HD.

106. Painter to Vito Alessio Robles, Aug. 31, 1947, UTPOR:HD.

107. Castañeda to FitzSimon, Sept. 10, 1947, KCCF/CAT.

Chapter 10

1. "Louis Joseph Reicher," in *New Handbook of Texas,* vol. 5, p. 510.

2. *Southern Messenger,* Apr. 8, 1948, IWCL.

3. *Southern Messenger,* Apr. 15, 1948; *Alamo Register,* Apr. 23, 1948, IWCL.

4. *Austin Statesman,* May 12, 1948, CBF.

5. *Southern Messenger,* May 13, 1948; *Alamo Register,* May 21, 1948, IWCL.

6. John D. Barnhart, "The Forty-First Annual Meeting of the Mississippi Valley Historical Association," *Mississippi Valley Historical Review* 35 (Sept., 1948): 239–62.

7. Castañeda to Most Reverend Laurence A. FitzSimon, Apr. 17, 1948, KCCF/CAT. Admittedly the transfer of the materials presaged inconveniences for future research, as Castañeda soon learned, but since Saint Edward's University Library no longer wanted the responsibility for documents it did not own, Bishop FitzSimon's offer seemed the best alternative.

8. Castañeda to FitzSimon, June 1, 1948, KCCF/CAT.

9. Ibid.

10. Castañeda to FitzSimon, Aug. 4, 1948, KCCF/CAT.

11. Castañeda to FitzSimon, Aug. 19, 1948, KCCF/CAT.

12. Castañeda to Eleuterio Escobar, Aug. 19, 1948, EEP, BLAC.

13. *La Prensa* [San Antonio, Tex.], Aug. 22, 1948, San Antonio College Library.

14. *San Antonio Express,* Sept. 1, 1948.

15. *San Antonio Evening News,* Sept. 1, 1948.

16. *San Antonio Express,* Sept. 2, 1948.

17. Castañeda to Escobar, Sept. 14, 1948, BTHC.

18. "School Improvement League," in *New Handbook of Texas,* vol. 5, pp. 925–26.

19. Castañeda to FitzSimon, Sept. 19, 1948, KCCF/CAT.

20. Rodríguez interview.

21. Castañeda to FitzSimon, Oct. 6, 1948, KCCF/CAT.

22. FitzSimon to Castañeda, Oct. 6, 1948, KCCF/CAT.

23. Castañeda to José Cisneros, Dec. 10, 1948, José Cisneros Correspondence File, El Paso, Tex.

24. Joe W. Neal, Director of International Office, UTA, to the author, Feb. 3, 1975, Almaráz Papers.

25. Ibid.

26. Minutes of the Budget Council Meeting, Dec. 7, 1948, Documents and Proceedings of the History Department, UTA, p. 1408, UTPOR:HD. In contrast to Castañeda's salary as a visiting professor in the summer, Charles W. Hackett, with the rank of distinguished professor and permanent member of the graduate faculty, earned $8,000, with an additional $1,200 set aside as supplemental income.

27. Castañeda to Francis Borgia Steck, Feb. 1, 1949, FBSP/QCBL.

28. Ibid.

29. Castañeda to FitzSimon, Feb. 17, 1949, KCCF/CAT. Actually, the appointment Carlos sought was to one of the Pontifical Institutes of Higher Learning that offered "special studies in theology, canon law, philosophy, missiology, ecclesiology, social sciences, and Church history" (Robert C. Broderick, *The Catholic Encyclopedia*, p. 478).

30. Castañeda to FitzSimon, Feb. 17, 1949, KCCF/CAT.

31. Castañeda to FitzSimon, Feb. 17 and 25, 1949, KCCF/CAT.

32. Castañeda to FitzSimon, Mar. 3, 1949, KCCF/CAT; *Southern Messenger*, Mar. 17, 1949, OLLU/SAT.

33. Castañeda to Cisneros, Mar. 10, 1949, Cisneros Correspondence File.

34. Castañeda to FitzSimon, Mar. 25 and Apr. 22, 1949, KCCF/CAT; M. J. Gilbert, ed., *Diamond Jubilee, 1874–1949: Archdiocese of San Antonio* (San Antonio: Schneidor Printing Company/Robert E. Lucey, 1949), pp. 1–16.

35. Castañeda to FitzSimon, Mar. 25, 1949, KCCF/CAT; Castañeda to Cisneros, Mar. 10, 1949, Cisneros Correspondence File.

36. "Professional Notes: Personal News," *HAHR* 29 (May, 1949): 291.

37. Castañeda to FitzSimon, Mar. 25, 1949, KCCF/CAT.

38. Castañeda to Cisneros, undated postcards from Argentina [circa Apr., 1949], Cisneros Correspondence File.

39. Félix D. Almaráz, Jr., "Carlos Eduardo Castañeda, Mexican-American Historian: The Formative Years, 1896–1927," *Pacific Historical Review* 42 (Aug., 1973): 319.

40. Castañeda to FitzSimon, Apr. 22, 1949, KCCF/CAT.

41. Castañeda to FitzSimon, May 4, 1949, KCCF/CAT.

42. Castañeda to FitzSimon, May 11, 1949, KCCF/CAT.

43. Castañeda to Steck, June 13, 1949, FBSP/QCBL.

44. Castañeda to FitzSimon, May 11, 1949, KCCF/CAT.

45. Ibid.

46. Castañeda to FitzSimon, May 31, 1949, KCCF/CAT.

47. Ibid.

48. Castañeda to Steck, June 16, 1949; Steck to Castañeda, July 2 and Sept. 13, 1949, FBSP/QCBL.

49. Ruth Lapham Butler, "Notes on the First Congress of Historians of Mexico and the United States," *HAHR* 24 (Nov., 1949): 634–36.

50. Castañeda to FitzSimon, Sept. 22, 1949, KCCF/CAT.

51. Castañeda to FitzSimon, Oct. 10, 1949, KCCF/CAT.

52. Castañeda to Steck, Oct. 15, 1949, FBSP/QCBL.

53. Steck to Castañeda, Oct. 20, 1949, FBSP/QCBL.

54. Neal to Almaráz, Feb. 3, 1975, Almaráz Papers.

55. Dabbs Recollections, Feb. 26, 1974.

56. Frantz interview.

57. *Southern Messenger*, Oct. 13, 1949, IWCL.

58. Minutes of the Budget Council, Nov. 1, 1949, Documents and Proceedings of the History Department, UTPOR:HD.

59. "Inter-American Notes: Annual Convocation of the Academy of American Franciscan History," *The Americas* 6 (Jan., 1950): 365; *Southern Messenger*, Dec. 29, 1949, IWCL; H. Bailey Carroll, ed., "Texas Collection," *Southwestern Historical Quarterly* 53 (Apr., 1950): 479.

60. Herbert E. Bolton, "The Confession of a Wayward Professor," *The Americas* 6 (Jan., 1950): 359–62.

61. Castañeda to Steck, Dec. 19, 1949, FBSP/QCBL.

62. Castañeda to FitzSimon, Feb. 15, 1950, KCCF/CAT.

63. Castañeda to FitzSimon, Mar. 13, 1950, KCCF/CAT.

64. Castañeda to FitzSimon, Mar. 30, 1950, KCCF/CAT. The legal name of the organization is The Catholic Church Extension Society of the United States of America.

65. Castañeda to FitzSimon, Apr. 6, 1950, KCCF/CAT.

66. Castañeda to FitzSimon, Apr. 28, 1950, KCCF/CAT. Monsignor William H. Oberste, who ultimately accepted the assignment, wrote *Knights of Columbus in Texas, 1902–1952* (Austin: Von Boeckmann-Jones, Co., 1952).

67. *Austin Statesman,* May 20, 1959, CBF. The young guests included Sonia Curd, Carol Cyrus, Joan Haag, and Mary Esther Haskell.

68. Castañeda to Sister Mary Paul Fitzgerald, May 31, 1950, Special Collections: College Commencements File, De Paul Library, Saint Mary College, Leavenworth, Kans. The Congregation of Sisters of Charity of Leavenworth operated Saint Mary College.

69. Castañeda to FitzSimon, June 6, 1950, KCCF/CAT; Castañeda to Sister Mary Paul Fitzgerald, May 31, 1950.

70. Castañeda to FitzSimon, July 8, 1950, KCCF/CAT.

71. Castañeda to FitzSimon, Aug. 3, 1950, KCCF/CAT.

72. Castañeda to FitzSimon, Aug. 17, 1950, KCCF/CAT.

73. Marc Simmons to Almaráz, Feb. 4, 1973, Almaráz Papers.

74. *Austin Statesman,* Oct. 15, 1950, CBF.

75. *Amarillo Register,* Oct. 13, 1950, CBF; *Southern Messenger,* Oct. 12, 1950, IWCL.

76. Castañeda to FitzSimon, Oct. 25, 1950, KCCF/CAT; *Amarillo Register,* Oct. 13, 1950.

77. Program, Ceremonies of Investiture of Carlos Eduardo Castañeda as Knight Commander in the Order of Isabella the Catholic, Oct. 19, 1950, CBF.

78. Castañeda to Bolton, Oct. 30, 1950, HEBP/BL/UCB.

79. Lilliana Owens, *Jesuit Beginnings in New Mexico.*

80. Carlos E. Castañeda, "Human Side of a Great Collection," p. 12.

81. Dabbs Recollections, Feb. 14, 1974.

82. Castañeda to FitzSimon, Oct. 25, 1950, KCCF/CAT.

83. Castañeda to FitzSimon, Nov. 8, 1950, KCCF/CAT.

84. Most Reverend Eugene J. McGuinnes to the Most Reverend John P. McCormick, Dec. 22, 1950, ROC,FS/DAM,CUA.

Chapter 11

1. Castañeda to Alexander Wyse, Feb. 7, 1951, AAFH/FST/BC; *Southern Messenger,* Feb. 1, 1951, IWCL.

2. Wyse to Castañeda, Feb. 14, 1951, AAFH/FST/BC.

3. Castañeda to Wyse, Feb. 7, 1951, AAFH/FST/BC.

4. Wyse to Castañeda, Feb. 14, 1951, AAFH/FST/BC.

5. Castañeda to Wyse, Feb. 24, 1952, and Mar. 3, 1953; Wyse to Castañeda, Feb. 29, 1952, and Jan. 15, 1953, AAFH/FST/BC. Two years later the editors published Nie-

meyer's essay, "Anti-Clericalism in the Mexican Constitutional Convention of 1916–1917" (*The Americas* 11 [July, 1954]: 31–49).

6. Castañeda to Wyse, Mar. 15, 1951, AAFH/FST/BC.

7. Budget Council Meeting, Mar. 8, 1951, Documents and Proceedings of the History Department, pp. 1505–1506, 1597, UTPOR:HD.

8. Castañeda to Wyse, Mar. 15, 1951, AAFH/FST/BC.

9. Ibid.

10. Wyse to Castañeda, Mar. 31, 1951, AAFH/FST/BC; Castañeda to Wyse, Mar. 28, 1951, AAFH/FST/BC; Carlos E. Castañeda, "In Memoriam," pp. 83–84.

11. Theophilus S. Painter to J. L. Mecham, Chairman, et al., Apr. 2, 1951, UTPOR:HD. The other members of the committee, besides Chairman John Lloyd Mecham, were Jefferson R. Spell, Eugene C. Barker, and Milton R. Gutsch.

12. Castañeda to Wyse, Mar. 15, 1951, AAFH/FST/BC.

13. Castañeda to Wyse, May 1, 1951, AAFH/FST/BC.

14. Castañeda to Wyse, Mar. 28, 1951, AAFH/FST/BC.

15. Clarence W. Walton, President, The Catholic University of America, to the author, Dec. 11, 1972, Almaráz Papers.

16. Most Reverend Patrick J. McCormick to the Most Reverend Eugene J. Mc-Guinnes, Jan. 5, 1951; McCormick to the Most Reverend Louis J. Reicher, Jan. 22, 1951; Reicher to McCormick, Feb. 17, 1951, CEC File, DAM/CUA. In canon law, the term *Ordinary* is used to designate a resident bishop "who exercises ordinary jurisdiction in the external form (as well as in the internal form)," which is attached to a diocesan office or chancery (Broderick, *Catholic Encyclopedia*, p. 439).

17. Castañeda to McCormick, Apr. 15, 1951, CEC File, DAM/CUA.

18. Castañeda to Wyse, Apr. 26, 1951, AAFH/FST/BC.

19. Castañeda to Wyse, Apr. 26 and May 24, 1951, AAFH/FST/BC. His Eminence, Amleto G. Cardinal Cicognani, served as apostolic delegate to the United States in Washington from 1933 to 1958 (*The Official Catholic Directory Anno Domini 1958* [Wilmette, Ill.: P. J. Kenedy & Sons, 1958], p. xx).

20. Castañeda to Wyse, Apr. 16, 1951, AAFH/FST/BC.

21. Wyse to Castañeda, Apr. 27, 1951, AAFH/FST/BC.

22. Castañeda to Wyse, May 1, 1951, AAFH/FST/BC.

23. *Daily Texan,* May 4, 1951, CBF. The first honoree in 1946 was Dr. Adolfo Urrutia of San Antonio, selected for his advocacy of health care for the "Spanish-speaking people." Gus García, a San Antonio attorney, and Dr. Héctor P. García, a Corpus Christi physician, received the accolade in 1947 and 1948, respectively, for their struggle in the public arena "fighting for the rights and privileges of Latin Americans" (*Daily Texan,* May 2, 1951, CBF).

24. *Amarillo Register,* May 18, 1951, CBF.

25. Castañeda to Wyse, May 17, 1951, AAFH/FST/BC.

26. Elisa R. Castañeda interview.

27. Wyse to Castañeda, May 19, 1951, AAFH/FST/BC.

28. Roy J. Deferrari, Secretary General, Catholic University of America, to Castañeda, May 11, 1951, CEC File, DAM/CUA.

29. Citation of Carlos Eduardo Castañeda, [June 6, 1951], CEC Papers, DAM/CUA. Catholic Action, in practice, is defined as being nothing "more than the cooperation with the bishop in the enterprises he sets forth." Catholic Action is not a political activity.

Rather, its work "is in the religious circle, the moral [realm], and those border areas where religion or morals are directly or indirectly related to the good of the individual or the community, or the universal good of the Church" (Broderick, *Catholic Encyclopedia*, pp. 98–99).

30. Elisa R. Castañeda interview.

31. Wyse to Castañeda, June 25, 1951, AAFH/FST/BC.

32. Castañeda to Wyse, June 25, 1951, AAFH/FST/BC.

33. Dabbs Recollections, Feb. 24, 1974.

34. Castañeda to Painter, June 25, 1951, UTPOR:HD.

35. 1950–51 M.A. and Ph.D. Committee Record of Members of the History Staff, July 9, 195[1], Documents and Proceedings of the History Department, p. 1543, UTPOR: HD; Castañeda to Wyse, July 26, 1951, AAFH/FST/BC. McLean's article, "Guillermo Prieto (1818–1897), a Forgotten Historian of Mexico," appeared in *The Americas* 10 (July, 1953): 79–88. Castañeda to Wyse, Feb. 24, 1952; Wyse to Castañeda, Feb. 29, 1952, AAFH/FST/BC. Two years later the editors published Niemeyer's essay "Anti-Clericalism in the Mexican Constitutional Convention of 1916–1917" (*The Americas* 11 [July, 1954]: 31–49). Estep interview, Mar. 1, 1974. Translated by Carlos A. Echánova Trujillo, *Lorenzo de Zavala: Profeta del Liberalismo de México,* "a 358-page volume," contained a preface by Castañeda ("Texas Collection," *Southwestern Historical Quarterly* 56 [Jan., 1953]: 557).

36. Castañeda to Wyse, June 27, 1951, AAFH/FST/BC.

37. Wyse to Castañeda, July 24, 1951; Castañeda to Wyse, July 26, 1951, AAFH/FST/BC.

38. Castañeda to Wyse, Aug. 9, 1951, AAFH/FST/BC.

39. Dabbs Recollections, Feb. 24, 1974.

40. See Lewis Hanke, *The Spanish Struggle for Justice in the Conquest of America* (Philadelphia: University of Pennsylvania Press, 1949) and Hanke, *Bartolomé de Las Casas, Historian: An Essay in Spanish Historiography* (Gainesville: University of Florida Press, 1952).

41. Sheridan interview.

42. Rodríguez interview.

43. Elisa R. Castañeda interview.

44. Maury Maverick to Harry Rogers, Oct. 3, 1951, EEP, BLAC.

45. Eleuterio Escobar to Castañeda, Oct. 5, 1951, EEP, BLAC.

46. Castañeda to Escobar, Oct. 6, 1951, EEP, BLAC.

47. Castañeda to Escobar, Nov. 8, 1951, EEP, BLAC.

48. *Daily Texan,* Jan. 10, 1952, CBF.

49. *Daily Texan,* Dec. 5, 1951, CBF; Castañeda to Wyse, May 1, 1951; Wyse to Castañeda, May 8, 1951, AAFH/FST/BC, BTHC. The directors of the Academy of American Franciscan History created the "coveted prize" in 1947 to recognize individuals who had performed "outstanding service in the promotion of inter-American cultural relations." Sumner Welles, undersecretary of state during the Franklin D. Roosevelt administration, received the first Serra Award in 1947, followed by Pablo Martínez del Río, Mexican historian (1948); Herbert Eugene Bolton, founder of the Borderlands school of historiography (1949); and Gabriela Mistral, poetess and diplomat of Chile (1950) (*Austin American,* Dec. 7, 1951, CBF).

50. "Inter-American Notes, Annual Convocation of the Academy of American Franciscan History," *The Americas* 8 (Apr., 1952): 515–16.

51. "Notes and Comments," *Catholic Historical Review* 37 (Jan., 1952): 485.

52. "Inter-American Notes," *The Americas* 8: 518.

53. Ibid.

54. Carlos E. Castañeda, "Why I Chose History," p. 483.

55. Ibid.

56. *Southern Messenger,* Jan. 24, 1952, IWCL.

57. Minutes of the Meeting of the Departmental Faculty, Feb. 13, 1952, Documents and Proceedings of the Department of History, UTA, [no page], UTPOR:HD.

58. *Southern Messenger,* Apr. 3, 1952, OLLU/SAT.

59. Castañeda to Painter, Mar. 10, 1952, UTPOR:HD; *San Antonio Express,* Apr. 3, 1952.

60. *Daily Texan,* Apr. 23, 1952, CBF; *Southern Messenger,* Apr. 17, 1952, OLLU/SAT.

61. Castañeda to the Most Reverend Laurence J. FitzSimon, May 21, 195[2], KCCF/CAT.

62. *Southern Messenger,* Apr. 17, 1952.

63. "The Texas Good Relations Association," circa 1952, copy in Almaráz Papers. Broadside.

64. *Southern Messenger,* May 22, 1952, OLLU/SAT.

65. Castañeda to FitzSimon, May 21, 195[2], KCCF/CAT.

66. Castañeda to FitzSimon, July 17, 1952, KCCF/CAT.

67. *Daily Texan,* Dec. 2, 1952, CBF; Dabbs Recollections, Feb. 24, 1974.

68. Bolton died on Jan. 30, 1953 (George P. Hammond, "In Memoriam: Herbert Eugene Bolton, 1870–1953," *The Americas* 9 [Apr., 1953]: 391).

69. Castañeda to Wyse, Mar. 3, 1953, AAFH/FST/BC. Disappointed in Castañeda's inability to complete the translation of Father Benjamín Gento Sanz's manuscript but wholly sympathetic to Carlos's preoccupation with "university work," the friars recruited Señora Fanchón Royer, an occasional contributor to *The Americas,* to take over the project (Wyse to Castañeda, May 14, 1953, AAFH/FST/BC).

70. Castañeda to Sam Liberto, Sr., Nov. 27, 1953, Liberto Papers; *Southern Messenger,* Nov. 19, 1953, IWCL; Carlos E. Castañeda, "Social Developments and Movements in Latin America," in *Church and Society: Catholic Social and Political Thought and Movements, 1789–1950,* ed. Joseph N. Moody (New York: Arts, Inc., 1953), pp. 733–73.

71. Documents and Proceedings of the Department of History, UTA, Oct. 14, 1953, UTPOR:HD.

72. Documents and Proceedings of the Department of History, Nov. 11, 1953, UTPOR:HD.

73. Minutes of the Meeting of the Departmental Faculty, Apr. 8, 1953, Documents and Proceedings of the Department of History, UTA, UTPOR:HD.

74. *Daily Texan,* Apr. 15, 1953, CBF.

75. *El Paso Times,* Mar. 22, 1953, CBF.

76. Ibid.

77. Castañeda to Logan Wilson, Apr. 9, 1953, UTPOR:HD.

78. Castañeda to Wilson, Apr. 9, 1953; Wilson to Castañeda, Apr. 13, 1953, UTPOR:HD.

79. *Daily Texan,* Apr. 15, 1953, CBF; *Senate Journal Texas,* 53rd Legislature Regular Session, 1953, p. 513.

80. *Senate Journal Texas,* 1953, pp. 512–13; *House Journal Texas,* Vol. 1 (Jan. 13, 1953, through Apr. 29, 1953), Regular Session 53rd Legislature, p. 1238.

81. *House Journal Texas,* 1: 1238.

82. "Address by Dr. Carlos E. Castañeda . . . to the Joint Session of the Legislature of Texas held on Apr. 14, 1953, to commemorate Pan American Day," p. 4, Texas State Archives, Austin, Tex.

83. Ibid., p. 7.

84. Ibid., pp. 9−10.

85. *Daily Texan,* Apr. 15, 1953, CBF.

86. Minutes of the 35th Regular Meeting of the Texas Knights of Columbus Historical Commission, Fort Worth, Tex., May 11, 1953, KCCF/CAT.

87. Castañeda to FitzSimon, May 14, 1953, KCCF/CAT.

88. Castañeda to FitzSimon, June 13, 1953, KCCF/CAT.

89. Castañeda to Mecham, July 21, 1953, KCCF/CAT. The publications were the *Calendar of the Hernández y Dávalos Collection* and *Diálogos de Cervantes de Salazar regarding the founding of the Royal and Pontifical University of Mexico.*

90. Castañeda to FitzSimon, July 28 and Aug. 28, 1953, KCCF/CAT; *Southern Messenger,* Nov. 19, 1953, IWCL; Carlos E. Castañeda, "God's Work in the Southwest," *Extension* 48 (Nov., 1953): 18−19, 56.

91. Castañeda to FitzSimon, July 28, 1953, KCCF/CAT.

92. Carlos A. Echánove Trujillo to Logan Wilson, July 25, 1953; Wilson to Echánove Trujillo, July 29, 1953; Castañeda to Wilson, July 30, 1953, UTPOR:HD.

93. Allan Shivers to Adolfo Ruiz Cortines, June 17, 1953; Shivers to Wilson, June 17, 1973, UTPOR:HD.

94. Castañeda to Wilson, July 24, 1953, UTPOR:HD.

95. Castañeda to Wilson, July 27, 1953; Wilson to Shivers, July 29, 1953, UTPOR:HD.

96. Castañeda to Henrietta Henry, Oct. 9, 1953, TOMFRA/HHP.

97. Castañeda to FitzSimon, Sept. 7, 1953, KCCF/CAT; Castañeda to FitzSimon, Sept. 11, 1953, KCCF/CAT; Castañeda to FitzSimon, Aug. 28, 1953, KCCF/CAT; Castañeda to FitzSimon, Oct. 9, 1953, KCCF/CAT.

98. Lane, "Catholic Archives of Texas," p. 71; Bernard Doyon, *The Cavalry of Christ on the Rio Grande, 1849−1883,* p. viii.

99. Lane, "Catholic Archives of Texas," p. 71.

100. Castañeda to FitzSimon, July 28, 1953, KCCF/CAT.

101. Castañeda to James Gibbons, July 31, 1953, KCCF/CAT.

102. Castañeda to FitzSimon, Oct. 9, 1953, KCCF/CAT.

103. Castañeda to Gibbons, July 31, 1953.

104. Lane, "Catholic Archives of Texas," p. 73.

105. Castañeda to Liberto, Nov. 27, 1953, Liberto Papers.

106. Rodríguez interview.

107. Howard M. Ehrmann, "Historical News: The Chicago Meeting, 1953," *American Historical Review* 59 (Apr., 1954): 796.

108. Frantz interview.

109. Carlos E. Castañeda, "Spanish Medieval Institutions in Overseas Administration: The Prevalence of Medieval Concepts," *The Americas* 15 (Oct., 1954): 115−29.

110. Ehrmann, "Historical News," 596−97.

111. Castañeda to FitzSimon, Dec. 15, 1953, KCCF/CAT.

112. Castañeda to Wyse, [circa Dec. 12, 1953], AAFH/FST/BC.

Chapter 12

1. Castañeda to Most Reverend Laurence J. FitzSimon, Jan. 13, 1954, KCCF/CAT.

2. Castañeda to Alexander Wyse, Mar. 27, 1954, AAFH/FST/BC.

3. Wyse to Castañeda, Apr. 29, 1954, AAFH/FST/BC.

4. Castañeda to Wyse, Mar. 27, 1954; Carlos E. Castañeda, "Introduction," in *Life in the Imperial and Loyal City of Mexico in New Spain and the Royal and Pontifical University of Mexico as Described in the Dialogues for the Study of the Latin Language Prepared by Francisco Cervantes de Salazar for Use in His Classes and Printed in 1554 by Juan Pablos,* trans. Minnie Lee Shepard (reprint ed., Westport, Conn.: Greenwood Press, 1970), pp. 1–20.

5. Castañeda to Wyse, May 10, 1954, AAFH/FST/BC.

6. Castañeda to Antonine S. Tibesar, Aug. 6, 1954, AAFH/FST/BC.

7. Tibesar to Castañeda, Sept. 14, 1954, AAFH/FST/BC.

8. Thomas E. Cotner and Carlos E. Castañeda, eds., *Essays in Mexican History,* p. vii. Thomas E. Cotner's brother Robert C. Cotner was Castañeda's colleague in the history department.

9. Castañeda to France V. Scholes, Oct. 9, 1954, FVSP/CSWR/SC/UNMGL.

10. Castañeda to Scholes, Feb. 16, 1955, FVSP/CSWR/SC/UNMGL.

11. Scholes to Castañeda, Feb. 21, 1955, FVSP/CSWR/SC/UNMGL.

12. Castañeda to Tibesar, Sept. 16, 1954, AAFH/FST/BC.

13. Tibesar to Castañeda, Sept. 18, 1954, AAFH/FST/BC.

14. Frantz interview.

15. Castañeda to Henrietta Henry, Sept. 19, 1955, TOMFRA/HHP.

16. Raymond Wheat to the author, Apr. 19, 1990, Almaráz Papers.

17. Artaza interview.

18. Charles E. Ronan, S.J., Loyola University of Chicago, to the author, Mar. 13, 1973, Almaráz Papers.

19. Folks and Artaza interview.

20. Dabbs Recollections, Feb. 24, 1974, Almaráz Papers.

21. Ibid.

22. Castañeda to Henrietta Henry, Sept. 3, 1955, TOMFRA/HHP.

23. H. Bailey Carroll, ed., "Texas Collection," *Southwestern Historical Quarterly* 59 (Oct., 1955): 224–25; Castañeda to Vice President C. P. Boner, May 28, 1955, UTPOR:HD.

24. Castañeda to Henry, Sept. 19, 1955, TOMFRA/HHP.

25. Castañeda to Barnes F. Lathrop, Oct. 26, 1955, UTPOR:HD.

26. Lathrop to Dean Harry H. Ransom, Nov. 18, 1955, UTPOR:HD.

27. Castañeda to Henry, Nov. 29, 1955, TOMFRA/HHP.

28. Castañeda to Henry, Dec. 7, 1955, TOMFRA/HHP.

29. Ibid.

30. Castañeda to Henry, Jan. 2, 1956, TOMFRA/HHP.

31. Castañeda to Henry, Jan. 7, 1956, TOMFRA/HHP.

32. Ibid.

33. *Austin American-Statesman,* Jan. 15, 1956, CBF.

34. Castañeda to Logan Wilson, Jan. 13, 1956, UTPOR:HD.

35. Castañeda to Wilson, Jan. 19, 1956, UTPOR:HD. Castañeda conveyed Wilson's

greetings to Dr. Pedro González Rincones, rector of Universidad Central de Venezuela (Caracas); Dr. Joaquín Mármol Luzardo, rector of Universidad de Los Andes (Mérida); Dr. J. M. Núñez Ponte, director of Academia Venezolana de la Lengua (Caracas); Dr. José Domingo Leonardi, rector of Universidad de Zulia (Maracaibo); Reverend Monsignor Nicolás E. Navarro, director of Academia Nacional de la Historia (Caracas); Dr. Simón Planas Suárez, president of Academia de Ciencias Políticas y Sociales (Caracas); and Dr. F. J. Duarte, president of Academia de Ciencias Físicas, Matemáticas y Naturales (Caracas).

36. *Daily Texan,* Feb. 25, 1956, CBF.

37. Amuay Venezuela, S.A., [1956], CBF.

38. Castañeda to Wilson, Feb. 15, 1956, UTPOR:HD; Alejandro J. Perera, Consul General of Venezuela (Houston), to the author, Jan. 23, 1995, Almaráz Papers.

39. Ibid.

40. Amuay Venezuela, S.A., 1956, CBF.

41. Joaquín Mármol Luzardo to Wilson, Feb. 21, 1956, UTPOR:HD.

42. Castañeda to Henry, Feb. 29, 1956, TOMFRA/HHP; Amuay Venezuela, S.A., 1956, CBF.

43. Castañeda to Wilson, Feb. 15, 1956, UTPOR:HD.

44. Wilson to Ambassador Fletcher Warren, Feb. 24, 1956, UTPOR:HD.

45. Warren to Wilson, Mar. 7, 1956, UTPOR:HD.

46. Wilson to Ex-Students of The University of Texas in Caracas and all Venezuela, Feb. 24, 1956, UTPOR:HD.

47. Warren to Wilson, Mar. 7, 1956, UTPOR:HD; Castañeda to Wilson, Mar. 5, 1956, UTPOR:HD; Warren to Wilson, Mar. 7, 1956, UTPOR:HD.

48. Castañeda to Wilson, Mar. 5, 1956, UTPOR:HD.

49. Nicolás E. Navarro to Wilson, Mar. 9, 1956, UTPOR:HD.

50. Pedro González Rincones to Wilson, Mar. 22, 1956, UTPOR:HD.

51. Castañeda to Wilson, Mar. 5, 1956, UTPOR:HD; Wilson to Castañeda, Mar. 12, 1956, UTPOR:HD.

52. George P. Hammond, review of *Independent Mexico in Documents: Independence, Empire, and Republic* by Carlos Eduardo Castañeda and Jack Autrey Dabbs, *HAHR* 16 (Aug., 1956): 404-405.

53. Castañeda to Henry, Aug. 3, 1956, TOMFRA/HHP.

54. Ibid.

55. Rodríguez interview.

56. Robert Kelly Acosta to the author, Mar. 2, 1973, Almaráz Papers.

57. William Soza to the author, Aug. 22, 1990, Almaráz Papers.

58. Castañeda to James P. Gibbons, [date unknown, circa 1956], KCCF/CAT.

59. Castañeda to Monsignor William H. Oberste, Nov. 2, 1956, KCCF/CAT.

60. Artaza interview.

61. Probate Record 19,624, Castañeda Estate, County Clerk's Office, Travis County Courthouse, Austin, Tex. In his stock portfolio Castañeda wisely diversified his investments among several enterprises: United Fruit Company; Nuntz T.V., Inc.; Public Service Electric and Gas Company; American Telephone & Telegraph Company; Sinclair Oil Corporation; Frito Company; and Texas Gulf Sulphur.

62. Oberste to Castañeda, Mar. 7, 1957; Oberste to Gibbons, Mar. 11, 1957; Oberste to Archbishop Lucey, Mar. 11, 1957, KCCF/CAT.

63. Castañeda to Oberste, Mar. 13, 1957, KCCF/CAT.

64. Ibid.

65. Castañeda to Sister M. Agatha Sheehan, Mar. 13, 1957, Mary Agatha Sheehan Letter Folder, Academy of the Incarnate Word, Houston, Tex.

66. Oberste to Castañeda, Apr. 10, 1957, KCCF/CAT.

67. Castañeda to Oberste, Apr. 16, 1957, KCCF/CAT.

68. Oscar O. Winther, "The Fiftieth Annual Meeting of the Mississippi Valley Historical Association," *Mississippi Valley Historical Review* 44 (Sept., 1957): 325.

69. Oberste to Lucey, June 20, 1957, KCCF/CAT.

70. Castañeda to Oberste, June 22, 1957, KCCF/CAT.

71. Castañeda to Oberste, July 8, 1957, KCCF/CAT.

72. Ibid.

73. Castañeda to Oberste, July 20, 1957, KCCF/CAT.

74. Oberste to Castañeda, July 27, 1957, KCCF/CAT.

75. Castañeda to Oberste, July 31, 1957, KCCF/CAT.

76. Oberste to Edwin D. Gunter, Aug. 5, 1957, KCCF/CAT.

77. Castañeda to Oberste, Aug. 8, 1957, KCCF/CAT. Oberste fully supported Castañeda's suggestion. In forwarding his nomination of Father Frank to the Chancery of San Antonio, Oberste summarized the priest's special qualifications: "He has these many years worked faithfully on the Commission, and he deserves some recognition" (Oberste to Lucey, Aug. 12, 1957, KCCF/CAT).

Rev. Joseph Maguire, C.S.C., president of Saint Edward's University, served as census deputatus for the first two volumes of *Our Catholic Heritage;* Reverend Patrick J. Haggerty, C.S.C., for volumes 3 and 4; Reverend Stanislaus F. Lisewski, C.S.C., for volume 5; and Reverend James J. O'Brien, C.S.C., for volume 6.

78. Castañeda to Oberste, Sept. 16, 1957, KCCF/CAT.

79. Castañeda to Oberste, Aug. 8, 1957, KCCF/CAT.

80. Castañeda to Oberste, Aug. 8, 1957; Oberste to Castañeda, Aug. 14, 1957, KCCF/CAT.

81. Castañeda to Oberste, Aug. 31, 1957, KCCF/CAT.

82. Oberste to Castañeda, Sept. 7, 1957, KCCF/CAT.

83. Lucey to Oberste, Sept. 3, 1957, KCCF/CAT.

84. Castañeda to Oberste, Sept. 16, 1957, KCCF/CAT.

85. Wheat to the author, Apr. 19, 1990, Almaráz Papers.

86. Ibid.

87. Castañeda to Wilson, Aug. 27, 1957, UTPOR:HD.

88. José Roberto Juárez to the author, Oct. 10, 1992, Almaráz Papers.

89. Castañeda to Wilson, Oct. 30, 1957; Wilson to Castañeda, Nov. 1, 1957, UTPOR:HD.

90. Antonio Castro Leal to Wilson, Dec. 19, 1957, UTPOR:HD.

91. Castañeda to Wilson, Dec. 27, 1957, UTPOR:HD.

92. Castañeda to Oberste, Jan. 4, 1958, KCCF/CAT.

93. Ibid.

94. *La Prensa* [San Antonio, Tex.], Dec. 31, 1957, and *Excelsor,* Dec. 29, 1957, quoted in Castañeda to Wilson, Jan. 7, 1958, UTPOR:HD.

95. Harry H. Ransom to Castañeda, Jan. 7, 1958, UTPOR:HD.

96. Castañeda to FitzSimon, Jan. 22, 1958, KCCF/CAT. In the seventeenth century

María de Agreda, abbess of a cloistered convent in the town of Soria in northeastern Spain, appeared to indigenous cultures in the Trans-Pecos region of west Texas and instructed them to seek the spiritual guidance of Franciscan missionaries in New Mexico.

97. Castañeda to Oberste, Feb. 12, 1958, KCCF/CAT.

98. Oberste to Anton J. Frank, Feb. 14, 1958, KCCF/CAT.

99. Oberste to Castañeda, Mar. 1, 1958, KCCF/CAT.

100. Castañeda to Oberste, Apr. 1, 1958, KCCF/CAT.

101. Rodríguez interview.

102. Frantz interview.

103. Rodríguez interview.

104. Certificate of Death No. 24774: Carlos Eduardo Castañeda, Texas Department of Health, Bureau of Vital Statistics, Austin, Tex., issued July 19, 1985.

105. *Austin American,* Apr. 5, 1958, CBF.

106. Juárez to the author, Oct. 10, 1992, Almaráz Papers.

107. Rodríguez interview.

108. E. Victor Niemeyer to the author, Jan. 10, 1975, Almaráz Papers.

109. Oberste to FitzSimon, May 27, 1958, KCCF/CAT.

110. *Daily Texan,* Apr. 5 and 9, 1958; *West Texas Register,* Apr. 13, 1958, CBF; *Alamo Messenger,* Apr. 10, 1958, OLLU/SAT.

Chapter 13

1. *Fort Worth Star-Telegram,* quoted in the *Austin American-Statesman,* Apr. 9, 1958, CBF.

2. *Dallas Morning News,* Apr. 7, 1958, quoted in *Daily Texan,* Apr. 10, 1958, CBF.

3. *Austin American-Statesman,* Apr. 7, 1958, BTHC.

4. *Lone Star Catholic,* Apr. 20, 1958, Catholic Archives of Texas.

5. *La Prensa* [San Antonio, Tex.], Apr. 10, 1958, San Antonio College Library.

6. J. Lloyd Mecham, "Obituary Notes: Carlos Eduardo Castañeda, 1896–1958," *HAHR* 38 (Aug., 1958): 383.

7. Ibid.

8. "Notes and Comments," *Catholic Historical Review* 44 (July, 1958): 246.

9. Mathias C. Kiemen, "In Memoriam: Carlos Eduardo Castañeda, 1896–1958," *The Americas* 15 (July, 1958): 61.

10. H. Bailey Carroll, ed., "Texas Collection," *Southwestern Historical Quarterly* 62 (Oct., 1958): 273–74.

11. Monsignor William H. Oberste to the Most Reverend Laurence J. FitzSimon, May 22, 1958, KCCF/CAT.

12. Oberste to FitzSimon, May 27, 1958, KCCF/CAT.

13. Oberste to the Most Reverend Louis J. Reicher, June 6, 1958, KCCF/CAT.

14. James Presley to the author, Jan. 27, 1975, Almaráz Papers.

15. Rodríguez interview.

16. *Daily Texan,* Apr. 9, 1958, CBF.

17. Marc Simmons to the author, Feb. 16, 1973, Almaráz Papers.

18. Archibald R. Lewis to Dean J. A. Burdine, Apr. 9 and 30, 1958, and May 29, 1958, UTPOR:HD.

19. Edwin D. Gunter to Oberste, Apr. 8, 1958, KCCF/CAT.

20. Oberste to Gunter, Apr. 10, 1958, KCCF/CAT.

21. Anton J. Frank to Oberste, Apr. 16, 1958, KCCF/CAT.

22. Oberste to Frank, Apr. 20, 1958, KCCF/CAT.

23. Oberste to Gunter, Apr. 20, 1958, KCCF/CAT. Archbishop Robert E. Lucey of San Antonio, invited by the Texas Philosophical Society to prepare a necrology for the "late beloved Carlos Castañeda," appealed for help to Bishop Garriga, who had known Don Carlos better than he. Garriga, wanting only the best biographical cameo for his deceased friend, borrowed the memorial Oberste had written to include in the last volume of *Our Catholic Heritage* and sent it to the chancery in San Antonio. Lucey immediately asked and received permission from Monsignor Oberste "to send it to the Texas Philosophical Society just as it is" (Most Reverend Robert E. Lucey to Oberste, Sept. 10, 1958; Oberste to Lucey, Sept. 15, 1958, KCCF/CAT).

24. Gunter to Oberste, May 5, 1958, KCCF/CAT.

25. Oberste to Gunter, May 7, 1958, KCCF/CAT.

26. Oberste to FitzSimon, June 6, 1958, KCCF/CAT.

27. Frank to Oberste, May 7, 1958, KCCF/CAT.

28. Oberste to Gunter, May 16, 1958, KCCF/CAT.

29. Report of William H. Oberste to the Knights of Columbus in Convention, San Antonio, Tex., May 18–20, 1958, KCCF/CAT.

30. Resolutions on the Death of Dr. Castañeda, May 20, 1958, KCCF/CAT.

31. Oberste to FitzSimon, June 6, 1958, KCCF/CAT.

32. Lane, "Catholic Archives of Texas," p. 74.

33. *West Texas Register,* June 5, 1959, CBF.

34. Lane, "Catholic Archives of Texas," p. 74.

35. *Alamo Messenger,* Feb. 12, 1960, CBF.

36. "Notes and Comments," *Catholic Historical Review* 44: 246.

37. *West Texas Register,* Feb. 12, 1960, CBF.

38. Ibid.

39. [Most Reverend Robert E. Lucey], "Carlos Eduardo Castañeda, 1886–1958," in *The Philosophical Society of Texas, Proceedings of the Annual Meeting at Austin, Dec. 13, 1958* (Dallas: Philosophical Society of Texas, 1959), p. 24.

40. Sam Liberto, Sr., interview with Félix D. Almaráz, Jr., tape recording, San Antonio, Tex., Dec. 28, 1972.

41. Frantz, *Forty-Acre Follies,* p. 289.

42. Ibid., p. 290.

43. Félix D. Almaráz, Jr., "Armistice Day Special to Texas History Scholar," *San Antonio Express-News,* Nov. 8, 1992.

44. *Daily Texan,* Nov. 21, 1977, KCCF/CAT.

Bibliography

Works by Carlos E. Castañeda

BOOKS

(with Jack Autrey Dabbs). *Calendar of the Manuel E. Gondra Manuscript Collection. The University of Texas Library.* Mexico City: Editorial Jus., 1952.

(with Frederick C. Chabot). *Early Texas Album: Fifty Illustrations with Notes.* Austin: Privately printed, 1929.

(ed.) *La Guerra de la Reforma Según el Archivo del General D. Manuel Doblado, 1857– 1860,* by Manuel Doblado. San Antonio: Casa Editorial Lozano, 1930.

(with Jack Autrey Dabbs). *Guide to the Latin American Manuscripts in the University of Texas Library.* Cambridge: Harvard University Press, 1940.

(ed.) *Historia de Todos los Colegios de la Ciudad de México desde la Conquista Hasta 1780,* by Félix de Osores y Sotomayor. Mexico City: Talleres Gráficos de la Nación, 1929.

(with Samuel Guy Inman). *A History of Latin America for Schools.* New York: Macmillan Company, 1944.

(trans. and ed.) *The History of Texas, 1673–1779, by Fray Juan Agustín Morfi, Missionary, Teacher, Historian.* 2 Vols. Albuquerque: The Quivira Society, 1935. Reprint. New York: Arno Press, 1967.

(with E. C. Delaney). *The Lands of Middle America,* ed. George I. Sánchez. New York: Macmillan Company, 1948.

(ed. and trans.) *The Mexican Side of the Texan Revolution (1836).* Dallas: P. L. Turner Company, 1928.

Our Catholic Heritage in Texas, 1519–1936. 7 vols. Austin: Von Boeckmann-Jones Company, 1936–58.

A Report on the Spanish Archives in San Antonio, Texas. San Antonio: Artes Gráficas and the Yanaguana Society, 1937.

(with Early Martin, Jr.) *Three Manuscript Maps of Texas by Stephen F. Austin.* Austin: Privately printed, 1930.

ARTICLES

"Archival Needs in Latin America." *Inter-American Bibliographical Review* 2 (Spring, 1942): 10–13.

"The Beginnings of University Life in America." *Catholic Review* 24 (July, 1938): 153–74.

"Broadening the Concept of History Teaching in Texas." *Proceedings of Inter American Conference on Intellectual Interchange* (1943): 97–108.

"Can Anyone Learn Spanish?" *Catholic School Interest* (March, 1924).

"Carta de la Emperatríz Carlota: Charlotte, Empress Consort of Maximilian, Emperor of Mexico, 1840–1927." *Revista de estudios hispánicos* 2 (January–March, 1929): 27–29.

"A Chapter in Frontier History." *Southwest Review* 28 (Autumn, 1942): 31–52.

"The Coming of the Augustinians to the New World." *Records of the American Catholic Historical Society of Philadelphia* 60 (December, 1949): 189–96.

"Communications Between Santa Fe and San Antonio in the Eighteenth Century." *Texas Geographic Magazine* 5 (Spring, 1941): 17–38.

"The Corregidor in Spanish Colonial Administration." *Hispanic American Historical Review* 9 (November, 1929): 446–70.

"Customs and Legends of Texas Indians." *Mid-America* 3 (July, 1931): 48–56.

"Did You Ever Stop to Think?" *America* (1924).

"Don Carlos de Sigüenza y Góngora." *Catholic Historical Review* 16 (April, 1930): 86–89.

"The Early Missionary Movement in Texas." *Missionary* 35 (December, 1921): 360–61.

"The Educational Revolution in Mexico." *Educational Review* 68 (October, 1924): 123–25.

"The First American Play." *Catholic World* 134 (January, 1932): 429–37.

"The First Chartered Bank West of the Mississippi: Banco Nacional de Texas." *Business History Review* 25 (December, 1951): 242–56.

"First European Settlement on the Rio Grande." *Texas Geographic* 9 (August, 1945): 28–31.

"The First Pan-American Congress." *North American Review* 223 (June, 1926): 248–55.

"The First Printing Press in Mexico." *Publisher's Weekly* 137 (January 6, 1940): 50–53.

"Fr. Antonio Margil de Jesús." *Missionary* 38 (June–July, 1924): 163–64, 197–99.

"Fray Juan de Zumárraga and Indian Policy in New Spain." *The Americas* 5 (January, 1949): 296–310.

"God's Work in the Southwest." *Extension* 48 (November, 1953): 18–19, 56.

"A Helping Hand to Mexico." *Commonweal* 5 (November 17, 1926): 37–38.

"The Human Side of a Great Collection." *Books Abroad* 14 (1940): 116–21.

"In Memoriam: Charles W. Hackett, 1888–1951." *The Americas* 8 (July, 1951): 83–84.

"Inter-American Cultural Relations." *Catholic Library World* 19 (October, 1947): 26–30.

"Introduction." In *Life in the Imperial and Loyal City of Mexico in New Spain and the Royal Pontifical University of Mexico as Described in the Dialogues for the Study of the Latin Language Prepared by Francisco Cervantes de Salazar for Use in his Classes and Printed in 1554 by Juan Pablos,* trans. Minnie Lee Barrett Shepard, pp. 1–20. Reprint. Westport, Conn.: Greenwood Press, 1970.

"Is Mexico Turning Bolshevik?" *Catholic World* 123 (June, 1926): 366–72.

"Latin America's First Great Educator." *Current History* 22 (May, 1925): 223–25.

"Los manuscritos perdidos de Gutiérrez de Luna." *Revista Mexicana de estudios históricos* 2 (September–October, 1928): 170–76.

"Modern Language Instruction in American Colleges, 1779–1800." *Catholic Educational Review* 23 (January–February, 1925): 3–9, 92–106.

"Modern Lighthouses of Culture." *Catholic Library World* 26 (November, 1944): 40–42.

"The Oldest University in America." *Pan-American Magazine* 43 (July, 1930): 54–57.

"Our Latin American Neighbors." *Catholic Historical Review* 25 (January, 1940): 421–33.

"Pioneers in Sackcloth." *Catholic Historical Review* 25 (October, 1939): 309–326.

"Pioneers of the Church in Texas." In *Diamond Jubilee, 1874–1949: Archdiocese of San Antonio,* edited by M. J. Gilbert, pp. 1–16. San Antonio: Schneider Printing Company/Robert E. Lucey, 1949.

"Relations of General Scott with Santa Anna." *Hispanic American Historical Review* 29 (November, 1949): 455–73.

"Silent Years in Texas History." *Southwestern Historical Quarterly* 38 (October, 1934): 122–34.

"The Six Flags of Texas." *Southern Messenger* (October 27, 1932).

"Social Developments and Movements in Latin America." In *Church and Society: Catholic Social and Political Thought and Movements, 1789–1950,* edited by Joseph N. Moody, pp. 733–73. New York: Arts, Inc., 1953.

"Some of Our Earliest Americans Await the Magic Touch." *Texas Outlook* 37 (January, 1937): 22–23.

"The Sons of St. Francis in Texas." *The Americas* 1 (January, 1945): 289–302.

"Sources for Spanish American Church History." *Catholic Library World* 10 (December, 1938): 99–102.

"Spanish Medieval Institutions in Overseas Administration: The Prevalence of Medieval Concepts." *The Americas* 15 (October, 1954): 115–29.

(trans. and ed.) "Statistical Report on Texas by Juan N. Almonte, 1835." *Southwestern Historical Quarterly* 28 (January, 1925): 177–222.

"The Teaching of History in the Secondary Schools of Mexico." *Historical Outlook* 24 (May, 1933): 246–52.

(trans. and ed.) "A Trip to Texas in 1828: José María Sánchez." *Southwestern Historical Quarterly* 29 (April, 1926): 249–88.

"Why I Chose History." *The Americas* 8 (April, 1952): 475–92.

"The Woman in Blue." *Age of Mary* (January–February, 1958): 22–29.

"World Peace Attainable Through Modern Language Study." *Texas Outlook* 17 (December, 1933): 9–10.

Other Sources

ARCHIVAL COLLECTIONS, DOCUMENTS, AND MANUSCRIPTS

Academy of American Franciscan History. Franciscan School of Theology. Berkeley, California.

Archive of the Southern Province of the Missionary Oblates of Mary Immaculate. San Antonio, Texas.

Austin-Travis County Collection. Austin Public Library. Austin, Texas.

Bancroft Library. University of California at Berkeley.

Barker, Eugene C., Texas History Center. University of Texas at Austin.

Benson, Nettie Lee, Latin American Collection. University of Texas at Austin.

Brenner Library. Quincy College. Quincy, Illinois.

Brewer, Tom Bowman. "A History of the Department of History of the University of Texas, 1883–1951." Master's thesis, University of Texas, Austin, 1957.

Brownsville Public Schools. Administrative Offices. Brownsville, Texas.

Castañeda, Carlos E., Certificate of Baptism No. 1, January 2, 1897. Immaculate Conception Church. Rio Grande City, Texas.

Castañeda, Gloria Irma, Certificate of Birth No. C-239-4132, Public Health Department, Office of Vital Statistics. San Antonio, Texas.

Catholic Archives of San Antonio. Archdiocese of San Antonio Chancery Office. San Antonio, Texas.

Catholic Archives of Texas. Diocese of Austin Chancery Office. Austin, Texas.

Center for Southwest Research. The University of New Mexico General Library. Albuquerque, New Mexico.

City Clerk's Office. Brownsville, Texas.

Collections Deposit Library. University of Texas at Austin.

County Clerk's Office. Bexar County Courthouse. San Antonio, Texas.

County Clerk's Office. Travis County Courthouse. Austin, Texas.

County Clerk's Office. Wilson County Courthouse. Floresville, Texas.

Daughters of the Republic of Texas Library at the Alamo. San Antonio, Texas.

DePaul Library. Saint Mary College. Leavenworth, Kansas.

District Clerk's Office. Brazoria County Courthouse. Angleton, Texas.

District Clerk's Office. Val Verde County Courthouse. Del Rio, Texas.

Immigration and Naturalization Service. U.S. Department of Justice. Washington, D.C.

Lane, Sister M. Claude. "Catholic Archives of Texas: History and Preliminary Inventory." Master's thesis, University of Texas, Austin, 1961.

Legislative Reference Library. Texas Capitol Complex. Austin, Texas.

Library of the University of Texas at Arlington. Arlington, Texas.

McMullen Library. The Catholic University of America. Washington, D.C.

Moloney, Louis C. "A History of the University Library at the University of Texas, 1883–1934." Ph.D. diss., Columbia University, New York, 1970.

National Archives of the United States. Washington, D.C.

News and Information Service. University of Texas at Austin.

Office of the Registrar, Official Transcript: Carlos Eduardo Castañeda. University of Texas at Austin.

Our Lady of the Lake University Library. San Antonio, Texas.

Peña, J. B. "A History of the San Felipe Independent School District and Its Influence on the Community, 1929–1951." Master's thesis, Sul Ross State College, Alpine, Texas, 1951.

San Antonio Independent School District. Administrative Offices. San Antonio, Texas.

Sapia-Bosch, Alfonso F. "The Role of General Lucio Blanco in the Mexican Revolution, 1913–1922." Ph.D. diss., Georgetown University, Washington, D.C., 1977.

Swem, Earl Gregg, Library. College of William and Mary. Williamsburg, Virginia.

Texas Collection. Incarnate Word College Library. San Antonio, Texas.

Texas Department of Health. Bureau of Vital Statistics. Austin, Texas.

Whisenhunt, Donald Wayne. "Texas in the Depression, 1929–1933: A Study of Public Reaction." Ph.D. diss., Texas Tech University, Lubbock, 1966.

INTERVIEWS

Artaza, Consuelo Castañeda de, interview with O. Wayne Poorman, tape recording, Houston, Texas, September 19, 1971.

Castañeda, Elisa R., interview with O. Wayne Poorman, tape recording, Austin, Texas, May 29, 1972.
Castañeda, Josefina E., interview with Diana Gómez, tape recording, Brownsville, Texas, December 15, 1970.
Estep, Raymond, interview with author, tape recording, Washington, D.C., March 1, 1974.
Folks, Rosemary Castañeda de, and Consuelo Castañeda de Artaza, telephone interview with author, Houston–San Antonio, Texas, September 3, 1990.
Frank, Rev. Monsignor Anton J., interview with O. Wayne Poorman, tape recording, Houston, Texas, December 29, 1972.
Frantz, Joe B., interview with O. Wayne Poorman, tape recording, Austin, Texas, May 23, 1972.
Liberto, Sam, Sr., interview with author, tape recording, San Antonio, Texas, December 28, 1972.
Moreno, José Rubén, interview with author, tape recording, San Antonio, Texas, June 26, 1990.
Peters, Edward H., interview with respondent, tape recording, Columbus, Ohio, [ca. June] 1972.
Rodríguez, Valdemar, interview with author, tape recording, San Antonio, Texas, January 24, 1974.
Sheridan, Philip J., interview with author, tape recording, San Antonio, Texas, January 26, 1973.
Tibesar, Antonine S., interview with author, transcribed, San Antonio, Texas, September 23, 1989.

BOOKS

Bailey, David C. ¡Viva Cristo Rey! The Cristero Rebellion and the Church-State Conflict in Mexico. Austin: University of Texas Press, 1974.
Bannon, John Francis, ed. Bolton and the Spanish Borderlands. Norman: University of Oklahoma Press, 1964.
———. Herbert Eugene Bolton: The Historian and the Man, 1870–1953. Tucson: University of Arizona Press, 1978.
Beaumont City Directory (1921). Beaumont Public Library, Beaumont, Texas.
Bravo Ugarte, José. Diócesis y Obispos de la Iglesia Mexicana (1519–1965). Mexico City: Editorial Jus, 1965.
Broderick, Robert C. The Catholic Encyclopedia. Huntington, Ind.: Our Sunday Visitor, Inc., 1975.
Carroll, H. Bailey, and Milton R. Gutsch (comp.). Texas History Theses: A Check List of the Theses and Dissertations Relating to Texas History Accepted at the University of Texas, 1893–1951. Austin: Texas State Historical Association, 1955.
Chabot, Frederick C. With the Makers of San Antonio. San Antonio: Artes Gráficas, 1937.
Chatfield, W. H. (comp.). The Twin Cities of the Border: Brownsville, Texas, [and] Matamoros, Mexico, and the Country of the Lower Rio Grande. New Orleans: E. P. Brandao, 1893; reprint, Brownsville: Harbert Davenport Memorial Fund, Brownsville Historical Association, and Lower Rio Grande Valley Historical Society, 1959.
Cotner, Thomas E., and Carlos E. Castañeda, eds. Essays in Mexican History. Austin: Institute of Latin American Studies, 1958; reprint, Westport, Conn.: Greenwood Press, 1972.

Cuevas, Mariano. *Historia de la Iglesia de México*. 5 vols. El Paso: Editorial Revista Católica, 1928.

Daniel, Clete. *Chicano Workers and the Politics of Fairness: The FEPC in the Southwest*. Austin: University of Texas Press, 1991.

D'Assemani, Michael H. Abraham. *The Cross on the Sword: A History of the Equestrian Order of the Holy Sepulchre of Jerusalem*. Chicago: Photopress, Inc., 1944.

Delaney, John J. *Dictionary of Saints*. Garden City, N.Y.: Doubleday & Company, Inc., 1980.

Diccionario Porrúa de Historia, Biografía y Geografía de México. 2 vols. Mexico City: Editorial Porrúa, S.A., 1971.

Doyon, Bernard. *The Cavalry of Christ on the Rio Grande, 1849–1883*. Milwaukee: Catholic Life Publishers/Bruce Press, 1956.

Dunn, William H. *Knights of Columbus in Texas: 1902–1977*. Austin: Texas State Council of the Knights of Columbus, 1978.

Espinosa, J. Manuel. *Inter-American Beginnings of U.S. Cultural Diplomacy, 1936–1948*. Washington, D.C.: U.S. Government Printing Office, 1976.

Frantz, Joe B. *The Forty-Acre Follies: An Opinionated History of the University of Texas*. Austin: Texas Monthly Press, 1983.

Griffin, Chula T., and Sam S. Griffin (comps.). *Record of Interments in the City Cemetery of Brownsville, Texas*. 5 vols. Brownsville: Privately published, 1987–98.

Gutiérrez, A. E. (comp.). *A History of San Felipe: San Felipe High School in the 1930s*. Del Rio: Whitehead Memorial Museum/San Felipe Ex-Students Association of California, 1978.

Gutiérrez Castillas, José. *Historia de la Iglesia en México*. Mexico City: Editorial Porrúa, S.A., 1974.

McLean, Malcolm Dallas (comp. and ed.). *Papers Concerning Robertson's Colony in Texas*. 19 vols. Arlington: University of Texas at Arlington, 1974–93.

The New Handbook of Texas. 6 vols. Austin: Texas State Historical Association, 1996.

Oberste, William H. *Knights of Columbus in Texas, 1902–1952*. Austin: Von Boeckmann-Jones Co., 1952.

The Official Catholic Directory Anno Domini 1988. Wilmette, Ill.: P. F. Kenedy & Sons, 1988.

Owens, Lilliana. *Jesuit Beginnings in New Mexico*. El Paso: Revista Católica, 1950.

Perales, Alonso S., ed. *Are We Good Neighbors?* San Antonio: Artes Gráficas, 1948.

Pool, William C. *Eugene C. Barker: Historian*. Austin: Texas State Historical Association, 1971.

Rossi, Ernest E., and Jack C. Plano. *Latin America: A Political Dictionary*. Santa Barbara: ABC-Clio, 1992.

Ruiz, Ramón Eduardo. *The Great Rebellion: Mexico, 1905–1924*. New York: W. W. Norton & Company, 1980.

Schmitz, Joseph William. *The Society of Mary in Texas*. San Antonio: Naylor Company, 1951.

Sitkoff, Harvard. *A New Deal for Blacks: The Emergence of Civil Rights as a National Issue—The Depression Decade*. New York: Oxford University Press, 1981.

Sonnichsen, C. L. *Pass of the North: Four Centuries on the Rio Grande*. El Paso: Texas Western Press, 1968.

Steck, Francis Borgia, ed. and trans. *Motolonía's History of the Indians of New Spain*. Washington, D.C.: Academy of American Franciscan History, 1951.

Taylor, T. U. *Fifty Years on Forty Acres*. Austin: Alec Book Company, 1938.

Walsh, Michael, ed. *Butler's Lives of the Saints*. San Francisco: Harper & Row, 1985.

Webb, Walter Prescott, and H. Bailey Carroll, eds. *The Handbook of Texas*. 2 vols. Austin: Texas State Historical Association, 1952.

Webster's Biographical Dictionary. Springfield, Mass.: G. & C. Merriam Co., 1963.

ARTICLES

"Affairs of the Association." *Southwestern Historical Quarterly* 31 (July, 1927): 86–88.

"Affairs of the Association." *Southwestern Historical Quarterly* 31 (April, 1928): 384.

"Affairs of the Association." *Southwestern Historical Quarterly* 32 (July, 1928): 100–102.

Almaráz, Jr., Félix D. "Carlos Eduardo Castañeda, Mexican-American Historian: The Formative Years, 1896–1927." *Pacific Historical Review* 42 (August, 1973): 319–34.

———. "The Making of a Boltonian: Carlos E. Castañeda of Texas—The Early Years." *Red River Valley Historical Review* 1 (Winter, 1974): 329–50.

———. "The Return of the Franciscans to Texas, 1891–1931." *Catholic Southwest: A Journal of History and Culture* 7 (1996): 91–114.

Barnhart, John D. "The Forty-First Annual Meeting of the Mississippi Valley Historical Association." *Mississippi Valley Historical Review* 35 (September, 1948): 239–62.

"Bibliographical Section: Various Bibliographical Items." *Hispanic American Historical Review* 18 (August, 1937): 357–69.

"Bibliographical Section: Additional Notes." *Hispanic American Historical Review* 18 (November, 1938): 600–606.

Bolton, Herbert E. "The Confession of a Wayward Professor." *The Americas* 6 (January, 1950): 359–62.

Butler, Ruth Lapham. "Notes on the First Congress of Historians of Mexico and the United States." *Hispanic American Historical Review* 24 (November, 1949): 634–36.

Carleton, Don E., and Katherine J. Adams. "'A Work Peculiarly Our Own': Origins of the Barker Texas History Center, 1883–1950." *Southwestern Historical Quarterly* 86 (October, 1982): 197–230.

Carroll, H. Bailey, ed. "Texas Collection." *Southwestern Historical Quarterly* 53 (April, 1950): 474–94.

———. "Texas Collection." *Southwestern Historical Quarterly* 59 (October, 1955): 222–36.

———. "Texas Collection." *Southwestern Historical Quarterly* 62 (October, 1958): 260–88.

"Dr. Carlos Eduardo Castañeda." *Catholic Library World* 9 (September–December, 1937): 132.

Ehrmann, Howard M. "Historical News: The Chicago Meeting, 1953." *American Historical Review* 59 (April, 1954): 768–802.

González Salinas, Ernesto. "El Colegio de San Juan: Remembranzas." In *Anuario de la Escuela Secundaria Federal Lic. y General Juan José de la Garza*, pp. 12–31. Matamoros, Tamaulipas, Mex.: n.p., 1960.

Gould, Lewis L. "The University Becomes Politicized: The War with Jim Ferguson, 1915–1918." *Southwestern Historical Quarterly* 86 (October, 1982): 255–76.

Hackett, Charles W. "Notes and Comments: The Special Institute of Latin-American

Studies at the University of Texas in the Summer of 1940." *Hispanic American Historical Review* 20 (November, 1940): 650–54.

Hammond, George P. "In Memoriam: Herbert Eugene Bolton, 1870–1953." *The Americas* 9 (April, 1953): 391–98.

"Historical News and Comments." *Mississippi Valley Historical Review* 31 (June, 1944): 177–78.

"Historical Notes." *Southwestern Historical Quarterly* 41 (January, 1938): 241–56.

"Inter-American Notes: Annual Convocation of the Academy of American Franciscan History." *The Americas* 6 (January, 1950): 363–68; 8 (April, 1952): 515–18.

Kiemen, Mathias C. "In Memoriam: Carlos Eduardo Castañeda, 1896–1958." *The Americas* 15 (July, 1958): 61–62.

Martin, T. P. "Notes and Comment: The Fifth Convention of Inter-American Bibliographical and Library Association." *Hispanic American Historical Review* 22 (May, 1942): 416–20.

McLean, Malcolm D. "E. D. Farmer International Fellowships." In *Papers Concerning Robertson's Colony in Texas, Introductory Volume: Robert Leftwich's Mexico Diary and Letterbook, 1822–1824.* 18 vols. Arlington: University of Texas Press/University of Texas at Arlington, 1986.

———. "Winnie Allen: The 'Mother of Texas History.'" *Texas Libraries* 50 (Winter, 1989–90): 124–29.

Mecham, J. Lloyd. "Obituary Notes: Carlos Eduardo Castañeda, 1896–1958." *Hispanic American Historical Review* 38 (August, 1958): 383–88.

"The Meeting of the American Historical Association at Richmond." *American Historical Review* 30 (April, 1925): 451–77.

"Miscellany: The Nineteenth Annual Meeting of the American Catholic Historical Association, Chicago, Illinois, December 28–30, 1938." *Catholic Historical Review* 25 (April, 1939): 59–70.

"Miscellany: The Twentieth Annual Meeting of the American Catholic Historical Association." *Catholic Historical Review* 26 (April, 1940): 78–91.

"A New Knight." *Commonweal* 35 (October 24, 1941): 4–5.

"News and Notes: Honors to Dr. Castañeda." *Catholic Library World* 13 (December, 1941): 78–86.

"Notes: Bibliographical Section." *Hispanic American Historical Review* 13 (November, 1933): 543–53; 15 (August, 1935): 403–424.

"Notes and Comment." *Hispanic American Historical Review* 10 (May, 1930): 237–46; 13 (May, 1933): 234–37.

"Notes and Comments." *Catholic Historical Review* 27 (January, 1942): 500–514; 29 (April, 1943): 118–32; 37 (January, 1952): 480–88; 44 (July, 1958): 237–46.

"Notes and Comments: Sociedad de Amigos de la Biblioteca de Lima." *Hispanic American Historical Review* 23 (August, 1943): 545–54.

Phillips, Charles. "The Trouble in Mexico: A Reply to the Foregoing Article." *Catholic World* 123 (June, 1926): 372–80.

Prindle, David P. "Oil and the Permanent University Fund: The Early Years." *Southwestern Historical Quarterly* 86 (October, 1982): 277–98.

"Professional Notes: Personal News." *Hispanic American Historical Review* 25 (November, 1945): 539–43; 26 (May, 1946): 267–83; 26 (August, 1946): 441–43; 26 (November, 1946): 633–43; 29 (May, 1949): 287–94.

"Professional Notes: Summer School, National University of Mexico, with the Cooperation of the Universities of California, Michigan, and Texas, and the Spanish Language Institute." *Hispanic American Historical Review* 26 (May, 1946): 269–83.

Santiestévan, Henry. "A Perspective on Mexican-American Organizations." In *Mexican-Americans Tomorrow: Educational and Economic Perspectives,* edited by Gus Tyler, pp. 164–202. Albuquerque: University of New Mexico Press, 1975.

Scholes, France. "Problems in the Early Ecclesiastical History of New Mexico." *New Mexico Historical Review* 7 (January, 1932): 32–74.

Slawson, Douglas. "The National Catholic Conference and the Church-State Conflict in Mexico, 1925–1929." *The Americas* 47 (July, 1990): 55–93.

Treviño, Roberto R. "Prensa y patria: The Spanish-Language Press and the Biculturation of the Tejano Middle Class, 1920–1940." *Western Historical Quarterly* 22 (November, 1991): 451–72.

Upton, Elsie. "A Knight of Goodwill." *St. Joseph Magazine* 44 (June, 1943): 12–14.

Villasana Haggard, J. Review of *History of Texas, 1673–1779* by Fray Juan Agustín Morfi, translated and edited by Carlos Eduardo Castañeda. *Southwest Review* 21 (Winter, 1936): 229–32.

Winther, Oscar O. "The Fiftieth Annual Meeting of the Mississippi Valley Historical Association." *Mississippi Valley Historical Review* 44 (September, 1957): 310–34.

Index